Housing Law Handbook

Diane Astin is a solicitor specialising in housing law. She is a Senior Lecturer and the Director of the Student Law Clinic at Westminster University and also a consultant with Scott-Moncrieff & Associates Ltd. She has many years' experience of all aspects of housing law both in private practice and in the voluntary sector.

Available as an ebook at www.lag.org.uk/ebooks

The purpose of the Legal Action Group is to promote equal access to justice for all members of society who are socially, economically or otherwise disadvantaged. To this end, it seeks to improve law and practice, the administration of justice and legal services.

Housing Law Handbook

THIRD EDITION

Diane Astin

Legal Action Group
2015

This edition published in Great Britain 2015
by LAG Education and Service Trust Limited
3rd floor, Universal House, 88–94 Wentworth Street, London E1 7SA
www.lag.org.uk

First edition published 2008
Reprinted 2010
Second edition 2012

Previously published as *Housing law: an adviser's handbook*

While every effort has been made to ensure that the details in this text are correct, readers must be aware that the law changes and that the accuracy of the material cannot be guaranteed and the author and the publisher accept no responsibility for any loss or damage sustained.

British Library Cataloguing in Publication Data
a CIP catalogue record for this book is available from the British Library.

This book has been produced using Forest Stewardship Council (FSC) certified paper. The wood used to produce FSC certified products with a 'Mixed Sources' label comes from FSC certified well-managed forests, controlled sources and/or recycled material.

ISBN   978 1 908407 56 6
E-ISBN   978 1 908407 57 3

Typeset by Regent Typesetting, London
Printed in Great Britain by Hobbs the Printers, Totton, Hampshire

Preface

The last edition of this book was published in 2011, the year after the 2010 general election, and this edition goes to press just weeks before the 2015 election. In the Law Society 'Sir Henry Hodge Memorial Lecture 2011' Lady Hale addressed the topic of 'Equal access to justice in the big society'. She identified the fundamental requirements of access to justice as being: a system of just laws, access to the law when you need it, access to the courts to enforce legal remedies and, when the issues and the law are complex, access to legal advice and representation. Anticipating the cuts to legal aid she was pessimistic but her unarguable conclusion was that 'Courts are and should be a last resort but they should be a last resort which is accessible to all, rich and poor alike'.

So, we knew that the Legal Aid, Sentencing and Punishment of Offenders Act 2012 (LASPO) was about to restrict access to legal aid but the government had conceded that to protect fundamental rights 'exceptional funding' would be available. It soon became clear that the 'Exceptional Cases Funding' scheme was being operated so restrictively as to exclude 94 per cent of those who applied for it.[1] And, in the last month, civil court fees have been increased dramatically making civil justice even less accessible to those of limited means. 'Fee remission' remains but the form and the guidance to complete the form is now no less than 31 pages long. Complexity of the law and procedure is increasing, as access to help diminishes.

The last few years has seen a sustained assault on access to justice for poor people. Thankfully, there are still many dedicated individuals committed to defending housing rights and I hope that this book helps them to continue to do so.

---

1 See *Gudanaviciene v Director of Legal Aid Casework and others* [2014] EWCA 1622, 15 December 2014 in which the Court of Appeal found the Legal Aid Agency guidance to be unlawful.

When the last edition appeared, in addition to LASPO, the Local-ism Act 2011 and the Welfare Reform Act 2012 were about to come into force. As predicted, the outcome of the changes has been that homes for the poor have become less secure and less affordable. Unsurprisingly, homelessness has increased, as has the number of households in temporary accommodation awaiting settled housing.[2] This may account for an unusual number of appeal cases about the homelessness duty since the last edition. The Court of Appeal has considered the issue of affordability of accommodation in several cases and the Supreme Court only this month considered the case of a family evicted from their private rented accommodation in London, because of the welfare reforms, accommodated by the local authority 50 miles away. The Court held that the accommodation was not suit-able. The reasoned judgment is pending.[3]

The Localism Act 2011 was clearly intended to reduce the rights of social tenants. It does this by enabling social landlords to grant fixed term tenancies, as opposed to the 'lifetime' tenancies, which were previously recognised as appropriate for low income households in need of stable housing. It also allows local authorities to end their duties to homeless applicants by way of the 'private rented sector offer' and gives more discretion to authorities to decide who can be placed on their waiting list for social housing.

But it is LASPO that has probably had the more significant impact in relation to the protection of housing rights, and the Welfare Reform Act 2012 has led to tenants being evicted from their homes. Many of the cases described in this book were generated by challenges to the lawfulness of the 'reforms' to legal aid and welfare benefits. These cases have had varying degrees of success and several appeals are still outstanding. Hopefully, these challenges will continue to be brought, despite the government's attempts to restrict access to judi-cial review.

When surveying the recent developments two things stood out: first, that removing welfare benefit law from the scope of legal aid is an excellent way of heading off challenges to draconian welfare reform. Secondly, politically motivated, piecemeal amendments to

2 See the Department of Communities and Local Government's quarterly homelessness statistics 'Statutory homelessness in England' published online: homelessness acceptances show a 6% increase for the last quarter of 2014, compared with the same period in 2013, and the number of households in temporary accommodation has increased by 9%, compared with the same period in 2013.

3 *TN v City of Westminster*, UKSC 2014/0275, 17 March 2015.

social welfare law has increased its complexity at the same time as the sources of legal help diminish. A prime example is housing benefit. Legal aid is no longer available to help with a housing benefit problem at an early stage (when help would be most effective). Instead, it is only when a person's home is at risk that legal aid becomes available. Unlike many areas of housing law, the relevant provisions are mostly contained in a single set of regulations: the Housing Benefit Regulations 2006. These can be found on the government website. However, they have been amended countless times since 2006 and only the original version of the regulations is available on the public website. To illustrate the difference, the original regulations run to 153 pages while the amended regulations are currently 376 pages long. Even if they were easy to understand by the average recipient of housing benefit (they are not), the amended version is only available by subscription to an expensive academic law library. If you know where to look, the decision makers' guidance is available online and this may be of some help but comprises four main volumes and the first of these alone is 357 pages long. One has to ask what use is a system of rules and appeals if both are inaccessible to the people affected by them.

Sadly, my audit of developments since the last edition, borrowing Lady Hale's criteria, reveals that for the poor, who are those mostly affected by 'housing law', our system of laws is less just and access to the law and to the courts has reduced. It does not appear that the next government will restore legal aid but surely to simplify and to provide free and open access to the law should be a priority for anyone who believes that justice should be accessible to rich and poor alike.

Main changes since the second edition

As indicated, we have seen the implementation and numerous legal challenges to the Localism Act 2011, LASPO and the Welfare Reform Act 2012.

In addition, the following statutes (or parts of them) have come into force: the Prevention of Social Housing Fraud Act 2013 (making sub-letting of social housing a criminal offence); the Anti-social Behaviour, Crime and Policing Act 2014 (consolidating anti-social behaviour provisions and introducing a new 'absolute' ground for possession for social tenants); the Immigration Act 2014 (restricting access to private housing by migrants by way of the new 'Right to Rent', which imposes financial penalties on private landlords who let to tenants without carrying out immigration checks); the Care Act

2014 (a sensible consolidation of community care law) mostly comes into force in April 2015; and, the Deregulation Act (DA) 2015 which came into force at the end of March 2015. The DA 2015 amends the tenancy deposit scheme provisions and the requirements for possession notices for assured shorthold tenancies as well as seeking to prevent 'retaliatory evictions'.

In addition to legislative changes, the Court of Appeal and the Supreme Court have been particularly active, in some cases in response to challenges to the government's legislative reforms. The challenge to the 'benefit cap' was dismissed by the Supreme Court in March 2015[4] and the challenge to the bedroom tax will be considered by the Supreme Court later in the year.[5] In a welcome judgment in March 2015 the Supreme Court set out how courts should deal with possession claims defended on the basis of disability discrimination under the Equality Act 2010.[6] For the first time the issue of vulnerability in homelessness was considered by the Supreme Court in December 2014 in three appeals heard together and judgment is expected later in 2015.[7]

Some important issues relating to landlord and tenant law were also decided by the Supreme Court: in *Sims v Dacorum BC*[8] the Court confirmed that a joint tenancy can be ended by one tenant's notice to quit; *CN v Lewisham LBC*[9] held that homeless applicants in temporary accommodation awaiting a decision have no protection from eviction; and *Loveridge v Lambeth LBC*[10] found that local authorities are liable to pay statutory damages for unlawful eviction in the same way as private landlords.

Unfortunately, the increasing complexity of the law and the fact that so many of the recent legislative changes apply only in England means that this book no longer covers all the relevant law in Wales.

Also, despite optimistic government announcements about the rolling out of Universal Credit, the date when this will be applied nationally is still uncertain so the proposed changes are not considered.

---

4 *R (SG and others) v Secretary of State for Work and Pensions* [2015] UKSC 16, 18 March 2015.

5 *R (MA and others) v Secretary of State for Work and Pensions* [2014] EWCA Civ 13, 21 February 2014.

6 *Akerman-Livingstone v Aster Communities Ltd* [2015] UKSC 15, 11 March 2015.

7 *Johnson v Solihull MBC, Hotak v Southwark LBC and Kanu v Southwark LBC*, SC 2014/ 0230, 0234 and 0233, heard on 15-17 December 2014.

8 [2014] UKSC 63, 12 November 2014.

9 [2014] UKSC 62, 12 November 2014.

10 [2014] UKSC 65, 3 December 2014.

I remain in debt to those who read and commented on chapters in the first edition and especially to those who have continued to offer help with the further editions. I am especially grateful to John Gallagher who, as always, patiently considered my numerous questions and equally numerous drafts and re-drafts, particularly in the later stages of the Deregulation Bill. I am also grateful to Tony Benjamin, Sally Morshead, Kathy Meade, Marc Mason and Hannah Camplin who either read drafts or fielded questions or both. Any errors are, of course, entirely mine.

I would also like to thank Esther Pilger at LAG, and Lesley Exton at Regent Typesetting, for putting everything into order so quickly and efficiently despite the numerous late amendments.

I have endeavoured to set out the law as at 31 March 2015, including the changes made by the Deregulation Act 2015, which made it in by only four days.

Diane Astin
31 March 2015

Contents

Table of cases

Table of statutes

Table of statutory instruments

Table of European and international legislation

EU Directives *continued*

Abbreviations

ADR	alternative dispute resolution
AIA 1999	Asylum and Immigration Act 1999
AJA 1970	Administration of Justice Act 1970
AJA 1973	Administration of Justice Act 1973
AOG	Adjudication Officers' Guide
ASBA 2003	Anti-social Behaviour Act 2003
ASBI	anti-social behaviour injunction
ASBO	anti-social behaviour order
BA 1984	Building Act 1984
CA 1989	Children Act 1989
CCA 1974	Consumer Credit Act 1974
CDA 1998	Crime and Disorder Act 1998
CFA	conditional fee agreement
CLA 1977	Criminal Law Act 1977
CLRA 2002	Commonhold and Leasehold Reform Act 2002
CPA 2004	Civil Partnership Act 2004
CPR 1999	Civil Procedure Rules 1999
CSDPA 1970	Chronically Sick and Disabled Persons Act 1970
CTA	Common Travel Area
DA 2015	Deregulation Act 2015
DCLG	Department of Communities and Local Government
DDA 1995	Disability Discrimination Act 1995
DFG	disabled facilities grants
DHP	discretionary housing payment
DoH	Department of Health
DPA 1972	Defective Premises Act 1972
DPA 1998	Data Protection Act 1998
DPS	Deposit Protection Services
DRO	displaced residential occupiers
DWP	Department for Work and Pensions
EA 2010	Equality Act 2010
ECHR	European Convention on Human Rights
ECtHR	European Court of Human Rights
ECJ	European Court of Justice
EEA	European Economic Area
EFTA	European Free Trade Association
EHO	environmental health officer
EHRC	Equality and Human Rights Commission
ELR	exceptional leave to remain

EPA 1990	Environmental Protection Act 1990
FACS	Fair Access to Care Services
FIA 2000	Freedom of Information Act 2000
FIT	family intervention tenancies
FLA 1996	Family Law Act 1996
FOS	Financial Ombudsman Service
FSA	Financial Services Authority
HA 1980	Housing Act 1980
HA 1985	Housing Act 1985
HA 1988	Housing Act 1988
HA 1996	Housing Act 1996
HA 2004	Housing Act 2004
HAT	housing action trust
HB	housing benefit
HB Regs 2006	Housing Benefit Regulations 2006
HBRB	Housing Benefit Review Board
HGCRA 1996	Housing Grants, Construction and Regeneration Act 1996
HHSRS	Housing Health and Safety Rating System
HHSRS Regs 2005	Housing Health and Safety Rating System Regulations 2005
HIA	Home Improvement Agency
HMO	house in multiple occupation
HOS	Housing Ombudsman Service
HRA 1998	Human Rights Act 1998
H&RA 2008	Housing and Regeneration Act 2008
HRT	habitual residence test
HSE	Health and Safety Executive
HSPHA 1968	Health Services and Public Health Act 1968
IA 1971	Immigration Act 1971
IA 1988	Immigration Act 1988
IAA 1999	Immigration and Asylum Act 1999
ILR	indefinite leave to remain
IPO	interim possession order
IS	income support
JSA	jobseeker's allowance
LA 2011	Localism Act 2011
LAA	Legal Aid Agency
LASPO 2012	Legal Aid, Sentencing and Punishment of Offenders Act 2012
LASSA 1970	Local Authority Social Services Act 1970
LGA 2000	Local Government Act 2000
LGO	Local Government Ombudsman
LHA	local housing allowance
LOTR	leave outside the rules
LPA 1925	Law of Property Act 1925
LRA 1967	Leasehold Reform Act 1967
LRA 2002	Land Registration Act 2002
LRHUDA 1999	Leasehold Reform, Housing and Urban Development Act 1993

LTA 1954	Landlord and Tenant Act 1954
LTA 1985	Landlord and Tenant Act 1985
LTA 1987	Landlord and Tenant Act 1987
LVT	Leasehold Valuation Tribunal
MCA 1973	Matrimonial Causes Act 1973
MCA 2005	Mental Capacity Act 2005
MCOB	Mortgage Conduct of Business Rules
MHA 1983	Mental Health Act 1983
MR(PT)A 2010	Mortgage Repossessions (Protection of Tenants) Act 2010
NAA 1948	National Assistance Act 1948
NASS	National Asylum Support Service
NHSA 1977	National Health Service Act 1977
NHSCCA 1990	NHS & Community Care Act 1990
NIA 2002	Nationality, Immigration and Asylum Act 2002
NOSP	notice of seeking possession
NSP	notice seeking possession
OFT	Office of Fair Trading
PEA 1977	Prevention from Eviction Act 1977
PFI	private finance initiatives
PHA 1997	Protection from Harassment Act 1997
PIO	protected intending occupier
PPO	postponed possession order
PR	personal representative
PRP	private registered provider
PSL	private sector leasing
PST	protected shorthold tenancy
RA 1977	Rent Act 1977
RMO	responsible medical officer
RSL	registered social landlord
SJE	single joint expert
SSCBA 1992	Social Security Contributions and Benefits Act 1992
TFEU	Treaty on the Functioning of the European Union
TLATA 1996	Trusts of Land and Appointment of Trustees Act 1996
TSA	Tenant Services Authority
UKBA	UK Border Agency
UTCCR 1999	Unfair Terms in Consumer Contracts Regulations 1999
YOI	young offenders institution

CHAPTER 1

Occupiers' rights: basic principles

continued

Key points

- In English law land is not 'owned'. Rather a person may have an estate or interest in land.
- A tenancy is an interest in land.
- A tenancy is distinct from a licence, which is a personal right.
- A tenancy may be created without a written agreement.
- The 'hallmarks of a tenancy' are: the grant of exclusive possession of premises; for a period of time; in return for the payment of rent.
- If these features are present an agreement will be a tenancy unless it falls into a specific category of recognised exceptions.
- A tenancy can be for a fixed term or periodic. A periodic tenancy runs automatically from one period to the next.
- Security of tenure is about the restriction on a landlord's right to evict. It may be 'procedural' (the landlord must follow a certain procedure to evict) or 'substantive' (the landlord cannot evict unless there are grounds).
- In the private sector, only tenants can enjoy substantive security of tenure.
- Licensees will enjoy procedural security of tenure unless they are 'excluded occupiers' as listed in the Protection from Eviction Act 1977.
- Excluded occupiers can be evicted without a court order.
- A tenant can end a tenancy either by serving notice to quit or by surrender. Notice to quit only operates to end a periodic tenancy. Surrender brings any sort of tenancy to an end but all parties must agree to a surrender.
- A notice to quit served by one joint tenant ends the joint tenancy.
- A person who does not have a legal interest in land may nevertheless have an equitable interest.

Introduction

1.1   Most of this book deals with the rights of those who occupy accommodation as a home. This is largely governed by statute. In some cases the statutory rights are in addition to rights set out in the agreement to occupy; in other cases the statutory rights override the agreement. The statutory intervention largely protects occupiers and restricts the rights of landlords. However, some occupiers fall outside statutory schemes of protection, which means that the parties' rights, such as the right to end an occupation agreement, are not restricted by statute. A significant part of the relationship between an occupier and a landlord is therefore governed by the occupation agreement or the general legal principles applying to rights over land.

1.2   This chapter examines some of these basic legal principles. The nature of a tenancy is examined and the different levels of security enjoyed by occupiers are explained, with particular reference to occupiers who are excluded from any protection. In addition, some difficult situations are explored, for example hotel and bed and breakfast accommodation and premises that are let for both business and residential use. Finally, the relevance of the law of trusts and equity to occupiers' rights is briefly explained.

Security of tenure

1.3   Before giving housing advice to any occupier it is necessary to identify the nature of their right to remain in occupation; in other words whether the person has 'security of tenure'. There are two levels of security of tenure. At the higher level an occupier may have the right not to be evicted unless the landlord can prove a statutory ground for possession; at the lower level an occupier may have the right not to be evicted unless the landlord follows a certain procedure (serving notice and obtaining a possession order).[1] These will be referred to as 'substantive security of tenure' and 'procedural security of tenure' respectively.

1.4   To decide whether an occupier has any security of tenure and, if so, whether this is procedural or substantive, requires the application of both:

---

1   The lower level of security of tenure is often referred to as 'basic protection' or 'protection from eviction'. However, such occupiers are sometimes also referred to as having 'unprotected tenancies' which causes confusion.

- the common law principles concerning rights over land; and
- the statutory rights enjoyed by occupiers.

Common law

1.5 The 'common law' refers to the legal principles and rules established by previous decisions of courts. These have developed to regulate relationships, such as that between a landlord and tenant, or between neighbouring occupiers. The system of law in England and Wales is a common law system. This means that the law is interpreted by judges and the decisions of the higher courts are binding on the lower courts.

1.6 Until the beginning of the twentieth century the relationship of landlord and tenant was almost entirely governed by the common law. It was determined by the principles of 'land law' and 'contract law' as they had developed through decided cases. Land law relates to the creation and transfer of legal interests in land. A tenancy is a legal interest in land. Contract law refers to the principles governing legally binding contracts, which can be enforced through the civil courts. A tenancy agreement is both an agreement creating an interest in land and a contract. An understanding of some of the principles of both land law and contract law is necessary before giving housing advice.

Statutory law

1.7 Statutory law refers to legislation made by Parliament. It includes 'primary legislation' which means statutes or Acts of Parliament and 'secondary legislation' (also called delegated or subordinate legislation). Secondary legislation is authorised to be made by primary legislation (known as enabling legislation). Most secondary legislation is made by way of a statutory instrument. In some cases secondary legislation merely sets out the detail of a requirement contained in primary legislation. In other cases the secondary legislation contains the substance of a provision. An example of the former is the statutory requirements for a valid notice seeking possession. The primary legislation provides that notice must be in 'prescribed form' and contain certain information but the detail of the prescribed form is set out in a statutory instrument: see para 6.32. An example of the latter would be the provisions about eligibility for homeless assistance, the substance of which is predominantly found in statutory instruments: see para 20.14.

1.8   Statutory law takes precedence over the common law but statutory rights are enforced through the courts and so judges must interpret the statutes. A court's decision about the interpretation of a statute will be binding on lower courts.

1.9   Since 1915 there has been extensive statutory regulation of the relationship of landlord and tenant. Mostly, statutes protect the rights of tenants.

1.10   Occupiers who are not tenants may also enjoy some statutory rights. For example, the eviction of many residential occupiers can be carried out only by using the civil courts.

1.11   The particular rights enjoyed by tenants depend on which statute applies to the agreement. The main statutes governing different types of tenancies are: the Rent Act (RA) 1977, the Housing Act (HA) 1985 and the Housing Act (HA) 1988. These are dealt with in chapter 2. This chapter describes some of the important legal principles that apply generally in relation to occupiers' rights and to the landlord and tenant relationship.

Interests in land

1.12   Although land and premises are 'bought' and 'sold', technically English law does not recognise the 'ownership' of land. It is said that the only true owner of land is the Crown. Rather, a person may have an 'interest' or 'estate' in land and the nature of the interest will determine how much control the person has over the land. Different 'interests' may exist in relation to the same land. This may sound artificial but it is essential to understand the nature of an 'interest' in land. The table below sets out the recognised legal interests and the rights that flow from the interest.

Interest	Rights
Freehold	This is the nearest thing to outright ownership – it is an interest or estate for unlimited duration. A freeholder may sell the freehold or may grant lesser interests to others, such as a lease or tenancy.
Legal charge/ mortgage	A person who lends money to another may secure the loan by taking a charge on property owned by the borrower. This entitles the lender to take possession if the borrower defaults.

Leasehold	A lease is a 'term of years', ie the grant of exclusive possession for a limited period of time. A person with a long lease may grant a shorter lease or may assign the remaining period of the lease to another person.
Tenancy	The terms tenancy and lease mean the same but the term 'tenancy' is commonly used to refer to a lease granted for a short period only.
Commonhold	Commonhold is a relatively new kind of interest created by statute: it enables those 'owning' parts of a building or estate to 'own' the common parts through a commonhold association. It is an alternative to a lease being held by one party and the freehold by another.

1.13　All of the above are 'legal interests' in land. This means that they can be transferred to another person.

1.14　　Land may be subject to a number of different interests at the same time. For example, a house 'owner' may have a mortgage and may grant a long lease to another person who in turn may grant a tenancy to another person. In such a case there will exist a freehold, a legal charge, a long lease and a short-term lease, all in respect of the same land.

1.15　　People may occupy premises without any legal interest but because they are permitted to do so, ie they have a 'licence' to occupy. They are known as 'licensees'. A licence is a personal interest and cannot be transferred to another person. Sometimes it can be difficult to ascertain whether a person occupies as a tenant or a licensee.

What is a tenancy?

1.16　A tenancy or lease is an interest in land for a period of time. The terms mean the same but 'tenancy' is usually used to refer to short-term tenancies whereas the term 'lease' is commonly used to describe a tenancy granted for a longer period of time.

1.17　　The period of time for which a tenancy may be granted is either:

- fixed; or
- periodic.

1.18　A fixed-term tenancy is created where, for example, the tenancy is granted for a period of six or 12 months. A periodic tenancy is created where no fixed period is identified or the tenancy is expressed to run from week to week or month to month, or to be a 'weekly tenancy' or a 'monthly tenancy'.[2]

1.19　At common law a tenancy for a fixed period ends at the end of the period or 'term'. A periodic tenancy continues from one period to the next until one party serves notice (a notice to quit) that he or she does not want the tenancy to continue beyond the end of the next complete period. However, if the tenant has security of tenure, a landlord's notice to quit does not mean that the tenant has to leave: either it is provided that the tenancy cannot be ended in this way, or the tenancy continues in another form after service of the notice, see: chapter 3 where the different mechanisms of security of tenure are explained.

1.20　An occupier who does not have an interest as a tenant but is permitted to occupy is a 'licensee', ie he or she has a 'licence' to occupy. The person who grants the permission is a 'licensor'.

1.21　The statutory protection introduced in 1915 (and continuing for the next 100 years) was enjoyed only by tenants. To avoid an occupier having statutory protection many landlords sought to create licences instead of tenancies. This practice led to a number of cases in which the courts considered the difference between a tenancy and a licence, the most important of which are discussed below at paras 1.25 and 1.56.

1.22　Much of this case-law is still important in understanding the nature of a tenancy. However, because most tenants in the private sector now have very limited rights there is less incentive for landlords to try to avoid creating a tenancy. Since 1997 the default private sector tenancy has been the assured shorthold tenancy and 'sham licences' are less common. Nevertheless, the difference between licences and tenancies still has some practical importance.

Difference between a tenancy and a licence

1.23　If a tenancy is created, regardless of the provisions of the actual agreement, additional statutory rights may be enjoyed by the tenant. Examples of these rights are:

- the right not to be evicted unless there are grounds, as set out in the statute;

2　In English law there is a rule that a tenancy cannot be granted for a term that is uncertain. Where the parties agree no finite term, but agree when the rent is payable (the 'rental period') a periodic tenancy is implied and this is the agreed period, see para 1.33 below. See, also *Berrisford v Mexfield Housing Co-operative Ltd* [2011] UKSC 52 at para 3.193.

- the right to have repairs carried out by a landlord;
- the right to pass on the tenancy to a family member on death.

1.24 Licensees do not have these rights. Usually the most a licensee will enjoy will be some protection against summary eviction.[3] A licence is a personal permission to occupy. It may be withdrawn by the licensor and cannot be transferred to another person.

1.25 Particularly in the 1970s and 1980s, when private tenants had extensive rights under the Rent Acts, landlords often attempted to circumvent the Rent Acts by describing an agreement as a licence agreement and/or including terms that were feature of licences rather than tenancies. Prior to the House of Lords decision in *Street v Mountford*[4] in 1985, the courts' approach had been to examine the terms of a disputed agreement and if, on balance, they suggested a licence rather than a tenancy the agreement was construed as a licence. However, in *Street v Mountford* the House of Lords rejected this approach.

> In *Street v Mountford* a house was divided into furnished rooms. Mrs Mountford signed an agreement entitled a 'licence agreement' to occupy the top floor. The landlord conceded that she had exclusive possession of this part of the house. However, the agreement included rules limiting how the accommodation was to be used. It referred to a licence fee and included a statement signed by Mrs Mountford stating: 'I understand and accept that a licence in the above form does not and is not intended to give me a tenancy protected under the Rent Acts'.
>
> The owner sought a declaration that Mrs Mountford did not have a tenancy. The county court held that she did but on the owner's appeal the Court of Appeal examined the express terms and decided that many were inconsistent with the grant of a tenancy. Furthermore, it held that the statement signed by Mrs Mountford was a clear indication of the parties' intentions. In the absence of misrepresentation, undue influence or mistake, the Court of Appeal held that the occupant had the burden of displacing the express statement of intention by showing that it was either a deliberate sham or at least an inaccurate summary of the true substance of the real agreement.

---

3 One exception to this is the 'secure licence' which is discussed at paras 3.109–3.112. However, such licences are very rare.

4 (1985) 17 HLR 402, HL.

The House of Lords allowed Mrs Mountford's appeal: it is the substance of the agreement and not the label attached to it that matters. In the words of Lord Templeman: 'The manufacture of a five pronged implement for manual digging results in a fork even if the manufacturer, unfamiliar with the English language, insists that he intended to make and has made a spade'.[5] To examine the terms to see which suggested a tenancy and which a licence was not the correct approach. Rather, if the 'hallmarks of a tenancy' were present, the agreement would be a tenancy agreement unless it fell within a class of recognised exceptions.

The hallmarks of a tenancy are:

- the grant of exclusive possession;
- for a period of time;
- in return for the payment of rent.

If these features are present, the agreement will be a tenancy unless it is of a type previously recognised by the courts as being exceptional. These exceptional kinds of agreements are:

- tied accommodation – accommodation occupied by employees;
- acts of charity and family arrangements – where there is no intention to enter into legally binding relations; and
- cases in which there is a legal relationship, but not that of landlord and tenant.

What is a lodger?

1.26   A lodger is someone who occupies part of a house but whose occupation is under the control of a landlord or his or her representative who resides in or retains possession or control over the house.[6]

1.27   In most cases a hotel occupier will also be a lodger or licensee.[7] However, exceptionally, it is possible for a person to occupy a 'dwelling' within a 'hotel' as a tenant, see paras 1.126 and 3.14 below.

1.28   A lodger is a licensee and will not enjoy long-term rights. Furthermore, if accommodation is shared with the landlord, he or she may be subject to eviction without a court order, see paras 1.100–1.107 below.

5   (1985) 17 HLR 402 at 411.
6   *Thompson v Ward* [1906] 1 KB 60.
7   *Luganda v Service Hotels* [1969] 2 Ch 209.

Hallmarks of a tenancy

Exclusive possession

1.29   The grant of 'exclusive possession' is essential to a tenancy. If an occupier does not have exclusive possession he or she cannot be a tenant.

1.30   Exclusive possession means more than being the only occupier; it means being the person in control of the premises. A tenant can exclude the whole world, including the landlord. In contrast, someone in exclusive 'occupation' can exclude the whole world, except the landlord. 'Possession' is distinct from 'occupation': a hotel guest may have exclusive occupation of a room but does not have exclusive possession because the hotel management retains control of the room.

1.31   Landlords sometimes include in a tenancy agreement terms which suggest that the occupier does not have exclusive possession. Examples include terms such as reserving a right of unlimited access and/or that the landlord has the right to move other occupiers into the premises or to move into the premises him or herself. Such terms may be 'pretences' or 'shams'. This is explained at paras 1.45–1.47 below.

1.32   It should be noted that a landlord's right of access for the purpose of inspection and repair does not mean that the tenant does not have exclusive possession. In fact, the inclusion of a term reserving such a right suggests that it is the tenant not the landlord who has control of the premises.

For a period of time

1.33   This may be expressly stated in the tenancy agreement. In most fixed-term tenancies there will be a written agreement setting out the fixed term, although it is possible to create a fixed-term tenancy for less than three years orally.[8] If there is no such agreed term, or perhaps no written agreement at all, the tenancy will be a periodic tenancy. The period will be implied by reference to the 'rental period'. If it is stated that 'the weekly rent is £x' or that the rent is '£x per week' the tenancy will be a weekly periodic tenancy. This is different from an agreement about the way in which rent is paid. For example, if a tenancy agreement states that 'the rent is £x per week, payable four weekly in advance', the period of the agreement is weekly, not four weekly.[9]

---

8 Law of Property Act 1925 s54(2).
9 *Ladies Hosiery and Underwear v Packer* [1930] Ch 304, CA.

At a rent

1.34   In *Street v Mountford* the House of Lords suggested that the payment of rent was essential to a tenancy agreement. However, it is theoretically possible to create a tenancy without the payment of rent.[10] In reality, where no rent is payable this will usually suggest that a legally binding tenancy has not been created. Furthermore, such agreements have always been outside statutory protection[11] and, since 1989, occupiers who pay no rent have been excluded from any sort of security and can be evicted without a court order (see para 1.111).

Exceptions

1.35   If there is no exclusive possession there can be no tenancy. However, there are some situations in which an occupier may appear to have exclusive possession but not be a tenant. These are:

- service occupiers;
- no intention to enter into a legal relationship;
- legal relationship but no tenancy.

Service occupiers

1.36   This is also known as 'tied accommodation'. Service occupation arises where:

- accommodation is provided by the occupant's employer; and
- it is a term of the employment contract that the employee occupies the accommodation in order to carry out the employment duties, or to better perform those duties.

1.37   Although an employee may enjoy exclusive occupation under such an agreement, this is deemed to be on behalf of the employer and the occupier is a licensee rather than a tenant.[12]

1.38   If there is a term in the employment contract stating that the employee is required to live in the premises, it is sufficient that this is for the better performance of the employment duties. Where the requirement to occupy is not an express term of the contract, the court may imply such a term but will only do so if it is necessary,

---

10 *Ashburn Anstalt v Arnold* [1988] 2 WLR 706, CA.
11 Tenancies for no rent, or at a low rent, are excluded from the Rent Act 1977 and the Housing Act 1988.
12 *Mayhew v Suttle* (1845) 4 El & Bl 347: the possession and occupation of the 'servant' is treated as being that of the 'master'.

ie the job cannot be performed without the employee living in the premises.[13]

1.39 Service occupiers have procedural security of tenure (unless they are also 'excluded occupiers', as listed at para 1.100). This means that a court order must be obtained by the landlord before the occupier can be evicted.

No intention to enter into a legal relationship

1.40 In a number of cases where the agreement was between family members or where the agreement was considered to be an 'act of charity' the courts have held that no tenancy was created. In *Street v Mountford*[14] the House of Lords held that these cases had been decided on the basis that there had been no intention between the parties to enter into a legally binding agreement.

Family arrangements

1.41 It is presumed that when an agreement is between family members there is no intention to create legal obligations. This presumption can, however, be overturned if there is sufficient evidence of an intention to be legally bound by the agreement, for example the drawing up of a formal tenancy agreement at a market rent.

1.42 The fact that the landlord and the occupier are related does not automatically prevent a tenancy arising.[15] However, the closer the relationship is, the stronger will be the presumption that the parties do not intend to be legally bound.

Acts of charity

1.43 Similarly, where the agreement has come about through an act of charity or generosity there is a presumption that no legal relationship was intended. It is not always easy to identify such situations. A person may offer to allow a friend to live in a property 'as a favour'. The surrounding circumstances will be relevant to decide whether a tenancy is created or the agreement is, exceptionally, an act of charity. Relevant factors will be the amount of 'rent' agreed and whether any kind of agreement is drawn up. The fact that a landlord may wish to gain possession at will does not mean that a tenancy has not been created. When deciding whether parties intend to be legally bound the question is not whether the parties intended to create a tenancy

---

13 *Glasgow Corporation v Johnstone* [1965] AC 609, HL.
14 (1985) 17 HLR 402, HL. See para 1.25 above.
15 *Nunn v Dalrymple* (1989) 21 HLR 569, CA.

but whether they thought they were bound by the arrangement, ie that one party was obliged to pay rent in return for which he or she had the right to live in the property. Cases in which the courts found that no tenancy was created include the following:

> *Booker v Palmer*,[16] in which an owner of a cottage agreed to allow a friend to place an evacuee in a cottage for the duration of the war.
>
> *Marcroft Wagons Ltd v Smith*,[17] where the tenant died and her daughter claimed to be entitled to succeed to the tenancy. The landlords expressly denied that she was so entitled but, while they considered their position, they allowed her to remain in occupation paying rent. The landlords indicated that, if they decided to take possession, the monies paid would be treated as 'mesne profits' (a form of damages for unlawful occupation) and, if they accepted her claim, as rent.
>
> When they did claim possession the Court of Appeal held that there had been no intention to enter into contractual relations during that period.
>
> *Heslop v Burns*,[18] in which an owner allowed friends to stay in a property rent free.

Legal relationship but no tenancy

1.44   In some cases the parties do intend to be legally bound by the agreement but the relationship is not that of landlord and tenant. An example is *Sopwich v Stuchbury*[19] in which a man selling a property let the prospective purchaser into occupation prior to the sale. This was held not to amount to the creation of a tenancy.

Shams and pretences

1.45   *Street v Mountford* re-asserted three principles:[20]

- parties to an agreement cannot contract out of statutory protection;

16 [1942] 2 All ER 674, CA.
17 [1951] 2 KB 496.
18 [1974] 1 WLR 1241.
19 (1984) 17 HLR 50, CA.
20 See also *AG Securities v Vaughan, Antoniades v Villiers* (1988) 21 HLR 79, Lord Templeman at 91.

- in the absence of special circumstances, the enjoyment of exclusive possession for a term in return for periodical payment, creates a tenancy; and
- where the language of the agreement suggests a licence rather than a tenancy, the facts prevail.

1.46 A court may decide that a term or a whole agreement is a 'sham' or 'pretence'. A sham is a term included in a contract which does not reflect the true agreement and which is intended to mislead a third party.[21] Where both parties do not intend to deceive another, the term will not be a sham but, if it does not reflect the true agreement, it may be a pretence.

1.47 It is usually the case that the landlord draws up the occupation agreement and those seeking accommodation will rarely be in a position to negotiate.[22] The occupiers may not read or understand the terms. If, however, a term is included that neither party ever intended would really apply, the term may be held to be a 'pretence'. The test is whether, had the parties had been asked at the time whether a particular term would apply, they would have answered that it would not. In deciding the issue, it is the intention of the parties *at the time the agreement was made* that is relevant. However, in deciding what that intention was, account may be taken of the way the parties have subsequently behaved. An example would be a term that permitted the landlord to move an occupier from one room to another. The fact that the landlord has never exercised the right does not, of itself, mean that the term is not genuine but may be relevant when deciding what the parties intended when they made the agreement. In such a case, the nature of the accommodation will also be relevant. A social landlord running a special needs hostel is more likely to need such control than a private landlord letting rooms in an ordinary house in multiple occupation (HMO).

Shared accommodation

1.48 In cases where accommodation is shared, it can be difficult to decide whether the occupiers are tenants or licensees. In such a case the legal arrangement may be:

- a joint tenancy of the whole of the premises;

---

21 *Snook v London and West Riding Investments Ltd* [1967] 2 QB 786.
22 In such a case the Unfair Terms in Consumer Contracts Regulations 1999 may also be relevant. See paras 4.163–4.173.

- individual tenancies of rooms with shared use of common parts, such as living room, kitchen and bathroom;
- a tenancy granted to one or more occupants, with others occupying as subtenants or lodgers of the tenant(s); or
- individual licensees.

Joint tenancies

1.49　A joint tenancy is a single agreement and the 'four unities' must be present:

- unity of title;
- unity of time;
- unity of interest; and
- unity of possession.

1.50　This means that each tenant claims his or her right to occupy under the same act or document (unity of title); that the interest of each tenant commences at the same time (unity of time); that the interest of each tenant is the same in extent, nature and duration (unity of interest); and each tenant is as much entitled to possession of the premises as any of the others (unity of possession).

1.51　Joint tenants jointly occupy the whole of the premises; one tenant cannot exclude another tenant from part of the premises.[23] Joint tenants are 'jointly and severally' liable for the rent and other obligations under the agreement. This means that a landlord is entitled to sue one or all of the joint tenants for the whole of the rent.

1.52　A joint tenancy will be created when more than one occupier signs the same tenancy agreement at the same time and together they occupy the whole of the premises. The fact that the joint tenants may choose to occupy different parts of the premises and agree individual contributions to the rent will not alter the nature of the agreement between the landlord and the tenants.

Individual tenancies of parts of the premises

1.53　In this case, each tenant must have an agreement with the landlord under which he or she has exclusive possession of part of the premises, for example, a particular room. In the private sector there is

---

23　This can only be done by virtue of a court order made under the Family Law Act 1996 because of domestic violence or relationship breakdown, see chapter 11.

specific provision for such a tenant to have security of tenure even where other accommodation is shared with other tenants.[24]

Tenancy with subletting

1.54 Where a tenancy of the whole of the premises is granted by the landlord to one or more tenants, the tenant/s may then sublet parts of the premises to others. An example would be where two joint tenants of a four-bedroom house sublet the unoccupied bedrooms to two others. In such a case, there will be no legal relationship between the two subtenants and the landlord. The landlord has a tenancy agreement with two tenants. They, in turn have a tenancy agreement with their subtenants (in fact it is more likely that the 'subtenants' are lodgers or licensees of the two tenants). Subtenancies are described in more detail in chapter 4.

Individual licensees

1.55 While it is possible to have a tenancy of a room with shared use of other parts of the premises, sometimes the arrangement is so fluid that this cannot be established. Unless there is a joint tenancy, it would be necessary for each occupier to have an agreement with the landlord for the letting of a specific room. In the absence of such an agreement, there can be no tenancy.

1.56 The following cases, heard together by the House of Lords, illustrate the correct approach to shared accommodation and the identification of genuine or sham terms.

In *AG Securities v Vaughan*[25] four men occupied a four-bedroom property with two living rooms, kitchen and bathroom. Each had signed a separate agreement with the landlord, at different times and at different rents. When a room became vacant the remaining occupiers would move so that the best rooms were occupied and the least attractive offered to the newest occupier.

The House of Lords rejected the occupiers' argument that they had a joint tenancy, because the four unities essential to a joint tenancy were not present. Furthermore, none of the occupiers had an agreement with the landlord identifying a specific room; therefore they could not be tenants of individual rooms. The occupiers were therefore licensees.

---

24 RA 1977 s22 and HA 1988 s3.
25 [1988] WLR 1205.

> The House of Lords considered at the same time, in *Antoniades v Villiers*,[26] the case of a co-habiting couple who occupied a small furnished flat comprising a bedroom, sitting room, kitchen and bathroom. When they moved in, each signed a separate 'licence agreement', which stated that neither enjoyed exclusive possession and that the landlord had the right to take up occupation or to nominate other occupiers to share with them. The identical agreements were signed on the same day at the same time. The occupiers also indicated that they would like a double bed to be provided rather than two single beds.
>
> The House of Lords held that there had been no genuine intention that the occupiers would be required to share with anyone else: the term was included by the landlord solely to avoid the protection of the Rent Act 1977 and the reality of the agreement was that the couple together enjoyed exclusive possession and were therefore joint tenants.

Termination of a tenancy

1.57   For tenants with security of tenure there are statutory limits on the landlord's right to end the tenancy and take possession: see chapters 3, 6 and 7. However, some tenancies fall outside the statutory provisions and termination is governed solely by the common law.

1.58   Under the common law a tenancy may be brought to an end in the following ways:

- Periodic tenancies may be ended by either the landlord or the tenant serving notice to quit.
- Fixed-term tenancies end automatically at the end of the agreed period (by 'effluxion of time').
- A periodic or a fixed-term tenancy may be ended by an agreement between the landlord and the tenant that the tenancy is surrendered.
- A fixed-term tenancy may be forfeited (ie the tenant forced to give up the tenancy) if the tenant breaches the agreement, provided the agreement permits this. This is usually drafted as a clause that allows the landlord to 're-enter' the premises.

1.59   The fact that legislation intervenes to protect residential tenants means that in most cases there are restrictions on a landlord's right

26 [1988] WLR 1205.

to serve notice to quit and to forfeit a tenancy. Also, at the end of a fixed term, a tenant who remains in occupation may automatically become a 'statutory periodic tenant'. This is because it is provided by statute that a periodic tenancy arises in such a situation. These restrictions, however, apply only to a landlord's right to terminate a tenancy.

1.60 There is no restriction on the termination of a tenancy by way of:

- tenant's notice to quit; or
- surrender.

Termination by the tenant

Tenant's notice to quit

1.61 A periodic tenancy can be ended by the tenant by serving a notice to quit on the landlord. A notice to quit is a notice indicating that the tenant intends to quit and give up possession to the landlord. At common law the minimum period of a notice to quit is a complete period of the tenancy. The notice can expire on either the last or the first day of the period. However, the Protection from Eviction Act (PEA) 1977 s5 provides that a valid notice to quit, including one served by a tenant, must be at least 28 days long. Shorter notice may be accepted by the landlord but this will take effect as a 'surrender' – the ending of the tenancy by agreement between the landlord and the tenant.

1.62 A tenant's notice to quit unilaterally ends the tenancy. The landlord need not agree: a valid notice to quit brings the tenancy to an end regardless. A fixed-term tenancy cannot be ended by notice to quit. However, the agreement may contain a 'break clause' allowing either party to serve notice to end the tenancy within the fixed period, see para 1.80 below.

1.63 A precedent for a tenant's notice to quit is included in the appendix to this chapter.

Notices to quit and joint tenancies

1.64 Where there is a joint periodic tenancy, one tenant can end the tenancy by serving notice to quit.[27] This is the case even if the other joint tenant is unaware of the notice and/or the termination of the tenancy

---

27 *Hammersmith and Fulham LBC v Monk* (1991) 24 HLR 206, HL. In *Sims v Dacorum BC* [2014] UKSC 63, 12 November 2014, the Supreme Court applied *Monk* and held that the principle is not inconsistent the European Convention on Human Rights. But it was significant that the district judge had reviewed the proportionality of an eviction before making a possession order.

is against his or her wishes. The notice to quit must be served on the landlord not the other tenant(s).[28] The failure of one joint tenant to consult the other(s) before serving notice is not a breach of trust.[29]

1.65   After expiry of the notice any person remaining in occupation is technically a trespasser, although in most cases the landlord cannot take possession without obtaining a possession order.[30] If the landlord is a public authority, consideration must be given to the right of the remaining occupier to respect for his or her home under the European Convention on Human Rights (see paras 7.146–7.156).

1.66   If a sole tenant serves notice that is technically deficient, for example not being for the required period, a landlord may nevertheless accept and act upon the notice, and the tenancy will end. However, this is not the case if the notice is served by one joint tenant. To terminate a joint tenancy, the notice must comply strictly with the legal requirements and, in particular, must be for the correct period, ie 28 days or a complete period of the tenancy, whichever is longer.[31]

Surrender

1.67   A surrender is an agreement between the landlord and the tenant that the tenancy shall come to an end. It can either be express or implied 'by operation of law'. Surrender is effective to end a periodic or a fixed-term agreement.

1.68   Because surrender is an agreement between the parties, all the joint tenants must agree to the surrender if the tenancy is a joint tenancy.[32]

Express surrender

1.69   Express surrender must be by deed.[33] A deed is an agreement in writing, clearly expressed to be a deed and which is properly executed, ie

---

28   Clearly, however, it would be good practice to send a copy of the notice to all affected parties.

29   See *Crawley BC v Ure* [1996] 1 All ER 724, CA and *Frank Brackley v Notting Hill Housing Trust and Julie Brackley* [2001] EWCA Civ 601, the latter case being decided after the Trusts of Land and Appointment of Trustees Act 1996 came into force.

30   See PEA 1977 s3.

31   *Hounslow LBC v Pilling* (1993) 25 HLR 305, CA; PEA 1977 s5.

32   *Leek and Moorlands Building Society v Clarke* [1952] 2 All ER 492, CA.

33   Law of Property Act 1925 ss52–53.

signed by all parties who intend to be bound by the provisions of the deed and whose signatures are witnessed.[34]

Implied surrender

1.70 In certain circumstances surrender may take effect by operation of law. This is also known as 'implied surrender'.

1.71 For surrender to be implied it is necessary that there is conduct by **both** parties that unequivocally amounts to an acceptance that the tenancy has ended. This may be either:

- relinquishment of possession and its acceptance by the landlord; or

- other conduct by both parties consistent only with the ending of the tenancy; as recently summarised by the Court of Appeal 'where both parties act on the basis that the tenancy has ended, the result will be that the tenancy has ended'.[35]

1.72 In each case, it is a question of fact for the court to decide whether these conditions are met.

Handing in the keys

1.73 If keys are returned and accepted by the landlord as ending the tenancy with immediate effect this will be an implied surrender. However, a tenant may give keys to the landlord for a reason other than wishing to surrender. Furthermore, a landlord is not bound to accept the return of keys as ending the tenancy.

> In *Laine v Cadwallader*[36] the tenants put the keys through the landlord's letter box. The landlord later made a claim against the tenant for four weeks' rent on the basis that the tenants had been required to give notice to terminate the agreement.
>
> The Court of Appeal held that the dropping in of keys cannot constitute more than an offer to surrender which a landlord is free to accept or reject. The landlord was entitled to treat the act as the giving of informal notice to quit or terminate the tenancy and the tenants were liable for the four weeks' rent following the delivery of the keys.

34 Law of Property (Miscellaneous Provisions) Act 1989 s1.
35 *QFS Scaffolding Ltd v Sable & Sable* [2010] EWCA Civ 682, 17 June 2010, Morgan J at [14]. See also *Proudcreed Ltd v Microgen Holdings plc* (1995) 72 P&CR 388 and *Bellcourt Estates Ltd v Adesina* [2005] EWCA Civ 208, 18 February 2005, see para 1.75 below.
36 (2000) 33 HLR 397, CA.

It should be noted that in *Laine v Cadwallader* the landlord would have been entitled to treat the tenancy as continuing indefinitely, in which case, the tenant would have had a continuing obligation for rent. If a tenant wishes to terminate a periodic tenancy, he or she must serve a formal notice to quit that complies with the common law and statutory requirements (see para 1.61 above). Such a notice operates unilaterally and does not depend on the landlord's agreement.

Tenants 'abandoning' premises

1.74   The fact that a tenant appears to have abandoned premises does not mean that the tenancy has been surrendered.

> In *Bellcourt Estates Ltd v Victoria Adesina*[37] a tenancy agreement was entered into for premises that comprised both residential and business units. The tenant paid part of the agreed deposit but no rent and subsequently complained about the state of the premises. She ceased to occupy the premises about three months after the start of the tenancy and asked the landlord to return the money she had paid. The landlord was aware that she had ceased to occupy and did not make any demand for the next rent payment. However, the landlord did inform the local authority's business rates department that Ms Adesina was the tenant and liable for the rates.
>
>   The county court judge held that the landlord's awareness that the tenant had left the premises, together with the failure to demand rent, amounted to surrender. However, the Court of Appeal upheld the landlord's appeal, holding that the landlord's conduct could not be held to be unequivocal conduct inconsistent with the continuation of the tenancy. All that the landlord had done was to omit to demand rent, service charges or arrears and to have failed to continue the correspondence with the tenant. This was not sufficient to establish surrender.

1.75   Many social landlords have procedures to take possession of dwellings they believe have been 'abandoned' by the tenants. However, the term 'abandonment' has no specific legal meaning and, even if a property has apparently been abandoned by the tenant and the landlord wishes to take possession, this is not enough to establish that the tenancy has ended.

37   [2005] EWCA Civ 208, 18 February 2005.

In *Preston v Fairclough*[38] the tenants of a local authority house invited another person to live in the house and then moved out, leaving arrears of rent. When the local authority became aware of this a claim for possession was made against the occupier.

The Court of Appeal held that the authority was not entitled to possession. It had taken no steps to end the tenancy and the abandonment by the tenants plus the arrears of rent were insufficient to establish surrender.

In the recent case of *Loveridge v Lambeth*[39] the local authority took possession of premises after a period of absence by the tenant. They were held to have committed an unlawful eviction and ordered to pay statutory damages of £90,500 to the former tenant, see para 8.90.

Conduct over a period of time

1.76 If there is an unequivocal act indicating a wish to surrender, the acceptance of the surrender by the landlord may be established by the landlord's conduct over a period of time rather than by a single act.

In *Brent LBC v Sharma and Vyas*[40] the sole tenant had lived in her home with her partner. She moved out and was granted a council tenancy elsewhere, following which she wrote to her landlords stating that she was no longer sharing the flat with her partner and would not object to a transfer of the tenancy into his name. At this stage there were rent arrears of £4,000. On receipt of the letter the landlords closed the rent account and served notice to quit, requiring the tenant's partner to leave. It was later held that the notice was ineffective. Several months later a claim for possession was made. A possession order was made on the basis that the tenant's letter was an unequivocal act showing that she wished to surrender and that this had been accepted by the landlords. The tenant and her partner appealed, arguing that there was no evidence of unequivocal conduct by the landlord to treat the tenancy as at an end and that the service of the notice to quit was consistent only with the continued existence of a tenancy.

The Court of Appeal dismissed their appeal, holding that the

---

38 (1982) 8 HLR 70.
39 [2014] UKSC 65, 3 December 2014.
40 (1992) 25 HLR 257.

court was entitled to look at the whole of the landlord's conduct before the claim for possession was made. The combination of no longer charging rent to the tenant and the service of the notice (a 'belt and braces effort by the council') clearly showed that from the expiry of the notice the landlords were treating the tenancy as at an end. By the time the proceedings were issued the landlords had unequivocally shown that the tenancy no longer existed.

1.77   A landlord who believes that premises have been abandoned by a tenant is not entitled to possession until the tenancy has ended. If surrender can be established, this ends the tenancy. If surrender is not established, but the tenant is no longer residing in the premises, a landlord may be able to end the tenancy by serving notice to quit. However, it should be noted that a tenant may be considered still to be resident even during an extended absence (see para 4.5).

Liability for rent

Fixed-term agreements

1.78   Where a tenant enters into a tenancy agreement for a fixed period, he or she is liable for the rent for the whole period, unless the agreement contains a 'break clause' (see para 1.80 below). Where a tenant wants to leave and end the tenancy early the landlord has no obligation to accept a surrender. Furthermore, if the tenant quits the premises and stops paying the rent, the landlord has no duty to treat the tenancy as at an end or to find another tenant in order to 'mitigate loss'. The landlord can sue the tenant for the whole of the rent for the remainder of the term.[41]

1.79   A tenant who wants to end a fixed-term tenancy early would be well advised to find someone who wishes to take on the tenancy. The landlord may then be more likely to agree to a surrender.

Break clauses

1.80   A break clause is a term that gives either party the right to end a fixed-term agreement early. The break clause will specify the length of

---

41   *Reichman & Dunn v Beveridge & Gauntlett* [2006] EWCA Civ 1659, 13 December 2006. A person claiming damages for breach of contract has a duty to mitigate (minimise) his or her losses. However, where a fixed-term tenancy is concerned, the landlord has no obligation to terminate the tenancy because by doing so the landlord would lose the right to rent for the remaining term or damages for loss of future rent.

notice that must be given and may be conditional on the tenant having complied with the obligations of the tenancy. This would mean that a tenant in rent arrears would be unable to trigger the break clause. If there is more than one tenant, all must agree to serve notice under a break clause unless the agreement specifies otherwise.

Periodic agreements

1.81 If a tenant serves notice to quit, the tenant's rent liability ends when the notice expires. If the tenant simply leaves the premises without serving an effective notice to quit, liability for rent continues. This is the case even if the landlord is informed that the tenant wants to end the tenancy or is moving out. The landlord is not obliged to treat the tenancy as at an end and may sue the tenant for unpaid rent until the date the tenancy is formally ended, see *Laine v Cadwallader* at para 1.73 above. If, however, the landlord takes possession or lets the premises to someone else, this would be taken as an acceptance of the tenant's surrender and the tenancy and rent liability would come to an end.

Subtenancies

1.82 Many tenants rent accommodation from landlords who are themselves tenants of higher landlords. For example, a long-leaseholder may let a flat to a tenant or a local authority may let a house to a tenant who then sublets a room to a subtenant. In such cases, the middle tenant is known as the 'mesne tenant'; he or she is both a tenant and a landlord. A mesne tenant cannot grant a subtenancy for a period that is longer than the tenancy he or she has. There may be more than one subtenancy in relation to the same premises.

1.83 The issues that arise when subtenancies are created are explained at para 4.92.

Statutory intervention

1.84 The legislation governing residential tenancies means that the particular statute that applies and the type of tenancy created depend on two things: the date the tenancy started and the identity of the landlord. The parties cannot contract out of the statutory protection given to tenants. So, regardless of the express terms of the tenancy agreement, certain statutory provisions will apply. For example, the tenancy agreement may state that a landlord can forfeit (end) the lease and take possession if the tenant is in arrears of rent. However, if the tenant has statutory protection, a landlord cannot enforce this right. The only way to take possession is to follow the procedure set out in the relevant statute. In relation to rents, under the Rent Act 1977 a certain contractual rent could be agreed but the tenant could immediately apply for a fair rent to be registered, which would then become the maximum rent that could be charged.

Private sector

1.85   Since the Increase of Rent and Mortgage Interest (War Restrictions) Act 1915 there has been extensive statutory intervention restricting the right of landlords to evict residential tenants.

1.86   The 1915 Act was introduced as an emergency wartime measure to prevent private landlords exploiting the shortage of rented accommodation in parts of the UK. The Act introduced for the first time security of tenure and rent control: tenants could not be evicted unless they failed to pay their rent or otherwise breached the tenancy agreement and landlords' rights to increase rents was restricted.

1.87   Clearly, security of tenure and rent control operate in tandem. Unless there is a restriction on a landlord's right to evict a tenant, a restriction on the right to increase the rent would be ineffective: a landlord would be able to evict a tenant and enter into an agreement with a new tenant at a higher rent.

1.88   The controls were intended only to last during the First World War. However, the scarcity of rented accommodation continued and successive governments found it impossible to remove the restrictions entirely. Various Rent Acts and Housing Acts were passed between 1914 and 1977 all providing differing levels of security of tenure and rent control. The Rent Act 1977 still governs tenancies granted by private landlords before 15 January 1989. Under the Rent Act 1977 tenants have a high level of security of tenure and rent is controlled by being limited to a 'fair rent' set by an independent rent officer (see para 4.186).

1.89   The Housing Act 1988 made it possible for private landlords to grant short-term tenancies by way of the assured shorthold tenancy. The assured shorthold tenancy is now the main form of tenure for private tenants. It gives only limited security and a landlord may obtain a possession order as of right, following service of two months' written notice. However, the courts would not make any possession order that would be effective before the end of six months from the start of the tenancy or before any fixed period has ended, whichever is longer. The Housing Act 1988 also effectively abandoned rent control for private tenants. While there are some limited rights to challenge very high rents and rent increases, the presumption is that rents should be 'market rents' as opposed to 'fair rents', as under the Rent Act 1977. Fair rents are set by deducting from the market rent any element deemed to be attributable to the scarcity of accommodation. Market rents are, by definition, set by the market, taking full account of the scarcity of accommodation. Rent control for different kinds of tenants is explained chapter 4.

Social housing

1.90   Social housing is 'low rent' accommodation provided by local authorities and other social landlords. Non-local authority social landlords were previously known as registered social landlords (RSLs). RSLs were not-for-profit housing providers, mainly housing associations and housing trusts registered and monitored by the Housing Corporation. The Housing and Regeneration Act 2008 abolished the Housing Corporation and set up the Tenants Services Authority (TSA). The term RSL was replaced by the term 'private registered provider of social housing'. However, on 1 April 2012, the TSA was itself abolished and replaced by a new regulator of social housing: the Regulation Committee of the Homes and Communities Agency (HCA). The Committee is the regulator for all social housing providers; both public sector providers (mainly local authorities) and private sector providers. In this book the term 'RSL' is sometimes used to refer to all not-for-profit PRPs as much of the legislation still refers to RSLs and the two terms, though not identical, are used interchangeably. See paras 2.95, 3.79 and 4.199 for more detail about the work of the HCA and the regulation of social housing.

1.91   Before 1980 the tenants of local authorities and housing associations did not enjoy statutory security of tenure. The tenants' rights were governed by the tenancy agreement which usually provided that the landlord would not take possession except in certain circumstances. These included failure to pay rent and other breaches of the tenancy agreement. Housing association tenants had rent control through the fair rent mechanism of the Rent Acts.

1.92   The Housing Act 1980 provided that the tenants of local authorities and housing associations would be 'secure tenants' with similar security of tenure to that of most private tenants. Secure tenants could only be evicted if one of the grounds for possession was proved. Additional statutory rights, including succession on the death of the tenant and the right to mutual exchange, were also granted to secure tenants. The secure tenants of local authorities also had a right to buy their home from the authority. The rights of secure tenants are now set out in the Housing Act 1985.

1.93   The Housing Act 1988 took new housing association tenancies outside the provisions of the Housing Act 1985. From 15 January 1989 they have been under the same regime as the tenancies created by private landlord.

1.94   Chapter 3 provides a summary of the different kinds of tenancy and the relevant statutes.

Security of tenure: levels of protection

1.95   As indicated above (para 1.3), there are two levels of security of tenure: substantive and procedural. Some residential occupiers have no security of tenure at all and can be evicted without a court order being obtained, although not forcibly.

1.96   The main statutes applying to residential tenancies are: the Rent Act 1977, the Housing Act 1985 and the Housing Act 1988. These Acts and the types of tenancies they govern are discussed in detail in chapter 2. Each Act sets out the conditions for a tenancy under which the tenant enjoys substantive security of tenure. In each Act the tenancy has a different name: under the Rent Act 1977, a 'protected' or 'statutory' tenancy (also known as a 'regulated' tenancy); under the Housing Act 1985, a 'secure' tenancy; and under the Housing Act 1988, an 'assured' tenancy (as distinct from an assured shorthold tenancy).

1.97   There are also tenancies under which a tenant has more limited rights such as the 'restricted contract' under the Rent Act 1977 and the assured shorthold tenancy under the Housing Act 1988, see paras 3.94 and 3.56. More recently, in the public sector, under anti-social behaviour provisions, the 'introductory' tenancy and the 'demoted' tenancy give tenants no substantive security of tenure but nevertheless impose some limits on the landlords' right to evict. These types of tenancy are explained in detail in chapter 3.

1.98   In addition to specific tenancies giving limited rights, some agreements simply fall outside the scope of statutory protection and the tenancy is referred to as, for example, a 'non-secure' tenancy or a 'contractual' tenancy.

1.99   A tenant who does not have substantive security of tenure may nevertheless have procedural security of tenure. The right to procedural security of tenure originates in the Protection from Eviction Act (PEA) 1977.[42] PEA 1977 s3 provides that certain occupiers can be evicted only by bringing possession proceedings in the County Court. The occupiers protected by section 3 are those who, when a tenancy or licence comes to an end, are lawfully residing in premises, where the letting was neither 'statutorily protected' nor 'excluded'. This means that a tenant who does not have substantive security of tenure but who is not an 'excluded occupier' will have the right to a court order before being evicted. PEA 1977 s3A lists the agreements that are excluded from the requirement to obtain a possession order. These are set out below (paras 1.100–1.120).

Excluded occupiers

1.100 Excluded occupiers can be lawfully evicted without the landlord obtaining a possession order. The following types of agreement are excluded:

- resident landlords with shared accommodation;
- licences granted to trespassers;
- holiday lets;
- rent-free accommodation;
- licensees of public sector hostel accommodation;
- accommodation provided to asylum-seekers.

Resident landlords with shared accommodation

Sharing accommodation with the landlord

1.101 A tenancy or licence is excluded if the following conditions are met:

- under the terms of the agreement the occupier shares any accommodation[43] with the landlord; and
- immediately before it was granted, and at the time when it comes to an end, the landlord was a resident landlord (ie he or she occupied the premises of which the shared accommodation forms part as his or her only or principal home).[44]

---

42 The provisions of PEA 1977 are described in detail in chapter 8.

43 'Accommodation' means any accommodation other than storage areas or means of access: PEA 1977 s3A(5).

44 See paras 4.15–4.22 for a detailed explanation of resident landlords.

Sharing accommodation with a resident landlord's family

1.102   A tenancy or licence is also excluded if the following conditions are met:

- under the terms of the agreement the occupier shares any accommodation with a member of the family of the landlord; and
- immediately before it was granted, and at the time when it comes to an end, the landlord was a resident landlord and the family member also occupied the premises as his or her only or principal home.

1.103   'Member of the family' is defined in HA 1985 s113. It includes the following: spouse, civil partner, co-habitees (those living together as spouse or civil partner), parent, grandparent, child, grandchild, brother, sister, uncle, aunt, nephew or niece. Relationships of marriage or civil partnerships are treated as relationships of blood, half-blood relationships are treated as whole blood relationships, stepchildren are treated as children and illegitimate children are treated as the legitimate children of the mother and reputed father.

1.104   The situation in para 1.102 is rare. It will arise only where there is a resident landlord in a different part of the building and a sharing of accommodation with a member of his or her family.

1.105   It should be noted that it is necessary for the landlord (and family member, if relevant) to occupy the premises at the beginning and at the end of the letting. It is not necessary that the landlord intends the occupation to be permanent or long-term and, where a landlord does not intend to continue to occupy after evicting the occupier, this does not change the status of the occupier.[45]

1.106   Before 1989 those who were lodging as part of the household of another were termed 'bare licensees' with no security of tenure. Since 1989 anyone sharing a person's home will necessarily be sharing accommodation with the landlord (or licensor) and will be an excluded occupier.

1.107   Advisers should always be aware of the possibility of agreements that are 'pretences', ie that do not reflect the reality of the situation. An agreement that states that the landlord resides in the premises and shares accommodation with the tenant will not make the occupier an excluded occupier if this is a pretence (see paras 1.45–1.47 above).

45   *Sumeghova v McMahon* [2002] EWCA Civ 1581, 24 October 2002.

Licences granted to trespassers

1.108 A tenancy or licence granted as a temporary expedient to someone who entered the premises as a trespasser is excluded.

1.109 This would be the case where a landlord discovers that an empty property is occupied by trespassers and agrees to allow the trespassers to stay on a temporary basis, paying a weekly fee, or rent, until the landlord needs possession.

Holiday lets

1.110 Where a tenancy or licence gives to a person the right to occupy premises for a holiday only, it is excluded. Again, advisers should be alert to the possibility that the agreement may be labelled a holiday let but that this may be a pretence (see paras 1.46–1.47).

Rent-free accommodation

1.111 A tenancy or licence granted otherwise than for money or money's worth is excluded.

1.112 The term 'money's worth' includes anything of value given or performed in return for the right or permission to occupy. A person who agrees to perform services, for example, cleaning, in return for 'rent-free' occupation would not be excluded, regardless of the value of the services.

Licensees of hostel accommodation

1.113 A licence is excluded if it grants the right of occupation in a public sector hostel.[46]

1.114 A 'hostel' is defined as

> ... a building in which is provided, for persons generally or for a class of persons:
> (a) residential accommodation otherwise than in separate and self-contained sets of premises, and
> (b) either board or facilities for the preparation of food adequate to the needs of those persons, or both.[47]

---

46 The public bodies that can grant excluded agreements are predominantly local authorities and charitable housing trusts and RSLs, plus a variety of development agencies. Other bodies can be specified by order made by the Secretary of State. To date orders have been made in favour of the London Hostels Association Ltd (1991 SI No 1943), the Shaftesbury Society (1999 SI No 1758) and Royal British Legion Industries Ltd (2003 SI No 2436).

47 HA 1985 s622.

1.115   To be excluded therefore the following conditions must be met:

- the landlord must be of a specified type;
- the agreement must be a licence agreement; and
- the premises must be a 'hostel' as defined above (para 1.114).

1.116   The mere fact that an accommodation provider describes the building as a 'hostel' or the agreement as a 'licence' does not determine the issue. An occupier may be able to establish that he or she is in reality a tenant, having been granted exclusive possession of a room. If this is the case, he or she will not be excluded. The key issue is whether the occupier or the landlord has control of the room (see paras 1.29–1.32 above). Many public sector hostels are for those with special needs and additional support may be provided. This does not of itself mean that the occupier will be excluded but makes it more likely that the landlord will genuinely retain overall control of an occupier's room.

Accommodation for asylum-seekers

1.117   Since April 2000 support and accommodation for asylum-seekers has been provided by the Home Office. Initially this was arranged by the National Asylum Support Service (NASS). Although NASS no longer exists the term 'NASS support' is still commonly used. Such accommodation is provided under the Immigration and Asylum Act (IAA) 1999 Part VI and any tenancy or licence granted under these provisions will be excluded.[48] See paras 20.194–20.199.

1.118   In fact, the providers of the accommodation are mostly private individuals and voluntary sector agencies under contracts with the Home Office. Regardless of the identity of the provider, occupiers will be excluded if the arrangements are made under IAA 1999 Part VI.

1.119   Some asylum-seekers are accommodated by local authority social services departments because they have community care needs or they are children. Such arrangements are not governed by IAA 1999 Part VI.

1.120   Asylum-seekers who are granted leave to remain in the UK cease to be asylum-seekers and become eligible for homeless assistance and social housing. Former asylum-seekers who are accommodated as homeless or allocated social housing have the same rights as others with the same type of tenancy or licence.

---

48 Accommodation provided under the Displaced Persons (Temporary Protection) Regulations 2005 SI No 1379 is also excluded.

Evicting excluded occupiers

1.121 Excluded occupiers can be evicted without a court order. The tenancy or licence must first be ended by giving either the notice specified in any agreement or, if there is no such agreement, reasonable notice.[49] After the notice has expired the occupier may be peaceably excluded from the premises, ie the locks may be changed. However, it is a criminal offence to use or threaten violence to gain entry to premises when there is someone inside who is opposed to entry.[50] This includes violence to property, so could cover breaking a window or door. See paras 8.38–8.41.

Reasonable notice

1.122 What is considered 'reasonable' depends on the circumstances. Because the minimum period of a notice to quit is 28 days, this is usually deemed to be sufficient notice. However, shorter notice may be reasonable if, for example, the occupier has not been in occupation for long or if he or she has behaved violently. Conversely, a longer period of notice may be appropriate in certain circumstances.

> In *Mehta v Royal Bank of Scotland*[51] it was held that an occupier of a room in a hotel was a contractual licensee and that the agreement between the parties was that the licence could be determined on 'reasonable notice'. Mr Mehta was bringing a claim for unlawful eviction and the court had to decide what reasonable notice would have been. Taking into account the references by the hotel owners to Mr Mehta being a 'long-term occupier' the court held that a period of four months would have constituted reasonable notice.

1.123 Where a person is excluded because he or she is sharing another person's home, enforcing a right to 'reasonable notice' may be impossible: a court will be reluctant to order someone to allow another person to occupy his or her home for a further period of time if the relationship has clearly broken down.

---

49 *Smith v Northside Developments Ltd* (1988) 55 P&CR 164.
50 Criminal Law Act 1977 s6.
51 (2000) 32 HLR 45, QBD.

Trespassers

1.124   The term 'trespasser' means any person in occupation of land unlawfully. It includes a person who was at one time lawfully occupying
but whose right to occupy has ended. This would include a subtenant
when his or her landlord's (the mesne tenant's) interest is brought
to an end or a joint tenant when the tenancy is ended by a tenant's
notice to quit.

1.125   Those who were occupying lawfully when a tenancy or licence is
brought to an end usually have procedural security of tenure (unless
they are excluded occupiers). However, trespassers who entered as
trespassers have no security of tenure. They can be evicted without a
court order, but not forcibly. Trespassing in residential premises is
now a criminal offence. This means that the trespasser can be arrested
by the police and that effectively they can be forcibly removed, see
para 8.46. Such trespassers are often referred to as 'squatters' but the
term squatter has no specific legal meaning.

Difficult situations

Hotels

1.126   A hotel is, according to the *Oxford English Dictionary*, 'an establishment providing accommodation and meals for travellers and
tourists'.

1.127   Some people 'live' in hotels. It is possible that accommodation
occupied within a hotel can constitute a letting of a 'dwelling' and
attract security of tenure.[52] More likely a hotel occupier will be a licensee with no more than procedural security of tenure, as in *Mehta v
Royal Bank of Scotland* at para 1.122 above). If the letting is for the
purpose of a holiday only, the occupier will be excluded from any
sort of protection (see para 1.100 above). So, depending on the circumstances surrounding the 'letting' an occupier of hotel accommodation could be a tenant with long-term rights, a licensee with
procedural rights only or an excluded occupier.

---

52   See *Uratemps Ventures Ltd v Collins* [2001] UKHL 43, 11 October 2001,
discussed at para 3.14.

'Bed and breakfast' establishments

1.128 Many hotels provide accommodation on a 'bed and breakfast' basis. Those occupying such accommodation for a holiday are excluded occupiers. Some owners of bed and breakfast establishments have arrangements with local authorities to provide emergency accommodation for those to whom the authority has a statutory accommodation duty. Such a duty may be owed by the homeless persons department or the social services department. Where the accommodation is provided on an emergency basis the occupier will have neither substantive or procedural security of tenure.[53]

1.129 Because it is possible to evict a person placed in bed and breakfast accommodation by a local authority without a court order, some accommodation providers designate all accommodation, including self-contained dwellings, 'bed and breakfast'. However, as is the case when identifying tenancies and licences, what determines the nature of a letting is the factual situation, not the label applied. Advisers should be alert to the possibility that describing accommodation as 'bed and breakfast' may be a pretence, and that occupiers may have a tenancy. While the tenancy is unlikely to attract substantive security of tenure, the occupier may have the right not to be evicted without a court order.

Hostels

1.130 Licensees in hostels run by specified public bodies are excluded occupiers. However, this only applies to licensees and not tenants. A person who has exclusive possession of a room in a hostel will usually be a tenant. If the hostel is run by an RSL, he or she will be an assured shorthold tenant (see para 3.56). If the hostel is run by a local authority he or she will be a secure tenant only if the premises let are self-contained, ie include cooking facilities (see paras 3.106–3.108).

1.131 If the hostel is not run by one of the specified bodies or does not satisfy the definition of 'hostel', as explained above (para 1.114), a licensee will have procedural security of tenure.

---

53 In *Mohammed v Manek and Kensington & Chelsea RLBC* (1995) 27 HLR 439 the Court of Appeal held that those placed in bed and breakfast accommodation pending a decision on a homeless application did not enjoy any procedural security of tenure. In fact, the Supreme Court has since confirmed that all occupiers accommodated on licences pending homeless decisions fall outside the protection of PEA 1977 s3: *R (ZH and CN) v Newham LBC and Lewisham LBC* [2014] UKSC 62, 12 November 2014. See para 8.18.

Mixed business and residential use

1.132   The Landlord and Tenant Act (LTA) 1954 Part II applies to 'any tenancy where the property comprised in the tenancy is or includes premises which are occupied by the tenant and are so occupied for the purposes of a business carried on by him or for those and other purposes'.[54]

1.133   If LTA 1954 Part II applies to a tenancy the tenant cannot be a protected or statutory tenant under the Rent Act 1977 and cannot be secure or assured. This is the case even if the premises include residential accommodation. However, the business use must be significant; if it is incidental to the use of the premises as a home, the tenant will not be excluded from residential security.

Is business use significant or incidental?

1.134   This is a question of fact to be determined by a court if at issue. The following two cases were heard at the same time by the Court of Appeal:[55]

> In *Cheryl Investments Ltd v Saldanha* a businessman rented residential premises but almost immediately began to use them for the purposes of his business. The business had no other premises, stationery was printed and a business telephone and other office equipment were installed at the premises. The court held that the tenancy was governed by the LTA 1954 Part II and not the Rent Act 1977.
>
> A different conclusion was reached in *Royal Life Saving Society v Page* in which a doctor took a lease of residential premises and, with the consent of the landlord, installed a consulting room where he occasionally saw patients. His principal practice and consulting rooms were elsewhere. The court held that the degree of business user was insufficient for the LTA 1954 to apply as the letting was residential.

1.135   Although a change of use may bring the tenancy within the Landlord and Tenant Act (LTA) 1954, spare-time activities, even for financial reward, do not necessarily change the character of the user from residential to business.

54   LTA 1954 s23(1).
55   [1978] 1 WLR 1329, CA.

In *Gurton v Parrot*[56] the main purpose of the tenant's occupation was to reside in the premises as his home and it was found that the running of a kennel business from the premises was incidental to that purpose.

Occupying for the purpose of a business

1.136 The above cases concerned residential premises also used for business purposes. The courts examined whether the business use was significant or incidental to the residential use. Where the stated purpose of a lease is for business use, the LTA 1954 will apply, even if the premises also include residential accommodation.

In *Broadway Investments Hackney Ltd v Grant*[57] the lease stated that the permitted use for the ground floor was for sale and catering for fish and the upper part was for residential purposes only. The tenant was obliged to keep the premises open as a shop throughout the year during business hours. Initially it had not been possible to conduct business because of the need for substantial works to the shop premises. In a claim for possession, the tenant argued therefore that the purpose of the letting had been residential.

The Court of Appeal held that, even if that had been the case initially, by the time the issue came to be determined the tenant was using the premises for the purpose of a business in accordance with the terms of the lease. The tenancy was governed by the LTA 1954.

1.137 However, the fact that tenants of mixed business and residential premises may not enjoy long-term security does not mean that they can be evicted without a court order.

In *Patel v Pirabakaran*[58] the Court of Appeal held that premises, including both business and residential premises, were 'let as a dwelling' for the purpose of the Protection from Eviction Act 1977. The landlord was required to obtain a possession order to evict the tenants lawfully.

56 (1990) 23 HLR 418, CA.
57 [2006] EWCA Civ 1709, 20 December 2006.
58 [2006] EWCA Civ 685, 26 May 2006.

Trusts and the law of equity

Trusts

1.138   A trust exists where one person holds property for the benefit of another person. The person who holds the property is the trustee and the person for whom the property is held is the beneficiary. Trusts are used for a variety of purposes, for example when a person wants to leave or transfer property for the benefit of a child or wishes to control the way property is used by another person. In such a case an express trust may be created, the terms of the trust and the powers of the trustees being set out in a deed of trust.

1.139   In addition to express trusts, certain arrangements result in the creation of a trust by implication of law. For example, where two people purchase property in the sole name of one but contribute equally to the purchase price, intending both parties to benefit equally, a trust is created, despite the absence of an express deed of trust. While the 'legal' ownership of the property is in the name of one party, the law implies a trust whereby the legal owner holds the property on trust for the benefit of both parties. The parties are joint 'equitable' owners: see paras 12.96–12.103.

1.140   Furthermore, under English law, jointly owned property is always owned under a 'trust of land'. The joint owners own the legal interest for the benefit of themselves. Such trusts are now governed by the Trusts of Land and Appointment of Trustees Act (TLATA) 1996. The fact that jointly held property is held by way of a trust enables one party to apply to a court for an order for sale. The presumption is that if one trustee no longer wants the property to remain in joint ownership the property should be sold and the 'equity' divided between the parties.

1.141   The matters that must be considered by the court when considering an application for sale are set out in TLATA 1996 s15 and are:

- the intentions of those who created the trust;
- the purposes for which the property is held;
- the welfare of any child who lives in the property or might reasonably be expected to;
- the interests of any secured creditor; and
- the circumstances and wishes of each of the beneficiaries who are entitled to occupy the property.

The law of equity

Implied trusts

1.142 Trusts are a creation of the 'law of equity'. The law of equity is a system of rules and principles which developed alongside the common law. It evolved through the decisions of the Court of Chancery (originally a court of equity) to remedy some of the defects of the common law.

1.143   Other equitable principles have developed so as to achieve fairness between parties. For example, where parties intend to create a certain legal relationship but fail to take the correct legal steps or there is some obstacle to the legal relationship intended, the law of equity may intervene to ensure a fair (equitable) outcome. An example is where a tenancy is granted to a minor. A minor cannot hold a legal tenancy but if a person purports to grant a tenancy to a minor the law of equity ensures a fair result by providing that the tenancy will be held on trust for the minor until he or she becomes an adult. The doctrine of 'implied' trusts is closely linked to the doctrine of 'estoppel': a party is prevented ('estopped') from denying his or her acts or representations where this would be unfair to the other party.

> In *Alexander-David v Hammersmith & Fulham LBC*[59] the Court of Appeal considered the effect of a local authority granting a tenancy to a 16-year-old child. The local authority used its standard form for granting a non-secure tenancy to a homeless applicant. Alleging breaches of the tenancy agreement, the authority served notice to quit to end the tenancy and a possession order was obtained.
>
>   The Court of Appeal held that the TLATA 1996 applied. This provides that where 'a person purports to convey a legal estate in land to a minor ... the conveyance – (a) is not effective to pass the legal estate, but (b) operates as a declaration that the land is held in trust for the minor ...'.[60] This meant that the legal tenancy was held on trust by the local authority; the service of the notice on the minor was a breach of trust; and, moreover, the notice was ineffective as the tenancy was held not by the minor but by the local authority as trustee.

59 [2009] EWCA Civ 258, 1 April 2009. The court suggested that local authorities should instead grant licences to minors, ensuring that they did not enjoy exclusive possession by including terms giving social workers a right to inspect the premises as part of their general duty to provide support.

60 TLATA 1996 Sch 1 para 1(1).

Estoppel

1.144 The following are examples of the operation of estoppel in landlord and tenant law:

- *Estoppel by conduct* (known as *'estoppel in pais'*) means that a tenant who has accepted a lease cannot dispute the landlord's title.
- *Promissory estoppel* refers to a situation in which a person makes unequivocal representations to another (whether by words or conduct), on which the other person relies to his or her detriment. The 'promissor' may be estopped from denying the representations. A tenant may raise such an argument against a landlord who represents that he or she will accept less than the full contractual rent but subsequently seeks possession on the ground of rent arrears.
- *Proprietary estoppel* prevents a person from denying another person's rights in property. An example would be where a person relies on another person's representations (whether by words or conduct) that he or she will have some interest in property. Where that person, relying on the representations, has spent money on the property he or she may gain an equitable interest in it, see paras 12.96–12.104.

The court's discretion

1.145 One central feature of the law of equity is that the court's remedies are discretionary. A person who relies on equity must come to the court with 'clean hands', which means that someone who has not behaved well or honestly in the transaction may be refused relief.

1.146 At one time claims based on the law of equity had to be brought in the Court of Chancery but an equitable claim can now be brought in any civil court.

APPENDIX

Tenant's notice to quit

NOTICE TO QUIT

To: [LANDLORD'S NAME AND ADDRESS]

I, [TENANT'S NAME], of [TENANT'S ADDRESS]

Give you Notice that I intend to quit and to deliver possession of the premises at [ADDRESS OF THE PREMISES]

On [INSERT DATE – should be the last or the first day of a period of the tenancy] or on the day on which a complete period of my tenancy expires next after the end of four weeks from the service of this notice.

Date:

Signed: [by tenant]

CHAPTER 2

Public law and housing

continued

Key points

- The Human Rights Act 1998 means that rights under the European Convention on Human Rights can be enforced in UK courts.
- There is a difference between 'public law' and 'private law'. Public law is about decision-making by public bodies. Private law is about disputes between individual legal persons.
- A public body, such as a local authority, is generally governed by public law when acting in its capacity as a public body (eg in relation to homeless applications) and by private law when acting in a private capacity (eg when carrying out repairs as a landlord).
- Most challenges to 'public law' decisions and duties are brought by way of judicial review.
- However, it is now possible to raise public law arguments, including under the Human Rights Act, in a defence to a claim for possession.
- Also, in homelessness cases although the legal challenge is in the County Court, this operates like judicial review.
- Most non-local authority social landlords are classed as public bodies and be bound by the Human Rights Act 1998 and subject to judicial review.
- Another way of challenging 'public law' decisions by local authorities and other social landlords is by making a formal complaint and, if not resolved, making an Ombudsman complaint.
- Public law is more about the way decisions are made rather than the merits of decisions.
- Important information about a public body's decision-making process can be obtained under the Data Protection Act 1998 and the Freedom of Information Act 2000.

Public law and private law

2.1   Housing law involves both private law and public law. Although the distinction between private and public law is becoming less clear, broadly speaking, private law is about the legal relationship between private individuals, including landlord and tenant, while public law governs the exercise of public functions by public bodies. A local authority is a public body but not all of its activities are public functions. For example, a local authority may enter into an employment contract or a tenancy agreement and when it does so it has the same rights and obligations as private individuals who are employers and landlords. Nevertheless, even in these spheres a local authority may be subject to additional obligations as a public body. For example, it must act in accordance with the Human Rights Act 1998 and under the Equality Act 2010 it must have due regard to the need to combat discrimination and promote equality of opportunity for protected groups.

2.2   In recent years 'housing law' has become more about public law and less about private law. Several factors have contributed to this, including the erosion of the rights of private tenants, an increase in the number of public sector tenants whose rights depend on the exercise of administrative discretion and, not least, the incorporation of the European Convention on Human Rights (ECHR) into domestic law by the Human Rights Act 1998.

2.3   Chapters 13 to 17 deal in detail with local authorities' duties in relation to homelessness and the allocation of accommodation. Such functions have always been public law functions and public law principles apply. Similarly, chapters 18 to 20 describe social services functions, again functions that clearly fall within the realm of public law. However, in addition to these areas of housing law, public law is increasingly relevant to activities that would previously have been identified as private law functions, most particularly those exercised by local authorities as landlords, including decisions to evict tenants. The application of public law and the Human Rights Act 1998 to possession claims is examined in chapters 6 and 7. This chapter seeks to summarise other key public law duties relevant in housing cases. This chapter examines the following:

- public law principles and judicial review;
- the effect of the Human Rights Act 1998;
- the effect of the Equality Act 2010;
- complaints and non-legal regulation of social landlords;
- rights of access to information held by public bodies and landlords.

Judicial review and public law principles

2.4   Judicial review means a claim to review the lawfulness of:

- an enactment; or
- a decision, action or failure to act in relation to the exercise of a public function.[1]

1   Civil Procedure Rules (CPR) 54.1(2)(a).

2.5 It is the way the courts exercise scrutiny over 'administrative action'. Claims are brought in the Administrative Court, a branch of the High Court. Claims may only be brought against bodies exercising public functions, including the government and local authorities. Many decisions relating to housing made by local authorities are challenged by judicial review.[2]

2.6 In judicial review the courts are exercising a supervisory function. A claim for judicial review is not an appeal or a challenge to the merits of a decision. The fundamental principle is that Parliament has given to certain bodies the power to make decisions and the court will intervene only if that body acts unlawfully.

2.7 Traditionally, public law disputes were dealt with in the Administrative Court by way of judicial review and the court's function was limited to considering the process of decision-making and did not extend to deciding factual disputes. However, the County Court now exercises judicial review functions in relation to homeless appeals[3] and can consider public law and proportionality defences to claims for possession, see paras 7.128–7.132. Furthermore, judicial review can encompass primary fact-finding (see *R (A) v Croydon LBC*,[4] below at para 2.57).

Grounds for judicial review

2.8 In its scrutiny of administrative decision-making, judicial review focuses on the process rather than the substance of decision-making.

2.9 Below is a summary of the grounds for judicial review, ie the reasons a decision, action or failure to act may be unlawful.

2.10 The House of Lords has suggested that the various grounds can be classified under three heads:[5]

- illegality;
- irrationality; and
- procedural impropriety/unfairness.[6]

---

2 See paras 15.13–15.14 and 17.62.
3 *Nipa Begum v Tower Hamlets LBC* (1999) 32 HLR 445, CA, see para 14.28.
4 [2009] UKSC 8, 17 February 2010.
5 *Council of Civil Service Unions v Minister for the Civil Service* [1985] 1 AC 374, HL (the 'CCSU' case).
6 In practice, the various 'grounds' of challenge tend to overlap and other forms of classification may be more appropriate for practitioners but this is a useful way of grouping certain types of challenge.

Illegality

2.11   This could include the following:

- a decision based on an incorrect interpretation of the law or a mistake of fact;
- a decision made when relevant matters have been ignored, or irrelevant matters taken into account;
- a decision taken by a body not authorised to make the decision, for example a body exceeding its powers or a decision unlawfully delegated to another person or body;
- fettering discretion, ie a decision taken in accordance with a rigid policy rather than being a true exercise of a discretion.

Examples

2.12   Reported cases about homelessness include many examples of decisions based on an incorrect understanding of the law or taken without regard to relevant matters. Examples can be found at paras 14.60–14.70 in relation to priority need decisions where parents have shared care. In some cases decisions were quashed because the authority had applied an incorrect test. But cases on similar facts were upheld where the authority had applied the correct test and decided, on the facts, that the children did not live with the applicant, or that, as a matter of judgment, it was not reasonable to expect the children to live with the applicant.

2.13   In relation to unlawful delegation, priority need decisions have been found to be flawed because a medical adviser rather than the housing authority effectively made the decision. The authority may take advice from a medical adviser but may not delegate the ultimate decision to the medical adviser.

2.14   The question of fettering discretion has often arisen in cases concerning the allocation of accommodation. In *R v Westminster CC ex p Nadhum Hussain*[7] a policy to suspend applicants from the waiting list for two years for unreasonably refusing an offer was challenged. The policy did not, in most cases, allow for exceptions, and was held to be an unreasonable fetter on the discretion of the authority.

---

7   (1998) 31 HLR 645, see para 17.73 below.

Irrationality

2.15 This is often referred to as '*Wednesbury* unreasonableness' after the case in which the concept was elaborated.[8] It is also referred to as 'perversity' and has been said to apply to 'a decision which is so outrageous in its defiance of logic or of accepted moral standards that no sensible person who had applied his mind to the question to be decided could have arrived at it'.[9]

2.16 However, in some recent cases the courts have held that the 'scope' of *Wednesbury* unreasonableness is too narrow and that the court's power to intervene should not be limited to such extreme degrees of unreasonable decision-making. When applying the Human Rights Act 1998 the courts are required to apply the test of proportionality, see paras 7.146–7.156 below. The proportionality test is applied more flexibility, depending on the nature of the rights at issue. The House of Lords has held that 'The depth of judicial review and the deference due to administrative discretion vary with the subject matter'.[10] So, in cases where fundamental rights are at issue the courts will be more willing to intervene in administrative decision-making and will apply a greater degree of scrutiny.

2.17 It is, however, rare that a challenge to an administrative decision succeeds on the ground of irrationality alone. More commonly, where a decision appears to be unreasonable it will also be found to be unlawful for other reasons, for example, failing to take account of relevant matters or to give adequate reasons for the decision. A recent example is the case of *R (IA) v Westminster CC*,[11] summarised in detail at para 13.35. The judge held that it was perverse for the authority to decide, on the basis of the evidence provided, that it did not have reason to believe the applicant may be in priority need. However, there were many other procedural flaws in the process and the decision was not on 'perversity' alone.

Procedural impropriety

2.18 This includes a failure to act in accordance with specific procedural rules as well as a failure to observe the basic rules of natural justice or fairness.

8 *Associated Provincial Picture Houses Ltd v Wednesbury Corporation* [1948] 1 KB 223, CA.
9 Lord Diplock in the CCSU case (see para 2.10 above) [1985] 1 AC 374, HL at 410G.
10 *R (Daly) v Secretary of State for the Home Department* [2001] UKHL 26.
11 [2013] EWHC 1273, 20 May 2013.

2.19   An example of the former would be an authority that fails to follow the statutory procedure when carrying out a homeless review (see paras 15.33–15.37).

2.20   The term 'rules of natural justice' refers to the general duty to act fairly. The extent of this duty varies according to the nature of the decision-making but two principles are usually held to be essential:

- the right to an unbiased decision-maker; and
- the right to be informed of and to comment on adverse information.

2.21   A decision taken in bad faith would clearly be unlawful as would a decision taken by an officer who was 'biased'. However, such challenges are rare and 'bias' usually refers to the existence of a personal interest in the decision rather than the general perception, sometimes alleged by clients, that the particular officer is biased or has approached the decision with a closed mind. In *Feld v Barnet LBC, Ali Pour v Westminster CC*,[12] the Court of Appeal rejected allegations of bias or lack of impartiality where the same reviewing officer conducted a second review following the quashing of the first review decision. Similarly, the court rejected alleged bias where the officer who made a negative homeless decision was also responsible for making the decision on whether interim accommodation should be provided pending a review of that decision.[13]

2.22   The duty to disclose adverse information often arises in the context of homelessness decision-making. Before making a decision an authority must offer an applicant the opportunity to comment on adverse information[14] and if the authority is unable to disclose the information it should be disregarded.[15]

Legitimate expectation

2.23   Legitimate expectation is an aspect of the duty of fairness. 'Where a public authority has made a promise or adopted a practice which represents how it proposes to act in a given area, the law will require the promise or practice to be honoured unless there is good reason not to do so.'[16] This is known as 'legitimate expectation'.

---

12 [2004] EWCA Civ 1307, 18 October 2004.
13 *Abdi v Lambeth LBC* [2007] EWHC 1565, 26 June 2007.
14 *R v Tower Hamlets LBC ex p Rouf* (1989) 21 HLR 294.
15 *R v Poole BC ex p Cooper* (1994) 27 HLR 605, QBD.
16 See *R (Nardarajah and Abdi) v Secretary of State for the Home Department* [2005] EWCA Civ 1363, 22 November 2005, Laws LJ at [68].

In the recent case of *R (Alansi) v London Borough of Newham*[17] the court summarised the principles applying in cases of legitimate expectation. The claimant sought to challenge the local authority's decision to change its allocation policy in a way that affected her priority. She had agreed to move from temporary homeless accommodation into the private sector on the basis that her priority for an allocation would not be affected. The council's new policy meant that she was no longer in a priority category and she sought to challenge the policy on the basis that the council's representation to her that her priority would not change created a legitimate expectation that her priority should remain the same. The court dismissed her claim summarising the law of legitimate expectation as follows:[18]

i) A claim to a substantive right based on a promise or assurance by a public authority requires the authority's statement to be clear, unambiguous and unqualified;

ii) The Court must ascertain the meaning the statements would reasonably convey to that person in light of all the background knowledge which the person had in the situation he or she was in at the time the statements were made;

iii) When considering a claim to a substantive right the court must consider whether the public authority has struck the correct balance between the public interest and the interests of the person relying on the promise or representation – it is not limited to a *Wednesbury* irrationality test.

iv) The test is whether frustrating the claimant's expectation is so unfair that to take a new and different course will amount to an abuse of power. Once the expectation has been established the court must weigh the requirements of fairness against any overriding interest relied on for the change of policy. Both procedural and substantive unfairness may be taken into account when applying this test.

v) Reliance and detriment are not essential pre-requisites to a finding of unlawful abuse of power but their presence or absence may be taken into account in deciding where the balance of fairness lies and whether the authority has acted unlawfully.

vi) The court must give due weight to the proper role of public authorities as agents of change and as having responsibility

---

17 [2013] EWHC 3722, 27 November 2013. The decision was upheld by the Court of Appeal [2014] EWCA Civ 786, 12 May 2014.

18 Stuart Smith J at [35]

for policies that are in the public interest even though they may conflict with the interest of private individuals, including those to whom assurances have been given.

Furthermore, in relation to allocations, being given priority is no guarantee of being awarded permanent accommodation either at all or within any particular timescale.

The judge found that the claimant had been given an unambiguous and unqualified assurance on which she had relied. She had suffered the detriment of being removed from the Priority Home Seeker band, but balanced against that was the fact that she had been occupying accommodation of a better standard by moving into the private sector. Furthermore, if she became homeless in the future she would have the right to make a new homeless application.

The judge found that the local authority had succeeded in establishing that their conduct was not unreasonable: 'it would be wrong to characterise the [council's] conduct as being an unlawful abuse of power. It is better characterised as a proportionate response to a pressing and widespread social problem which struck a proper balance between the competing claims of many different interests'.[19]

Reasons

2.24   A decision may be challenged on the ground that the decision-maker has failed to explain adequately the reasons for the decision. In homelessness decision-making there is a statutory duty to give reasons for any adverse decision.[20] Such reasons must be 'proper, adequate and intelligible and enable the person to know why they have won or lost'.[21]

2.25   There is no general duty to give reasons for administrative decisions. However, even where there is no express duty to give reasons, in some circumstances a particular decision may call for an explanation, for example where a decision-maker is rejecting an expert opinion or an account of events given by the person concerned. In *R v Westminster CC ex p Nadhum Hussain*, a further reason for

---

19 Stuart Smith J at [51].
20 Housing Act (HA) 1996 s184(3). There are also specific decisions made in relation to allocations which require reasons to be given. See chapter 17.
21 *R v Brent LBC ex p Baruwa* (1997) 29 HLR 915, CA at 920.

quashing the decision was the authority's failure to offer any reasons for not following the recommendation of its social services department (see para 17.73). While it was open to the authority not to follow the recommendation, the decision was unlawful because the assessment appeared to have been ignored completely.

Judicial review remedies

2.26 The court can make one of the following orders:
- a mandatory order – requiring a body to carry out some act;
- a prohibiting order – prohibiting a body from carrying out some act;
- a quashing order – an order cancelling a decision.

2.27 In addition, the court may grant an injunction to restrain a person from acting in any office in which he or she is not entitled to act.

2.28 Damages can also be awarded but a claim for judicial review cannot be based on a claim for damages alone.

2.29 The most common order is a quashing order. This means that the body must make a new decision since the original decision no longer stands. This reflects the court's role: not to substitute its own finding but to review the lawfulness of the decision.

Which bodies can be challenged by judicial review?

2.30 Local authorities are clearly public bodies and may be challenged by a claim for judicial review when making public law decisions.

2.31 Most registered providers of social housing will also be public bodies for the purposes of judicial review, depending on the nature of the provider and the particular decision under challenge, see *R (Weaver) v London & Quadrant Housing Trust*,[22] at para 2.72 below.[23]

Who may bring a claim for judicial review?

2.32 The claimant must have 'sufficient interest' in the matter to which the application relates. Usually this will mean the person directly affected by the decision. However, it is possible for campaigning organisations to bring claims or to intervene in claims already before

22 [2009] EWCA Civ 587, 18 June 2009.
23 The tests for whether a body is subject to judicial review and whether it is bound by the Human Rights Act 1998 are not identical but they are very closely linked.

the court, particularly where they have access to information useful to the court or represent a particular interest group.[24]

Procedure

2.33   In all but the most urgent cases a pre-action protocol letter must be sent before the claim is issued, see appendix 2 to chapter 18.

2.34   Unless an urgent order is sought (see 2.36 below), the first step is applying for permission to bring the claim. After issuing the permission application, the court papers must be served on the respondent. The respondent must file an acknowledgement of service within 21 days. This indicates whether the claim is contested and provides summary grounds of defence. In urgent cases these time limits can be shortened.

2.35   The permission application is considered by a single judge, without a hearing (a 'paper application'). If permission is refused, an application may be made for reconsideration at a hearing. If permission is again refused the applicant may appeal to the Court of Appeal.

2.36   In urgent cases the claimant may be seeking 'interim relief', eg an order that emergency accommodation is provided until the claim is heard. If so, a certificate of urgency must be completed and the papers will be referred to a judge for urgent consideration within a specified period. If necessary a judge can consider an application for an injunction by telephone before the claim has been issued. In such an application the applicant must give full and frank disclosure. See para 16.9 for a summary of the case of *R (F) v Westminster CC*[25] where this was not done and the court ordered the lawyers to show cause why a wasted costs order should not be made against them.

Time limits

2.37   A claim must be brought promptly, and, in any event, within three months of the date when grounds first arose.[26] This is usually the date of the decision that is being challenged.

2.38   The court has the power to extend the time limit where there is good reason to do so. The parties cannot extend the time limit by agreement.

---

24   At the time of writing the government is seeking to introduce measures to restrict interventions and claims being brought by 'pressure groups.'
25   [2012] EWCH 1357 (Admin), 21 March 2012.
26   CPR 54.5(1).

Legal aid

2.39 Subject to a means and merits test, public funding remains available for judicial review proceedings. However, since April 2014 the payment of the fees to a legally aided claimant's legal representative is conditional on permission being granted, subject to a discretion by the Legal Aid Agency, see chapter 22.

Human Rights Act 1998

Effect of the Human Rights Act 1998

2.40 The Human Rights Act (HRA) 1998 came into force on 2 October 2000. It incorporated into UK law most of the rights contained in the European Convention on Human Rights (ECHR or 'the Convention'). The Convention is an international treaty of the Council of Europe, ratified by the UK in 1951. The human rights protected by the ECHR are referred to as 'Convention rights' and the Human Rights Act 1998 means that these rights can be enforced in UK courts. Previously, Convention rights could only be enforced by application to the European Court of Human Rights (ECtHR) in Strasbourg.

Enforcement of Convention rights in UK courts

2.41 The Human Rights Act 1998:

- lists the Convention rights which are made part of UK law;
- makes it unlawful for any 'public authority' to act in a way that is incompatible with Convention rights;
- enables a person alleging a breach of a Convention right to bring a claim in the UK courts against the relevant public authority; and
- allows such a person to claim compensation for a breach of Convention rights.

UK law must be compatible with the Convention

2.42 The Human Rights Act 1998 provides that:

- the courts are public authorities and must not act in a way that is incompatible with Convention rights;
- UK courts and tribunals must take account of decisions made by the ECtHR when making decisions about Convention rights;

- legislation must be interpreted in a way that is compatible with Conventions rights 'so far as it is possible to do so';[27] and
- if this is not possible the higher courts can make 'declarations of incompatibility', stating that legislation is not compatible with Convention rights.[28]

Convention rights that are part of UK law

2.43   The following Convention rights are now part of UK law:[29]

- article 2: the right to life
- article 3: the prohibition on torture and inhuman or degrading treatment or punishment
- article 4: the prohibition on slavery and forced labour
- article 5: the right to liberty and security
- article 6: the right to a fair trial
- article 7: protection from punishment for acts that were not offences at the time they were committed
- article 8: the right to respect for private and family life, home and correspondence
- article 9: freedom of thought, conscience and religion
- article 10: freedom of expression
- article 11: freedom of assembly and association
- article 12: the right to marry and found a family
- article 14: the prohibition of discrimination in relation to the enforcement of Convention rights.

Under Protocol 1 to the Convention:

- article 1: the right to property
- article 2: the right to education
- article 3: the right to free and fair elections.

Under Protocol 13 to the Convention:

- article 1: abolition of the death penalty and prohibition on condemnation to death.

---

27   HRA 1998 s3(1).
28   HRA 1998 s4(2).
29   Articles 1 and 13 of the Convention have not been incorporated. Article 1 is an obligation on the state to ensure that everyone within its jurisdiction has his or her rights safeguarded and article 13 is an obligation to ensure that there is a way of enforcing Convention rights in the state's own courts or institutions. The reason these articles have not been incorporated is that the very purpose of the HRA 1998 is to secure those rights.

How Convention rights work

Absolute and qualified rights

2.44 Some Convention rights are 'absolute' and others 'qualified'. What this means is that, in relation to qualified rights, individual rights are balanced against collective rights. The state may be justified in restricting the exercise of qualified rights. Article 3 is an absolute right: there can be no justification for subjecting a person to torture, inhuman or degrading treatment. Article 8 is a qualified right: it is the right to 'respect' for private and family life, home and correspondence. The state may interfere with article 8 rights if necessary in certain circumstances.

Derogation and reservation

2.45 A state may enter a 'reservation' about particular Convention rights and may, in times of war or public emergency 'derogate' from the Convention. It can do this only if the situation 'strictly requires' the suspension of the rights. Reservation and derogation are not possible in relation to absolute rights.

Convention rights and housing cases

2.46 The Convention rights most relevant to housing law are articles 6, 8, 14 and article 1 of the 1st Protocol. In addition, article 3 has been used to challenge the government's policy of refusing housing and subsistence to asylum-seekers and failed asylum-seekers, see para 2.51 and chapter 20 below.

2.47 These Convention rights are examined below (paras 2.49–2.67) with reference to case-law.

Article 3

2.48 Article 3 provides:

> No one shall be subjected to torture or to inhuman or degrading treatment or punishment.

2.49 Torture is deliberate inhuman treatment which causes very serious suffering.[30] Inhuman treatment or punishment is less severe than torture and need not be deliberately inflicted. The threat of torture

---

30 *Selmouni v France*, ECtHR AG0000970, 28 July 1999.

and very poor conditions of detention may amount to inhuman treatment. Degrading treatment is that which 'grossly humiliates' or 'debases' the victim. To establish a breach of article 3 the treatment must reach a minimum level of severity.[31]

> In *Pretty v UK*[32] the ECtHR considered the types of 'treatment' that fell within the scope of article 3 holding that it is:
>
> ... ill-treatment that attains a minimum level of severity and involves actual bodily injury or intense physical or mental suffering. Where treatment humiliates or debases an individual showing a lack of respect for, or diminishing, his or her human dignity or arouses feelings of fear, anguish or inferiority capable of breaking an individual's moral and physical resistance, it may be characterised as degrading and also fall within the prohibition of article 3.[33]

Treatment

2.50   As a general rule the withholding of a service, such as benefits or housing, does not amount to 'treatment'. However, if it is part of a system under which people are prevented from fending for themselves it may amount to treatment that constitutes a breach of article 3.

> *R (Limbuela) and others v Secretary of State for the Home Department*[34] concerned the Nationality, Immigration and Asylum Act (NIAA) 2002 s55. This applies to asylum-seekers who, in the opinion of the Home Office, did not make their claim for asylum as soon as reasonably practical. Section 55 prevents accommodation or support being provided pending consideration of the asylum claim. This is subject to the proviso that support should be provided if necessary to avoid a breach of Convention rights. Asylum-seekers cannot work and are ineligible for benefits or homeless assistance.
>
> The House of Lords determined that although the withdrawal of support does not of itself amount to treatment that is a breach of article 3, it will do so 'once the margin is crossed between destitution

---

31 *Ireland v UK* (1979–80) 2 EHRR 25 at para 162, 18 January 1978.
32 ECtHR (2346/02), 26 April 2002.
33 At [52].
34 [2005] UKHL 66, 3 November 2005.

[as defined in the asylum support legislation] and the condition that results from inhuman or degrading treatment'.[35]

The fact that the asylum support system prohibited asylum-seekers from working and claiming mainstream benefits meant that the provision did not just amount to the refusal of a service but was 'treatment' under article 3.

The question was whether the degree of suffering endured, or about to be endured imminently, reached the severity prohibited by article 3. The threshold is high but the court held that to place asylum-seekers in a situation of having to endure the indefinite prospect of being without shelter or money for food and clothing was both inhuman and degrading.

2.51   In contrast, in *Bernard v Enfield LBC*[36] the claimant failed to establish a breach of article 3 but succeeded in establishing a breach of article 8 where a local authority had failed to provide suitable disability-adapted accommodation after accepting a duty to do so.

Article 6

2.52   Article 6(1) provides:

> In the determination of his civil rights and obligations or of any criminal charge against him, everyone is entitled to a fair and public hearing within a reasonable time by an independent and impartial tribunal established by law.

Internal reviews

2.53   There are many cases in which civil rights are determined outside of a court or tribunal. Since 1996 in many areas of housing rights the courts' role has diminished. Instead, for many decisions there is a right to request an internal review by the local housing authority. This applies to most decisions about homelessness and the allocation of housing. Similarly, introductory, demoted and flexible tenants may challenge decisions to seek possession by requesting an internal review. The same right to an internal review applies to the new absolute anti-social behaviour possession ground. See paras 6.95–6.101.

2.54   In relation to a decision about accommodation offered to a homeless applicant, the House of Lords held that the availability of a

---

35 Lord Hope at [57].
36 [2002] EWHC 2282 (Admin), 25 October 2002. See para 18.24.

procedure akin to judicial review to challenge the lawfulness and/or fairness of the review means that the process, considered as a whole, complies with article 6:

In *Runa Begum v Tower Hamlets LBC*[37] the House of Lords considered a challenge to a decision about the suitability of accommodation offered under HA 1996 Part VII. The applicant argued that her right to an internal review did not satisfy the article 6(1) requirement of an independent and impartial tribunal.

The House of Lords held that the reviewing officer was not an independent tribunal but that it was the composite procedure for this kind of administrative decision-making that must be considered. The fact that an appeal lay to the county court, albeit on a point of law only, meant that the requirements of article 6 were satisfied. The scope of conventional judicial review (which is the basis of the county court's jurisdiction in homelessness appeals) was sufficient to comply. It was not necessary for there to be independent fact finding or a full appeal. The court decided that the review and appeal taken together satisfied the requirements of article 6, so that it was not necessary to decide if 'civil rights' were at stake in such cases.

However, whether judicial review provides an adequate safeguard 'for the resolution of sensitive factual questions' has been doubted by the ECtHR[38] (see para 2.56 below).

2.55   In housing cases article 6 is closely connected with article 8: an interference with rights under article 8 may be justified (proportionate) but, if there is no forum for an occupier to have the proportionality of the decision considered by an independent and impartial decision-maker, the rights under both articles 6 and 8 may be breached. A recognition of the limits of traditional judicial review is reflected in two recent developments. First, it is now accepted that article 8 and public law defences to claims for possession must, in principle, be considered by the County Court (see paras 7.135–7.139). Second, the court's remit when considering claims for judicial review has been expanded to involve making determinations of fact in certain cases.[39]

37 [2003] UKHL 5, 13 February 2003.
38 See *McCann v UK* ECtHR App No 19009/04, 13 May 2008 and *Tsfayo v UK*, para 2.58 below.
39 Specifically, in relation to age disputes concerning unaccompanied asylum-seeking children, see para 2.57.

2.56   These developments reflect the decisions of the ECtHR, which has examined the extent to which judicial review in the UK is sufficient to cure any inadequacies of an internal review process.

> In *Tsfayo v UK*[40] the ECtHR considered a decision by a housing benefit review board that an applicant had failed to establish good cause for a late claim.
> The ECtHR decided that the review board was not independent and impartial. The issue was a simple question of fact and the board not only lacked independence but was directly connected to one of the parties to the dispute. Furthermore, the availability of judicial review did not correct the deficiency because the issue went to the credibility of the applicant and the Administrative Court had no jurisdiction to rehear evidence or substitute its own finding on the applicant's credibility.

2.57   Housing benefit appeals are now heard by the independent Social Security and Child Support Tribunal. However, in other areas of decision-making about housing rights, the UK courts have held that the 'rights' at issue are not 'civil rights' for the purpose of article 6.

> In *R (A) v Croydon LBC; R (M) v Lambeth LBC*[41] the Supreme Court considered challenges to social services decisions that certain 'unaccompanied asylum-seeking minors' were not, as a matter of fact, children. It held that in cases of dispute the issue must be determined by the court: the authority's statutory powers depended on the establishment of a factual situation therefore a court must be the ultimate arbiters of whether those facts existed. The Administrative Court can therefore operate as a fact-finding tribunal in such cases. Having found that the court's role in judicial review was wide enough to encompass fact finding, the Supreme Court held, as in *Runa Begum*, that the lack of an independent decision-maker was cured by the availability of judicial review; it therefore declined to determine whether the right to accommodation and support under the Children Act 1989 were civil rights for the

---

40 ECtHR (60860/00), 14 November 2006.
41 [2009] UKSC 8, 17 February 2010. Such challenges are now mostly referred by the Administrative Court (following the grant of permission) to the Upper Tribunal (Immigration and Asylum Chamber) for a fact finding hearing to determine age.

purpose of article 6. However, the court did suggest that if the rights were civil rights at all they were on the periphery of such rights.

Similarly, in *Birmingham City Council v Ali*[42] the Supreme Court held that a decision about whether or not the homelessness duty had ended was not a determination of civil rights. The issue between the parties was whether the appellants had received a crucial letter informing them of the consequences of refusing offers made under HA 1996 s193. The council maintained that it had sent the letters but both applicants claimed not to have received them. The appellants sought a review but the reviewing officer found, as a matter of fact, that they had received the letters. Their appeals to the county court were rejected on the basis that there was no 'point of law' that justified interfering with the reviewing officer's decision.

The Supreme Court held that the appellants' cases were outside the scope of article 6: this was not a determination of civil rights. Having reviewed the relevant ECtHR judgments, Lord Hope held:

> I would be prepared now to hold that cases where the award of services or benefits in kind is not an individual right of which the applicant can consider himself the holder, but is dependent upon a series of evaluative judgments by the provider as to whether the statutory critera are satisfied and how the need for it ought to be met, do not engage article 6(1). In my opinion they do not give rise to 'civil rights' ... for the purpose of article 6(1).[43]

Article 8

2.58   Article 8 is the Convention right most directly relevant to housing. It provides:

(1) Everyone has the right to respect for his private and family life, his home and his correspondence.

(2) There shall be no interference by a public authority with the exercise of this right except such as is in accordance with the law and is necessary in a democratic society in the interests of national security, public safety or the economic well-being of the country, for

42 [2010] UKSC 8 (the case is also known as *Tomlinson v Birmingham City Council*).
43 At [49].

the prevention of disorder or crime, for the protection of health or morals, or for the protection of the rights and freedoms of others. Recent developments regarding article 8 and possession proceedings are summarised at paras 7.146–7.159.

2.59 Article 8 is relevant to many issues that arise in relation to the provision of accommodation as well as decisions to evict. See, for example, *Bernard v Enfield LBC*, above, para 2.51, and summarised at para 18.25.

2.60 Where the person seeking accommodation is subject to immigration control, and thereby prevented from having access to social housing, benefits or employment, the effect of a refusal to provide 'safety net' community care services is more likely to breach the person's rights under article 8. And note that article 8 is about respect not only for a person's home but also for his or her private and family life.

2.61 A recent trend in immigration cases has been to give greater focus to the rights of children to private and family life under article 8 and to the UN Convention on the Rights of the Child (UNCRC). This has led to changes in Home Office practice in relation to the granting of leave on the basis of the right to family life. These developments are described in chapter 20 at paras 20.31–20.34.

In *ZH (Tanzania) v Secretary of State for the Home Department*[44] the Supreme Court considered a decision to remove a woman whose immigration history had 'rightly been described as "appalling"'.[45] She had been in the UK since 1995 and had made a number of unsuccessful claims for asylum, two using false identities. She had had a long-standing relationship with a British man, which ended in 2005, with whom she had two children. The children, aged 9 and 12 at the date of the hearing, were also British and had lived all their lives in the UK. The Immigration Tribunal had held that the removal of the mother and children to Tanzania would be a breach of article 8. However, the question was whether it would be proportionate. The tribunal held that the removal of the mother would not represent a disproportionate interference with the children's family life because they could either remain in the UK with their father or return to Tanzania with their mother, and their father could visit them there.

The Supreme Court considered not just the family's rights under article 8 but also the general principles of international law and in

44 [2011] UKSC 4, 1 February 2011.
45 Baroness Hale at [5].

particular article 3 of the UN Convention on the Rights of the Child (UNCRC) which provides that:

In all actions concerning children, whether undertaken by public or private social welfare institutions, courts of law, administrative authorities or legislative bodies, the best interests of the child shall be a primary consideration.

This is a binding obligation in international law and is translated into national law under Children Act 2004 s11.

The Supreme Court held that, although nationality is not a 'trump card', it is of particular importance in assessing the best interests of any child. The children in this case

... are British children; they are British, not just through the 'accident' of being born here, but by descent from a British parent; they have an unqualified right of abode here; they have lived here all their lives; they are being educated here; they have other social links with the community here; they have a good relationship with their father here.[46]

Furthermore, in relation to their rights under article 8:

In making the proportionality assessment under article 8, the best interests of the child must be a primary consideration.[47]

2.62   The interests of the child as a primary consideration, under section 11 of the Children Act 2004, has been asserted in support of establishing rights to reside under EU law but without success in the cases of *Harrison v Secretary of State for the Home Department*[48] and *Hines v Lambeth LBC*,[49] see para 20.153. It was also raised unsuccessfully in a challenge to a decision on intentional homelessness in *Huzrat v Hounslow LBC*,[50] see para 14.143.

Article 14

2.63   Article 14 provides:

The enjoyment of the rights and freedoms set forth in this Convention shall be secured without discrimination on any ground such as

---

46   [2011] UKSC 4, Baroness Hale at [31].
47   Baroness Hale at [33].
48   [2012] EWCA Civ 1736, 21 December 2012.
49   [2014] EWCA Civ 660, 20 May 2014.
50   [2013] EWCA Civ 1865, 21 November 2013.

sex, race, colour, language, religion, political or other opinion, national or social origin, association with a national minority, property, birth or other status.

2.64   The right not to be discriminated against under article 14 is not free-standing. Article 14 is engaged only if there is discrimination in relation to Convention rights and freedoms.

2.65   *Mendoza v Ghaidan*[51] provides a good example of the operation of article 14 and of the courts' duty to interpret domestic law in accordance with the Convention. It also illustrates the way articles 8 and 14 may be engaged in a dispute between individuals, as opposed to one between an individual and a public authority.

In *Mendoza v Ghaidan* a same-sex partner claimed the right to succeed to a Rent Act (RA) 1977 tenancy. RA 1977, at the time, limited the right of succession to a spouse or a person living with the deceased tenant as husband or wife. Cases determined prior to the Human Rights Act 1998 had held that a same-sex partnership could not fall within this definition.

Although the dispute was between two private individuals, the House of Lords held that once the state has chosen to intervene in a factual area involving those rights protected by article 8, article 14 is engaged if there is relevant discrimination in the mode of that intervention. The question was whether the discrimination could be justified. The landlord argued that the discrimination fell within the legitimate ambit of the state's discretion to arrange its housing schemes and the disposition of its housing stock. Alternatively it was argued that the policy of distinguishing between heterosexual and homosexual couples was legitimate and reasonable.

The court held that once discrimination has been demonstrated it is for the discriminator to establish an objective and reasonable justification for that discrimination. It is not enough to claim that what has been done falls within the permissible ambit of Parliament's discretion.

The House of Lords rejected the argument that the policy of the Rent Act was the protection of the family or that the exclusion of homosexuals from succession to a statutory tenancy would, in any event, be necessary to pursue such a policy.

To remedy this breach of the Convention the court must, if it can, interpret the Rent Act so that its provisions are rendered compatible with the Convention rights of the survivors of same-sex

51 [2004] UKHL 30, 21 June 2004.

partnerships. That duty can be properly discharged by reading the words 'as his or her wife or husband' to mean 'as if they were his or her wife or husband'.[52] This included a same-sex partner of a relationship that had the characteristics of a marriage.

2.66   Article 14 has also been relied on in most of the challenges to the welfare reform measures. In *Burnip v Birmingham CC and Secretary of State for Work and Pensions, Trengrove v Walsall MC and Secretary of State for Work and Pensions and Gorry v Wiltshire Council and Secretary of State for Work and Pensions*[53] the Court of Appeal held that the new Local Housing Allowance formula which failed to take account of a disabled person's need for an extra bedroom was unlawful as it discriminated on the grounds of disability. However, in *R (MA and Others) v Secretary of State for Work and Pensions*[54] a similar challenge to the 'bedroom tax' failed: the Court of Appeal held that the measure was discriminatory but, taking into account the availability of discretionary housing payments, the government had been able to justify the discrimination. The Supreme Court also dismissed the challenge in *R (SG) v Secretary of State for Work and Pensions*[55] which was a challenge to the benefit cap. The Supreme Court held that although the benefit cap did discriminate against women, the discrimination was justified as there was no alternative way of pursuing the legitimate aims of the policy.

2.67   The claimants in *R (MA and others) v Secretary of State for Work and Pensions* have been granted permission to appeal to the Supreme Court and the appeal should be heard in 2015. All of these cases are discussed in more detail in paras 9.87–9.88.

Article 1 of the 1st Protocol

2.68   Article 1 of the 1st Protocol provides:

> Every natural or legal person is entitled to the peaceful enjoyment of his possessions. No one shall be deprived of his possessions except in

---

52 In fact the Rent Act 1977 was amended by the Civil Partnership Act 2004 to provide specifically that partners living together as if they were civil partners are entitled to succeed, see para 4.33.

53 [2012] EWCA Civ 629, 15 May 2012.

54 [2014] EWCA Civ 13, 21 February 2014.

55 [2015] UKSC 16, 18 March 2015.

the public interest and subject to the conditions provided for by law and by the general principles of international law.

The preceding provision shall not, however, in any way impair the right of a state to enforce such laws as it deems necessary to control the use of property in accordance with the general interest or to secure the payment of taxes or other contributions or penalties.

2.69   In relation to rented premises the term 'possessions' includes the interest of both the landlord and the tenant.

In *Chapman and others v UK*[56] the applicants wanted to live in caravans on their own land but were refused planning permission by the local authorities. They complained that there had been a violation of their rights under article 8 and Protocol 1 article 1.

Their claims were dismissed. The ECtHR held that the decisions to refuse planning permission were in accordance with the law and pursued the legitimate aim of protecting the rights of others through the preservation of the environment. Domestic authorities must be given a wide margin of appreciation in planning decisions. The interference with the claimants' right to respect for the home under article 8 and the right to peaceful enjoyment of their property under Protocol 1 article 1 was proportionate and struck a fair balance between individual rights and the public interest.

Public authorities

2.70   The Human Rights Act (HRA) 1998 applies to the decisions and actions of public authorities. Under HRA 1998 s6(6) a public authority includes:[57]

- a court or tribunal; and
- any person certain of whose functions are functions of a public nature.

2.71   But, in relation to a particular act, a person is not a public authority by virtue only of this provision if the nature of the act is private.[58]

---

56   (2001) 33 EHRR 18, 18 January 2001, ECtHR.
57   HRA 1998 s6(6).
58   HRA 1998 s6(5).

Registered providers of social housing (formerly registered social landlords)

2.72   Local authorities, when making decisions about homelessness and the allocation of accommodation, or about community care services, are clearly public authorities. However, whether other providers of social housing are public authorities for the purpose of the HRA 1998 is a more complex issue. It will depend on the nature of the provider and the particular function being performed.

In *Poplar Housing and Regeneration Community Association Ltd v Donaghue*[59] the Court of Appeal considered a possession claim against an assured shorthold tenant. The claimant had become the defendant's landlord following a stock transfer by the local authority. The defendant had been granted the tenancy by the authority, originally as interim accommodation pending a homeless decision. On the stock transfer her tenancy became an assured shorthold tenancy. Following the authority's decision that she was intentionally homeless the claimant served notice under the Housing Act 1988 s21 and sought possession. The defendant argued that the association was a public authority for the purpose of the HRA 1998 and therefore under a duty to act in a way compatible with Convention rights, and the provisions of section 21 were incompatible with articles 6 and 8 of the ECHR.

The Court of Appeal held:

1) HRA 1998 s6 requires a generous interpretation of what is a public authority. It is inspired by the approach previously developed by the courts as to which bodies are susceptible to judicial review. The emphasis on public functions reflects the approach adopted in judicial review cases.

2) When the authority transferred its housing stock to the association it did not transfer its primary public duties. The association was no more than the means by which the authority sought to perform those duties.

3) The act of providing accommodation for rent, without more, is not a public function for the purpose of HRA 1998 s6.

4) The fact that a body is a charity or not-for-profit organisation means it is likely to be motivated by what it perceives to be the public interest but that does not point to it being a public authority. Even if it performs functions that would be considered

59   [2001] EWCA Civ 595, 27 April 2001.

to be of a public nature if performed by a public body, such acts may nevertheless remain of a private nature.

5) It is a feature or combination of features that gives 'public character' to the act so as to make it public when it would otherwise be private. Statutory authority for what is done can help to mark the act as being public, as can the extent of control over the function exercised by a public authority. The more closely the acts are enmeshed in the activities of a public body, the more likely they are to be public. However, the fact that acts are supervised by a public regulatory body does not necessarily mean the acts are of a public nature.

6) In this case, the closeness of the relationship between the authority and the association was relevant: the association was created by the authority to take a stock transfer; five of its board members were also members of the authority; and it was subject to the guidance of the authority in the way it acted towards the defendant.

7) That the defendant was a tenant of the authority before the transfer and was advised that she would be treated no better or worse as a result of the stock transfer was also relevant. While she remained a tenant the association stood in much the same position as that previously occupied by the authority.

The Court of Appeal held that in the circumstances the association was a public authority. However, the way HA 1988 s21 operates did not conflict with the defendant's rights under article 6 or article 8. Section 21 which gives an automatic right to possession is necessary in a democratic society to ensure there is a procedure for recovering possession at the end of a tenancy. The question is whether the restricted power of the court is legitimate and proportionate.[60] This is the area of policy where the court should defer to the decision of Parliament.

2.73   The issue was again considered by the Court of Appeal in relation to a trust that was not the recipient of a large-scale stock transfer.

---

60 Since *Poplar* case-law developments regarding the court's remit when considering possession claims mean that an assured shorthold tenant could now, in principle, defend a claim on the grounds that the decision to seek possession was disproportionate under article 8, or otherwise unlawful on public law grounds. See paras 7.128–7.132.

In *R (Weaver) v London and Quadrant Housing Trust*[61] the applicant
was an assured tenant of the trust which sought to evict her using
Ground 8 (the mandatory ground). She argued that the trust was
acting unlawfully; that she had a 'legitimate expectation' that, in
accordance with Housing Corporation guidance referred to in
the tenancy terms and conditions, it would pursue all reasonable
alternatives before resorting to a Ground 8 claim. She argued
that the decision was in breach of her rights under article 8 and
Protocol 1 article 1 (see para 2.66 above). As a preliminary issue
it was necessary for the court to decide whether the trust was
amenable to judicial review and whether it was a public authority for
the purposes of the HRA 1998.

The judge held that the management and allocation of housing
stock by the trust was a function of a public nature and the trust
should be regarded as a public authority under HRA 1998 s6(3)(b).
Although the court had rejected the tenant's arguments on the facts,
the trust appealed to the Court of Appeal on the issue of whether
or not it was exercising public functions for the purposes of the
HRA 1998. The trust argued that although it was a hybrid authority
(a body, certain of whose functions are of a public nature), the act
in question, the termination of the tenancy, was an act of a private
nature and therefore not within the scope of the HRA 1998.

The Court of Appeal held that the key issue where the body in
question was a hybrid authority was whether the act in question
was a private act. The starting point was to consider both the
source and the nature of the activities of the body before deciding
whether a function was public or private. The issue was fact
specific. The following factors were relevant: the extent to which the
body was publicly funded and the extent to which it was exercising
statutory functions, or taking the place of central government or
local authorities or was providing a public service. Here, the trust
relied significantly on public funding and, while not taking the place
of local government, operated in close harmony with it. Providing
subsidised housing was a government function. The trust was
providing a public service, it was acting in the public interest
and had charitable objectives. It was also subject to regulations
designed in part to ensure that the government's objectives
regarding a vulnerable group were fulfilled. All of these factors
brought the provision of social housing by the trust within the

> realm of a public function. The grant and termination of a tenancy were part and parcel of determining who should be allowed to take advantage of the public benefit of social housing. Accordingly, the act of terminating the tenancy did not constitute an act of a private nature and was in principle subject to human rights considerations.

2.74 So, while not all registered providers of social housing are public authorities for the purposes of the HRA 1998, it now seems likely that almost all not-for-profit providers will be treated as public authorities for the purposes of the HRA 1998, judicial review and in relation to the Equality Act public sector equality duty (see para 2.84 below).

Contracted out functions of social services

2.75 In contrast to *Weaver*, in *R (Heather) v Leonard Cheshire Foundation and another*,[62] the Court of Appeal reached a different conclusion when considering whether a registered social landlord providing long-term residential accommodation for disabled residents was a public authority for the purpose of the HRA 1998. The residents retained their article 8 rights against the local authority which had the duty to accommodate but the defendant was not a public authority for the purpose of the HRA 1998. And in *YL v Birmingham CC*[63] the House of Lords held (by a majority of three to two) that the HRA 1998 did not apply to a private care home even though the home was providing accommodation under arrangements made under the National Assistance Act 1948 (NAA 1948).

2.76 The position in relation to private care homes has now been dealt with by legislation. A registered care provider providing care and support to an adult in residential accommodation will be taken to be exercising a function of a public nature for the purpose of section 6(3)(b) of the HRA 1998 provided the care or support is arranged by a local authority or paid for by a local authority. However, this will not apply if the person is paying privately and the local authority has not made the arrangement.[64]

---

62 [2002] EWCA Civ 366, 21 March 2002.
63 [2007] UKHL 27, 20 June 2007.
64 Care Act 2014 s73. This will also apply to a registered care provider providing care and support in a person's home but only if the arrangement is made by or paid for by the local authority.

Declarations of incompatibility

2.77 Where an action is brought against a public authority for breach of a Convention right, it is a defence if the public authority can show that it was bound to act the way that it did because of primary legislation.[65]

2.78   In such a case the issue then becomes whether the legislation itself is incompatible with the Convention and the government will be joined as defendant.[66] In *R (Morris) v Westminster City Council*[67] the Court of Appeal declared that HA 1996 s185(4) was incompatible with article 14 of the Convention to the extent that it required that a dependent child subject to immigration control be disregarded when deciding whether a British citizen had a priority need for accommodation: it was discrimination on the grounds of nationality.

2.79   A declaration of incompatibility does not affect the 'validity, continuing operation or enforcement of a provision' and it is not binding on the parties to the proceedings in which is it made.[68] The government is not bound to take action to amend the law to ensure that it is compatible but will usually do so to avoid claims for damages in the ECtHR. The legislative amendments to resolve the incompatibility identified in *Morris* are set out at paras 20.175–20.178.[69]

Remedies

2.80 Human Rights Act 1998 s8(1) provides that:

> ... in relation to any act (or proposed act) of a public authority which the court finds is (or would be) unlawful, it may grant such relief or remedy, or make such order, within its powers as it considers just and appropriate.

In other words, the court may grant any remedy it considers appropriate provided the court already has the power to grant such a remedy.

2.81   Many of the housing cases in which the HRA 1998 has been used have been possession cases where the occupier argued that an eviction would involve an unjustified breach of article 8. In such a case the remedy sought is the refusal of a possession order.

---

65 HRA 1998 s2.
66 Civil Procedure Rules 19.4A(1) provides that notice must be given to the Crown before a declaration of incompatibility can be made.
67 [2005] EWCA Civ 1184, 14 October 2005, and see para 20.174.
68 HRA 1998 s4(6).
69 In fact, in *Bah v UK* App No 56328/07, 27 December 2011, the ECtHR held that the discrimination identified in *Morris* was justified so that the legislation was not, in fact, incompatible with the Convention.

2.82   In judicial review proceedings the court can quash (cancel) any decision deemed to be in breach of the HRA 1998 and can order a public authority to do something or to refrain from doing something to avoid a breach.

2.83   It is also possible to claim damages under the HRA 1998 from a court that has the power to award damages.[70] A court can only award damages if satisfied that such an award is necessary 'to afford just satisfaction to the person in whose favour it is made'. The court must take into account:

> ... all the circumstances of the case, including:
> (a) any other relief or remedy granted, or order made, in relation to the act in question (by that or any other court), and
> (b) the consequences of any decision (by that or any other court) in respect of that act.[71]

Equality Act 2010

2.84   The Equality Act (EA) 2010 brought together, in a single Act, the provisions relating to equality and discrimination regarding race, gender and disability and extended equality duties to encompass other 'protected characteristics'. In relation to public bodies, a key feature is that it is not enough to avoid direct and indirect discrimination; public bodies must, in all their functions, have due regard to the need to promote equality of opportunity and combat discrimination and harassment. A failure to do so may make their decisions and policies unlawful. This is known as the public sector equality duty ('PSED').

Protected groups

2.85   Prior to the EA 2010, equality duties applied only in relation to race, gender and disability.[72] The new duties apply to 'protected characteristics': age, disability, gender reassignment, pregnancy and maternity, race, religion or belief, sex and sexual orientation. In relation to disability, the duty may mean treating disabled persons more favourably than others.

---

70 HRA 1998 s8(3).
71 HRA 1998 s8(3).
72 Under Sex Discrimination Act 1975, Equal Pay Act 1970, Race Relations Act 1976 and Disability Discrimination Acts 1995 and 2005.

Public sector equality duty (PSED)

2.86   The duty is found in EA 2010 s149. This provides that in relation to all protected groups:

(1) A public authority must, in the exercise of its functions, have due regard to the need to –

(a) eliminate discrimination, harassment, victimisation and any other conduct that is prohibited by or under this Act;

(b) advance equality of opportunity between persons who share a relevant protected characteristic and persons who do not share it;

(c) foster good relations between persons who share a relevant protected characteristic and persons who do not share it.

2.87   In relation to advancing equality of opportunity, this means having due regard to the need to remove or minimise disadvantage suffered by protected groups, taking steps to meet their needs, where different, and encouraging participation in public life where such participation is disproportionately low. And, in relation to disabled people, it means taking steps to take account of disabled people's disabilities.

2.88   The duty applies to public authorities[73] and to other bodies exercising public functions. This would include most registered providers of social housing. Similar factors will be relevant as under the HRA 1998, see paras 2.70–2.74 above, including: the extent of public funding the organisation has; whether it is exercising statutory powers; whether it is doing things that a public body would otherwise have to do; and whether it is providing a public service.

2.89   There is extensive case-law on the nature of the PSED and the extent of the duty to have 'due regard'. Information and guidance is available on the website of the Equalities and Human Rights Commission (EHRC): www.equalityhumanrights.com. The statutory Codes of Practice which should be followed by public bodies are also available from the commission's website.

2.90   Most of the cases in which the courts have considered the duty have been about the development of policies and decisions about such issues as the funding of services and voluntary organisations by local authorities and other public bodies. However, the courts have held that the disability equality duty also applies to decisions about individuals, including decisions on homeless applications and eviction.[74]

---

73 EA 2010 Sch 19 provides a list of public authorities subject to s149. In addition to the general duty set out in s149, the listed public authorities also have specific equality duties set out in regulations.

74 See *Barnsley MBC v Norton* [2011] EWCA Civ 834, 21 July 2011.

In *Pieretti v London Borough of Enfield*[75] the Court of Appeal
considered the PSED in the context of a homeless application. The
application forms had included indications that Mr and Mrs Pieretti
were disabled. They were found to be intentionally homeless as their
private landlady stated she had evicted them because of rent arrears.
The decision was upheld on review. At the county court appeal they
argued that Enfield had been in breach of the PSED. The general rule
is that a person can only raise an issue at the county court appeal if
it has been raised in the review. The county court judge dismissed
the appeal on this basis. A further appeal was made to the Court of
Appeal. Enfield argued that the duty to have due regard to the need
to take steps to take account of a person's disability did not apply
to the decision that the applicants were intentionally homeless for
three reasons: (1) the duty only applies to the general formulation
of policy and not to its decisions on individual cases; (2) Part VII
of the Housing Act 1996 addresses the rights and needs of the
disabled comprehensively through the priority need categories,
the 'good faith' provision under intentionality and the suitability of
accommodation provisions; and (3) when making such a decision
a local authority is not carrying out 'functions' to which the duty
applies.

The Court of Appeal rejected all of these arguments holding that:

- The duty applies both when a local authority is planning its
  services and drawing up criteria and also when applying them in
  individual cases. While the duty does not create new individual
  rights it is designed 'to secure the brighter illumination of a
  person's disability so that, to the extent that it bears upon his
  rights under other laws, it attracts a full appraisal'.
- When introducing the PSED Parliament intended that there
  be 'a culture of greater awareness of the existence and legal
  consequences of disability, including the fact that a disabled
  person may not be adept at proclaiming his disability'.
- The reviewing officer was in breach of the duty as she failed to
  take the appropriate steps to take account of the disability; she
  failed to make further inquiry into the evidence that suggested
  that the applicant was disabled in a way relevant to whether he
  was acting 'deliberately' as is necessary for a person to be found
  intentionally homeless. The review decision was quashed.

75 [2010] EWCA Civ 1104, 12 October 2010.

2.92   However, in *Kanu v Southwark LBC*[76] the Court of Appeal held that the position is different in relation to priority need inquiries. The definition of priority need requires the authority to decide whether a person's disability renders them vulnerable and the PSED 'adds nothing to the [housing] duty ... so far as the issue of priority need is concerned, it was not in fact necessary for [the reviewing officer to consider it further at all'.[77] The applicant's appeal was heard by the Supreme Court in December 2014 and judgment is pending at the time of writing.

Complaints

Local authorities

2.93   Statutory complaints procedures operate in relation to social services duties to adults and children and are described in chapters 18 and 19.

2.94   There is no statutory complaints procedure in relation to housing decisions by local authorities but all local authorities operate general complaints procedures and some may have procedures specific to a particular department. Most local authority complaints procedures follow a similar pattern, beginning with informal resolution, formal investigation and a final appeal or panel hearing. If the internal complaints procedure does not resolve the issue, further complaint may be made to the Ombudsman, see below at para 2.96.

Regulation of social landlords

2.95   The Regulatory Committee of the Homes and Communities Agency now regulates all providers of social housing, including local authorities, see para 1.90. The Committee has published the 'Regulatory Framework for Social Housing in England from April 2012' which sets out seven standards, including 'the consumer standard'. Providers are responsible for complying with these standards and the Committee will only intervene in relation to a breach of the consumer standard where the failure to comply could lead to 'serious detriment' to the tenants. If an internal complaint to a registered provider

---

76 [2014] EWCA Civ 1085, 29 July 2014.
77 [2014] EWCA Civ 1085, Underhill LJ at [55].

does not resolve an issue, the complainant can refer the matter to the Housing Ombudsman.

Ombudsman complaints

2.96 Since 1 April 2013, complaints by tenants alleging maladministration by registered providers of social housing, including local authorities, are dealt with by the Housing Ombudsman.[78] Previously, the Local Government Ombudsman (LGO) dealt with complaints made by local authority tenants. The LGO still deals with complaints about issues such as homelessness including accommodation provided under Part VII of the HA 1996, housing benefit, housing allocations and home improvement grants. But complaints about the local authority as landlord are mostly dealt with by the Housing Ombudsman. In some cases both Ombudsman schemes have jurisdiction and in such cases the two services should work together.

2.97 Before a complaint can be made to the Housing Ombudsman the complainant must first exhaust the provider's complaints procedure. Even after this has been done, the complainant cannot immediately go to the Housing Ombudsman but must either refer it to a 'designated person' (an MP, local councillor or recognised Tenant Panel) or must wait eight weeks before referring it to the Housing Ombudsman.[79] The ostensible aim is that the designated person may assist to resolve the complaint. This does not apply to complaints to the LGO.

2.98 Information about both Ombudsman services can be downloaded from their respective websites, as can the complaints forms. The website of the Housing Ombudsman is: www.housing-ombudsman.org.uk and the LGO's is: www.lgo.org.uk.

2.99 The following are common to both Ombudsman schemes:

- Complaint can usually only be made after the internal complaints procedure has been exhausted.[80]
- Complaints must be made within 12 months from the date the complainant first knew about the relevant matters. The Ombudsman can extend this time limit if he or she considers it reasonable to do so.
- The service is free.

78 Localism Act 2011 s181.
79 Localism Act 2011 s180.
80 There are exceptions however: the LGO will investigate complaints by homeless persons without requiring them to exhaust the authority's complaints procedures and will 'fast-track' complaints from children and young people, see paras 19.65–19.67.

- The Ombudsman may decline to deal with a complaint if a legal remedy is available or the issue is one of legal interpretation. However, there is some overlap and complaints are frequently made to the Ombudsman about such issues as disrepair or a failure to assist a homeless person when the complainant has a clear right to issue legal proceedings.
- The Ombudsman can recommend compensation but this is usually much less than a court would award where there is a legal remedy.
- The Ombudsman may make other recommendations, for example, that the particular body changes a policy or ensures that staff are properly trained.

2.100   The main disadvantage of the complaints and Ombudsman procedure is that there is usually considerable delay before the complaint is resolved and effective action taken. Also, the Ombudsman accepts only a very small proportion of complaints for full investigation. The advantage is that it is free and legal representation is not necessary.

Obtaining information

2.101   There are two statutes under which information can be obtained from a public body such as a local authority:

- the Data Protection Act 1998 concerns information held about an individual;
- the Freedom of Information Act 2000 concerns other information held by a public authority.

Data Protection Act 1998

2.102   The Data Protection Act 1998 (DPA 1998) governs the holding and processing of personal data (information) by businesses and organisations in the public and private sector. Under the Act an individual has the right to be informed whether data is being held on him or her and to have communicated 'in an intelligible form' the information held and the source of the information.[81] Such information must be given provided the following conditions are satisfied:[82]

---

81 Certain information is exempt, for example information that may cause distress to the recipient or that may disclose the identity of a third party who does not consent.
82 Data Protection Act 1998 s7(1)–(3).

- the request is made in writing;
- sufficient information is provided as to the identity of the individual concerned; and
- the fee (currently a maximum of £10 in most cases) is paid.[83]

2.103 If the request is made on behalf of another individual that person's consent must also be provided. A model letter requesting information under the DPA 1998 is contained in the appendix to this chapter.

2.104 Provided those conditions are satisfied, the information (usually in the form of photocopies) must be provided no later than 40 calendar days after the request is received.[84] This does not mean that organisations should routinely take 40 days to provide the information: DPA 1998 s7(8) provides that: '... a data controller shall comply with a request under this section promptly and in any event before the end of [the 40-day period].'

2.105 Complaints about breaches of the DPA 1998 may be made to the Information Commissioner's Office via the website: www.ico.org.uk. An application may also be made in the County Court for an order compelling an organisation to comply with its obligations under DPA 1998.

Freedom of Information Act 2000

2.106 The Freedom of Information Act (FoIA) 2000 gives a person the right to obtain information from a public authority.

2.107 Public authorities include:

- central and local government;
- the health service;
- schools, colleges and universities;
- the police; and
- many other non-governmental organisations, committees and advisory bodies.

2.108 Most requests are free but a person may be asked to pay a fee for photocopies or postage. However, if the public authority thinks it will cost more than £450 to comply with the request (or £600 for a central government department) the request can be refused.

2.109 A request under FoIA 2000 must be made in writing and should identify the person making the request and give an address for reply.

---

83 Data Protection (Subject Access) (Fees and Miscellaneous Provisions) Regulations 2000 SI No 191 reg 3. Different fees apply in relation to credit agencies and health records.

84 Data Protection Act 1998 s7(8) and (10).

It is not necessary to identify the request as one made under the Act but it is usually helpful to do so. It is also not necessary to state why the information is required. The public body has 20 working days to respond to the request, so the request should be dated. Requests to local authorities may be sent to the relevant department or to the Chief Executive or designated information officer/department. It may be possible to make the request online.

2.110   The information required should be identified as precisely as possible. So, for example, it is better to request copies of minutes of meetings or internal policies and guidance on a specific issue rather than requesting all information held in relation to that issue. A request that is too vague may be impossible to respond to or a public body may argue that it would be too expensive to do so. A precedent letter is contained in the appendix to this chapter.

2.111   A public body may refuse a request because, for example, the information is already in the public domain (much information can now be found on the websites of public authorities, eg committee minutes and agendas) or because it may prejudice national security or damage commercial interests.

2.112   If there is a dispute about whether information should be provided or not, an internal review should be requested. If this does not resolve the issue (or if the body does not offer an internal review) the complaint may be made to the Information Commissioner.

The Information Rights Tribunal

2.113   If complaint to the Information Commissioner does not resolve the issue and/or the person wishes to challenge the decision of the commissioner, an appeal can be made to the First-tier Tribunal, General Regulatory Chamber. The tribunal's website is at: www.justice.gov. uk/tribunals/general-regulatory-chamber.

2.114   The tribunal deals with disputes about both DPA 1998 and FoIA 2000 disputes.

APPENDIX 1

Request under Data Protection Act 1998

Dear Sir or Madam,

Re: Mr/Ms Client (DOB: ....)

Request under Data Protection Act 1998

We are advising the above named with regard to [.............].

On his/her behalf we request that you provide to us a complete copy of [his/her housing/social services file].

We enclose our client's signed authority for the release of this information together with a cheque in the sum of £10.

We look forward to receiving the information as soon as possible [include any reason for needing the information urgently, eg required for homeless submissions] and in any event within the statutory period of 40 days.

Yours faithfully,

A.N. Adviser

APPENDIX 2

Request under Freedom of Information Act 2000

To: A Local Authority [depending on the subject area, address to either Chief Executive/Director of relevant department or, if appropriate the Freedom of Information Officer] •

Dear Sir or Madam,

Request under Freedom of Information Act 2000

We request that you supply the following information:

Copies of the minutes of the Cabinet meetings since [date] at which the new [housing allocations policy/homeless prevention strategy etc] was discussed;

Copies of any internal policies or guidance regarding the implementation of the [....] policy/strategy.

Please acknowledge this request.

We look forward to receiving the information as soon as possible and, in any event, within the statutory period of 20 working days.

Yours faithfully,

A.N. Adviser

Different kinds of tenancies

continued

Key points

- Most residential tenancies are governed by a particular statutory scheme.
- The statute that applies, and the type of tenancy a person has, will generally be determined by the identity of the landlord and the date the tenancy started.
- Tenancies within a particular statutory scheme will give to tenants statutory rights, principally some form of 'security of tenure'.
- As a general rule to have security of tenure a tenant must live in premises as a home.
- Each statutory scheme contains a list of tenancies that fall outside statutory protection.
- A tenant with long-term rights ('substantive security of tenure') cannot be evicted unless there is a reason (ground for possession). The landlord must apply to the court for a possession order.
- Almost all private lettings are now assured shorthold tenancies Assured shorthold tenants do not have long-term rights and can be evicted after the first six months unless the tenancy is for a longer period. The landlord must obtain a possession order but does not need a reason to evict.
- Anti-social behaviour legislation created several new types of tenancy under which the tenants do not have long-term rights, including introductory and demoted tenancies.
- Since 2012 local authorities are able to grant fixed-term tenancies instead of long-term periodic tenancies: so called 'flexible tenancies'.

Introduction

3.1 Different schemes of statutory protection apply to residential tenancies depending on whether the landlord is a private or social landlord and the date the tenancy commenced. Each scheme sets out the conditions that must be met for the tenant to enjoy substantive security of tenure and lists those tenancies that fall outside statutory protection. The main Acts and types of tenancies granted under each are summarised in the table below.

The Act	Type of tenancy	Type of landlord and date of grant
Rent Act 1977	Protected tenancy and statutory tenancy – both also known as regulated tenancies	Tenancies granted by private landlords before 15 January 1989.
Housing Act 1985	Secure [periodic] tenancy ('lifetime tenancy')[1]	Tenancies granted by local authorities whenever granted; and tenancies granted by housing associations before 15 January 1989.
Housing Act 1988	Assured tenancy and assured shorthold tenancy	Tenancies granted by private landlords and housing associations on or after 15 January 1989.
Housing Act 1996	Introductory tenancy	Probationary tenancies granted by local authorities.
Anti-social Behaviour Act 2003 (amended Housing Act 1996)	Demoted tenancy	Previously secure tenancies granted by local authorities but demoted by the court.
Housing and Regeneration Act 2008	Family intervention tenancy	Tenancies granted by local authorities and other social landlords to provide behaviour support for tenants guilty of anti-social behaviour.
Localism Act 2011 (amends the Housing Act 1985)	Flexible tenancy	A type of secure tenancy granted by local authority for a fixed term with the possibility of an extension at the end of the fixed term.

1   The term 'lifetime' tenancy is used to denote a periodic secure tenancy, as opposed to the 'flexible' tenancy, which is a fixed-term secure tenancy. Prior to 2012 almost all secure tenancies were periodic.

Housing Act 1988: assured and assured shorthold tenancies

3.2 The Housing Act (HA) 1988 introduced a new regime in the private sector. Most tenancies granted by private landlords on or after 15 January 1989 will be either:

- an assured tenancy; or
- an assured shorthold tenancy.

3.3 The HA 1988 also brought non-local authority social housing within the private sector regime. Tenancies granted by social landlords (now known as 'registered providers of social housing', see para 2.91) are also assured and assured shorthold tenancies if granted on or after 15 January 1989. Before then housing associations could grant secure tenancies and housing association secure tenancies granted before 15 January 1989 remain secure tenancies.

3.4 Assured tenants enjoy substantive security of tenure while assured shorthold tenants have security only for an initial period of six months. Both have very limited rent control. In practice, there are few assured tenancies in the private sector; most are granted by registered providers to tenants nominated for an allocation of social housing (see chapter 17). However, registered providers also use assured shorthold tenancies, mainly when operating 'starter' or 'probationary' tenancy schemes, or accommodating homeless applicants by arrangement with a local authority. Since 2012 the use of assured shorthold tenancies by registered providers has been encouraged, to mirror the 'flexible tenancies' offered by local authorities, see para 3.103 below.

3.5 When assured shorthold tenancies were introduced, landlords had to comply with certain formal requirements. Failing to comply would result in an assured tenancy by default. The Housing Act 1996 changed this: after 28 February 1997 any new tenancy created by a private landlord or a registered provider will be an assured shorthold tenancy unless it is expressly stated that it is not an assured shorthold tenancy.

3.6 An assured shorthold tenancy is a type of assured tenancy. If a tenancy cannot be an assured tenancy it cannot be an assured shorthold tenancy. This section is therefore in three parts:

- the necessary conditions for the creation of any assured tenancy, including an assured shorthold;
- the specific characteristics of assured tenancies (not shortholds);
- the specific characteristics of assured shorthold tenancies.

Conditions for all assured tenancies

3.7   To create an assured tenancy the following conditions must be satisfied:[2]

- The tenancy must be of a dwelling-house 'let as a separate dwelling'.
- The tenant must be an individual, or if there are joint tenants all must be individuals.
- The tenant must occupy as his or her only or principal home. If joint tenants at least one must occupy as his or her only or principal home.
- The tenancy must not be one excluded by HA 1988 Sch 1.

3.8   In all cases there must be a tenancy. An occupier who does not have exclusive possession of at least some part of the premises cannot be a tenant, see paras 1.29–1.32.

'Dwelling-house let as a separate dwelling'

3.9   Housing Act 1988 s1(1) provides that there must be:

A tenancy under which a dwelling-house is let as a separate dwelling.

3.10   This condition has two separate elements.

A 'dwelling-house'

3.11   This includes part of a dwelling-house.[3] Whether a particular letting is of a dwelling-house depends on the facts of the case. A caravan was held to be a dwelling-house where the wheels had been raised and it had been connected to mains services.[4] However, if a caravan is let as moveable property it cannot be a dwelling-house.[5] A houseboat does not have sufficient degree of attachment and annexation to the land to become part of it and cannot be a dwelling-house.[6] Even where a houseboat had been placed on a wooden platform it was held not to have become annexed to the land so as to become a dwelling-house.[7] In any particular case, the relative degrees of permanence and mobility will be relevant.

---

2 HA 1988 s1.
3 HA 1988 s45.
4 R v Guildford Area Rent Tribunal ex p Grubey (1951) (unreported), DC.
5 R v Rent Officer of Nottingham Registration Area ex p Allen (1985) 17 HLR 481, QBD.
6 Chelsea Yacht and Boat Co Ltd v Pope [2001] 2 All ER 409.
7 Mew & Just v Tristmire Ltd [2011] EWCA Civ 912, 28 July 2011.

'Let as a separate dwelling'

3.12 This means that the main purpose of the letting must be to provide a home for the tenant.

3.13 The requirement that for a tenant to have substantive security of tenure premises must be let as a separate dwelling is well established in the statutory schemes. It was originally intended to prevent a tenant who shared accommodation with the landlord from having long-term security. However, express provision is now made for the following situations:

- a tenant sharing accommodation with a landlord, see para 1.102;
- a tenant sharing accommodation with other tenants, see paras 3.51–3.53.

3.14 The early case-law is therefore of limited relevance. More recently the issue of whether a tenant occupies 'a dwelling-house let as a separate dwelling' has been considered in the context of accommodation in hotels and hostels. The phrase 'let as a separate dwelling' had previously been interpreted by the courts as meaning that the premises let had to be capable of being lived in and that the absence of a kitchen meant that premises were not let as a separate dwelling.[8] However, the House of Lords rejected this approach:

> In *Uratemps Ventures Ltd v Collins*[9] Mr Collins occupied a hotel room which was basically furnished and did not include any cooking facilities, although there was a power point. Breakfast had initially been available in the restaurant and included in the rent. Mr Collins brought in a pizza warmer, a toasted sandwich maker, a kettle and a warming plate. The landlords sought possession, arguing that that Mr Collins could not be an assured tenant under the Housing Act 1988 as there was no 'letting of a dwelling-house as a separate dwelling'.
>
> The House of Lords held that the word 'dwelling' is not a term of art with a specialised legal meaning. It is 'the place where [an occupier] lives and to which he returns and which forms the centre of his existence ... No doubt he will sleep there and usually eat there; he will often prepare at least some of his meals there.'[10]

---

8 This is in contrast to the sharing of facilities such as bathroom and toilet which did not prevent there being a letting of a separate dwelling.

9 [2001] UKHL 43, 11 October 2001.

10 Millet LJ at [31].

> However, there is no legislative requirement that cooking
> facilities must be available for premises to qualify as a dwelling. In
> deciding whether an occupant has security of tenure:
>
> > The first step is to identify the subject-matter of the tenancy
> > agreement. If this is a house or part of a house of which the
> > tenant has exclusive possession with no element of sharing, the
> > only question is whether, at the date when proceedings were
> > brought, it was the tenant's home. If so, it was his dwelling ...
> > The presence or absence of cooking facilities in the part of the
> > premises of which the tenant has exclusive occupation is not
> > relevant.[11]
>
> The House of Lords held that Mr Collins was an assured tenant.

Tenant(s) must be individual(s)

3.15   A letting to a company cannot be an assured tenancy.

Tenant(s) must occupy as only or principal home

3.16   Note that this condition is stricter than under the Rent Act 1977
where the equivalent requirement is that the tenant occupies the
premises as a residence. For an assured tenancy the premises must
be the tenant's only or main home.

3.17   The residence condition may still be met even during the tenant's
absence provided there is:

- an intention by the tenant to return; and
- some physical sign of that intention.[12]

3.18   This issue is discussed in detail at paras 4.2–4.11.

Agreements that cannot be assured

3.19   Schedule 1 of HA 1988 sets out those agreements that cannot be
assured tenancies. They are listed below at paras 3.20–3.38.

Tenancies entered into before HA 1988: para 1

3.20   A tenancy entered into before 15 January 1989, or pursuant to a contract made before that date.

---

11   Millet LJ at [58].
12   *Brown v Brash* [1948] 2 KB 247.

High value tenancies: para 2

3.21 Any tenancy entered into on or after 1 April 1990 under which the rent is more than £100,000 a year.[13] 'Rent' does not include any sum expressed to be payable in respect of rates, council tax, services, management, repairs, maintenance or insurance.

3.22 The threshold was increased from £25,000 on 1 October 2010 but applies retrospectively to tenancies granted after 1 April 1990 in England. This means that a tenancy that was outside the Housing Act 1988 by virtue of a rent in excess of £25,000 will have become an assured tenancy provided the rent does not exceed £100,000.[14] If it was granted on or after 28 February 1997 it will be an assured shorthold tenancy which means that any deposit held by the landlord must be protected (see paras 4.144–4.170).

Tenancies at a low rent or no rent: para 3

3.23 This means either:

• a tenancy under which, for the time being, no rent is payable; or
• a tenancy entered into on or after 1 April 1990 under which the rent for the time being payable is £1,000 or less if the premises are in Greater London, and £250 or less elsewhere.[15]

3.24 Where services are provided in return for the accommodation, the tenancy will not be a 'no rent' tenancy provided the value of the services is capable of quantification. If so, the value of the services must exceed £1,000 per year for the tenancy to be an assured tenancy. If the nature of the services means their value cannot be quantified or the value is less than £1000 a year, the tenancy cannot be assured.

3.25 If no rent is paid and no services provided, the tenancy will also be an 'excluded tenancy' which means that the tenant can be evicted without a court order.[16]

Business tenancies: para 4

3.26 A tenancy of premises occupied primarily for business purposes is governed by the Landlord and Tenant Act 1954 and not the Housing

---

13 For tenancies entered into between 15 January 1989 and 31 March 1990 the test is set by the rateable value. If the rateable value was in excess of £1,500 in Greater London or £750 elsewhere, the tenancy cannot be an assured tenancy.

14 See Assured Tenancies (Amendment) (England) Order 2010 SI No 908.

15 For tenancies entered into between 15 January 1989 and 31 March 1990, the tenancy is a low rent tenancy if the rent for the time being payable is less than two-thirds of the rateable value on 31 March 1990.

16 Protection from Eviction Act 1977 s3A and para 1.112.

Act 1988. See paras 1.132–1.135 regarding premises occupied for mixed business and residential use.

Licenced premises: para 5

3.27   A tenancy of premises or part of premises licensed for the sale of intoxicating liquor for consumption on the premises.

Tenancies of agricultural land: para 6

3.28   A tenancy under which agricultural land, exceeding two acres, is let together with the dwelling-house.

Agricultural holdings: para 7

3.29   A tenancy under which the dwelling-house is comprised of:

- an agricultural holding occupied by the person responsible for the control of the farming of the holding; or
- a holding held under a farm business tenancy occupied by the person responsible for the control of the management of the holding.[17]

Specified student lettings: para 8

3.30   A tenancy granted to a student pursuing or intending to pursue a course of study, provided by a specified educational institution, granted either by that institution or by another specified institution or body of persons. 'Specified' means specified by regulations.[18]

Holiday lettings: para 9

3.31   A tenancy the purpose of which is to give the tenant the right to occupy for a holiday. Such tenancies are also 'excluded tenancies' and a landlord need not obtain a court order to evict.

Resident landlords: para 10

3.32   Tenants with a resident landlord. See paras 4.16–4.29 below for the definition of 'resident landlord' and the other necessary conditions.

---

17 The term 'agricultural holding' is defined in the Agricultural Holdings Act 1986 and the terms 'farm business tenancy', and 'holding' are defined in the Agricultural Tenancies Act 1995.

18 The current regulations are the Assured and Protected Tenancies (Lettings to Students) Regulations 1998 SI No 1967 which have been amended frequently to add specific providers of student accommodation.

Crown tenancies: para 11

3.33 A tenancy under which the landlord is Her Majesty or a government department or where the premises are held in trust for Her Majesty for the purpose of a government department.

Local authority and other tenancies granted by specified public bodies: para 12

3.34 A tenancy under which the landlord is a local authority[19] or one of a list of other public bodies. Tenancies granted by most of these bodies will be secure tenancies. However, the list also includes 'fully mutual housing associations' who cannot grant either assured or secure tenancies, see paras 3.192–3.195.

Accommodation for asylum-seekers: para 12A

3.35 A tenancy granted by a private landlord under arrangements made for the provision of support for asylum-seekers and their dependants under Immigration and Asylum Act 1999 Part VI. Such tenancies are also excluded tenancies and the occupiers can be evicted without a court order.

Family intervention tenancies: para 12ZA

3.36 See para 3.191 below. However, a family intervention tenancy can become an assured tenancy if the landlord notifies the tenant expressly that it is to be regarded as an assured tenancy.

Accommodation for people with temporary protection: para 12B

3.37 A tenancy granted by a private landlord under arrangements for the provision of accommodation for people with temporary protection made under the Displaced Persons (Temporary Protection) Regulations 2005.[20]

Transitional cases: para 13

3.38 The following tenancies are not assured because they are governed by different statutes, all of which are explained below:

- a protected tenancy, within the meaning of the Rent Act 1977;

---

19 Local authorities include the London Fire and Emergency Planning Authority and police authorities.

20 SI No 1379. These regulations bring into force a European Directive (2001/55/EC) requiring member states to apply minimum standards for giving temporary protection to persons in the event of a mass influx of displaced persons.

- a housing association tenancy granted before 15 January 1989;
- a secure tenancy;
- a protected occupier under the Rent (Agriculture) Act 1976.

Features of an assured tenancy

Security of tenure

3.39   An assured tenant (in contrast to an assured shorthold tenant) has substantive security of tenure: he or she can be evicted only if the landlord obtains a possession order and an order will only be made if a ground for possession is proved. A landlord cannot terminate an assured tenancy other than by obtaining a possession order; it is the possession order that brings the tenancy to an end.

3.40   HA 1988 s5(1) provides that:

- an assured tenancy cannot be brought to an end by the landlord except by obtaining an order of the court; and
- the service by the landlord of a notice to quit shall be of no effect in relation to a periodic assured tenancy.[21]

3.41   In the case of a fixed-term tenancy containing a power for the landlord to determine the tenancy (a landlord's 'break clause'),[22] the landlord can end the fixed term by exercising that power. However, HA 1988 s5(2) provides that where a fixed-term assured tenancy comes to an end, other than by an order of the court or the tenant's surrender, the tenant is entitled to remain in possession as a 'statutory periodic tenant'.

3.42   This means that when a fixed-term assured tenancy ends, either by the landlord exercising a break clause or by 'effluxion of time' (ie, the fixed period expiring), a tenant who remains in occupation automatically becomes a statutory periodic tenant.

3.43   The only way a landlord can end a periodic assured tenancy (including a statutory periodic tenancy) is by obtaining a possession order, and HA 1988 s7 provides:

> ... the court shall not make an order for possession of a dwelling-house let on an assured tenancy except on one or more of the grounds set out in Schedule 2 to this Act.

---

21 Note, however, that this does not prevent a tenant, including a joint tenant, ending a tenancy by serving notice to quit.
22 This does not include a power of re-entry or forfeiture: s45(4). Re-entry and forfeiture are explained at paras 5.7–5.22.

3.44   So, although a landlord may have the right to end a fixed-term assured tenancy, the statutory periodic tenancy that then arises can only be ended by obtaining a possession order.

3.45   The grounds for possession are explained in detail in chapter 6.

Periodic assured tenancies

3.46   An assured tenancy may be a periodic tenancy from the outset. This will be the case if it is expressed to be a weekly or monthly tenancy. If no term is specifically agreed, the period will be implied from the 'rental period'. This is not the same as the way rent is paid. The rental period refers to the way rent is calculated, not the way rent is actually paid, although in most cases these will be the same.[23] So, if the tenancy agreement states that the rent is a certain amount per month the tenancy will be a monthly periodic tenancy. This is regardless of the fact that the rent may actually be paid, for example, four-weekly in arrears (as is usual when a tenant receives housing benefit).

3.47   If the tenancy was originally a fixed-term tenancy it becomes a statutory periodic tenancy on the expiry of the fixed term. It is deemed to be granted by the same landlord to the same tenant in relation to the same dwelling-house as under the fixed-term agreement.[24]

3.48   Registered providers have generally granted periodic assured tenancies with fixed-term agreements more common in the private sector. However, in future registered providers may routinely grant fixed-term tenancies to mirror the 'flexible tenancy', see paras 3.76–3.80.

The terms of a statutory periodic assured tenancy

3.49   Housing Act 1988 s5(3) provides:

- The statutory periodic tenancy takes effect immediately on the coming to an end of the fixed-term tenancy.
- The periods of the tenancy are the same as those for which rent was last payable under the fixed-term tenancy.
- The other terms are the same as under the fixed-term tenancy.[25] However, any term that makes provision for the landlord or tenant

---

23 See para 1.33.

24 HA 1988 s5(3)(a)–(c).

25 Though any rent review clause within the fixed-term agreement will not be a term of the periodic tenancy. This means that HA 1988 s13 will apply to rent increases under the statutory periodic tenancy: *London District Properties Management Ltd and Others v Goolamy & Goolamy* [2009] EWHC 1367 (Admin), 16 June 2009, see paras 4.186–4.190.

to end the agreement is of no effect while the tenancy remains assured.

3.50   A statutory periodic tenancy does not arise if a new tenancy of the same or substantially the same dwelling-house is granted at the end of the fixed-term tenancy.

> In *Church Commissioners for England v Gisele Meya*[26] the fixed-term agreement had been for a term of one year less a day. Rent had been expressed to be a certain amount per annum, payable by equal quarterly payments in advance on the usual quarter days. The issue was the period of the statutory assured tenancy arising at the end of the fixed term.
>
> At common law a periodic tenancy arising by implication would be an annual tenancy. However, the Court of Appeal held that HA 1988 s5(3)(d) meant that, the period was to be calculated by reference to the way rent was payable, not to the way rent was calculated. The statutory tenancy which arose at the end of the fixed term was therefore a quarterly periodic tenancy and not, as the tenant contended, an annual tenancy.

Tenant sharing accommodation with others

3.51   Even if a tenant shares accommodation with others, he or she may still be an assured tenant. However, there must be some accommodation of which the tenant has exclusive possession.

3.52   HA 1988 s3(1) provides that a person may have an assured tenancy of 'the separate accommodation' (ie, the room(s) of which exclusive possession is granted) despite the fact that the agreement provides for the sharing of other accommodation with other people, not including the landlord.[27]

3.53   The landlord cannot restrict use of the shared accommodation: as long as the tenant remains in possession of the separate accommodation, any term of the tenancy modifying or terminating the right to use the shared accommodation will be of no effect.[28] However, a

---

26   [2006] EWCA Civ 821, 21 June 2006.
27   For the position of tenants who share accommodation with their landlords see para 1.101.
28   HA 1988 s3(3).

term permitting variation or increase in the number of people with whom the tenant shares accommodation is enforceable.[29]

Tenant subletting part of the accommodation

3.54   Where a tenant has sublet part of his or her premises to another person this will not prevent the tenancy from remaining an assured tenancy even though the tenant now shares accommodation with others.[30]

3.55   However, subletting is prohibited in most assured tenancy agreements. It could therefore result in a claim for possession on the grounds of a breach of the tenancy agreement. See paras 4.98–4.99.

Features of an assured shorthold tenancy

Security of tenure

3.56   An assured shorthold tenant has no substantive security of tenure after the first six months, unless the tenancy is for a longer fixed period. So, after the intial six months the landlord is entitled to possession but must serve notice and obtain a possession order. No ground or reason for requiring possession is needed. The procedure for obtaining possession of premises let on an assured shorthold tenancy is described in chapter 6.

Formalities prior to 28 February 1997

3.57   Any assured tenancy granted on or after 28 February 1997 is an assured shorthold tenancy unless it is expressly provided otherwise. In contrast, to create an assured shorthold tenancy before 28 February 1997 the following conditions had to be satisfied:[31]

- the tenancy had to be for a fixed term of not less than six months, with no provision for the landlord to end the tenancy within the first six months;[32] and
- notice in a prescribed form had to be served by the landlord on the tenant before the tenancy was entered into.

---

29   HA 1988 s3(4).
30   HA 1988 s4.
31   HA 1988 s20.
32   This does not include a term for re-entry or forfeiture, see paras 5.7–5.22 below.

3.58   If these conditions were not met, the tenancy was an assured tenancy and the tenant had substantive security of tenure.

3.59   In most cases where it was argued that there had been a failure to comply with the formalities, the issue was the validity of the prescribed notice, known as the 'section 20 notice'.

HA 1988 section 20 notice

3.60   The notice served by the landlord had to be in a 'prescribed form' (HA 1988 s20(3)). 'Prescribed' means prescribed by regulations.[33] However, it was sufficient if the notice was in 'a form substantially to the same effect' as the prescribed form.[34] This meant that forms incorrectly completed or containing omissions could be valid if it was 'substantially to the same effect' as a properly completed prescribed form.

3.61   In some of the early cases about section 20 notices, the test applied was whether the error was obvious to the tenant so that he or she did not suffer detriment as a result of the error; such an error did not invalidate the notice.[35] However, where important information for the tenant was missing it was held that the notice was invalid.[36]

3.62   However, the Court of Appeal later rejected an approach that focuses on whether an error is obvious and whether it has caused detriment to the tenant. Rather, it has been held that there is only one question: whether the notice accomplished the statutory purpose of warning the tenant of the special nature of an assured shorthold tenancy.[37]

> In *Osborne & Co Ltd v Dior and Marito Holdings SA v Deneche and Lundborg*[38] the Court of Appeal considered two notices challenged by the tenants.
>
> In the first case the notice was signed by an employee of the managing agents and the space for the landlord's details left blank. In the second case the notice was also signed by the agent. The

---

33 Assured Tenancies and Agricultural Occupancies (Forms) Regulations 1988 SI No 2203 contain a schedule of prescribed forms, including that under section 20.

34 Regulation 2.

35 *Brewer v Andrews* (1997) 30 HLR 203 and *York v Ross & Casey* (1998) 31 HLR 209, CA.

36 See *Manel v Memon* (2001) 33 HLR 24, CA, which was approved in relation to a tenant's notice converting an assured tenancy into an assured shorthold tenancy; see *Kahlon v Isherwood* [2011] EWCA Civ 602 at para 3.70 below.

37 *Ravenseft Properties Ltd v Hall* [2001] EWCA Civ 2034, 19 December 2001.

38 [2003] EWCA Civ 281, 22 January 2003.

name of a company was entered into the box for the landlord's details but the company was not, in fact, the landlord. The Court of Appeal held, following *Ravenseft*, that the question is whether, notwithstanding any errors or omissions that have been demonstrated, the notice is 'substantially to the same effect' as a notice in the proper form which has been duly completed. In reaching its conclusion, the court must bear in mind the statutory purpose of the notice, ie telling the proposed tenant of the special nature of an assured shorthold tenancy.[39] Both notices were held to be valid and the tenancies were assured shorthold tenancies.

3.63 Section 20 notices are only required for tenancies created prior to 28 February 1997. However, the Court of Appeal's approach to prescribed notices is relevant to other kinds of notices such as possession notices see chapter 6.

Service of the notice

Joint landlords and tenants

3.64 The section 20 notice could be served by any one of two or more joint landlords[40] but had to be served on all the joint tenants.[41]

Agency

3.65 Section 20 notices (like many other notices) were often served by agents acting on behalf of landlords (see *Osborne & Co Ltd v Dior* at para 3.62 above). However, a section 20 notice could also be served *on* an agent instructed by a tenant to negotiate the tenancy agreement.[42]

Timing

3.66 The notice had to be served before the tenancy was entered into. This is a question of fact in each case.[43] A landlord who had failed to serve notice at the appropriate time may seek to remedy this by delivering a backdated notice to the tenant. The simple production of a copy notice that apparently complies with section 20 is not determinative. In a possession claim the burden is on the landlord to satisfy the

39 Arden LJ at [37].
40 HA 1988 s20(6).
41 HA 1988 s45(3).
42 *Yenula Properties Ltd v Naidu* [2002] EWCA Civ 719, 23 May 2002.
43 *Bedding v McCarthy* (1993) 27 HLR 103.

court 'on balance of probabilities' that any necessary conditions were satisfied. A tenant who disputes service of the notice must state this in the reply or defence and will be able to give oral evidence about what happened when the tenancy was granted; if the court cannot decide who is telling the truth, the claim should be dismissed.

New tenancies granted to existing tenants

Existing assured tenants

3.67   Where a tenant is already an assured tenant the signing of a new assured shorthold tenancy will be of no effect. This is the case even if the landlord grants the tenant a tenancy of different premises.

3.68   Housing Act 1988 s20(3) provides that if:

> ... immediately before a [new] tenancy is granted, the persons to whom it is granted or, as the case may be, at least one of [them], was a tenant under an assured tenancy which was not a shorthold tenancy, and the new tenancy is granted by the person who, immediately before the beginning of the tenancy, was the landlord under the assured tenancy ... the new tenancy cannot be an assured shorthold tenancy.

3.69   Therefore, a landlord cannot remedy a failure to follow the proper procedure after the start of the tenancy. Simply getting the tenant to sign a new tenancy agreement that is a shorthold agreement will not 'convert' an assured tenancy into an assured shorthold tenancy. However, the circumstances may be such that the old tenancy is deemed to have ended before the commencement of the new tenancy.

> In *Dibbs v Cambell*[44] it was held that tenants who signed a deed of surrender one day and entered into a new tenancy agreement the following day, were not tenants immediately before the grant of the new agreement. This was so even though the tenants had not vacated the premises.

Tenant's notice that a new tenancy is a shorthold

3.70   An exception to the rule that a new tenancy granted to an existing assured tenant cannot be a shorthold is where the tenant serves on the landlord a notice in prescribed form (or form substantially to the

---

44   (1988) 20 HLR 372, CA. The case was about similar anti-avoidance provisions preventing landlords from converting protected tenancies into protected shorthold tenancies, see below at paras 3.202–3.205.

same effect) stating that the new tenancy is to be assured.[45] Despite being a notice served by a tenant, the form begins with bullet points warning the tenant that he or she is giving up rights as an assured tenant and includes an exhortation to take advice if in doubt about whether to sign the form.

In *Kahlon v Isherwood*[46] the Court of Appeal considered a case in which an assured tenant had entered into a consent order in possession proceedings. The agreed terms were that the landlord would waive the rent arrears, the parties would enter into a new 12-month assured shorthold tenancy, and that the landlord would not claim any rent in excess of the tenant's housing benefit.

The parties did enter into such an agreement but when the landlord sought possession at the end of the term the tenant argued that the tenancy was not an assured shorthold tenancy because he had not served notice on the landlord in prescribed form.

The Court of Appeal rejected the landlord's argument that the schedule to the order, setting out the terms of the agreement, was effectively a form substantially to the same effect as the prescribed form. Although commenting that the tenant's defence was 'deeply unattractive', the court held that, as in *Manel v Manon* (see above, para 3.61) similar bullet points containing information for the tenant were crucial. Furthermore, there was nothing corresponding to paragraph 4 of the form which confirms that the tenant understands the nature of the tenancy he or she is giving up and the limited rights under an assured shorthold tenancy. The notice is 'the means of providing a clear record that the tenant has been appraised of his rights and the loss of security which the new arrangements will entail'.[47] The new tenancy was not an assured shorthold tenancy.

Existing assured shorthold tenants

3.71   Where an assured shorthold tenant simply remains in occupation after the end of the fixed term, he or she becomes a statutory periodic assured shorthold tenant. It is not necessary for the parties to enter into a new agreement (or, where the tenancy commenced before 28 February 1997, for a new section 20 notice to be served). Nevertheless

---

45   HA 1988 s19A and Sch 2A para 7(2). The prescribed form is Form 8 and is set out in Assured Tenancies and Agricultural Occupancies (Forms) Regulations 1997 SI No 194.

46   [2011] EWCA Civ 602, 19 May 2011.

47   Patten LJ at [24].

it is common for an assured shorthold tenant to be given a succession of fixed-term agreements by a landlord.[48]

Existing Rent Act tenants: HA 1988 s34

3.72 As described below (paras 3.81–3.95), tenants under the Rent Act 1977 have the strongest rights: the grounds for possession are the most restrictive and rents are subject to the fair rent system. A landlord would have a strong incentive for wishing to 'convert' a Rent Act tenancy into an assured or assured shorthold tenancy. There is no express protection in terms similar to HA 1988 s20(3) (see para 3.68 above). Rather, the position is governed by HA 1988 s34(1) which provides that tenancies entered into on or after 15 January 1989 cannot be protected (under the Rent Act 1977) except in certain circumstances. These circumstances include a tenancy which 'is granted to a person (alone or jointly with others) who, immediately before the tenancy was granted, was a protected or statutory tenant and is so granted by the person who at that time was the landlord (or one of the joint landlords) under the protected or statutory tenancy'.[49]

3.73 Although the terms of HA 1998 s34 suggest only that it is *possible* to create a new protected tenancy in such a situation, the courts have held that any new tenancy *will* be a protected tenancy, provided the landlord and tenant are the same, even if the tenancy is of different premises.[50]

> In *Rajah v Arogol Co Ltd*[51] the defendant had been a Rent Act tenant of a room on the ground floor of a property since 1982. In 1990 he moved to occupy the entire floor. In possession proceedings the landlord argued that he was no longer a protected tenant. The county court made an order for possession, holding that there had been a surrender of the protected tenancy when the parties entered into a tenancy for the whole floor.
>
> The Court of Appeal upheld the tenant's appeal: the protection of HA 1988 s34(1)(b) was not limited to the same or substantially the same premises. The move did not constitute surrender and the defendant retained the protection of the Rent Act.

---

48 Many local authorities insist, incorrectly, that housing benefit cannot be paid unless a new tenancy agreement is drawn up.
49 HA 1998 s34(1)(b).
50 *Laimond Properties Ltd v Al-Shakarchi* (1998) 30 HLR 1099.
51 [2001] EWCA Civ 454.

3.74 It is, however, always necessary that the tenant is a protected or statutory tenant 'immediately before the [new] tenancy was granted'.

> In *The Governing Body of Rugby School v Edwards*[52] the defendant had
> been a protected tenant of the claimant. Possession proceedings
> were brought on the grounds of substantial rent arrears. The
> proceedings were compromised by a consent order providing
> that the defendant give up possession in consideration for the
> claimant agreeing not to enforce payment of the agreed rent arrears
> of £7,885. It was also agreed, although not part of the consent
> order, that the claimant would grant to the defendant a three-year
> assured tenancy of a smaller property. Rent arrears accrued in the
> new property and a claim for possession was made. The defendant
> argued that he was a protected tenant as HA 1988 s34(1) applied;
> as such, his case was that rather than being in arrears of £4,500 he
> had overpaid rent of about £15,000.
>   The district judge, however, found that the tenant had
> surrendered his previous tenancy as part of the agreement *before*
> being granted a new tenancy of the smaller property. Therefore, he
> was not a protected or statutory tenant immediately before the grant
> of the new tenancy and section 34 did not apply. The decision was
> upheld by a circuit judge.

3.75 The Housing Act 1988 s34 also enables new protected tenancies to be granted when a possession order is made on the ground that suitable alternative accommodation is available to the tenant. However, such a tenancy is not automatically protected; rather, section 34(1)(c) permits the court to order that any new tenancy be a protected tenancy if that is necessary for it to constitute a suitable alternative to the existing accommodation. See paras 7.109–7.111.

Assured shorthold tenancies granted by private registered providers of social housing (PRPSH)

3.76 The Localism Act 2011 and the new guidance issued by the housing regulator (see paras 1.90 and 2.95) encourages all social landlords to consider granting tenancies for fixed periods, rather than 'for life'. For local authorities, the new flexible tenancy has been created for this purpose. For private registered providers no new type of tenancy is needed since they can grant assured shorthold tenancies.

52 July 2004 *Legal Action* 17, Mayors & City County Court.

3.77   The current regulatory guidance[53] provides that for general needs tenants landlords should grant either periodic assured tenancies, or fixed-term (ie, assured shorthold) tenancies for a minimum of five years, or, exceptionally, for a minimum of two years (in addition to any probationary period). There are also additional notice requirements which are described in chapter 6.

3.78   Most private registered providers are classed as public bodies and if they fail to follow the regulatory guidance or fail to adhere to the principles of good administrative decision-making, they may be challenged by judicial review or subject to public law and/or human rights defences when claiming possession. See chapter 7.

3.79   In addition to the requirements regarding the minimum term of assured shorthold tenancies, the regulatory guidance also provides that landlords must publish clear and accessible policies outlining their approach to tenancy management, setting out:[54]

- the type of tenancies they will grant;
- if they grant fixed-term tenancies, the length of the terms;
- any exceptional circumstances in which they will grant terms of less than five years for 'general needs housing';
- the circumstances in which they may or may not grant a further tenancy at the end of the fixed term;
- the way a tenant may appeal against or complain about the term of the tenancy or a decision not to grant another tenancy at the end of the fixed term; and
- their policy on taking into account household needs for a reasonable degree of stability because of vulnerability by reason of age, disability or illness or because of children in the household.

3.80   This type of assured shorthold tenancy can also be demoted, on the grounds of anti-social behaviour, see para 6.85. If demoted it will become a periodic assured shorthold tenancy.

Rent Act 1977: protected and statutory tenancies

3.81   The Rent Act (RA) 1977 governs tenancies granted by private landlords before 15 January 1989. The contractual tenancy that gave substantive security of tenure under the RA 1977 is called a 'protected tenancy'.

53   HCA Regulatory Framework for Social Housing in England from April 2012, para 2.2.
54   See para 2.

3.82 The RA 1977 has a similar structure to the HA 1988: it sets out the conditions for a protected tenancy and contains a schedule listing tenancies that cannot be protected. However, the way security of tenure operates is different. Under the HA 1988 a landlord cannot bring an assured tenancy to an end except by a court order. Under the RA 1977 there is no restriction on the landlord's right to bring the tenancy to an end but, after it ends, a 'statutory tenancy' comes into existence, provided the tenant is residing in the premises. So, under the RA 1977 the tenancy was known as a 'protected tenancy' during the contractual term and a 'statutory tenancy' after the contractual term had ended. The term 'regulated tenancies' refers to both protected and a statutory tenancies.[55]

Conditions for protected tenancies

3.83 The tenancy must be one 'under which a dwelling-house (which may be a house or part of a house) is let as a separate dwelling'.[56] See paras 3.9–3.14 above for a discussion of the case-law on this condition.

Sharing with other tenants

3.84 As with assured tenancies, there is specific provision that sharing accommodation with other tenants does not prevent the tenancy being protected. RA 1977 s22 provides that where a tenant has exclusive occupation of separate accommodation but the terms of the agreement include the use of other accommodation in common with others, not including the landlord, the separate accommodation shall be deemed a dwelling-house let on a protected or statutory tenancy. Any term terminating or modifying the right to use the shared living accommodation shall be of no effect but the terms may provide for a variation and/or increase in the number of persons with whom the tenant must share.

Ending the protected tenancy

3.85 As the RA 1977 places no restriction on a landlord's right to end a tenancy, the service of a notice to quit operates to end a periodic protected tenancy.

---

55 RA 1977 s18(1). Under RA 1977 s18A and Sch 17 tenancies governed by previous Rent Acts, known as 'controlled tenancies' were converted into regulated tenancies.
56 RA 1977 s1(1).

3.86   A fixed-term protected tenancy ends when the fixed term expires ('by effluxion of time'). It could also end by the landlord triggering a contractual break clause or by way of forfeiture if the agreement provides for this.

3.87   However the protected tenancy ends, a tenant who remains in residence becomes a statutory tenant and can be evicted only if a possession order is obtained. A possession order will be made only if one of the statutory grounds is proved.

3.88   Furthermore, a notice of rent increase operates to convert a periodic protected tenancy into a statutory tenancy.[57]

3.89   Even where a tenant serves notice to quit on a landlord this only ends the protected tenancy; if the tenant remains in residence, he or she becomes a statutory tenant. However, there is a ground for possession where the landlord has relied on the tenant's notice and contracted to sell or let the premises or is otherwise prejudiced.[58]

The statutory tenancy

3.90   Rent Act 1977 s2(1)(a) provides that:

> ... after the termination of a protected tenancy of a dwelling-house the person who, immediately before that termination, was the protected tenant of the dwelling-house shall, if and so long as he occupies the dwelling-house as his residence, be the statutory tenant of it.

Security of tenure

3.91   A protected or statutory tenant cannot be evicted by a landlord unless either:[59]

- one of the grounds for possession is proved to a court; or
- suitable alternative accommodation is available to the tenant.

3.92   As is the case under the Housing Acts 1985 and 1988 security of tenure is enjoyed only if a person is occupying the premises as a home. Under the RA 1977 the statutory tenant must be occupying premises as his or her residence[60] whereas under the Housing Acts the assured or secure tenant must occupy premises as his or her only

---

57   RA 1977 s49(4).
58   RA 1977 Sch 15, Case 5, see appendix to chapter 7.
59   RA 1977 ss98 and 99.
60   A protected tenancy exists even if the tenant does not reside in the premises. Few tenancies will still be protected: the original contract would still have to be in existence with no notice to quit or notice of rent increase being served since the tenancy started.

or principal home. The residence condition is discussed in detail at paras 4.2–4.11.

Exceptions to Rent Act protection

3.93 The Rent Act 1977 lists those tenancies that cannot be protected:

- tenancies with a high rateable value (s4);[61]
- tenancies under which no rent or a low rent is paid. A low rent is a rent of less than two-thirds of the rateable value (s5);[62]
- dwelling-houses let with more than two acres of agricultural land (ss6 and 26);
- tenancies which include payments for board or attendance, provided the payment forms a substantial part of the rent (s7); board means the provision of food (as in 'board and lodgings'), attendance means the provision of services personal to the tenancy, such as room cleaning and the supply of clean linen;
- certain tenancies granted to students by specified educational institutions (s8); the conditions are the same as under the HA 1988, see para 3.30 above;
- holiday lets (s9);
- tenancies of agricultural holdings and farm business lets (s10), see paras 3.206–3.210 below;
- tenancies of licensed premises (s11);
- tenancies where there is a resident landlord (s12); this is discussed in detail at paras 4.16–4.29;
- Crown tenancies (s13);
- business tenancies (s24); mixed business and residential tenancies are discussed at paras 1.132–1.137;
- tenancies granted by exempt landlords such as local authorities, housing associations and housing co-operatives (ss14, 15 and 16).

If a tenancy cannot be protected for one of the above reasons, it will usually be a contractual tenancy and the tenant's rights will depend on the agreed terms. In most cases the tenant will be protected from eviction without a court order, see paras 8.10–8.15.

61 What constitutes a high rateable value depends on when the tenancy was granted and whether the property is in Greater London or elsewhere. See RA 1977 s25. Rates on domestic premises were abolished in 1990. Few local authorities keep old ratings lists but archived lists may be held by local libraries.

62 Again, the relevant rateable value depends on when and where the tenancy was granted and it may be necessary to consult archived ratings lists.

Restricted contracts

3.94   Under the RA 1977 some tenancies were 'restricted contracts' under which tenants had limited rights: the possible postponement of a notice to quit and some rent control. A restricted contract was created in two situations:

- where there was a resident landlord; and
- where the tenant made payments for board but where the payments were not substantial.

The majority of restricted contracts were granted by resident landlords. No new restricted contracts could be granted after 15 January 1989 and any change in the terms of the agreement, including a rent increase, after that date will mean that the tenancy is no longer a restricted contract but is governed by the HA 1988 (or, more correctly falls outside HA 1988 and is simply a contractual tenancy).

Fair rents

3.95   Under the RA 1977 all protected and statutory tenants have the right to have a 'fair rent' registered. This is the maximum rent that can be charged. The fair rent system is explained below at paras 4.185–4.188.

'Sitting tenants' and being 'bought out'

3.96   The term 'sitting tenant' refers to a tenant who is entitled to remain in occupation of premises so that if ownership of the premises changes the new owner takes the premises subject to the tenant's interest. Tenancies, being interests in land, bind a purchaser.[63] A landlord cannot evict a tenant simply because he or she wishes to sell, or because he or she has just purchased the premises and wishes to obtain vacant possession.

3.97   Clearly, some tenancies can be ended more easily than others; an owner with an assured shorthold tenant in occupation can evict the tenant by serving two months' notice and obtaining and enforcing a possession order before selling with vacant possession. Similarly, a purchaser can obtain possession in the same way following completion of the purchase. Because a statutory tenant under the RA 1977 has the strongest rights possible, the term 'sitting tenant' is usually used to refer to such tenants. An owner of premises subject to a

---

63   Land Registration Act 2002 Schs 1 and 3.

statutory tenancy may wish to pay the tenant a sum of money to give up his or her tenancy. The question arises: how is such an interest valued?

3.98 There is no statutory formula for determining the value of a tenant's interest. Any agreement will depend on how much the landlord is prepared to pay and how much the tenant is prepared to accept. A tenant who intends to move in with family members may accept less than someone who needs to secure alternative accommodation. If the tenant is elderly the landlord may prefer to keep the property until the death of the tenant rather than pay a substantial sum to gain vacant possession.

3.99 If a tenant is negotiating such an agreement, expert valuation evidence will assist because the increased value of the property with vacant possession is often underestimated. However, agreement always depends on reaching a compromise and if a landlord is unwilling to pay the amount asked by the tenant, the tenant will remain in occupation as a statutory tenant. It should be remembered that a possession order may be made by a court if suitable alternative accommodation is available to the tenant. A landlord may choose to offer alternative accommodation rather than pay the tenant to leave. Suitable alternative accommodation as a ground for possession is discussed at paras 7.104–7.122.

Local authority tenancies

3.100 Tenancies under which the landlord is a local authority may be one of the following:

- a secure periodic tenancy (a 'lifetime' tenancy);
- a secure 'flexible'(fixed-term) tenancy;
- an introductory tenancy;
- a demoted tenancy;
- a family intervention tenancy; or
- a non-secure tenancy.

Housing association secure tenancies

3.101 Before 15 January 1989 housing associations also granted secure tenancies, governed by the Housing Act (HA) 1985. Tenants of housing associations whose tenancy started before that date remain secure tenants, while tenants whose tenancy was granted on or after that date will be assured tenants.

3.102   Secure tenants of housing associations have the same rights as secure tenants of local authorities with two main differences: (1) secure tenants of housing associations do not have the 'right to buy' and (2) secure tenancies of housing associations are subject to the fair rent scheme under the Rent Act 1977; this is described at paras 4.186–4.187.

The new 'flexible' secure tenancy

3.103   Until 2012, the predominant tenancy in the social rented sector, whether granted by a local authority or a housing association (private registered provider), would give the tenant long-term security of tenure: the tenant could only be evicted if there was a ground for possession, eg rent arrears or anti-social behaviour. Probationary tenancies could be used for an initial period but provided the tenant was not evicted in the probationary period, he or she would become a secure or assured tenancy with substantive security of tenure. The Localism Act 2011 created a new type of tenancy for local authorities: the so-called 'flexible tenancy'. In order to use flexible tenancies, local authorities must adopt a policy of doing so and the principles they will apply must be set out in their 'housing strategy'.[64] The strategy will set out whether the particular authority uses flexible tenancies, their policies when offering flexible tenancies (eg the circumstances in which they will grant flexible tenancies as opposed to 'lifetime tenancies'), the length of the fixed term that will be offered, and the policy for granting further flexible tenancies following expiry. Unlike introductory tenancies (see below at paras 3.168–3.173) it is not necessary for an authority to offer all new tenants a flexible tenancy. An authority may have a policy of offering flexible tenancies to most tenants but offering lifetime tenancies to certain groups, eg people over a certain age, or people with dependent children. The policy must be specified in the housing strategy and must not discriminate unlawfully against protected groups under the Equality Act 2010, see paras 2.84–2.86 and 7.183–7.201.

3.104   A flexible tenancy is a secure tenancy that is:

- for a fixed period of not less than two years, and
- before it was granted written notice was served on the tenant stating that it would be a flexible tenancy.

---

64   Under the Localism Act 2011 local authorities were given until January 2013 to publish their housing strategies.

3.105 A flexible tenancy is a type of secure tenancy so the conditions for secure tenancies, set out at para 3.106 below, must also be met.

Conditions for all secure tenancies

3.106 The HA 1985 Part IV sets out the conditions for creating secure tenancies and the rights of secure tenants. The conditions apply to secure periodic tenancies and secure flexible tenancies. The conditions for the creation of a secure tenancy are that:[65]

- the premises are 'let as a separate dwelling';
- the landlord condition is satisfied;
- the tenant condition is satisfied; and
- the tenancy is not excluded by HA 1985 Sch 1.

Separate dwelling

3.107 HA 1985 s79(1) provides that the tenancy must be one 'under which a dwelling-house is let as a separate dwelling'.

3.108 All of the statutes providing for security of tenure include this condition. See paras 3.9–3.14 above for a more detailed explanation of the condition. Note that unlike tenancies in the private sector there is no provision for a secure tenancy where a tenant has possession of a room only, with shared use of other accommodation. Such a letting cannot be a secure tenancy because there is no letting of a separate dwelling.

Secure licences

3.109 HA 1985 s79(3) provides that the rights of secure tenants, not including the right to buy, apply also to licensees of dwelling-houses (except those granted to trespassers as a temporary measure, see para 3.112 below). So, under the Housing Act 1985 there is the possibility of a 'secure licence'.

3.110 One situation in which a secure licence may be granted is when a right to occupy is granted to someone under the age of 18. A minor cannot legally hold a tenancy but there are two possible ways of granting a right to occupy to a child. Either a secure licence can be given until the child turns 18 when it will become a tenancy, or a secure tenancy can be granted, to be held on trust by some other person for the benefit of the child, until he or she turns 18. See paras 1.138–1.143 for an explanation of such trusts.

---

65 HA 1985 ss79–81.

3.111   In addition, an occupier of a single room who shares facilities with others may have a secure licence provided he or she has exclusive possession of the room.[66]

3.112   A licence may also be granted to a trespasser as a 'temporary expedient' pending the recovery of possession. Such a licence will not be secure and the trespasser/licensee is an excluded occupier, who can be evicted without a court order after the licence is ended.[67]

Landlord and tenant conditions

3.113   A tenancy can be secure only if the landlord and the tenant conditions are satisfied. HA 1985 s79 provides that the tenancy will be secure 'at any time when' those conditions are satisfied. The same tenancy may therefore be at one time secure and at another time not secure if the conditions are not met, for example, if there is a change of landlord or the tenant ceases to live in the premises.

Landlord condition

3.114   HA 1985 s80 provides that the landlord must be one of a list of specified authorities or bodies. The first, and main, type of body is 'a local authority'. However, certain other public bodies can be the landlords of secure tenancies.[68]

3.115   Before 15 January 1989 most housing trusts and housing associations could grant secure tenancies. A secure tenancy granted by such a body before that date will remain secure and the following paragraphs therefore apply also to the secure tenants of housing trusts and housing associations.

Tenant condition

3.116   HA 1985 s81 provides that the tenant must be an individual who occupies the dwelling-house as his or her only or principal home. If there are joint tenants each must be an individual and at least one must occupy the premises as his or her only or principal home.

---

66 *Westminster CC v Clarke* (1992) 24 HLR 360, HL.
67 HA 1985 s79(4) and Protection from Eviction Act 1977 s3A, and see paras 1.101–1.122.
68 The list is subject to frequent amendment to reflect the creation of new public bodies, and abolition of old ones. The current list includes: a development corporation, a housing action trust, a Mayoral development corporation, an urban development corporation, the Homes and Communities Agency, the Greater London Authority or the Welsh Ministers, the Regulator of Social Housing, a housing trust that is a charity, a housing association and certain types of housing co-operative.

3.117 If at any time the tenant condition is not met, ie, the tenant is not occupying the premises as his or her only or principal home, the tenant stops being a secure tenant. He or she enjoys only a non-secure contractual tenancy at this time. However, the secure status can be regained if the tenant resumes occupation as his or her only or principal home, provided there has not been a subletting or parting with possession of the whole of the premises, see para 4.107.

Exceptions: tenancies that cannot be secure

3.118 Certain tenancies cannot be secure. These are set out in HA 1985 Sch 1 and are as follows.

Long leases: para 1

3.119 A 'long tenancy' is defined in HA 1985 s115 and includes a lease granted for a fixed period of more than 21 years and any lease granted under the right to buy or right to acquire provisions.[69]

Introductory tenancies: para 1A

3.120 Introductory tenancies are governed by HA 1996 Part V, see paras 3.168–3.183 below. Also excluded are tenancies that have ceased to be introductory following the death of the tenant or where the tenant is not occupying as his or her only or principal home.

Demoted tenances: para 1B

3.121 See paras 3.184–3.190 below.

Tenancies granted to employees: para 2

3.122 Tenancies granted to employees of the landlord or certain specified bodies where it is a condition of the employment contract that the employee occupies the dwelling-house for the better performance of his or her duties.[70]

3.123 Those required to occupy accommodation owned by an employer for the better performance of the employment duties will, under the common law, be licensees and not tenants (see chapter 1). However,

---

69 The 'right to buy' enjoyed by secure tenants is set out in HA 1985 Part V. The 'right to acquire' for assured tenants of RSLs is set out in HA 1996 ss16–17. Both schemes are outside the scope of this book.

70 The employment contract may be express or implied and an express contract may be an oral contract. However, a term requiring occupation will only be implied into the employment contract if occupation is necessary in order for the employee to do the job: *Hughes & Hughes v Greenwich LBC* (1993) 26 HLR 99.

this exception to secure status extends to those who are employed by one specified body and accommodated by another. The specified bodies are listed in para 2 and include the governors of an aided school.

3.124   In all cases the employment contract must specify that the employee must live in the particular accommodation.

3.125   This exclusion also deals specifically with rent-free accommodation provided to the police and fire authority employees.

3.126   Where the landlord is a local housing authority the tenancy does not become secure unless the authority notifies the tenant that it is secure. Where the landlord is not a local housing authority the tenancy will become secure automatically if the conditions are not met for a period of three years in aggregate.

Short-life tenancies on land acquired for development: para 3

3.127   Tenancies granted to provide temporary accommodation on land acquired for development, pending the development.[71]

3.128   Although the provision is for 'temporary' accommodation the occupiers may be in occupation for long periods, and even under long fixed-term lettings, provided development is pending. The exception applies even if the identity of the landlord changes. However, if the development plans are rejected or abandoned and no alternative development plan is pending the exception will cease to apply and any tenants will become secure.[72]

Homeless accommodation: para 4

3.129   Tenancies granted to homeless applicants under HA 1996 Part VII. This includes accommodation pending inquiries and accommodation provided under HA 1996 s193 following acceptance of a housing duty.

Family intervention tenancies: para 4ZA

3.130   See para 3.191 below.

---

71 'Development' means: 'the carrying out of building, engineering, mining or other operations in, on, and over or under land, or the making of any material change in the use of buildings or other land': Town and Country Planning Act 1990 s55.

72 *Lillieshall Road Housing Co-operative Ltd v Brennan & Brennan* (1991) 24 HLR 195, CA.

Asylum-seekers: para 4A

3.131 Accommodation provided to asylum-seekers under the Immigration and Asylum Act 1999 Part VI (ie, by arrangement with the Home Office, see para 20.194). However, the landlord may notify the tenant that the tenancy is to become secure. This will only happen if the asylum-seeker is granted some form of leave and becomes entitled to an allocation under HA 1996 Part VI (see chapter 17).

Accommodation for people with temporary protection: para 4B

3.132 See para 3.37 above – this provision is the same as for tenancies excluded from the HA 1988.

Temporary accommodation to people taking up employment: para 5

3.133 This exception applies to schemes under which an authority offers temporary accommodation to those taking up employment in the district or surrounding area. The tenant must be informed in writing, before the grant of the tenancy, that the exception applies. Unless the landlord is a local housing authority the tenancy will automatically become secure one year after the start of the tenancy. In the case of a local housing authority the tenancy will only become secure if the authority notifies the tenant. Such schemes are now rare.

Short-term subleasing schemes: para 6

3.134 Where the accommodation has been leased to the landlord for use as temporary housing accommodation, with a provision that vacant possession will be given back after a certain period. This exception covers 'private sector leasing' arrangements in which private landlords let vacant property to a local authority which then sublets the accommodation on a temporary basis to homeless applicants.

Temporary accommodation during works: para 7

3.135 Where a tenancy is offered to a person on a temporary basis to enable works to be carried out to the tenant's home. This exception does not apply if the tenant was already a secure tenant of the home being repaired. In such a case the tenant will become a secure tenant of the temporary accommodation but a discretionary ground for possession is available to enable landlord to compel the tenant to return to the repaired property.

3.136 This provision enables an authority to provide temporary accommodation to private tenants to facilitate carrying out major works. In the past some authorities had a policy of doing this when serving

repair or improvement notices on private landlords where vacant possession was needed to complete the major works. Given the shortage
of local authority accommodation such policies are now rare.

Agricultural holdings: para 8

3.137   Tenancies granted to tenants engaged in farming land where the
accommodation is part of an agricultural holding. Such tenancies are
governed by the Agricultural Holdings Act 1986 and the Agricultural
Tenancies Act 1995 (see paras 3.206–3.210 below).

Licenced premises: para 9

3.138   A tenancy of premises or part of premises licensed for the sale of
intoxicating liquor for consumption on the premises.

Specified student lettings: para 10

3.139   A tenancy granted to a student to enable the tenant to attend a designated course at a university or further education establishment is
not a secure tenancy. In this case a written notice must be served
on the tenant before the tenancy is granted, stating that the tenancy
falls within this exception and specifying the proposed educational
establishment.

3.140   Unless the landlord is a local authority the tenancy will automatically become secure six months after the tenant ceases to attend the
designated course (or, if the tenant fails to take up the course, six
months from the date of grant). If the landlord is a local authority the
tenancy will only become secure if the landlord notifies the tenant.

Business tenancies: para 11

3.141   A tenancy of premises occupied primarily for business purposes is
governed by the Landlord and Tenant Act 1954. See paras 1.132–
1.135 for issues arising when there is mixed business and residential
use.

Almshouses: para 12

3.142   A licence to occupy an almshouse dwelling will not be a secure tenancy. Almshouse occupiers are licensees and not tenants because the
grant of the right of occupation is a charitable act.[73] The licence must
have been granted by or on behalf of a charity authorised to maintain the dwelling-house as an almshouse and which has no power to
grant a tenancy of the dwelling-house.

---

73   *Gray v Taylor* [1998] 1 WLR 1093, CA.

Secure tenancies 'by default'

3.143 Note that where there is provision for tenancies to become secure by default after a certain period (under HA 1985 Sch 1 paras 2, 5 and 10) where the landlord is a local authority the tenancy will only become secure if the authority notifies the tenant. This ensures that only those who qualify for an allocation of accommodation under HA 1996 Part VI become tenants of the local authority.

Features of a secure periodic tenancy

Security of tenure

3.144 In contrast to the flexible secure tenant the periodic secure tenant has security of tenure indefinitely. Such tenancies are commonly now referred to as 'lifetime tenancies'. Flexible tenants have 'security of tenure' only during the fixed term. On the expiry of the fixed period, they can be evicted, providing the landlord follows the correct procedure, set out below at paras 3.160–3.167. So, the paragraphs below, 3.145–3.146, apply to flexible tenants during the fixed term and to periodic secure tenants throughout the tenancy.

3.145 HA 1985 s82(1) provides that a secure periodic tenancy can only be brought to an end by a landlord by obtaining and executing a possession order, or by obtaining a demotion order under s82A, see para 6.86. A landlord's notice to quit therefore has no effect on a secure periodic tenancy. The tenancy ends on the date when the order is executed, ie when the tenant is actually evicted.

3.146 A possession order will only be made if one of the statutory grounds for possession is proved. These are set out in the appendix to chapter 7. The most commonly used grounds ('tenant's fault' grounds) are discretionary. In addition, there are grounds that depend on the landlord offering suitable alternative accommodation to the tenant, some of these are discretionary and some mandatory. These grounds enable public sector landlords to exercise control over the occupancy of accommodation designed for those with special needs and to forcibly re-house tenants to facilitate development. In addition, as from October 2014 there is a new 'mandatory' anti-social behaviour ground, see para 7.49.[74]

---

74 This ground operates differently from all of the other grounds in that there is a right of internal review prior to the claim being issued, see paras 6.95–6.101 and appendix 2 to chapter 6.

Other statutory rights

3.147   Secure tenants also have the following additional statutory rights:

- succession – the right to pass the tenancy to a partner or family member after death;[75]
- transfer of the tenancy – in limited circumstances;
- mutual exchange – the right to 'swap' the tenancy with another tenant of a social landlords;
- the right to take in lodgers;
- the right to make improvements;
- the right to buy the property.

3.148   Flexible secure tenants enjoy all these rights but any transfer or succession will be to a flexible tenancy only.

3.149   The right to buy is outside the scope of this book. The other rights listed above are discussed in chapter 4.

Variation of secure periodic tenancies

3.150   A feature peculiar to the secure tenancies is that the landlord has the right to vary the terms of a periodic secure tenancy. The general rule is that once a contract has been entered into, both parties are bound by the agreed terms and can only vary them by agreement. However, the HA 1985 provides that a landlord can unilaterally vary the terms of the tenancy agreement by following the procedure set out in section 103. This requires service of notice of proposed variation on the tenant in advance. The variation cannot take effect sooner than four weeks from the date of the notice. This right does not apply to flexible tenancies.

Features of a secure flexible tenancy

3.151   Local authorities can now grant tenancies for a fixed period, after which a further tenancy can be granted or possession can be obtained, without any statutory ground for possession being needed. These are called flexible tenancies and they are a type of secure tenancy. A flexible tenancy must be for a minimum period of two years and written notice must have been served before the tenancy commenced stating that the tenancy would be a flexible tenancy.[76]

---

75 For secure tenancies granted after 1 April 2012 the statutory right of succession is limited to a spouse, civil partner or cohabitee, see para 4.33.
76 HA 1985 s107A(2).

3.152   The regulatory guidance recommends that in most cases the length of the term should be at least five years.[77]

3.153   A flexible tenancy may be granted to someone who has never before held a local authority tenancy or may be granted to existing demoted and family intervention tenants.[78]

3.154   Authorities that use introductory tenancies must serve notice prior to the grant of the introductory tenancy stating that at the end of the introductory tenancy the secure tenancy that arises will be a flexible tenancy and the term of that tenancy.[79]

3.155   All local authorities must publish their 'tenancy strategy'.[80] This must set out:

- the matters to which registered providers of social housing in the area (including the local authority itself) must have regard when formulating policies about the kinds of tenancies they grant;
- the circumstances in which they will grant particular kinds of tenancies;
- if they grant fixed-term tenancies, the lengths of the terms; and
- the circumstances in which they will grant a further tenancy at the end of the initial tenancy.

3.156   Flexible tenants do not have substantive security of tenure beyond the fixed term: at the end of the period the landlord can obtain a possession order as of right, provided the correct notices have been served. There are three notices that must be served by a landlord on a flexible tenant: (1) before the tenancy begins; (2) six months before the end, stating that no new tenancy is to be granted (unless the landlord does intend to grant a new flexible or periodic tenancy); and (3) giving two months notice that possession is required.

3.157   A landlord wishing to evict a flexible secure tenant before the fixed term has ended, can do so provided one of the statutory grounds is made out. As is the case for periodic secure tenancies, notice of possession must (in most cases) be served before the proceedings can be commenced. The Notice of Possession is a prescribed form, but is

---

77 See para 2 of the HCA Regulatory Framework for Social Housing in England from April 2012, referred to above at para 3.77.

78 HA 1985 s107(3) and (6).

79 HA 1985 s(6) and HA 1996 s137A.

80 In devising a housing strategy, certain matters must be taken into account (for example, the existing allocation scheme and homelessness strategy) and certain bodies must be consulted, for example, the private registered providers in the area.

not the same prescribed form as for periodic secure tenants, see para 6.32.[81]

3.158   The issue has not yet been tested before the courts, but it would appear to be the case that the landlord can only claim possession within the fixed period if the tenancy agreement includes a provision entitling the landlord to terminate the agreement before the end of the fixed term. Furthermore, such a clause will usually be conditional on there being arrears of rent or a breach of the agreement by the tenant, ie a forfeiture clause. This will mean (as the prescribed notice states) that the tenant will have the common law right to seek relief against forfeiture, see para 5.19.

3.159   A flexible secure tenancy can also be demoted and, if this happens, the tenancy becomes a periodic demoted tenancy.

Flexible tenancy notices

3.160   The first notice is served before the tenancy starts and states that the tenancy is to be a flexible tenancy and the length of the term.[82] If the landlord decides not to grant a new tenancy at the end of the flexible tenancy, a further notice must be served giving at least six months notice informing the tenant of this decision with reasons. The final notice is a two-month notice stating that the landlord requires possession. This notice may be given before or on the day the tenancy comes to an end.[83]

3.161   It is unclear what will happen if the landlord fails to serve the six-month notice before the fixed period ends. No provision is made for the tenancy to become periodic by default but since the notice is to explain why a new tenancy will not be offered after the end of the term, it is clearly expected that the notice, and any review conducting at the tenant's request, must precede the last day of the fixed term.

3.162   Similarly no provision is made if the two-month notice is not served before the tenancy ends. A tenant may argue that the landlord has lost the right to seek possession as of right. However, in light of the recent case-law on notices served under section 21 of HA 1988, it is likely that the courts will interpret the provision as enabling a

---

81 The prescribed notice is the one set out in Part II of the Schedule to the Secure Tenancies (Notices) Regulations 1987 SI No 755.

82 If the authority operates a policy of introductory tenancies, this notice will inform the tenant that when the introductory tenancy ends it will become a flexible tenancy.

83 HA 1985 s107D(5).

landlord to serve the two-month notice either before or after the end of the fixed period.

3.163 The tenant has the right to seek a review of each of these three notices, including the one served before the tenancy begins. However, in relation to the first notice any review is limited to the decision about the term of the tenancy. An example would be where a landlord grants a five-year term to most tenants but a shorter term in exceptional circumstances. The tenant may argue that the decision to grant a shorter term is not justified. The tenant has 21 days to request the review and the outcome must be notified in writing with reasons. Given the need to reduce empty properties, it is likely that the tenant will have to accept the offer and sign the tenancy agreement pending the review, or face losing the property being offered. Alternatively, local authorities may serve notice about the proposed term of any tenancy before a particular property has been identified.

3.164 The six-month and two-month notices are dealt with at paras 6.89–6.94.

Flexible tenants terminating within the fixed term

3.165 For secure periodic tenancies a tenant can always bring the tenancy to an end unilaterally by serving notice to quit on the landlord. However, a notice to quit does not end a fixed-term tenancy (see para 1.62). HA 1985 s107C gives the tenant the right to serve a minimum four-week written notice terminating the tenancy, although a landlord may dispense with the requirement that the notice be in writing or be at least four weeks long. Oddly, section 107C(5) provides that the tenancy ends on the date specified or agreed 'only if on that date – (a) no arrears of rent are payable under the tenancy and (b) the tenant is not otherwise materially in breach of a term of the tenancy'.

3.166 In theory, therefore, a tenant in rent arrears cannot terminate the tenancy in order to bring to an end an unaffordable liability. In practice, it is likely that landlords will be only too glad to accept termination by tenants in arrears or who have breached the tenancy agreement; an agreement to end the tenancy early by surrender is not prohibited, see paras 1.167–1.172.

Flexible tenants: possession at the end of the term

3.167 On a claim for possession at the end of the flexible tenancy, the court has limited powers: a possession order will only be refused if a review of either notice has been requested and the landlord has not carried out the review or if the decision made on the review is 'otherwise wrong in law',[84] which will encompass the public law and human rights defences described paras 7.128–7.177.

Introductory tenancies

3.168   The 'introductory tenancy' was created by the Housing Act (HA) 1996.[85] Local authorities may adopt a scheme whereby all new tenancies, which would otherwise be secure, are 'probationary' tenancies for an initial period of one year. These are called 'introductory tenancies'. If an authority operates an introductory tenancy scheme it must grant introductory tenancies to *all* new tenants.[86] An authority cannot offer introductory tenancies to particular tenants or types of tenants and unless a scheme has been adopted it has no power to grant any form of introductory or probationary tenancy.

3.169   However, where a new tenancy is granted to someone who was already a secure tenant, or assured tenant of a registered provider, of the same or another dwelling he or she will not become an introductory tenant.[87]

Conditions of an introductory tenancy

3.170   If a housing authority operates a regime of introductory tenancies, every new periodic tenancy shall, if it would otherwise be secure, be an introductory tenancy.[88] So, if a tenancy could not be a secure tenancy, because the necessary conditions are not met, it cannot be an introductory tenancy. The conditions for a secure tenancy are described at paras 3.106–3.117 above.

Features of an introductory tenancy

3.171   An introductory tenant has limited security of tenure; the landlord may serve notice that it has decided to apply to the court for a possession order. The notice must give reasons and advise the tenant of the right to request a review of the decision (see para 6.88). The conduct of the review is governed by regulations (see appendix 2 to chapter 6).

84   HA 1985 s107D(6)(b).
85   The introductory tenancy scheme is set out in HA 1996 Part V and came into force on 12 February 1997.
86   HA 1996 s124(2).
87   HA 1996 s124(2)(a) and (b).
88   HA 1996 s124(2).

3.172   If no review is requested or the decision is confirmed on review, the landlord may apply for a possession order. Provided the correct notice has been served and a review carried out in accordance with the relevant regulations, the tenant will have no defence to the possession claim, other than on public law or human rights grounds. Such a defence will only be arguable in exceptional cases, see para 7.157.

3.173   Introductory tenancies were introduced as part of a raft of measures to tackle anti-social behaviour. However, most introductory tenancies are terminated because of rent arrears.

Licences[89]

3.174   Where an authority uses introductory tenancies, any licences granted will be subject to the same rules. However, this does not apply to licences granted to trespassers as a temporary expedient. Such licensees remain excluded occupiers (see paras 1.108–1.109).

The 'trial' period

3.175   The tenancy will remain an introductory tenancy until one year has passed unless:[90]

- the circumstances are such that the tenancy would no longer be secure, eg the tenant no longer lives in the dwelling-house as his or her only or principal home;
- a person or body other than the authority becomes the landlord;
- the election (to operate a scheme of introductory tenancies) is revoked;
- the tenant dies and there is no-one entitled to succeed:
- the period of the introductory tenancy is extended by the authority (see para 3.179 below);
- the landlord starts a claim for possession.

3.176   At the end of the one-year period, if none of the above has happened, the tenancy automatically becomes secure, either periodic or flexible (if the local authority use flexible tenancies and served the relevant notice in advance of the granting of the introductory tenancy). The one-year period is calculated from:

- the date the tenancy is entered into; or
- if later, the date on which the tenant becomes entitled to possession; or,

---

89 HA 1996 s126.
90 HA 1996 s125(5).

- if the tenancy is adopted by the authority, from the date of the adoption.[91]

Previous probationary tenancies

3.177   Any time immediately prior to a new tenancy during which the tenant was an introductory tenant of another landlord or another property, or an assured shorthold tenant of a registered provider,[92] will count towards the trial period, provided there is no interruption in the cumulative period.[93]

3.178   Where the introductory tenants are joint tenants the trial period starts at the earliest date when any of the joint tenants was a probationary tenant under a previous tenancy agreement.[94]

Extending the trial period

3.179   A landlord may extend the introductory tenancy for six months. Notice must be served on the tenant giving reasons and the tenant has the right to seek a review of the decision.[95]

Statutory rights of introductory tenants

3.180   Introductory tenants have rights similar to those of secure tenants in relation to succession but more limited rights of assignment. These are described at paras 4.84–4.85. No specific provision is made regarding lodgers and subletting. Introductory tenants also have the same rights to have repairs carried out as all other short-term tenants, see chapter 10.

Information about introductory tenancies

3.181   Authorities operating introductory tenancies must periodically publish information about such tenancies, in whatever form it considers

---

91 A tenancy is adopted if the landlord changes because of a disposal or surrender. Such a tenancy will only become an introductory tenancy if it was not a secure or assured tenancy. See HA 1996 s124(2) and (4).

92 Private registered providers cannot grant introductory tenancies. If they want to use 'probationary' or 'starter' tenancies they can grant assured shorthold tenancies for an initial period. Such tenancies do not automatically become assured after the initial period: the landlord must serve a notice stating that the tenancy is no longer an assured shorthold tenancy or a new assured tenancy agreement must be entered into.

93 HA 1996 s125(3).

94 HA 1996 s125(4).

95 HA 2004 s179 see HA 1996 ss125A and 125B.

most suitable, and 'so far as it considers it appropriate' to explain in simple terms:[96]

- the express terms of its introductory tenancies;
- the law relating to introductory tenancies;
- the implied repairing obligations.

3.182 This information should be supplied to an introductory tenant together with a written statement of the terms of the tenancy. It should be given to the tenant on the grant of the tenancy, 'or as soon as practicable afterwards'.

Consultation

3.183 An authority using introductory tenancies must maintain arrangements to consult introductory tenants regarding matters of housing management likely to substantially affect such tenants.[97]

Demoted tenancies

3.184 A demoted tenancy is one that was previously secure but was 'demoted' by the court, on the landlord's application. Demotion may be sought as an alternative to possession. A demotion order has the effect of bringing to an end a secure tenancy and replacing it with a demoted tenancy. Both a periodic secure tenancy and a flexible secure tenancy can be demoted.

3.185 The nature of a demoted tenancy is similar to an introductory tenancy.

Features of a demoted tenancy

3.186 A demoted tenancy remains demoted for 12 months before becoming secure again, unless during the 12 months the landlord applies for possession.[98] If the secure tenancy prior to demotion was a flexible tenancy, the new secure tenancy will also be a flexible tenancy and the landlord must serve notice before the end of the demoted tenancy informing the tenant of the length of the term of the new flexible tenancy, which must be a minimum of two years.[99]

---

96 HA 1996 s136.
97 HA 1996 s137.
98 HA 1996 s143B(1). The tenancy also ceases to be a demoted tenancy if the landlord or tenant conditions are not met, if the demotion order is quashed, or the tenant dies and there is no one to succeed to the tenancy: HA 1996 s143B(2).
99 HA 1985 s107(6)(b) and HA 1996 s143MA.

3.187   There is a right to succeed to a demoted tenancy if the tenant dies, but the conditions are slightly different from those applying to secure or introductory tenancies,[100] see para 4.33. A demoted tenant may only assign the tenancy pursuant to a court order made in the event of relationship breakdown or for the benefit of children.[101]

3.188   A demoted tenant does not have substantive security of tenure: a landlord need not prove a statutory ground for possession in order to obtain a possession order. A notice of intention to seek possession must be served setting out the reasons for the decision and informing the tenant of the right to request an internal review of the decision. The review procedure is governed by regulation.[102]

3.189   If the review confirms the decision, or the tenant fails to request a review, the court must make a possession order against a demoted tenant unless the proper procedure has not been followed by the landlord. However, this does not prevent a tenant raising a public law or article 8 defence, see paras 7.128–7.179.

3.190   The procedure for seeking possession of a demoted tenancy is explained at para 6.87 and at appendix 2 to chapter 6.

Family intervention tenancies

3.191   Family intervention tenancies (FITs) were introduced by the Housing and Regeneration Act 2008. They can be offered to existing social tenants guilty of anti-social behaviour as an alternative to the tenant being evicted. The purpose must be so the landlord can provide 'behaviour support'. They are extremely rare.

Tenancies granted by housing co-operatives

3.192   Most housing co-operatives are 'fully mutual' associations registered under the Industrial and Provident Societies Act 1965.[103] Such co-operatives cannot grant secure or assured tenancies. However, if the co-operative ceases to be fully mutual, then their tenancies will either

---

100 HA 1996 ss143H–143J.

101 HA 1996 s143K.

102 Demoted Tenancies (Review of Decisions) (England) Regulations 2004 SI No 1679 and Demoted Tenancies (Review of Decisions) (Wales) Regulations 2005 SI No 1228, W86.

103 The registering authority for such societies is currently the Registrar of Friendly Societies at the Financial Conduct Authority (FCA). The website, www.fca.org.uk, gives information about the registration requirements.

become secure, assured, or assured shorthold tenancies, depending on when they were granted.

3.193 Fully mutual housing co-operatives are non-profit-making organisations run by the members who are also tenants of the co-operative. A tenant's rights will be set out in the tenancy agreement and the rules of the association. It is common for the tenancy agreement and/or rules of the association to limit the circumstances in which the tenancy can be ended by a landlord's notice to quit, eg for rent arrears or ceasing to be a member of the association.

In *Berrisford v Mexfield Housing Co-operative Ltd*[104] the Supreme Court considered the position of a tenant with a periodic tenancy where the agreement stated that the tenancy could only be determined by the landlord in specified circumstances. It was held that such a term operated to prevent the tenancy being a periodic tenancy at all since the landlord's right to terminate was 'fettered'. The effect of the agreement was the same as granting a 'tenancy for life'. However, section 149(6) of the Law of Property Act 1925 provides that tenancies for life are to be treated as tenancies for a fixed term of 90 years. So, Ms Berrisford had a fixed-term tenancy for a period of 90 years and the notice to quit was ineffective to end the tenancy.

3.194 This case will have many unforeseen consequences for co-operative tenancies. Such tenancies may have to be registered with the Land Registry and the decision may affect entitlement to housing benefit (which is not available for long leases) and repairing obligations (which are only implied into tenancies for periods of less than seven years). Housing co-operatives will no doubt draft new tenancies that are effectively 'unfettered' but they will not be able to change the nature of their existing tenancies without the tenant's consent.

3.195 Note that housing co-operatives sometimes manage properties owned by local authorities. In such a case the housing co-operative is the local authority's agent and the tenancies can be secure because the landlord is the local authority and not the co-op. The tenancy agreement should make this clear but, in cases of doubt, a tenant is entitled to be informed of the identity of his or her landlord, see paras 4.131–4.132 below.

104 [2011] UKSC 52, 9 November 2011.

Other types of tenancy

3.196　Most residential tenancies fall into one of the categories described above. However, advisers may also come across the following types of tenancy:

- assured tenancies created under the Housing Act 1980; and
- protected shorthold tenancies.

3.197　'Old style' assured tenancies created under the Housing Act 1980 will have automatically converted into assured tenancies under HA 1988.[105]

3.198　　Protected shorthold tenancies are described briefly below (paras 3.202–3.204).

3.199　　In addition there are different statutory schemes governing tenancies of agricultural land and agricultural holdings. These are also described briefly below (paras 3.207–3.210).

'Unprotected' and 'non-secure' tenancies

3.200　Many tenancies cannot be any of the main types of tenancy because they fall outside the provisions of the RA 1977 and the Housing Acts 1985 and 1988. The most common reasons for this are:

- the tenant does not reside in the premises (see paras 4.2–4.4);
- the tenant has a resident landlord (see paras 4.16–4.30);
- the tenant has been granted a 'non-secure' tenancy by a local authority following a homeless application;
- the tenancy is excluded for some other reason, such as, for example, a very low or very high rent, or because the premises are licensed for the sale of alcohol.[106]

3.201　Such tenancies are referred to as 'unprotected tenancies', 'non-secure tenancies' or 'contractual tenancies'. The tenant has only the rights under the tenancy agreement. He or she does not enjoy substantive security of tenure: the landlord can end the tenancy and is entitled to possession when the tenancy ends. However, a landlord who wishes to evict must serve notice to quit to end the tenancy and obtain a possession order unless:

- the letting is 'excluded' from the Protection from Eviction Act 1977, see para 1.100; or

---

105　HA 1988 ss1(3) and 37.
106　All of the exceptions under the various statutes are listed above at paras 3.19–3.38, 3.93 and 3.118–3.142.

- the letting is to a homeless applicant pending a decision, see para 8.18.

Such tenants still enjoy the rights implied into all tenancies, such as the right to have repairs carried out (see para 10.9) and the right to 'quiet enjoyment' (see para 8.51).

Protected shorthold tenancies

3.202 The protected shorthold tenancy (PST) was an early attempt to enable private landlords to grant short-term tenancies. They are now very rare. Under the Housing Act 1980 the following conditions had to be met to create a PST:[107]

- The tenancy was for a fixed term of between one and five years.
- There was no provision for the landlord to end the tenancy before the expiry of the fixed term.[108]
- Before the grant of the tenancy, the landlord must have given to the tenant a prescribed notice stating that the tenancy was to be a protected shorthold, though the court has the power to waive this requirement if it is just and equitable to make a possession order.[109]
- If there was not already a registered rent, the landlord had to apply for rent registration within 28 days of the start of the tenancy.

3.203 If those conditions were not met, the tenancy created would be a protected tenancy under RA 1977, provided the relevant conditions were satisfied.

A PST becoming an assured shorthold tenancy

3.204 The Housing Act 1988 provides that no new PST can be created on or after 15 January 1989.[110] Furthermore, any new tenancy entered into after that date by the same landlord and tenant will be an assured shorthold tenancy.[111]

---

107 HA 1980 s52(1).
108 Excepting a right of forfeiture or re-entry.
109 See appendix to chapter 7.
110 HA 1988 s34(1).
111 HA 1988 s34(3).

Claiming possession of a PST

3.205   A mandatory ground for possession is available for existing PSTs but the landlord must serve notice on the tenant before bringing a claim for possession. The notice must be served within three months of the anniversary of the end of the PST.[112]

Occupiers of agricultural land

3.206   A distinction is made between those who occupy agricultural land by virtue of their employment in agriculture (farm workers) and those who occupy agricultural land as farmers or farm managers. The occupation rights of farm workers are governed by statutory schemes similar to RA 1977 and HA 1988 while the rights of farmers and farm managers are similar to those of business tenants.

Farm workers and former farm workers

3.207   The key features of the statutory schemes are as follows:

- Special protection is given to tenants and licensees who work in agriculture and forestry. Such occupiers are referred to as 'agricultural occupiers'.
- An agricultural occupier may be protected even though he or she pays a low rent, or no rent at all.
- The rights of most agricultural occupiers whose agreement began before 15 January 1989 are governed by the Rent (Agriculture) Act 1976 which is similar to Rent Act 1977. Protected agreements are called 'protected occupancies' and 'statutory tenancies'.
- For those whose agreement began on or after 15 January 1989, HA 1988 Part I Chapter III applies. Sections 24–26 provide that an assured tenancy, other than an assured shorthold tenancy, will be an 'assured agricultural occupancy'.
- Many agricultural occupiers are required to live in the premises as a condition of their employment for the better performance of their employment duties. Under the common law such an occupier cannot be a tenant, see paras 1.36–1.39. However, under both the Rent (Agriculture) Act 1976 and the Housing Act 1988 protection extends to agricultural licensees (ie service occupiers), provided they have exclusive possession.

112   RA 1977 Sch 15 Case 19.

- Under both Acts certain conditions must be met regarding the employment of the occupier in agriculture or forestry for a minimum period.[113]
- Protection may continue even after the agricultural occupier has retired. However, to facilitate efficient management of agricultural land, the landlord will have a right to possession if suitable alternative accommodation is available, provided either by the landlord or the local authority.
- Special provision is made for unprotected agricultural occupiers in the Protection from Eviction Act 1977 s4: a court may suspend the execution of a possession order for up to six months.

Farmers and farm managers

3.208   Protection under the Rent (Agriculture) Act 1976 and under HA 1988 ss24–26 is given to a person who is employed in agriculture. The tenants of agricultural holdings, who are in control of the holding, do not enjoy this protection. They are excluded from the RA 1977 and the Housing Acts 1985 and 1988.

3.209   Such agreements will usually be governed by the Agricultural Holdings Act 1986 or the Agricultural Tenancies Act 1995; these operate on a similar basis to the Landlord and Tenant Act 1954, which applies to business tenancies.

3.210   In addition, under RA 1977 and HA 1988 a tenancy cannot be protected or assured if it includes more than two acres of agricultural land, even if the main purpose of the letting is to provide a home.

113 See Rent (Agriculture) Act 1976 s1(1) and HA 1988 Sch 3.

CHAPTER 4

Common issues for tenants

continued

Key points

- To enjoy substantive security of tenure a tenant must satisfy a residence condition: he or she must live in a dwelling as his or her home. During an extended absence a person may continue to satisfy the residence condition if there is an intention to return and physical evidence of this.

- Tenants with resident landlords do not enjoy substantive security of tenure but the landlord must be resident when the tenancy starts and continuously throughout.

- If a tenant dies the tenancy may be passed to a family member who lives with the tenant by 'succession'. Each scheme of protection has different conditions for succession.

- Assignment of a tenancy means transferring it to someone else. Mostly this is prohibited except in specific circumstances.

- Subletting is when the tenant grants a [sub]tenancy to someone else but retains his or her tenancy. Subletting is mostly prohibited in short-term residential tenancies.

- A tenant has a statutory right to certain information about the identity of his or her landlord. Failure to provide this information may be a criminal offence.

- There is a mandatory scheme for the protection of rent deposits paid by assured shorthold tenants. A landlord who has not protected the deposit cannot serve a possession notice. And a court can order the landlord to return the deposit and pay up to three times the deposit.

- Unfair terms in tenancy agreements may be unenforceable. Only a court can declare a term to be unenforceable.

- Assured tenants have little rent control: rents are set at market levels. Tenants under the Rent Act and housing association secure tenants have strong rent control: fair rents are set by the rent officer.

- Local authority landlords must set a 'reasonable rent'. These tend to be much lower than market rents.

- New restrictions on the right of migrants to rent private accommodation are currently being rolled out.

Introduction

4.1   This chapter examines issues that commonly arise in relation to residential tenancies and explains how the rules apply to each type of tenancy. The following issues are considered:

- the tenancy condition – residing in the premises;
- resident landlords;
- succession (the tenancy passing to another on the death of the tenant);
- assignment (transfer of the tenancy);
- subletting;
- obtaining information about a landlord;
- rent deposits;
- unfair contract terms;
- rent control;
- new 'right to rent' rules.

The tenancy condition – residing in the premises

4.2   At common law a tenant is not required to live in the premises let. However, statutory security of tenure is to protect a tenant's home; only a tenant who resides in premises can enjoy security of tenure.

4.3   Under the Rent Act (RA) 1977 when the (contractual) 'protected' tenancy ends the tenant remains a statutory tenant if and so long as he or she occupies the premises as a residence. A statutory tenant can be evicted only if a possession order is made and an order will be made only if a statutory ground for possession is proved. The Housing Acts 1985 and 1988 provide that a tenancy is only 'secure' or 'assured' when the tenant is occupying the premises as his or her only or principal home; the only way a landlord can end a secure or assured tenancy is by obtaining a possession order; and, an order will only be made if a statutory ground for possession is proved.

4.4   The condition under the RA 1977 is not as strict as under the Housing Acts: occupation as *a residence* is required as opposed to occupation as the tenant's *only or principal home*. In several cases concerning Rent Act tenants it has been held that a person can occupy more than one dwelling as a residence. Under the Housing Acts the dwelling must be the person's only or main home to enjoy security of tenure.

Absence of the tenant

4.5 Clearly, a tenant need not be physically present at all times to be residing in premises. It is recognised that a tenant may continue to be resident in premises even during an extended absence. In such a case the tenant may continue to reside in or occupy premises as a home provided that:

- the tenant intends to return; and
- there is some physical evidence of that intention.[1]

> In *Amoah v Barking and Dagenham*[2] a secure tenant was sentenced to 12 years' imprisonment. He left some furniture in his flat and appointed a relative to act as a 'caretaker' in his absence. The council served notice to quit and obtained a possession order on the basis that the tenant had lost his secure status.
>
> On appeal it was held that he had retained his secure status. The correct approach was that a prolonged absence raised a presumption that a tenant no longer occupied. That presumption must be rebutted by the tenant who must establish:
>
> 1) an intention to return;
> 2) a practical or real possibility of fulfilment of the intention within a reasonable time; and
> 3) some outward and visible sign of the intention.
>
> In this case, in spite of the length of the expected absence, the tenant had continued to reside in the premises as his only or principal home and could only be evicted if a ground for possession could be proved.

4.6 It is common for prisoners to lose their tenancies but this is usually because the rent is not paid during their absence: housing benefit can only be paid for a limited period during an absence (see paras 9.31–9.39). Subletting the whole of premises let on a secure or assured social tenancy will result in the loss of security (see para 4.107 below) and an arrangement between family members will only be possible if the family member looking after the premises for the tenant can pay the rent without reliance on housing benefit.[3]

---

1 *Brown v Brash* [1948] 2 KB 247.
2 (2001) 82 P&CR DG6, CA.
3 This is because housing benefit will not normally be paid where the occupier is a family member of the 'landlord': see para 9.20 below.

4.7   Another common situation is when an elderly tenant goes into hospital or a residential home for respite care. Provided the tenant intends to return home he or she should be considered to be continuing to reside there.[4] However, a problem may arise if the tenant's physical or mental health deteriorates so that return becomes unlikely or impossible. When the intention to return ends the tenant can no longer be said to reside in the premises. However, care must be taken to ascertain the tenant's enduring intention.

Hammersmith & Fulham LBC v Clarke[5] concerned a frail, elderly tenant who had, since 1981, lived in disabled-adapted council accommodation. In 1997 her grandson and his wife moved in to look after her and in 1998 a joint right-to-buy application was submitted. The tenant was subsequently admitted to a nursing home suffering from depression and physical disabilities. While at the nursing home she signed a note prepared by a council social worker stating that she had decided to become a permanent resident of the nursing home and that she no longer intended to return home. The next month the authority served notice to quit and sought possession. The tenant returned home before the trial. Her evidence was that she had gone to the nursing home intending to return home and had signed the note at a time when she was depressed and when her medication had just been sorted out. The claim for possession was dismissed.

The authority appealed, arguing that the tenant's earlier intention was irrelevant, that the material date was the date of the expiry of the notice to quit and that the social worker's note was the best evidence of this. The Court of Appeal accepted that the relevant time for determining the tenant's intention was the date of the expiry of the notice but held that the court should focus on 'the enduring intention of that person' and not 'fleeting changes of mind'. This was particularly true of an elderly tenant in poor health whose intentions may have fluctuated from day to day. The judge was entitled to find that the note did not represent the tenant's more general and enduring intention which was borne out by her evidence, the continuing presence of her family and furniture and all the other circumstances.

---

4 See paras 9.35–9.36 for an explanation of housing benefit entitlement during such an absence.

5 (2002) HLR 37, CA.

In contrast, in *Beech v Birmingham CC*[6] the elderly tenant had signed a notice to quit at a meeting with a council officer. After her death, her daughter and husband, who remained in occupation, tried to argue that the notice should be presumed to have been procured by the undue influence of the council. The Court of Appeal rejected this. There was no evidence of undue influence and the relationship of a landlord's agent (the council employee) and tenant was not one that gave rise to such a presumption.

4.8   Secure tenants can assign their tenancy to a person who would be entitled to succeed to the tenancy in the event of the tenant's death (see below at paras 4.62 and 4.78–4.79). However, such an assignment will only be effective to transfer a secure tenancy if, at the date of the assignment, the tenant is still secure, ie still occupying the premises as his or her only or principal home. If assignment is only considered after the tenant has been absent for an extended period and no longer intends to return home the tenancy will no longer be secure.

Statutory tenancies

4.9   A statutory tenancy arises when a protected tenancy ends provided the tenant is in occupation. Such a tenant 'shall, if and so long as he occupies the dwelling-house as his residence, be the statutory tenant of it'.[7]

Assured tenancies

4.10   The same wording is used in the Housing Act (HA) 1988: a tenancy is only assured 'if and so long as' the conditions, including occupation as only or principal home, are met.[8]

Secure tenancies

4.11   A secure tenant is secure 'at any time when' the relevant conditions are met; this includes the condition that the tenant occupies the dwelling as his or her only or principal home.[9] This means that a tenant who has lost secure status by moving out may regain it by resuming occupation. A tenancy that is no longer secure can be ended by

6   [2014] EWCA Civ 830, 17 June 2014.
7   RA 1977 s2(1)(a).
8   HA 1988 s1(1).
9   HA 1985 ss79(1) and 81.

a landlord's notice to quit but if a tenant resumes occupation before the notice to quit expires, it will have no effect; the tenant will have again become a secure tenant and a secure tenancy can only be ended by a court order.[10]

Subletting the whole premises: secure and assured tenants

4.12 If a secure or an assured tenant of social housing sublets or parts with possession of the whole of the premises the tenancy ceases to be secure or assured and cannot subsequently become secure or assured.[11]

New criminal offence of subletting

4.13 Furthermore, under the Prevention of Social Housing Fraud Act (PSHFA) 2013 it is also now a criminal offence for secure tenants and assured tenants of social housing to unlawfully sublet.[12] The offence is committed where:

- in breach of an express or implied term of the tenancy
- the tenant sublets the whole or part of the premises let
- the tenant ceases to occupy the premises as only or principal home, and
- the tenant knows that the subletting is in breach of the tenancy.

On conviction, the tenant is liable for a fine of up to £5,000. However, if the offence is committed 'dishonestly' the maximum penalty is imprisonment for up to two years and/or a fine.

Occupation by spouse/civil partner

4.14 The occupation of the spouse or civil partner of the tenant is sufficient to satisfy the tenant condition. This is the case whether the tenancy is assured, statutory or secure. However, this ceases to be the case after the marriage or civil partnership ends. If the tenant is out of occupation, it is therefore essential that any transfer of the tenancy takes place before the decree absolute or dissolution of the civil partnership (see chapter 12).

---

10 *Hussey v Camden LBC* (1995) 27 HLR 5, CA.
11 HA 1985 s93(2) and HA 1988 s 15A. For assured tenants this provision was added by the Prevention of Social Housing Fraud Act 2013 and came into force on 5 November 2013.
12 See PSHFA 2013 ss1 and 2. Defences are available where the subletting was because of threats of violence or was to a person entitled to apply for a transfer of the property (eg an estranged spouse or civil partner). The offences do not apply to shared ownership leases.

Resident landlords

4.15   Under both RA 1977 and HA 1988 tenants who have a resident land-lord, as defined below (paras 4.16–4.22), do not have substantive security of tenure: they cannot be protected or assured. Under RA 1977 such a tenant had a 'restricted contract', see below (para 4.28), which gave the tenant very limited rights. Under HA 1988 there is no specific provision; the tenancy cannot be assured and is therefore an unprotected or basic contractual tenancy. In both cases, although the tenant does not have substantive security of tenure, he or she cannot be evicted without a court order, unless the agreement was made on or after 15 January 1989 *and* the landlord and tenant share accom-modation (see para 1.101).

Meaning of 'resident landlord'[13]

4.16   A tenant has a resident landlord where:

- the premises let form part of a building, and that building is not a purpose-built block of flats;
- the landlord lives in other premises in the same building; and
- he or she has done so since the tenancy began and continuously throughout the tenancy.

The premises

4.17   A landlord may be a resident landlord even if the premises he or she occupies are completely separate from those occupied by the tenant, if they are in the same building. Only purpose-built flats are excluded, so a landlord residing in a converted house may be a resi-dent landlord, regardless of when the conversion was completed and even if the premises have separate entrances.

Landlord's residence

4.18   The landlord must be a resident landlord when the tenancy com-mences; a landlord who begins to reside in the building after the ten-ancy started does not become a resident landlord for these purposes. The occupation by any one of joint landlords is sufficient to retain the resident landlord status.[14]

---

13 The conditions are set out in RA 1977 s12 and HA 1988 Sch 1 para 10.
14 *Cooper v Tait* (1984) 15 HLR 98, CA and HA 1988 Sch 1 para 10(2).

4.19 A tenant who is already protected, statutory or assured, who is granted a new tenancy by the same landlord (whether of the same or different premises in the building) will remain a protected, statutory or assured tenant.[15]

4.20 The residence condition is different under RA 1977 and HA 1988: under RA 1977 the landlord must 'occupy the premises as a residence'; under HA 1988 the landlord must occupy the premises as his or her 'only or principal home'. A landlord who has more than one home may qualify as a resident landlord under RA 1977 whereas under HA 1988 the premises in the shared building must be the only or main home of the landlord.

4.21 If a landlord ceases to satisfy the residence condition, the tenancy will no longer be excluded from the provisions of RA 1977 or the HA 1988, see below para 4.29.

4.22 However, as for tenants, physical absence alone does not mean that a landlord no longer resides in premises. A landlord may continue to satisfy the residence condition provided he or she intends to resume occupation and there is physical evidence of that intention (see para 4.5 above).

Transfer of ownership

4.23 If ownership of the premises changes, certain periods of time are disregarded for the purposes of determining continuous residence. These are known as 'periods of disregard'.[16]

Lifetime transfer

4.24 Where ownership of the premises changes during the resident landlord's life, the new owner has 28 days in which to take up occupation. This can be extended to six months if the new landlord gives notice in writing that he or she intends to reside in the premises. This notice must be given within the 28-day period.

4.25 A new landlord cannot serve a notice to quit during this period unless he or she actually takes up residence. If he or she fails to take up residence within the 28 days, or six months if extended, the tenancy ceases to be excluded from the protection of either RA 1977 or HA 1988.

---

15 RA 1977 s12(2) and HA 1988 Sch 1 para 10(3).
16 See RA 1977 Sch 2 and HA 1988 Sch 1 Pt III.

Death of resident landlord

4.26   Where the landlord dies and the property passes to personal representatives (PRs)[17] the residence requirement is deemed to be satisfied for a period of up to two years, commencing with the death of
the landlord.

4.27   The difference between a lifetime transfer and a transfer on death
should be noted: the PRs of a deceased resident landlord may serve
notice to quit to end the tenancy within the two-year period of disregard.[18] If there is a lifetime transfer, the new landlord must actually
take up occupation to retain the resident landlord status. Notice to
quit cannot be served by a non-resident landlord during the period
of disregard: during this period the tenant may only be evicted on a
statutory ground, as if he or she were a statutory or assured tenant.

Restricted contracts

4.28   No new restricted contracts may be granted after 15 January 1989.
Most will now have ceased to be restricted contracts and become
unprotected tenancies, outside the scope of HA 1988. HA 1988
s36(2)(a) provides that if there has been an increase of rent (other
than by reference to the rent tribunal), the agreement is treated as
though made at the date of the increase and therefore ceases to be a
restricted contract. Similarly, a fundamental variation of other terms
would mean that a new agreement was entered into at the date of the
variation.

Landlord ceasing to be resident

4.29   If the resident landlord condition ceases to be met, the tenant is no
longer excluded from the provisions of the relevant Act. However,
one issue remains unclear: whether the type of tenancy is determined
by the date of the commencement of the original tenancy or the date

17   Personal representatives means executors named in the will or, where there is
no will, anyone who applies, as next of kin, for authority to deal with the estate
(known as 'letters of administration').

18   The situation is more complicated under RA 1977 in that if the landlord's
interest is vested in trustees (including the trustee in bankruptcy) or the
Public Trustee (as happens if the landlord dies without a will) up to two years
is disregarded, during which no notice to quit can be served. If the premises
then pass to PRs appointed to deal with the estate, there is a further period of
up to two years during which the resident landlord condition is deemed to be
satisfied so that notice to quit can be served.

it ceased to be excluded. This will be significant if the tenancy commenced before 15 January 1989, or between 15 January 1989 and 28 February 1997 and the landlord ceases to be resident after 28 February 1997. If the date of commencement of the tenancy is decisive it will be an assured tenancy unless the landlord complied with the relevant formalities to create an assured shorthold tenancy when the tenancy was granted. However, it is unlikely that a landlord would have done so as, at the date of the grant, the tenancy would have been excluded from the HA 1988 and therefore could not have been an assured shorthold tenancy.

Succession

4.30   Succession means one person becoming entitled to something after another person's entitlement ends, eg inheriting the property of someone who dies. A tenancy, being an interest in land, is property that can be inherited. However, each statutory scheme provides that a person can succeed to a tenancy with security of tenure only if certain conditions are satisfied. In all cases the successor must have been living with the deceased tenant at the time of or immediately before death. In some cases, the successor must have been living with the deceased tenant for a specified period before death.

4.31   Under RA 1977 more than one succession was permitted. Two successions are still possible but the second can only be to an assured and not a statutory tenancy. Under the Housing Acts 1985 and 1988 there can be only one succession. HA 1988 has only ever allowed succession to a spouse, civil partner or co-habitee. For secure tenancies granted before 1 April 2012, HA 1985 allows succession by other family members. The Localism Act 2011 amended HA 1985: for secure tenancies granted on or after 1 April 2012 statutory succession can only be to a spouse, civil partner or co-habitee, as is the case for tenancies granted under HA 1988. However, local authorities and private registered providers (PRPs) of social housing may grant more extensive rights of succession through the tenancy agreement; they could extend succession to a relationship outside that of spouse, civil partner and co-habitee and/or could grant more than one right of succession in relation to the same tenancy. If such rights are granted in the tenancy agreement and the successor fulfils the conditions then the succession operates as a statutory succession.

4.32   Statutory succession happens by 'operation of law' and is not something 'granted' by a landlord. However, disputes often arise between landlords and tenants about whether the necessary conditions are met. Unless agreement can be reached any dispute must be resolved by a court. This may happen when the landlord claims possession against the occupiers. Alternatively, an occupier may seek a declaration from the County Court that he or she is a tenant by succession.

Summary of succession rights

4.33   The following tables set out the rules relating to succession in each statutory scheme.

Private sector and private rented providers of social housing

	Rent Act 1977[19]	**Housing Act 1988**[20]
Type of tenancy	Protected and statutory tenancies.	Assured tenancies, including assured shorthold tenancies.
Who can succeed?	Spouse, civil partner, co-habitee, member of family (not defined).	Spouse, civil partner, co-habitee.
Conditions	Spouse/civil partner/co-habitee must be residing in premises immediately before death. Family member must be residing in premises for two years before death.	The successor must be occupying as only or principal home immediately before death.
What kind of tenancy does successor get?	Spouse/civil partner/co-habitee gets statutory tenancy. Family member gets assured tenancy.	The tenancy of the deceased: assured or assured shorthold tenancy.
Number of successions	Two possible only if first succession (to a statutory tenancy) is by spouse/civil partner/co-habitee and second succession (to an assured tenancy) is by a person who is a family member of both original and the successor tenant.	One only. Only a sole assured tenancy carries a right of succession.

19   RA 1977 Sch 1 Pt 1.
20   HA 1988 s17

Local authority tenancies

Type of tenancy	Pre-1 April 2012 Secure or introductory tenancy	Post-1 April 2012 Secure, introductory and all flexible tenancies[21]	Demoted tenancies[22]
Who can succeed?	Spouse, civil partner, member of family (defined, and includes co-habitee).	Spouse, civil partner, co-habitee. But tenancy agreement can extend to other relationships	Any family member (including spouse, civil partner, co-habitee)
Conditions	Spouse/civil partner must be occupying as only or principal home at the time of death. Co-habitee/ family member must have been residing with the deceased for 12 months before death and be occupying premises as only or principal home at time of death.	Must be occupying as only or principal home at the time of death.	Must be occupying as only or principal home at the time of death and have resided with the tenant for 12 months ending with the tenant's death.
What kind of tenancy does successor get?	The tenancy of the deceased: secure or introductory tenancy.	The tenancy of the deceased: secure, introductory or flexible tenancy.	Demoted tenancy

---

21 HA 1985 ss86A–89. The Localism Act 2011 s160(6)(a) makes clear that the changes do not apply to secure tenancies granted prior to 1 April 2012.

22 HA 1996 s143H(1).

Type of tenancy	Pre-1 April 2012 Secure or introductory tenancy	Post-1 April 2012 Secure, introductory and all flexible tenancies	Demoted tenancies
Number of successions	One only. Joint tenancy becoming sole tenancy = one succession. If there has been an assignment to a potential successor no 'further' successions possible.	One only unless tenancy agreement states otherwise. Joint tenancy becoming sole tenancy = one succession. If there has been an assignment to a potential successor no 'further' successions possible.	One only.

4.34   In the tables the term 'co-habitee' refers to a person who is living with the tenant as the tenant's husband or wife or as if they were civil partners.

Demoted tenants and succession

4.35   If there is more than one potential successor, the spouse or civil partner is preferred; if there is no spouse or civil partner, a co-habitee (defined as one who lived with the deceased as a couple in an enduring family relationship, whether of the opposite or same sex) is preferred. Family members are defined in the same way as for secure tenants[23] (see paras 4.41 below). If the potential successors cannot agree who shall succeed the landlord will select the successor.[24]

Joint tenancies

4.36   Under the Housing Acts 1985 and 1988 it is specifically provided that where a joint tenant has become a sole tenant he or she is treated as a successor and no further succession is possible. When a joint tenant dies the other tenant becomes the sole tenant not by succession but

23   HA 1996 s143P.
24   HA 1996 s143H(5)(b).

by 'survivorship' (ie he or she was already a joint tenant and becomes a sole tenant simply by having survived the other joint tenant). This is not a succession but the surviving sole tenant is treated as a successor.[25] This means that whenever there is a joint tenancy there is no possibility of a statutory succession, unless the tenancy was granted after 1 April 2012 and the tenancy agreement provides otherwise.

4.37   Under RA 1977 there is nothing to prevent a succession to a sole statutory tenancy where the deceased tenant had previously been a joint statutory or protected tenant with another person.

Meaning of 'residing with' the deceased tenant

4.38   'Staying with' the deceased tenant or being physically present in the premises is not sufficient: 'residing with' means making a home with the deceased tenant.

In *Freeman v Islington LBC*[26] the deceased tenant's daughter claimed the right of succession. She had owned her own flat for many years but had let it out from time to time. When her father became ill she started staying with him to care for him, initially three nights a week but eventually she was staying with him full time. For most of the year before her father died she had left her own flat unoccupied but let it out on an assured shorthold tenancy shortly before he died. Despite finding that the daughter had stayed with her father full time for the year before his death a possession order was made on the basis that she had not established that she was 'residing with' him during that period.

The Court of Appeal upheld the judge's decision: residing with a person meant making one's home in the premises, and '... the retention of another home, whilst not fatal, can be a significant factor in deciding that a person was not making their home in the premises in question'.[27] Although it was accepted that by the time of her father's death the appellant has made the premises her home, it had been found that she could not establish that it had been her home for the previous 12 months. Her appeal was dismissed and the possession order upheld.

25   HA 1985 s88(1)(b); HA 1988 s17(2)(b). Note that this does not apply where a secure tenancy became a sole tenancy before the Housing Act 1980 came into force: *Birmingham CC v Walker* [2007] UKHL 22, 16 May 2007.

26   [2009] EWCA Civ 536, 11 June 2009.

27   Jacob LJ at [22].

Common problems

Evidence of residence

4.39   When a tenant dies the potential successor should notify the landlord and will be asked to provide evidence of residence. For family members, a specific period of residence is necessary: for pre-1 April 2012 secure and introductory tenancies this is 12 months and for statutory tenancies it is two years. Landlords sometimes indicate that only certain kinds of documentary evidence will be accepted. However, the issue is a factual one and any evidence confirming a person's residence should be obtained and submitted. Letters and witness statements from neighbours and friends may be obtained although evidence from more neutral and/or official sources, such as doctors or teachers, the Department for Work and Pensions (DWP) or HM Revenue and Customs (HMRC), are likely to be more persuasive.

4.40   Occupiers in receipt of housing benefit must declare who is in occupation of the premises. Because this usually results in a reduction of benefit some occupiers falsely declare that they live alone. Local authority landlords with access to this information may suggest that this is decisive and proves that the potential successor was not living in the property. Obviously such evidence is relevant but there may be other evidence strong enough to persuade an authority (or a court) that the declaration was untrue and that the succession conditions are satisfied. In *Freeman v Islington LBC*, above, para 4.38 above, the fact that the deceased tenant had stated in his housing benefit application that he lived alone was one of several factors that led to the finding that his daughter had not, at that time, made her home with him despite staying with him on a regular basis.

Relationship between successor and deceased tenant

4.41   Where the relationship is that of spouse or civil partner, documentary evidence of identity and marriage or civil partnership will be required. For pre 1 April 2012 secure and introductory tenancies and demoted tenancies, the family members are defined in HA 1985 s113. They are: a person living with the tenant as husband and wife or as civil partner; parents, grandparents, children and grandchildren; brothers and sisters; uncles, aunts, nephews and nieces. 'Children' does not include foster children.[28]

---

28 *Sheffield CC v The Personal Representatives of June Wall, Steven Wall, Robert Ingham and Theresa June Butler* [2010] EWCA Civ 922, 30 July 2010.

4.42   Relationships of marriage or civil partnership are treated as relationships of blood. This means that the relative of a person's spouse or civil partner is treated as a relative of that person. Half (blood) relatives are included, step-children are treated as children of the step parent and illegitimate children are treated as the legitimate children of the mother and the reputed father.

4.43   In relation to succession claimed under a post-1 April 2012 tenancy agreement, the tenancy agreement itself will specify the relationship that gives the right to succession (and any other conditions such as length of residence in the premises). The defined relationships need not accord with s113 of the HA 1985.

4.44   Disputes may arise with regard to 'co-habitees'. It is not enough to be residing in the premises and to be in an intimate relationship with the deceased tenant; the quality of the relationship must be similar to that of marriage or civil partnership.

In *Nutting v Southern Housing Group*[29] the gay partner of a deceased assured tenant claimed to succeed to the tenancy. The case was heard before the Civil Partnership Act 2004 was in force but it had been established that gay couples could live together as if they were husband and wife and thereby qualify for succession.[30] However, the county court rejected the claim finding that the relationship did not have the necessary characteristics such that it could be said that they were living together as if they were husband and wife. The two men had lived together for just over two years before the tenant's death. The relationship was characterised by alcohol abuse and the tenant had once obtained a non-molestation order against the appellant. It was accepted that the appellant was living with the tenant immediately before his death.

The decision was upheld on appeal. The tests applied by the judge, and approved by the appeal court, included: whether the relationship was one of mutual lifetime commitment rather than one of convenience, friendship, companionship or the living together as lovers; and whether the relationship was one that had been presented to the outside world openly and unequivocally so that society considers it to be of permanent intent. The judge had been entitled to find that the appellant had failed to demonstrate that the relationship displayed a sufficient commitment to permanence to meet the test.

29 [2004] EWHC 2982 (Ch).
30 *Mendoza v Ghaidon* [2004] UKHL 30, 21 June 2004.

More than one potential successor

4.45   It is possible for more than one person to be qualified to succeed to a tenancy. In such cases, the way the successor is selected is different in each Act.

HA 1985: secure and introductory tenancies[31]

4.46   For pre-1 April 2012 tenancies, the tenant's spouse or civil partner is preferred over other members of the family. If there is no spouse or civil partner the family members should agree who will be the successor and, if no agreement is possible, the landlord may select the successor.

4.47   For pre-1 April 2012 tenancies, a co-habitee is treated as a member of the family. For post-1 April 2012 tenancies, only a spouse, civil partner or co-habitee is entitled to succeed. In the unlikely event of more than one potential successor, this should be agreed between the potential successors, and if no agreement is possible the landlord will decided which is 'to be treated ... as the tenant's spouse or civil partner'.

HA 1988: assured and assured shorthold tenancies[32]

4.48   The issue is determined by agreement between the potential successors and, in the absence of agreement, by the County Court.

RA 1977: statutory tenancies[33]

4.49   The tenant's spouse or civil partner is preferred over other members of the family. If more than one person is entitled to succeed, the potential successors should agree who will be the successor and, if no agreement is possible, the issue will be determined by the County Court.

Succession by children

4.50   A child can succeed to a tenancy provided the relevant conditions are satisfied. If the deceased tenant leaves a will appointing a personal representative or trustee, the tenancy is held on trust by that person until the child becomes an adult. The child holds an equitable tenancy that automatically becomes a legal tenancy when he or she reaches the age of 18. Where no person is expressly appointed as

---

31   HA 1985 s89(2).
32   HA 1988 s17(5).
33   RA 1977 Sch 1 Pt 1 para 2.

trustee the tenancy will usually be held on trust by the landlord until the child is 18. See para 1.138 for an explanation of trusts and legal and equitable interests.

> In *Kingston upon Thames RLBC v Prince*[34] the tenant of a three-bedroom house died, leaving in occupation his adult daughter who had lived with him for six months and his 13-year-old granddaughter who had lived with him for three years. The local authority served notice on the daughter requiring her to vacate. Possession proceedings were issued against the daughter and a possession order made. An application was made to join the granddaughter and to set aside the possession order. The application was granted and the circuit judge dismissed the authority's appeal, making a declaration that the tenancy was held by the daughter on trust for the granddaughter until she reached the age of majority; further, the tenancy had been so held since the death of the tenant. The authority appealed, arguing that a minor could not hold a legal estate and the 1985 Act made no provision for secure equitable tenancies.
>
> The Court of Appeal held that a minor can hold an equitable tenancy of any property, including a council house. Property law provided that where a legal estate in land was granted to or devolved to a child it operated as a trust, with the legal estate held by a trustee for the benefit of the child and that there was nothing to stop a local authority granting to a child a tenancy effective in equity.[35] The authority's appeal was dismissed.

Succession and rent arrears

4.51 Where the tenant dies owing rent arrears these do not become the responsibility of the successor.[36] The debt is, however, owed by the deceased tenant's estate and it may be the case that the successor is also the personal representative and beneficiary of the estate as next of kin. If so, he or she is responsible for paying the arrears from

---

34 (1999) 31 HLR 794.
35 The tenant had died before the Trusts of Land and Appointment of Trustees Act 1996, which now governs such trusts, was in force. However, the Court of Appeal held that this did not change the previous position. See also *Alexander-David v Hammersmith and Fulham LBC*, summarised at para 1.143, which deals with the position when an authority expressly grants a tenancy to a minor.
36 See *Tickner v Clifton* [1929] 1 KB 207.

the estate. A landlord cannot make it a condition of succession that arrears are paid as the succession takes effect as a matter of law and is not 'granted' by the landlord. However, if a suspended or postponed possession order exists at the date of death the successor tenant is bound by the terms of the order and may be evicted if any instalments of arrears of rent are not paid and the arrears cleared.

Succession and housing benefit

4.52   Even if the landlord disputes that the conditions for succession are satisfied, if the conditions are satisfied, the tenancy vests in the successor automatically on the death of the tenant. Anyone claiming a right to succeed who qualifies for housing benefit should submit an application as soon as possible. Where the succession is disputed the application may be suspended but, if the right to succeed is subsequently established, benefit will be payable from the date of the application.[37]

'Non-statutory' succession

4.53   Some social landlords have operated what are usually called 'non-statutory' succession schemes. This means an agreement or policy that 'succession' will be allowed in certain circumstances even where there is no right to statutory succession. For example, some local authorities operate policies in relation to adult children of deceased tenants who would be entitled to succeed if the original tenancy had not been a joint tenancy.

4.54   Furthermore, under large-scale voluntary transfers of local authority properties to non-local authority providers, tenants who were originally secure become assured with less generous succession rights. Most such tenants are given enhanced rights by way of 'non-statutory' succession to those family members who would have been entitled to succeed to the secure tenancy. Despite the name a tenancy granted to such a person is not 'succession' at all; it is the grant of a new tenancy.

4.55   Where local authorities operate such policies they should be reflected in the allocation policy since the grant of a new tenancy is an allocation governed by HA 1996 Part VI (see chapter 17).

---

37   Housing benefit should be paid regardless of whether the succession is established where the 'successor' occupies the premises as a home. Such an occupier has a liability to make payments equivalent to rent even if in unlawful occupation, see paras 9.8–9.11.

4.56   The Localism Act (LA) 2011 changes include restricting statutory succession to spouses, civil partners and co-habitees. However, the Act also gives to both local authorities and PRPs of social housing the right to grant more generous 'statutory succession' by way of the tenancy agreement. It is important to distinguish between more generous succession rights granted in relation to tenants whose tenancies started prior to 1 April 2012 and those granted after that date (which are governed by the LA 2011). In the case of the former, the 'non-statutory succession' takes effect as a new tenancy. This means that there will in fact be a further right of succession. In contrast, if the tenancy is governed by the LA 2011 a right of succession provided for in the tenancy agreement is still a 'statutory succession' and so there will be no further rights of succession when the successor tenant dies. Disputes as to whether the conditions are met will be resolved in the County Court, either as a defence to a possession claim or by the successor tenant applying for a declaration.

Assignment

4.57   An assignment is the transfer of the tenancy during the life of the tenant. The person who transfers the tenancy is the 'assignor' and the person to whom the tenancy is transferred is the 'assignee'. The effect of an assignment is that the assignee becomes the tenant of the landlord under the same tenancy agreement. For this reason, in most well drafted leases assignment is permitted only with the landlord's consent.

4.58   An assignment transfers the legal interest in land and to be valid must be done by deed.[38] An attempt to assign by deed that does not comply with the relevant formalities may, however, still be effective between the parties to the assignment although it will not bind the landlord.[39] References in this section to assignor and assignee refer to the parties to a valid assignment by deed.

4.59   The general rule is that tenancies, as legal interests in land, are capable of being assigned. However, that does not necessarily mean that the statutory security of tenure enjoyed by the tenant can also be assigned. Each Act specifies the limited situations in which a tenancy

---

38 Law of Property Act 1925 s52.
39 Law of Property (Miscellaneous Provisions) Act 1989 s2: if evidenced in writing it may take effect as an enforceable contract for the assignment.

can be transferred to someone else so that that 'statutory security' is also transferred.

Rent Act 1977

4.60   A protected tenancy is capable of assignment but, if assignment is prohibited under the terms of the tenancy, the landlord may have a ground for possession against the assignee.

4.61   A statutory tenancy, being personal to the statutory tenant, is not capable of assignment, other than in matrimonial proceedings, see paras 12.73–12.85.[40]

Housing Act 1985

4.62   The Housing Act 1985 provides that a secure tenancy (including a flexible secure tenancy) is not capable of assignment save in three situations.[41] These are set out in HA 1985 s91(3):

- assignment by way of mutual exchange;
- assignment made pursuant to a court order in certain matrimonial, civil partnership or Children Act proceedings;
- assignment to a potential successor.

4.63   Any assignment in circumstances other than those expressly permitted under HA 1985 s91(3) will be ineffective to transfer the secure tenancy; the assignee will become the tenant but the tenancy will no longer be secure. The assignee will have a contractual tenancy only which the landlord can terminate by service of notice to quit. Furthermore, as the original secure tenant will have parted with possession of the whole of the premises he or she cannot regain secure status by taking back possession of the premises assigned (see para 4.108).

Mutual exchange

4.64   It is a term of every secure tenancy that the tenant has the right to exchange his or her tenancy with another secure tenant or with an assured tenant of a social landlord provided both parties have the written consent of their respective landlords, see paras 4.66–4.73. The general rule with assignments, including mutual exchange, is

40   RA 1977 also provides for the transfer of a statutory tenancy by written agreement with the landlord: Sch 1 para 13. However, it is impossible to imagine why a landlord would enter into such an agreement.

41   HA 1985 s91(1).

that the assignee takes the tenancy of the assignor. So, a secure tenant who does a mutual exchange with an assured tenant will take an assured tenancy.

4.65 Special provision is made for the 'exchange' of tenancies where one is a flexible secure tenancy or a fixed term assured tenancy with a social landlord, and the other tenancy is not. The conditions that apply are complex and are set out in sections 158–159 of the Localism Act 2011. This type of 'exchange/transfer' takes effect by way of each tenant surrendering their tenancy and being granted a new tenancy. The purpose is to facilitate transfers and enables a non-flexible secure or assured tenant to retain their tenancy status in a new property.

Consent

4.66 The landlord can only withhold consent to an assignment of a secure tenancy on certain grounds, set out in HA 1985 Sch 3. If the landlord withholds consent for reasons not set out in HA 1985 Sch 3, consent is deemed to be given.[42] The grounds upon which consent can be refused are:

1) Either tenant is obliged to give up possession under a court order.

2) Proceedings have been commenced under Grounds 1–6, or notice of seeking possession under one or more of those grounds has been served (Grounds 1–6 are the 'tenant's fault' grounds, see appendix to chapter 7).

2A) A suspended anti-social behaviour possession order (under the discretionary Grounds 2 of HA 1985 and 14 of HA 1988)) or a suspended riot possession order (under the discretionary grounds 2ZA of HA 1985 or 14ZA of HA 1988), or a 'relevant order' is in force. A 'relevant order' means one of a number of different anti-social behaviour injunctions and orders. Alternatively, an application is pending for one of those orders or a demotion order.[43]

2B) The dwelling-house is subject to a closure notice or closure order under the Anti-social Behaviour, Crime and Policing Act (ASBCPA) 2014.

3) The accommodation is substantially more extensive than is reasonably required by the assignee.

4) The extent of the accommodation is not reasonably suitable to the needs of the assignee and family.

42 HA 1985 s92(3).
43 See para 6.81.

5) The accommodation was let to the tenant in consequence of employment, relating to non-housing purposes.

6) The assignment would conflict with the purposes of a landlord who is a charity.

7) The premises are adapted for a disabled person.

8) The assignment would conflict with the purposes of a landlord who is a specialist housing association or trust.

9) The accommodation is sheltered accommodation.

10) The property is managed by a housing association and the assignee refuses to become a member of the housing association.

4.67   If consent is sought and the landlord wishes to withhold consent the landlord must give notice to the tenant stating the ground upon which consent is withheld and giving particulars. This notice must be served within 42 days of the tenant's application. If no notice is served within the 42 days the landlord loses the right to withhold consent on any of the specified grounds. However, in the absence of any response, consent is not deemed to have been given. The tenant must therefore persuade the landlord to give consent, on the basis that the landlord has lost the right to refuse consent, or apply to the court for an order that the landlord must give consent. The tenant cannot simply proceed as if consent had been given.

4.68   The County Court has jurisdiction to resolve issues regarding secure tenancies, including issues about the giving or withholding of consent under HA 1985 Sch 3.[44]

4.69   Where the tenant is in arrears of rent or is otherwise in breach of the tenancy agreement the landlord can give conditional consent, requiring the tenant to pay the outstanding rent or remedy the breach: HA 1985 s93(5). A landlord can give such conditional consent even after the 42-day period has expired: HA 1985 s93(6). Otherwise, the landlord is not entitled to impose a condition on the giving of consent and any condition imposed can be disregarded by the tenant.

4.70   So a tenant can proceed if:

- the landlord gives written consent;
- consent is withheld for reasons other than those specified in HA 1985 Sch 3;
- consent is given subject to conditions other than relating to arrears of rent or the remedying of a breach of the tenancy agreement;
- conditions attached relating to rent arrears or other breach are met.

44 HA 1985 s110.

4.71 In all cases the other tenant must also have the written consent of his or her landlord.

4.72 The tenant cannot proceed if the landlord has failed to respond to the request for consent.

Rent arrears

4.73 Landlords will always insist that rent arrears are cleared before an exchange can proceed. It is sometimes the case that the exchanging tenant is so keen to move that he or she will offer money so that the other tenant can clear his or her arrears. Advisers should be aware that if payment is made by either tenant as part of the agreement to exchange this provides the landlord with a ground for possession.[45] The ground is a discretionary one and if a landlord was aware of the transaction made to clear arrears the court is unlikely to grant a possession order.

Matrimonial or Children Act assignment

4.74 In divorce or judicial separation proceedings the court can, under the Matrimonial Causes Act 1973, order one party to assign a tenancy to the other party, see chapter 12. It is more common for a transfer of tenancy to be ordered under the Family Law Act 1996. Under Family Law Act 1996 it is the court order that actually transfers the tenancy. Under Matrimonial Causes Act 1973 the transfer happens when the parties enter into a deed of assignment and if they fail to do this the tenancy is not transferred.[46]

4.75 The Matrimonial and Family Proceedings Act 1984 also gives the court the power to order assignments where divorce proceedings take place abroad.

4.76 Under the Children Act 1989 Sch 1 a court can make orders for the assignment of tenancies for the benefit of children (see chapter 12).

4.77 Assignments pursuant to court orders made under these Acts are effective to transfer the secure tenancy into the name of the assignee.

Assignments to potential successors

4.78 It is possible to assign a secure tenancy to a person who would, if the tenant died, be qualified to succeed (see para 4.33 above). This enables a tenant who wishes to move out of the premises to transfer

---

45 HA 1985, Sch 2, Ground 6 – see table in chapter 7.
46 *Crago v Julian* (1991) 24 HLR 306, CA.

the tenancy to a family member before doing so. The assignment must be done before the person moves out since the tenancy must be secure at the date of the assignment. If the tenant has ceased to occupy the premises as his or her only or principal home the tenancy will no longer be secure and this right will have been lost (see paras 3.116–3.117 and 4.5–4.8 above).[47]

4.79   If an assignment to a potential successor is made there can be no succession when the assignee tenant dies.[48]

Landlord's consent

4.80   Other than for mutual exchange, there is no requirement under HA 1985 that the tenant must obtain the landlord's consent to an assignment. However, the tenancy agreement itself may require that the landlord's consent be obtained. If so, an assignment without the landlord's consent will be effective to transfer the secure tenancy but will be a breach of the tenancy agreement. This will give the landlord the right to seek possession against the assignee. The ground is discretionary so the court would have to be satisfied not only that the assignment was in breach of the agreement but also that making a possession order was reasonable.

4.81   Where a tenancy agreement provides that consent must be sought, the landlord must not withhold consent unreasonably.[49]

4.82   If a secure tenancy has been assigned without the landlord's consent a request for consent can be made retrospectively. The landlord must still consider the request and, if reasonable, give consent. If a landlord refuses to respond to a request and seeks possession against the assignee, the court would take this into account when considering whether it was reasonable to make a possession order. The likely outcome is that the court would refuse to make an order if it found that the landlord would not have had any reasonable grounds on which to refuse consent.[50]

4.83   Even if the tenancy agreement prohibits assignment absolutely, if the necessary conditions are satisfied, the assignment will be effective to transfer the secure tenancy to the assignee. However, the landlord could claim possession against the assignee tenant for breach of

---

47   HA 1985 s95 specifically provides that the restrictions on assignment under HA 1985 s91 apply also to a tenancy that ceases to be secure because the tenant condition is not satisfied.
48   HA 1985 s88(16)(d).
49   Landlord and Tenant Act 1927 s19(1).
50   *Leeward Securities Ltd v Lilyheath Properties Ltd* (1983) 17 HLR 35, CA.

the tenancy agreement.[51] Again, an order would be made only if the court considered it reasonable to make a possession order.

Introductory tenancies

4.84   Introductory tenancies cannot be assigned except in the following circumstances:[52]

- an assignment on relationship breakdown or for the benefit of children, as for secure tenancies;
- an assignment to a potential successor.

4.85   An introductory tenant does not have the right to mutual exchange.

Demoted tenancies

4.86   A demoted tenancy cannot be assigned except on relationship break-down or for the benefit of children.[53]

4.87   A demoted tenant does not have the right to mutual exchange or to assign to a potential successor.

Housing Act 1988

4.88   For assured tenants considering assignment the starting point is the tenancy agreement. Most written agreements will either prohibit assignment absolutely or permit assignment only with the landlord's consent. If the agreement is silent, or there is no written agreement, HA 1988 will usually imply a term prohibiting assignment.

4.89   HA 1988 s15(2) provides that where a periodic tenancy agreement makes no provision about assignment it is an implied term that the tenant cannot assign the tenancy without the consent of the landlord. However, this does not apply if the tenant has paid a premium.[54] Where such a term is implied the landlord can refuse consent for any reason.[55]

---

51 See *Peabody Donation Fund v Higgins* (1983) 10 HLR 82, CA.
52 HA 1996 s134.
53 HA 1996 s143K.
54 This is a payment made for the grant of the tenancy but also includes a deposit that is more than two months' rent: HA 1988 s15(4).
55 Under Landlord and Tenant Act 1927 s19 where the landlord's consent is required it is an implied term that such consent shall not be unreasonably withheld. However, this is specifically excluded by HA 1988 s15(2).

4.90   So the situation for assured and assured shorthold tenancies is:

Terms of agreement	Means
Agreement prohibits assignment	Assignment not possible.
Agreement permits assignment with the consent of the landlord	Consent required and must not be unreasonably withheld.
Agreement is silent	Periodic tenancy (no premium paid): assignment not possible without landlord's consent and landlord may withhold consent for any reason. Fixed-term tenancy or periodic tenancy where premium paid: assignment is possible and the landlord's consent is not required.

4.91   Even where assignment is absolutely prohibited a landlord may agree to an assignment. However, the landlord is entitled to refuse and need not have any reason.

Subletting

What is subletting?

4.92   Subletting is when a tenant creates a tenancy out of his or her interest, but remains in the position of tenant against a higher landlord. This is distinct from an assignment where the tenant transfers the whole of his or her interest to someone else. In an assignment the assignee becomes the tenant of the landlord; this is not the case for a subtenant. The relationship between the parties is shown in the diagram opposite:

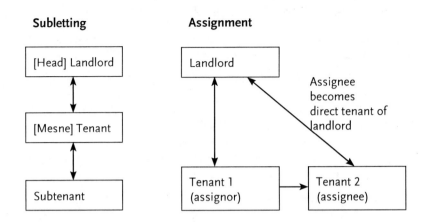

4.93   There is no limit to the number of subtenancies of the same premises so long as each subtenancy is for a shorter term than the tenancy out of which it is created. There may also be joint tenants or joint landlords at each level.

4.94   Subletting is distinct from lodging (which creates a licence). For subletting the hallmarks of a tenancy must be present: the grant of exclusive possession, for a period of time, in return for rent (see paras 1.29–1.34). In situations where the tenant shares the accommodation with another person it is more likely to be an arrangement of lodging than subletting (see para 1.26).

4.95   For the purpose of this section it is assumed that there are three parties only: the head landlord; the mesne tenant;[56] and the subtenant.

The issues

4.96   The questions that arise are:
- Is a tenant allowed to sublet?
- What happens if a tenant who isn't allowed to sublet does so?
- What happens to a subtenant when the mesne tenancy ends?

4.97   The answers to these questions depend on the terms of the tenancy agreement and the statutory provisions that apply to the tenancy. There is a distinction between subletting part of the premises and subletting the whole of the premises.

---

56 'Mesne' means 'intermediate'. It is pronounced 'mean'.

Is the tenant allowed to sublet?

4.98   Apart from secure tenancies where the position is governed by statute, the starting point is the tenancy agreement:

- if the tenancy agreement permits subletting, it is allowed;
- if the tenancy agreement permits subletting only with the landlord's consent, consent must be sought but the landlord must not unreasonably withhold consent;
- if the tenancy agreement prohibits subletting, it is not allowed;
- if the tenancy agreement is silent (or there is no tenancy agreement) the answer depends on the type of the tenancy.

4.99   It should be noted that where a tenant sublets in breach of the tenancy agreement the landlord may 'waive' the breach if he or she, aware of the breach, confirms the existence of the tenancy. This may make an unlawful subletting lawful. Waiver is generally only established by positive, intentional acts and not by a failure to act.

Rent Act tenancies

Subletting part

4.100 A protected or statutory tenant may sublet part of the premises. However, if subletting is prohibited or subject to the landlord's consent and consent is not obtained, it will be a breach of a term of the tenancy agreement. This gives the landlord a ground for possession but the ground is discretionary so the court would have to be satisfied that it is reasonable to make a possession order.

Subletting the whole

4.101 Subletting of the whole of the dwelling is only possible if the tenancy is protected, ie still within the contractual period. However, there is a ground for possession where a tenant has sublet the whole without the landlord's consent. This applies even if the tenancy agreement does not prohibit subletting, see appendix to chapter 7.

4.102 If the tenancy has become statutory, subletting the whole will result in the loss of the tenancy: a statutory tenancy lasts only if and so long as the statutory tenant resides in the premises.

Secure tenancies

4.103 The right of a secure tenant to sublet is entirely governed by statute.

Subletting part

4.104 A secure tenant may take in lodgers without the consent of the land-lord[57] and has a right to sublet part of the premises with the written consent of the landlord.[58]

4.105 HA 1985 s94 sets out detailed provisions regarding consent and provides:

- consent cannot be unreasonably withheld: s94(2);
- consent cannot be given subject to conditions: s94(5);
- if the tenant applies in writing for consent and the landlord refuses consent, a written statement of reasons must be given: s94(6)(a);
- in deciding whether to give consent, relevant issues include whether the subletting would lead to overcrowding and any proposed works that would affect the subtenant's accommodation: s94(3);
- if the landlord neither gives nor refuses consent, or fails to reply within a reasonable time, consent is treated as being withheld: s94(6)(b);
- in contrast, if a landlord refuses consent unreasonably, or gives consent subject to a condition, consent is treated as being given unconditionally: s94(2) and (5).

4.106 Any issue regarding consent may be dealt with by the County Court.[59] A tenant may apply for an injunction or declaration or the issue may arise in possession proceedings. If there is an issue as to whether consent was withheld unreasonably, it is for the landlord to show that it was not: HA 1985 s94(2).

Subletting the whole

4.107 HA 1985 s93(2) provides that a secure tenant who sublets or parts with possession of the whole premises ceases to be secure and cannot subsequently become secure.[60] Furthermore, such subletting is now a criminal offence, see para 4.13 above.

---

57 HA 1985 s93(1)(a).
58 HA 1985 s93(1)(b).
59 HA 1985 s110.
60 This is in contrast to a tenant who ceases to be secure because of not occupying the premises as only or principal home. Such a tenant can become a secure tenant again by re-occupying but a tenant who sublets the whole cannot regain secure status.

Introductory tenancies

Subletting part

4.108   Whether an introductory tenant can sublet part of the premises will depend on the terms of the tenancy agreement. In most cases it will be prohibited or subject to the landlord's consent.

Subletting the whole

4.109   Although there is no specific prohibition on subletting for introductory tenancies HA 1996 s124(5) provides that an introductory tenancy ceases to be an introductory tenancy if the circumstances are such that a secure tenant would no longer be secure. Subletting of the whole would therefore mean that the tenancy ceased to be introductory. The Prevention of Social Housing Fraud Act 2013 makes no reference to any offence in relation to subletting by an introductory tenant.

Assured tenancies and assured shorthold tenancies

4.110   Whether or not subletting is allowed depends on the terms of the tenancy agreement. If the agreement is silent, in most cases HA 1988 implies a term prohibiting subletting. The term is not implied into fixed-term tenancies or to tenancies where the tenant has paid a premium to the landlord for the grant of the tenancy.[61] In most of those cases the tenancy agreement will make specific provision about subletting.

4.111   So for a periodic assured tenancy where there is no written agreement or no specific provision, subletting is prohibited and a landlord may refuse consent to subletting for any reason.[62]

4.112   For most assured and assured shorthold tenants, therefore, subletting, whether of part or the whole, will be prohibited, either expressly in the tenancy agreement or by implication, under HA 1988 s15.

4.113   For assured tenants of PRPs of social housing, parting with possession or sub-letting the whole means that the tenant ceases to be assured and cannot subsequently become assured. This puts assured tenants of social housing into the same position as secure tenants.[63]

---

61   HA 1988 s15(3).
62   HA 1988 s15(1)(b) and (2).
63   HA 1988 s 15A. This was added by the Prevention of Social Housing Fraud Act 2013 and came into force on 5 November 2013. The subletting/parting with possession must be in breach of an express or implied term of the tenancy, which it almost always will be.

What happens if a tenant who is not allowed to sublet does so?

4.114   If a tenant is prohibited from subletting this does not mean that a subtenancy created by the tenant is invalid or void. The subtenancy will create the relationship of landlord and tenant between the mesne tenant and the subtenant. However, if it is in breach of the mesne tenancy agreement this will usually give the head landlord the right to end the mesne tenancy and take possession. In most cases the subtenant will have no right to remain in possession against the head landlord.

4.115   The positions of the tenant and the subtenant must be considered separately.

The tenant

4.116   A subletting in breach of the tenancy agreement gives the landlord a ground for possession: breach of a term of the tenancy agreement. Furthermore, for secure and assured tenants a subletting of the whole will mean that the mesne tenant no longer occupies the premises and thereby loses the secure or assured status. A landlord may therefore serve notice to quit on the mesne tenant and claim possession on the basis that the contractual tenancy has ended following expiry of the notice to quit.

The subtenant

4.117   The fact that the subletting is in breach of the mesne tenancy agreement does not give the head landlord a right to possession against the subtenant without first ending the mesne tenancy. Landlords who discover that their tenant is no longer in occupation sometimes serve notice on the occupiers/subtenants, indicating that they are in unlawful occupation and must leave. This is not the case; the subtenant is lawfully occupying under the subtenancy until the point at which the mesne tenancy is brought to an end. A landlord cannot take any action, whether through the courts or otherwise, to take possession against a subtenant until the mesne tenancy is terminated.

4.118   Moreover, the fact that the subtenancy is in breach of the mesne tenancy agreement does not give the mesne tenant the right to possession against the subtenant. The mesne tenant has created a binding subtenancy agreement. Unless the subtenant agrees to give up possession the mesne tenant can only obtain possession by serving the appropriate notice and obtaining a possession order against the subtenant.[64] An attempt to gain possession forcibly will be unlawful under the Protection from Eviction Act 1977, see paras 8.21 and 8.72.

What happens to a subtenant when the mesne tenancy ends?

4.119   The general rule is that when a mesne tenancy ends, any subtenancies or licences also come to an end and the head landlord is entitled to possession of the premises.

4.120   However, for subtenants in this situation, there are two common law exceptions. A subtenant may become the direct tenant of the head landlord in the following situations:

- where the mesne tenancy is ended by surrender (see para 4.122 below);[65]
- where the mesne tenancy is ended by forfeiture (see paras 4.123–4.124 below).

4.121   In addition, the Rent Act 1977 and the Housing Act 1988 make specific provision for subtenancies and set out the circumstances in which a subtenant may become a direct tenant, with statutory protection, against a head landlord (see paras 4.125–4.128 below).

Surrender

4.122   Surrender is an agreement between a tenant and a landlord that the tenancy is given up, see paras 1.67–1.77. The landlord must agree to the surrender and, in doing so, takes back the premises subject to any rights and interests created by the tenant. For this reason when a mesne tenant surrenders the tenancy, any subtenant becomes the direct tenant of the head landlord. This applies whether or not the subtenancy is in breach of the tenancy agreement.

> The unusual case of *Basingstoke and Deane BC v Paice*[66] illustrates how this doctrine operates. The tenancy was of commercial premises owned by the local authority. The tenant of the commercial

---

64   A subtenancy granted by a private individual to another private individual after 28 February 1997 will usually be an assured shorthold tenancy. See paras 6.47 and 7.2 for information about possession claims against assured shorthold tenants.

65   *Parker v Jones* [1910] 2 KB 32.

66   (1995) 27 HLR 433, CA.

premises carried out works to create a dwelling within the premises which he then sublet. The authority subsequently accepted the surrender of the tenancy of the commercial premises, at which point the subtenant became the direct tenant of the authority. As the landlord and tenant conditions were satisfied the tenancy was a secure tenancy.

Forfeiture

4.123 Forfeiture is described in more detail at paras 5.7–5.23. It is a common law remedy giving the landlord the right to end a fixed-term tenancy if the tenant breaches the terms of the agreement. If the tenant is able to remedy the breach he or she may apply to a court for 'relief against forfeiture' which restores the lease. Subtenants may also apply for relief against forfeiture and the court may make an order effectively transferring the tenancy to the subtenant.

4.124   However, relief against forfeiture depends on the tenant or subtenant being able to remedy any breach. If the breach complained of is the unlawful subletting (as opposed to, say, rent arrears owed to the head landlord), relief will not be granted to the subtenant because the breach cannot be remedied by the subtenant.

Rent Act tenancies

4.125 RA 1977 s137 provides that if certain conditions are met a subtenant may become the protected or statutory tenant of the head landlord when the mesne tenancy ends. The conditions are that:

- the tenancy (ie, the agreement between the head landlord and the mesne tenant) must be a 'statutory protected tenancy';
- the subtenancy (ie, the agreement between the mesne tenant and the subtenant) must be a protected or statutory tenancy; and
- the subtenancy must be lawful.

4.126 These conditions will rarely be satisfied for the following reasons:

- if the head tenancy is a statutory tenancy under RA 1977 this will end if the statutory tenant no longer resides in the premises;
- if the statutory tenant shares the premises with the subtenant he or she will be a resident landlord which means that the subtenancy cannot be protected or statutory;
- most written tenancy agreements prohibit subletting so that the subtenancy will not be lawful.

Housing Act 1988 tenancies

4.127　If there is a lawful subletting to an assured subtenant he or she becomes the assured tenant of the head landlord when the mesne tenancy ends.[67] If the subtenancy is an assured shorthold tenancy the subtenant will become the assured shorthold tenant of the head landlord.

4.128　　The subtenancy must be a lawful assured subtenancy, ie one which is permitted under the mesne tenancy agreement.

Obtaining information about the landlord

4.129　Tenancies may be created with little formality; no documentation is necessary and negotiations are often conducted by agents. A tenant may therefore be in a legally binding relationship but have little information about the identity of his or her landlord.

4.130　　Various statutory provisions give a tenant the right to be informed of the name and address of his or her landlord (paras 4.131–4.134 below). Other ways of obtaining information are described at paras 4.139–4.141.

Requesting information

4.131　The Landlord and Tenant Act (LTA) 1985 s1 provides that a tenant of a dwelling can make a written request for the landlord's name and address to any person demanding rent or who last received rent, or to anyone acting as the landlord's agent. The person receiving the request must supply to the tenant a written statement of the landlord's name and address within 21 days.

4.132　　If the landlord is a company the tenant may make a further written request for the name and address of every director and the secretary of the company: LTA 1985 s2. The request may be made to the company landlord, to the agent or the person who demands rent and must be forwarded to the landlord 'as soon as may be'. The landlord must provide this information within 21 days of receiving the request.

67　HA 1988 s18. This is not possible, however, if the tenancy is excluded by Schedule 1 to the Act.

Change of landlord

4.133   If the property is sold or the landlord's interest otherwise transferred the new landlord must inform the tenant of his or her name and address no later than two months after the transfer, or if rent is not payable within that two-month period, no later than the next day on which rent is payable: LTA 1985 s3.[68]

4.134   If the tenant is not informed of the new landlord's name and address the previous landlord remains liable for any breach of the tenancy agreement (eg, disrepair) up to the date when notice is given.[69]

Criminal penalties

4.135   The sanction for failure, without reasonable excuse, to give information to tenants about the identity of the landlord is that the landlord, rent collector or agent, can be prosecuted. The penalty for offences under LTA 1985 ss1, 2 and 3 is the same: a fine, not exceeding level four, currently £2,500. Such cases are not prosecuted by the police but by local authorities.

4.136   A tenant may be seeking information about the landlord because of complaints about disrepair. Local authorities' environmental health or housing standards departments may assist the tenant but prosecutions are rare. The withholding of rent will often force a landlord to provide the information but tenants must be aware that any rent withheld becomes payable as soon as the landlord gives the information, see below, para 4.137.

Withholding rent

4.137   Under LTA 1987 s48 a landlord must provide a tenant with an address in England and Wales at which notices may be served on the landlord by the tenant. If the landlord fails to do so any rent or service charge otherwise due to the landlord shall be treated as not being due 'at any time before' the landlord complies. The tenant's liability for the rent is not extinguished by the landlord's failure to give this information: the moment the landlord provides the information the whole of any unpaid rent or service charge becomes payable.

---

68   Some tenants have the 'right of first refusal' and must, under LTA 1985 s3A, be served with notice to that effect.
69   LTA 1985 s3(3A).

4.138   The information need not be given in a specific notice; it is sufficient if the information is stated in the tenancy agreement or in a
possession notice.[70]

The Land Registry

4.139   Most land in England and Wales is registered at the Land Registry.
The Land Registry records the name and address of the registered
proprietor and any registered charges (mortgages). Note that the registered proprietor may not be the landlord. Any member of the public can request this information for any address and the search can
be done online at: www.gov.uk/search-property-information-land-
registry. The current fee is £6.00.

Data Protection Act 1998

4.140   For tenants of social landlords (or other large-scale landlords) useful
information may be obtained under the Data Protection Act 1998.
However, the right is to information held relating to the 'data subject', ie the person making the request, rather than the landlord. See
paras 2.101–2.105 and the appendix to chapter 2.

Housing Act 1985 – housing applications

4.141   Under HA 1985 s106(5) a person may obtain information held by a
housing authority in relation to an application for housing.

Tenancy deposits

4.142   In the private sector most landlords require rent in advance plus a
returnable deposit at the start of the tenancy. Because of the difficulty faced by many tenants in recovering the deposit at the end of
the tenancy, the Housing Act 2004 made it compulsory for private
landlords granting assured shorthold tenancies to protect deposits in
'an authorised scheme'. The relevant provisions came into force on 6
April 2007.

4.143   The provisions are set out in HA 2004 ss212–215. These sections
were amended in 2012 by the Localism Act (LA) 2011 ('the 2012

---

70 *Rogan v Woodfield Building Services Ltd* (1994) 27 HLR 78; *Drew-Morgan v
Hamid-Zadeh* (2000) 32 HLR 316.

amendments') and in March 2015 by the Deregulation Act (DA) 2015.

Tenancy deposit schemes

4.144 The relevant sections provide that:

- any deposit received must be dealt with in accordance with an authorised scheme, ie protected; and
- the landlord must give to the tenant prescribed information.

Both must be done within 30 days of receiving the deposit.

4.145 There are two types of authorised scheme:[71]

- *Custodial schemes:* the landlord pays the deposit into a deposit protection scheme.
- *Insurance based schemes:* the landlord keeps the deposit but pays a premium for an insurance policy against which the tenant can claim if the landlord fails to return the deposit.

4.146 The 2012 amendments came into force on 6 April 2012. Landlords of existing tenancies were given a 'window' in which to comply: they had 30 days from 6 April 2012 to protect a deposit and give the prescribed information.[72]

4.147 There are two sanctions for a landlord's failure to comply:

- under section 214 the tenant can apply to a county court for an order that the landlord pays a sum between one and three times the amount of the deposit (in addition to returning the deposit); and
- under section 215 the landlord may not claim possession under HA 1988 s21 'at a time when' the deposit is not protected.

These are explained in more detail at paras 4.154–4.156 and 4.158–4.162 below.

Deposit paid by third party

4.148 The same rights are also given to 'any relevant person'. This is defined as 'any person who, in accordance with arrangements made with the tenant, paid the deposit on behalf of the tenant'.[73] This could include a local authority operating a tenancy deposit scheme or a

---

71 Information about authorised deposit schemes can be found at: www.gov.uk/tenancy-deposit-protection/overview.

72 See Localism Act 2011 (Commencement No 4 and Transitional, Transitory and Saving Provisions) Order 2012 article 16.

73 HA 2004 s213(10).

relative acting as guarantor and paying the deposit on behalf of the tenant. Prescribed information must be given to the 'relevant person' who may also make an application to the county court for a 'money order' under section 214.

The landlord's obligations

4.149 'Tenancy deposit' is defined as 'money intended to be held ... as security for – (a) the performance of any obligations of the tenant, or (b) the discharge of any liability of his, arising in connection with the tenancy.'[74]

4.150 There are two parts to the landlord's obligations:

- **Protection of deposit in an authorised scheme: s213(3)**
  '... the initial requirements of an authorised scheme [ie the protection of the deposit in accordance with the scheme being used] ... within 30 days' of receiving the deposit.

- **Giving of prescribed information: s213(5) and (6)**
  A landlord must give prescribed information to the tenant [and any person who paid the deposit on the tenant's behalf] within 30 days of receiving the deposit

4.151 The landlord must comply with the particular requirements of whatever protection scheme is being used. In addition to protecting the deposit the landlord must give prescribed information to the tenant and any relevant person within 30 days of receiving the deposit.

4.152 The information the landlord must provide is:[75]

- contact details of the scheme administrator where the deposit is held;
- information provided by the scheme administrator to the landlord explaining the requirements of the HA 2004 in relation to deposits;
- the procedures for recovering the deposit at the end of the tenancy, including the procedures applying if either the landlord or tenant cannot be contacted;

---

74 HA 2004 s212(8).
75 HA 2004 s213(5) and (6); Housing (Tenancy Deposits) (Prescribed Information) Order 2007 SI No 797. Note that a particular scheme may require additional information to be given to the tenant. Section 30 of the DA 2015 makes clear that the information can be given by either the landlord or the landlord's agent and that the contact details given in the prescribed information can be those of the agent.

- the procedures applying where there are disputes about the amount to be returned and the facilities available for resolving disputes;
- information about the tenancy and the deposit: the amount paid, the address of the property, and the contact details of the landlord and the tenant which will be used by the administrator of the scheme at the end of the tenancy;
- the circumstances in which all or part of the deposit may be retained by the landlord;
- confirmation by the landlord that the information given is accurate to the best of his or her knowledge or belief and that he or she has given the tenant the opportunity to sign to confirm that the information is accurate to the best of the tenant's knowledge and belief.

Dispute resolution

4.153   Tenancy deposit schemes assist tenants to recover their deposits at the end of a tenancy. Disputes may arise about whether the landlord is entitled to withhold the deposit or part of it because of damage caused by the tenant or unpaid bills. The authorised schemes provide dispute resolution mechanisms to resolve such issues.

Sanctions for non-compliance

County court action for money order: s214

4.154   An application in relation to a deposit received on or after 6 April 2007 can be made on the grounds that:

- The landlord has not complied with section 213(3) or (6), ie the landlord has failed to protect the deposit or failed to give the prescribed information to the tenant, *or*
- The landlord has given such notice but no written confirmation from the scheme administrator can be obtained to confirm the deposit is being held.

The application may be made either by the tenant or the person who paid the deposit[76] and can be made after the tenancy has ended.[77]

---

76 Section 214(1).
77 This was changed in 2012 to reverse the effect of *Gladehurst Properties Ltd v Hashemi & Johnson* [2011] EWCA Civ 604, 19 May 2011.

4.155   If the court:

- is satisfied that s213(3) or (6) has not been complied with; or
- is not satisfied that the deposit is being held in accordance with an authorised scheme,

the court *must* make an order that:

- the person who appears to be holding the deposit either repays it to the applicant, or pays it into the designated account of an authorised custodial scheme;[78] *and*
- the landlord pays to the applicant a sum equivalent to between one and three times the amount of the deposit, within 14 days.

Note that the court's discretion is limited to the amount of the money order, which can be between one and three times the amount of the deposit. If satisfied of the matters set out above, the court must make a money order of some kind, and order the return or protection of the deposit.

4.156   Section 213 provides that the landlord must comply with the requirements of a particular scheme and give the prescribed information within 30 days of receiving the deposit. So, even where a landlord has complied by the date of the hearing, or even before the application, the court must make an order of between one and three times the deposit.[79] Clearly, if the omission was a genuine error and the landlord complies as quickly as possible after being made aware of it the court is likely to award the lower sum but this is still in addition to the return of the deposit (assuming the deposit scheme confirms that it must be returned in full).

Non-monetary deposits

4.157   It is unlawful for a landlord to require a deposit that consists of property other than money in connection with an assured shorthold tenancy.[80] However, if such a deposit is taken, the property is 'recoverable' from the person holding it.[81] There is no specific provision

---

78   However, if the application is made after the tenancy has ended, the landlord can only repay the deposit to the applicant: s214(3A).

79   The amended s214 reverses the effect of the decisions in *Tiensa v Vision Enterprises Ltd; Honeysuckle Properties v Fletcher, McGrory and Whitworth* [2010] EWCA Civ 1224, 12 November 2010, in which the Court of Appeal held that the relevant date was the date of the hearing so that a landlord could always defeat a claim by complying before the actual hearing of the tenant's claim.

80   HA 2004 s213(7).

81   HA 2004 s214(5).

for sanctions under ss214 in such a case. Such a deposit must be returned to the tenant before a s21 notice can be served.

Restriction on possession proceedings

4.158 In relation to all tenancy deposits, whether paid before or after 6 April 2007, 'no section 21 notice may be given in relation to the tenancy at a time when the deposit is not being held in accordance with an authorised scheme'.[82] If the tenancy deposit was paid on or after 6 April 2007 'no section 21 notice may be given in relation to the tenancy at a time when section 213(3) has not been complied with',[83] ie the deposit was not protected within 30 days of receipt. In both cases a landlord can rely on section 215(2A), see below at para 4.160.

4.159 Note that in addition to protecting the deposit, if received on or after 6 April 2007, the landlord must also give the prescribed information and no section 21 notice can be served until this has been done, again subject to section 215(2A).[84]

4.160 Section 215(2A) provides that the sanctions in relation to the service of a s21 notice do not apply if:

- the deposit has been returned in full, or subject to agreed deductions; or
- an application under s214 has been decided by the court, withdrawn, or settled between the parties.

4.161 In summary then, if a landlord received a deposit prior to 6 April 2007, he or she must either protect it in an authorised scheme or return it to the tenant (subject to the exceptions in s215(2A)). If the deposit was received on or after 6 April 2007 and was not protected within 30 days (and has not been the subject of an application under s214) the only way the landlord can serve a section 21 notice is by first returning the deposit to the tenant in full, or subject to agreed deductions.

4.162 It is the *giving* of the notice that is prohibited during a period of non-compliance. Therefore if a notice has already been served, the landlord cannot make the notice good by protecting or repaying the deposit. This must be done before a fresh s21 notice is served. The provisions do not prevent a landlord from serving notice seeking possession under s8 of the HA 1988, based on grounds for a possession (eg rent arrears or nuisance).

---

82 HA 2004 s215(1).
83 HA 2004 s215(1A).
84 HA 2004 s215(2).

Case-law developments and the Deregulation Act 2015 amendments explained

4.163   The 2012 amendments resolved two problems created by poor drafting and ensured that (1) applications under section 214 can be made after the tenancy has ended and (2) a landlord could not defeat the sanction of a money judgment by complying with the requirements at a late stage.

4.164   However, further Court of Appeal decisions created new problems in relation to (1) tenancies that commenced prior to the HA 2004 coming into force and (2) new tenancies following on from the original tenancy. The Deregulation Act 2015 amendments remedy these problems.

> In *Superstrike v Rodrigues*[85] the Court of Appeal considered a tenancy which had started as a fixed term tenancy before the HA 2004 came into force. After the fixed term ended, in 2008, the tenant remained in occupation as a statutory periodic tenant. Six months later the landlord served a notice under HA 1988 s21 and obtained a possession order. The Court of Appeal held that the statutory periodic tenancy that arose in 2008 was a new tenancy and that at that point the landlord should have protected the deposit. As the deposit was unprotected when the section 21 notice was served, the possession order should not have been made.

> In *Charalambous v Ng*[86] the tenancy had commenced in August 2002 and was for a fixed term of one year. It was renewed each year until August 2005 when a statutory periodic tenancy arose. The tenants remain in occupation and a section 21 possession notice was served in October 2012. A deposit had been paid in August 2002 but had never been protected. This was unsurprising since the tenancy deposit scheme was not in existence when the deposit was paid or when the statutory periodic tenancy arose. The Court of Appeal nevertheless held that for the purposes of section 215, the deposit should have been protected. Section 215 provides that no section 21 notice may be given at a time when 'the deposit is not being held in accordance with an authorised scheme, or section 213(3) has not

85   [2013] EWCA Civ 669, 14 June 2014.
86   [2014] EWCA Civ 1604, 16 December 2014.

been complied with in relation to the deposit.' The court held that this was not a retrospective application of the provisions since it only affects section 21 notices served after they came into force. A landlord in such a situation can serve a section 21 notice if he or she first repays the deposit to the tenant.

4.165 In order to remedy what was seen as an unfair, retrospective application of the provisions, the Deregulation Act 2015 amends the tenancy deposit provisions by making specific provision for deposits paid prior to 6 April 2007 and also for cases in which a landlord has complied with the requirements in relation to the original tenancy but new tenancies have since come into being. These are summarised below at paras 4.166–4.169.

Deposits received before 6 April 2007

4.166 The new section 215A applies where prior to 6 April 2007 a tenancy deposit was received by a landlord in relation to a fixed term assured shorthold tenancy and, after that date, the tenancy became a statutory periodic tenancy (a *Superstrike* situation, see para 4.164 above). In such a case the landlord has 90 days from 26 March 2015 to protect the deposit and to give the prescribed information to the tenant, ie this must be done on or before 24 June 2015. If, before 24 June 2015, there is a hearing to determine either an application under section 214 (money judgment) or to consider whether to make a possession order based on a s21 notice, the landlord must comply before the date of the hearing (or the date of any appeal in relation to an order already made).

4.167 Section 215 has been amended to address the situation in which a deposit was received prior to 6 April 2007 and no new tenancy, including a statutory periodic tenancy, has arisen since that date (a *Charalambous* situation, see para 4.164 above). In such a case the landlord must protect the deposit before he or she can serve a valid s21 notice. However, there is no requirement to serve the prescribed information and the landlord is not subject to any sanction under s214 (money judgment).

4.168 In both cases, instead of paying the deposit into an authorised scheme, the landlord can instead repay the deposit to the tenant under s215(2A) above at para 4.160.

Deposits received after 6 April 2007

4.169   The new section 215B applies where a landlord complied with the requirements when the initial tenancy commenced but new tenancies have arisen since (whether expressly agreed or automatically under HA 1988 s5). In such a case, provided:

- the landlord and the tenant are the same
- the premises let are the same or substantially the same, and
- the deposit continues to be held in the same authorised scheme as when the prescribed information was last given,

the requirements are deemed to have been complied with in relation to the new tenancy.

Transitional provisions

4.170   The new section 215C sets out the transitional provisions that apply only to claims that have been commenced but not determined as at 26 March 2015. Any claim under section 214, or possession claim relying on HA 1988 s21, determined before 26 March 2015 is not affected by the changes. However, claims issued but not finally determined will be affected by the changes, ie the landlord can rely on the provisions of the DA 2015. But if a landlord successfully defeats a claim under section 214, or defeats a defence to a claim for possession because of the DA 2015 amendments the tenant will not be ordered to pay the landlord's costs. Note that proceedings are considered to be determined after the date on which an appeal could be brought. This is 21 days from the date of the decision. A landlord wishing to benefit from this will have to lodge an appeal within the 21 days after the decision.

Unfair contract terms in tenancy agreements

4.171   The Unfair Terms in Consumer Contracts Regulations (UTCCR) 1999[87] apply to contracts between 'suppliers' and 'consumers', including tenancy agreements. To apply, the following conditions must be met:

---

87 UTCCR 1999 SI No 2083 came into force on 1 October 1999. They replaced the 1994 Regulations SI No 3159, which applied to all contracts entered into on or after 1 July 1995. The purpose of the 1994 Regulations was to give effect to a European Community Directive, effective from 1 January 1995. There is therefore an argument that the 1994 Regulations (and the 1999 Regulations) apply to contracts entered into by emanations of the state, including local authorities, as from 1 January 1995.

- The tenant must be an individual not acting in the course of a trade, business or profession.
- The landlord may be an individual or a company, but must be acting for purposes relating to his or her trade, business or profession, whether publicly or privately owned.
- The agreement or particular term must not have been individually negotiated. Where an agreement is in a pre-formulated standard contract the terms will always be regarded as not having been individually negotiated. However, if a particular term has been agreed expressly between the parties that term will not be subject to the regulations. If it is argued that a term was individually negotiated the burden is on the landlord to show that it was.

4.172 UTCCR 1999 apply to tenancies granted by registered providers and local authorities as well as private landlords.[88]

When is a term 'unfair'?

4.173 Under the regulations: 'A contractual term ... shall be regarded as unfair if, contrary to the requirements of good faith, it causes a significant imbalance in the parties' rights and obligations arising under the contract to the detriment of the consumer.'[89] But, significant imbalance alone is not sufficient: the term must also be contrary to the requirements of good faith, for example a term that is expressed unclearly or where the consumer's inexperience or lack of understanding is exploited.

UK Housing Alliance (North West) Ltd v Francis[90] concerned a sale and leaseback scheme under which the property was sold and a tenancy granted by the purchaser to the seller for a period of 10 years. 70 per cent of the purchase price was to be paid on completion with 30 per cent paid at the end of the tenancy. The tenant (consumer) argued that a term under which the final payment could be withheld if the tenancy ended early (because of the tenant's breach) was an unfair term.

The Court of Appeal held that the term was not unfair: it did not create a significant imbalance between the parties and, as it was

---

88 *Newham LBC v Khatun, Zeb, Iqbal & OFT* [2004] EWCA Civ 55.
89 UTCCR 1999 reg 5(1).
90 [2010] EWCA Civ 117, 8 February 2010.

> 'fully, clearly and legibly' expressed, the tenant could not say that he
> had been taken advantage of unfairly.[91]

4.174   The assessment of fairness does not apply to:[92]

- the definition of the main subject matter of the contract (for
  example, the extent of the letting); or
- the 'adequacy of the price or remuneration, as against the goods
  or services supplied' – in the context of tenancy agreements this
  would exclude an argument that the rent is excessive. Other provisions may be used to challenge excessive rents, see below, paras
  4.189–4.196.

Plain language

4.175   The landlord must ensure that any written tenancy agreement is
expressed in plain, intelligible language. If there is any doubt about
the meaning of a written term, the interpretation most favourable to
the consumer shall prevail.[93]

Effect of unfair terms

4.176   An unfair term is not binding on the tenant. However, the remainder
of the tenancy agreement continues to be binding provided it can
operate in the absence of the unfair term.

Enforcing the regulations

4.177   The regulations are now enforced by the Competition and Markets
Authority (CMA) and the Financial Conduct Authority, the Office of
Fair Trading (OFT) having ceased to exist on 1 April 2014. Guidance on terms that will be considered to be unfair can be downloaded
from the FCA website: www.fca.org.uk.

4.178   In September 2005 the OFT produced guidance on terms considered potentially unfair in assured and assured shorthold tenancies. The guidance has been adopted by the CMA. Complaint may be
made to the CMA about particular standard agreements but it cannot

---

91 Longmore LJ at [29].
92 UTCCR 1999 reg 6(2), although such terms must be in 'plain intelligible
    language' and could be challenged under the regulations if not.
93 UTCCR 1999 reg 7.

become involved in individual disputes. Only the court can declare that a particular term is unenforceable.

4.179 For tenants it is more likely that the issue will arise in court proceedings when a landlord is seeking to rely on the disputed term. The tenant must state in the defence that the particular term is alleged to be unfair. If the court finds that the term is an unfair term under UTCCR 1999, it is unenforceable.

Examples of unfair terms in tenancy agreements

4.180 In the following cases the courts have considered the application of UTCCR 1999 to tenancy agreements.

In *Camden LBC v McBride*,[94] Central London County Court considered the application of the previous regulations to a 'nuisance' clause in a local authority tenancy agreement. The clause prohibited the tenant from doing anything which in the landlord's opinion might be or become a nuisance.
   The court held that the term was unenforceable and unfair because the question of its breach was to be determined subjectively by the landlord.

In *Cody v Philps*[95] the tenancy agreement contained a clause that prevented the tenant from making any 'set-off' or deduction whatsoever against rent. The tenant had a claim for damages for disrepair and wished to set off the damages awarded against the agreed rent arrears.
   West London County Court found that the clause was contrary to good faith and caused significant imbalance between the parties. It was therefore unfair and unenforceable; the tenant was entitled to set off the damages against the arrears of rent.

4.181 UTCCR 1999 Sch 2 sets out a non-exhaustive list of terms that may be regarded as unfair. Furthermore, the OFT guidance from 2005 suggested a number of terms in tenancy agreements that would be considered unfair. These include clauses:

94 [1999] 1 CL 284.
95 January 2005 *Legal Action* 28.

- allowing the landlord to determine whether the tenant is in breach of contract;
- giving the landlord the final decision as to whether repairs have been properly done, or whether work is rechargeable to the tenant;
- requiring the tenant to go through an arbitration process before he or she can go to court;
- giving the landlord an excessive right of access to the property;
- requiring a tenant to pay a 'penalty' charge for breach that is in excess of the landlord's loss; this would include excessive interest charged on late rent;
- applying excessive restrictions on day-to-day use of the property.

Rents

4.182   Under a tenancy agreement the amount of rent payable is agreed between the parties and, if there is a written agreement, the rent will be stated in the agreement. Provision may be made for rent to be increased in the future. This may be expressed to be by a fixed amount or to be calculated by a specific formula. Alternatively, the agreement may simply give the landlord the right to increase rent on a periodic basis, the amount to be determined by the landlord.

4.183   If the agreement provides that no rent is payable it is unlikely to be a tenancy. But if a rent-free tenancy *is* created the tenant will have few rights (see paras 1.100 and 1.111–1.112).

4.184   In all cases where a tenant has substantive security of tenure it is a ground for possession that the tenant has failed to pay rent 'lawfully due'. It is therefore crucial to understand how rents are set and increased.

Rents in the private sector

4.185   Rent control was effectively abandoned by the Housing Act 1988: the rents for assured and assured shorthold tenancies are expected to be market rents. Assured shorthold tenants have the right to challenge a rent that is significantly higher than the market rent, but the fact that such tenants have no long-term security means that such challenges are rare. Assured tenants may challenge rent increases only if there is no provision for rent increases in the tenancy agreement, see below at para 4.194. Furthermore, a challenge can only be on the basis that the proposed increase is in excess of a market rent.

Rent Act 1977: fair rents

4.186   Prior to 15 January 1989 private and housing association tenants enjoyed a high level of rent control. Under the Rent Act (RA) 1977, regardless of any express agreement, either the tenant or the landlord could apply for the rent to be 'registered' by a rent officer. The rent registered would be a 'fair rent', assessed by discounting from the appropriate market rent any sum deemed attributable to the scarcity of accommodation. The registered rent became the maximum rent a landlord could charge. Furthermore, the only way a landlord could increase the rent was by applying for a registered rent, or for an increase in a rent previously registered. Most remaining Rent Act tenants already have a registered rent. If not, a Rent Act tenant can apply for a fair rent to be registered for the first time.

4.187   Both private tenants (protected or statutory) and housing association (secure) tenants whose tenancy began before 15 January 1989 have the right to fair rents under RA 1977 Parts III and IV. The features of fair rents are as follows:

- A registered rent for a particular property is the maximum rent that the landlord can recover.[96] A rent registered in respect of a previous tenancy is binding even if the parties to a later tenancy are completely different.
- If there is no registered rent, the maximum rent the landlord can recover is the original contractual rent. The only way this can be increased is by an agreement complying with RA 1977 s51: see below, or by applying to the rent officer for a new (fair) rent to be registered.
- An agreement to increase the rent is only valid if it is in writing and complies with RA 1977 s51: it must include a statement that the tenant's security of tenure will not be affected by a refusal to sign and that the agreement does not prevent a future application for a registered rent.[97]
- If a landlord purports to increase the rent, otherwise than by a s51 agreement or an application for a new registered rent, the tenant can recover from the landlord any rent overpaid over the previous two years.[98] Recovery may be made by deductions from future

---

96   RA 1977 s44(1).
97   Furthermore, this information must be set out in 'characters not less conspicuous than those used in any other part of the agreement'.
98   RA 1977 s57. Where the overpayment of rent was because of a failure to comply with the technical requirement of section 51 the recovery period is one year: s54.

rent or by bringing a claim in the County Court. Because of the limit on the period for which recovery can be made a claim should be made without delay.

- Where there is a registered rent the landlord can apply for an increase two years after it was last registered, unless there are other reasons justifying an increase, such as improvement works, or an increase in rates or service charges payable by the tenant. In such a case the landlord must still apply for a new rent to be registered and the decision as to the new rent will be made by a rent officer.

- Rent officers were employed by the Rent Service but are now part of the Valuation Office Agency. They value property both for the purposes of the registration of rents and for the setting of housing benefit levels. Usually a rent officer inspects a property before setting or increasing a fair rent. For records since 2003, there is an electronic rent register, available via the VOA website.

- Since 1999 there has been a cap on the level of increases to fair rents.[99] An increase cannot exceed a sum calculated as follows: the difference in the Retail Price Index at the date of last registration and the date of the current registration plus 7.5 per cent on the first increase after February 1999 and 5 per cent on any subsequent increase. However, this does not apply if repairs or improvements carried out by the landlord justify an increase in the rent.[100]

- If rent is increased following an application to a rent officer, the increased rent does not become payable until the landlord has served a valid notice of increase on the tenant in prescribed form.[101]

4.188   The rents for tenancies granted by housing associations, housing trusts and the Housing Corporation that would have been protected tenancies, if it were not for the identity of the landlord, are also subject to the fair rent scheme.[102] Such tenancies must have been created before 15 January 1989.

---

99 Rent Acts (Maximum Fair Rent) Order 1999 SI No 6.
100 Rent Acts (Maximum Fair Rent) Order 1999 art 2(7).
101 RA 1977 s45(2)(b) and (3).
102 RA 1977 s86.

Housing Act 1988: assured and assured shorthold tenancies

Challenging the agreed rent

4.189 An assured shorthold tenant can apply to the Residential Property Tribunal for a determination of the rent.[103] An application can only be made in the first six months of the tenancy and must be made in prescribed form. If successive agreements are entered into by the same parties this does not revive the right to apply to the committee. Given that a landlord can evict an assured shorthold tenant as of right after six months, this right is seldom enforced. An assured tenant has no right to challenge the agreed rent but may be able to challenge proposed increases, see paras 4.192–4.196 below.

4.190 The tribunal will make a determination only if:

- there are a sufficient number of similar dwellings let on similar tenancies in the locality; and
- the rent payable is 'significantly higher' than the market rent, having regard to the rents for those other dwellings.

4.191 If the tribunal makes a determination, that becomes the maximum rent the landlord can recover.

Rent increases and HA 1988 s13

4.192 HA 1988 s13 gives to some assured tenants[104] the right to refer proposed rent increases to a rent committee. It applies to:

- a statutory periodic assured tenancy; and
- any other periodic tenancy which is an assured tenancy, other than one in relation to which there is a provision, for the time being binding on the tenant, under which the rent for a particular period of the tenancy will or may be greater than the rent for an earlier period.[105]

4.193 So, HA 1988 s13 applies to a periodic tenancy that comes into being at the end of a fixed term. Any rent increase term in the fixed-term agreement does not become a term of the statutory periodic tenancy so as to displace section 13.[106] Where the tenancy has always been a periodic tenancy, section 13 applies only if there is no term in the agreement that provides for future rent increases.

103 HA 1988 s22.
104 This includes assured shorthold tenants but, because of their lack of security, is rarely used by such tenants.
105 HA 1988 s13(1)(b).
106 *London District Properties Management Ltd & Others v Goolamy & Goolamy* [2009] EWHC 1367 (Admin), 16 June 2009.

4.194   To exclude HA 1998 s13 it is not necessary that the term makes provision for a specified increase, or an increase calculated by a set formula, at a future date. Any provision giving the landlord the right to increase the rent in the future is sufficient.

> In *Contour Homes Ltd v Rowen*[107] the agreement was a periodic tenancy with a term stating: 'The rent will be reviewed by the Association in April of each year. The Association shall give to the tenant no less than four weeks notice of the revised amount payable. The revised Net Rent shall be the amount specified in the notice of increase.' The tenant tried to challenge the rent increase by applying to the Rent Assessment Committee under s13.
>   The Court of Appeal held that section 13 did not apply if there was any provision in the tenancy agreement for the rent to be increased if certain events occur, in this case the service by the landlord of a notice.

4.195   So, if the tenancy agreement makes provision for the landlord to increase the rent a tenant will have no right to challenge an increase on the basis that it exceeds a market rent. However, where a rent increase is imposed for the purpose of removing a tenant's security by taking the tenancy outside the provisions of the Housing Act 1988 it may be held to be unenforceable.[108]

4.196   If HA 1988 s13 does apply, a landlord must serve a prescribed notice on the tenant stating the proposed new rent. The increased rent cannot take effect before a certain date, being no earlier than one year since the last increase. Furthermore, a certain period must elapse between service of the notice and the increase taking effect.[109] If the tenant wishes to object, he or she can refer the notice to the Residential Property Tribunal. The referral must be made (ie, received by the tribunal[110]) before the increase takes effect. The tribunal will determine an open market rent which will be the maximum rent the landlord can charge. This may be done at a hearing. A tenant challenging the rent as being in excess of a market rent will need to provide evidence of market rents for similar properties in the locality.

---

107 [2007] EWCA Civ 842, 26 June 2007.
108 *Bankway Properties Ltd v Pensfold Dunsford* [2001] EWCA Civ 528.
109 This varies, depending on the period of the tenancy, see HA 1988 s13(2)–(3).
110 *R on the application of Lester v London RAC* [2003] EWCA Civ 319, 12 March 2003.

Varying the rent by agreement

4.197 A landlord and tenant under an assured tenancy agreement may agree a rent increase or any other variation of terms.[111]

Rents set by social landlords

Local authorities

Setting 'reasonable rents'

4.198 Local authorities may make such reasonable charges for the occupation of their dwellings as they determine and must from time to time review their rents: HA 1985 s24. However, this apparently wide discretion is subject to the housing regulator's guidance.[112]

The new 'Rent Standard'

4.199 A new Rent Standard, published in May 2014, applies as from 1 April 2015. This sets out a complex formula for the setting and increasing of rents by all registered providers, including local authorities and private registered providers. The basis of the formula is that:

• 30 per cent of a property's rent should be based on relative property values compared to the national average

• 70 per cent of a property's rent should be based on relative local earnings compared to the national average, and

• a bedroom factor should be applied so that, all things being equal, smaller properties have lower rents

Rents for 'low cost' rental accommodation should be set so as to achieve a number of aims, including that rents should not exceed 80 per cent of estimated market value. The annual increases on rents for existing tenancies is capped at CPI (Consumer Price Index) + 1 per cent each year.

4.200 Note, however, that the Rent Standard will not apply to lettings by private registered providers to 'a social housing tenant household during a financial year where the household income was £60,000 or more in the [relevant] tax year'.

4.201 Rents across the social sector can be expected to rise in the year 2015/16.

---

111 HA 1988 s13(5).

112 Under section 24 authorities must have regard to any relevant standards set under section 193 of the Housing and Regeneration Act 2008. Section 193 provides for the regulator of social housing to set standards for all registered providers, including local authorities.

Increasing rents and challenging increases

4.202   Most local authorities increase rents on an annual basis. In respect of all periodic tenancies a notice of variation may be served on the tenant to increase the rent. The increased rent cannot take effect before the end of a complete period of the tenancy, or four weeks, whichever is the longer period. A tenant who does not want to pay the increased rent can serve notice to quit on the landlord to bring the tenancy to an end. However, the tenant would then lose his or her tenancy. Unlike other variations of terms the authority is not required to consult before increasing the rent (see para 3.150).

4.203   For flexible tenancies, which are for a fixed term, the tenancy agreement will need to make express provision for rent increases.

4.204   If an authority has acted unlawfully in setting the rent levels an application for judicial review may be made. A tenant has 'sufficient interest' to bring such an action. The decision must be shown to be unlawful under the usual principles of public law (see chapter 2). Alternatively, a challenge to the validity of a rent increase may be raised as a defence to possession proceedings.[113]

Registered social landlords

Setting rents

4.205   Housing association secure tenants have access to the fair rent regime under the Rent Act 1977, see above, paras 4.186–4.188.

4.206   For the assured and assured shorthold tenants of private registered providers the mechanism for challenging rents and rent increases is the same as for private tenants. However, the landlords are also subject to the same regulatory regime as local authorities: currently the regulator is the Homes and Communities Agencies (HCA).

4.207   The Rent Standard, explained briefly above at para 4.199 above, also applies to rent setting and rent increases by private registered providers.

4.208   Lettings by private registered providers on so-called 'affordable rents' have been possible since April 2010. 'Affordable rents' can be set at up to 80 per cent of market rents. They are only available where the landlord has entered into a 'delivery agreement' for 'new supply' social housing with either the HCA or the Greater London Authority (GLA) under the 'Affordable Homes Programme Framework'. They are exempt from the Rent Standard.

---

113 *Wandsworth LBC v Winder (No 1)* [1984] UKHL 2, 29 November 1984.

4.209   Most private registered providers will be amenable to a challenge by way of judicial review if they act unlawfully when making decisions about the rents they charge, see paras 2.30–2.31 and 2.71.

Rent increases

4.210   Private registered providers usually grant periodic assured and assured shorthold tenancies and agreements will generally include a term providing for annual rent increases. If so, the landlord need not serve a prescribed notice of increase under HA 1988 s13 and a tenant will have no right to challenge an increase by applying to the Residential Property Tribunal. [114]

4.211   However, if the agreement contains no provision for rent increases, the landlord must follow the procedure set out in HA 1988 s13 and the tenant can challenge the proposed increase (see above para 4.192). However, it is unlikely that a tribunal will uphold a challenge as their jurisdiction is limited to rents exceeding market rents.

New immigration controls: the 'right to rent'

4.212   Part 3 of the Immigration Act (IA) 2014, deals with 'Access to Services', including 'residential tenancies'. Section 22 provides that 'a landlord must not authorise an adult to occupy premises under a residential tenancy agreement if the adult is disqualified as a result of their immigration status'. These provisions are partially in force. At the the time of writing they are being piloted in the West Midlands and are expected to come into force nationally in April 2015. A Code of Practice was issued in October 2014 setting out landlords' obligations and giving guidance on the nature of the documentary evidence needed to show that an occupier has a right to rent.[115] The provisions will apply only to tenancy agreements entered into after the date on which the scheme is implemented in the relevant area.

4.213   In summary the provisions mean that private landlords must carry out initial and follow-up checks on their tenants to ensure that they are not disqualified persons. Civil penalties apply if a landlord breaches the requirements: 'fines' of up to £3,000 may be applied, depending on the nature of the breach.

---

114 *Contour Homes Ltd v Rowen* [2007] EWCA Civ 842.

115 *Code of Practice on illegal immigrants and private rented accommodation, Civil penalty scheme for landlords and their agents*, published by the Home Office and available on the www.gov.uk website.

Disqualified persons

4.214   Disqualified persons are people who are not British citizens, EEA or Swiss nationals, who require leave to enter or remain in the UK but do not have it, or who have leave to enter or remain in the UK but the leave is subject to a condition preventing him or her from occupying residential premises. Permission to rent may be granted by the Home Office. A 'limited right to rent' may be granted to someone with leave for a limited period or a person with an enforceable right under EU law to enter or remain in the UK (this means a '3rd country national' who has rights as the family member of an EEA national). See chapter 20 for a fuller explanation of EU rights.

4.215   A landlord must carry out 'follow up' checks to ensure that an occupier continues to have a right to rent. If the checks indicate that the occupier no longer has the right to rent, the landlord is not compelled to evict the occupiers but must make a report to the Home Office.

4.216   Some types of agreements are excluded from the scheme, including:

- accommodation arranged by local authorities;
- social housing;
- care homes, hospitals and hospices and continuing healthcare provision;
- hostels and refuges;
- mobile homes;
- tied accommodation;
- student accommodation; and
- long leases.

4.217   The Code of Practice, and a separate 'anti-discrimination Code of Practice' gives advice to landlords on how to operate checking processes that are non-discriminatory and in accordance with statutory equalities duties. The Code states that 'Landlords should check all prospective occupiers' right to rent before granting a residential tenancy agreement'. This will involve asking for documents such as passports, driving licences, letters from prisons and colleges and benefits agencies to confirm identity and status. In spite of the exhortations to apply the same checks to all prospective tenants, it seems likely that landlords may avoid letting to prospective tenants who are not obviously British or EEA nationals.

Leaseholders' rights

continued

Key points

- A 'long lease' for most purposes is a lease granted for a term of at least 21 years.
- A long lease may be ended (forfeited) by a landlord if the lease-holder breaches the lease. For residential premises the right of forfeiture can only be enforced by obtaining a possession order.
- A landlord's right to forfeit the lease is restricted by statute: formal notice must be served and a lease cannot be forfeited for small amounts of arrears unless they have been outstanding for more than three years. Other breaches must be agreed or determined by a court or tribunal before the landlord can start the forfeiture procedure.
- In all cases a leaseholder can apply to a court for relief against forfeiture.
- Long leases will set out the landlord's obligation to insure, repair and maintain the premises and the right to recover the cost of doing so from the leaseholder by way of service charges and administration charges.
- Leaseholders can challenge demands for service charges and administration charges. Only charges that are reasonable can be recovered.
- At the end of the lease a leaseholder may be able to remain in occupation as a statutory tenant.
- A leaseholder may also be able to extend the lease or force the landlord to sell the freehold.

Introduction

5.1   A 'lease' is an interest in land granted for a fixed period. The term 'lease' and the term 'tenancy' have the same meaning. The person who grants a lease may be referred to as the lessor or landlord and the person to whom the lease is granted, the lessee, leaseholder or tenant. In this chapter the terms 'landlord' and 'leaseholder' will be used.

5.2   A long lease is the same as any tenancy for a fixed period: the grant of exclusive possession for a specified period of time. However, many of the statutory rights of periodic tenants or tenants with short fixed-term agreements (described in chapters 3 and 4) are not enjoyed by long leaseholders.[1] Most of the rights and obligations of the landlord and the leaseholder are set out in the lease. However, long-leaseholders also have some statutory rights over and above those contained in the lease. Mostly, these apply to leases for a fixed period of at least 21 years.

5.3   The rights of long-leaseholders are complex and contained in a number of different statutes. This chapter contains only an overview. Advice and information on leaseholders' rights may be obtained from LEASE, the Leasehold Advisory Service. LEASE is funded by the Department for Communities and Local Government, and the Welsh Government. The website is at www.lease-advice.org and useful leaflets on different aspects of leaseholders' rights can be downloaded. In addition the website contains a list of solicitors and surveyors who claim expertise in leaseholders' rights.

5.4   This chapter examines briefly the following issues:

- forfeiture;
- service charges and administration charges;
- security of tenure at the end of the lease; and
- enfranchisement – the right to purchase the freehold or to extend the lease.

Key features of long leases

5.5   Some of the key features of a 'long lease', as distinct from a short-term tenancy, are summarised below:

- A fixed-term tenancy or lease for a period of three years or more must be created by deed.[2] See para 1.69 for the requirements of a deed.
- A long lease has a value and can be transferred (assigned) to another person (the assignee) in return for a sum of money (a premium).
- The 'rent' payable under a long lease is usually a nominal sum, sometimes as little as £10 per year, referred to as 'ground rent'.

---

1   Such tenancies are excluded from the Rent Act 1977 and the Housing Act 1988 because they are at a low rent. They are expressly excluded from the Housing Act 1985.
2   Law of Property Act 1925 ss52 and 54. However, these provisions are disapplied in relation to 'flexible' fixed-term tenancies, see paras 3.151–3.159.

- Most long leases will permit the assignment of the lease during the fixed term with the consent of the landlord. The landlord's consent must not be unreasonably withheld.
- Most long leases will also permit the leaseholder to sublet, again with the landlord's consent which must not be unreasonably withheld.
- The respective repairing obligations of the landlord and the leaseholder are set out in the lease. Section 11 of the Landlord and Tenant Act (LTA) 1985 (the landlords' implied repairing obligation (described in chapter 10)) does not apply to leases for a fixed period of seven years or more.[3]
- A long lease will provide that the landlord carries out certain works of repair and maintenance and will also provide that the leaseholder must reimburse the landlord's costs by way of a service charge. Unreasonable service charges can be challenged by application to the First-tier Tribunal (Residential Property) ('the tribunal').[4]
- The main cost of a long lease is the purchase price or premium which will usually be funded by a mortgage and the lender will have the right to take possession if the terms of the mortgage are breached, see chapter 7.
- Leaseholders do not have statutory security of tenure during the term of the lease; their right to possession is by virtue the lease. However, at the end of the lease a statutory tenancy may come into being if the leaseholder is residing in the premises.
- Most long leases include a 'forfeiture' clause which entitles the landlord to end the lease and/or re-enter the premises if the leaseholder breaches the terms of the lease. The leaseholder has the right to apply to a court for 'relief against forfeiture' to have the lease re-instated.
- Many disputes between a landlord and a leaseholder can be determined by the tribunal. However, claims for possession and relief against forfeiture are dealt with in the County Court or the High Court.

---

3 Again, this does not include flexible fixed-term tenancies; section 11 LTA 1985 does apply even if the fixed term is longer than seven years, see para 10.14.
4 This used to be the Leasehold Valuation Tribunal (LVT).

Right to information

5.6   A leaseholder has the right to obtain information about the landlord in the same way as any other tenant. These rights include the right to be notified of the landlord's name and address and to be informed of a change of landlord. They are described in paras 4.131–4.136. Demands for rent and service charges must also contain the landlord's name and address, see paras 5.28 below and 4.157.

Forfeiture

5.7   A landlord only has a right to forfeit a lease if this is expressly provided in the lease. Most long leases contain a forfeiture clause. The clause will usually state that if the tenant commits a breach of covenant or fails to pay rent the landlord may re-enter the premises and the lease will come to an end. Alternatively, a lease may provide that it is granted 'on condition that' or 'provided that' the tenant fulfils certain obligations. This also gives the landlord a right of forfeiture.

5.8   At common law, a landlord could enforce the right of forfeiture by 're-entering' the land and taking possession. However, if there is a residential occupier in the premises it is unlawful for a landlord to re-enter without obtaining a possession order.[5] Furthermore, there are now statutory restrictions on the right of forfeiture, described below at paras 5.10–5.15.

5.9   A landlord may claim the right of forfeiture for the non-payment of rent or for other breaches of the lease. The procedure for each differs.

Forfeiture for rent arrears

Formal demand

5.10   The common law position was that a landlord who wished to forfeit for the non-payment of rent must have made a formal demand for payment. However, a lease could, and usually would, provide that the landlord was exempt from this requirement. This loophole was closed by the Commonhold and Leasehold Reform Act (CLRA) 2002

---

5   Protection from Eviction Act 1977 s2. If there is a residential occupier, taking possession without obtaining a court order is both a civil wrong and a criminal offence. A further criminal offence would be committed under Criminal Law Act 1977 s6 if a landlord forcibly takes possession while a person is physically in the premises. These offences are described in paras 8.2–8.11 and 8.38–8.41.

which provides that a long-leaseholder is not liable to pay rent unless the landlord has served notice demanding payment.[6] The notice must be in prescribed form and must state:

- the amount of the payment and the date by which it is payable;[7]
- the name of the leaseholder to whom notice is given;
- the period to which the rent demanded is attributable;
- the name of the person to whom payment is to be made and the address for payment;
- the name of the landlord who is giving notice and the landlord's address;
- the information for landlords and tenants contained in the prescribed form.[8]

Restriction on forfeiture for small arrears

5.11   CLRA 2002 also provides that a landlord cannot forfeit a lease for unpaid rent, service charges or administration charges unless the total amount exceeds a prescribed sum, currently £350[9] or unless the total amount includes a sum that has been outstanding for more than a prescribed period, currently three years.[10]

Unpaid service charges and administration charges

5.12   Further protection is given by the Housing Act (HA) 1996 s81 which prevents a landlord from exercising a right of re-entry or forfeiture of premises let as a dwelling for the non-payment of service charge demands unless the amount claimed is either agreed or determined by a court or tribunal.[11]

---

6   CLRA 2002 s166(1).
7   The date payment is due must be no sooner than 30 days and no later than 60 days after the notice is served and cannot be earlier than payment is required under the lease: CLRA 2002 s166(3).
8   See CLRA 2002 s166 and Landlord and Tenant (Notice of Rent) (England) Regulations 2004 SI No 3096 and Landlord and Tenant (Notice of Rent) (Wales) Regulations 2005 SI No 1355.
9   This sum excludes any 'default' charge imposed for a failure to pay on time: CLRA 2002 s167(3).
10 CLRA 2002 s167(1) and Rights of Re-entry and Forfeiture (Prescribed Sum and Period) (England) Regulations 2004 SI No 3086 and Rights of Re-entry and Forfeiture (Prescribed Sum and Period) (Wales) Regulations 2005 SI No 1352.
11 The provision applies to all proceedings started on or after 24 September 1996.

Forfeiture for unpaid rent – tenant's rights

5.13   Where the landlord is applying to the court to enforce a right of re-entry or forfeiture for non-payment of rent, the County Courts Act 1984 s138 gives the tenant the following rights:

- The tenant can pay all of the rent arrears and costs into court at least five days before the first hearing date. If this is done the lease continues as if proceedings had not been issued.
- At the hearing the court must delay possession for at least four weeks during which the tenant has the opportunity to pay the arrears and costs. If the tenant pays in full, there is 'relief against forfeiture' and the lease continues.
- Within six months of the landlord actually taking possession, the tenant can apply to the court for relief against forfeiture.

Forfeiture for other breach

5.14   The Law of Property Act (LPA) 1925 s146 provides that before exercising a power of forfeiture for breaches other than the non-payment of rent a landlord must serve notice on the tenant, known as a 'section 146 notice'.

5.15   Under the Commonhold and Leasehold Reform Act 2002 s168 a landlord under a long lease cannot serve a section 146 notice unless:

- it has been finally determined on an application by the landlord to the tribunal that the alleged breach has occurred; or
- the tenant has admitted the breach; or
- a court or tribunal has finally determined that the breach has occurred.

Section 146 notice

5.16   Where a landlord is claiming forfeiture for breaches other than the non-payment of rent the section 146 notice must:

- specify the breach complained of;
- if the breach is capable of remedy, require the leaseholder to remedy the breach;
- require the tenant to pay compensation to the landlord if required; and
- give the tenant a reasonable time to comply with the notice.[12]

---

12 LPA 1925 s146(1).

Tenant's response

5.17 If the tenant remedies the breach within the specified period the landlord will be unable to exercise the right of forfeiture. Even if the tenant cannot remedy the breach or pay any compensation within the period, the tenant may still apply to the local County Court for relief against forfeiture. However, if there is a residential occupier a claim for possession must be made in the County Court, so it is more common for the leaseholder to make the claim for relief against forfeiture in response to the possession claim.

5.18 The section 146 notice must be served on any subtenant who also has the right to seek relief against forfeiture.[13]

Relief against forfeiture

5.19 The right to relief is generally dependent on the leaseholder paying the arrears and the landlord's costs or otherwise remedying any breach.

5.20 However, the court's discretion when considering an application for relief against forfeiture is very wide and relief may be granted on terms. LPA 1925 s146(2) provides that:

> ... the court may grant or refuse relief, as the court, having regard to the proceedings and conduct of the parties ... and to all other circumstances, thinks fit; and ... may grant [relief] ... on such terms, if any, as to costs, expenses, damages, compensation, penalty, or otherwise, including the granting of an injunction to restrain any like breach in the future, as the court, in the circumstances of each case, thinks fit.

5.21 The courts have been generally reluctant to lay down principles to be applied in the exercise of the discretion.[14]

5.22 The court can order relief on terms that the lease be sold so that the leaseholder can benefit from the value of the lease and the landlord recover any monies outstanding.[15]

Waiver

5.23 A landlord may 'waive' the right to forfeit the lease by taking positive steps to confirm the existence of the lease while aware of the breach.

---

13 LPA 1925 s146(5).
14 See *Greenwood Reversions Ltd v World Environment Foundation Ltd and Madhav Mehra* [2008] EWCA Civ 47, in which the Court of Appeal dismissed the leaseholder's appeal against the refusal of relief.
15 *Khar v Delbounty Ltd* [1996] NPC 163, CA.

However, this does not prevent a landlord from taking other action to enforce a covenant.

Service charges and administration charges

5.24   In addition to the payment of ground rent the lease will specify that the leaseholder must pay other sums as 'service charges' and 'administration charges'. Such charges are a common source of conflict between landlords and leaseholders. Service charges and administration charges are only recoverable to the extent that they are reasonable and this may be determined by the tribunal.

5.25   A landlord may only charge the leaseholder for costs incurred if the lease expressly provides this. A lease will usually set out a landlord's obligation for maintenance, repairs and other services and the right to be reimbursed by the leaseholder for the costs incurred. It will also set out how the charges are apportioned between different leaseholders in the same building or estate.

Service charges

5.26   A service charge is:

> an amount payable by a tenant of a dwelling as part of or in addition to the rent ... for services, repairs, maintenance, improvements or insurance or the landlord's costs of management ... the whole or part of which varies or may vary according to the relevant costs.[16]

Administration charges

5.27   An administration charge is an amount payable by a leaseholder as part of or in addition to rent that is payable, directly or indirectly for costs relating to:[17]

- the consideration of and grant of approvals under the lease, for example, consent to alterations or subletting;
- the provision of information or documents by or on behalf of the landlord or a person who is party to the lease, other than between the landlord and leaseholder (for example, in connection with the sale of the leasehold);
- a failure by the leaseholder to make payments due under the lease;
- a breach or alleged breach of covenant or condition in the lease.

16   LTA 1985 s18(1).
17   CLRA 2002 Sch 11 para 1.

Demand for payment

5.28 Service charges and administration charges are not payable until a demand has been served on the leaseholder, accompanied by a summary of the rights and obligations of the leaseholder.[18] The demand must contain the name and address of the landlord. If the address is not in England or Wales an address in England or Wales must be given at which notices may be served on the landlord.[19]

Reasonableness of service charges

5.29 The Landlord and Tenant Act 1985 s19(1) provides that service charges can be recovered from the tenant:

(a) only to the extent that they are reasonably incurred; and
(b) where they are incurred on the provision of services or the carrying out of works, only if the services or works are of a reasonable standard;

and the amount payable shall be limited accordingly.

5.30 Furthermore, where a landlord can charge in advance of the costs being incurred, only a reasonable amount is payable and the landlord must make an adjustment after the costs have been incurred, including repayment where appropriate.[20]

5.31 In relation to a service charge demand the leaseholder may apply to the tribunal for a determination as to:[21]

• whether costs incurred for services, repairs, maintenance, insurance or management were reasonably incurred;
• whether services or works for which costs were incurred are of a reasonable standard; or
• whether an amount payable before costs are incurred is reasonable.

5.32 In addition, either a landlord or a leaseholder may apply in advance to the tribunal for a determination as to whether:

• costs for services, repairs, maintenance, insurance, or management of a specified description would be reasonable;

---

18 LTA 1985 s21B and CLRA 2002 Sch 11 para 4. The prescribed information is set out in the Service Charges (Summary of Rights and Obligations, and Transitional Provisions) (England) Regulations 2007 SI No 1257. The Welsh regulations are contained in 2007 SI No 3160.
19 LTA 1987 s47. See para 4.157.
20 LTA 1985 s19(2).
21 LTA 1985 s19(2A).

- services provided or works carried out to a particular specification would be of a reasonable standard; or
- what amount payable before costs are incurred would be reasonable.

5.33   However, no application to the tribunal can be made in respect of a matter that has been agreed or admitted by the tenant, or which is subject to resolution by arbitration or where a court or tribunal has already made a determination.[22]

5.34   If the demand for payment includes a demand for costs incurred more than 18 months before the demand, those costs are not payable by the leaseholder. However, the costs are not 'incurred' at the date when the services are provided or the repairs carried out but when a landlord is presented with an invoice or when the landlord makes payment.[23]

Information about service charges

5.35   Landlords must supply to leaseholders a statement of account for the charges made, no later than six months after the end of the accounting period.[24] This must be accompanied by an accountant's certificate and a summary of the leaseholder's rights and obligations (see para 5.28 above).

5.36   A leaseholder may request a summary of the charges that make up a service charge demand and the landlord must provide the summary within one month of the request (or within six months of the end of the relevant period if later).[25] The leaseholder may then, within six months of receiving the summary, request facilities to inspect documents supporting the statement of account, such as receipts and estimates and the landlord must make those facilities available within two months of the request.[26] However, a tenant cannot obtain an injunction to force the landlord to provide the information since the Act sets out a criminal sanction for a landlord's breach.[27] The 'remedy' a leaseholder has if the landlord fails to provide the

---

22 LTA 1985 s19(2C).
23 See LTA 1985 s20B(1), *OM Property Management Ltd v Burr* [2013] EWCA Civ 479,3 May 2013, *Paddington Walk Management Ltd v Governors of Peabody Trust* (2009) Central London County Court, 16 April 2009 and *Brent LBC v Shlum B Association Ltd* [2011] EWHC 1663 (Ch), 29 June 2011.
24 LTA 1985 s21.
25 LTA 1985 s21.
26 LTA 1985 s22.
27 *Morshead Mansions v Di Marco* [2014] EWCA Civ 96, 12 February 2014.

information required under the LTA 1987 s21 is to withhold payment of the services charges to which the leaseholder's request relates. However, the full amount will become payable on receipt of the information, subject to any challenge as to the reasonableness of the charges. Where the leaseholder withholds payment for this reason, any penalties for late payment do not apply.[28]

What is reasonable?

5.37 There is no definition of what is reasonable in the relevant legislation. Where the dispute is about whether works were necessary or about the standard of work carried out, expert evidence will usually be needed.

5.38 Costs are not necessarily unreasonable because it may have been possible to do works or provide services more cheaply. The question is whether the costs would have been incurred if the landlord had been responsible for bearing the cost. The issue of whether costs are reasonable is therefore decided from the landlord's perspective.

5.39 It should be noted that, even if it is decided that charges are unreasonable or the works not done to a reasonable standard, this does not mean that nothing is payable. The tribunal will assess what is a reasonable amount.

Right-to-buy leases

5.40 There are additional restrictions on service charge demands for 'right-to-buy' leaseholders. During the right-to-buy process a landlord must provide information to the leaseholder about service charges including an estimate of the likely cost of repairs or improvements over the next five years.[29] For the five-year period the leaseholder cannot be required to pay service charges in excess of the estimated costs. Right-to-buy leaseholders may also be entitled to a loan from the landlord if the service charges exceed a certain amount.[30]

5.41 Additionally, there is now a cap on major works service charges levied by social landlords, see below at para 5.46.

28 LTA 1985 s21A.
29 HA 1985 s125.
30 HA 1985 s450A.

Reasonableness of administration charges

5.42   The Commonhold and Leasehold Reform Act 2002 introduced similar controls in relation to administration charges. It provides that a variable administration charge is payable only to the extent that the amount of the charge is reasonable.[31]

5.43   A leaseholder can also apply to the tribunal to vary the lease on the grounds that any administration charge specified in the lease is unreasonable or that any formula in the lease for calculating the administration charge is unreasonable.[32]

Consultation

5.44   Landlords must consult leaseholders before carrying out works above a certain value or entering into a long-term agreement for the provision of services.[33] If a landlord fails to consult in accordance with the regulations, the landlord must apply to the tribunal for dispensation from the requirements, failing which the services charges recoverable will be capped at £250 per leaseholder.

In *Daejan Investments Ltd v Benson and others*[34] the landlords had failed to comply with the consultation requirements for a major works contract. The LVT held that it was not reasonable to dispense with the requirements and as a result the landlords could not recover the £270,000 they had spent, the amount recoverable being capped at £250 per leaseholder. This was upheld by the Court of Appeal but the Supreme Court held that where there had been a failure to consult, the outcome was not necessarily 'binary' (ie full recovery or capping at £250 per leaseholder). A landlord must apply to the LVT for dispensation under s20(1)(b). If it is shown that the leaseholders will suffer some prejudice as a result of the landlord's failure, the LVT must, when granting the dispensation, do so on condition that the landlords reduce the amount of the service charges so as to compensate the leaseholders for that prejudice. The duty of consultation reflects the twin aims of s19: to protect leaseholders from having to pay for unnecessary services, or services provided to an unacceptable standard and from having

31   CLRA 2002 Sch 11 para 2.
32   CLRA 2002 Sch 11 para 3.
33   LTA 1985 s20 and Service Charges (Consultation Requirements) (England) Regulations 2003 SI No 1987. The current value is £250 per leaseholder.
34   [2013] UKSC 14, 6 March 2013.

to pay more than they should for necessary services provided to an acceptable standard.

5.45 Many local authorities enter into 'qualifying long-term agreements'[35] with independent contractors for the provision of repairs and major works. In such cases leaseholders must be consulted on the decision to enter into such an agreement but once the agreement is concluded the leaseholders' rights to be consulted about the actual works to particular properties are less prescriptive. For example, the leaseholders cannot propose alternative contractors since the freeholder has already entered into a contract for the provision of particular works and services for the relevant period.

Social landlords: cap on major works costs

5.46 As from 12 August 2014 there is a cap on the charges that social landlords can make for major works where the landlord has received government funding for the works. The total amount that can be charged to individual leaseholders who occupy the dwelling as their only or principal home for works of repair, maintenance or improvement is £15,000 for dwellings in London authorities and £10,000 outside of London.[36] In addition, social landlords have a discretion to reduce or waive service charges for such works on the grounds of exceptional hardship.[37]

Unfair contract terms

5.47 Further protection for leaseholders may be found in the Unfair Terms in Consumer Contracts Regulations 1999. The regulations are described at paras 4.171–4.181 above.

35 A qualifying long-term agreement is an agreement entered into by the landlord with a wholly independent organisation or contractor for a period of more than 12 months: LTA 1985 s20ZA(2).

36 This was already the case in relation to works funded under Private Finance Initiatives (PFI). However, most major works schemes are not funded in this way. The Social Landlords Mandatory Reduction of Service Charges (England) Directions 2014 directs all social landlords to apply this cap as from 12 August 2014 works funded under the Decent Homes Backlog Funding (part of the 2013 Spending Round) or other government assistance. It will only apply where the application for the government assistance is made on or after 12 August 2014.

37 The Social Landlords Discretionary Reduction of Service Charges (England) Directions 2014; these set out the criteria social landlords should have regard to when exercising the discretion.

The First-tier Tribunal (Residential Property)

5.48   Disputes about the amount of service charges are mostly dealt with by the First-tier Tribunal (Residential Property) (the tribunal). The forms used to make applications to the tribunal are available online. Most cases are resolved at a hearing but the parties can agree to a determination without a hearing. The hearing will be conducted by a judge sitting alone or along with one or two 'panel' members. Hearings in London usually take place at the tribunal office in central London. Outside London hearings are arranged near the location of the property in public buildings such as church halls and town halls.

5.49   There is no legal aid for representation at the tribunal hearing or for advice and assistance about leasehold problems, unless the issue is disrepair in residential premises of such severity as to pose a serious risk of harm to the health or safety of the occupiers, see para 10.213. As a general rule the tribunal will not order an unsuccessful party to pay the legal costs of the other party but it can order a party to reimburse other fees incurred. It can also make an order to prevent a landlord from enforcing a term in the lease to recover legal costs incurred in taking or defending a claim in the tribunal.[38]

5.50   An appeal from a First-tier Tribunal decision is made to the Upper Tribunal (Lands Chamber). Permission to appeal must be sought from the tribunal within 28 days of the reasons for the decision being sent to the parties. If permission is refused an application may be made directly to the Upper Tribunal (Lands Chamber) for permission. Decisions of the Upper Tribunal are appealed to the Court of Appeal.

Security of tenure at the end of the lease

5.51   Subject to the landlord's right of forfeiture a leaseholder has exclusive possession and therefore a right of occupation during the term of the lease. When the lease expires the leaseholder may continue to occupy under a statutory tenancy provided certain conditions are met. The main condition is that the leaseholder is occupying the premises as a 'home'. Whether the statutory tenancy is governed by the Rent Act 1977 or the Housing Act 1988 depends on when the lease commenced or expired. In each case the kinds of agreement that are excluded from the Act apply (see paras 3.19 and 3.92) save for the provision that excludes tenancies at a low rent.

38   LTA 1987 s20C.

5.52   If the lease expired before 15 January 1999 the tenant will be a statutory tenant under RA 1977.[39] If the lease commenced after 1 January 1990 or expires after 15 January 1999 the statutory tenancy will be an assured tenancy under HA 1988.[40]

5.53   There are complex provisions regarding the service of notices by the landlord and the leaseholder. A landlord may serve notice either proposing the terms of a new assured tenancy or indicating an intention to seek possession. The leaseholder should respond by serving a counter notice. The leaseholder may wish to exercise the right to a lease extension or to purchase the freehold, see para 5.57 below. If so, it is essential that the relevant notices are served within the time limits otherwise the rights may be lost. Furthermore, if the landlord is proposing a new assured tenancy and the leaseholder fails to serve a counter notice, the leaseholder will be bound by the terms proposed by the landlord.

5.54   If no notice is served the lease continues on the same terms until the landlord does serve notice.

5.55   If the parties wish to enter into a new assured tenancy agreement but cannot agree on a new rent, an application can be made to the Rent Assessment Committee.

5.56   If the landlord wishes to obtain possession, an application must be made to the court and grounds must be proved before a possession order will be made.

Enfranchisement

5.57   Enfranchisement refers to the right of a leaseholder to force a freeholder to extend the lease or to grant a new one, or to sell the freehold. Rights of enfranchisement have developed and expanded over the last 40 years and a number of different statutes apply. The qualifying conditions and procedures are extremely complex and outside the scope of this book. A leaseholder who wishes to exercise the right will need help from a specialist solicitor or surveyor. This section contains only a brief summary.

---

39 LTA 1954 Pt X.
40 Local Government and Housing Act 1989 Sch 10.

Leaseholds of houses

5.58   Most long leases are of flats. However, it is also possible to hold a long lease of a house and leasehold houses are common in some parts of the UK. The rights of leaseholders of houses are set out in the Leasehold Reform Act 1967. It gives leaseholders of houses the following rights:

- the right to an extension of the lease for 50 years at no cost; or
- the right to purchase the freehold at an agreed price or a price fixed by the tribunal.

5.59   The Leasehold Reform Act 1967 applies to leases of 21 years or more (when originally granted) and to some right-to-buy leases for a shorter term.[41]

Leaseholds of flats

5.60   Most flats are held on long leases because they form part only of a building. The Leasehold Reform, Housing and Urban Development Act 1993 gives to the leaseholders of flats:

- the right to a new lease of 90 years for an agreed price or a price set by the tribunal; and
- the collective right of a group of leaseholders to purchase the freehold of the building – collective enfranchisement.

Collective enfranchisement

5.61   Where there are a number of leaseholders in a building, the right to purchase the freehold depends on there being a minimum number of 'qualifying tenants', a minimum proportion of whom must want to exercise the right. The purchase will usually be made by a company formed by the leaseholders for this purpose.

5.62   Long-leaseholders may also rely on the rights in the Landlord and Tenant Act 1987 Part I. This gives to qualifying leaseholders the right of first refusal if the landlord proposes to dispose of the freehold. In addition, under Part III of the Act there is a right to apply to a court for a compulsory 'acquisition order' if the following conditions are met:

- the freeholder is in breach of the obligations under the lease; or
- the freeholder cannot be found.

41 CLRA 2002 s76(2).

Commonhold

5.63 The Commonhold and Leasehold Reform Act (CLRA) 2002 created a new type of property ownership: commonhold. This allows for the ownership of individual commonhold units within a building or estate, the common parts being owned and managed jointly by the unit-holders through a commonhold association.

Right to manage

5.64 The CLRA 2002 also provides for a right to manage by way of a 'right to manage company' set up by leaseholders of flats. The leaseholders can force a transfer of the landlord's management functions to the company. The right is not dependent on the landlord being in default of the obligations under the lease.

Possession claims – procedure

continued

Key points

- Most residential occupiers cannot be evicted without a court order. Exceptions are 'excluded occupiers', trespassers who entered premises as trespassers and homeless applicants awaiting a decision.
- In most cases formal notice must be given to the occupier before making an application for a possession order.
- Failure to serve valid notice may mean that the possession claim is struck out or dismissed.
- For occupiers with substantive security of tenure a possession order will only be made if a statutory ground for possession is proved.
- There are two types of ground for possession: mandatory and discretionary. For discretionary grounds the court must find that it is reasonable to make a possession order.
- If the court makes an order on a discretionary ground it may also adjourn the claim, postpone possession or suspend enforcement when making the order or at any time up to the date of eviction.
- To enforce a possession order a 'warrant' must be obtained from the court. The warrant authorises court bailiffs to evict the occupiers.
- Even after eviction a warrant may be set aside on the grounds of fraud, abuse of process or oppression.

Introduction

6.1 Chapters 1 and 3 explain which tenants have substantive security of tenure, which occupiers have procedural security of tenure and which occupiers can be evicted without a possession order (see paras 1.100–1.120). Even occupiers with no substantive defence to a possession claim may avoid eviction if the correct procedure has not been followed by the landlord. Furthermore, it is possible to rely on public law and the Human Rights Act 1998 to challenge evictions by public bodies, including registered providers of social housing. Such challenges are examined in paras 7.128–7.179. This chapter focuses on the procedural requirements, including:

- steps before serving notice;
- possession notices;

- issuing the possession claim;
- the hearing;
- the possession order;
- enforcing the order;
- possible action after eviction.

Steps before serving notice

6.2   Any landlord intending to take legal action against a tenant because of rent arrears or nuisance or who simply wants a tenant to vacate premises will usually contact the tenant before serving formal notice. However, there is no requirement on a private landlord to do so. But it may be relevant if the court is considering whether it is reasonable to make a possession order. In contrast, social landlords must follow certain procedures when managing both rent arrears and complaints of nuisance.

Nuisance and anti-social behaviour

6.3   Under the Anti-social Behaviour Act (ASBA) 2003 social landlords must publish their policies on dealing with complaints of nuisance.[1] Usually this will include the investigations they will undertake before serving notice, the support that will be given to vulnerable tenants, both the perpetrators and the victims of anti-social behaviour. However, note that where serious anti-social behaviour is alleged, a claim for possession may be started at the same time as serving notice of seeking possession, see para 6.30 below.

Rent arrears

Pre-Action Protocol

6.4   For social landlords claiming possession on the grounds of rent arrears, there is a Pre-Action Protocol under the Civil Procedure Rules. This should be followed before the claim is issued. The Protocol can be downloaded from: www.justice.gov.uk/courts/procedurerules/civil/protocol/prot_rent.

6.5   The Protocol applies to all claims for possession of residential premises brought by social landlords (local authorities, registered providers and Housing Action Trusts) solely on the ground of rent

1 See Housing Act (HA) 1996 s218A inserted by ASBA 2003 s12.

arrears. It does not apply to claims in respect of long leases or where the occupier has no security of tenure (this includes assured shorthold tenants and non-secure tenants even if the reason for taking action is the existence of rent arrears). The Protocol has four sections, summarised below (paras 6.6–6.19).

(1) Initial contact

6.6 The landlord should contact the tenant when the tenant falls into arrears. The landlord and tenant should try to agree affordable sums for the tenant to pay towards the arrears. The landlord should provide quarterly rent statements and, if aware of any difficulties in reading or understanding information, should take reasonable steps to ensure that the tenant understands any information given.

Tenants who are under 18 or vulnerable

6.7 If the landlord is aware that a tenant is under 18 or particularly vulnerable, the landlord should consider at an early stage:

- whether the tenant has capacity and, if not, an application for a litigation friend should be made;
- whether any issue arises under the Disability Discrimination Act 1995 (now the Equality Act 2010); and
- if the landlord is a local authority, whether there is a need for a community care assessment.

Housing benefit

6.8 The landlord should offer to help the tenant in any claim the tenant may have for housing benefit. The landlord should not start possession proceedings against a tenant who can demonstrate that he or she has provided the authority with all evidence required to process the claim, that he or she has a reasonable expectation of eligibility and has paid other sums due not covered by housing benefit.

6.9 The landlord should make every effort to establish effective ongoing liaison with housing benefit department, and should, with the tenant's consent, make direct contact with the housing benefit department prior to taking enforcement action.

6.10 The landlord and tenant should work together to resolve any housing benefit problems.

6.11 The landlord should arrange for arrears to be paid directly by the Department for Work and Pensions (DWP) by instalments if the releant criteria are met.

(2) After service of statutory notices

6.12   After service of notice but before issue of proceedings the landlord should make reasonable attempts to contact the tenant to discuss the amount of arrears, the cause of the arrears, repayment of the arrears and the housing benefit position.

6.13   If the tenant complies with an agreement the landlord should agree to postpone court proceedings as long as the tenant keeps to the agreement.

6.14   If the tenant fails to comply with the agreement the landlord should warn the tenant of the intention to bring proceedings and give the tenant clear time limits within which to comply.

(3) Alternative dispute resolution (ADR)

6.15   The Protocol provides that the parties should consider whether it is possible to resolve the issues by discussion and negotiation without recourse to litigation. Compliance with the protocol is a form of ADR. This section stresses that litigation should be a last resort, and that claims should not be issued prematurely when a settlement is still actively being explored.

(4) Court proceedings

6.16   No later than ten days before the hearing, the landlord should:

- provide to the tenant up-to-date rent statements;
- disclose what the landlord knows about the tenant's housing benefit.

6.17   The landlord should inform the tenant of the date and time of any court hearing and the order being applied for. The landlord should advise the tenant to attend the hearing and should record such advice.

6.18   If the tenant complies with an agreement made after the issue of proceedings the landlord should agree to postpone the proceedings so long as the tenant keeps to the agreement.

6.19   If the tenant ceases to comply with the agreement, the landlord should warn the tenant of the intention to restore the proceedings and give clear time limits within which to comply.

Sanctions for non-compliance

6.20   If the landlord unreasonably fails to comply with the terms of the protocol the court may:

- make an order for costs;

- adjourn, strike out or dismiss claims (except where the claim is brought solely on a mandatory ground).

6.21 However, note that if a social landlord fails to comply with the protocol in a claim based on the mandatory rent arrears ground, the tenant could raise a public law or proportionality defence to the claim for possession, see paras 7.128–7.179.

6.22 If the tenant unreasonably fails to comply with the terms of the protocol, the court may take that into account when considering whether it is reasonable to make a possession order.

Possession notices

6.23 If a possession order is required the landlord must usually give formal notice to the occupier before the claim is issued. The type of notice depends on the type of tenancy or agreement. The Housing Acts (HA) 1985 and 1988 provide that a landlord can terminate certain kinds of tenancy only by obtaining a possession order; before a possession order can be applied for a statutory notice must be served. For tenancies that fall outside the Housing Acts (including Rent Act 1977 tenancies), the common law applies: a periodic tenancy must be ended by service of a notice to quit. A 'notice to quit' is a common law instrument that brings a contractual periodic tenancy to an end. There are some statutory requirements for the content and period of a notice to quit served on a residential occupier. A notice to quit that does not comply with these requirements will not be effective to end the tenancy.

6.25 In the case of notices to quit and notices served on assured shorthold tenants, a failure to serve valid notice means the claim must be dismissed.[2] For statutory 'notices seeking possession' served on assured and secure tenants the court has the power to hear a claim for possession even where no notice has been served and can permit the landlord to amend the notice, unless the ground relied on is 'absolute' or 'mandatory' (see below at paras 6.41–6.44).

6.26 In addition, legislation aimed at combatting anti-social behaviour requires different kinds of notice to be served in addition to, or instead of the possession notices referred to above. Introductory, demoted and flexible tenancies all require notices which give reasons and which can be the subject of a statutory internal review. The

---

2 However, a court may decide that a minor error does not invalidate the notice. See paras 6.38–6.39.

new absolute anti-social behaviour ground also requires a notice which carries a right of review. These notices are dealt with at paras 6.87–6.107.

6.27   The detailed requirements for each kind of notice are set out below at paras 6.28–6.96. A summary of the different kinds of notice is contained in the table in appendix 1.

Secure and assured tenants – notices seeking possession[3]

6.28   Secure and assured tenants have substantive security. This operates in the same way for both types of tenant: a landlord can only bring the tenancy to an end by obtaining a possession order. Before a claim for possession can be brought a statutory notice must be served. The notice must:

- be in prescribed form, or form substantially to the same effect;
- state the ground(s) on which the court will be asked to make a possession order;
- give particulars of the ground(s) (ie, an explanation of why each ground is being is relied on); and
- state the earliest date on which the claim can be commenced.

6.29   The prescribed forms give information about the procedure to be followed, the requirements of particular grounds and the tenant's rights. The prescribed forms for periodic secure tenancies and assured tenancies are similar but there are some important differences. In both cases the court has the power to waive the notice requirement if it is 'just and equitable' and can permit the landlord to amend the notice.

Secure periodic tenants

6.30   The prescribed form for a secure periodic tenant is usually a notice of seeking possession[4] (referred to as an NSP or NOSP). In most cases the earliest date the proceedings can commence is no earlier than the tenancy could be ended by a notice to quit (usually four weeks). However, if the landlord is relying on the nuisance ground (Ground 2) proceedings can be started immediately but the tenant cannot

---

3 This section refers to secure periodic tenancies only, secure fixed-term tenancies are dealt with at para 6.89 below.

4 See Secure Tenancies (Notices) Regulations 1987 SI No 755 and Secure Tenancies (Notices) (Amendment) Regulations 1997 SI No 71.

be required to give up possession earlier than the tenancy could be ended by a notice to quit. The notice expires 12 months after the date specified as the earliest date on which proceedings can commence.

6.31 However, if the landlord is relying on the new absolute anti-social behaviour ground a different kind of notice is served: one that combines the features of an NSP and a review notice,[5] see paras 6.95–6.99.

Secure flexible tenants

6.32 A flexible tenancy is a fixed-term tenancy. Flexible tenancies are relatively new and as yet there are no reported cases in which the courts have considered the notice requirements. The tenancy agreement must contain a provision for the landlord to bring the tenancy to an end before the fixed term expires, to enable a landlord to seek a possession order. However, because the tenancy is a secure tenancy, the landlord must in addition serve a Notice Seeking Possession (setting out the ground and particulars) and obtain a possession order. The prescribed form is similar to that for a periodic tenancy but is the one set out in Part II of the relevant regulations.[6]

Assured tenants

6.33 The prescribed form for an assured tenant is a notice seeking possession (NSP).[7] The earliest date the proceedings can commence depends on the grounds relied on. If the nuisance ground (Ground 14) is relied on proceedings may be commenced immediately. Otherwise, the proceedings may be commenced two weeks or two months after service of the notice. For all of the rent arrears grounds two weeks' notice must be given. The notice expires 12 months after the date it is served (not, as with secure tenants, 12 months after the date proceedings can be commenced).

6.34 Note that, as is the case for secure tenancies, a different kind of notice is required where the landlord is relying on the new absolute anti-social behaviour ground for possession, see below at paras 6.95–6.99.

---

5 See HA 1985 s84A and s83ZA.
6 Secure Tenancies (Notices) Regulations 1987 SI No 755.
7 See Assured Tenancies and Agricultural Occupancies (Forms) Regulations 1997 SI No 194.

Challenging notices seeking possession

Errors in the notice

6.35   The notice must be in prescribed form or in a form substantially to the same effect. A notice completed incorrectly may nevertheless be held to be 'substantially to the same effect' as a properly completed notice. The cases regarding errors in notices served under Housing Act 1988 s20 (see paras 3.60–3.63), suggest that where the prescribed information for tenants is omitted the notice will be held to be invalid. Whether the notice is 'substantially to the same effect' as a properly completed notice will depend on the nature of any error or omission. Although the court has a discretion to waive the requirement to serve notice and to permit amendments, a notice that is not properly completed or not in the prescribed form may be held to be invalid and the proceedings struck out. Much will depend on the merits of the claim. Where there is evidence of serious and continuing nuisance a court will be more likely to exercise its discretion than in a claim involving less serious allegations or alleging a low level of rent arrears.[8]

6.36   If the grounds relied on are summarised incorrectly this may invalidate the notice.

In *Mountain v Hastings*[9] a private landlord sought possession on Ground 8. At the time Ground 8 required rent to be at least three months in arrears at the date of the notice <u>and</u> at the date of the hearing.[10] In the notice Ground 8 was summarised as follows: 'at least three months rent is unpaid'. The court made an order for possession at the first hearing on the tenant admitting the level of arrears. The tenant appealed.

The Court of Appeal held that the notice was invalid as the purpose of the notice

... is to give to the tenant the information ... to enable the tenant to consider what she should do and, with or without advice, to do that which is in her power and which will best protect her against the loss of her home.[11]

The failure to specify that the ground required the level of arrears to exist at the date of the hearing meant that it was not substantially

---

8   See *Kelsey Housing Association v King* (1995) 28 HLR 270, CA.
9   (1993) 25 HLR 427.
10   The requirement is now only two months' rent arrears.
11   (1993) 25 HLR 427, Ralph Gibson LJ at 433.

> to the same effect as a notice correctly setting out Ground 8. The possession order was set aside and the case remitted to the county court.

However, although it is clearly sensible to recite the actual words of the ground as set out in the statute, it is not necessary to do so. In *Masih v Yousaf*[12] the Court of Appeal considered a notice that stated that Ground 8 reads '… the tenant owed at least two months' rent' rather then referring to rent being 'lawfully due', as Ground 8 does. The notice did state that the rent must be owed both when the notice was served and at the date of the hearing. The Court of Appeal held the notice to be valid.

6.37   Similarly, insufficient particulars of the allegations against the tenant may mean the notice is invalid:

> In *Torridge District Council v Jones*[13] the rent arrears ground was correctly set out. However, the only particulars given were: 'the reasons for taking this action are non-payment of rent'.
>
> The Court of Appeal upheld the tenant's appeal against the possession order, holding: 'nothing short of a specification of the amount which is claimed as being in arrears could … amount to a proper particular of the ground upon which possession was sought'. What is required is 'a specification sufficient to tell the tenant what it is he has to do to put matters right before the proceedings are commenced'.[14]

6.38   However, this does not mean that if the figure given is incorrect, the notice will necessarily be invalid.

> The notice in *Dudley MBC v Bailey*[15] stated that the tenant was in arrears of a certain amount as at the date of the notice. Subsequently, the local authority accepted that the figure stated included arrears of rates and water rates as well as rent.
>
> The Court of Appeal held that an error in the particulars made in good faith would not invalidate the notice providing there is a

12 [2014] EWCA Civ 234, 6 February 2014.
13 (1985) 18 HLR 107.
14 Oliver LJ at 114.
15 (1990) 22 HLR 424.

statement in summary form of the facts which the landlord intends to prove to support the claim for possession.

6.39 Furthermore, it has been held that even if the arrears at the date of the notice are not specified, the notice will be valid if the figure can easily be ascertained by the tenant.

> In *Marath v MacGillivray*[16] the particulars stated only that 'at a meeting between the landlord and tenant on 24 July 1994 the arrears were agreed at £103.29 ... Since that date no payments of rent have been made'. The total arrears at the date of the notice were not stated.
>
> The Court of Appeal held that the notice was valid and that HA 1988 s8 was satisfied, provided
>
> > ... it is made clear ... that more than three months' rent is at the date of that notice unpaid and due and provided also that in some way or other that notice makes it clear either how much, or how the tenant can ascertain how much, is alleged to be due.

Courts' power to waive notice

6.40 For both secure and assured tenants 'the court shall not entertain proceedings' for possession unless notice has been served on the tenant, or 'the court considers it just and equitable to dispense with the requirement of such a notice'.[17]

> In *Kelsey Housing Association v King*[18] the defendants were alleged to have been violent, abusive and threatening towards neighbours and there had been a conviction for actual bodily harm. In February 1994 the housing association served a notice to quit. The correct notice was a notice seeking possession. The case was commenced in May 1994 and possession was claimed on Grounds 12 and 14 of HA 1988. The allegations were detailed in an appendix to the summons. A defence was served denying the allegations. In November 1994 the defendants applied for the summons to be dismissed because of the failure to serve a notice seeking possession. The court

16 (1996) 28 HLR 484, CA.
17 HA 1985 s83 and HA 1988 s8.
18 (1995) 28 HLR 270.

refused, holding that it was just and equitable to waive the requirement. The defendants appealed.

The Court of Appeal dismissed the appeal holding that: 'in deciding whether the requirement should be waived the court should weigh all of the factors, taking into account the view of the landlord and the tenant'. Even if the failure to give notice created prejudice to the tenant that was not itself decisive. The court was entitled to take account of things that occurred after the proceedings had commenced and was right to conclude that the defendants had suffered no prejudice; by the time of the hearing the defendants had had time to put things right. Furthermore, an application to dismiss a claim for possession must be made promptly, at about the same time as serving the defence or even before.

Mandatory grounds

6.41   Note that the court does not have the power to waive the notice requirement when possession is sought on the mandatory Ground 8 under HA 1988.[19] The ground is only made out if the arrears of rent exist at the date of the notice and at the date of the hearing, see para 7.31 below.

6.42   Similarly, where a landlord is relying on the new 'mandatory antisocial behaviour' ground there is no power to dispense with the service of the possession notice.[20]

Courts' power to allow amendments

6.43   The court can only make an order for possession on any ground if that ground and particulars of it are specified in the notice. However, the court may give permission for the specified grounds to be altered or added to.[21] This includes a power to add or amend the particulars of the ground.[22]

6.44   Whether a court will exercise this discretion will depend on the nature and extent of the proposed amendment. Moreover, the time when the application is made will be relevant. A minor amendment may be permitted at a late stage but, if the amendment significantly

19   HA 1988 s8(5).
20   See paras 6.95 and 7.51.
21   HA 1985 s84(3); HA 1988 s8(2).
22   *Camden LBC v Oppong* (1996) 28 HLR 701, CA, 22 February 1996.

changes what is at issue between the parties, permission may be refused. An application for permission to amend at an early stage, before the defence has been filed, is more likely to succeed.

Service of the notice

6.45   No special method of service is required but the burden is on the claimant to satisfy the court, on balance of probabilities, that the notice was received by the tenant.

> In *Tadema Holdings v Ferguson*[23] the Court of Appeal held that notice of rent increase and notice of seeking possession were both validly served on a tenant who did not have capacity to either understand the notice or to defend a claim without the appointment of a litigation friend.
>   The Court held that service under both s8 and s13 of the Housing Act 1988 simply meant delivering the notice and that it was not necessary that the notice was understood by the tenant.

The issue of disabilty discrimination was not argued in the case and the outcome would probably have been different if it had been, see *Haworth v HMRC*[24] at para 7.198. Furthermore, under the Rent Arrears Protocol, in a rent arrears case where a social landlord is aware that a tenant has difficulties in reading or understanding information, the landlord must take reasonable steps to ensure he or she understands any information given (see para 6.6 above).

6.46   Social landlords will be bound by the disability equality duty under the Equality Act 2010 s149 (see paras 2.86–2.92) and must make reasonable adjustments in relation to disabled people to ensure that they do not suffer disadvantage by virtue of their policies and procedures (see paras 7.192–7.197). Also the Rent Arrears Protocol expressly provides that a social landlord who is aware that a tenant may be vulnerable must consider whether a litigation friend should be appointed, see para 6.7. Moreover, the tenant's understanding of a notice will always be relevant if the court is considering whether it is reasonable to make a possession order.

---

23 *Tadema Holdings v Ferguson* (2000) 32 HLR 866.
24 [2011] EWHC 36 (Ch).

Assured shorthold tenants – 'section 21 notice' (notice requiring possession)

6.47 The possession notice for an assured shorthold tenant is not a pre-scribed notice.[25] The requirements are set out in HA 1988 s21 and the notice is commonly referred to as a 'section 21 notice' or 'notice requiring possession'.

6.48 An assured shorthold tenancy is a form of assured tenancy and so cannot be ended by a landlord other than by obtaining a court order (see para 3.39). HA 1988 s21 sets out the conditions that must be satisfied for the court to make a possession order, one of which is that the landlord must have given notice to the tenant.

6.49 HA 1988 s21(1) provides as follows:

(1) ... on or after the coming to an end of an assured shorthold tenancy which was a fixed term tenancy, a court shall make an order for possession ... if it is satisfied –
  (a) that the assured shorthold tenancy has come to an end and no further assured tenancy (whether shorthold or not) is for the time being in existence, other than an assured shorthold periodic tenancy (whether statutory or not); and
  (b) the landlord or, in the case of joint landlords, at least one of them has given to the tenant not less than two months' notice in writing stating that he requires possession of the dwelling-house.

6.50 Section 21(2) goes on to state that the notice served under section 21(1) 'may be given before or on the day on which the tenancy comes to an end; and ... shall have effect notwithstanding that on the coming to an end of the fixed-term tenancy a statutory periodic tenancy arises.'

6.51 Section 21(4) provides that:

Without prejudice to any such right referred to in subsection (1) above, a court shall make an order for possession of [a periodic assured shorthold tenancy] if the court is satisfied–
  (a) that the landlord, or in the case of joint landlords, at least one of them has given to the tenant a notice in writing [of no less than two months] stating that, after a date specified in the notice, being the last day of a period of the tenancy ... possession of the dwelling-house is required by virtue of this section.

6.52 So, the requirement under section 21(1) is simply for a written notice of at least two months stating that the landlord requires possession. In contrast, the requirement under section 21(4) is for a notice that is

---

25 However, the Deregulation Act 2015 enables regulations to be made to introduce a prescribed form for s21 notices.

at least two months long but also mimics a notice to quit by requiring possession after the last day of a period of the tenancy.[26]

Section 21(1) and section 21(4)

6.53   Until the Court of Appeal decision in *Spencer v Taylor*[27] (below) it was widely understood that section 21(1) applied if the landlord gave notice before the end of a fixed-term tenancy and that section 21(4) applied to all periodic assured shorthold tenancies – both those that had always been periodic and those that were statutory periodic tenancies arising automatically at the end of a fixed term.

In *Spencer v Taylor* the fixed term was originally for six months and commenced on a Monday. Rent was payable weekly so that the statutory periodic tenancy that arose at the end of the fixed term was a weekly tenancy running from Monday to Sunday. The landlord served a section 21 notice that required possession after a specified date that was a Saturday. However, the notice went on to add 'or ... at the end of your period of tenancy which will end next after the expiration of two months from the service upon you of this notice'.

In accordance with the previous case-law and general understanding of the law, both parties proceeded on the basis that the notice had to comply with section 21(4). The landlord accepted that the date identified had not been the correct date but argued that the 'saving clause' made the notice valid. The tenant argued that the giving of two dates, a specific date and an alternative, invalidated the notice.

The Court of Appeal held that it was wrong to interpret section 21(2) as meaning that the landlord may *only* serve such a notice up to the last day of the fixed period. Rather, the provision was 'permissive': a landlord may serve a notice before the fixed term ends or after the fixed term ends. So, the requirements of section 21(4) did not apply where a statutory periodic tenancy had arisen at the end of a fixed-term agreement.

Spencer v Taylor appears to contradict the Court of Appeal decisions in *McDonald v Fernandez* and *Notting Hill Housing Trust v Roomus*

---

26 For assured shorthold tenancies commencing on or after 26 March 2015 (and, after 26 March 2018, for all assured shorthold tenancies whenever they commenced) section 21(4) will not apply: Deregulation Act 2015 ss35 and 41.

27 [2013] EWCA Civ 1600.

referred to at para 6.55 below. However, in *Spencer v Taylor* the Court of Appeal held that the specific issue of whether section 21(4) applied had not been decided in those cases since the parties had proceeded, incorrectly, on the basis that it did.

6.54   The Supreme Court refused permission for an appeal in *Spencer v Taylor* so the decision was binding.

6.55   *Spencer v Taylor* means that s21(4) applies only when the original tenancy was a periodic tenancy and not to statutory periodic tenancies arising at the end of a fixed term. Also, that the use of a 'saving clause' ensures that the notice will be valid even if the date specified is not the last day of a period of the tenancy. However, where a section 21(4) notice is required, a notice that identifies the wrong date will be invalid unless a properly drafted saving clause is used. A notice requiring possession 'on' the last day of a period of the tenancy rather than 'after' the last day was held to be invalid in *McDonald v Fernandez*.[28] However, a notice that required possession 'at the end of' the period of the tenancy was held to be valid in *Notting Hill Housing Trust v Roomus*.[29] Note, however, that for tenancies commencing on or after 26 March 2015 the changes made by the Deregulation Act 2015 mean that section 21(4) will not apply whether the tenancy is a fixed term or a periodic tenancy. And after 26 March 2018 this will be the case for all assured shorthold tenancies, whenever they commenced, see below at para 6.57.

6.56   Section 21(4) will apply where the landlord and the tenant had agreed to a completely new tenancy after a fixed term tenancy had ended (though this is a very unlikely scenario). It is generally not to apply where the new periodic tenancy was referred to in the original fixed term tenancy as being one that would automatically arise at the end of the fixed term, and/or one that is identified as being a 'continuation tenancy'.

Changes made by Deregulation Act 2015

6.57   The Deregulation Act 2015 amends section 21 (in England only) by removing the requirement in s21(4)(a) for the date specified to be the last day of a period of the tenancy. So, the notice will simply need to be in writing giving the tenant a minimum of two months. In addition, the amendments provide that a landlord cannot give a section 21 notice within the first four months of the tenancy (in the case of a replacement tenancy, the four months runs from the start of the

28 [2003] EWCA Civ 1219.
29 [2006] EWCA Civ 407.

original tenancy). Furthermore, the landlord must start proceedings within six months of service of the notice. If the notice requires possession more than two months after service, the proceedings must be commenced no later than four months after the date specified in the notice. So, where a tenant receives a section 21 notice he or she will know that the claim for possession must be started within six months, or if a period longer than two months is given, within four months of the date requiring possession. If the landlord fails issue a claim within that period a fresh section 21 notice must be served.[30] These provisions will initially only apply to new assured shorthold tenancies granted on or after 26 March 2015. However, after 26 March 2018 they will apply to all section 21 notices regardless of when the tenancy commenced: ss36 and 41 Deregulation Act 2015.

6.58   No appeal court cases have examined the requirement in HA 1988 s21(4) that the notice should state that possession 'is required by virtue of this section' but in the county court case of *Adamson v Mather*[31] a notice that made no reference to section 21 was held to be defective and the possession claim dismissed. If section 21(4) does apply, then this defence could be raised.

6.59   Under section 21(5) where a tenancy is a periodic tenancy from the outset, a possession order cannot 'take effect' earlier than six months after the tenancy commenced. This suggests that notice could be served and a claim for possession started before the first six months has expired. However, a landlord who did this would be unlikely to recover the costs of the claim from the tenant.[32]

Grounds for possession

6.60   The section 21 procedure requires no grounds or reasons for seeking possession: the landlord is entitled to possession as of right. However, an assured shorthold tenancy is a form of assured tenancy and all of the statutory grounds relevant to assured tenancies are avail-

---

30 The DA 2015 also makes provision for the Secretary of State to introduce a prescribed form of notice under section 21. Additionally, regulations may be made requiring a landlord to give prescribed information about the rights and responsibilities of a landlord and a tenant under an assured shorthold tenancy, with a prohibition on service of a section 21 notice where the landlord is in breach of this requirement.

31 November 2004 *Legal Action* 26, Harrogate County Court, 24 September 2004.

32 Note that for tenancies commencing after 26 March 2015, a landlord cannot serve a section 21 notice within the first four months of the period, see para 6.57 above.

able. A landlord can seek an order for possession within the first six months if he or she can prove that a possession ground is made out. In this case the landlord must serve a notice seeking possession under HA 1988 s8, see above, paras 6.33–6.34.

Section 21 notices and rent deposits

6.61 On 6 April 2007 the mandatory tenancy deposit requirements came into force: any landlord of an assured shorthold tenancy who receives a deposit must protect the deposit in an authorised scheme and give prescribed information to the tenant about the protection of the deposit (see paras 4.149–4.152). The requirements may also apply even where the original tenancy began prior to 6 April 2007, see paras 4.158–169 for details.

6.62 The sanctions for non-compliance are described at paras 4.154–4.169 and include a provision that no section 21 notice may be given by a landlord at a time when the deposit is not being held in accordance with an authorised scheme.[33]

6.63 So, it is a defence to a claim for possession brought under HA 1988 s21 that the landlord had not, at the date notice was served, protected a deposit paid by the tenant. If the deposit was paid before 6 April 2007 the landlord can either protect the deposit or return it in full (or subject to agreed deductions) before a valid section 21 notice can be served. If the deposit was paid after 6 April 2007 the landlord must have protected it within 30 days of receipt so will be unable to satisfy the requirements. In such a case the deposit must be refunded in full (or subject to agreed deductions) before a section 21 notice can be served. The landlord will also be subject to the possible sanction under HA 2004 s214. See paras 4.154–4.169.

Social landlords granting fixed-term assured shortholds: additional requirements

6.64 Until April 2012, the regulatory guidance for social landlords was that tenants should be given tenancies with the maximum levels of security, ie assured tenancies, where possible. However, the current guidance provides that for general needs tenants PRPs should grant either a periodic assured (ie not an assured shorthold) tenancy or a tenancy for a minimum fixed term of five years, or exceptionally, no less than two years. This period excludes any period during which

33 HA 2004 ss215–215B.

the tenant is a 'probationary' tenant.[34] This is to mirror the 'flexible' tenancies that local authorities can now grant, see para 3.103. Such a tenancy would be an assured shorthold tenancy.

6.65   While no legislative amendment was necessary to introduce a new type of tenancy, section 21 has been amended to provide for the additional notice provisions for these fixed-term tenancies granted by social landlords.

Notice of non-renewal

6.66   The amended section 21(1A–1B) provides that where a private registered provider of social housing has granted a fixed-term assured shorthold tenancy of not less than two years, the court will not make a possession order unless (in addition to the two-month notice requiring possession) the landlord has 'given to the tenant not less than six months' notice in writing – (a) stating that the landlord does not propose to grant another tenancy on the expiry of the fixed term, and (b) informing the tenant of how to obtain help or advice about the notice and, in particular, of any obligation of the landlord to provide help or advice.'

6.67   Note that, unlike the equivalent six-month notice served on secure flexible tenants, the landlord is not required to give reasons for the decision not to grant a new tenancy and there is no statutory right of review. However, the Regulatory Framework requires private registered providers to publish 'clear and accessible policies' setting out such things as: 'the circumstances in which they may or may not grant another tenancy on the expiry of the fixed term, in the same property or in a different property' and 'the way in which a tenant or prospective tenant may appeal against or complain about the length of fixed-term tenancy offered and the type of tenancy offered, and against a decision not to grant another tenancy on the expiry of the fixed term'.[35] This does not mean that the landlord *must* offer a right of appeal but a failure to offer any opportunity to challenge a decision not to grant a new tenancy will leave the landlord open to a defence based on public law and/or proportionality grounds, see paras 7.128–7.134.

---

34 See para 2.2 of *The Regulatory Framework for Social Housing in England from April 2012*.
35 Regulatory Framework para 2.15–2.16.

Notices to quit

6.68 A notice to quit is a notice given by either landlord or tenant to bring a periodic tenancy to an end. A periodic tenancy continues automatically from one period to the next unless one party indicates that he or she wants the tenancy to end. A notice to quit is an indication that, at the end of the next complete period of the tenancy, either the tenant intends to leave or the landlord requires the tenant to leave. Landlords' notices to quit have no effect in respect of secure and assured tenancies; the only way a landlord can determine a secure or assured tenancy is by obtaining a possession order.[36] However, any contractual periodic tenancy that is not secure or assured must be ended by notice to quit before a landlord can make a claim for possession. All periodic tenancies can be ended by a *tenant's* notice to quit (see para 1.62).

6.69 A notice to quit must be served by a landlord to end the following types of tenancy:

- tenancies that have ceased to be secure or assured because the tenant no longer resides in the premises;
- tenancies that are excluded from the secure and assured schemes, for example, tenancies with a resident landlord, tenancies of licensed premises, non-secure tenancies granted to homeless applicants;[37]
- protected and statutory tenancies under Rent Act 1977.

6.70 Furthermore, a contractual licensee is entitled to a notice to quit before a claim for possession can be brought, provided the licence is not an excluded letting (see para 1.100).[38]

Form of notice to quit

6.71 There is no prescribed form for a notice to quit but the Protection from Eviction Act (PEA) 1977 requires that the notice is in writing and includes prescribed information about the tenant's rights.[39]

Time limits

6.72 A notice to quit must give a minimum of 28 days' notice or a complete period of the tenancy, whichever is longer.

36 See chapter 3.
37 See paras 3.19 and 3.117.
38 PEA 1977 s3(2B).
39 PEA 1977 s5.

6.73   The notice must expire either on the last or first day of a period of the tenancy. However, a notice may include a saving phrase such as: 'I require you to quit and deliver up possession on [date] or the day on which a complete period of your tenancy expires next after the end of four weeks from the service of this notice.'

6.74   There is no statutory time limit on how long a notice to quit can be relied upon following service. However, the landlord must prove that the contractual tenancy has ended. Usually a notice to quit will be served shortly before the claim is issued since otherwise the tenant may argue that a new tenancy implicitly came into being at some point after expiry of the notice to quit.

6.75   A claim for possession cannot be commenced before a notice to quit has expired.[40]

Errors in a notice to quit

6.76   Minor errors relating to the description of the premises or the name of the tenant will not invalidate the notice provided the tenant is not prejudiced by the error. An error in the date for the giving up of possession will invalidate the notice.

6.77   If the court finds the notice invalid any claim for possession must fail since the tenancy or licence must have ended before a claim for possession is made. The court cannot waive the requirement to serve notice to quit.

Service

6.78   The notice may be served by post, 'by hand' delivery to the address of the tenant or by personal service on the tenant. The burden is on the landlord to prove that the notice was received by the tenant, so most landlords will deliver or personally serve the notice.

6.79   Problems may arise when a tenant has left premises and the landlord wishes to end the tenancy before taking possession. A tenant 'abandoning' the premises does not of itself give the landlord a right to possession: the tenancy must be brought to an end.[41] However, a notice to quit left at premises when the tenant is absent will not be effective unless the tenancy agreement specifically permits this (or refers to a requirement that the lanldord serves a notice to quit). If so, the notice can be served by leaving it at the tenant's last known place of abode or business.[42]

---

40 *Plaschkes v Jones* (1983) 9 HLR 110.
41 See paras 1.70–1.77.
42 *Wandsworth LBC v Atwell* (1995) 27 HLR 536; Law of Property Act 1925 s196(5).

Introductory, demoted and flexible tenancies – notice requirements

6.80 An introductory tenancy is a local authority 'probationary' tenancy. A demoted tenancy is a tenancy that was once secure but has been demoted by a court. These are described at paras 3.168–3.190. A landlord must obtain a possession order before evicting such tenants and notice must be served before the claim is issued. Flexible tenancies are fixed-term secure tenancies, see paras 3.103–3.105 and 3.151–3.159+. For such tenancies there are specific notice requirements, described below.

Demoted tenancies

6.81 Demoted tenancies are similar to introductory tenancies in that the tenant has limited security for a specified period. However, before the tenancy is demoted notice must be served and the court must make an order demoting the secure or assured tenancy. Therefore, for demoted tenancies two kinds of notices must be considered:

- the notice served prior to applying for demotion (see paras 6.82–6.86 below); and
- the notice served prior to applying for a possession order to evict a demoted tenant (see paras 6.87–6.88).

Notice of intention to apply for a demotion order

6.82 A landlord seeking a demotion order must serve notice of the intention to apply to demote the tenancy. As for notices seeking possession, the court may dispense with the requirement if it is just and equitable to do so.[43] This applies whether the tenant is secure or assured.

6.83 An application may be solely for a demotion order but most applications will be within an application for possession; the demotion order being sought as an alternative to a possession order. In such a case two notices must be served: notice of seeking possession and notice of intention to apply for a demotion order.

---

43 HA 1985 s83(1)(b); HA 1988 s6A(5)(b).

Secure tenants

6.84   For secure tenants the notice must be in prescribed form.[44] It is similar to a notice of seeking possession and requires the following information be given:[45]

- particulars of the conduct that has caused the landlord to seek a demotion order;
- the earliest date on which the proceedings may be begun, (this is at least 28 days, as for an NSP).

The notice lapses 12 months after the date specified.

Assured tenants

6.85   A landlord must serve a notice of intention to apply for a demotion of the tenancy before commencing proceedings. There is no prescribed form of notice but HA 1988 s6A(6) provides that the notice must:

- give particulars of the conduct complained of;
- state that proceedings will not begin before the date specified in the notice, being at least two weeks from the date of the notice; and
- state that proceedings will not begin later than 12 months after the notice was served.

6.86   Demotion means that a secure tenant of a local authority becomes a demoted tenant; assured and secure tenants of a registered providers of social housing become 'demoted assured shorthold tenants'.

Notice before applying for possession – introductory and demoted tenancies

6.87   Although demoted and demoted assured shorthold tenants have limited security of tenure, a landlord who wishes to evict the demoted tenant must obtain a possession order and must give further notice to the tenant before starting the possession claim.

6.88   For both introductory and demoted tenancies the requirements of the notice of intention to seek possession are essentially the same.[46] There is no prescribed form of notice but the notice must:

---

44   HA 1985 s83(2) and the Secure Tenancies (Notices) (Amendment) (England) Regulations 2004 SI No 1627.
45   HA 1985 s83 as amended by ASBA 2003.
46   HA 1996 s128(1) and ASBA 2003 s143E.

- state that the court will be asked to make an order for possession;
- set out the reasons for the decision to apply for possession;
- specify the date after which possession proceedings may be begun, being no earlier than the date the tenancy could be terminated by notice to quit;
- inform the tenant of the right to request a review of the decision and the time within which the request must be made (14 days); and
- inform the tenant that if he or she needs help or advice about the notice, he or she should take it immediately to a citizens' advice bureau, housing aid centre or a solicitor.

The court has no power to waive the notice requirement or to permit an amendment.

Notices before applying for possession – flexible tenancies

6.89   Two different notices must be served on a flexible tenant before possession proceedings can be commenced: a six-month notice informing the tenant that no further tenancy will be granted and a two-month notice stating that possession will be sought.

6.90   HA 1985 s107D provides that a possession order will be made if the court is satisfied of three conditions: that the tenancy has come to an end and that the six-month and the two-month notices have been served.

The six-month notice

6.91   Under HA 1985 s107D(3) the requirement is that 'the landlord has given to the tenant not less than six months' notice in writing – (a) stating that the landlord does not propose to grant another tenancy on the expiry of the flexible tenancy, (b) setting out the landlord's reasons for not proposing to grant another tenancy, and (c) informing the tenant of the tenant's right to request a review of the landlord's proposal and of the time within which such a request must be made.' See below at paras 6.100–6.101 for details regarding the review process.

6.92   It is not stated when this notice must be served but arguably it must be served at least six months before the fixed-term tenancy ends.

The two-month notice

6.93   This notice must be served in addition to the six-month notice and the requirement is that 'the landlord has given the tenant not less than two months' notice in writing stating that the landlord requires possession of the dwelling-house.' This notice 'may be given before or on the day on which the tenancy comes to an end.'[47]

6.94   This may suggest that the notice must be served no later than the last day of the flexible tenancy. However, in light of recent Court of Appeal decisions on notices served under section 21 of HA 1988, see para 6.5, this is likely to be interpreted as an 'enabling' provision, ie the landlord may serve the notice before the fixed term ends, ie after it has ended.

The absolute anti-social behaviour ground – possession notice

6.95   The new anti-social behaviour ground is set out in detail in the appendix to chapter 7. It applies to both secure (periodic and flexible) tenancies and to assured tenancies, including fixed-term assured shorthold tenancies.[48] The ground is based on there having been a previous court finding that confirms anti-social behaviour by a tenant, resident or visitor to the premises (ie a conviction for a serious offence, for breach of a criminal behaviour order or for breach of a noise abatement notice, or a proven breach of an anti-social behaviour injunction, and/or the making of a closure order). The tenant must have been served with notice under HA 1985 s83ZA or HA 1988 s8(3A)–(4E).

6.96   For secure tenancies, section 83ZA states that the notice must:

- state that the court will be asked to make an order on the absolute anti-social behaviour ground;
- set out the reasons for the decision, including the condition or conditions (ie the court finding) the landlord relies on;
- inform the tenant of the right to request a review and the time within which the request must be made;
- if possession is also being sought on other grounds, the notice must also specify the ground/s and give particulars of the ground/s;

---

47   HA 1985 s107D(4)–(5).
48   It is found in HA 1985 s84A and Schedule 2, Ground 7A of HA 1988.

- inform the tenant that if he or she needs help or advice about the notice they should go to a Citizens Advice Bureau, a housing aid centre, a law centre or a solicitor; and
- specify the date on which proceedings for possession may commence

Note that if the landlord is also relying on other grounds, no separate NSP need be served: the other grounds and particulars of the grounds should be set out in the section 83ZA ground.

Time limits

6.97   If relying on a conviction the notice must be served within 12 months of the conviction or final disposal (ie any appeal). If the notice relies on a closure order it must be served within three months of the making of the closure order or final disposal.

6.98   The notice ceases to be in force 12 months after the date on which the proceedings could have been commenced.

6.99   For assured tenants section 8 provides that the notice should be in prescribed form. At the time of writing no form has yet been prescribed but presumably the contents will mirror the requirements of section 83ZA.

Reviews of decisions to seek possession

6.100   Introductory tenants, demoted tenants, flexible tenants and tenants facing possession on the absolute anti-social behaviour ground all have a right to a review of the decision to seek possession (strictly, the right of the flexible tenant is to a review of the decision not to grant a new tenancy – the subsequent two-month notice of possession carries no right of review).

6.101   For each scheme, the requirements of the review are fundamentally the same:

- the tenant must request a review within a specified time limit
- the review can be at a hearing or without a hearing
- the tenant must indicate if he or she wants an oral hearing – if so there must be a hearing
- the tenant can be accompanied or represented at a hearing, can call evidence and challenge the evidence put forward by the landlord
- the person conducting the review must have had no involvement in the original decision

- if the review is conducted by an officer or employee, he or she must be senior to the decision-maker
- the review decision must be communicated to the tenant in writing, with reasons.

The precise details and time limits for the reviews do differ and these are summarised in the table at the end of this chapter.

Challenging the review process or the decision to evict

6.102   In all cases, the court does not have to be satisfied that it is reasonable to evict and cannot scrutinise the landlord's reasons for the decision. If the correct procedure has been followed by the landlord a possession order must be made, unless the tenant can successfully defend the claim on public law or article 8 grounds, see para 7.128.

6.103   The statutory framework for both introductory and demoted tenancies set out to limit the power of the court by providing that the court *must* make a possession order unless the procedural requirements of notice and review had not been complied with by the landlord.[49] However, it is now clear that this does not preclude the County Court from considering a defence on public law grounds (which could include a challenge to the fairness of the review process) or based on article 8 of the European Convention on Human Rights (asserting that the decision to evict was not proportionate and therefore unlawful). See paras 7.135–7.139.

6.104   For flexible tenancies, section 107D(6) states that the court may only refuse to grant an order if the tenant has requested a review and the landlord has failed to carry out the review in accordance with the relevant provisions, or 'the court is satisfied ... that the decision on the review is otherwise wrong in law'.

6.105   For the absolute anti-social behaviour ground, HA 1985 s84A and HA 1988 s7(3) state that the court must make an order if the conditions are satisfied 'subject to' the landlord failing to comply with the obligations in relation to a review, 'and to any available defence based on the tenant's Convention rights, within the meaning of the Human Rights Act 1998'.

Demoted assured shorthold tenancies

6.106   A demoted assured shorthold tenancy is similar to an ordinary assured shorthold tenancy and a landlord must serve a notice complying with HA 1988 s21.

49   See HA 1996 ss127(2) and 128 and HA 1996 s143D.

6.107 A demoted assured shorthold tenant does not have a statutory right to a review of the decision but the landlord may have a policy of offering a review or appeal. There is also no obligation to give reasons in the notice but the landlord may have a policy of doing so particularly where there is a right of appeal. Social landlords who do not offer any opportunity to challenge the decision to evict will be open to defences based on public law and/or proportionality grounds, see below and para 7.128.

Issuing a possession claim

6.108 Part 55 of the Civil Procedure Rules (CPR) sets out the procedure for issuing possession claims. Failure to comply with Part 55 may be grounds for a claim to be struck out or adjourned. Part 55 and the Part 55 practice direction (PD) to can be downloaded from the website of the Ministry of Justice: www.justice.gov.uk/courts/procedure-rules/civil.

6.109 Chapter 22 provides a general explanation of civil claims in the County Court.

6.110 Claims for possession will usually be issued in the County Court.[50] Each County Court covers a geographical area and possession claims must be issued in the County Court with jurisdiction for the area where the premises are situated. This can be checked for particular addresses by using the court service search facility: https://courttribunalfinder.service.gov.uk.

6.112 Under CPR Part 55 there are three types of possession claim:

- **ordinary claims** against tenants, licensees and trespassers and mortgage possession claims, when the claim is dealt with at a hearing (CPR Part 55 Section I);
- claims under **the accelerated procedure** when a possession order may be made without a hearing. This procedure is only available against assured shorthold tenants (CPR Part 55 Section II);
- claims for **interim possession orders** against trespassers when the claim is dealt with at a hearing but with very short notice to the occupiers (CPR Part 55 Section III).

---

50 Only in exceptional circumstances can a possession claim be brought in the High Court, see CPR PD 55A, 1.1 and 1.3.

Ordinary possession claims – CPR Part 55 Section I

6.113   CPR 55.I applies where the claim for possession is against:

- a tenant with substantive security of tenure;
- an occupier with procedural security of tenure;
- an assured shorthold tenant where the landlord also seeks a money judgment for unpaid rent or where there is no written tenancy agreement;
- a borrower (mortgagor) by a lender (mortgagee).

6.114   The claim is commenced by the landlord (claimant) sending to the court the following:

- claim form (N5) and copies (one for each defendant);
- particulars of claim and copies;[51]
- written evidence relied on or required by CPR; and
- court fee.

6.115   On receipt the court will:

- give the case a court reference number;
- set a date for the first hearing;
- post to the defendant copies of the following:
  - the claim form, endorsed with the hearing date,
  - particulars of claim,
  - a 'defence form'[52] with guidance notes;
- post to the claimant notice confirming issue and giving notice of the hearing date.

6.116   In some County Courts some possession claims can be issued online.[53]

Particulars of claim

6.117   In any civil claim the particulars of claim set out 'a concise statement of the facts on which the claimant relies'.[54] For particular kinds of claim Practice Directions (PDs) specify certain information that must be included in the particulars of claim. The PD to CPR 55 provides that the particulars of claim must:[55]

---

51   The particulars of claim is on form N119 if based on rent arrears and N120 if the claim is a mortgage possession claim.
52   Form N11R if rent arrears and N11M if mortgage possession claim.
53   PD 55B applies to possession claims issued online.
54   CPR 16.4(a).
55   PD 55A.4, para 2.1. The claims forms N5, N11R and N11M, which can be accessed online, are designed to elicit the required information.

- identify the land to which the claim relates;
- state whether the claim relates to residential property;
- state the ground on which possession is claimed;
- give full details about any mortgage or tenancy agreement; and
- give details of every person who, to the best of the claimant's knowledge, is in possession of the property.

6.118 If the claim relies on statutory grounds for possession the particulars of claim must set out the ground/s relied on.[56]

Rent arrears cases

6.119 If the claim includes a claim for non-payment of rent the particulars of claim must also set out specific information about the arrears. In particular, a schedule of arrears must be provided. This must cover the two-year period immediately before issue, or, if the first date of default occurred less than two years before the date of issue, from the first date of default. The schedule must give a running total of the arrears.

6.120 If the claimant relies on a history of arrears that is longer than two years, this should be stated in the particulars of claim and a full or longer schedule attached to a witness statement.[57]

6.121 The following information must also be given:

- information about the defendant's circumstances, if known, including whether he or she is in receipt of social security benefits and whether any direct payments are made to the claimants from benefit;
- details of any previous steps taken to recover the arrears, including previous proceedings.[58]

Nuisance and anti-social behaviour cases

6.122 If the claim for possession relates to the conduct of the tenant, details of the conduct alleged must be included in the particulars of claim.[59]

---

56 PD 55A.4, para 2.4B.
57 PD 55A.4, para 2.3A.
58 Note also that if the landlord is a social landlord the steps set out in the Pre-Action Protocol should have been followed and should be described in the particulars of claim.
59 PD 55A.4, para 2.4A.

Mortgage arrears cases

6.123   If the claim for possession is brought by a mortgagee (lender of a secured loan) the particulars of claim must state whether certain notices and charges have been registered under the Matrimonial Homes Act 1967, the Matrimonial Homes Act 1983 or the Family Law Act 1996.[60]

6.124   Full details of the mortgage account must be given, including the amount of the advance; any periodic payments; any interest payments required; the amount needed to redeem the mortgage at a stated date not more than 14 days after issue, including any adjustment for early settlement and specifying the amount of solicitors' costs and administration charges that would be payable. If the claim is brought because of failure to pay the periodic payments when due, detailed information must be given about the arrears, as for rented properties, in schedule form.

6.125   If the claimant relies on a history of arrears longer than two years, this should be stated in the particulars of claim and a full or longer schedule attached to a witness statement.[61]

6.126   If the loan is a regulated consumer credit agreement (see paras 7.232–7.234), this must be stated.

6.127   The following information must also be given:

- information about the defendant's circumstances, if known, including whether he or she is in receipt of social security benefits and whether any direct payments are made to the claimants from benefit;
- details of any previous steps taken to recover the arrears, including previous proceedings.[62]

Statements of truth

6.128   The claim form, the particulars of claim and defences are 'statements of claim' and must be endorsed with a statement of truth. This should be signed by a person able to verify the truth of the facts stated in the document.[63]

---

60   PD 55A.4, para 2.5. These refer to the occupation rights of spouses and civil partners, see chapter 11.
61   PD 55A.4, para 2.5A.
62   A pre-action protocol also applies to mortgage possession proceedings.
63   CPR Part 22.

Service of the claim by the court

6.129 The claim form and particulars of claim are served on the defendant by the court usually by first class post. The papers are deemed received by the defendant on the second day after posting. At least 21 days' notice of the hearing must be given and the hearing should be within eight weeks of issue.[64] However, the court has the power to shorten the time before the hearing of the claim.[65]

Defendant's response to the claim

6.130 The court guidance sent to the defendant advises the defendant to complete the defence form and to attend the hearing.

6.131 However, failure to file a defence form does not prevent the defendant from attending the hearing and contesting the claim; there is no provision for default judgment under CPR Part 55.[66] However, a defendant who fails to indicate that the claim is contested before the hearing may be ordered to pay any legal costs wasted by the claimant.[67]

6.132 To avoid this, a defendant intending to defend a claim but who cannot file a full defence before the hearing, should inform both the claimant and the court as soon as possible before the hearing.

6.133 Where a defence is to be filed it may be possible for the parties to agree what case management directions the court should make (see para 6.138 below). Agreed case management directions can be submitted to the court in advance and if the court approves the directions the parties may avoid having to attend the first hearing.

The first hearing

6.134 Most courts list a large number of possession claims for hearing during a morning or afternoon session. This means that each claim will be allocated very little court time (sometimes as little as five or ten minutes). This usually means that only very simple cases and undefended claims are decided at the first hearing.

6.135 Possession claims concerning rent arrears, mortgage arrears and applications to suspend possession warrants are held in private, ie

---

64 CPR 55.5(3).
65 CPR 3.1(2)(a) and (b). PD 55A.5, para 4.2 refers specifically to situations in which the defendant has committed or threatened to commit assault or damage to property but the power is not limited to such situations.
66 Unlike most other civil claims, see chapter 22.
67 CPR 55.7.

members of the public cannot sit in court. Confusingly, however, rent arrears cases are in theory heard in 'open court' rather than 'in chambers', as is the case for mortgage claims and warrant applications. Rights of audience depend on whether a case is in open court or in chambers. See para 22.85 below.

Evidence

6.136   Unless the claimant knows that the claim is defended and cannot be finally decided at the first hearing (usually for lack of time), the claimant should attend court with the necessary evidence to prove the case. This means the evidence needed to prove any ground for possession and, if necessary, that it is reasonable to make possession order.

6.137   In most cases the claimant will arrange for an appropriate witness to attend court to give evidence orally. A private landlord may present his or her own case *and* give evidence. However, it is possible to rely on written evidence such as the particulars of claim and any witness statements, provided these have been served in advance.[68] Nevertheless, if the defendant challenges the truth of a written statement the hearing will usually be adjourned for the maker of the statement to attend court.[69]

Possible outcome of first hearing

6.138   At the first hearing the possible outcomes are:

- some form of possession order is made;[70]
- the claim is dismissed or struck out;
- the claim is adjourned generally (possibly on terms), or to a date in the future; or
- case management directions are given, setting out the steps the parties must take before the claim comes back before the court.

The accelerated possession procedure – CPR Part 55 Section II

6.139   The accelerated possession procedure is available only for assured shorthold tenancies, including demoted assured shorthold tenancies

---

68   See CPR 55.8(4): witness statements should be served two clear days before the hearing, unless the claim is against trespasssers when they should be served with the claim form.

69   PD 55A.8, paras 6.1–6.4.

70   Different kinds of possession orders are explained at para 6.143 below.

and fixed-term 'flexible' assured shorthold tenancies (see paras 6.106–6.107 and 6.64–6.67 above). It can only be used where:

- the original tenancy agreement is a written agreement;
- the only remedy sought is a possession order – rent arrears or any other form of relief cannot be claimed under the accelerated procedure.[71]

6.140 The procedure means a landlord can obtain a possession order without a court hearing. The stages of the procedure are as follows:

- The landlord completes and sends to the court: the claim form (form N5B) which must be endorsed with a statement of truth; copies of the documents relied on (ie, the tenancy agreement, the notice requiring possession, the demotion order in the case of a demoted assured shorthold tenancy, the licence or application in the case of a house in multiple occupation that requires a licence);[72] and the court fee.
- The court then sends to the tenant a copy of the completed form N5B and copy documents with a form of reply (form N11B). The tenant has 14 days to return the completed form N11B. Even if a tenant does not contest the making of a possession order he or she may use the reply to ask the court to postpone the order for up to 42 days on the grounds of 'exceptional hardship'.
- The tenant may also ask for time to pay the court costs (the court fee and the fixed costs which can be claimed if solicitors complete the form N5B). If the tenant files a reply a copy is sent to the landlord and the papers are referred to a judge.
- If the tenant does not file a reply within 14 days the landlord should file a request for a possession order and this will be referred to a judge. On considering the landlord's application and (if filed) the tenant's reply, the judge will do one of three things: make a possession order; fix a hearing for the parties to attend; or dismiss the application. The judge may order a defended claim to proceed under CPR 55.I.
- Where the tenant requests a postponement the court must fix a hearing unless the landlord has indicated (on the claim form) that he or she is content for the court to decide the issue of postponement without a hearing.

---

71 However, s40 of the Deregulation Act 2015 inserts a new s21C to the HA 1988 enabling the court to order a landlord to repay rent paid in advance where the landlord is seeking possession before the end of a period of the tenancy. Until 26 March 2015 this will only apply to tenancies granted on or after that date.

72 See paras 11.67–11.76.

- If a hearing is fixed the parties should be given at least 14 days notice and the judge may direct the parties to take certain steps before the hearing.
- If a possession order is made without a hearing the tenant can apply for the order to be set aside within 14 days. This may be appropriate where the tenant failed to file a reply in time, or in any other case where the tenant contends that the landlord has failed to establish the right to a possession order.

Interim possession orders – CPR Part 55 Section III

6.141   A quicker procedure for obtaining an interim possession order (IPO) against trespassers is available under CPR Part 55 Section III. It does not apply to all claims against trespassers, only cases where the occupiers entered as trespassers. So, for example, it cannot be used against someone who entered the premises with permission but who has subsequently became a trespasser (e.g. a sub-tenant after the tenancy comes to an end). Strict time limits apply in relation to making and service of the application.

6.142   Now that trespass on residential premises is a criminal offence[73] the IPO procedure is unlikely to be used in relation to residential premises; most trespassers can be arrested and removed by the police and possession secured without the need for a court order.

Possession orders

The extended discretion

6.143   When considering a claim for possession on a discretionary ground[74] the court has the 'extended discretion'[75] under which it may:

- adjourn the proceedings for such period or periods as it thinks fit; and
- when making an order for possession or at any time before the order is executed the court may:
  - stay or suspend the execution of the order; or
  - postpone the date of possession;
  - for such period or periods as it thinks fit.

---

73 Legal Aid, Sentencing and Punishment of Offenders Act 2012 s144.
74 See appendix to chapter 7 for a full list of all of the discretionary grounds for possession.
75 RA 1977 s100, HA 1985 s85 and HA 1988 s9.

Conditions

6.144   On any such adjournment, stay, suspension or postponement the court must impose conditions regarding the payment of rent arrears and rent (unless to do so would cause exceptional hardship or otherwise be unreasonable) and may impose such other conditions as it thinks fit.

6.145   The court may discharge or rescind the order for possession if it thinks it appropriate to do so, having regard to the conditions imposed and the conduct of the tenant in connection with the conditions.

6.146   If the claim for possession is established on a mandatory ground, or where no grounds are required (for example, claims against assured shorthold tenants or against non-secure tenants) the court does not have the extended discretion. It must make an 'outright' order fixing the date for possession, subject to any public law or proportionality defence that the occupier may raise: see para 7.128.

6.147   In such a case section 89 of the Housing Act 1980 provides that the court may postpone the effect of the possession order for a maximum of six weeks if the tenant can show exceptional hardship if an earlier order were made.

6.148   Section 89 does not limit the court's powers if the tenant can persuade the court that the making of a possession order would breach his or her rights under article 8 of ECHR.[76]

Conditional possession orders

6.149   Where an order is made on a discretionary ground, most commonly rent arrears, it is common for the court to make some kind of conditional order which gives the tenant the opportunity to avoid being evicted. The most common kind of conditional order is the 'suspended possession order' (form N28). Such an order provides that the landlord is granted the right of possession but that enforcement of the order is suspended on terms that the tenant must repay the arrears (and costs) by instalments, until they are cleared.

6.150   Until May 2009 the effect of such an order was that the tenancy ended if the tenant breached the terms of the order. At that point the former tenant became a 'tolerated trespasser', who did not enjoy most of the rights of a secure tenant but who could not be evicted without a further application to the court. In fact, certain kinds of suspended orders resulted in the tenant becoming a 'tolerated trespasser' even

---

76   See the judgment of Lord Neuberger at para [103] in *Hounslow v Powell* [2011] UKSC 8, 23 February 2011, see paras 7.130–7.132.

without breaching the order.[77] The Housing and Regeneration Act 2008 resolved the problem of tolerated trespass by amending the Housing Act 1985 so that a secure tenancy ends at the point of eviction and not the date on which the landlord became entitled to possession. Furthermore, those occupiers who were tolerated trepassers were to become tenants again on the date the Act came into force: 20 May 2009.[78] As from that date the tenants had 'replacement tenancies'; effectively tolerated trespass was abolished. For most purposes the tenancy is treated as having continued throughout the period of 'tolerated trespass'. However, this is not the case in relation to claims for damages for disrepair, see paras 10.4–10.93.

6.151   The problem of tolerated trespass could be avoided by the court making a different kind of order: this could take the form of an 'adjournment on terms'; here the court does not make a possession order but adjourns the claim for possession for so long as the tenant complies with terms, usually the repayment of arrears by instalments (though such orders can also be made in relation to other breaches, including nuisance and anti-social behaviour). Alternatively, a two-stage postponed order could be made. Under a postponed possession order (form N28A) the landlord is given the right to make an application for a date to be fixed but that right is postponed provided the tenant complies with the terms of the order. In the event of an alleged breach, the tenant is notified by the landlord of the intention to apply for a date to be fixed, with details of the alleged breach. The tenant has a right to reply and both the notice and reply must be sent by the landlord to the court when making the application. Most applications are dealt with without a further hearing. If a date for possession is fixed, the landlord may then proceed to obtain a warrant of eviction.

6.152   So, the court may, when wishing to make a conditional order:

• make a suspended possession order;
• make a two-stage postponed possession order; or
• adjourn on terms.

---

77 *Harlow v Hall* [2006] EWCA Civ 156, 28 February 2006.
78 The Housing and Regeneration Act 2008 provided that both former secure and former assured 'tolerated trespassers' would again become tenants and amended both the HA 1985 and the HA 1988. However, prior to the Act receiving Royal Assent, the House of Lords determined that a suspended possession order did not have the effect of creating a tolerated trespasser under the HA 1988: *Knowsley Housing Trust v White* [2008] UKHL 70, 10 December 2008. So, in fact, assured tenants subject to suspended possession orders had not become tolerated trespassers.

6.153 The effect of a suspended order is that if the tenant breaches the conditions the landlord may apply for a warrant of possession without notice to the tenant. The tenant will be notified of the application for the warrant and may apply to suspend or stay the warrant, see below at para 6.168. However, if the tenant does not make any application the warrant will be executed and the tenant evicted. The advantage of the postponed possession order or an adjournment on terms is that the landlord must make a further application, on notice to the tenant.

6.154 Sometimes claims for possession remain adjourned on terms (or generally with libertey to restore) for many years. Where the landlord wishes to pursue the claim for possession, the landlord can make an application to restore the claim but need not notify the tenant. The tenant will receive notice from the court but sometimes the notice simply gives a hearing date without explanation. It is essential that the tenant attends the hearing as the court will usually be asked to make a possession order.

Enforcing possession orders

6.155 Possession orders of residential premises must be enforced by application for a warrant from the court.[79] The warrant is executed by court bailiffs and there may be a delay of several weeks from the application for a warrant to the date of eviction.

6.156 The landlord may apply for a warrant after the date for the giving of possession. This will usually be the date fixed by the order (if an outright order) or the date of any breach (if a suspended order). In the case of a postponed order (see above at para 6.151) the landlord must apply for the date of possession to be fixed before applying for the warrant. Issuing a warrant is an administrative act. No further hearing will take place; the completion of a form requesting the issue of a warrant is sufficient. The court sends notice to the occupier that a warrant has been issued, indicating the date and time of the eviction. If the possession order was made on a discretionary ground the occupier may apply for the warrant to be suspended or stayed. If no application is made the court bailiffs will attend the premises and can use reasonable force to secure entry.

---

79 *Haniff v Robinson* (1994) 26 HLR 386, CA.

Challenging the possession order

6.157   After a possession order is made a defendant may:

- appeal against the order;
- apply to set the order aside; or
- apply to vary the order.

Appeals

6.158   A defendant can appeal against the making of a possession order but an appeal will only succeed if it can be established that the decision was:

- wrong; or
- unjust because of a serious procedural or other irregularity in the proceedings in the lower court.[80]

6.159   In all cases the permission of the court is needed. Permission may be obtained from the judge who made the order or from the judge or court to which the appeal is made.[81] An appeal against a district judge's order is heard by a circuit judge and an appeal against a circuit judge's order by the Court of Appeal.

6.160   CPR Part 52 governs the procedure for bringing appeals. The deadline for starting the appeal is 21 days from the date of the order. This means applying for permission if it was not granted at the hearing or, if permission was granted, lodging the grounds of appeal.

6.161   Note that lodging an appeal does not prevent enforcement of the order.[82] Unless the landlord agrees not to enforce the order until the appeal is heard, a separate application must be made for a stay of execution.

6.162   The unsuccessful party in an appeal will usually be ordered to pay any legal costs of the other party, see chapter 22. A landlord who has not instructed solicitors to obtain the possession order may do so if an appeal is lodged. A tenant considering an appeal must be advised of the increased liability for costs. If possible, legal aid should be

---

80 CPR 52.11(3).

81 Where a party wishes to appeal, permission should be sought orally at the hearing, immediately after the judge has made the order. However, the party may be unrepresented or it may not be clear that there are grounds to appeal until after the hearing. If permission is not requested or is refused by the judge who made the order, permission must be sought on the 'Appellant's Notice' (form N161) which is submitted to the appeal court.

82 CPR 52.7.

obtained so as to provide some protection against being ordered to pay further costs, see para 22.135.

Setting aside an order

6.163   In any case where a party does not attend the trial of a claim, the court may proceed with the hearing and make an order. In such a case the absent party may apply to set aside the order.

6.164   CPR 39.3 provides that the application must be supported by evidence (a statement endorsed on the application notice will suffice) and that the following conditions must be satisfied:

- the applicant must have acted promptly when he or she found out about the order;
- the applicant must have had a good reason for not attending the hearing; and
- the applicant must have had a reasonable prospect of success at trial.

6.165   Applications to set aside possession orders made in a tenant's absence were, until 2009, treated as applications under CPR 39.3.

However, in *Forcelux Ltd v Binnie*[83] the Court of Appeal held that a possession order made at the first hearing was not an order made 'at trial'. Therefore, when the court was considering setting aside the possession order it was not exercising its power under CPR 39.3 but under CPR 3.1(2)(m), which gives to the court very wide case management powers, including a power to 'take any other step or make any other order for the purpose of managing the case and furthering the overriding objective'. The court held that this power was broad enough to include the setting aside of a possession order.

The case was followed by *Hackney LBC v Findlay*[84] in which the Court of Appeal confirmed that when considering an application to set aside a possession order made at the first hearing, the court was exercising the wide powers under CPR Part 3, but that the court should nevertheless apply the CPR 39.3 criteria. However, taking into account the wide powers of the court under the Housing Act 1985 (including the power to vary a possession order) the criteria

83   [2009] EWCA Civ 854, 21 October 2009.
84   [2011] EWCA Civ 8, 20 January 2011.

> should be applied less rigorously. So, when considering why the tenant did not attend court the court can take into account the Rent Arrears Pre-Action Protocol and best practice among social landlords. Where a landlord has failed to comply with the Protocol and/or follow best practice, the possession order may be set aside even if the conditions under CPR 39.3 are not strictly made out.

6.166　In relation to the CPR 39.3 criteria as applied to possession claims, a reasonable prospect of success would include having a reasonable chance of avoiding an outright possession order even if some form of possession order would have been made. Also, in practice, the court may accept as good reasons for not attending, genuine mistakes such as going to the wrong court or arriving at court late. What will not usually be accepted is a deliberate decision not to attend, unless this was pursuant to advice from the landlord that attendance was not necessary, which would be a breach of the Rent Arrears Protocol, see para 6.17.

6.167　A possession order may be set aside even after it has been executed, ie after eviction,[85] see below, paras 6.171–6.173.

Variation, stay or suspension

6.168　Where an order has been made on a discretionary ground, the court retains the 'extended discretion' (see para 6.143 above) up to the date of eviction. Under the extended discretion the possession order may be varied if the court thinks it reasonable to do so. In addition the enforcement of the order may be suspended or stayed.

6.169　Where an outright order has been made in the tenant's absence an application may be made to set aside the order and, as an alternative in the same application, to postpone the date of possession or to suspend enforcement on terms.

6.170　Where the court does not have the extended discretion the only arguments that could be raised to support a stay or suspension of a possession order would be under public law or article 8 grounds. The Court of Appeal has held that in most cases it would be an abuse of process to ask the court to conduct a 'proportionality review' for the first time at the stage of enforcement.[86] However, it may be possible

---

85　*Peabody Donation Fund Governors v Hay* (1986) 19 HLR 145, CA.
86　See *R (JL) v Secretary of State for Defence* [2013] Civ 449, 30 April 2013, at para 7.168.

to persuade a court that it would not be an abuse of process where the tenants were unrepresented and without advice when the possession order was made, see paras 7.168–7.169.[87]

After eviction

6.171　After eviction the court no longer has a discretion to stay or suspend execution or to vary the possession order. However, there are two possible ways for the tenant to regain occupation:

- setting aside the possession order, see paras 6.163–6.167 above; or
- setting aside the warrant.

6.172　If the possession order is set aside, the warrant itself 'falls away' and the tenant is entitled to re-occupy. Because of the need to act promptly on finding out about the order it may be difficult to satisfy the criteria of CPR 39.3 (see para 6.164 above) in a case in which the order has already been enforced.

6.173　In any case when a person has been evicted it is essential to act quickly in applying to the court. Since it may take some time to prepare the application, the landlord should be contacted immediately, informed of the intended application and requested not to re-let the premises until it has been heard. If premises are let to someone else before the court considers the application it will be too late to obtain an order allowing the occupier to return.

Setting aside a warrant

6.174　A court may set aside a warrant of possession after eviction if satisfied that:

- the warrant was defective;
- the warrant was obtained by fraud; or
- there has been an abuse of process or oppression in the execution of the warrant.[88]

Abuse of process

6.175　A breach of the court rules would usually be an abuse of process.

87　In *Lawal v Circle 33 Housing Trust* [2014] EWCA Civ 1514, 24 November 2014, the Court of Appeal dismissed the tenants' appeal when they had been unrepresented initially but in that case there had in fact been a proportionality review by a judge, see para 7.169.

88　*Hammersmith & Fulham LBC v Hill* (1994) 27 HLR 368, CA.

In *Hackney LBC v White*[89] the local authority had obtained a possession order in 1986. Subsequently several warrants had been issued and suspended on the tenant's application. In 1995 a further warrant was issued and the tenant evicted. The tenant applied to set aside the warrant because the court rules require that permission to issue a warrant is needed when the possession order was made more than six years earlier.

The Court of Appeal upheld the tenant's appeal: the warrant had been improperly issued and was an abuse of process.

Oppression

6.176   A warrant can be set aside if there has been oppression in its execution. Misleading information given by a landlord to a tenant may constitute oppression.

In *Lambeth LBC v Hughes*[90] a warrant was issued, following which the council wrote to the tenant giving the date for eviction and stating that the only way to stop the eviction was to pay the arrears in full. The tenant went to see his housing officer who said the same thing but said he could take legal advice. The tenant tried but failed to get advice. He went to the court office but they could not find his file and told him to wait for a letter from the court bailiff which would contain the eviction date and details of how to stop the eviction. The bailiff's letter was sent on 22 October by second class post. It arrived on 28 October as the eviction was taking place.

The Court of Appeal held that:

- the council's message that only payment in full could prevent eviction was misleading and oppressive, in the absence of any reference to an application to the court;
- the oppression was not cured by the reference to taking legal advice without indicating what he could seek advice about;
- the failure of the court office to advise of the procedure was also oppressive; and
- the failure to post the bailiff's letter in sufficient time for it to be acted upon also made the execution oppressive.

89   (1995) 28 HLR 219, CA.
90   (2001) 33 HLR 33, CA.

6.177 It is not necessary that the 'oppression' is deliberate and it may not be caused by the landlord.

In *Hammersmith & Fulham LBC v Lemeh*[91] the occupier was aware of the impending eviction and attended court the day before it was scheduled. The court told him, mistakenly, that no warrant had been issued and advised him to contact the council. The following day he was evicted and applied to have the warrant set aside on the grounds of oppression.

The Court of Appeal held that there is no reason why misleading information given by the court cannot amount to oppression. It is a question of fact and it was clear that if the court had not given the wrong information to Mr Lemeh he would have been able to make his application to stay or suspend execution and have it heard before the eviction took place.

6.178 On receiving notice of eviction, occupiers often contact their landlord to reach agreement. While a landlord is not bound to accept the tenant's proposals the landlord may be guilty of oppression if it is suggested that the only way to stop the eviction is to pay the whole of the arrears. Instead, a landlord may indicate that it is not willing to withdraw the warrant but should make clear that the tenant may apply to the court and that it is for the court to decide whether the eviction can go ahead.

6.179 To establish oppression it is necessary for the tenant to be misled with the effect that that no application is made to the court before the eviction takes place.

In *Jephson Homes Housing Association v Moisejevs*[92] the occupier received notice of eviction and took advice from a citizens' advice bureau. The bureau drafted an application to suspend the warrant for the occupier to take to court. However, instead of lodging the application, she decided to pay to the landlord an amount equal to the shortfall under the terms of the order plus the costs of obtaining the warrant. Despite this, the landlord proceeded with the eviction.

91 (2001) 33 HLR 23, CA.
92 [2001] 2 All ER 901, CA. See also *Circle 33 Housing Trust Ltd v Ellis* [2006] HLR 106, CA. However, in *Southwark LBC v Augustus*, February 2007 *Legal Action* 29, Lambeth County Court, 24 November 2006, a warrant was set aside on the basis of oppression where the landlord had failed to follow its stated rent arrears policy requiring it to use eviction only as a last resort.

The occupier applied to set aside the warrant but her application was dismissed and permission to appeal refused. The court accepted that she was under a genuine misapprehension about what she needed to do to prevent the eviction but held that it did not have a free-standing power to remedy the unfairness of the eviction.

The Court of Appeal held that if the court process has been properly used without fault on the part of the landlord or the court, a warrant will not be set aside.

Effect of setting aside a warrant after eviction

6.180 Following the amendments to the HA 1985 and HA 1988 by the Housing and Regeneration Act 2008 the tenancy does not end until the warrant is executed, so the setting aside of a warrant will automatically restore the tenancy.

APPENDIX 1

Summary of possession notice requirements

The table below summarises the notices applicable to each type of tenancy or agreement under the Housing Acts 1985, 1988 and 1996, Protection from Eviction Act (PEA) 1977 and common law.[93]

Type of occupier	Notice	Law	Requirements	Length of notice
'Ordinary' Assured shorthold tenancy	Notice requiring possession/ 'section 21 notice'	HA 1988 s21	No prescribed form. Must be in writing. For contractual periodic tenancies, must require possession after last day of a period of the tenancy, (or use appropriate 'saving clause).[94]	At least two months.
Assured tenancy	Notice seeking possession/ 'section 8 notice'	HA 1988 s8	Prescribed form or form substantially to the same effect. NB – different requirements if absolute anti-social behaviour ground is being used, see below.	Depends on grounds: if nuisance, proceedings can start immediately. Otherwise, either two weeks or two months.
Secure periodic tenancy	Notice of seeking possession/ 'NOSP'	HA 1985 s83	Prescribed form or form substantially to the same effect. NB – different requirements if absolute anti-social behaviour ground is being used, see below.	Depends on grounds: if nuisance, proceedings can start immediately. Otherwise, at least 28 days.

93 In addition, family intervention tenancies (see para 3.191) require both a notice of an intention to serve a notice to quit, giving reasons and informing the tenant of the right to a review, followed by the service of a notice to quit. These notices are not dealt with in any detail as such tenancies are extremely rare.

94 But note that for tenancies granted on or after 26 March 2015, the Deregulation Act 2015 amends the Housing Act 1988 to remove the reference to the last day of a period of the tenancy and after 26 March 2018 this will apply to all tenancies whenever they commenced, see para 6.57.

Type of occupier	Notice	Law	Requirements	Length of notice
Introductory tenancy	Notice of proceedings	HA 1996 s128	No prescribed form but must contain certain information including reasons, right of review, time limit for requesting review and where to get help with notice. Tenant has statutory right to request review by landlord.	At least 28 days. Review must be completed before claim started.
Demoted tenancy (previously secure)	Notice of proceedings	HA 1996 s143E	No prescribed form but must contain certain information including reasons, right of review, time limit for requesting review and where to get help with notice. Tenant has statutory right to request review by landlord.	At least 28 days. Review must be completed before claim started.
Demoted assured shorthold tenancy (previously assured)	Notice requiring possession/ 'section 21 notice'	HA 1988 s21	No prescribed form and no prescribed information. Must be in writing. If periodic tenancy, must require possession after last day of period.[95] No right of review. Landlord may have policy offering right of review/appeal.	At least two months.
Flexible secure tenancy – within fixed term[96]	Notice of seeking possession/ 'NOSP'	HA 1985 s83 And s107D	Prescribed form or form substantially to the same effect. Form of NOSP is different from that for periodic secure tenants.	Depends on grounds: if nuisance, proceedings can start immediately. Otherwise, at least 28 days.

95 But see footnote 94.

96 Note that there is some uncertainty as to whether a notice of forfeiture also needs to be served to end the fixed term: see paras 3.158 and 5.16.

Type of occupier	Notice	Law	Requirements	Length of notice
Flexible tenant – at end of fixed term	Two notices required (1) notice of non-renewal (2) notice of intention to seek possesion	HA 1985 s107D	(1) No prescribed form but must state that landlord does not propose to grant new tenancy, and contain certain information including reasons, right of review, time limits for requesting review and where to get help with notice. (2) No prescribed form – must be in writing and give notice that possession required.	(1) Not less than six months. (2) Not less than two months.
'Flexible' assured shorthold tenancy – minimum 2 years, granted by private registered provider	(1) notice of non-renewal; and (2) notice requiring possesion (s21 notice)	HA 1988 s21(1B)	(1) No prescribed form. Must be in writing. Must state that landlord does not propose to grant a new tenancy and where to get help with notice. No reasons required. No statutory right of review but landlord may have policy offering right of review/appeal. (2) As for ordinary s21 notice: must be in writing, no prescribed information.	(1) Not less than six months. . (2) Not less than two months.
Rent Act periodic tenancy (protected or statutory) and other contractual tenancies not governed by HA 1985 or HA 1988 and not excluded letting	Notice to quit	Common law and PEA 1977 s5	Notice not in prescribed form but must be in writing and contain prescribed information.	A complete period of the tenancy or 28 days, whichever is longer.
Contractual licensee (not 'excluded occupier')	Notice to quit	Common law and PEA 1977 s5	Notice not in prescribed form but must be in writing and contain prescribed information.	What the contract provides or 28 days, whichever is longer.

Type of occupier	Notice	Law	Requirements	Length of notice
Special provisions where landlord is relying on new absolute anti-social behaviour ground				
Can apply to 'secure', 'assured', 'introductory' and 'flexible' tenants Also to the new 2–5-year ASTs granted by private registered providers	Notice of intended proceedings on absolute anti-social behaviour ground	HA 1985 s83ZA and 84A and HA 1988 s8	Must be in writing and state that court will be asked to make possession order under s84A/ground 7A. Must set out the specific conditions (criminal convictions/ recorded breaches etc) relied on. Must be served within 12 months of conviction or proven breach or within 3 months of closure order. If other grounds also relied on must give ground and particulars.	At least 28 days

APPENDIX 2

Tenants' right to a review of the decision to seek possession – procedural requirements

Tenancy/ reason for notice	Introductory	Demoted	Flexible	Absolute ground for possession
Relevant statutory provisions	Introductory Tenants (Review) Regulations 1997 SI No 72 HA 1996 ss128, 129	Demoted Tenancies (Review of Decisions) (England) Regulations 2004 SI No 1679 HA 1996 s143F	Flexible Tenancies (Review Procedures) Regulations 2012 SI No 695 HA 1985 ss107B and 107D	Absolute Ground for Possession for Anti-social Behaviour (Review Procedure) (England) Regulations 2014 SI No 2554 HA 1985 ss83ZA and 85ZA
Time limit for landlord's notice	Before introductory tenancy ends – 12 months – extendable to 18 months (otherwise will become secure by default)	Before end of 12 months (otherwise will become secure by default)	Landlord must give at least 6 months notice of decision not to grant new tenancy (two-month notice – no right of review)	Within 12 months of conviction/ breach or within 3 months of closure order.
Time limit for tenant to request review	Within 14 days of receiving notice	Within 14 days of receiving notice	Within 21 days of service of notice	Within 7 days of service of notice

Tenancy/ reason for notice	Introductory	Demoted	Flexible	Absolute ground for possession
Form and content of tenant's request for review	No specific form or content required. Tenant must 'request a review'. If tenant wants an oral hearing, must indicate this within 14 days of receiving landlord's notice.		In writing and must include: • applicant's name and address; • description of original decision including date; • statement of grounds on which review sought; • statement as to whether applicant requires oral hearing; • statement as to whether applicant agrees to email communications (and, if so, email address to use).	
No hearing requested	Landlord must inform tenant of date by which written reps must be received. Cannot be less than five clear days after tenant informed.	Landlord must give to tenant at least five clear days notice of date of review. Whether or not there is an oral hearing, tenant may make written reps – must be received by landlord at least two clear days before date of review.	Landlord must send written notice re right to make written reps within certain time which cannot be less than five days. Must take into account reps made.	
Hearing requested	Landlord must give notice of date, time and place – not less than five days after receiving request for hearing.	Landlord must give to tenant at least five clear days' notice of date of review – if oral hearing, must give notice of time and place.	Landlord must send written notice of date, time and place of hearing. At least five days' notice.	
Who conducts the review	Someone appointed by the landlord. If an officer or employee must be senior to person who made decision and not involved in decision.			

Tenancy/ reason for notice	Introductory	Demoted	Flexible	Absolute ground for possession
Representations at review hearing	Reviewer decides on procedure. Applicant can: • make oral or written reps, and be accompanied or represented by someone else; • call people to give evidence; • put questions to anybody giving evidence.		Hearing should be conducted with minimum amount of formality. Applicant can: • make oral or written reps, and be accompanied or represented by someone else; • call people to give evidence; • put questions to anybody giving evidence. Decision-maker can also attend and same rights apply.	
Adjournments/ postponements	Reviewer can postpone, adjourn or proceed in absence of tenant.			
Notice of decision	Landlord must notify tenant of decision on review. If decision confirmed, reasons must be given.		Decision must be by person who conducted hearing. If original decision confirmed, reasons must be given.	
Time limit for completion	Review must be carried out and tenant notified before date specified in notice as day after which claim may be begun (minimum 28 days).			

Defending possession claims

continued

Key points

- There are broadly three types of possession claims for rented property: claims based on discretionary grounds, claims based on mandatory grounds, and claims for which no ground is needed.
- If the ground is discretionary the court cannot make a possession order unless it is reasonable to do so.
- The most commonly used grounds are those relying on rent arrears and nuisance/anti-social behaviour.
- Most rent arrears grounds are discretionary: it must be reasonable to make a possession order.
- For assured tenants there is a mandatory rent arrears ground where more than eight weeks' rent is in arrears.
- The nuisance ground for possession is discretionary but a new mandatory 'anti-social behaviour' ground has been introduced by the Anti-social Behaviour, Crime and Policing Act 2014.
- Even where no ground for possession is needed, in exceptional cases a tenant may defend a claim on public law and/or human rights grounds.
- In mortgage cases, the lender usually has a right of possession under the mortgage, so mortgage possession claims are usually about the borrower getting time to repay arrears or time to sell the property.
- The court can postpone or suspend possession in a mortgage case if the borrower can repay mortgage arrears within a reasonable period of time.
- The tenants of landlords who default on a morgtgage will usually be evicted by the lender unless the tenancy was created before the mortgage was taken out.

Introduction

7.1   Chapter 6 deals with the procedural requirements of possession claims, including notice requirements. This chapter examines the most commonly used grounds and defences, possible human rights and public law defences, the impact of the Equality Act 2010 and other provisions affecting vulnerable tenants. Claims for possession of mortgaged property are briefly described. The appendix lists all of the statutory possession grounds for tenants.

Possession claims against private assured shorthold tenants

7.2   Since 28 February 1997 almost all tenancies granted by private land-lords are assured shorthold tenancies: see para 3.57. An assured shorthold tenant has very limited security of tenure; he or she may be evicted after the first six months unless a longer fixed period is granted. The possible defences to a claim for possession against an assured shorthold tenant are:

- the tenancy is not an assured shorthold tenancy;[1]
- the notice requiring possession is not valid (see paras 6.47–6.59);
- the landlord cannot rely on the notice because of a failure to com-ply with the mandatory tenancy deposit and/or HMO (houses in multiple occupation) licencing requirements, see paras 4.142–4.153 and 11.67–11.73;
- the requirements of the Civil Procedure Rules (CPR) have not been met.[2]

Under the Deregulation Act 2015 a new defence may be available based on the provisions to prevent 'retaliatory evictions'. See paras 11.90–11.102.

7.3   Additionally, where the landlord is a public body (ie most social landlords) in exceptional cases it may be possible to defend a claim for possession on public law or proportionality grounds (see paras 7.128–7.132 below).

Grounds: rent arrears

7.4   Most claims for possession based on statutory grounds are brought because of rent arrears. Public sector landlords, including private registered providers, must follow the rent arrears protocol before claiming possession on rent arrears grounds.[3] See para 6.4.

---

1 Eg a tenancy granted before 28 February 1997 where the necessary formalities were not complied with or where the anti-avoidance provisions of Housing Act (HA) 1988 s20(3) apply, see paras 3.67–3.70.
2 For example where a landlord brings a claim under the accelerated procedure but fails to produce a written tenancy agreement. See para 6.139.
3 Unless the tenant has no security of tenure.

Discretionary rent arrears grounds

7.5   For regulated, secure and assured tenants there is a discretionary ground for possession where 'rent lawfully due from the tenant' has not been paid.[4]

7.6   In addition, for assured tenants only, there is a further discretionary ground (Ground 11) where the tenant has persistently delayed in paying rent.

Mandatory rent arrears ground

7.7   For assured tenants only, there is a mandatory rent arrears ground: where at least eight weeks' rent (or, if rent is paid monthly, two months' rent) is in arrears both when the notice seeking possession is served and at the date of the hearing.

7.8   All of the rent arrears grounds are set out in full in the appendix to this chapter.

Rent arrears – defending claims for possession

7.9   In all cases the following elements must be established:

- rent;
- lawfully due;
- has not been paid (or there has been persistent delay in payment).

Rent

7.10   Many social landlords collect other charges as part of the rent, including water rates, heating and hot water charges and insurance contributions. Whether such charges can properly be treated as rent for the purpose of a claim for possession is undecided.

> In *Lambeth LBC v Thomas*[5] the Court of Appeal considered a claim for possession brought because of arrears of water rates collected by the council. The court held that it was not necessary to decide whether such sums constituted rent because Ground 1 was made out if there were arrears of rent or other breaches of the tenancy agreement. However, the court indicated that there was force in the

---

4   Rent Act (RA) 1977, Case 1; HA 1985, Ground 1; HA 1988, Ground 10.
5   (1998) 30 HLR 89, CA.

argument that the term 'rent' should be given the meaning adopted in earlier Rent Act cases: all sums payable to the landlord.[6]

7.11 If the tenancy agreement makes provision for the payment of the other charges, failure to pay will constitute a breach of the tenancy agreement and therefore a ground for possession in any event. However, the amount of the total debt made up of non-rent charges will be relevant and advisers should, where possible, ensure that these are distinguished from the arrears of net rent.

7.12 In a Ground 8 claim, where the court *must* make an outright order if a certain level of arrears is proved, the narrow definition of rent should be applied and the court should exclude from the arrears figure any sums due to charges other than the net rent.

Lawfully due

7.13 In all cases the landlord must prove that the unpaid rent is 'lawfully due'.

Rent increases

7.14 The way landlords can increase rents is described at paras 4.182–4.198. If the landlord has not followed the correct procedure, the tenant may have a defence that the rent claimed was not 'lawfully due'. Advisers should ascertain the correct rent (ie the rent payable before any unlawful increase) and calculate whether there would be arrears in any event. Even if so, the court may be prepared to dismiss the claim, depending on the true level of arrears, or to adjourn the claim for the landlord to prepare an amended rent schedule.

Landlord and Tenant Act 1987 s48

7.15 Under the Landlord and Tenant Act (LTA) 1987 s48 rent is not treated as due where a landlord has not given to the tenant an address in England and Wales at which notices may be served. However, it should be noted that as soon as the landlord gives the information, the whole of any rent due becomes payable (see para 4.137).

---

6 This was the view taken in the county court case of *Lewisham LBC v Simba-Tola*, June 1993 *Legal Action* 14, Bromley County Court, in which a possession order was made based on arrears entirely attributed to general rates, water rates and other charges, full housing benefit having been paid throughout the tenancy. See also *Rochdale BC v Dixon* [2011] EWCA Civ 1173, 20 October 2011.

Has not been paid

7.16   Where the landlord relies on one of the discretionary grounds that some rent is unpaid, the ground is made out if there were arrears both when notice was served and at the date of issue. Clearing the arrears before the date of the hearing does not mean the ground is not made out. However, a judge is unlikely find it reasonable to make a possession order in such a case but will usually order the tenant to pay the landlord's legal costs.

7.17   If Ground 11 is used against an assured tenant the allegation is of 'persistent delay'. It is not necessary that there are arrears at the date of the notice or the date of issue, only that there is a history of late payment or the repeated accrual of arrears before payment is made, and that it is reasonable to make an order.

Rent schedules

7.18   The landlord must prove that the rent is unpaid. CPR Part 55 requires a schedule to be attached to the particulars of claim (see paras 6.119–6.120). The requirement is mandatory and a failure to comply may mean the claim is struck out or at least adjourned. An adjournment can be crucial as it may enable a tenant to resolve outstanding benefit issues and to make regular payments before the possession claim is considered by the court.

7.19   The rent schedules must be carefully examined with any evidence the tenant has of payment. Recent payments may not appear on the schedule. Also, large public sector landlords often operate separate accounts to recover arrears for previous tenancies and payments may be wrongly credited to those accounts.

Offers of rent

7.20   Where rent is offered and refused by the landlord, this provides the defence of 'tender'. Private landlords sometimes refuse to accept payments of rent, or fail to present cheques, with the aim of establishing a ground for possession. Having offered payment gives the tenant a defence but the liability for rent is not extinguished even if the offer of payment has been refused. Tenants must therefore ensure that the rent is set aside and available at the date of any hearing.

7.21   Where a cheque is accepted by the landlord the rent is treated as being paid on the date the cheque is delivered provided the cheque is subsequently honoured (see below at para 7.38).

Housing benefit problems

7.22 Chapter 9 summarises the housing benefit system. Many claims for possession are triggered by problems in relation to housing benefit claims, particularly in the social rented sector.

7.23 Arrears may accrue entirely as a result of an authority's inefficiency in administering housing benefit claims. However, more often there is a combination of maladministration and some failure on the part of the tenant, eg failing to comply with requests for information or evidence or to submit claims in time.

7.24 The introduction of the 'benefit cap' and the 'bedroom tax' has forced many tenants into rent arrears. The government's response to legal challenges to these provisions has been to argue (successfully) that the Discretionary Housing Payment (DHP) scheme must be seen as part of the whole benefit system, see paras 9.80–9.92. Where DHP applications are pending, the courts should be asked to adjourn any claims for possession until the applications have been decided.

7.25 It is important to obtain as much information as possible about any housing benefit problems before a possession hearing. The court will expect detailed information about the outstanding issues, in particular what action is needed to resolve the issues, how long it is likely to take and how much housing benefit is likely to be paid.

7.26 The following housing benefit issues commonly cause or contribute to the accrual of rent arrears.

Issue	Suggested action
Tenant delays or fails to make or renew claim	Consider request to backdate. See paras 9.111–9.116.
Local authority delays processing claim for private tenant	Consider legal action to compel payment on account. See paras 9.109–9.110.
Overpayment recovery	Consider whether decision on recoverability can be challenged; request reduction of rate of recovery. See paras 9.117–9.124.

Issue	Suggested action
Non-dependant deductions	Check deduction correctly applied and at correct rate; advise tenant of need to claim contribution from non-dependant and/or to obtain information on non-dependant's income; advise tenant on right to evict non-dependant who refuses to contribute. See paras 9.99–9.102.
Local authority claims tenant failed to provide evidence	Obtain information from authority as to what is required/request copy letters sent to tenant;[7] advise tenant on what to provide and to obtain receipts; consider backdating request if claim closed.
Unexplained delay in processing claim/backlog in HB department	Consider issuing witness summons requiring housing benefit manager to attend court.[8] Alternatively a claim for judicial review could be made to challenge the delay, see paras 2.4–2.10.
Eligible rent or local housing allowance is less than current rent	Apply for discretionary housing payment. See paras 9.80–9.86.
For some other reason housing benefit does not meet the full rent	Ascertain reason and consider appeal against assessment of entitlement and/or advise tenant of amount he or she must pay each week for non-eligible charges and/or because income is too high to receive full housing benefit.
Benefit cap or bedroom tax applied and tenant cannot make up difference	Apply for discretionary housing payment. Advise on other options: benefit cap not applied to 'in-work' benefit recipients; obtain support from family, take in lodger. See paras 9.66–9.79.

7 Local authority landlords sometimes list such letters in the particulars of claim in the section on information about previous steps taken to recover the arrears. A party may make a written request for a copy of any document referred to in a statement of case and, provided an undertaking to pay reasonable costs is given, copies must be provided within seven days of the request: see CPR 31.14–31.15.

8 The procedure is set out in CPR Part 34.

7.27 Where rent arrears have accrued as a result of local authority inefficiency or error, an application may be made for the authority to be joined to the proceedings and ordered to pay the costs.[9] Where the landlord *is* the local authority an application for costs can be made against the authority as claimant.

The relevance of housing benefit problems

7.28 In most cases housing benefit problems are relevant to the issue of whether it is reasonable to make a possession order rather than whether rent lawfully due is unpaid. There is an argument that rent is not 'unpaid' in the case of a local authority tenant who receives a rent rebate which the authority subsequently decides he or she was not entitled to.[10] However, it is rare for the whole of a tenant's arrears to be caused by the recovery of an overpayment. Furthermore, this will not assist a tenant of a non-local authority landlord.[11]

7.29 A tenant awaiting a decision on a housing benefit claim should always pay the non-rebated charges (eg water rates and other charges). If the tenant's entitlement can be assessed, he or she should also pay any expected shortfall. Where there will be arrears even after housing benefit has been paid, instalments towards the arrears should also be paid. A failure to do this may mean that there are significant arrears when the housing benefit issues are resolved and a possession order may be made. If adjournments are granted to resolve housing benefit problems, the court may make it a condition of the adjournment that the tenant pays the non-rebated charge plus a sum towards the arrears.

7.30 It should be noted that in Ground 8 (mandatory) claims it may not assist a tenant that the arrears have accrued as a result of housing benefit problems.[12] Advisers must try to ensure that all outstanding issues are resolved before the hearing of the possession claim and that the arrears are below the mandatory level of eight weeks.

Mandatory rent arrears ground: assured tenants only

7.31 Ground 8 is a mandatory ground for possession where at least eight weeks' rent (for a weekly or fortnightly tenancy) or two months' rent

---

9 See *Asra v Coke* June 2001 *Legal Action* 31. See para 22.149 below.
10 See Social Security Administration Act 1992 s134(2).
11 See Housing Benefit Regulations (HB Regs) 2006 SI No 213 reg 95(2).
12 See *North British Housing Association Ltd v Mathews and Others* [2004] EWCA Civ 1736 at para 7.34 below.

(for a monthly tenancy) is in arrears both at the date the notice seeking possession was served and at the date of the hearing.[13]

7.32   If Ground 8 is proved, the court has no discretion: an outright possession order must be made. This will usually be a 14-day order but if it appears to the court that this would cause exceptional hardship this may be extended to a maximum of six weeks.[14] But, see paras 7.128–7.132 below on the possibility of a public law or proportionality defence where the landlord is a public body.

7.33   Rent means rent lawfully due from the tenant so advisers should consider the issues referred to above at paras 7.13–7.21. Landlords usually rely on Grounds 8, 10 and 11 at the same time so that if Ground 8 is not made out, the court can still make an order under one of the discretionary grounds. However, under Grounds 10 and 11 the court may make a conditional order instead of an outright order (see para 6.149).

7.34   The court does not have an 'extended discretion' when Ground 8 is made out. Possession orders cannot be postponed or suspended. A possession order should clearly state whether it has been made on Ground 8. If it does not, the court can, at a later date, exercise its discretion.[15]

Adjournments

7.35   In 2004 the Court of Appeal considered whether an adjournment could be granted to enable a tenant to resolve housing benefit problems and clear the arrears in a Ground 8 claim:

> *North British Housing Association Ltd v Matthews and Others, London & Quadrant Housing Limited v Morgan*[16] concerned four tenants of social landlords against whom possession was claimed on Ground 8. In each case the ground was made out but the arrears had accrued because of maladministration by the local authority housing benefit departments. The judges hearing the claims refused to adjourn to give the tenants time to resolve the housing benefit problems.

---

13   For yearly or quarterly tenancies, the figure is at least three months' rent or one quarter's rent, in arrears for at least three months. The ground is set out in full in the appendix to this chapter.

14   HA 1980 s89.

15   *Diab v Countrywide Rentals 1 plc*, ChD, (2001) *Independent* 5 November, CH/2001/PTA/494, 10 July 2001.

16   [2004] EWCA Civ 1736.

The Court of Appeal held that the power to adjourn a hearing to enable a tenant to reduce the arrears to below the Ground 8 threshold may only be exercised in exceptional circumstances and the fact that the arrears are attributable to maladministration on the part of the housing benefit authority was not an exceptional circumstance.

However, the court did refer to circumstances in which the court may properly exercise its discretion to adjourn. One of these was

... where the landlord is a public body, and the tenant may have an arguable defence based on abuse of power ... A yet further example is where, before or at the hearing date, the landlord accepts a cheque from the tenant for a sufficient sum to bring the arrears below the Ground 8 threshold, but the cheque is conditional payment, it may be a proper exercise of discretion to adjourn the claim for possession to see whether the cheque will be honoured.[17]

7.36   This does not, however, mean that in the absence of such exceptional circumstances a court can never adjourn such a hearing. The court has an inherent power to control its own procedure. If a tenant raises a defence or procedural argument that the court does not have time to resolve, an adjournment may be granted for the case to be listed for a longer hearing. Or, where a tenant intends to bring a counterclaim for damages for disrepair, the court may give case management directions. What the court cannot do is adjourn for the express purpose of giving the tenant an opportunity to reduce the arrears below the minimum level so as to defeat the ground.

7.37   When asking for an adjournment in such a case it is essential to make the application before the court has heard evidence. Otherwise, the court may decide that, being satisfied the ground is made out, it has no option but to make a possession order.

---

17 [2004] EWCA Civ 1736, Dyson LJ at [12]. It should be noted that the House of Lords/Supreme Court has since ruled that such public law and proportionality defences can be raised in the county court; the defendant need not seek an adjournment to apply for judicial review. Also, it is not necessary to establish 'abuse of power'; a defence on ordinary public law grounds or proportionality would be sufficient, though the court will only permit such defences exceptionally. See paras 7.128–7.132.

Payment by cheque

7.38   If, before the hearing, the tenant makes a payment to reduce the arrears to less than eight weeks the ground will not be made out.

> In *Coltrane v Day*[18] a cheque for the full amount of the arrears was sent by the tenant's solicitors to the claimant's solicitors five days before the hearing. Had it been paid into the landlady's account on the day of receipt it would not have cleared before the hearing. In fact, the cheque was given to the claimant by her solicitors on the day of the hearing and she subsequently paid it into her account. The district judge adjourned the hearing for 56 days. The circuit judge upheld the landlady's appeal holding that at the date of the hearing the rent was unpaid and an order for possession was made.
>
>   The Court of Appeal allowed the tenant's appeal. It is an established principle of contract law that if a cheque is delivered and is not returned by the creditor the debt is discharged as at the date of delivery, provided the cheque is met on first presentation. In this case rent had always been paid by cheque, the landlady had accepted the cheque and paid it into her account where it was met on first presentation. However, if in such a case the cheque does not clear on first presentation an order for possession must be made, the date of the hearing being, for the purposes of Ground 8, the earlier and not the adjourned hearing date. Furthermore, in the absence of express or implied agreement regarding the payment of rent by cheque a landlord is not bound to accept a last-minute cheque from the tenant.
>
>   The district judge had been right to adjourn the hearing but the appropriate adjournment would have been seven or 14 days; 56 days was excessive.

So, unless there is an agreement that rent is paid by cheque, a tenant who wishes to make payment shortly before or at the hearing must do so by paying cash.

Ground 8 and registered social landlords

7.39   In *R (Weaver) v London and Quadrant Housing Trust*[19] the tenant sought to judicially review the trust's use of Ground 8 arguing that she had a 'legitimate expectation' that the trust would follow Housing

18 [2003] EWCA Civ 342, 14 March 2003.
19 [2008] EWHC 1377 (Admin), 24 June 2008.

Corporation guidance. The guidance suggested that RSLs should use all reasonable alternatives to recover rent arrears before using Ground 8. The court dismissed the claim, holding that the tenant, having been unaware of the guidance, could not establish any legitimate expectation. Furthermore, on the facts, the trust could not be said to have failed to use reasonable alternatives before pursuing the claim for possession under Ground 8.

7.40   However, since *Weaver* the courts have made clear that public law and article 8 defences can, in exceptional cases, be considered by the county court, and paras 7.170–7.171 refers to cases in which defences have succeeded where public bodies have failed to follow their own policies.

Counterclaims

7.41   The defence of 'set-off' may be available to a possession claim based on rent arrears. Set-off means that the defendant acknowledges monies owed but claims the right to set off against the debt an amount due from the claimant to the defendant. The most common defences of set-off will be based on the claimant's breach of the repairing obligation. Even where damages are yet to be assessed the defendant has a right to equitable set-off.[20] However, the defendant's right of action must exist at the date the claim was issued. Chapter 10 describes in detail the repairing obligations of landlords and the way compensation is assessed. A disrepair counterclaim will exist only where:

- there is 'disrepair' as opposed to poor conditions caused, for example, by poor design or overcrowding;
- the repairs are the landlord's responsibility;
- the landlord has had notice of the need for repairs;
- the landlord has failed to carry out the repairs within a reasonable period; and
- the tenant has suffered loss and inconvenience.

7.42   If the assessed damages do not extinguish the arrears the court may make a possession order.[21] A tenant should pay current rent plus a sum towards the arrears until the proceedings are disposed of.

7.43   The court has the power to order that a counterclaim be heard separately. Provided the court is satisfied that the defendant has a genuine claim this is unlikely but it is a risk if the issue is raised at

20 *British Anzani (Felixstowe) Ltd v International Marine Management (UK) Ltd* [1979] 2 All ER 1063.
21 See *Haringey v Stewart* (1991) 23 HLR 557.

the first hearing without any evidence of the disrepair (such as photographs or a report) or where the counterclaim is unlikely to result in more than minimal damages and the arrears are substantial.

Grounds: nuisance

7.44   Since 1996 a range of legislative measures have been introduced to address 'anti-social behaviour', including specific powers given to the providers of social housing. The Anti-social Behaviour, Crime and Policing Act (ASBCPA) 2014 introduces further new provisions consolidates some existing provisions.

7.45   In summary, providers of social housing have the following powers to deal with anti-social behaviour committed in and around the premises they let:

- the use of 'probationary tenancies' granting less security for the first 12 months of a new tenancy, see para 3.168;
- obtaining possession orders on nuisance grounds to evict tenants;
- obtaining orders 'demoting' secure or assured tenancies, see para 3.184;
- obtaining injunctions to restrain anti-social behaviour;
- obtaining orders excluding perpetrators of anti-social behaviour from defined areas (where there are lettings of social housing);
- obtaining orders excluding perpetrators from their own homes;
- obtaining 'closure orders' to prevent premises being used in relation to persistent anti-social behaviour, particularly related to illegal drugs.

7.46   In addition, a local authority, as a public authority, has general powers to address anti-social behaviour in its area, generally exercised in conjunction with the police.

Grounds for possession based on nuisance and anti-social behaviour

7.47   Until the ASBCPA 2014, the only nuisance grounds for possession were discretionary grounds. These grounds remain and for secure and assured tenants the ground is the same. It is set out in the appendix to this chapter: Ground 2 for secure tenants and Ground 14 for assured tenants. In summary, the ground is made out if the tenant, a resident or visitor to the premises:[22]

22   HA 1985 Sch 2 Ground 2; HA 1988 Sch 2 Ground 14.

(Nuisance)

- has been guilty of conduct causing or likely to cause a nuisance or annoyance to:
  - someone residing, visiting or otherwise engaging in a lawful activity in the locality, or to the landlord, or
  - someone employed in connection with the landlord's housing management functions (not necessarily employed by the landlord), where the conduct is related to or affects the landlord's management functions

or

(Conviction)

- has been convicted of:
  - using or allowing the premises to be used for immoral or illegal purposes, or
  - an indictable offence committed in, or in the locality of, the premises.

7.48   Note that:

- It is not necessary to prove that nuisance or annoyance has been caused to another person, only that the conduct was *likely* to cause nuisance or annoyance. This means that it is not necessary for there to be a 'victim' of the behaviour.
- The conduct may be that of a visitor to the premises.
- The likely nuisance and annoyance need not be to neighbouring occupiers. It may be to someone visiting or engaged in a lawful activity in the locality, or to the landlord or landlord's employees or contractors. The conduct need not be in the locality of the dwelling.
- Any indictable[23] offence committed in or near the premises is sufficient. The offence need not be such as to be likely to cause nuisance.
- There must be a conviction for such an offence, not merely an allegation or charge.

New grounds for possession: riot and the mandatory anti-social behaviour ground

7.49   ASBCPA 2014 introduces two additional grounds: (1) a discretionary ground where there have been convictions for riot-related offences,

---

23   An indictable offence does not include an offence that can only be tried in the magistrates' court under section 22 of the Magistrates' Courts Act 1980 ('either way' offences where the value involved is small).

and (2) a mandatory anti-social behaviour ground, based on convictions or previous court findings. These are explained in detail below at paras 7.50–7.61.

Conviction for rioting

7.50   This new ground was introduced in response to the riots that took place in 2011. It is Ground 2ZA for secure tenants and 14ZA for assured tenants, and is made out if the tenant or another adult living in the premises has been convicted of an indictable offence during, and at the scene of a riot in the UK. It is discretionary so the court must be satisfied that it is reasonable to make a possession order.

Mandatory ground for serious offences

7.51   The ground is described as an 'absolute' ground (ie the court must make a possession order if proved and cannot suspend a possession order on terms). It is unlike other grounds (discretionary or mandatory) in that a local authority landlord must offer the tenant a right to a review of the decision to seek possession and this must be set out in a notice served before the proceedings are commenced. Provided the landlord has followed the proper procedure, if the ground is made out, the court must make a possession order subject to any available human rights defences raised by the tenant. See paras 6.95–6.101 for details of the notice and review procedure.

7.52   The ground requires that at least one of five conditions is met and that the landlord has followed the proper procedure. For secure tenants the ground is in section 84A of HA 1985. For assured tenants it is Ground 7A in Schedule 2 of HA 1988. Ground 7A is set out in the appendix to this chapter. The ground under section 84A for secure tenants is in identical terms.

The conditions for the mandatory anti-social behaviour ground

7.53   Conditions 1–3 and 5 are that the tenant, a member of the tenant's household, or a person visiting the property has been:

- convicted of a serious offence (condition 1);
- found by a court to have breached a civil injunction made under the ASBCPA 2014, see below at paras 7.77–7.80 (condition 2);
- convicted for breaching a criminal behaviour order (CBO), see below at para 7.92 (condition 3);
- convicted for breaching a noise abatement notice or order (condition 5).

7.54 For conditions 1, 3 and 5 there must be a conviction (it is not sufficient to have been arrested and/or charged). Furthermore, the offence or conduct constituting the breach must have been committed in, or in the locality of, the property, or have affected a person with a right to live in the locality of the property or have affected the landlord or the landlord's staff or contractors. The relevant 'serious offences' are listed in Schedule 2A to HA 1985 and include violent and sexual offences and those relating to offensive weapons, drugs or damage to property.

7.55 Condition number 4 is:

- the premises have been closed for more than 48 hours under a closure order for anti-social behaviour.

The notice and review procedure for the mandatory anti-social behaviour ground

7.56 **For conditions 1–3 and 5**: 'Notice of Proceedings' must be served on the tenant within 12 months of the relevant conviction or finding of the court (ie of a relevant breach). It there is an appeal, the notice must be served within 12 months of the appeal being finally determined, abandoned or withdrawn.

7.57 **For condition 4 (closure order)**: the notice must be served within three months of the making of the order (or, of any appeal being finally determined, abandoned or withdrawn).

7.58 The minimum period of the notice is four weeks for periodic tenancies and one month for a fixed-term tenancy.

7.59 The notice is similar to a notice served on an introductory or demoted tenancy and must contain the following information:

- the landlord's intention to seek possession under the new absolute ground;
- the reasons why the landlord is seeking possession;
- which of the five conditions the landlord proposes to rely on;
- the relevant conviction, finding of the court, or closure order the landlord proposes to rely on;
- details of the tenant's right to request a review of the landlord's decision, and the time within which the request must be made;[24]
- the date after which a possession claim may be started.

7.60 If the landlord intends to seek possession on one or more of the existing discretionary grounds as well, this must also be specified and

---

24 Note that there is only a *statutory* right of review if the landlord is a local authority.

details given of the relevant ground/s. Only the single notice need be served, see para 6.69.

7.61　These provisions only came into force in October 2014 and, at the time of writing, are only partially in force. It remains to be seen how the ground is used by landlords and how the courts deal with Human Rights Act 1998 defences which are expressly referred to in the grounds.

Discretionary nuisance ground

7.62　The discretionary nuisance ground remains available where the new absolute ground is not made out (and a landlord may rely on both in the same proceedings).

7.63　As for all discretionary possession grounds, when considering a claim for possession the court must first decide whether it is reasonable to make a possession order and, if so, should then consider whether to suspend the order.

7.64　When deciding whether to make a possession order the judge must focus on the effect of the nuisance on others. This is referred to as the 'structured discretion' under which:[25]

> The court must consider, in particular – the effect that the nuisance or annoyance has had on persons other than the person against whom the order is sought; any continuing effect the nuisance or annoyance is likely to have on such persons; the effect that the nuisance or annoyance would be likely to have on such persons if the conduct is repeated.

7.65　Once the court has decided to make a possession order the onus is on the tenant to persuade the court that it is reasonable to suspend the order, not on the landlord to show that is should not be suspended.[26]

7.66　For the court to exercise its discretion to suspend an order '... there must always be a sound basis for the hope that the anti-social behaviour will cease'.[27]

7.67　Paras 7.68–7.75 below summarise some of the principles set out in the cases on nuisance claims decided since 1996. Note that the case-law on nuisance tends to be very 'fact specific'; where a court has made or refused to make a possession order on particular facts may

---

25　See HA 1985 s85A and HA 1988 s9A.
26　See *Birmingham City Council v Ashton* [2012] EWCA Civ 1557, Treacy LJ at [42].
27　Treacy LJ at [30].

not set any kind of precedent. However, the cases do illustrate the way the courts approach claims for possession based on nuisance.

7.68   A serious breach of the tenancy agreement means that a possession order is likely to be made.

> In *Bristol CC v Mousah*[28] a sole tenant was granted a tenancy with an express term that the tenant must not supply controlled drugs from or in the neighbourhood. Within the first nine months of the tenancy the premises were raided by police several times and it was clear that drugs were being sold from the premises. The tenant's evidence was that he had not been present at the time of the raids and had not been aware of what had been going on. He also gave evidence that he had previously received psychiatric treatment. The county court judge found that the tenant had been aware of the drug dealing but declined to make a possession order taking into account his medical circumstances and that he would be unlikely to be housed as a homeless person if evicted.
>
> The Court of Appeal allowed the council's appeal. The proper approach was that where there was a very serious breach of the tenancy agreement, it was reasonable to make a possession order unless there were exceptional circumstances.

However, this does not reverse the burden of proof and a possession order may be suspended even where there has been a serious breach, including possession and supply of drugs.

> In the county court case of *Tai Cymdogaeth Cyfngedig v Griffiths*[29] the landlord tried to appeal against an order suspending possession where the tenant's partner had been convicted four times for possession of Class B drugs and once of possession with intent to supply.
>
> The judge had rejected the landlord's argument that the Court of Appeal's judgment in *Bristol CC v Mousah* meant that where a serious crime was committed, in the absence of exceptional circumstances, a possession order must be made. Most of the

---

28 (1998) 30 HLR 32, CA. For other cases where the Court of Appeal upheld a landlord's appeal against the refusal of a county court judge to make a possession order, see: *Darlington BC v Sterling* (1997) 29 HLR 309, CA; *West Kent Housing Association Ltd v Davies* (1999) 31 HLR 415, CA and *Newcastle upon Tyne CC v Morrison* (2000) 32 HLR 891, CA.

29 February 2003 *Legal Action* 36, Swansea County Court.

convictions were for possession only, the drugs were restricted to Class B, and there was no evidence of users coming to the premises or causing nuisance; there had been no breach of any terms of the tenancy agreement in the 12 months before the hearing. Furthermore, the tenant herself was not involved save to the extent of allowing the premises to be used; the tenant had not breached any other term, had always paid the rent and was was suffering from depression. Her nine-year-old granddaughter lived with her and her partner had left the premises although it was possible that he might return. The Court of Appeal refused the landlord permission to appeal the order which suspended possession for 12 months on condition that the tenant complied with the terms of the tenancy agreement.

7.69　Cases such as *Mousah* and *Griffiths*[30] involved convictions for indictable offences. Now, under ASBCPA 2014 the absolute ground for possession would be available. In such a case the tenants could request a review of the decision to seek possession and put their mitigating arguments forward at the review. But if the landlord confirmed the decision to seek possession, the tenant would have no defence, save under the Human Rights Act. Furthermore, the court would have no power to suspend an order.

7.70　In all cases when the court is being asked to suspend an order the tenant needs to show that there is a real possibility of an improvement in the conduct of the tenant or their family members. Where tenants deny all allegations and only after findings are made against them promise change or offer undertakings, the court is unlikely to suspend an order.

In *Manchester CC v Higgins*[31] a suspended possession order was made against a tenant whose 12-year-old son had been guilty of 'appalling misbehaviour' targetted at a neighbour's disabled sons. An injunction against the tenant had had little effect and an ASBO had been made against her son who was in secure accommodation at the time of the trial. The tenant also had a two-year-old child with serious health problems. The judge found the tenant's evidence was 'inadequate' and that her approach was that if her son told her he

30　See also the more recent case of *London Borough of Barking and Dagenham v Bakare* [2012] EWCA Civ 750, 2 May 2012, at para 7.70.

31　[2005] EWCA Civ 1423, 21 November 2005.

had not done something then he had not done it. Nevertheless, the judge indicated that the family needed support and that it would be wrong to give up on any chance that the tenant's son could make some sort of improvement in his behaviour.

The Court of Appeal upheld the council's appeal against the decision to suspend the order: the judge had failed to take sufficient account of the effect of the behaviour on the neighbours and there was no evidence to support the view that the nuisance may cease. Ward LJ stated:

> Previous unheeded warnings point one way: genuine remorse the other. The level of support available to a parent who is making proper efforts to control an errant child will be relevant. There must, however, always be a sound basis for the hope that the anti-social behaviour will cease.[32]

In *Barking & Dagenham LBC v Bakare*[33] the court refused to suspend an order where the tenant's 19-year-old son had been convicted of several offences concerning the possession and supply of drugs. At a late stage the tenant offered to be bound by a condition that her son be excluded from the block. The judge held that this was 'too little too late' and made an immediate possession order. The Court of Appeal dismissed the tenant's appeal holding that the only issue had been whether or not to suspend the order and that the judge had exercised the discretion on a proper and sound basis.

Leeds & Yorkshire HA v Vertigan[34] did not involve criminal convictions. The tenant was found to have been guilty of repeated breaches of his tenancy agreement over many years. This included sawing through floorboards to gain access to a cellar which was not part of his tenancy, damaging padlocks placed by the landlord, erecting a metal structure outside the flat (which he had refused to dismantle), allowing his dogs to foul the communal areas and refusing to clean it up regularly. The judge refused to suspend a

32 [2005] EWCA Civ 1423, Ward LJ at [37].
33 [2012] EWCA Civ 750, 2 May 2012.
34 [2010] EWCA Civ 1583, 9 December 2010.

possession order to give him the opportunity to remedy the breaches on the basis that his attitude to previous requests for compliance made it unlikely that he would comply. After an immediate order for possession was made he offered undertakings to comply with the terms of a suspended order. The Court of Appeal rejected his appeal against an immediate possession order:

> Those who commit persistent breaches of their tenancy agreements, albeit that the breaches may not individually be serious, must understand that they are at risk of an immediate order for possession in an appropriate case. They should not assume that, because an individual breach is not serious, the outcome will inevitably be a suspended order, however many or repeated breaches.[35]

Other measures

7.71   It is sometimes argued that the availability of other measures to control anti-social behaviour, such as injunctions and ASBOs, means that an outright possession order is not necessary. However, the fact that the behaviour warrants such measures may support the argument that the conduct is so serious that a possession order must be made.

7.72   As was pointed out in *Manchester CC v Higgins*:

> In one case the facts giving rise to the making of an ASBO may be so serious that both the making [of] a possession order and the refusal to suspend it will be self evident. In another case the making of the ASBO may have served its purpose of restraining future misbehaviour so that although past conduct might make it reasonable to order possession yet suspension might be possible.[36]

7.73   In summary, where there is evidence of conduct causing, or likely to cause, significant nuisance and/or repeated breaches of the tenancy agreement, the kinds of exceptional factors that may help avoid an outright order are:

- the person causing the nuisance has left the premises;
- the tenant has shown genuine remorse and a willingness to modify his or her behaviour at an early stage;

---

35   Norris J at [19].
36   [2005] EWCA Civ 1423, Ward LJ at [35]. See para 7.70 above.

- other measures, such as injunctions or ASBOs, have proved effective.

7.74 Tenants accused of nuisance must be realistic about the strength of the evidence relied on by the landlord. If a tenant's defence is that all of the allegations are untrue, if the nuisance is proved it will be very difficult to persuade a court that the tenant is willing to change his or her behaviour and that a possession order should be suspended or postponed.

> In *Canterbury CC v Lowe*[37] the court heard evidence of serious harassment of neighbours, including threats to kill. The judge suspended an order for possession, taking into account the fact that there had been no incidents since injunctions had been granted eight days before the hearing and that the tenant's partner had belatedly indicated that 'common sense should prevail'. The council appealed, seeking an outright order.
>
> The Court of Appeal allowed the council's appeal. The judge had treated compliance with the injunction as decisive rather than one of a number of relevant facts. Given that it had only been in force for eight days, its importance had been overestimated. Also, the statement attributed to the partner had been made in a closing speech by his barrister at a time when he was still denying the harassment. Given the evidence of serious harassment and its impact on the neighbour's family, the only proper conclusion was an outright possession order.

Tenants with mental health problems

7.75 Complaints of nuisance may be made against tenants with mental health problems. In such cases the tenant's health problems will be relevant to whether or not it is reasonable to make an order for possession,[38] as will the effect on neighbours, the tenant's ability to change his or her behaviour and the steps taken by the landlord to support the tenant. Where a tenant causing nuisance is vulnerable it will be particularly important to consider the landlord's policies for dealing with anti-social behaviour.[39] A failure to act in accordance with its

---

37 (2001) 33 HLR 53, CA.
38 See *Croydon LBC v Moody* (1999) 31 HLR 738.
39 Social landlords must publish their policies for dealing with anti-social behaviour: ASBA 2003 s12, see para 6.3.

stated policies and/or to take proper account of the tenant's disability may also amount to disability discrimination and form the basis of a public law defence, see *Barber v Croydon LBC*[40] at para 7.170 below.

Other anti-social behaviour provisions

7.76 Social landlords have other powers to deal with anti-social behaviour, in addition to or as an alternative to claiming possession. The main ones relevant to housing are: anti-social behaviour orders (ASBOs), anti-social behaviour injunctions (ASBIs) and closure orders. The various powers given to local authorities and other social landlords are currently found in a number of difference statutes, mostly introduced since 1996. ASBCPA 2014 will 'streamline' these powers, reducing 19 different powers to six powers. Those relevant to housing management are:

- a **civil injunction** to prevent nuisance and annoyance – this replaces the ASBO and the ASBI;
- an order on conviction to prevent behaviour which causes harassment, alarm or distress: the **criminal behaviour order;**
- **closure of premises** associated with nuisance and annoyance (this will replace the existing power to make closure orders).[41]

Civil injunctions under ASBCPA 2014

7.77 General civil injunctions are available in court proceedings, including possession proceedings. However, the aim of such an injunction is usually to restrain unlawful behaviour or behaviour that is in breach of the tenancy agreement until the final hearing, eg pending a possession order being made. Under the ASBCPA 2014 a civil injunction is a 'stand-alone' remedy and the applicant for such an injunction can be a local council, a local housing provider, the police, Transport for London, the Environment Agency and NHS Protect. There are two types of injunction under the Act, non-housing related and housing related.

7.78 A **non-housing related injunction** is aimed at anti-social behaviour in a public place where the behaviour does not affect the housing management functions of a social landlord or people in their homes.

---

40 [2010] EWCA Civ 51, 11 February 2010.
41 The other three are: the Dispersal Power, the Community Protection Notice and the Public Spaces Protection Order.

Anti-social behaviour means conduct that has caused, or is likely to cause, **harassment, alarm or distress** to any person.[42]

7.79 **A housing related injunction** is where the anti-social behaviour consists of conduct that has caused, or is likely to cause, **nuisance or annoyance** to a person 'in relation to that person's occupation of residential premises, or ... conduct capable of causing housing-related nuisance or annoyance to any person'.[43] Only social landlords, local authorities or the police can apply for such injuctions.

7.80 The injunctions can be made against anyone over the age of 10 provided the court is satisfied, on the balance of probabilities, that it is 'just and convenient' to grant the injunction to prevent the respondent engaging in anti-social behavour (as defined above).[44]

Terms of the injunctions

7.81 Injunctions will include prohibitions to prevent the continued anti-social behaviour. However, they can also include positive requiredments to address the underlying cause of the behaviour, eg to attend alcohol awareness classes, dog training classes or mediation sessions with neighbours or victims.

7.82 Where the anti-social behaviour consists of or includes the use or threatened use of violence against other perons, or there is a significant risk of harm to other persons, the injunction may have the effect of excluding the person from the place he or she nornally lives.[45]

7.83 The statutory guidance states that 'We do not expect the power of exclusion to be used often and the court will pay special attention to proportionality in light of the Article 8 ... implications. As such, applications should only be made for exclusion in extreme cases that meet the higher threshold ... .'[46]

7.84 For adults the injunctions can be for a fixed or indefinite period. For children the maximum term is 12 months.[47]

Urgent cases

7.85 Interim injunctions can be obtained pending a full hearing. They can be obtained 'without notice' (but see para 7.98). 'Without notice'

---

42 ASBCPA 2014 s2(1)(a).
43 ASBCPA 2014 s2(1)(b)–(c).
44 ASBCPA 2014 s1(1)–(3).
45 ASBCPA 2014 s13.
46 *Reform of anti-social behaviour powers – Statutory guidance for frontline professionals*, July 2014, p24, available at www.gov.uk.
47 ASBCPA 2014 s1(6).

injunctions can only include prohibitions and not positive requirements. Applicatons for interim injunctions can be made 'without
notice' in exceptional cases to prevent serious harm to victims.

Power of arrest

7.86   The court can attach a power of arrest to any prohibition or requirement other than a positive requirement (ie participating in some
kind of activity).[48] A power of arrest can only be attached to an order
if the anti-social behaviour which the respondent has engaged in, or
threatens to engage in, consists of or includes the use, or threatened
use, of violence against other persons; or there is a significant risk of
harm to a person from the respondent.

7.87   'Harm' is defined as 'serious ill-treatment or abuse, whether
physical or not',[49] so can include emotional or psychological harm.

7.88   Where a power of arrest is attached a police officer can arrest the
respondent without a warrant if there is reasonable cause to believe
that a breach has occurred. The police must present the respondent
to a court within 24 hours of the arrest (except on a Sunday, Christ-
mas Day or Good Friday).

7.89   It is possible to obtain a power of arrest (or warrant if there is no
power of arrest) by presenting written evidence including hearsay
and professional witness evidence.

7.90   Breach of an injunction is not a criminal offence. It is a contempt
of court, punishable by up to two years imprisonment and/or an
unlimited fine.[50] For children, proceedings for breach will be dealt
with in the youth court and may result in a supervision order with
a supervision, curfew or activity requirement. In the most serious
cases the court may impose a detention order on a young person for
breaching the terms of the injunction, including breaching a positive requirement. However, children aged 13 and younger cannot be
detained for breaching injunction. Only those aged between 14 and
17 years can be detained and then for no longer than three months.
The standard of proof when applying for a penalty to be imposed for
a breach is beyond reasonable doubt.

---

48   ASBCPA 2014 s4(1).

49   ASBCPA 2014 s20.

50   Note that where the court has found that an injunction has been breached this
means that the mandatory anti-social behaviour ground for possession is made
out, see para 7.53 above.

Variation and discharge

7.91 Either party can apply to vary or discharge the order. Variation may include removing or adding a prohibition or positive requirement, reducing or extending the period for which the injunction has effect, or attaching a power of arrest

Criminal behaviour orders

7.92 In addition to civil injunctions, under ASBCPA 2014 the court can also make a criminal behaviour order (CBO).[51] A CBO may be made when the perpetrators of the anti-social behaviour are convicted of a criminal offence. A CBO will also include prohibitions to prevent further anti-social behaviour and can include positive requirements to force an offender to address the underlying causes of the behaviour. Breach of CBO is a criminal offence and the standard of proof to obtain such an order is the criminal standard: beyond reasonable doubt.

Closure power

7.93 The closure power allows the police or local authority to close premises that are being used, or are likely to be used, to commit nuisance and disorder.[52]

7.94 A **closure notice** lasts for up to 48 hours and can be granted if nuisance to the public or disorder near the premises has occurred.

7.95 A **closure order** for up to six months can be granted where there has been disorderly, offensive or criminal behaviour, serious nuisance to the public, or disorder near the premises.

7.96 A closure notice is issued out-of-court initially and thereafter a closure order can be applied for through the courts. The closure notice does not prevent the owner or those who habitually live there from gaining access to the premises. A closure order, in contrast, can restrict all access including by the residents.

7.97 Breach of a closure notice or order are criminal offences (punishable by up to thre months and six months respectively). Appeals can be made by any person on whom the closure notice was served and/or by any person with an interest in the premises. Also, where a local authority or the police issued a notice but a closure order was not made by the court, they may also appeal.

---

51 ASBCPA 2014 s22.
52 ASBCPA 2014 ss76–83.

7.98   Note that the courts should only grant 'without notice' injunctions when absolutely necessary and only to the extent necessary.

In *Moat Housing Group-South Ltd v Harris and Hartless*[53] the Court of Appeal considered the making of an anti-social behaviour injunction (ASBI), an ASBO and an outright possession order (under the pre-ASBCPA powers).

An ASBI with power of arrest had been granted without notice against a tenant with four dependent children. The ASBI required her to vacate her home and excluded her from the neighbourhood. The order was served at 9.00 pm on a Friday evening, three hours after the time specified for compliance with the order. The tenant was able to obtain a stay on the order from the High Court until the matters could be considered at a hearing the following week in the county court.

No previous warnings had been given to the tenant by the landlord about allegations of anti-social behaviour by herself and two of her children. Most of the evidence of anti-social behaviour in the neighbourhood concerned a different family. Notice of seeking possession was subsequently served and at the possession hearing, which took place four weeks after the ASBI had been served, an outright possession order was made together with an ASBO for a period of four years. Much of the evidence presented to the court was hearsay, some from anonymous witnesses.

Considering the granting of the ASBI without notice, the Court of Appeal reiterated the long-standing principle that 'to grant an injunction without notice is to grant an exceptional remedy' and that:

> As a matter of principle no order should be made in civil or family proceedings without notice to the other side unless there is a very good reason for departing from the general rule that notice must be given. Needless to say, the more intrusive the order, the stronger must be the reasons for the departure.[54]

Making an exclusion order without notice was neither proportionate nor necessary to the harm sought to be avoided. The without notice ASBI should have been limited only to that which was necessary, ie an injunction against approaching witnesses. Furthermore, it should not have been made for a period of six months but only until the

53 [2005] EWCA Civ 287, 16 March 2005.
54 [2005] EWCA Civ 287, Brooke LJ at [71] and [63].

further hearing. There was no justification for an ASBO for a four-year period and the judge had failed to consider the alternative of an ordinary injunction or undertakings that could be enforced by committal proceedings. In making the outright possession order the judge had failed to have regard to the needs of the tenant and her family.

The Court of Appeal set aside the ASBO, ordering that an injunction or undertakings should be substituted. Furthermore, the outright possession order was set aside and replaced by an order suspended on terms.

Demotion orders

7.99 The nature of the demoted tenancy is dealt with at paras 3.184–3.190. Only 'social' landlords can apply for the demotion of tenancies.[55]

7.100 The court must not make a demotion order unless it is satisfied that the tenant or a person residing in or visiting the dwelling has engaged or threatened to engage in:

- 'housing-related anti-social conduct'. This means conduct capable of causing nuisance or annoyance to any person and which directly or indirectly relates to or affects the housing management functions of the relevant landlord; or
- conduct which consists of or involves using or threatening to use housing accommodation for an unlawful purpose.[56]

The court must also be satisfied that it is reasonable to make the order.

7.101 A freestanding application for a demotion order is unusual: it is more common for a landlord to apply for a demotion order as an alternative within a claim for possession on the nuisance ground. The court may make a demotion order instead of making a suspended or postponed possession order.

7.102 Where a secure tenancy is demoted it becomes a demoted tenancy, under section 143A of HA 1996. If an assured tenancy is demoted it becomes a demoted assured shorthold tenancy under section 20B of HA 1988.

---

55 This is primarily local authorities and private registered providers of social housing.
56 See HA 1985 s82A, HA 1988 s6A and HA 1996 ss153A and 153B.

7.103   In most cases the terms of the demoted tenancy, including the period of the tenancy, remain the same as prior to demotion. However, if the secure or assured [shorthold] tenancy were for fixed terms (ie flexible tenancies or assured shorthold tenancies for a minimum of two years) on demotion the tenancies become periodic.

Grounds: suitable alternative accommodation

7.104   For regulated tenants and assured tenants the availability of suitable alternative accommodation provides a discretionary ground for possession.[57] For secure tenants there are two classes of grounds under which, in addition to other matters being proved, suitable alternative accommodation must be available to the tenant.

7.105   In all cases, it is sufficient that suitable accommodation will be available for the tenant when the [possession] order takes effect.[58] It is not a refusal of an offer of suitable accommodation that establishes the ground for possession. So, if a tenant has previously refused an offer he or she will not be rendered homeless if a possession order is made on this ground; rather there will be the option of taking up the alternative accommodation. This may be the same accommodation previously offered or different accommodation. A court can make an order that accommodation not yet identified will, in principle, be suitable:

> In *Holt v Reading BC*[59] the Court of Appeal considered an order made against the daughter of a deceased tenant who had succeeded to the tenancy but was under-occupying. The order was made under Ground 16, now 15A, see para 7.118 below. The Court held that: (1) the court must be satisfied that suitable accommodation will be available when the possession order takes effect; (2) there is no requirement that an offer has been made before the date of the hearing or that the accommodation is available at the date of the hearing; (3) however, the court will have to be satisfied on the basis of the evidence presented at the hearing; and (4) there is nothing in the legislation which says that the court must be satisfied that the requirements are met by reference to a particular property.

---

57   RA 1977 s98(1)(a); HA 1988, Ground 9.
58   For regulated and assured, the ground is that suitable accommodation is available for the tenant *or* will be when the order takes effect.
59   [2013] EWCA Civ 641, 7 June 2013.

> Nevertheless, it is important that the court retains the power to scrutinise the suitability of any particular property and to vary or even discharge its order. So, if the court does not make its order on the basis of a particular property available to the tenant, it may either make a conditional possession order or adjourn the final application until a particular property has been identified.

7.106 However, where a tenant unsuccessfully challenges the suitability of the accommodation offered, or to be offered, he or she will usually be ordered to pay the costs of the landlord.

How is suitability assessed?

7.107 Each statute sets out the necessary conditions and the relevant matters to be taken into consideration when assessing suitability.[60]

Private tenants

7.108 A local authority certificate that it will provide suitable alternative accommodation on a specified date is conclusive evidence that suitable alternative accommodation will be available by that date. Such certificates are now rare.

Level of security

7.109 In all cases the alternative accommodation must be let as a separate dwelling. The kind of tenancy offered must be the same kind of tenancy or one with 'equivalent security'.

7.110 For an existing protected or statutory tenant a new protected tenancy may be granted.[61] However, an assured tenancy is capable of offering 'equivalent security' to a protected or statutory tenancy.[62]

7.111 The new protected or assured tenancy cannot be one which would be subject to a mandatory notice ground (see appendix to this chapter) or an assured shorthold tenancy.

Other factors

7.112 The accommodation must be reasonably suitable to the needs of the tenant and the tenant's family in relation to proximity to a workplace.

60 RA 1977 Sch 15 Pt IV, HA 1985 Sch 2 Pt IV and HA 1988 Sch 2 Pt III.
61 HA 1988 s34(1)(c).
62 *Laimond Properties Ltd v Al-Shakarchi* (1998) 30 HLR 1099.

7.113   The accommodation must also be either:

- similar to accommodation let by the local authority to those with similar needs, in terms of the rent and the size of the accommodation; or
- reasonably suitable to the means and needs of the tenant and the tenant's family in terms of the extent and character of the accommodation.

7.114   Accommodation cannot be suitable if it would be statutorily over-crowded.

Secure tenants

7.115   Note that for secure tenants there is no 'free standing' suitable alternative accommodation ground for possession. The condition is one element of several grounds, some of which are discretionary. Most of the grounds are to facilitate development or to ensure that special needs or adapted accommodation is occupied by those who need it. However, for secure tenants, a ground exists for tenancies obtained by succession, where the successor is 'under-occupying'. Until April 2012 this was Ground 16 but is now Ground 15A in England (Ground 16 still applies in Wales). Apart from this ground, which is only available for a limited period after the succession, see below at para 7.120, under-occupation is not a ground for possession.

7.116   In all cases regard must be had to the following factors:

- the nature of the accommodation the landlord normally allocates to persons with similar needs;
- the distance from the places of work or education of the tenant and the tenant's family;
- the distance from the home of any other family members if proximity is 'essential' to the well-being of the tenant or other family member;
- the needs (as regards the extent of accommodation) and means of the tenant and the tenant's family;
- the terms on which the accommodation is available and the terms of the secure tenancy.

Level of security

7.117   In most cases the authority will offer the tenant another secure tenancy. However, it is possible for an assured tenancy (but not one subject to mandatory grounds or a shorthold) to be deemed suitable alternative accommodation.

Ground 15A (under-occupation by successor tenant)

7.118   Note that this ground is not available if the successor was the spouse or civil partner of the deceased tenant.

7.119   Where the landlord is relying on Ground 15A certain additional matters must be taken into account in deciding whether it is reasonable to make an order. These are:

- the tenant's age;
- how long the tenant has occupied the dwelling-house as his or her only or principal home;[63] and
- any financial or other support given by the tenant to the deceased tenant.

7.120   To rely on Ground 15A the authority must serve notice of seeking possession between six and 12 months after the previous tenant's death or, if the court so directs, the date on which, in the opinion of the court, the landlord became aware of the previous tenant's death.[64]

7.121   If the successor tenant accepts suitable alternative accommodation he or she will be treated as a successor in that accommodation, unless the landlord agrees otherwise.

7.122   The date for assessing whether the accommodation is under-occupied is the date of the hearing, not the date of the succession.[65]

Discretionary grounds – reasonableness

7.123   Whenever the court is considering a claim for possession on a discretionary ground the landlord has the burden of proving that:

- the ground is made out; and
- it is reasonable to grant possession.

7.124   The court must always consider whether it is reasonable to grant possession in the particular circumstances. It is for the judge to decide which are the most significant factors:

---

63 See *Bracknell Forest v Green* [2009] EWCA Civ 238, 20 March 2009, in which the court refused to order possession of a three-bedroom house occupied by the adult son and daughter of the deceased tenant. The son who succeeded to the tenancy was 50 years old and had lived in the premises his whole life. The Court of Appeal dismissed the landlord's appeal.

64 The ground was amended to resolve the problem for a landlord where the successor does not inform it of the death of the tenant. See *Newport City Council v Charles* [2008] EWCA Civ 1541, 11 August 2008.

65 *Wandsworth LBC v Randall* [2007] EWCA Civ 1126, 7 November 2007. See also *LB Brent v Tudor* [2013] EWCA Civ 157, 6 March 2013.

The duty of the judge is to take into account all relevant circumstances as they exist at the date of the hearing. That he must do in what I venture to call a broad common-sense way giving weight as he thinks right to the various factors in the situation. Some factors may have little or no weight others may be decisive.[66]

7.125　Although it may suspend or postpone an order for possession, the court must first be satisfied that it is reasonable to make a possession order at all. It must then consider whether it is reasonable to suspend or postpone the order. Because of this requirement, a possession order (whether or not suspended or postponed) cannot be made by consent.[67] If the tenant does not oppose an order he or she must specifically admit all the necessary facts for the court to be satisfied that it is reasonable to grant possession.

7.126　Consideration of an occupier's right to respect for the home under article 8 of the European Convention on Human Rights (ECHR) is part of the overall consideration of the question of whether it is reasonable to make an order.[68]

7.127　Note that when the court is exercising its discretion in relation to the nuisance ground it must take certain specific factors into account, namely the effect of the nuisance on other people (see para 7.64 above).

Public law and article 8 defences

Introduction

7.128　Since 1997 legislative developments have led to increasing numbers of people in social housing having no substantive security of tenure. The Housing Act 1996 reformulated the accommodation duty to the homeless: the 'full housing duty' became a duty to secure temporary accommodation pending the allocation of a long-term tenancy through the authority's allocation scheme. Homeless applicants may remain for many years non-secure tenants, assured shorthold tenants or, in some cases licensees. At the same time measures aimed at combatting anti-social behaviour included the creation of new kinds of tenancies with limited security: principally the introductory

---

66　Lord Greene MR in *Cumming v Danson* [1942] 2 All ER 653 at 655.
67　See *Plaschkes v Jones* (1983) 9 HLR 110; *R v Bloomsbury & Marylebone County Court ex p Blackburne* (1985) 14 HLR 56; *Wandsworth LBC v Fadayomi* (1987) 19 HLR 512; and *Baygreen Properties v Gill* [2002] EWCA Civ 1340, 5 July 2002.
68　*Gallagher v Castle Vale Action Trust Ltd* [2001] EWCA Civ 944, 23 February 2001.

tenancy and the demoted tenancy (see paras 3.168 and 3.184). In all these cases when a landlord wants possession no statutory 'ground' is needed and there is no requirement that it is 'reasonable' to make an order for possession.

7.129 The Human Rights Act 1998 came into force in October 2000 and incorporated European Convention on Human Rights (ECHR) rights into domestic law (see para 2.40). Previously, an occupier relying on Convention rights had to apply to the European Court of Human Rights (ECtHR)to assert a breach. However, since October 2000 the UK courts must take account of ECtHR decisions when considering Convention rights. The key issue in housing law has been the extent to which an occupier with no security of tenure could resist a claim for possession by relying on article 8 of ECHR.

7.130 The way the law developed has been described as 'ping pong';[69] with the same issues, and sometimes the same cases, going back and forth between the UK appeal courts and the ECtHR. However, by 2011 certain principles were established and these were set out by the Supreme Court in *Hounslow LBC v Powell; Leeds CC v Hall; Birimingham CC v Frisby*.[70] This section summarises those principles, considers some recent cases and offers some practical tips for occupiers without security of tenure.

7.131 The same developments in relation to tenants' rights also led to the appeal courts considering the closely related issue of 'public law defences' to possession claims. Previous case-law had suggested that public law arguments in possession claims should generally be raised by way of judicial review and could not form the basis of a defence in the county court. However, this is no longer the case.

7.132 The following principles are now established:

- Public law and 'human rights' defences can be raised in the county court in response to claims for possession by public bodies.
- This is the case even where statute expressly limits the powers of the court.
- The county court must, in principle, be able to review the 'proportionality' of an eviction under article 8 but only in exceptional cases will 'proportionality defences' be arguable.
- The personal circumstances of the occupier can be considered by the court when considering proportionality and may be relevant to a public law defence.

---

69 Nic Madge, 'La Lutta Continua' [2009] JHL 43.
70 [2011] UKSC 8, 23 February 2011.

- Where, under domestic law, an occupier has no security of tenure it will be assumed that the public body/landlord is pursuing a legitimate aim in seeking to evict the occupier.
- The burden is on the occupier to show that an eviction would be a disproportionate interference with the his or her rights under article 8 or unlawful on public law grounds.

Human rights defences and public law defences: what is the difference?

7.133 A public law defence is one alleging that the decision to bring and/or pursue the claim for possession is unlawful on established public law principles. These principles are summarised in paras 2.4–2.25. Such a defence focuses on the conduct of the public body rather than the effect of an eviction on the occupier. However, the personal circumstances of the occupier may be relevant, provided the public body is made aware of them.

7.134 An article 8 or 'proportionality' defence is one in which it is argued that an eviction is not a necessary measure in pursuance of one of the legitimate aims set out in article 8(2). In other words, that evicting the occupier would be disproportionate to the aims pursued. Whether or not the eviction is proportionate depends on balancing the aim pursued by the landlord against the effect of the eviction on the particular occupier. So the occupier's personal circumstances will always be relevant. And, in raising such a defence, the occupier is asking the court to review the proportionality of the eviction, ie to carry out that balancing exercise for itself, not confine itself to considering the lawfulness of the landlord's decision-making, as in a public law defence.

Public law and human rights arguments in the county court

7.135 It was established some time ago that a public law defence can in certain circumstances be brought in the county court. In *Wandsworth LBC v Winder*[71] the House of Lords held that a tenant who argued that the council had acted unlawfully when increasing council rents

---

71 *Wandsworth LBC v Winder (No 1)* [1984] UKHL 2. Note that although Mr Winder established the right to raise his defence in the county court, the defence was ultimately unsuccessful: *Wandsworth LBC v Winder (No 2)* (1988) 20 HLR 400.

could defend a claim for possession on that basis and could do so in the county court. The lawfulness of the rent increase was crucial to whether the ground for possession was made out. In such a case it was not an abuse of process to raise a public law argument by way of a defence, rather than by bringing a claim for judicial review.

7.136　Even after the decision in *Wandsworth v Winder* the more common practice, where a tenant challenged the decision to evict on public law grounds, was to adjourn the possession claim to enable the tenant to bring a claim for judicial review in the Administrative Court. In *Buscott & others v Avon County Council*[72] the Court of Appeal held that where the challenge to the decision was that it was 'Wednesbury unreasonable', the correct procedure was to bring the challenge by way of judicial review. *Wandsworth v Winder* was distinguished on the basis that Mr Winder's defence challenged the merits of the claim for possession and related to his private law rights, ie whether or not he was in arrears of rent.

7.137　In several early cases where introductory and demoted tenants sought to resist possession on public law grounds the Court of Appeal held that the correct procedure was for the court to adjourn the possession claims to enable the tenants to bring judicial review claims. This was because the relevant statutory regimes purported to limit the county court's powers to a consideration of whether the notice and review procedure had been followed by the landlord.[73]

7.138　However, the Supreme Court subsequently held that this approach failed to offer the procedural safeguards necessary to meet the requirements of article 8. Article 8 is engaged whenever the court is considering a claim for possession of a person's home and it is essential when article 8 is engaged that there is the *possibility* of an independent and impartial review of the decision to evict. This must encompass not only challenges on points of law but also disputed issues of fact.[74] Furthermore, the extent of this review is 'is best left to the good sense and experience of judges sitting in the county court'.[75]

72　[1988] QB 656.

73　See *Manchester CC v Cochrane* [1999] 1 WLR 809, CA; *McLellan v Bracknell Forest BC* [2001] EWCA Civ 1510 and *R (Gilboy) v Liverpool CC* [2008] EWCA Civ 751.

74　See the House of Lords/Supreme Court decisions in *Kay v Lambeth LBC and Leeds CC v Price* [2006] UKHL 10, 8 March 2006; *Doherty v Birmingham* [2008] UKHL 57, 30 July 2008; *Manchester CC v Pinnock* [2010] UKSC 45, 3 November 2010 and *Hounslow LBC v Powell* [2011] UKSC 8, 23 February 2011. However, how the court should deal with disputed issues of fact is still not entirely clear: see Lord Hope at [37] contrasted with Lord Phillips at [93] in *Hounslow LBC v Powell* [2011] UKSC 8, 23 February 2011.

75　*Manchester CC v Pinnock* [2010] UKSC 45, Lord Neuberger at 57.

7.139   So, reflecting the decisions of the ECtHR,[76] the Supreme Court has held that it is no longer necessary to adjourn a claim for possession and bring a claim for judicial review: the county court must consider a defence founded on public law or proportionality ground.

Public law defences

7.140   The principles of public law are described at paras 2.4–2.25. Essentially, a public body landlord must act lawfully, which means:

- in accordance with the law/legally;
- fairly; and
- reasonably.

Legality

7.141   Public bodies are creatures of statute and must act in accordance with the purpose of the legislation under which they exercise their powers. When exercising their public functions, including the allocation and management of social housing, they must also act in accordance with statutory guidance and other legislation, such as the Equality Act 2010 (see paras 2.84–2.92 and 7.183–7.201).

7.142   If a public body fails to take account of relevant matters (including its statutory duties as a public body) when making a decision, this may render the decision unlawful. See, for example, *Pieretti v Enfield LBC*[77], at para 2.90. In addition, public bodies should act in accordance with their own stated policies.

Fairness

7.143   Procedural fairness usually requires a public body to give notice of any adverse information taken into account when making a decision and to give the person affected the opportunity to comment. Furthermore, it must comply with any statutory procedural requirements (eg the conduct of reviews of decisions to seek possession) and act in accordance with its own published polices. It may also be bound to act in accordance with its established practice and, if it proposes to depart from its policies or practices, to consult those affected before doing so.[78]

---

76 See *Connors v UK* App No 66746/01, 27 May 2004; *McCann v UK* App No 19009/04, 13 May 2008 and *Kay v UK* App No 37341/06, 21 September 2010.
77 [2010] EWCA Civ 1104.
78 This is known as 'legitimate expectation', see para 2.23.

Reasonableness

7.144   It is generally very difficult to challenge a public body decision on the grounds that the decision is 'unreasonable'. 'Traditional' public law defines unreasonableness as 'perversity', or 'irrationality'. The *Wednesbury*[79] test suggests that only a decision that 'no reasonable decision-maker could reach' is capable of being unlawful on this ground.

7.145   However, one effect of the HRA 1998 is that the concept of 'reasonableness' is applied in a more flexible way, depending on the nature of the rights at issue. Where fundamental rights are at stake the courts will apply 'anxious scrutiny' of decisions, whereas in the sphere of economic rights the courts will be less willing to intervene. Furthermore, article 6 of ECHR requires an independent and impartial review in the determination of a person's civil rights. This means that in some circumstances the court's review must extend to issues of fact and cannot be restricted to issues of law.[80]

Article 8 defences

7.146   Article 8 of the ECHR provides:

1)   Everyone has the right to respect for his private and family life, his home and his correspondence.
2)   There shall be no interference by a public authority with the exercise of this right except such as is in accordance with the law and is necessary in a democratic society in the interests of national security, public safety or the economic well-being of the country, for the prevention of disorder or crime, for the protection of health or morals, or for the protection of the rights and freedoms of others.

7.147   To succeed in an article 8 defence, the following must be established:

- the premises are the occupier's 'home';
- the decision to evict is an interference with the occupier's right to respect for his or her home; and
- the interference is either not in accordance with the law or is not necessary in pursuance of one of the interests set out in article 8(2), ie is disproportionate to the legitimate aims.

---

79   *Associated Provincial Picture Houses Ltd v Wednesbury Corporation* [1948] 1 KB 223, CA. See paras 2.15–2.17.

80   See Lord Hope at [110] in *Kay v Lambeth LBC and Leeds CC v Price* [2006] UKHL 10, and later when reviewing the scope of the conventional public law challenge in *Doherty v Birmingham* [2008] UKHL 57 at [55] and again at [7] in *Hounslow v Powell* [2011] UKSC 8.

The 'home'

7.148   This is a question of fact and does not depend on a legal right of occupation. The ECtHR has held: 'Whether or not a particular habitation constitutes a "home" which attracts the protection of article 8(1) will depend on the factual circumstances, namely, the existence of sufficient and continuous links with a specific place.'[81] A man who was technically a trespasser following service of a notice to quit by his ex-wife who was a joint tenant was held to be occupying as his home.[82] However, where a family had occupied a traveller's site for only two days before proceedings were issued the House of Lords held that it was 'all but unarguable that [the land on which they parked their caravans] was ever their home within the meaning of article 8(1)'.[83] Nevertheless, the Supreme Court has held that 'in most cases it can be taken for granted that a claim by a person who is in lawful occupation to remain in possession will attract the protection of article 8'.[84]

Interference

7.149   Article 8 is a qualified right: interference may be justified if it is in accordance with the law and is necessary in a democratic society in pursuance of the legitimate interests set out in article 8(2).

7.150   To evict a person from his or her home will always involve an interference with rights under article 8. 'Loss of one's home is a most extreme form of interference with the right to respect for the home'.[85]

7.151   However, when the court is considering the eviction of an occupier with no security of tenure, the starting point is that the interference is assumed to be lawful and necessary:

> The legislature has excluded [certain] types of tenancy from the statutory scheme which applies to secure tenancies for very good reasons, which are firmly rooted in social policy. In seeking democratic solutions to the problems inherent in the allocation of social housing, Parliament has sought to strike a balance between the rights of the occupier and the property rights and public responsibilities of the public authority.[86]

---

81   *Kryvitska v Ukraine* ECtHR App No 30856/03, 9 November 2010 at [40].
82   *Harrow LBC v Qazi* [2003] UKHL 43, 31 July 2003.
83   *Leeds CC v Price* [2006] UKHL 10, 8 March 2006, Lord Bingham at [48].
84   *Hounslow LBC v Powell* [2011] UKSC 8, 23 February 2011, Lord Hope at [33].
85   *Kryvitska v Ukraine* ECtHR App No 30856/03, 9 November 2010 at [41]. See also, *McCann v UK* ECtHR App No 19009/04 at [50].
86   *Hounslow v Powell* [2011] UKSC 8, 23 February 2011, Lord Hope at [10].

7.152 If an occupier is arguing that the legislation itself breaches his or her article 8 rights and cannot be read in a way that is compatible with those rights, the courts can make a declaration of incompatibility (see para 2.77). However, the following regimes relating to housing rights have been held to be compatible with the Convention:

- the use of non-secure tenancies for homeless applicants accommodated by local authorities;[87]
- the use of assured shorthold tenancies, and the section 21 notice procedure, for homeless applicants accommodated by social landlords;[88]
- the introductory tenancy regime;[89]
- the rules allowing the issuing of warrants without a hearing following a possession order;[90]
- the provisions restricting those members of the family entitled to succeed to a secure tenancy.[91]

The margin of appreciation

7.153 The cases referred to at para 7.152 above illustrate what is called the 'margin of appreciation'. As the ECtHR held in *Kay v UK*:

> In making their initial assessment of the necessity of the measure, the national authorities enjoy a margin of appreciation in recognition of the fact that they are better placed than international courts to evaluate local needs and conditions.[92]

7.154 And in *Connors v UK*:

> The margin will tend to be narrower where the right at stake is crucial to the individual's effective enjoyment of intimate or key rights ... On the other hand, in spheres involving the application of social or economic policies, there is authority that the margin of appreciation is wide ...[93]

7.155 As Lord Hope said in *Powell*:

> There are clear policy reasons why Parliament has denied security to certain classes of occupier.[94]

87 *Sheffield CC v Smart, Central Sunderland Housing Co Ltd v Wilson* [2002] EWCA Civ 4.
88 *Poplar Housing v Donaghue* [2001] EWCA Civ 595, see para 2.72.
89 *McLellan v Bracknell Forest* [2001] EWCA Civ 1510 and *Merton LBC v Williams* [2002] EWCA Civ 980.
90 *Sheffield CC v Hopkins* [2001] EWCA Civ 1023.
91 *Michalak v Wandsworth LBC* [2002] EWCA Civ 271.
92 ECtHR App No 37341/06, 21 September 2010 at [66].
93 ECtHR App No 66746/01, 27 May 2004 at [82].
94 *Hounslow LBC v Powell* [2011] UKSC 8, 23 February 2011 at [10].

Article 8 defences: summary of key principles

7.156   In the case of *Southend-on-Sea v Armour,* below at para 7.162, the Court of Appeal summarised the principles applicable to article 8 defences as follows:[95]

> (i) It is a defence to a claim by a local authority for possession of a defendant's home that the recovery of possession is not necessary in a democratic society within article 8 (2), that is to say it would be disproportionate in all the circumstances. An order for possession in such a case would be an infringement of the defendant's rights under article 8 to respect for his or her home and so unlawful within the Human Rights Act 1998 section 6(1).
>
> (ii) The test is whether the eviction is a proportionate means of achieving a legitimate aim.
>
> (iii) The threshold for establishing an arguable case that a local authority is acting disproportionately and so in breach of article 8 where repossession would otherwise be lawful is a high one and will be met in only a small proportion of cases.
>
> (iv) The reasons why the threshold is so high lie in the public policy and public benefit inherent in the functions of a local authority in dealing with its housing stock, a precious and limited public resource. Local authorities, like other social landlords, hold their housing stock for the benefit of the whole community and they are best equipped, certainly better equipped than the courts, to make management decisions about the way such stock should be administered.
>
> (v) That is why the fact that a local authority has a legal right to possession, aside from article 8, and is to be assumed to be acting in accordance with its duties (in the absence of cogent evidence to the contrary), will be a strong factor in support of the proportionality of making an order for possession without the need for explanation or justification by the local authority.
>
> (vi) An article 8 defence on the grounds of lack of proportionality must be pleaded and sufficiently particularised to show that it reaches the high threshold of being seriously arguable.
>
> (vii) Unless there is some good reason not to do so, the court must at the earliest opportunity summarily consider whether the article 8 defence, as pleaded, and on the assumption that the pleaded facts relied upon are correct, reaches that threshold.
>
> (viii) Even where an article 8 defence is established, in a case where the defendant would otherwise have no legal right to remain in the property, it is difficult to imagine circumstances in which the defence

---

95 [2014] EWCA Civ 231, 12 March 2014. Lewison LJ at [14], summarising the judgment of Etherton LJ in the earlier case of *Thurrock BC v West* [2012] EWCA Civ 1435, 8 November 2012.

could operate to give the defendant an unlimited and unconditional right to remain.

Exceptionality

7.157 The courts have repeatedly stressed that it will only be in highly exceptional cases that a proportionality defence will be arguable where, under domestic law, the occupier has no right to remain in occupation. However, this does not mean that that proportionality arguments should be limited to 'very highly exceptional cases'. In *Pinnock* it was held that it would be:

> ... both unsafe and unhelpful to invoke exceptionality as a guide ... exceptionality is an outcome and not a guide. ... The question is always whether the eviction is a proportionate means of achieving a legitimate aim ... in virtually every case where a residential occupier has no contractual or statutory protection, and the local authority is entitled to possession as a matter of domestic law, there will be a very strong case for saying that making an order for possession would be proportionate. However, in some cases there may be factors which would tell the other way.[96]

What this means is that a case does not necessarily have to have highly exceptional features to be arguable but that the cases in which an eviction is disproportionate are likely to be highly exceptional.

The personal circumstance of the tenants/vulnerability

7.158 Whenever a court is considering whether an eviction is proportionate it must balance the legitimate aims being pursued by the public body landlord with the effect of the eviction on the occupier. This necessarily involves considering the personal circumstances of the occupier: the harsher the effect of an eviction, the more likely it is to be disproportionate. However, there is a limit to the extent of the consideration:

> The court need be concerned only with the occupiers' personal circumstances and any factual objection she may raise and, in the light only of what view it takes of them, with the question whether making the order for possession would be lawful and proportionate.[97]

7.159 But, as the Supreme Court made clear in *Pinnock* (approving the submissions made by the Equalities and Human Rights Commission):

---

96 *Manchester CC v Pinnock* [2010] UKSC 45, 3 November 2010, Lord Neuberger at [51], [52] and [54].
97 *Hounslow LBC v Powell* [2011] UKSC 8, 23 February 2011, Lord Hope at [37].

... proportionality is more likely to be a relevant issue 'in respect of occupants who are vulnerable as a result of mental illness, physical or learning disability, poor health or frailty' and that 'the issue may also require the local authority to explain why they are not securing alternative accommodation in such cases.[98]

Note that where the tenant is alleging that the eviction constitutes disability discrimination the presumption that the defence should be dealt with on a summary basis does not apply. And the proportionality review places a greater burden on the landlord to justify the eviction: see *Akerman-Livingstone* at para 7.190.

Examples of article 8 defences

7.160　In most of the reported cases the article 8 defences have not succeeded on the facts. However, what the reported cases do not reflect is how often a pubic body may be persuaded to change a decision or to 'give the tenant another chance' when faced with representations based on article 8.

7.161　Usually, a defence will raise both article 8 and conventional public law grounds and in most of the cases it has been the conventional public law defence that has succeeded.[99]

7.162　However, in *Southend-on-Sea BC v Armour*[100] the Court of Appeal upheld a decision to dismiss a claim for possession on proportionality grounds alone:

> Mr Armour had an introductory tenancy which commenced on 31 January 2011. Shortly after the tenancy started there were three complaints about anti-social behaviour and notice of possession was served with a review taking place on 21 April 2011. The review decision was to dismiss Mr Armour's appeal and a possession claim was commenced on 7 June 2011. Various procedural delays meant the matter was not tried until 2 March 2012. By the time of the trial there was evidence that Mr Armour lacked capacity to conduct the litigation, having been diagnosed with depression and

98　*Manchester CC v Pinnock* [2010] UKSC 45, 3 November 2010, Lord Neuberger at [64].

99　See *Croydon v Barber* and *McGlynn v Welwyn Hatfield DC* (see para 7.115). However, these cases were decided before the Supreme Court made clear that the county court could conduct a proportionality review and would most likely have succeeded if argued on the ground that the eviction was disproportionate under article 8.

100　[2014] EWCA Civ 231, 12 March 2014.

Asperger's syndrome. However, his previous conduct had not been attributable to those conditions. The main factor was that despite his mental health problems he had kept to the terms of his tenancy for nearly a year. There had been no complaints of anti-social behaviour after the service of the possession notice. The judge observed that he would still be at risk of eviction if there was any repetition of the anti-social behaviour and that his desire to keep the tenancy was supported by his probation officer, community worker and other members of his family. She held that the council's decision to initiate possession proceedings had been a reasonable decision and that if the case had been heard on the date it was issued, Mr Armour would have had no defence. However, the issue of proportionality must be determined at the date of trial. She held that a possession order was no longer proportionate and dismissed the claim. This had the effect of making Mr Armour a secure tenant.

The council appealed unsuccessfully to the High Court and then to the Court of Appeal. The council argued that a tenant complying with the terms of the tenancy could not amount to the kind of exceptional circumstances that would justify a successful article 8 defence: compliance should be regarded as the norm, not the exception.

The Court of Appeal dismissed the appeal: an improvement in the tenant's behaviour is capable of being a factor in deciding whether a possession order is disproportionate and the weight to be given to that factor is a matter for the judge. She was entitled to conclude that by the date of the trial, a possession order was disproportionate.

> The question is not whether the circumstances are exceptional because as the Supreme Court pointed out in *Pinnock* exceptionality is an outcome rather than a test. Where, as here, the tenant under an introductory tenancy gets off to a shaky start, but mends his ways for almost all of the one-year period, I consider that that improvement in behaviour is capable of being a factor in deciding whether it is disproportionate for the landlord to continue to insist on recovering possession.[101]

The significance of the case is that an eviction may be dispropor-tionate at the date of trial because of an improvement in the ten-ant's behaviour, even where the landlord could not be criticised for issuing the claim. This makes clear the difference between a public

101 Lewison LJ at [30].

law defence and the proportionality review. However, the grounds for the proportionality defence must be set out at an early stage and should be dealt with on a summary basis, see above at para 7.156. So, opportunities to use any delay between issue and trial to improve the tenant's position will be limited.

Unsuccessful article 8 defences

7.163   Note that in *Manchester CC v Pinnock* and *Birmingham CC v Frisby*, the Supreme Court held that on the facts the decisions to evict had been proportionate. In *Hounslow LBC v Powell* the court held that there might have been grounds to remit the case for consideration by the county court for a proportionality review but this was not necessary as an offer of alternative accommodation had been made. And in *Leeds CC v Hall* it was held that no grounds had been put before the court to suggest that Mr Hall had a seriously arguable defence. However, as he too had been offered a secure tenancy by Leeds CC, the appeal was upheld and the possession order set aside.

7.164   In a recent series of cases the Court of Appeal has not only rejected proportionality defences but also criticised the county court judges for not dealing with the issue at an early stage on a summary basis.[102]

> In *Thurrock v West*[103] the claim for possession was against a man whose grandparents had been the joint tenants of a three bedroom house. He had lived with them since 2007 but had no right to succeed to the tenancy. After they had both died the council sought possession and he defended the claim on article 8 grounds. By the date of the proceedings he, his partner and young son were living in the house and they argued that it was ideal for them in terms of location, family ties and local employment. As they were on a low income they could not afford to rent or buy privately so would have to apply as homeless if evicted.
>   The claim was allocated to the multi-track but in fact the hearing was short and evidence was by way of written statements. The judge declined to make an order for possession holding that it would be

---

102   See for example: *Corby BC v Scott and West Kent HA v Haycraft* [2012] EWCA Civ 276, 13 March 2012; *Birmingham CC v Lloyd* [2012] EWCA Civ 969, 4 July 2012; and *Fareham BC v Miller* [2013] EWCA Civ 159, 6 March 2012.

103   [2012] EWCA Civ 1435, 8 November 2012.

disproportionate to evict a family with a young child who then may have to be re-housed in a property that is one bedroom smaller. The Court of Appeal upheld the council's appeal. Having set out the principles to be applied in relation to article 8 defences, (adopted in *Armour* and set out above, at para 7.156) it was held:

Having regard to the above principles it is quite clear that the Article 8 defence in the present case, as pleaded, does not even reach the threshold of being reasonably arguable. The defence should have been struck out summarily at the earliest opportunity.[104]

The burden is on the occupier

7.165 The courts have consistently held that the burden is on the occupier to establish that an eviction would be disproportionate:

The basic rules are now not in doubt. The court will only have to consider whether the making of a possession order is proportionate if the issue has been raised by the occupier and it has crossed the high threshold of being seriously arguable.[105]

7.166 When a landlord is seeking possession against an occupier with no security of tenure, the presumption is that the landlord is acting lawfully and that the decision to evict is proportionate. As stated in *Pinnock*:

... in virtually every case where a residential occupier has no contractual or statutory protection, and the local authority is entitled to possession as a matter of domestic law, there will be a very strong case for saying that making an order for possession would be proportionate. However, in some cases there may be factors which would tell the other way.[106]

So, the occupier must prove the presumption wrong; it is not for the landlord to prove that the eviction is proportionate.

7.167 However, although the burden is not on the landlord in every case to 'justify its application for a possession order or to plead the reason for seeking this', in most cases when a public body landlord is seeking to evict a tenant with no security of tenure 'the tenant must be informed of the reason for the authority's action so that he

---

104 Etherton LJ at [32].

105 *Hounslow LBC v Powell* [2011] UKSC 8, 23 February 2011, Lord Hope at [33].

106 [2010] UKSC 45, 3 November 2010, Lord Neuberger at [62].

can, if so minded, attempt to raise a proportionality challenge'.[107] For introductory and demoted tenants notice must be served giving reasons but in relation to other non-secure tenancies there is no such requirement.[108] In *Powell* the court declined to indicate whether reasons should be given before the service of a notice to quit suggesting that any procedural requirements were best set out in a practice direction.[109]

When must an article 8 defence be made?

7.168   Within a possession claim, the occupier must put forward the particulars of the article 8 defence at an early stage. However, the question arises: can the occupier rely on article 8 after a possession order has been made but before an eviction?

> In *R (JL)v Secretary of State for Defence*[110] the Court of Appeal considered a most unusual situation: in 2007 the ocupiers had tried to defend a claim for possession relying on article 8. The claim was transferred to the Administrative Court. The court held that the state of the law was such that an article 8 defence could not defeat an unqualified right of possession, even where the owner was a public body. By the time the possession order came to be enforced, the case of *Pinnock*, see para 7.138 above, had been decided. The occupiers sought judicial review of the decision to evict but the claim was dismissed, with the judge holding that the enforcement of the possession order was not disproportionate. On the issue of whether article 8 could be relied on at the enforcement stage, the Court of Appeal held that:
>
> > In the overwhelming majority of cases the occupant's article 8 rights will be appropriately and sufficiently respected by the provision at the occupant's request of a proportionality review during the possession proceedings themselves, and usually at the hearing of them. ... The court hearing the possession proceedings is not obliged to conduct a proportionality review of its own motion. It must do so if, but only if, that review is requested by

---

107 *Hounslow LBC v Powell* [2011] UKSC 8, 23 February 2011, Lord Phillips at [116].

108 And for demoted assured shorthold tenancies there is no such requirement. See paras 6.106–6.107.

109 See *Hounslow LBC v Powell* [2011] UKSC 8, 23 February 2011 at [117].

110 [2013] EWCA Civ 449, 30 April 2013.

> the occupant, by the raising of an article 8 defence. ... Generally, an attempt to re-litigate the article 8 issue at the enforcement stage, or to litigate it for the first time when it could and should have been raised at the defence in the possession proceedings, would have been an abuse of process by the occupant. ... But there will be exceptional cases, and the present is a very unusual but powerful example, where the raising of article 8 rights at the enforcement stage will not be an abuse. ... It follows that the judge was correct in the wholly exceptional circumstances of the present case, to accede to the appellant's request to conduct a proportionality review of the requested eviction, even though it will be a very rare case where it is appropriate to do so at the enforcement stage.[111]
>
> Nevertheless, the Court of Appeal dismissed the occupiers' appeal against the judge's finding that the eviction was not disproportionate.

7.169 In the case of *Lawal v Circle 33 Housing Trust*[112] the Court of Appeal rejected an appeal by occupiers who had been litigants in person at the relevant possession hearing. However, the complicated procedural history of the case meant that a challenge to the proportionality of the eviction had in fact been considered by a judge and rejected. It remains to be seen whether a case where the occupiers are legally advised for the first time at the enforcement stage can succeed in arguing that it would not be an abuse of process to ask the court to conduct a proportionality review when considering the execution of the warrant.

Examples of successful public law defences

7.170 As indicated above, examples of successful defences based solely on proportionality are few. However, there is usually an overlap between the proportionality issue and the lawfulness of the public body's conduct on 'traditional' public law grounds. In the following cases the public law challenge was successful.

---

111 Briggs LJ at [39]-[41] and [45].
112 [2014] EWCA Civ 1514, 24 November 2014.

In *Barber v Croydon LBC*[113] a non-secure tenant appealed against a possession order. The tenant had been accommodated as a homeless applicant. He had learning difficulties and a personality disorder and it was accepted that he was a disabled person within the meaning of the Disability Discrimination Act 1995. It was alleged that he had sworn at, spat at and kicked the caretaker of his block of flats. He denied spitting or assaulting the caretaker but admitted there had been an argument and he subsequently accepted a police caution for a public order act offence (causing harassment, alarm or distress by the use of threatening and abusive language). The council started possession proceedings. Medical evidence about his disability and the likely effect of an eviction was submitted. The council considered the evidence but decided to proceed with the eviction.

The Court of Appeal found that the council had failed to follow its own anti-social behaviour policy which stressed the need to work in partnership with other agencies when dealing with vulnerable persons and to seek alternatives to eviction. The council had also failed to give due weight to the psychiatrist's report and its decision to evict was one that no housing authority, faced with these facts, could reasonably have taken.

A similar decision was taken in relation to an assured shorthold 'starter' tenant who fell into rent arrears. In *Eastlands Homes Partnership Ltd v Sandra Whyte*[114] the tenancy agreement provided that after one year the tenancy would convert into an assured tenancy as long as certain events had not happened, including possession proceedings being brought. Because of rent arrears, a further starter tenancy was entered into but the landlords subsequently decided not to offer an assured tenancy and to proceed with an eviction. The landlords operated an appeals process in relation to such decisions.

The court found that the landlords had not followed their own appeals procedure properly and had acted unfairly in the way the appeal was conducted. Furthermore, they had failed to adhere to their own rent arrears policy which stated that eviction would be treated 'as a last resort when clear and deliberate failure to pay is

113 [2010] EWCA Civ 51, 11 February 2010. See also the similar case of *McGlynn v Welwyn Hatfield DC* [2009] EWCA Civ 285, 1 April 2009.
114 [2010] EWHC 695 (QB), 31 March 2010.

apparent'. Taking those failings into account, the court concluded that the decision was one that no reasonable authority could have reached and dismissed the claim for possession. Since the landlords' policy was that assured shorthold tenancies became full assured tenancies after one year, the effect of the court's decision was that Ms Whyte was an assured tenant.

7.171   In an unusual decision concerning a family living in a house they could not succeed to, the Court of Appeal found that the local authority had acted unlawfully in failing to consider whether the property could be allocated to them under the allocation scheme:

In *Leicester CC v Shearer*[115] a family was occupying a property they had no right to succeed to. Ms Shearer had suffered from domestic violence and her husband had committed suicide. She was left to care for their two young daughters. She and the daughters were living in the house which had been her late husband's tenancy by succession and were awaiting an allocation of accommodation. They argued that they should be allowed to remain in the accommodation they were occupying. The council sought possession on the basis that Ms Shearer was a trespasser. The defence did rely on article 8 but was principally a public law defence: that the decision to evict was flawed because the council had not properly considered the possibility of allocating of the property by way of a direct let under their allocations policy. The judge found that because Ms Shearer had never been a tenant and did not have the council's permission to live in the property, she could not establish an article 8 defence. However, the council had failed to consider the option of a direct let. The council argued at the trial that because Ms Shearer had not provided the evidence required to support a direct let, they could not consider it. However, although they had asked for certain evidence to be provided, they had led Ms Shearer to believe that a direct let of the accommodation was impossible. They then relied on her failure to provide the evidence to justify not considering this option. The judge refused to make a possession order and the council appealed. The council argued that despite the misleading information, which was the result of Ms Shearer dealing with two different departments, if she had persevered she would have received correct advice from the Housing Options Department regarding the need for evidence

115 [2013] EWCA Civ 1467, 19 November 2013.

to support the application for a direct let. The Court of Appeal dealt with this as follows:

> I am afraid this will not do. The defendant was a vulnerable person who has suffered much during her adult life. I need not recount the details. The culmination of her troubles was the suicide of her husband. The defendant found the body after he had hanged himself. The defendant was living on benefits and bringing up two young children as a single mother with, it would seem, little outside help. The defendant cannot be expected to appreciate that one housing department of the Council was giving her wrong advice, but that another housing department of the same council might give her different and correct advice.[116]

The council's appeal was dismissed. However, although the family's circumstances were compassionate, this was a case decided on public law grounds, not under article 8. The council had acted unlawfully in failing to properly consider a direct let: had they not informed her this was impossible, Ms Shearer would have submitted the necessary evidence and a direct let may have been agreed.

The above cases illustrate the nature of 'public law' defences, as distinct from article 8 defences: the focus is on the landlord's failure to act lawfully on traditional 'public law' grounds.

7.172   The failure of a public body to follow its own policies may also be relevant when seeking to avoid eviction *after* the making of a possession order. In *Southwark LBC v Augustus*[117] a warrant was set aside on the basis of oppression where the authority had failed to follow its rent arrears policy which stated that eviction would only be used as a last resort. However, this case concerned a secure tenancy which meant that the court had the 'extended discretion' at the enforcement stage and could consider the reasonableness of the eviction.

7.173   Although the issue is the lawfulness of the public body's decision-making, the occupier's personal circumstances are relevant in so far as the court is scrutinising the way the public body has taken those circumstances into account and the extent to which it has applied its own policies.

116 Jackson LJ at [58].
117 February 2007 *Legal Action* 29, Lambeth County Court, 24 November 2006.

7.174   When running a public law defence it is essential to ensure that the landlord is made aware of the occupier's personal circumstances. This is particularly so when the tenant is vulnerable since the basis of the defence is likely to include an argument that the landlord has failed to take sufficient account of those circumstances or to abide by a policy or statutory requirement regarding vulnerable tenants.[118]

The outcome of a successful defence

7.175   If the court holds that an eviction is not proportiontate or that the decision to evict was unlawful on public law grounds, it will refuse the make a possession order.[119] In some cases a refusual to make a possession order at a particular time may result in the person gaining a long-term tenancy.[120] In *Hounslow LBC v Powell*[121] the fact that denying a claim for possession against an introductory tenant would result in the tenant becoming secure was identified as a factor highly relevant in any assessment of proportionality. In *Armour*,[122] see para 7.162 above, the trial judge acknowledged this but commented that this reflects the purpose of the probationary tenancy: to give limited security for a trial period after which the tenancy becomes secure. And, under a secure tenancy there is still the risk of eviction if anti-social behaviour is repeated.

7.176   In most cases the refusal of a possession order will not have this effect. For those with no right to occupy (eg trespassers, including occupiers with no succession rights) the courts have found that article 8 cannot be used for anything other than to postpone the date for eviction, or to ensure that alternatives are considered before a possession order is made.[123] In all cases, a refusal to make a possession order at a particular time does not prevent a possession order being made in the future, in different circumstances.

118   Note that to establish disability discrimination it is necessary that the alleged discriminator is aware that the person is a disabled person, see paras 7.187–7.189 below.

119   Section 89 of the HA 1980 permits a postponement for a maximum of six weeks in cases where orders are made against those with no right to remain under domestic law. The courts have tended to approach this as being a bar on any longer postponement so that if a six-week postponement would not make the eviction proportionate an order of any kind will be refused.

120   See *Eastlands Homes Partnership v White*, para 7.171. and *Southend-on-Sea BC v Armour*, para 7.162.

121   [2011] UKSC 8, 23 February 2011, Lord Hope at [19].

122   [2014] EWCA Civ 231, 12 March 2014.

123   See, for example, *Leicester CC v Shearer* at para 7.171.

Practical tips

7.177 To succeed in public law and article 8 arguments it will help to:

- Be familiar with the relevant policies of the public body. Failing to follow its own policy may make a landlord's decision unlawful.
- Provide information and put forward realistic proposals at an early stage. If it is argued that a person should not be evicted because of their particular circumstances (eg, a recent bereavement, loss of employment), the public body cannot be criticised if it is not informed of those circumstances. A blunt refusal to consider such information or a reasonable proposal may make the decision to evict unlawful on public law grounds.
- Advise the occupier realistically: improved behaviour is the best way to persuade the landlord to postpone action and/or to persuade the court that an eviction is not proportionate.
- Remember that the case will be listed for a very short hearing in the possession list. A draft defence, witness statement or at least a summary of the defence should be available at the first hearing and sent to the landlord before the hearing if possible.[124]

Which landlords are subject to article 8 and public law defences?

7.178 As is the case for judicial review, most registered providers of social housing will be classed as public bodies for the purposes of both article 8 and judicial review (ie subject to public law arguments). See paras 2.70–2.74 for an explanation of the test. Some small social landlords may not be classed as public bodies, but most will be.

Private landlords

7.179 Arguments have been made that article 8 defences can be raised against private landlords because the court itself is a public authority (often referred to as the 'horizontal application' of article 8). However, these arguments have not succeeded. Most recently in the case of *McDonald v McDonald*[125] the Court of Appeal held that the decisions of the ECtHR do not support the argument. Furter, the challenge was to a claim brought under section 21 of HA 1988, which has already been found compatible with article 8.[126] Permission to appeal to the

---

124 See paras 6.130–6.133 for an explanation of the rules about filing defences in possession claims.

125 [2014] EWCA Civ 1049, 24 July 2014.

126 See para 7.152 above, and the case of *Poplar Housing* at para 2.73.

Supreme Court was granted in December 2014 but at the time of writing the hearing has not been listed.

Disability discrimination in possession proceedings

7.180   It is unlawful to discriminate against disabled people in several spheres of activity, including renting or buying land or property. The Disability Discrimination Act (DDA) 1995 has now been replaced by the Equality (EA) Act 2010. Under DDA 1995 it was unlawful to discriminate against a person by evicting them. Discrimination was when a person, 'for a reason which relates to the disabled person's disability', treated a disabled person less favourably than he or she would treat others 'to whom that reason did not apply'. An eviction that amounted to discrimination could however be justified on the ground that the eviction was necessary in order not to endanger the health or safety of any person.[127]

7.181   In a number of cases under the DDA 1995 claims for possession based on anti-social behaviour were defended by tenants who argued that their behaviour was related to their disability. The issue was whether it was discrimination to evict a tenant because of behaviour related to a disability when a non-disabled tenant would be evicted for the same behaviour. In other words, was the proper 'comparator' a non-disabled person who behaved in the same way or a non-disabled person who did not behave in the same way? If the latter, to evict the disabled person behaving in an anti-social way would amount to discrimination. And such discrimination could only be justified on health and safety grounds.

In *Lewisham LBC v Malcolm*[128] the House of Lords considered a claim for possession against a tenant with a previous diagnosis of schizophrenia who had unlawfully sublet his flat. This led to the loss of the secure tenancy (see para 4.12).

The House of Lords held, by a majority of three to two, that in deciding whether an eviction amounted to disability discrimination the proper comparator was a non-disabled person who had sublet his or her flat. As the authority would have sought possession against such a person, Mr Malcolm was not being treated less favourably and the eviction did not constitute disability

127   See DDA 1995 ss22(3)(c), 24(1) and 24(3).
128   [2008] UKHL 43, 25 July 2007.

> discrimination. Furthermore, it was also held that an eviction could not be discriminatory if the landlord was not aware of the occupier's disability.

7.182   This decision effectively abolished indirect discrimination, not only in housing cases but in other areas such as employment. The EA 2010 has largely reversed the effect of *Lewisham LBC v Malcolm*. The EA 2010 consolidates discrimination legislation into a single Act and extends the protection from discrimination (previously confined to race, gender and disability) to all those with 'protected characteristics'.

Equality Act 2010

7.183   The Act protects from discrimination people with 'protected characteristics'. Protected characteristics are: age; disability; gender reassignment; pregnancy and maternity; race; religion or belief; sex; and sexual orientation.

Definition of disability[129]

7.184   A person with a disability is defined as a person with a physical or mental impairment that has a substantial and long-term adverse effect on the person's ability to carry out normal day-to-day activities. 'Long-term' means it has lasted or is likely to last at least 12 months or for the rest of the person's life. Some conditions are specifically defined as disabilities so it is not necessary to establish evidence of their effect on the ability to carry out normal day-to-day activities. Some conditions, mostly relating to personality disorders or self-inflicted behaviour, are specifically excluded.

Conditions specifically identified as a disability are:

• progressive conditions such as cancer, HIV infection and multiple sclerosis;
• visual impairments certified by a consultant ophthalmologist.

---

129 See EA 2010 s6 and Sch 1, Equality Act 2010 (Disability) Regulations 2010 SI No 2128 and *The Equality Act 2010 Guidance: guidance on matters to be taken into account in determining questions relating to the definition of disability*, May 2011.

Conditions/impairments specifically excluded are:

- addiction to alcohol, nicotine or other substances (though not if the addiction is the result of initially prescribed medication);
- a tendency to set fires, steal, physically or sexually abuse others, exhibitionism or voyeurism;
- hay fever (but not to the extent it aggravates another condition);
- severe disfigurement which consists of tattoos or piercings.

What is discrimination?

7.185   The EA 2010 provides that a person (A) discriminates against another (B) if because of a protected characteristic A treats B less favourably than A treats or would treat others.[130] This is 'direct discrimination'. However, in relation to disability, it is not discrimination to treat a disabled person *more* favourably than a non-disabled person.[131] There are also certain qualifications that are specific to particular protected characteristics.

7.186   Disability discrimination is more specifically defined in EA 2010 s15(1): a person (A) discriminates against a disabled person (B) if A treats B unfavourably *because of something arising in consequence of* B's disability and A cannot show that the treatment is a proportionate means of achieving a legitimate aim. However, the treatment is not discrimination if A can show that A did not know, and could not reasonably have been expected to know, that B had the disability.[132]

Discrimination by eviction

7.187   Section 35 of the EA 2010 deals with the management of premises, including evictions, and provides that a person must not discriminate against an occupier with a relevant protected characteristic by evicting the occupier or taking steps to secure the eviction.

7.188   So, to establish disability discrimination the person alleging discrimination must prove that:

- the person is a disabled person as defined in the EA 2010. In most cases medical evidence will be needed;
- he or she was treated unfavourably (no comparison with a non-disabled person is necessary);

---

130   EA 2010 s13(1). In relation to age however, less favourable treatment is lawful if it is a proportionate means of achieving a legitimate aim: s13(2).

131   EA 2010 s13(3).

132   EA 2010 s15(2).

- the unfavourable treatment was because of something 'arising in consequence of' the disability.

An eviction or proposed eviction is, on the face of it, discriminatory if it is because of something 'arising in consequence of' the occupier's disability.

7.189   If this is established, the treatment will amount to discrimination unless the alleged discriminator can show that:[133]

- the treatment is a proportionate means of achieving a legitimate aim; or
- he or she was not aware and could not reasonably be expected to know about the disability.

The 'proportionality' test

7.190   The Supreme Court recently considered how the court should deal with disability discrimination defences to claims for possession. The Court of Appeal had held that they should be treated in the same way as article 8 defences, ie in the first instance on a summary basis (see para 7.156). The Supreme Court held that this was wrong; an occupier's rights under the EA 2010 are different from the rights protected by article 8:

> In *Akerman-Livingstone v Aster Communities Ltd*[134] the tenant was occupying temporary accommodation under s193 of the Housing Act 1996. He suffered from a severe prolonged duress stress disorder and had been unable to cope with the process of responding to offers of a permanent tenancy from the local authority. The local authority decided that its housing duty was ended by the defendant's refusal or failure to respond to its offers. It instructed the social landlord to evict him. The tenant argued that the possession proceedings amounted to disability discrimination under EA 2010 ss35 and 15 and a breach of his rights under article 8. The county court judge held that the landlord's aim in seeking possession was to comply with the council's direction and meant that there was no seriously arguable case under either article 8 or the EA 2010. An immediate possession order was made.
>
> On the tenant's appeal the Court of Appeal considered how the court should deal with a disability discrimination defence and held

133 EA 2010 s136 deals with the burden of proof in discrimination cases. See *Akerman-Livingstone v Aster Communities Ltd* below for an explanation of how this applies.

134 [2015] UKSC 15, 11 March 2015.

that the judge had been right to approach it in the same way as an article 8 defence.

However, the Supreme Court held that this was not the correct approach to a defence based on disability discrimination. The right to equal treatment and the rights protected by article 8 are different. Section 35 of the Equality Act 2010 applies to all landlords regardless of status. No landlord can adopt a discriminatory policy towards eviction. It is clear than that the substantive right to equal treatment protected by the EA 2010 is different from the substantive right protected by article 8. All occupiers have a right to respect for their home but Parliament has expressly provided for an extra right to equal treatment; people are protected against direct or indirect discrimination in relation to eviction.

Furthermore, s136 EA 2010 deals with the burden of proof in discrimination cases. A person alleging discrimination must show that there are facts from which, in the absence of some other explanation, the court could conclude that there was discrimination. But if this is shown then the alleged discriminator bears the burden of showing that the pursuit of the proceedings is 'a proportionate means of achieving a legitimate aim'. The obligations on a landlord are not absolute. A landlord is entitled to evict a disabled tenant if he or she can show that it is a proportionate means of achieving a legitimate aim.

A consideration of proportionality normally required the consideration of four questions: (1) whether the aim was sufficiently important to justify limiting a fundamental right, (2) whether the measure was rationally connected to the aim, (3) whether the means was no more than was necessary to accomplish the aim, and (4) whether the infringement was disproportionate to the likely benefit. In the cases of Pinnock and Powell the Supreme Court rejected this 'structured' approach to proportionality in relation to article 8 because in most cases the 'twin aims' being pursued by the landlord are overwhelming (ie the vindication of the landlord's property rights and the need for a local authority landlord to comply with its statutory duties in relation to the allocation and management of social housing), see para 7.156. However, 'It simply does not follow that, because those twin aims will almost always trump the right to respect which is due to the occupier's home, they will always trump the occupier's equality rights.'[135] When

---

135 Lady Hale at [30].

considering a defence under the EA 2010 the court must adopt
a structured approach to the question of whether the eviction is
appropriate and must ask whether there is any lesser measure that
might achieve the landlord's aims.

A balance must be struck between the seriousness of the impact
on the tenant and the importance of the landlord's aims. The impact
of a person having to move from particular accommodation may be
such that it is not outweighed by the benefits to the local authority
or social landlord from being able to regain possession.

Although both an article 8 defence and a disability discrimination
defence require the court to consider the proportionality of making
an order for possession, the protection under s35 EA 2010 is 'plainly
stronger' than the protection afforded by article 8. Section 35 affords
protection to a limited class of occupiers, who are considered by
Parliament to deserve special protection. The protection is to avoid
a specific wrong in a number of fields, not just in relation to the
occupation of property, namely discrimination against disabled
persons. Furthermore, once the possibility of discrimination is
made out, the burden of proof is firmly on the landlord to show
that there was no discrimination or that an order for possession is
proportionate. And the proportionality exercise involves focusing on
a very specific issue, namely the justification for discrimination.

This does not mean that it will never be appropriate to deal with
such a defence in a summary way. This could be the case if the
landlord could establish that (i) the occupier had no real prospect
of establishing that he or she was disabled, (ii) it was plain that
possession was not being sought 'because of something arising in
consequence of the disability', or (iii) the claim and its enforcement
plainly represented 'a proportionate means of achieving a legitimate
aim'.

However, the problem will be that each of those kinds of issues
will usually give rise to disputed facts or assessments such that
summary judgment will rarely be appropriate.

Despite overruling the Court of Appeal and finding the trial
judge had been wrong to make an order on a summary basis, the
Supreme Court nevertheless dismissed the appeal because by the
time of the hearing the social landlord's interest in the property had
been brought to an end by the private freeholder so a possession
order was inevitable.

7.191   By defining disability discrimination as unfavourable treatment because of something 'arising in consequence of' the disability, without reference to a comparision with how someone who is not disabled would be treated, the EA 2010 has removed the problem created by *Lewisham LBC v Malcolm* (see para 7.181). An eviction may be discriminatory because it is based on conduct arising in consequence of the disabilty, but, a landlord seeking to justify such an eviction has an easier test to meet than under the DDA 1995: the eviction will be lawful if it is a proportionate way of achieving a legitimate aim. As the Supreme Court made clear in *Akerman-Livingstone*, in deciding whether the eviction is 'proportionate' consideration must be given to whether there is any alternative to eviction that might achieve the landlord's aims.

Indirect discrimination

7.192   Also relevant in housing cases are two other forms of potential indirect discrimination:

- by way of the operation of a 'provision, criterion or practice' which places a disabled person at a disadvantage (EA 2010 s19); and
- by way of a failure make 'reasonable adjustments' for disabled persons (EA 2010 s20).

These two forms of discrimination are closely connected and are explained in detail at paras 7.193–7.197 below.

Provision, practice or criterion

7.193   EA 2010 s19 provides that a person (A) discriminates against another (B) if A applies to B a provision, criterion or practice which is discriminatory in relation to a relevant protected characteristic of B's. The provision, criterion or practice will be discriminatory if it puts people who share B's protected characteristic at a particular disadvantage when compared with people who do not share the particular characteristic (and it does or would put B at that disadvantage) and A cannot show that it is a proportionate means of achieving a legitimate aim.

7.194   Note that it is the application of a 'provision, criterion or practice' not the enforcement of legal rights or duties that may be discriminatory. So, to rely on a statutory ground for possession against the disabled person (eg the rent arrears or nuisance ground) is not discrimination under EA 2010 s19. However, the 'practice' adopted by the landlord in doing so is capable of being discriminatory. An example may be where a landlord communicates about a proposed eviction only in writing to a tenant known to have a learning disability which affects his or her ability to read or understand written communications.

7.195   This provision is closely connected to the duty to make reasonable adjustments.

Reasonable adjustments[136]

7.196   Section 20 of EA 2010 sets out the duty to make 'reasonable adjustments' for disabled people. A failure to do so may itself amount to disability discrimination. The duty to make reasonable adjustments for disabled persons applies to landlords, to those providing public services and to those exercising public functions.[137] There are three ways the duty may apply:

1) where a provision, criterion or practice puts a disabled person at a substantial disadvantage in comparison with persons who are not disabled;
2) where a physical feature puts a disabled person at a substantial disadvantage in comparison with persons who are not disabled; and
3) where a disabled person would, but for the provision of an auxiliary aid, be put at a substantial disadvantage.

7.197   For (1) and (2) the duty is to take such steps as it is reasonable to have to take to avoid the disadvantage; for (3) the duty is to take such steps as it is reasonable to have to take to provide the auxiliary aid.

7.198   A case about a bankruptcy order obtained against a woman with known mental health problems illustrates how a failure to make reasonable adjustments may amount to disability discrimination.

> In *Haworth v Cartmel and HMRC*[138] an anonymous allegation was made to HM Revenue & Customs (HMRC) that Ms Haworth was running a profitable business breeding horses. She had a history of mental health problems and claimed to keep the horses for therapeutic reasons. Following letters sent to her by HMRC requesting her to submit a tax return Ms Haworth's mother

---

136 EA 2010 s20.
137 EA 2010 ss36(1) and 29(7).
138 [2011] EWHC 36 (Ch), 4 February 2011. The case concerned very similar provisions contained in the DDA 1995 as most of the EA 2010 was not then in force.

contacted HMRC and made them aware of her daughter's mental health problems, indicating that she found it very difficult to deal with correspondence and often failed to open official letters.

Ms Haworth also contacted them and said the same. As she failed to file a tax return, HMRC then sent to her a statutory demand for payment of the estimated tax due and subsequently served a bankruptcy petition. A bankruptcy order was granted at a hearing which Ms Haworth did not attend. Two years later an application was made to annul the order on the grounds that Ms Haworth had not had capacity under the Mental Capacity Act 2005 to deal with the issues at the time and that HMRC had discriminated against her under the DDA 1995.

The court considered the medical evidence in relation to the relevant period two years earlier and annulled the order on the ground that Ms Haworth had lacked capacity to deal with the notices and court proceedings. But the court went on to consider whether HMRC's actions amounted to disability discrimination. The court held that HMRC had failed to make reasonable adjustments in relation to a 'policy, practice or procedure', namely the way in which they had made the application for a bankruptcy order. In particular, the court found that HMRC should have informed Ms Haworth's mother about when they planned to serve the statutory demand and the petition and should have informed the court about her disability. If they had done so, her mother could have made sure that the envelopes were opened and the documents dealt with. Furthermore, the court would have been likely to adjourn for further steps to be taken to ensure that Ms Haworth was aware of the hearing and to investigate the extent of her disability.

7.199 It is easy to see how this could apply in relation to a landlord's conduct when seeking a possession order. What the EA 2010 provides, and *Haworth v Cartmel* illustrates, is that where a landlord is aware that a tenant is disabled the landlord must take steps to ensure:

- that he or she is not disadvantaged by the procedures normally followed;
- that appropriate support is offered or adjustments made; and
- that alternatives to eviction are considered.

If not, an eviction may be held to be discriminatory.

7.200 Note that any landlord may be guilty of disability discrimination but where the landlord is a public body the arguments relating to disability discrimination are likely to overlap with defences relying on public law and rights under article 8 of the ECHR (see paras 7.128–7.132 above). Furthermore, a public body is also subject to the public sector equality duty set out in EA 2010 s149. This requires a public body to have due regard to the need to eliminate discrimination and promote equality of opportunity when exercising its public functions. See paras 2.86–2.89.

7.201   Where disability discrimination is likely to be relevant, the following matters should also be borne in mind:

- **Reasonableness** If a claim for possession is on a discretionary ground the court must be satisfied that it is reasonable to make a possession order. If the tenant has a disability this will be a relevant factor, whether or not the disability is related to the grounds on which possession is sought. If the landlord is a unitary local authority it will be particularly relevant that it also has duties to provide support under community care law (see chapter 18).

- **The rent arrears protocol** A social landlord seeking possession against a 'vulnerable tenant' on the grounds of rent arrears must consider at an early stage the issues of capacity, possible disability discrimination and (for local authority landlords) the possible need for a community care assessment (see para 6.7).

- **Public law defences** Where the landlord is a public body, there may be a defence based on public law or proportionality even where the landlord has an absolute right to possession. The tenant's circumstances, the landlord's policies on vulnerable tenants, the support offered by the landlord and alternatives to eviction will all be relevant. See paras 7.128–7.132.[139]

- **Capacity** Where a person lacks capacity, the CPR require a 'litigation friend' to be appointed. A landlord bringing a claim must apply for the appointment if aware of the disability. A failure to inform the court of the person's disability may result in orders being set aside (see *Haworth v HMRC*, para 7.198 above). Capacity is dealt with in more detail in paras 7.202–7.212 below.

---

139 See for example *McGlynn v Welwyn Hatfield DC* [2009] EWCA Civ 285, 1 April 2009 and *Barber v Croydon* [2010] EWCA Civ 51, 11 February 2010, see para 7.170 above.

Capacity

7.202 The Mental Capacity Act (MCA) 2005 sets out the framework for assessing capacity and for dealing with the affairs of those who lack capacity. The detailed provisions of the Act are outside the scope of this book. In summary, the central principles of the MCA 2005 are:[140]

- A person is assumed to have capacity unless it is established that the person lacks capacity.
- A person is not to be treated as unable to make a decision unless all practicable steps to help the person to do so have been taken, without success.
- A person is not to be treated as unable to make a decision merely because the person makes an unwise decision.

Inability to make decisions

7.203 Capacity is to be assessed not in general terms but in relation to particular decisions[141] and MCA 2005 s3 provides that a person is unable to make a decision if unable:

- to understand the information relevant to the decision;
- to retain that information;
- to use or weigh that information as part of the process of making the decision; or
- to communicate the decision (whether by talking, using sign language or any other means).

7.204 A person is not to be regarded as unable to understand relevant information if he or she can understand an explanation given in an appropriate way, using, for example, simple language, visual aids or other means.

7.205 The fact that a person is able to retain relevant information only for a short period does not prevent a person being regarded as able to make a decision.

---

140 These are set out in MCA 2005 s1.
141 *Haworth v Cartmel & HMRC* (at para 7.198) illustrates this well. The court examined capacity specifically in relation to three specific steps in the process: the service of the statutory demand, the service of the petition and the court application.

The Court of Protection

7.206   The Mental Capacity Act (MCA) 2005 also governs the powers and procedures of the Court of Protection which makes decisions about the property and affairs, healthcare and personal welfare of those without capacity. The Court of Protection has powers equivalent to the High Court and can decide whether someone has the capacity to make a particular decision. The Court of Protection can appoint people to act for those without capacity, including 'litigation friends'.

Court proceedings: litigation friends

7.207   Under the CPR a 'protected party' must have a litigation friend appointed to conduct proceedings on his or her behalf.[142] A protected party means 'a party, or an intended party, who lacks capacity to conduct the proceedings'.[143]

7.208   If proceedings are issued against a protected party, a person may not take any steps in the proceedings until the party has a litigation friend.

7.209   In most cases medical evidence will be needed to establish a lack of capacity and therefore the need for a litigation friend. However, CPR Part 21 does not require this and the opinion of a friend or family member who offers to act as a litigation friend may be sufficient. However, MCA 2005 specifically provides that:

> A lack of capacity cannot be established merely by reference to a person's age or appearance, or a … condition or an aspect of [the person's] behaviour, which might lead others to make unjustified assumptions about his [or her] capacity.[144]

7.210   A person appointed by the Court of Protection may conduct proceedings on behalf of the protected party. Otherwise, anyone can put themselves forward as a litigation friend by filing and serving on all parties a 'certificate of suitability' (form N235) stating that the necessary conditions are met. The conditions are that the person must be able fairly and competently to conduct proceedings on behalf of the party and has no interest adverse to that of the party.[145] The certificate

---

142   CPR Part 21.
143   CPR 21.1(2).
144   MCA 2005 s2(3).
145   CPR 21.4–21.5. If a claim is *brought* by a litigation friend (as opposed to being defended) the person must also undertake to pay any costs the protected party may be ordered to pay, subject to any right to be repaid from the party's assets. If the protected party is entitled to legal aid the litigation friend enjoys costs protection in the same way, see para 22.135.

must also state the grounds of the person's belief that the party lacks capacity and, if based on a medical or other expert opinion, must attach relevant documents.[146]

7.211 An application for the appointment of a litigation friend may be made by the person who wishes to be the litigation friend or by one of the parties to the proceedings.

7.212 If a claim is made *against* a protected party without a litigation friend the claimant *must* apply for an order appointing a litigation friend.

Mortgage possession claims

7.213 A mortgage operates as the grant of an interest in land giving the right of possession to the lender. Unlike claims for possession against tenants, a lender already has a right of possession by virtue of the mortgage. It does not depend on the court to *grant* the right. Rather, the lender applies to the court to *enforce* the right of possession. In relation to residential premises, the court has statutory powers to postpone the exercise of the right of possession.

7.214 The mortgage agreement will usually provide that the lender's right of possession cannot be *enforced* unless the borrower breaches the terms of the mortgage, and so the lender will have to prove the breach. The Civil Procedure Rules (CPR) require very specific information to be provided by the lender in the court documents (see paras 6.123–6.127). There is also a Pre-Action Protocol for Possession Claims based on Mortgage Arrears which requires most of the information to be given to the borrower before proceedings are commenced. This is to encourage the parties to reach agreement and, if possible, avoid proceedings.

7.215 This section examines briefly the court's powers to restrict a lender's right of possession and some situations in which an application may be made to set aside a mortgage to defeat the claim for possession.

Regulation of mortgages

7.216 Since October 2004, the Financial Services Authority (FSA) has been responsible for regulating the sale of mortgages. The Mortgage Conduct of Business Rules (MCOB) came into effect on 31 October

146 CPR Part 21, PD para 3.2(c).

2004 and applies to 'regulated mortgage contracts' entered into on or after 31 October 2004. Previously the 1997 Voluntary Mortgage Code applied.

7.217   The MCOB includes rules for:

- responsible lending, ie giving proper consideration to a borrower's ability to pay;
- the giving of information in prescribed format throughout the life of the loan;
- the giving of prescribed information, including an official FSA leaflet, to borrowers who fall into arrears; and
- the way lenders deal with arrears and possession cases.

7.218   The MCOB rules can be downloaded from the FSA website: www.fsahandbook.info/FSA/html/handbook/MCOB.

7.219   The FSA operates a dispute resolution procedure through the Financial Ombudsman Service (FOS) and awards of compensation can be made.

7.220   A lender's failure to follow the MCOB and/or the Pre-Action Protocol does not prevent a claim for possession being made but may be taken into account by the court when considering whether to exercise its discretion to allow a borrower more time to repay the arrears.

Claims for possession

7.221   There are two separate regimes governing the courts' powers in relation to possession claims of residential property subject to a mortgage:

- The Consumer Credit Act (CCA) 1974[147] governs 'regulated agreements'. Previously, the CCA 1974 only applied to agreements where the amount of credit did not exceed £25,000. However, this limit was removed by the CCA 2006. Agreements exempt from the CCA 1974 include those entered into with banks and building societies and all loans which are regulated mortgage contracts.
- The Administration of Justice Acts (AJA) 1970 and 1973 govern other mortgages of residential premises that are not regulated under the CCA 1974.

Administration of Justice Acts

7.222   Where a lender (mortgagee) seeks a possession order of residential premises against a borrower (mortgagor) the court has powers similar

147 As amended by CCA 2006.

to those under the extended discretion in relation to tenants (see para 6.143): the court can adjourn, postpone or suspend an order. However, the power depends on the borrower being able to pay 'the sums due' or remedy the default within a reasonable period.

7.223 The courts' powers are contained in the Administration of Justice Acts 1970 and 1973. AJA 1970 s36 of provides that where a mortgagee makes a claim for possession of a dwelling-house:

(1) ... the court may exercise any of the powers conferred on it by subsection (2) below if it appears to the court that in the event of its exercising the power the mortgagor is likely to be able within a reasonable period to pay any sums due under the mortgage or to remedy a default consisting of a breach of any other obligation arising under or by virtue of the mortgage.

(2) The court–
   (a) may adjourn the proceedings, or
   (b) on giving judgment, or making an order, for delivery of possession of the mortgaged property, or at any time before the execution of such judgment or order, may–
       (i) stay or suspend execution of the judgment or order, or
       (ii) postpone the date for delivery of possession, for such period or periods as the court thinks reasonable.

(3) Any such adjournment, stay, suspension or postponement as is referred to in subsection (2) above may be made subject to such conditions with regard to payment by the mortgagor of any sum secured by the mortgage or the remedying of any default as the court thinks fit.

(4) The court may from time to time vary or revoke any condition imposed by virtue of this section.

7.224 AJA 1973 s8(2) makes it clear that the borrower must be able to pay not only the amount in arrears but the further amounts due, including interest, during the life of the agreement. Effectively, the borrower must be able to show that he or she can maintain payment of the current instalments plus regular payment towards the arrears (or a lump sum payment of the arrears) so that at the end of the reasonable period the arrears will have been cleared.

7.225 Section 36(1) AJA 1970 operates so as to provide a 'juridictional gateway' to the court exercising its powers to stay, suspend or postpone possession. It is conditional on a borrower satisfying the court that he or she is likely to be able to pay the sums in question within a reasonable period. If not, the court has no power to stay or suspend the order.[148] If the borrower can satisfy the court of this, then the

148 *Royal Trust Co of Canada v Marckham* [1975] 1WLR 1416 and *Zinda v Bank of Scotland*, see para 7.225.

court has a wide discretion under s36(2) and (3) to attach 'conditions with regard to payment by the mortgagor of *any sum* secured by the mortgage'.

In *Zinda v Bank of Scotland*[149] the borrower defaulted on an interest only mortgage. A suspended possession order was made in the standard terms.[150] Subsequently the bank agreed to consolidate the arrears with the principal loan, which meant a new sum for the monthly instalments. The borrower again defaulted. His applications for further suspension of the enforcement of the order were refused. In the Court of Appeal he argued that the consolidation, which resulted in a short period when he was not in arrears, meant that the order was effectively extinguished. The Court of Appeal dismissed his appeal. Section 36 of AJA 1970 and section 8 of the AJA 1973 operate so as to impose two conditions for a borrower to stave off eviction: (1) the borrower must pay off the arrears by monthly instalments, and (2) he must also pay the current instalments (relating to the principal sum). Doing one without the other will avail him nothing. And the fact that the arrears may have been discharged in their entirety by the consolidation is not enough if there is nonetheless a failure to comply with the second leg of the condition.

7.226　Although the Pre-Action Protocol 'does not alter the parties' rights and obligations' the court will take account of a failure to comply when exercising its discretion under the Administration of Justice Acts. The Protocol stresses the need for the exchange of information about the arrears at an early stage, in a way that is 'clear, fair and not misleading' and the consideration of alternatives to court proceedings.

What is a reasonable period?

7.227　This is decided having regard to the rights and obligations of both the lender and the borrower. The Court of Appeal considered the issue in *Cheltenham & Gloucester Building Society v Norgan*.[151] The court held that in determining the 'reasonable period' the court 'should take as its starting point the full term of the mortgage and at the outset

---

149 [2011] EWCA Civ 707, 23 June 2011.
150 The standard form for a mortgage possession order is form N31.
151 [1996] 1 All ER 449.

pose the question: would it be possible for the mortgagor to clear the arrears by instalments over that period?'.[152] The relevant factors in determining the reasonable period were summarised as follows:[153]

- how much the borrower can reasonably afford to pay currently and in the future;
- if the borrower is in temporary difficulty, how long the difficulty is likely to last;
- the reason for the arrears;
- the period of the remaining term;
- the contractual terms, ie the type of mortgage and when the principal sum is due to be repaid;
- whether it is appropriate to disregard any provision in the agreement for the lender to demand early repayment;
- whether it is reasonable to expect the lender to recoup the arrears of interest over the whole term, within a shorter period or even within a longer period;
- whether it is reasonable to expect the lender to capitalise the interest or not;
- any reasons affecting the security which should influence the length of the period for repayment.

Much will depend on the amount of equity in the property. Where there is substantial equity the court is more likely to be willing to permit a longer period for the borrower to repay the arrears.

7.228 Clearly, when the court is being asked exercise its powers under AJA 1970 evidence of the borrower's ability to pay the amounts due within a reasonable period must be provided. If the borrow cannot satisfy the court of this, the court does not have any power under the AJAs 1970 or 1973.[154] Evidence of the value of the property, and therefore the amount of equity, should also be obtained.

7.229 The power under section 36 does not apply where the agreement is regulated under the Consumer Credit Act 1974.[155]

Adjourning or suspending to permit a sale by the borrower

7.230 The court can grant an adjournment or suspension to allow the borrower time to sell the property. To do so the court must be satisfied

152 Waite LJ at 458.
153 Evans LJ at 463A.
154 See *Jameer v Paratus AMC* [2012] EWCA Civ 1924, 29 October 2012, where the Court of Appeal stressed the need for full, frank and up-to-date information about the borrower's income and expenditure.
155 AJA 1970 s38A.

that the proceeds of sale will be sufficient to discharge the whole of the mortgage debt, including the arrears, within a reasonable period. If the borrower is in negative equity the court cannot suspend possession to permit the borrower to sell unless he or she has other funds to make up the shortfall.[156]

7.231   A borrower may want the property to be sold when the lender does not. This may happen where the amount owed exceeds the value of the property and the lender wants to wait until the value increases. In such a case the borrower can make an application under the Law of Property Act 1925 s91(2). Under section 91 the court has a wide discretion as to whether to order a sale and, if so, on what terms. However, the court is unlikely to order a sale where the proceeds of sale are likely to be substantially less than the amount owed.

Regulated agreements under the Consumer Credit Act 1974

7.232   The Consumer Credit Act (CCA) 1974 deals with a large range of credit agreements and prescribes the way regulated agreements are entered into. Under CCA 1974 the court has more extensive powers than under the Administration of Justice Acts. In particular, a borrower can apply for a 'time order' under which the court can extend the time for repayment of the loan and can reduce the contractual interest rate.

7.233   There is also provision for a court to 'reopen the credit agreement so as to do justice between the parties' where there is an 'unfair relationship'.[157]

7.234   Some types of loans are specifically exempt from the CCA 1974. Because of the strict procedural requirements regarding regulated agreements it should be clear from the court documents whether or not an agreement is regulated.

Substantive defences to mortgage possession claims

7.235   A lender has the right to possession by virtue of the mortgage. An application to the court to exercise its discretion is not a 'defence' to a claim for possession. The substantive defences that may be raised are summarised below (paras 7.236–7.241).

---

156 *Cheltenham and Gloucester plc v Krausz* [1997] 1 All ER 21, CA.
157 Under the 1974 Act this applied in relation to an 'extortionate credit bargain' but this was amended by the Consumer Credit Act 2006.

Spouse or civil partner in occupation who did not consent to the mortgage

7.236　Where a mortgage is entered into by a sole owner of premises, a spouse or civil partner who is in occupation of the premises has an 'overriding interest' under the Land Registration Act (LRA) 2002.[158] This means the lender's interest is subject to the right of occupation. Unless the person consented to the mortgage, it will not be binding on him or her.[159] Most lenders will make specific enquiry of such a person and obtain consent before entering into a mortgage.

Forgery

7.237　Where one spouse or civil partner forges the signature of the other the mortgage is ineffective. However, an equitable charge is granted to the lender in relation to the share of the premises owned by the party who entered into the mortgage agreement. In such a case the lender can apply for a money judgment against the borrower and can then apply for a charging order and subsequently an order for sale under section 13 of the Trusts of Land and Appointment of Trustees Act 1996. Section 15 sets out the relevant factors to be considered when the court is considering an order for sale (see para 1.141).

Misrepresentation/undue influence

7.238　It will be difficult for a borrower to establish that a lender has misrepresented the effect of the mortgage or placed undue pressure on the borrower to enter into the mortgage. Where a borrower can establish that the lender has been negligent in representing the terms of the mortgage (negligent misstatement) this may give rise to a claim for damages but does not usually mean that the mortgage will be set aside, unless it can be shown that the lender has taken unfair advantage of the borrower.[160]

7.239　　Defences based on undue influence are usually raised where a party has acted as surety. The allegation is that the principal debtor has placed undue influence on the person who agreed to act as surety. Most of the reported cases have concerned husbands persuading wives to enter into agreements to secure business debts on the shared home. To establish undue influence as a defence it is necessary to prove not only that there has been misrepresentation, undue influence or other wrong but also that the lender would be affected

158　See Sch 3 para 2.
159　Unless inquiry was made and the interest not disclosed.
160　*Cornish v Midland Bank plc* [1985] 3 All ER 513.

by the wrong. For this it must be proved that the lender had actual or constructive notice of the wrong.[161]

7.240   The House of Lords considered the issue in the cases of *Barclays Bank v O'Brien*[162] and *Royal Bank of Scotland v Etridge (No 2)*[163] and gave guidance on the steps a lender should take to satisfy itself that a wife's agreement has been properly obtained. In *O'Brien* the House indicated that a lender should:

- take steps to ensure the wife is aware of the risks she is running; and
- advise her to take independent advice.

In *Etridge* the court elaborated on the duty to communicate with the wife directly or with her solicitor and on the duty of the solicitor who is advising the wife.

7.241   Although these cases concerned husbands and wives, the same principles apply wherever there is an emotional relationship between the parties, including a same-sex partnership.

Unfair terms

7.242   The Unfair Terms in Consumer Contracts Regulations 1999 apply to mortgage agreements (see paras 4.171–4.176). If a term is deemed unfair by the court it is unenforceable.

Tenants of borrowers

7.243   Where a landlord borrows money on a mortgage, the power to grant a tenancy can only be exercised where no contrary intention is expressed in the mortgage deed.[164] Most mortgage deeds contain a term preventing the borrower from granting a tenancy.

7.244   The position of the tenant of a borrower depends on two factors:

- whether the tenancy commenced before or after the property was mortgaged; and
- whether the lender gave consent.

---

161   Or, unusually, that the wrongdoer was acting as the lender's agent.
162   [1994] 1 AC 180, HL.
163   [2001] 4 All ER 449, HL.
164   Law of Property Act 1925 s99.

Tenancy granted before the mortgage

7.245 A tenancy granted by the landlord/borrower before the mortgage was created is valid as against the lender.

7.246 Even if the mortgage deed prohibits the creation of a tenancy, this does not prevent an existing tenancy from binding the lender: if the lender obtains possession against the landlord/borrower, the tenant becomes the direct tenant of the lender.

7.247 A lender may take advantage of certain of the possession grounds available to landlords.[165] Furthermore, if the tenancy is an assured shorthold tenancy the lender will be able to obtain possession by serving two months' notice and obtaining a possession order against the tenant, provided any fixed term has ended.

Tenancy granted after the mortgage

7.248 If the tenancy is granted with the lender's consent it is binding on the lender.

7.249 If the tenancy is granted without the lender's consent it will not be binding on the lender and when the lender obtains a possession order the tenants can be evicted.[166] However, such 'unauthorised' tenants have the right to seek a postponement of possesion, see paras 7.250–7.252 below.

Notifying occupiers/postponing possession

7.250 The position of 'unauthorised' tenants of borrowers was strengthened by the Mortgage Repossessions (Protection of Tenants etc) Act (MR(PT)A) 2010. The Act applies where there is an 'unauthorised tenancy', ie, an assured, protected or statutory tenancy that does not bind the lender. Any lender who is applying for possession must send a notice to the property (addressed to 'the tenant or the occupier') within five days of receiving notice of the hearing. The notice must state that a possession claim has started, give the name and address of the claimant, the defendant and the court, and details of the hearing.[167] This is to give the occupiers the chance either to apply to be joined, if they assert that their tenancy is binding on the lender,

---

165 Under RA 1977 if the tenancy is subject to possession under Case 11, Case 12 or Case 20, and under HA 1988, if the tenancy is subject to possession under Ground 1, a lender may obtain possession under Ground 2. See appendix to this chapter.

166 *Dudley and District Building Society v Emerson* [1949] 2 All ER 252, CA.

167 See CPR 55.10(2). A similar notice must also be served on the local housing department for the area in which the premises are situated.

or to make an application for a postponement under the MR(PT)A 2010. At the hearing the lender must produce copies of the notice and evidence it was sent.

7.251   If an application is made by unauthorised tenants for a postponement, the court has the power to postpone the date for the giving of possession by up to two months. Alternatively, an application can be made to stay or suspend the warrant of execution by up to two months. However, the court may only stay or suspend the warrant if it did not postpone the possession order and only if the unauthorised tenants have first asked the lender for an undertaking in writing not to enforce the order for two months.

7.252   Where a possession order has been made and the lender is applying for a warrant, the lender must send to the property, at least 14 days before applying to the court, a notice in prescribed form, informing any unauthorised tenants of the right to make such an application.[168] The lender must certify that notice has been given when applying for the warrant.[169]

---

168 Dwelling Houses (Execution of Possession Orders by Mortgagees) Regulations 2010 SI No 1809.
169 See CCR Order 26 rule 17(a)(2A).

APPENDIX

Grounds for possession under Housing Act 1985, Housing Act 1988 and Rent Act 1977

This sets out a summary of the grounds for possession in each Act. In some cases the provisions are condensed and/or paraphrased.

Housing Act 1985 Sch 2

STATUTORY GROUNDS FOR POSSESSION

Part I: discretionary grounds – grounds on which the court may order possession if it considers it reasonable

Ground 1 – rent arrears or breach of tenancy agreement

Rent lawfully due from the tenant has not been paid or an obligation of the tenancy has been broken or not performed.

Ground 2 – nuisance and annoyance

The tenant or a person residing in or visiting the dwelling-house–
(a) has been guilty of conduct causing or likely to cause a nuisance or annoyance
 – to a person residing, visiting or otherwise engaging in a lawful activity in the locality, or
 – to the landlord, or
 – to a person employed (whether or not by the landlord) in connection with the exercise of the landlords' housing management functions, and that is directly or indirectly related to these functions, or
(b) has been convicted of using the dwelling-house or allowing it to be used for immoral or illegal purposes, or an indictable offence committed in, or in the locality of, the dwelling-house.

Ground 2ZA – riot offences

The tenant or an adult residing in the dwelling-house has been convicted of an indictable offence which took place during, and at the scene of, a riot in the United Kingdom.

Ground 2A – domestic violence

The dwelling-house was occupied (whether alone or with others) by a married couple or civil partnership couple (or a couple living together as either) and–
(a) one or both of the partners is a tenant of the dwelling-house,
(b) one partner has left because of violence or threats of violence by the other towards–
  (i)   that partner, or
  (ii) a member of the family of that partner who was residing with that partner immediately before the partner left, and
(c) the court is satisfied that the partner who has left is unlikely to return.

Ground 3 – damage to property

The condition of the dwelling-house or common parts has deteriorated owing to acts of waste, neglect or default of the tenant or a person residing in the dwelling-house. If the acts are those of a subtenant or lodger, the tenant has not taken such steps as he or she ought reasonably to have taken to remove that person.

Ground 4 – damage to furniture

As for Ground 3 but the deterioration is to furniture provided by the landlord.

Ground 5 – tenancy granted because of false statement

The tenant is the person, or one of the persons, to whom the tenancy was granted and the landlord was induced to grant the tenancy by a false statement made knowingly or recklessly by–
(a) the tenant, or
(b) a person acting at the tenant's instigation.

Ground 6 – mutual exchange for payment

The tenancy was assigned to the tenant by way of mutual exchange and a premium was paid in connection with the assignment.

The ground is also available if the assignment (for which payment was made) was to a member of the tenant's family, who lives with the tenant, and who passed the tenancy to the current tenant.

Ground 7 – employment-related accommodation and inappropriate conduct

The dwelling-house is part of or within the grounds of a building held by the landlord mainly for non-housing purposes and consists mainly of accommodation other than housing accommodation, and
(a) was let to the tenant in consequence of the tenant being employed by the landlord, or a local authority, a development corporation, a housing action trust, a Mayoral development corporation an urban development corporation or the governors of an aided school, and
(b) the tenant or another person living in the dwelling-house has been

guilty of conduct such that, having regard to the purpose for which the building is used, it would not be right for the tenant to continue in occupation.

The ground also applies if a previous tenant, who passed the tenancy to the current tenant was the person to whom the tenancy was granted in consequence of employment.

Ground 8 – temporary accommodation pending works

The tenancy was granted to a secure tenant of another property as temporary accommodation pending works to the other property and the works have been completed and the other dwelling-house is available for occupation.

Part II: grounds on which the court may order possession if suitable alternative accommodation is available

Ground 9 – statutory overcrowding

The dwelling-house is statutorily overcrowded, as defined in HA 1985 so as to make the occupier guilty of an offence.

Ground 10 – demolition or reconstruction

The landlord intends, within a reasonable time, to demolish or reconstruct the building or part of the building comprising the dwelling-house, or to carry out works and cannot do so without obtaining possession.

Ground 10A – redevelopment schemes

The dwelling-house or part of it is in an area which is the subject of a redevelopment scheme and the landlord intends within a reasonable time to dispose of the dwelling-house in accordance with the scheme and for that purpose reasonably requires possession.

Ground 11 – charities

The landlord is a charity and the tenant's continued occupation of the dwelling-house would conflict with the objects of the charity.

Part III: grounds on which the court may order possession if it is reasonable to make a possession order and suitable alternative accommodation is available

Ground 12 – non-housing employment-related accommodation

The dwelling-house forms part of, or is within the grounds of, a building held mainly for non-housing purposes and consists mainly of non-housing accommodation, or is in a cemetery, and:

(a) it was let to the tenant in consequence of employment by the landlord, or a local authority, a development corporation, a housing action trust, a Mayoral development corporation an urban development corporation or the governors of an aided school; and that employment has ceased;

and

(b) the landlord reasonably requires the dwelling-house for occupation by a new employee.

The ground also applies if a previous tenant, who passed the tenancy to the current tenant, was the person to whom the tenancy was granted in consequence of employment.

Ground 13 – disabled adapted accommodation

The dwelling-house has features which are substantially different from those of ordinary dwelling-houses and which are designed to make it suitable for occupation by a physically disabled person who needs such accommodation and–

(a) there is no longer such a person residing in the dwelling-house; and

(b) the landlord needs it for occupation by such a person.

Ground 14 – special needs accommodation – housing associations and trusts

The landlord is a housing association or housing trust which lets dwelling-houses only for occupation by persons whose circumstances make it especially difficult to obtain housing, and:

(a) either there is no longer such a person residing in the dwelling-house or the tenant has received an offer of a secure tenancy of a separate dwelling; and

(b) the landlord needs the dwelling-house for another person with such needs.

Ground 15 – special needs accommodation – close to special facilities

The dwelling-house is one of a group of dwelling-houses which the landlord lets for occupation by persons with special needs and–

(a) a social service or special facility is provided near to the group of dwelling-houses to assist persons with those special needs; and

(b) there is no longer a person with those special needs residing in the dwelling-house; and

(c) the landlord needs the dwelling-house for occupation by a person who has those special needs.

Ground 15A – succession and under-occupation (England only)

The accommodation is more extensive than reasonably required by the tenant who became the tenant by succession not as spouse or civil partner [but as family member] and notice of proceedings was served (or if no notice was served, the proceedings were begun) more than six months but less than twelve months after the 'relevant date'.

The relevant date is the date of the previous tenant's death or, if the court so directs, the date on which, in the opinion of the court, the landlord became aware of the previous tenant's death.

The matters to be taken into account by the court in deciding whether it is reasonable to make a possession order include:

(a) the age of the tenant;

(b) the period during which the tenant has occupied the dwelling-house as his or her only or principal home; and

(c) any financial or other support given by the tenant to the previous tenant.

Absolute Ground for Possession for anti-social behaviour

This ground is set out in s84A of the HA 1985 and is in identical terms to ground 7A under the HA 1988, set out below.

For the purposes of the absolute ground for possession against both secure and assured tenants, the relevant 'serious offences' are set out in Schedule 2A of HA 1985.

They include murder, manslaughter, kidnapping, false imprisonment, a range of offences under the Offences against the Persons Act 1861, the Explosive Substances Act 1883, the Firearms Act 1968, the Theft Act 1968 (robbery, burglary and aggravated burglary), criminal damage, a range of offences against children, including sexual offences, drugs offences,

Housing Act 1988 Sch 2

MANDATORY GROUNDS

Notice Grounds 1–5

Since, in the private sector, the default tenancy under the HA 1988 is the assured shorthold, Grounds 1–5 are rarely needed and therefore dealt with only briefly.

Ground 1 – landlord is previous owner-occupier or needs premises as home

Notice must have been served at the start of the tenancy or it must be just and equitable to dispense with the notice.

Ground 2 – tenancy subject to Ground 1 and lender taking possession

This applies where a lender has a power of sale and needs to sell with vacant possession.

For each of Grounds 3, 4 and 5 below, notice must be served at the start of the tenancy and there is no provision for dispensation.

Ground 3 – out-of-season holiday let

The tenancy is a fixed-term tenancy for no longer than eight months and within the 12 months preceding the start of the tenancy it was occupied as a holiday let.

Ground 4 – student accommodation let to non-students

The tenancy is a fixed-term tenancy for no longer than 12 months and within the 12 months preceding the start of the tenancy it was occupied as student accommodation under HA 1988 Sch 1 para 8.

Ground 5 – minister of religion

The dwelling-house is for occupation by a minister of religion to perform the duties of that office and it is required for occupation by a minister of religion as such a residence.

Mandatory grounds not requiring advance notice

Ground 6 – demolition or reconstruction

The landlord intends to demolish or reconstruct the whole or a substantial part of the dwelling-house or to carry out substantial works on it or any part of it or the building of which it is a part.

The following conditions must be met:

The intended work cannot reasonably be carried out without the tenant giving up possession because:
• the tenant is not willing to agree a variation of the tenancy to enable the work to be carried out, or
• the nature of the work is such that no such variation is practicable, or
• the tenant is not willing to accept an assured tenancy of a 'reduced part' of the dwelling-house to enable the works to be carried out, or
• the nature of the work is such that such a tenancy is not practicable.

The ground is not available if:
• the landlord acquired the interest after the grant of the tenancy; or
• the assured tenancy came into being on succession to a previous Rent Act tenancy.

Where the immediate landlord is a registered provider of social housing or a charitable housing trust the ground is made out if the demolition or reconstruction is intended by the superior landlord.

Ground 7 – tenant dies and no right of succession

Where a periodic or fixed-term tenancy devolves under the will or intestacy of the previous tenant. Possession proceedings must be commenced no later than 12 months after the death of the former tenant, or, if the court so directs, after the date on which, in the opinion of the court, the landlord became aware of the former tenant's death.

For the purpose of Ground 7, the acceptance of rent from the new tenant is regarded as creating a new tenancy unless the landlord agrees in writing to a change in the amount of the rent, the period of the tenancy, the premises that are let or any other term of the tenancy.

Note that the ground does not apply if someone is entitled to succeed to the tenancy (see para 4.31). Also, it does not apply to a fixed-term tenancy where a premium has been paid or the tenant is entitled to a payment referable to the value of the dwelling.

Ground 7A – new mandatory ground for serious offences/anti-social behaviour

Any of the following conditions will make out this ground:

Condition 1 – conviction for serious offence:

(a) the tenant or a person residing in or visiting the dwelling-house, has been convicted of a serious offence, and

(b) the serious offence:
  (i) was committed (wholly or partly) in or in the locality of the dwelling-house,
  (ii) was committed elsewhere against someone with a right to reside in or occupy housing accommodation in the locality of the dwelling-house, or
  (iii) was committed elsewhere against the landlord or someone employed in connection with the exercise of the landlord's housing management functions, and directly or indirectly related to or affected those functions.

Condition 2 – breach of ASB injunction:

The court has found the tenant or a person residing in or visiting the dwelling-house, has breached an injunction made under the ASB, Crime and Policing Act (ASBCPA) 2014 (other than one requiring participation in a particular activity).

Condition 3 – breach of ASB criminal behaviour order:

The tenant or a person residing in or visiting the dwelling-house, has been convicted of an offence under s30 of the ASBCPA 2014 (breach of a criminal behaviour order).

For conditions 2 and 3, the breach must have occurred in or in the locality of the dwelling-house, or if elsewhere, must have been a breach of a provision intended to prevent anti-social behaviour in relation to other residents, the landlord or employees assisting in the landlord's management functions.

Condition 4 – closure order

The dwelling-house is or has been subject to a closure order under s80 of the ASBCPA 2014, and access has been prohibited pursuant to such an order for a continuous period of more than 48 hours.

Condition 5 – Offence under the Environmental Protection Act (EPA) 1990

The tenant or a person residing in or visiting the dwelling-house, has been convicted of an offence under ss80(4)or 83((8)of the EPA and the nuisance concerned was noise nuisance.

In all the above cases, the condition is not met if there is pending appeal or if the final determination of the appeal results in the conviction, finding or order being overturned.

Ground 8 – mandatory rent arrears ground

Both at the date of the service of the notice under section 8 of this Act relating to the proceedings for possession and at the date of the hearing:
(a) if rent is payable weekly or fortnightly, at least eight weeks' rent is unpaid;
(b) if rent is payable monthly, at least two month's rent is unpaid;
(c) if rent is payable quarterly, at least one quarter's rent is more than three months in arrears; and
(d) if rent is payable yearly, at least three months' rent is more than three months in arrears;
and for the purpose of this ground 'rent' means rent lawfully due from the tenant.

Discretionary grounds – grounds on which the court may order possession if it considers it reasonable

Ground 9 – suitable alternative accommodation

Suitable alternative accommodation is available for the tenant or will be available for him when the possession order takes effect.

Ground 10 – rent arrears or breach of tenancy agreement

Some rent lawfully due from the tenant is unpaid on the date on which the proceedings for possession are begun; and [except where the court considers it just and equitable to dispense with the notice requirement] was in arrears at the date of the service of the notice seeking possession.

Ground 11 – persistent delay in paying rent

Whether or not any rent is in arrears on the date on which proceedings for possession are begun, the tenant has persistently delayed paying rent which has become lawfully due.

Ground 12 – other breach

Any obligation of the tenancy (other than one related to the payment of rent) has been broken or not performed.

Ground 13 – damage to premises

The condition of the dwelling-house or any of the common parts has deteriorated due to acts of waste, neglect or default of the tenant or a person residing in the dwelling. If the acts are those of a subtenant or lodger, the tenant has not taken such steps as he or she ought reasonably to have taken to remove that person.

Ground 14 – nuisance and annoyance

The tenant or a person residing in or visiting the dwelling-house–
(a) has been guilty of conduct causing or likely to cause a nuisance or annoyance

- to a person residing, visiting or otherwise engaging in a lawful activity in the locality, or
- to the landlord, or
- to a person employed (whether or not by the landlord) in connection with the exercise of the landlords' housing management functions, and that is directly or indirectly related to these functions, or

(b) has been convicted of using the dwelling-house or allowing it to be used for immoral or illegal purposes, or an indictable offence committed in, or in the locality of, the dwelling-house.

Ground 14ZA – riot offences

The tenant or an adult residing in the dwelling-house has been convicted of an indictable offence which took place during, and at the scene of, a riot in the United Kingdom.

Ground 14A – domestic violence

The dwelling-house was occupied (whether alone or with others) by a married couple or civil partnership couple (or a couple living together as either) and–

(a) one or both of the partners is a tenant of the dwelling-house,
(b) the landlord who is seeking possession is a registered provider of social housing or a charitable housing trust,
(c) one partner has left because of violence or threats of violence by the other towards–
  (i) that partner, or
  (ii) a member of the family of that partner who was residing with that partner immediately before the partner left, and
(d) the court is satisfied that the partner who has left is unlikely to return.

Ground 15 – deterioration of furniture

The condition of furniture provided under the tenancy has deteriorated due to ill-treatment by the tenant or other person living in the dwelling-house and, if the ill-treatment is by a lodger or subtenant, the tenant has not taken reasonable steps to remove that person.

Ground 16 – employment-related accommodation

The dwelling-house was let to the tenant in consequence of employment by the landlord, or a previous landlord, and the tenant has ceased to be in that employment.

Ground 17 – tenancy granted because of false statement

The tenant is the person, or one of the persons, to whom the tenancy was granted and the landlord was induced to grant the tenancy by a false statement made knowingly or recklessly by–

(a) the tenant, or
(b) a person acting at the tenant's instigation.

Rent Act 1977: Sch 15

Suitable alternative accommodation

In addition to the 'cases' set out in Schedule 15, section 98(1)(a) provides that a possession order may be made if suitable alternative accommodation is available to the tenant.

Part I: discretionary grounds – cases in which the court **may** order possession

Case 1 – rent arrears or breach of tenancy agreement

Where any rent lawfully due from the tenant has not been paid, or any obligation of the protected or statutory tenancy has been broken or not performed.

Case 2 – nuisance and annoyance

Where the tenant or any person residing or lodging with him or any subtenant of his has been guilty of conduct which is a nuisance or annoyance to adjoining occupiers, or has been convicted of using the dwelling-house or allowing the dwelling-house to be used for immoral or illegal purposes.

Case 3 – damage to the premises

Where the condition of the dwelling-house has deteriorated owing to acts of waste by, or the neglect or default of, the tenant or any person residing or lodging with him or any subtenant of his. Where the acts or neglect is that of a lodger or subtenant, the court must be satisfied that the tenant has not taken reasonable steps to remove the lodger or subtenant.

Case 4 – damage to furniture

Where the condition of any furniture provided for use under the tenancy has deteriorated owing to ill-treatment by the tenant or any person residing or lodging with him or any subtenant of his. Where the ill-treatment is by a lodger or subtenant, the court must be satisfied that the tenant has not taken reasonable steps to remove the lodger or subtenant.

Case 5 – tenant's notice to quit

Where the tenant has given notice to quit and, in consequence of that notice, the landlord has contracted to sell or let the dwelling-house or taken any other steps as the result of which he would, in the opinion of the court, be seriously prejudiced if he could not obtain possession.

Case 6 – subletting or assignment without consent

Where, without the consent of the landlord, the tenant has assigned or sublet the whole of the dwelling-house or sublet part of the dwelling-house, the remainder already being sublet.[170]

---

170 For certain kinds of tenancies the subletting or assignment must have taken place after a certain date, the latest of which is 14 August 1974.

Case 7 [repealed]

Case 8 – employment-related accommodation, needed for new employee

Where the dwelling-house is reasonably required by the landlord for occupation as a residence for a full-time employee, where the tenancy was let to a previous employee, who is no longer employed.[171]

Case 9 – accommodation needed as residence for landlord or family

There are three specific conditions that must be met under Case 9:
• The dwelling-house must be reasonably required by the landlord for occupation as a residence for:
 – the landlord;
 – any adult son or daughter of the landlord;
 – the landlord's father or mother; or
 – the father or mother of the landlord's wife, husband or civil partner.
• The landlord did not become landlord by purchasing the dwelling-house.[172]
• An order may not be made if the court is satisfied that greater hardship would be caused by making the order than by refusing it. The court must have regard to all the circumstances, including the availability of other accommodation to the landlord and to the tenant.

Furthermore, as the ground is discretionary the court must also be satisfied that it is reasonable to make an order.

Case 10 – tenant subletting for excessive rent

Where the tenant is subletting part of the premises and is charging a rent in excess of a registered fair rent.

*Part II: mandatory grounds – cases in which the court **must** order possession*

Under RA 1977 for all mandatory cases, other than those relating to farm tenancies (cases 16 to 18), the landlord must have served prior notice on the tenant unless the court dispenses with the requirement. The detailed grounds are complex with different requirements depending on the date the tenancy commenced. These grounds are only briefly summarised here.

Notice grounds – Cases 11–16, 19 and 20

In all these cases the following conditions must be satisfied:

---

171 Note that if an employee is *required* to live in premises for the better performance of the job there will be no tenancy: see para 1.36.
172 This condition applies to purchases after a certain date, the latest of which is 24 May 1974, depending on the particular type of tenancy and how it came to be governed by RA 1977.

- the landlord gave notice in writing to the tenant that possession might be recovered under the particular ground; or
- the court is satisfied it is just and equitable to dispense with the notice requirement.

Case 11 – returning owner-occupier + notice

The landlord must have previously occupied the premises as a residence and it must be required as a residence or for sale with vacant possession to enable the landlord to purchase a residence. Alternatively, the owner has died and the person who has inherited wants to sell with vacant possession or a mortgagee is entitled to possession.

Case 12 – accommodation purchased for retirement + notice

The landlord must have intended to occupy the dwelling-house as a residence on retirement and it must be required as a residence or for sale with vacant possession to enable the landlord to purchase a residence. Alternatively, the owner has died and the person who has inherited wants to sell with vacant possession or a mortgagee is entitled to possession.

Case 13 – out-of-season holiday let + notice

The dwelling-house is let on a fixed-term tenancy not exceeding eight months and has previously been occupied as a holiday let.

Case 14 – out-of-term student accommodation + notice

The dwelling-house is let on a fixed-term tenancy not exceeding 12 months and has been previously occupied as student accommodation.

Case 15 – letting to minister of religion + notice

The dwelling-house is let to a minister of religion as a residence to perform the duties of the office; and is required for occupation by a minister of religion as such a residence.

Case 16 – accommodation used for agricultural employees + notice

The dwelling-house was at any time occupied by an agricultural employee; and the tenant is not so employed, nor ever was and is not the widow of someone who was so employed; and it is required for occupation by an agricultural employee.

Cases 17 and 18

Further grounds applying where the dwelling-house is needed for an agricultural occupier.

Case 19 – protected shorthold tenancy

This ground applies only to protected shorthold tenancies.

Notice must have been served when the tenancy was created, though this requirement can be dispensed with if it is just and equitible.

In addition to the notice requirements when the tenancy was created, the landlord must have served a possession notice at least three months long and served within a three-month period immediately preceding the anniversary of the last day of the fixed period.

Case 20 – landlord was in armed forces and needs accommodation + notice

The dwelling-house was let after 28 November 1980 by someone who, at the time of acquisition and at the time of the letting, was a member of the regular armed forces; and it must be required as a residence or for sale with vacant possession to enable the landlord to purchase a residence. Alternatively, the owner has died and the person who has inherited wants to sell with vacant possession or a mortgagee is entitled to possession.

CHAPTER 8

Unlawful eviction and harassment by landlords

continued

Key points

- An unlawful eviction means excluding an occupier from his or her home without following the proper procedure. In most cases the proper procedure includes serving a notice, obtaining a possession order and enforcing the order by the court bailiffs.
- Some occupiers can be evicted without following this procedure but violent eviction is always a criminal offence.
- Harassment means acts likely to interfere with the occupiers' peace and comfort or withdrawing essential services. The acts must be done knowing they are likely to make the occupier leave, or to deter the occupier from asserting his or her legal rights.
- Unlawful eviction and harassment are criminal offences. They are usually prosecuted by local authorities but because of limited resources, prosecutions are rare. However, the threat of prosecution may persuade a landlord let a tenant back into occupation.
- Unlawful eviction and harassment by a landlord also give a tenant the right to take civil action – to seek damages and/or an injunction.
- Substantial damages may be awarded if an unlawfully evicted tenant had security of tenure. These damages are based on the difference in the value of the premises with the tenant in occupation and with vacant possession.
- Significant damages may be awarded to tenants without long-term security who have been harassed and/or unlawfully evicted. The court can also order the landlord to let the occupier back into the premises. In an emergency an order may be obtained very quickly, sometimes on the day of the eviction.

Criminal offences

Unlawful eviction and harassment

8.1   The criminal offences of unlawful eviction and harassment were introduced in 1964 and 1965 respectively and are now found in the Protection from Eviction Act (PEA) 1977, as amended by the Housing Act (HA) 1988.

8.2　　Under PEA 1977 there are two offences:

- unlawful eviction of a residential occupier; and
- harassment of a residential occupier.

Residential occupier

8.3　　Understanding the definition of 'residential occupier' is crucial. A residential occupier is:

> ... in relation to any premises ... a person occupying the premises as a residence, whether under a contract or by virtue of any enactment or rule of law giving him the right to remain in occupation or restricting the right of any other person to recover possession of the premises.[1]

8.4　　There are two aspects to the definition: (1) the factual issue of whether the person is occupying as a residence; and (2) the nature of the person's right to occupy (see paras 8.8–8.12) or any restriction on the right of another person to recover possession (see paras 8.14–8.15).

Occupying premises as a residence

8.5　　This is always a question of fact. To be a residential occupier there must be a substantial degree of regular personal occupation.[2] However, it is possible to reside in more than one place.[3]

8.6　　A person may be physically absent from premises yet retain the status of residential occupier. If there is an extended absence the occupier will need to prove that he or she intended to return to the premises and that there was physical evidence of the continued occupation (for example, belongings, furnishings, or friends or family 'looking after' the premises).[4] See paras 4.5–4.8 for a summary of the cases concerning the extended absence of an occupier and the case of *Loveridge v Lambeth LBC*[5] at para 8.90 below.

8.7　　However, a landlord has a defence both in criminal and civil proceedings if he or she reasonably believed that the residential occupier had ceased to occupy.

1　PEA 1977 s1(1).
2　*Herbert v Byrne* [1964] 1 All ER 882, CA.
3　*Langford Property Co v Athanassoglou* [1948] 2 All ER 722, CA. Note that it is not necessary to occupy as only or principal home to be a residential occupier, as is the case to retain secure or assured status.
4　*Brown v Brash* [1948] 1 All ER 922, CA.
5　[2014] UKSC 65, 3 December 2014.

The right to occupy

8.8   In addition to the fact of occupation, the residential occupier must occupy:

- under a contract; or
- by virtue of some enactment or rule of law that either gives the occupier the right to remain in occupation or restricts the right of any other person to recover possession.

8.9   Clearly, all tenants are residential occupiers as they occupy under a contract. Furthermore, for tenants with security of tenure there is a restriction on the landlord's right to recover possession after the tenancy comes to an end. Those who are married or in a civil partnership have a statutory right to occupy accommodation even if the agreement is in the name of their spouse/civil partner provided the premises have been their shared home.[6] All such occupiers then are 'residential occupiers' under PEA 1977. In addition, the PEA 1977 itself provides that for other occupiers (save those specifically excluded – see para 8.12) when an agreement to occupy has been ended an eviction may only be carried out by taking court proceedings. This too is a restriction on the right to recover possession and means that the person is a 'residential occupier'; an eviction other than by taking court proceedings will be unlawful.

PEA 1977 s3: restriction on eviction other than by court proceedings

8.10   PEA 1977 s3 applies where 'premises have been let as a dwelling under a tenancy which is neither a statutorily protected tenancy nor an excluded tenancy'. It also applies to 'premises occupied as a dwelling under a licence' provided it is not an excluded licence. Section 3 provides that where the tenancy or licence has come to an end but the occupier continues to reside in the premises, or a part of them, it is not lawful for the owner to enforce the right of possession otherwise than by possession proceedings in the court.

Statutorily protected tenancies

8.11   The term 'statutorily protected tenancy' is defined in PEA 1977 s8 and means the following kinds of tenancies:

- protected and statutory tenancies under the Rent Act (RA) 1977 and the Rent (Agriculture) Act 1976;

6   See paras 12.35–12.39.

- statutory tenancies arising at the end of a long lease;[7]
- tenancies which include premises occupied for business purposes, to which Part II of the Landlord and Tenant Act 1954 applies;
- agricultural tenancies;[8] and
- assured and assured shorthold tenancies.

'Excluded occupiers'

8.12   The following are excluded occupiers:[9]

- occupiers with a resident landlord who share accommodation with the resident landlord, or with a member of the family of the resident landlord;
- former trespassers granted a temporary licence;
- occupiers granted the right to occupy for a holiday only;
- occupiers granted the right to occupy other than 'for money or money's worth';
- asylum-seekers accommodated under the Immigration and Asylum Act 1999 and displaced persons accommodated under the Displaced Persons (Temporary Protection) Regulations 2005;
- occupiers of hostel accommodation where the landlord is a public sector body and the occupation is under a licence and not a tenancy.

8.13   Excluded occupiers are described in detail at paras 1.100–1.120.

Application of PEA 1977 s3

8.14   PEA 1977 s3 therefore provides that, with limited exceptions, after terminating a right to occupy under a licence or tenancy a landlord must use court proceedings to evict the occupier, unless the occupier is an excluded occupier. This then is an enactment that restricts the right of another person to recover possession: a person protected by PEA 1977 s3 is a 'residential occupier'.

---

7 These are governed by Landlord and Tenant Act 1954 Pt I and Local Government and Housing Act 1989 Sch 10, see paras 5.51–5.56.
8 Including tenancies of agricultural holdings under the Agricultural Holdings Act 1986, assured agricultural occupancy agreements under the Housing Act 1988 and farm business tenancies within the meaning of the Agricultural Tenancies Act 1995, see para 3.206–3.210.
9 PEA 1977 s3A.

8.15   Note that PEA 1977 applies only to occupiers who are 'lawfully residing in the premises or part of them at the termination of the former tenancy or licence'.[10]

Evicting excluded occupiers without a court order

8.16   Before an excluded occupier can be evicted any occupation agreement must be brought to an end. If the agreement is a tenancy, a notice to quit must be served. If the agreement is a licence the contractual period of notice must be given. For excluded tenants the requirement that a notice to quit is at least 28 days long does not apply;[11] the only requirement is the common law rule that the notice must be for at least a period of the tenancy (eg, one week or one month, usually depending on the rental period). If there is no tenancy and no express provision about notice, 'reasonable notice' must be given to end the agreement[12] (see paras 1.122–1.123 for consideration of what constitutes reasonable notice).

8.17   After notice has expired the owner may exclude the occupier without obtaining a court order. However, the forcible eviction of an occupier will usually be a criminal offence under the Criminal Law Act 1977 (see para 8.38 below). What this means is that physical possession can be taken when the occupier is out of the premises but physical force cannot be used to remove the occupier from the premises.

An exception: temporary accommodation pending homelessness decision

8.18   A common situation in which occupiers have no protection under the PEA 1977 is when they are occupying as licensees pending a decision on a homeless application.

---

10 PEA 1977 s3(2) and (2B). The fact that the protection is given to those lawfully residing in the premises means that the unlawful tenants of a borrower have no protection against a lender entitled to possession: *Bolton Building Society v Cobb and others* [1965] 3 All ER 814. The position of unlawful subtenants as against the 'head landlord' is more complex and is dealt with at paras 4.92–4.128.

11 PEA 1977 s5.

12 *Smith v Northside Developments Ltd* (1988) 55 P&CR 164.

368 Housing law handbook / chapter 8

In *R (ZH and CN) v Newham LBC and Lewisham LBC*[13] two women
and their children were accommodated by their respective local
authorities, pending decisions on their homeless applications. Both
were found to be intentionally homeless and given notice to leave
their temporary accommodation. They brought claims for judicial
review to challenge the local authorities' decisions to evict them
without first obtaining possession orders. The Supreme Court held
that they were not entitled to the protection of section 3 of the PEA
1977. Previous case-law was considered and the majority found that
the term 'dwelling' denoted 'a greater degree of settled occupation
than "residence"'.[14] The nature of the temporary accommodation
was considered: it was provided on an interim basis pending a
decision; by arrangement with others who providing 'nightly-let' or
'spot booked' accommodation; the applicants were often moved
from one property to another; and did not cease to be 'homeless'
while accommodated in interim accommodation. By a majority
of 5:2 it was decided that they were not 'premises occupied as a
dwelling under a licence.' The Court also referred to the fact that it
would cause local authorities great inconvenience and expense if
they were required to obtain court orders every time they wanted
to evict occupiers after deciding that no housing duty was owed,
although this alone would not justify finding that they fell outside
the protection of the Act. Lord Neuberger and Lady Hale dissented
observing that Parliament could have added such licences to the list
of excluded licences but had not done so.

The majority also held that there was no breach of article 8
since the process of homelessness decision-making, taken as a
whole, offered sufficient opportunity for applicants to challenge the
decision to evict.

The majority decision means that all occupiers in interim
accommodation pending decisions under the various parts of
Part VII (and also pending a decision on an assessment under the
Children Act 1989) can be evicted without receiving a formal notice
to quit and without a court order. If it is argued in an individual case

---

13 [2014] UKSC 62, 12 November 2014. The judgment confirms the earlier
    decisions of the Court of Appeal in the cases of *Roma Desnousse v Newham
    LBC, Paddington Churches HA, Veni Properties Ltd* [2006] EWCA Civ 547, 12
    May 2006 and *Mohammed v Manek and RLBC Kensington & Chelsea* (1995) 27
    HLR 439, 30 March 1995.
14 Lord Hodge at [26].

that an eviction would be unlawful because of the short notice or the disproportionate impact on the family, any challenge would be by judicial review.[15]

It is not therefore necessary to obtain a possession order to evict a licensee occupying accommodation pending a homeless decision. However, the situation will be different if the person remains in the same accommodation *after* a housing duty has been accepted even though the nature of the occupation agreement and the parties may remain the same. As Lady Hale pointed out in her dissenting judgment in *CN v Lewisham LBC* above at para 8.18, it is hard to understand how the position can change fundamentally when the nature of the occupation and terms of the agreement remain the same. But this is the outcome of the majority decision in *CN v Lewisham LBC*.

8.19 So, the following occupiers of residential accommodation may be evicted by a landlord without a court order:

- excluded occupiers listed in PEA 1977 s3A;
- homeless applicants granted a licence pending a homeless decision;
- trespassers who entered as trespassers.

8.20 For other residential occupiers an eviction without a court order will be unlawful, giving rise to a civil claim for damages and an injunction. It may also be a criminal offence. The criminal offences are summarised below (paras 8.21–8.27).

Unlawful eviction

8.21 The offence is committed if:

Any person unlawfully deprives the residential occupier of any premises of his or her occupation of the premises or any part of the premises, or attempts to do so.[16]

8.22 No offence is committed if the person believed, and had reasonable cause to believe, that the residential occupier had ceased to reside in the premises.

---

15 Lord Hodge suggested at [71] that a proportionality review might be undertaken as part of an appeal under HA 1996 s204 but the county court's jurisdiction is very limited, see para 15.63.
16 PEA 1977 s1(2).

Harassment

8.23 There are two different offences under the PEA 1977: one committed by a landlord or landlord's agent and one committed by any person.

Harassment by landlord or agent

8.24 The offence is committed if:

- a landlord or landlord's agent does acts likely to interfere with the peace or comfort of the residential occupier or members of the household, or persistently withdraws or withholds services reasonably required for the occupation of the premises as a residence; and
- he or she knows, or has reasonable cause to believe, that the conduct is likely to cause the residential occupiers to give up occupation of the whole or part of the premises or to refrain from exercising any right or pursuing any remedy in respect of the whole or part of the premises.[17]

8.25 The first part of the definition describes the two kinds of act that make out the offence. Note that a single act likely to interfere with peace or comfort of the occupier is sufficient. However, if the complaint is about the withdrawal or witholding of services this must be 'persistent'. This means there must be more than a single act or there must be 'deliberate continuity' (for example, a refusal to reconnect a service).[18]

8.26 In either case there must also be the necessary intention; the act or acts must be done by someone who knows that the likely outcome is that the occupier will leave or refrain from exercising rights in relation to the premises.[19]

8.27 For the offence of harassment it is not necessary that the likely outcome is that the occupier leaves the premises. It is sufficient that it is likely to deter an occupier from pursuing a complaint to the council or from taking legal action about disrepair. An intention to force an occupier to give up occupation temporarily while building works are carried out is not sufficient.[20]

---

17 PEA 1977 s1(3A).
18 *R v Varol* [1972] Crim LR 318, CA.
19 *R v Burke* (1990) 22 HLR 433, HL, and *R v Yuthiwattana* (1984) 16 HLR 49, CA.
20 *Schon v Camden LBC* (1986) 18 HLR 341, QBD.

Definition of landlord and agent[21]

8.28 The 'landlord' means the immediate landlord and any superior land-lord (ie a landlord who granted to the immediate landlord his or her interest). The immediate landlord is the person who would be entitled to possession but for the occupier's right to remain in occupation. This includes a person to whom the original landlord sold or transferred ownership.

8.29 An 'agent of the landlord' is not defined in PEA 1977. An agent is any person who acts on behalf of the landlord. It includes someone who has an express agreement to do so, whether written or oral. This would include a lettings agent or rent collector. It can also include any person who implicitly acts on behalf of the landlord. This may be difficult to prove but in practice the evidence often makes it clear that the acts were carried out on behalf of the landlord. However, note that even if the acts were done on behalf of the landlord it is the agent and not the landlord who commits the offence.[22]

Defence

8.30 For harassment it is a defence if the landlord or agent can prove that he or she had reasonable grounds for doing the acts or withdrawing or withholding the services in question.

Harassment by 'any person'

8.31 An offence of harassment under PEA 1977 may also be committed by any person, not necessarily the landlord or agent. In this case the person must *intend* to cause the occupier to give up occupation of the whole or part or to refrain from exercising any right or remedy in respect of the premises: PEA 1977 s1(3).

21 PEA 1977 s1(3)(c).
22 See *R v Qureshi (Mohammed)* [2011] EWCA Crim 1584, 17 May 2011.

Local authority powers

Prosecutions

8.32   Local authorities have the power to prosecute offences committed under the PEA 1977. However, prosecutions are rare.[23] This is partly because of the limited resources of local authorities, which must carry out all of the investigations and evidence gathering and, to succeed, must prove the case beyond reasonable doubt. Even if a prosecution is successful, the penalties imposed by the courts are usually insufficient to operate as a deterrent. Few local authorities now employ specialist officers (usually known as tenancy relations officers) to deal with such cases. Although the police can prosecute such offences they rarely do so, leaving enforcement of the Act to local authorities.

8.33   Nevertheless, local authorities may use the threat of an eviction to persuade a landlord to resolve a dispute, for example, to allow a tenant back into premises, to re-connect services or stop committing acts of harassment.

Criminal penalties

8.34   The offences under the PEA 1977 may be tried in a magistrates' court or the Crown Court. If tried in a magistrates' court the maximum penalty is six months in prison and/or a fine of up to £5,000. In the Crown Court the maximum term of imprisonment is two years and/or an unlimited fine. The court also has the usual range of sentencing powers and may grant an absolute or conditional discharge, make a community order, or suspend a sentence of imprisonment.

8.35   In addition, the court can order that compensation be paid to the victim 'for personal injury, loss or damage' resulting from the offence.[24] However, awards of compensation by the criminal courts are confined to simple and straightforward cases.[25] Where an offence under the PEA 1977 has been committed, the victim will almost certainly have a strong claim for damages in the county court (see paras 8.107–8.116 below).

8.36   Under the PEA 1977 the criminal courts cannot order that a victim of unlawful eviction be re-instated or restrain future unlawful

---

23 The number of prosecutions has declined since the early 1990s. In 2008 the total number of prosecutions nationally under PEA 1977 was 34, in 2009, 49 and in 2010, 37: Hansard HC, 7 June 2011, col 164W.

24 Powers of the Criminal Courts (Sentencing) Act 2000 s130.

25 *Herbert v Lambeth LBC* (1991) 24 HLR 299, QBD.

behaviour by the landlord. Where a landlord is prosecuted, a civil action may be also be brought by the victim to claim damages and an injunction. Levels of damages awarded by the civil courts will usually be much higher than compensation awarded in the criminal courts.

Re-connecting services

8.37 Local authorities also have the power to arrange for the restoration or continuance of gas, water or electricity supplies where the supplies have been or are likely to be cut off because of failure by the owner to pay for the services.[26] Authorities are reluctant to use these powers as it involves expenditure which it may be difficult or impossible to recover from the landlord. Some authorities only use the powers as a last resort if the occupiers include young children or the elderly. Nevertheless, local authorities should be asked to exercise their powers. If an authority refuses to do so this may assist a person applying as homeless to the same authority: he or she can argue that it is not reasonable to continue to occupy accommodation without necessary services.

Offences under the Criminal Law Act 1977

8.38 Even where there is no requirement to obtain and enforce a possession order to lawfully evict an occupier, it is a criminal offence to use violence to secure entry to premises.

8.39 Section 6(1) of the Criminal Law Act (CLA) 1977 provides that it is an offence if:

... any person who, without lawful authority, uses or threatens violence for the purpose of securing entry into any premises for himself or for any other person ... provided that:
(a) there is someone present on those premises at the time who is opposed to the entry which the violence is intended to secure; and
(b) the person using or threatening the violence knows that is the case.

8.40 The violence may be directed against the person or against property.[27] Forcing open a door or window is therefore an offence, if there

---

26 Local Government (Miscellaneous Provisions) Act 1976 s33.
27 CLA 1977 s6(4)(a).

is someone in the premises opposed to the entry and this is known to the perpetrator.

8.41   The offence is committed when violence is used to 'secure entry' into the premises. It is immaterial whether it is intended to secure possession or for some other purpose.[28]

Lawful authority

8.42   'Lawful authority' means the authority to use reasonable force to secure entry, not having the legal right to possession.

8.43   The CLA 1977 specifies situations in which no offence is committed by the use of force to secure entry to premises, ie the situations in which a person does have lawful authority to use reasonable force. These situations are described below in paras 8.46–8.56.

Displaced residential occupiers (DROs) and protected intending occupiers (PIOs)

8.44   The CLA 1977 sets out procedures to enable those occupying (or intending to occupy) residential premises to take possession as against trespassers. However, trespass in residential premises is now a criminal offence which means that the occupiers can be arrested and removed so these procedures are now redundant.

Court bailiffs

8.45   A court bailiff executing a possession order may use reasonable force to secure entry.

Police officers

8.46   A police officer exercising a power of arrest or search under the criminal law may use reasonable force to secure entry. There are certain specific criminal offences relating to trespass for which an officer may use these powers thereby effectively removing the trespasser. These include removing:

- a person who is in 'a residential building' as a trespasser, having entered as a trespasser, who knows or ought to know that they are a trespasser, and who is living in the building or intending to live in the building for any period;[29]

---

28 CLA 1977 s6(4)(b).
29 See LASPO 2012 s144.

- a person who is on premises as a trespasser, having entered as a trespasser, who has with him or her on the premises an offensive weapon;[30]
- a person who is evicted following the making of an interim possession order who re-enters the premises.[31]

Prosecutions for offences under CLA 1977

8.47 Unlike under the PEA 1977, local authorities have no power to prosecute offences under the CLA 1977. Such offences are investigated by the police and prosecuted by the Crown Prosecution Service. The maximum penalties for convictions under CLA 1977 s6 are the same as for PEA 1977 offences described in para 8.36 above. Note that the penalties for the 'trespassing offences' described above are more severe: for the offence of trespass in a residential building under section 144 of Legal Aid, Sentencing and Punishment of Offenders Act (LASPO) 2012 the maximum penalty is imprisonment for up to 51 weeks or a fine of up to £5,000.

Civil proceedings

8.48 When a landlord has harassed or unlawfully evicted an occupier there will usually be a number of potential causes of action, based in contract and in tort. See paras 22.8–22.18 for an explanation of causes of action.

Contract

8.49 A tenancy agreement is a legally binding contract. If one party breaches the contract the other party can bring an action for damages and can also ask the court to grant an injunction to restrain future breaches of the contract. A tenancy agreement may contain an express term that the tenant will enjoy 'quiet enjoyment' of the premises. If not, such a term will be implied.

---

30 CLA 1977 s8.
31 Criminal Justice and Public Order Act 1994 s76.

Implied terms of the tenancy agreement

8.50 There are two terms implied into all tenancy agreements that are relevant in claims based on harassment or unlawful eviction by landlords:

- the covenant of quiet enjoyment; and
- the covenant not to 'derogate from grant'.

Quiet enjoyment

8.51 It is an implied term of all tenancy agreements (but not licence agreements), whether written or oral, that the landlord covenants to allow the tenant quiet enjoyment of the premises. This term will always be relied on in a civil claim for unlawful eviction or harassment brought by a tenant.

8.52 Conduct by a landlord that interferes with the right to occupy undisturbed will usually be a breach of the covenant of quiet enjoyment.[32] This can range from minor interference to an actual eviction.

Derogation from grant

8.53 It is also implied into all tenancy agreements that the landlord covenants not to 'derogate' from the grant of the tenancy. This covenant may be relevant if the landlord retains possession of part of the premises, such as the common parts, or of neighbouring premises. A landlord will breach the covenant if he or she does anything in relation to premises in the landlord's control which makes the tenant's premises materially less fit for the purpose of the letting. This could include letting the other premises for a purpose that interferes with peaceful residential use of the tenant's home.

Common law torts

8.54 A tort is a civil wrong. Some torts exist because they are recognised by the courts ('common law torts') and others are created by statute ('statutory torts'). The following common law torts will often be relied on in civil actions for unlawful eviction and harassment:

- nuisance (see paras 8.55–8.56);
- trespass (see paras 8.57–8.66);

---

32 However, there may be instances where the landlord's conduct does disturb the tenant's quiet enjoyment but is not a breach of the covenant, eg carrying out necessary repairs provided reasonable steps are taken to minimise the disturbance, see para 10.70.

- assault and battery (see paras 8.64–8.66); and
- intimidation (see para 8.67).

The relevant statutory torts are set out at paras 8.68–8.95.

Nuisance

8.55   Nuisance is a state of affairs, condition or activity that interferes with the use of neighbouring land. It includes causing physical damage to premises as well as interference with the use or enjoyment of premises, such as loud noise or obnoxious smells.

8.56   Whether acts amount to a nuisance must be judged according to the standard of a reasonable person[33] and what is judged to be a nuisance depends on the circumstances. Noise caused by home improvements may not constitute a nuisance if carried on for a limited period at a reasonable time. The same level of noise may constitute a nuisance if caused intentionally in order to annoy or if the activities are conducted at unsocial times such as early in the morning or late at night.[34]

Trespass

8.57   There are three kinds of trespass: trespass to land; trespass to goods; and trespass to the person.

Trespass to land

8.58   Trespass means entering premises without the permission of the person entitled to possession, or remaining on premises after permission has been withdrawn.

8.59   Only a person entitled to possession can sue in trespass. Therefore, a tenant can make a claim in trespass but a licensee cannot since a licensee does not have a legal right to possession.

8.60   A landlord who enters premises without the tenant's consent commits the tort of trespass.

Trespass to goods

8.61   This means the unlawful interference with goods belonging to someone else. If the goods are taken and used without permission this is known as 'conversion'.

8.62   Action can be taken by the person who owns the goods and does not depend on rights in relation to the premises.

33 *Robinson v Kilvert* (1889) 41 ChD 88, CA.
34 *Christie v Davey* [1893] 1 ChD 316.

8.63   A landlord who simply disposes of an occupier's belongings or removes them and leaves them outside the premises may face an action for damages in trespass, even if the eviction itself was not unlawful.[35] Damages can be awarded to compensate for the loss or damage to the goods.

Trespass to the person

8.64   This is also known as 'assault and battery'. As well as being a criminal offence, an assault is a tort.

8.65   An assault is an act that puts the victim in immediate and reasonable fear of being physically attacked. Battery is the actual application of physical force to another person.

8.66   Action can be taken by the victim regardless of their rights in relation to the premises.

Intimidation

8.67   The tort of intimidation is committed when a person makes a demand accompanied by an unlawful threat which results in damage to the person threatened or to some other person. The threat may be verbal or by acts but must be contrary to the criminal or civil law. An example would be a threat to unlawfully evict or assault a person if rent was not paid by a certain date or time.

Statutory torts

8.68   There are two statutory torts relevant to claims for unlawful eviction and harassment against landlords:

- unlawful eviction under the Housing Act 1988 (see paras 8.71–8.80);
- harassment under the Protection from Harassment Act 1997 (see paras 8.91–8.95).

8.69   In both cases the relevant Act also sets out a particular remedy available if the tort is proved.

---

35 Under the law of bailment a person who comes into possession of another person's belongings has a duty to take reasonable care of them for a reasonable period and to give the person a reasonable opportunity to collect them.
For local authorities there is statutory provision regarding former tenants' belongings, under the Local Government (Miscellaneous Provisions) Act 1982 s41.

Housing Act 1988: unlawful eviction

8.70   Section 27 of the Housing Act (HA) 1988 created a specific tort of unlawful eviction. The definition mirrors the criminal offences under the PEA 1977. There are two ways in which the tort can be committed:

- unlawful eviction; or
- attempted eviction or harassment.

Unlawful eviction

8.71   Under HA 1988 s27(1) the tort of unlawful eviction is committed when a landlord or any person acting on behalf of the landlord unlawfully deprives a residential occupier of his or her occupation of the whole or part of the premises.

Attempted eviction or harassment

8.72   The tort under HA 1988 s27(2) is committed where a landlord or any person acting on behalf of the landlord either:

- attempts to unlawfully evict a residential occupier; or
- harasses a residential occupier;

with the result that the occupier gives up occupation.[36]

8.73   An example of the tort under HA 1988 s27(2) would be where a landlord attempts to exclude the tenant by changing the locks but the tenant is able to gain entry. If the tenant subsequently gives up occupation because of the landlord's conduct, the tort under section 27(2) would be committed. If the landlord had successfully excluded the tenant, the tort under section 27(1) would have been committed.

8.74   Harassment is defined in the same terms as for the criminal offence. The tort is committed where the landlord or any person acting on behalf of the landlord does acts likely to interfere with the peace or comfort of the residential occupier or members of his or her household, or persistently withdraws or withholds services reasonably required for the occupation of the premises as a residence. Furthermore, he or she must know or have reasonable cause to believe that the conduct is likely to cause the residential occupier to give up occupation of the premises or any part, or to refrain from exercising any right or pursuing any remedy in respect of the premises or any part.

36 HA 1988 s27(2).

8.75   If the harassment does not result in the occupier giving up occupation, the statutory tort is not committed. However, the tenant can still bring a civil claim relying on the torts described above at paras 8.54–8.67, as well as breach of contract.

8.76   As is the case for the criminal offence of harassment, it is not necessary that the behaviour is intended or likely to make the occupier leave the premises. It is sufficient that the perpetrator knows it is likely to dissuade an occupier from exercising rights, such as taking action about disrepair or complaining to the local authority about the premises or the landlord.

Who to sue

8.77   Although the tort may be committed by someone acting on the landlord's behalf, it is the landlord who is liable to pay damages.[37] This is in contrast to a prosecution of a criminal offence under the PEA 1977 which is brought against the person committing the acts, for example, the landlord's agent.

Defences

8.78   The defences available to a landlord are the same as for the criminal offences.[38] It is a defence if the landlord can prove the following:

- that he or she believed and had reasonable cause to believe that the person had ceased to reside in the premises; or
- if harassment is alleged, that he or she had reasonable grounds for doing the acts complained of or withdrawing or withholding the services.

8.79   'Reasonable grounds' would include disconnecting services because they were dangerous or where necessary works of repair interfered with the occupier's peace or comfort. It would not extend to harassment by a landlord who had a legitimate claim for possession or rent arrears against an occupier.

8.80   If the tort under HA 1988 s27 is proved the damages will be calculated according to the formula set out in HA 1988 s28.

Section 28 damages

8.81   HA 1988 section 28 damages are assessed on the basis of the difference between:

37   HA 1988 s27(3).
38   HA 1988 s27(8).

- the landlord's interest, valued on the basis that the residential occupier continues to have the same right to occupy the premises as before giving up occupation or being evicted; and
- the interest valued on the basis that the residential occupier has ceased to have that right.

8.82 To determine the relevant values expert evidence will usually be needed.[39]

Reduction of section 28 damages

8.83 The amount of damages may be reduced by the court in the following circumstances:[40]

- where, *prior to the acts complained of,* the victim was guilty of conduct which makes it reasonable to reduce the amount of damages; or
- where, *before the start of the proceedings,* the landlord offered to reinstate the victim, who unreasonably refused the offer.[41]

8.84 The offer of re-instatement must be genuine: handing the tenant a key to a lock which did not work and where the room previously occupied had been wrecked was held not to be an offer of re-instatement for these purposes.[42]

8.85 In both cases the court may reduce the damages 'as it thinks appropriate'.

Re-instatement of occupier

8.86 No damages can be awarded under HA 1988 s28 if, *before court proceedings are finally disposed of,* the victim is re-instated so as to become a residential occupier again. This may be by agreement or by order of the court.[43]

---

39 The relevant values are assessed as at the time immediately before the person ceased to occupy. Certain assumptions are made for the purposes of the valuation, namely that the landlord is selling on the open market to a willing buyer, that neither the residential occupier nor a member of his or her family wish to buy, and any potential development value of the land is disregarded: HA 1988 s28(3).

40 HA 1988 s27(7).

41 Furthermore, damages may be reduced even if the victim has obtained alternative accommodation before the offer was made, if the court considers that it would have been unreasonable to refuse the offer had he or she not obtained alternative accommodation: HA 1988 s27(7)(b).

42 *Tagro v Cafane and Patel* (1991) 23 HLR 250, CA.

43 HA 1988 s27(6).

8.87   So, a tenant who is granted an injunction for re-instatement and re-occupies cannot be awarded section 28 damages.

Offers to re-instate

8.88   The consequences of offers to re-instate can be summarised as follows:

- If an offer to re-instate is made *before* the claim for unlawful eviction is *commenced,* an unreasonable refusal may result in a reduction of damages.
- If the offer is made *after* the claim for unlawful eviction is *commenced* the offer may be refused without any consequence in relation to the award of section 28 damages.
- A tenant who *accepts* an offer of re-instatement, before the proceedings are *concluded,* cannot be awarded section 28 damages. Damages for other causes of action, such as breach of contract, nuisance, trespass etc may still be awarded.

Valuing the tenant's interest

8.89   The valuation must be carried out on the basis of the tenant's actual interest and not on a notional basis. This means that the level of HA 1988 s28 damages in relation to tenants with no long-term security will be limited.

> In *King v Jackson*[44] an assured shorthold tenant was unlawfully evicted. In the county court she was awarded £11,000 under section 28.
>
>   The Court of Appeal upheld the landlord's appeal: where a property was let to a tenant with little security at a market rent the difference in the value of the premises with the tenant in occupation and with vacant possession would be minimal, if anything. An award of £1,500 was substituted.

8.90   In *Wandsworth LBC v Osei-Bonsu*[45] the Court of Appeal considered how damages should be assessed and the power to reduce damages where the victim is guilty of conduct that justifies a reduction.

---

44   (1997) 30 HLR 541, CA.
45   (1998) 31 HLR 515, CA.

Mr Osei-Bonsu was a joint secure tenant with his wife, who had left the premises because of his violence. The authority evicted him following the service by his wife of a defective notice to quit. He succeeded in his claim for unlawful eviction under HA 1988 s27 and was awarded £30,000 on the basis of agreed valuation evidence.

The Court of Appeal reduced this by two-thirds to £10,000 on the basis of the husband's violence towards his wife. It was also held that the valuers had failed to have regard to the actual circumstances existing at the time of the eviction, namely that the tenancy was precarious and could be ended by the wife serving a correct notice to quit. Appropriate damages would have been £2,000. However, the court did not interfere with the valuation evidence as this had been agreed by the parties.

In *Kalas v Farmer*[46] the landlord took possession during a period when an assured tenant was in prison, and put the property up for sale. On his release from prison the tenant claimed damages for unlawful eviction under HA 1988 ss27–28. He was awarded £49,500 plus £3,200 in special damages. The landlord's defence was that the premises had been abandoned and the tenancy ended or alternatively that he believed the premises to have been abandoned. Both arguments were rejected on the evidence. On appeal the landlord also argued that the damages should have been reduced on the basis of the tenant's conduct: he had been found guilty of theft and storing stolen goods in the premises, which resulted in the police breaking down the door following his arrest. This was also rejected as it had not been pleaded or raised at trial.

In *Loveridge v Lambeth LBC*[47] the secure tenant occupied a one-bedroom flat. His tenancy agreement required that he inform the local authority landlord if he was absent from the premises for more than eight weeks. He travelled to Ghana in July 2009 and did not return until December 2009. Although he continued to pay the rent by standing order he did not inform the authority of his absence. Concerned that he may have died in the premises the authority

---

46 [2010] EWCA Civ 108, 29 January 2010.
47 [2014] UKSC 65, 3 December 2014.

forced entry in September 2009 and, finding it empty, cleared it
of his possessions and let it to a new introductory tenant. On his
return, the tenant claimed damages for unlawful eviction and the
unlawful disposal of his property. The issue was whether he was
entitled to damages under HA 1988 s27, in addition to the common
law damages for the unlawful eviction and the special damages for
the lost possessions. At trial he was awarded £90,500 calculated
under section 28 as the difference in value between the flat with
vacant possession and with a secure tenant in occupation. The
Court of Appeal reversed this decision holding that no damages
under section 28 should be awarded because the court had to take
account of the fact that if the local authority sold the premises it
would be to a private buyer and this would 'convert' the secure
tenancy into a less secure assured tenancy which would be at
a market rent. The Court of Appeal therefore decided that the
difference in value was nil. The Supreme Court upheld the tenant's
appeal. The formula in section 28 was clear: the premises had to be
valued on the basis of the tenant being in occupation immediately
before the eviction enjoying the 'same right' of occupation as at
that time. Though local authorities would rarely perpetrate unlawful
evictions deliberately, ss27–28 apply to local authority landlords as
well as private landlords. The award of £90,500, calculated under
section 28, was re-instated.

Protection from Harassment Act 1997

8.91   The Protection from Harassment Act (PHA) 1997 provides that harassment is both a criminal offence and a tort. It was introduced to
address the problem of stalking, where someone's behaviour towards
another may not be explicitly threatening or intended to cause fear
but nevertheless causes alarm or distress.

What is harassment?

8.92   PHA 1997 does not define the term 'harassment' but section 1(1)
provides that a person must not pursue a course of conduct which
amounts to harassment of another, and which he or she knows or

ought to know amounts to harassment of the other.[48] PHA 1997 s7 offers the following definitions:

- a 'course of conduct' must involve conduct on at least two occasions;[49]
- references to harassing a person include alarming or causing the person distress;
- 'conduct' includes speech; and
- aiding, abetting, counselling or procuring harassment by another person is also prohibited.

8.93 It is a defence to show that:[50]

- the conduct was pursued to prevent or detect crime – this would include the actions of not only police officers but also tenancy relations officers and private individuals;
- the conduct was pursued under any statute or rule of law or to comply with a statutory condition or requirement – this could include sending a statutory demand for a debt or a notice to quit; or
- the pursuit of the conduct was reasonable in the circumstances.

Enforcement

8.94 Since the behaviour prohibited under the PHA 1997 is both a tort and a criminal offence, the victim has two options: a civil claim against the perpetrator for damages and an injunction or complaint to the police for investigation and prosecution of the perpetrator.

8.95 Unusually, the civil and criminal remedies overlap: breach of a civil injunction is a criminal offence; and the criminal courts can make restraining orders to prevent future harassment.

---

48 PHA 1977 s1(1). A person 'ought to know that it amounts to harassment of another if a reasonable person in possession of the same information would think the course of conduct amounted to harassment of the other': s1(2).

49 See *Boylin v Christie NHS Foundation* [2014] EWHC 3363 (Admin), 17 October 2014.

50 PHA 1997 s1(3). In addition to these defences, certain acts, certified by the Home Secretary, and done on behalf of the Crown, relating to national security, the economic well-being of the UK or to prevent or detect serious crime are excluded from the PHA 1997: s12.

Criminal offences under PHA 1997

Harassment

8.96   Harassment, as defined in para 8.102 above, is a criminal offence punishable by a fine of up to £5,000 and/or up to six months' imprisonment.[51] However, if the offence was 'racially or religiously aggravated' the maximum penalty is two years' imprisonment.[52]

Violent harassment

8.97   The offence of 'violent harassment' is committed where a person pursues a course of conduct which 'causes another to fear, on at least two occasions, that violence will be used against him ... if he know or ought to know that the course of conduct will cause the other so to fear on each of those occasions'.[53]

8.98   The offence is punishable in the magistrates' court by a fine of up to £5,000 and/or imprisonment for up to six months, and in the Crown Court by an unlimited fine and/or imprisonment for up to five years. If the offence was 'racially or religiously aggravated' the maximum penalty is seven years imprisonment.

8.99   The defences available to a charge of violent harassment are the same as the defences to an allegation of harassment (listed above in para 8.103) save that it is not a defence to a charge of violent harassment that the conduct was reasonable; the defendant must show that the conduct was reasonable 'for the protection of himself or another or for the protection of his or another's property'.[54]

Breach of a restraining order

8.100   Following a conviction for either offence the criminal courts can impose restraining orders to protect the victim from further harassment or conduct causing a fear of violence.[55]

8.101   Breach of a restraining order without reasonable excuse is also a criminal offence. The maximum penalty in the magistrates' court is

---

51   PHA 1997 s2.
52   Crime and Disorder Act (CDA) 1998 s32. A crime is racially or religiously aggravated if, at the time the offence is committed, there is evidence of a hostility based on the victim's membership or presumed membership of a racial or religious group, or the offence is motivated by such hostility: CDA 1998 s28.
53   PHA 1997 s4(1).
54   PHA 1997 s4(3).
55   PHA 1997 s5.

a fine of up to £5,000 and/or imprisonment of up to six months and in the Crown Court an unlimited fine and/or imprisonment of up to five years.

Breach of a civil injunction

8.102   Where a civil injunction has been granted to restrain the defendant from pursuing a course of conduct that amounts to harassment, it is a criminal offence to do anything prohibited by the injunction without reasonable excuse.[56]

8.103   The offence is punishable in the magistrates' court by a fine of up to £5,000 and/or imprisonment for up to six months and in the Crown Court by an unlimited fine and/or imprisonment for up to five years.[57]

8.104   Civil injunctions are enforced in the civil courts by application for committal to prison for contempt of court. The PHA 1997 provides that the civil courts may issue a warrant for the arrest of a person if there is evidence of breach of the injunction[58] and contempt of court may be punished by up to two years' imprisonment. However, a person can only be convicted of the offence of breaching a civil injunction *or* punished for contempt of court, not both.[59]

Other remedies in the civil courts

8.105   The above paragraphs (8.70–8.80 and 8.91–8.95) describe the particular remedies available to a claimant who proves the statutory torts of unlawful eviction under the HA 1988 or harassment under the PHA 1997. However, even if such claims are not made, the usual civil remedies are available to a claimant alleging harassment or unlawful eviction by a landlord.

8.106   A claim may be made for:

- damages; and
- an injunction – to prevent future harassment and/or to force a landlord to re-admit.

---

56 PHA 1997 s3(6).
57 PHA 1997 s3(9).
58 PHA 1997 s3(3)–(5).
59 PHA 1997 s3(7) and (8).

Damages

8.107 A claimant may claim the following types of damages:

- special damages;
- general damages;
- aggravated damages;
- exemplary damages.

Special damages

8.108 Special damages are for quantifiable loss or expenditure incurred as a result of the landlord's unlawful actions. They may include sums for the value of damaged goods, the cost of temporary accommodation and any other loss that can be quantified.

General damages

8.109 General damages are assessed by the court to compensate the claimant for unquantifiable loss or inconvenience.

8.110 General damages may include amounts to compensate a claimant for the anxiety, distress and inconvenience suffered as a result of a landlord's unlawful behaviour, as well as any personal injury suffered. Examples of damages awards are set out below.

> In *Addison v Croft*[60] the claimant was an assured shorthold tenant whose landlady was selling the property. When the landlady entered the premises without warning, accompanied by an estate agent and prospective purchaser, there was an argument between the landlady and the tenant's girlfriend. Later the landlady came to the premises and insisted that the girlfriend leave. Two weeks later the front door was kicked in and four men threw the tenant and his girlfriend out into the street. One of the men was the landlady's former boyfriend. The tenant suffered bruises and scratches. The landlady refused to re-admit the tenant until after he obtained an injunction. He slept in his van for 20 nights.
>
> The tenant was awarded general damages of £3,000 for the actual eviction and the fact that he was deprived of his home and belongings for 20 days. He was also awarded aggravated damages of £1,000 and exemplary damages of £1,000.

60 June 2008 *Legal Action* 31, Preston County Court, 17 April 2008.

8.111 General damages are intended to compensate the claimant but it is common in claims for unlawful eviction and harassment for additional damages to be claimed under the heads of aggravated damages and exemplary damages.

Aggravated damages

8.112 These may be awarded if the defendant has behaved in a particularly unpleasant or violent way or where he or she has ignored the orders of the court.

> In *Youziel v Andrews*[61] the claimant was an assured shorthold tenant of a one-bedroom flat. The defendant was initially his landlord but then transferred his interest to a third party. Notice of this was not given to the tenant and the defendant continued to manage the property. Rent arrears accrued because the defendant was an asylum-seeker not eligible for benefits. Over a six-week period the defendant subjected the claimant to a campaign of harassment. On ten occasions he threatened the claimant, by entering the flat, telephoning and shouting threats, including that the claimant 'would pay with his life'. The claimant and two friends also assaulted the claimant, slapping and kicking him and throwing him to the ground. He sustained an injury to his knee and suffered stress, anxiety and weight loss.
> At Lambeth County Court the claimant was awarded general damages of £13,000 for the personal injuries sustained, £4,300 in aggravated damages for the tort of assault and £2,700 in respect of breach of covenant of quiet enjoyment. The total award was £20,000 plus interest of £200.

Exemplary damages

8.113 Exemplary damages may be awarded if the defendant intended to profit from the unlawful act. Such damages are in addition to compensatory damages and are intended to punish or set an example in order to deter unlawful behaviour.[62] They are calculated to ensure that any financial gain resulting from the unlawful action is paid in damages to the victim.

8.114 The following case is a good example of an award of exemplary damages in an unlawful eviction claim.

---

61 March 2003 *Legal Action* 30, Lambeth County Court, 23 January 2003.
62 *Rookes v Barnard* [1964] 1 All ER 367, HL.

> In *Drane v Evangelou*[63] the tenant's rent was reduced following an
> application to the rent officer. In response, the landlord moved
> other people into the premises, changed the locks and moved the
> tenant's belongings into the back yard. An injunction was granted
> but the tenant was not able to return to the premises for ten weeks.
> Exemplary damages of £1,000 were awarded for what was described
> as the landlord's 'monstrous behaviour'.
>
> The Court of Appeal dismissed the landlord's appeal: it was
> appropriate to award exemplary damages where the defendant's
> conduct had been calculated to make a profit and those damages may
> exceed the compensation ordinarily payable. It was said: 'To deprive a
> man of a roof over his head in my judgment is one of the worst torts
> which can be committed. It causes stress, worry and anxiety.'[64]

8.115   The statutory damages awarded under HA 1988 s28 are calculated in
a similar way and exemplary damages will not be awarded in addition
to section 28 damages.[65]

8.116   Although many of the reported cases concern tenants with long-
term rights, damages may be substantial even where the occupier
occupies under a short-term agreement.

> In *Lee v Lasrado*[66] an assured shorthold tenant lived in a bedsit in
> a House in Multiple Occupation (HMO). She moved in summer
> 2008 and made a number of allegations of harassment and in June
> 2009 returned home to find the locks changed and a notice stating
> that she had been evicted. She issued proceedings including an
> application for an injunction to be re-admitted. The respondent did
> not comply with the orders served on him and a committal order
> was made sentencing him to 18 months imprisonment, although
> this order was not executed. The tenant was awarded £16,800
> general damages, calculated at £200 per day for 84 days from date
> of the eviction to her finding alternative accommodation in a hostel.
> She was also awarded £400 as the repayment of her deposit, plus
> £1,200 under section 214 of the HA 2004 (three times the deposit,
> see paras 4.154–4.156), general damages of £1,000 for the

63 [1978] 2 All ER 437.
64 Lawton LJ at 461.
65 HA 1988 s27(5).
66 July 2011 *Legal Action* 19, Clerkenwell & Shoreditch County Court, 10 March
2011.

harassment during the tenancy, special damages of £2,200 for items of property not returned to her, aggravated damages of £1,500 and exemplary damages of £1,500. The total award was £24,600. The landlord appealed on various grounds, including that the award was excessive. His appeal was dismissed. The judge found that the various awards were not outside the appropriate ranges.

Injunctions

8.117   An injunction is a court order compelling a person to do something or to stop doing something. The terms of an injunction must be clear so that the respondent knows exactly what he or she must do and any time limit. If a person does not comply with an injunction an application may be made to the court for the person to be committed to prison for contempt of court (see para 8.125 below).

8.118   Injunctions are discretionary remedies. This means that the court may refuse to grant an injunction even if satisfied that the defendant has behaved unlawfully. In deciding whether to grant an injunction the court can take account of the claimant's behaviour.

Interim injunctions

8.119   It is common to seek an interim injunction to ensure that the occupier is re-instated and/ or to restrain further acts of harassment until the claim can be tried by the court.

8.120   To obtain an interim injunction the applicant must show that:[67]

- damages are not a sufficient remedy;
- there is a serious issue to be tried; and
- the 'balance of convenience' favours the making of an injunction.

8.121   In most cases of unlawful eviction it is clear that the action is unlawful and the court will order the landlord to allow the occupier back into the premises. However, this may not be possible if the premises have been re-let (see below, para 8.127).

---

67 *American Cynamid Co v Ethicon* [1975] AC 396, HL.

Cases of urgency

8.122   Three days' notice must usually be given when applying for an interim injunction.[68] However, a 'without notice' injunction may be obtained where there is 'exceptional urgency'.[69] If the case is too urgent to give three days' notice, the landlord should nevertheless be informed of the application if possible.

8.123   In addition, where there is a risk of violence to the claimant from the defendant, a without notice application may be made to protect the claimant before the defendant is notified of the proceedings.

8.124   Where a without notice order is obtained, the defendant must be served with the order, the application notice, evidence, and notice of any further hearing as soon as possible. Injunctions should always be personally served on the defendant.

8.125   An order made on a without notice application will usually be for a very limited period. The court may list a further 'on notice' hearing with the injunction lasting until that hearing. Alternatively, the order may allow the defendant to apply to discharge it at short notice. In any event the injunction will be reconsidered at any final hearing.

Enforcing injunctions

In *Saxby v McKinley*[70] a landlord unlawfully evicted tenants by changing the locks. The tenants' solicitors informed the landlord that he was not entitled to evict the tenants in this way and that he had committed a criminal offence. This was confirmed in writing. The landlord did not re-admit the tenants. The tenants then obtained an injunction without notice. The injunction required the landlord to provide keys and permit them to re-enter. The landlord failed to comply. At a further hearing, of which the landlord was given notice, the landlord did not appear and the injunction was continued. It was not until 21 days later that the landlord allowed the tenants back into the premises. The tenants applied to commit the landlord to prison for contempt of court.

The judge found that there had been a serious contempt and ordered an immediate sentence of imprisonment of 28 days. The landlord appealed but his appeal was dismissed. It was held that there had been a serious contempt of court and the consequence for

68   Civil Procedure Rules (CPR) Part 23, PD 23A para 4.1.
69   See CPR 3.1(2) and 23.4(2).
70   (1996) 29 HLR 569, CA.

the tenants was potentially, if not actually, disastrous. The landlord had shown cynical disregard for the order over a substantial period of time.

Homeless applications

8.126 A person with a right to occupy but who cannot secure entry to premises is homeless.[71] Emergency accommodation should be provided by the local authority if the person appears to be eligible and in priority need. Usually an authority will provide emergency accommodation only until an injunction can be obtained and enforced. However, if the landlord's conduct is such that it would be unreasonable to continue to occupy the premises, a long-term housing duty may be owed, see para 14.47.

Where premises have been re-let

8.127 Where premises have already been let to innocent third parties the court will not make an injunction against the landlord: for the landlord to comply he or she would have to evict the new tenants unlawfully. Rather, if the unlawfully evicted tenants wish to regain possession they can take possession proceedings against the new tenants on the basis that they are in fact trespassers, the landlord having no lawful authority to let the premises.

In *Love v Herrity*[72] a landlord served notice to quit because of rent arrears and then changed the locks and re-let the premises. A without notice injunction was obtained for re-entry but later discharged on the basis that the balance of convenience favoured waiting until final trial to decide the issues.

The Court of Appeal held that the court had been wrong to find that there was any serious issue to be tried because it was admitted that there was an assured tenancy that could only be determined by a court order; the tenants had clearly been unlawfully evicted. However, as the premises had been re-let it would be pointless to grant an injunction.

A declaration was granted that, as against the landlord, the tenants were entitled to possession and the tenants were given

71 HA 1996 s175(2)(a).
72 (1991) 23 HLR 217.

permission to join the new tenant as a defendant to enable them to claim possession against her. It would have been possible for the tenants to apply for a possession order against the new tenant directly using the summary procedure, on the basis that she was a trespasser.

Legal aid

8.128   Under the Legal Aid, Sentencing and Punishment of Offenders Act 2012 the following remains in scope for civil legal aid: 'services provided to an individual in relation to the unlawful eviction from the individual's home of the individual or others.'[73] 'Home' includes a house, caravan, houseboat or other vehicle or structure that is the individual's only or main residence. However, this does not include homes occupied by trespassers where the occupation commenced as trespass, and where it cannot be argued otherwise.

8.129   Also included are 'civil legal services provided in relation to an injunction under sections 3 or 3A of the Protection from Harassment Act 1977.'[74]

8.130   What this means is that legal aid will be available to bring proceedings for an injunction to get back into a property and to prevent harassment under the PHA 1977 but not solely to pursue a claim for damages. So, if an occupier does not want to return but instead pursues a claim for damages for unlawful eviction, no legal aid will be available. The same will apply if a claim for an injunction and damages is commenced but the occupier is re-admitted leaving only a claim for damages. Such claims may be funded under a Conditional fee agreements (CFAs) – see para 10.217.

8.131   See paras 22.154–22.172 for a fuller explanation of public funding and civil proceedings.

---

73 LASPO Schedule 1, para 33(6)(b).
74 LASPO Schedule 1, para 37(1)(a).

CHAPTER 9

Housing benefit

continued

Key points

- Housing benefit is paid to help people on low incomes meet rent payments. It does not cover mortgage payments. It can only be paid for accommodation occupied as a home.
- Not all people are eligible for housing benefit, including most people from abroad and some full-time students.
- Some agreements are excluded from the housing benefit scheme, eg some agreements between relatives and other agreements considered not to be commercial.
- Housing benefit does not cover certain charges such as water rates and heating and hot water charges.
- For increasing numbers of tenants the 'maximum housing benefit' is less than the rent they are legally obliged to pay. This used to be the case only for tenants of private landlords. Because of the 'welfare reform' measures (eg the bedroom tax and the benefit cap) many private and social tenants face significant shortfalls between the rent they have to pay and the housing benefit they receive. This includes tenants on 'safety net' benefits.
- Discretionary housing payments (DHPs) may be awarded by local authorities to help a person make up the shortfall between housing benefit and the rent payable. Funding for DHPs has been increased to alleviate the impact of some of the welfare reforms. However, DHPs are discretionary and are usually awarded only to help in the short term.
- There have been several legal challenges to the welfare reform measures and some are pending. As a result the regulations have been amended several times already and are likely to be further amended.
- Housing benefit claims can be backdated for up to six months if there is continuous good cause.
- Most housing benefit decisions can be appealed and local authorities may also revise a decision. Housing benefit regulations and procedures are very complex and local authorities often make errors.
- More changes will be necessary if and when Universal Credit is 'rolled out' for most benefit claimants.
- Legal aid is no longer available for housing benefit problems unless a challenge is made by judicial review.

Introduction

9.1 Housing benefit (HB) is a means-tested benefit available to help those on a low income to pay for a dwelling occupied as a home. It is administered by local housing authorities. The rules about entitlement and the assessment of claims are complex. This chapter contains an overview of the housing benefit system with a focus on the problems commonly experienced by claimants. Housing benefit problems often lead to rent arrears and possession claims and a basic understanding of the housing benefit system is essential for housing advisers.

9.2 The Social Security Contributions and Benefits Act (SSCBA) 1992 provides for the payment of HB. The details of the HB scheme are found in regulations, principally the Housing Benefit Regulations (HB Regs) 2006.[1] For those over the retirement age the relevant regulations are the Housing Benefit (Persons who have attained the qualifying age for state pension credit) Regulations (HB(PC) Regs) 2006[2] which mirror the provisions of the HB Regs 2006. This chapter refers only to the HB Regs 2006.

9.3 Although administered by local authorities, the scheme is a national scheme set out in regulations. The *Housing Benefit Guidance Manual* and the *Local Housing Allowance Guidance Manual* though not law, summarise the regulations and the way they should be applied by local authorities.[3]

9.4 Housing benefit cannot be paid to cover mortgage payments[4] or other housing costs paid by owner-occupiers, such as service charges and insurance payments.

9.5 Owner-occupiers who receive income support or pension credit may receive some 'housing costs' as part of their benefit. Such housing costs can include interest on home loans (but not capital repayments), service charges and insurance. Again, the rules are complex and are outside the scope of this book.

---

1 SI No 213. These regulations have been subject to multiple amendments and currently run to 393 pages!
2 SI No 214.
3 The manuals can be downloaded from: www.gov.uk/government/collections/housing-benefit-claims-processing-and-good-practice-for-local-authority-staff and www.gov.uk/government/publications/local-housing-allowance-guidance-and-good-practice-for-local-authorities
4 SSCBA 1992 s130(2).

Entitlement to HB

9.6   Entitlement to HB depends on the following conditions:[5]

- the claimant must be liable to make payments in respect of a dwelling in Great Britain;
- the dwelling must be occupied as a home;
- there is a maximum amount of HB that will be paid;
- the claimant's income and savings must be below a certain level.

9.7   Some people cannot claim HB because of their immigration status or because they are full-time students. Each of the qualifying conditions is dealt with below.

Liability to make payments

9.8   Mostly HB is paid in respect of a person's liability for rent. However, a liability other than rent may qualify for HB and a person other than the tenant (or the person legally liable to make the payment) can be treated as liable.

9.9   HB can be paid in respect of:[6]

- rent;
- licence payments;
- mesne profits;
- use and occupation charges;
- service charges, where payment is a condition on which the right to occupy depends;[7]
- mooring charges for a houseboat;
- site payments for a caravan or mobile home;
- certain costs charged by housing associations and charities for the maintenance of almshouses and essential services;[8]
- payments under a rental purchase agreement.

---

5 SSCBA 1992 s130(1).
6 HB Regs 2006 reg 12(1).
7 See para 9.14 below.
8 Because the provision of almshouses is charitable, the occupiers cannot be tenants, see para 1.43. However, there will be occupation charges for which housing benefit is payable.

Mesne profits and charges for use and occupation

9.10   Mesne profits are damages for which a trespasser is liable. They are usually assessed on the basis of rent because this represents the income lost by the landlord/owner as a result of the unlawful occupation. Use and occupation charges are charges made or agreed when an occupier has no legal right to occupy land. The terms 'mesne profits' and 'use and occupation charges' are often used interchangeably. Owners who deny that a person has any legal right to occupy may state that payments made will be accepted as mesne profits or use and occupation charges only. This is to avoid an argument that the acceptance of 'rent' proves that a tenancy exists. This is common after the expiry of a notice to quit or when a landlord disputes a claim to succeed to a tenancy, see paras 4.28–4.47.

9.11   Often, where trespass is alleged the owner refuses to accept any payment, either as rent or use and occupation charges, while pursuing a claim for possession. However, the person in occupation remains liable and an application for HB should be made. The authority may suspend actual payment but, provided a timely application has been made, HB may be paid when the dispute has been resolved, either as rent (where a right to occupy is established) or mesne profits (if the unlawful occupation is established).

9.12   Housing benefit is not paid in respect of:[9]

- payments under a long tenancy[10] except a shared ownership tenancy granted by a housing association or housing authority;
- payments under a co-ownership scheme;
- payments by an owner;
- payments under a hire purchase, credit sale or conditional sale agreement, except to the extent that the conditional sale is in respect of land;
- payments by a Crown tenant;[11]
- payments for a dwelling owned by the claimant's partner; and
- payments for some night shelters.[12]

---

9   HB Regs 2006 reg 12(2).
10   A long tenancy is defined as a tenancy for a fixed period of 21 years or more: HB Regs 2006 reg 2.
11   See para 3.33 for the definition of a Crown tenant. Crown tenants on income support or pension credit can claim housing costs. Crown tenants may also claim a rent rebate from the landlord under a voluntary scheme. Inquiries should be made to the landlord.
12   See *OR v Secretary of State for Work and Pensions and Isle of Anglesey* [2013] UKUT 65 (AAC), 15 January 2013. The particular nightshelter for rough

Non-eligible charges

9.13   Where the weekly amount paid as 'rent' includes sums that are for charges other than the right to occupy the accommodation, the other charges will usually be 'non-eligible charges' and HB will not cover those charges.

9.14   Non-eligible charges include water rates, heating and hot water charges for the premises (as opposed to the common parts) and some service charges. Service charges that must be paid as a condition of occupation are eligible charges for which HB can be paid. These include charges for such services as general management costs, lifts, entry phones and rubbish removal. Services charges that are not eligible include services that are personal to the occupier. Some service charges in supported accommodation may be paid for by the local authority's social services department, depending on the occupier's means.

Who can claim housing benefit?

9.15   Housing benefit will normally be paid to the person who is liable to make the payments, for example, the tenant or licensee.[13] However, the following may be treated as being liable so as to be eligible to receive HB:[14]

- a partner of the person who is liable;
- a person who has to make the payments in order to continue to live in the home because the 'liable person' is not doing so (the person must be a former partner of the liable person or it must be reasonable to treat the person as liable to make the payments);
- a person whose rent liability has been waived by the landlord as compensation for works of repair which are the landlord's responsibility but which were carried out by the tenant, for a maximum period of eight weeks;
- a partner of a student who cannot claim HB (see para 9.19).

sleepers offered dormitory accommodation on a nightly basis and the shower facilities were in another building a quarter of a mile away.

13   HB Regs 2006 reg 8(1)(a).
14   HB Regs 2006 reg 8(1)(b)–(e).

Persons ineligible for housing benefit

Persons from abroad

9.16   Housing benefit cannot be paid to certain people because of their immigration status or because they are not habitually resident in the UK.

9.17   There are three classes of people ineligible for HB because of being 'from abroad':

- persons subject to immigration control;
- European Economic Association (EEA) nationals with no right to reside; and
- persons who are not habitually resident.

9.18   Under the HB regulations such people are defined as 'not liable' but this is just a convoluted way of expressing the fact that they are not entitled to HB. They may of course be 'liable' to pay rent under the terms of a tenancy agreement. See chapter 20 for a fuller description of the way these rules operate in relation to HB, homelessness assistance and housing allocations.

Students

9.19   The general rule is that full-time students[15] are ineligible for HB.[16] However, the certain full-time students *are* eligible for HB, including people in receipt of income support or income-based jobseeker's allowance (JSA) or income-based Employment and Support Allowance (ESA), lone parents and those in receipt of certain disability benefits. The full list is set out in regulation 56(2) of the HB Regs 2006.

Agreements that are excluded from housing benefit

9.20   In addition to individuals being ineligible, certain kinds of agreements are also excluded. A person who is liable to make payment is treated as not being liable in the circumstances set out below.[17]

---

15   'Full-time student' is defined as a person attending a full-time course of study including a sandwich course. See HB Regs 2006 reg 53 which provides extensive definition of all terms relevant to students.

16   HB Regs 2006 reg 56(1).

17   HB Regs 2006 reg 9.

Non-commercial agreements

- The tenancy or other occupation agreement is not on a commercial basis (see paras 9.24–9.26).

Liability to family members/partners

- The liability under the agreement is to a person also living in the dwelling who is a close relative[18] of the claimant or his or her partner.[19]

Accommodation previously owned by claimant or partner

- The claimant or the claimant's partner previously owned the dwelling within the last five years. However, this will not apply if the claimant can show that it was necessary to relinquish ownership in order to continue in occupation.

Employment-related accommodation

- Occupation by the claimant or the claimant's partner is a condition of employment.

Religious orders

- The claimant is a member of a religious order and is wholly maintained by the order.

Care homes

- The claimant is in a care home or independent hospital.

9.21 Note that a liability to a close relative is only automatically excluded where he or she shares the dwelling. But a tenancy agreement between close relatives may be considered not to be on a commercial basis even where the accommodation is not shared. If the claim does not fall within one of the specific situations listed above in para 9.20, the question of whether an agreement is a commercial agreement is a question of fact in each case.

---

18 HB Regs 2006 reg 2(1): 'close relative' means a parent, parent-in-law, son, son-in-law, daughter, daughter-in-law, step-parent, step-son, step-daughter, brother, sister, or if any of the preceding persons is one member of a couple, the other member of that couple.

19 Also excluded are arrangements under which the liability is to a former partner for a previously shared home, and to a person who shares responsibility for a child. See regulaton 9 of the HB Regs 2006 for the full list.

Agreements created to take advantage of the HB scheme

9.22   In addition to the specific exclusions above in para 9.20, an agreement will be excluded if the liability was created to take advantage of the HB scheme.

9.23   The following are excluded unless the claimant can satisfy the authority that the liability was not intended to take advantage of the HB scheme:

- An agreement under which the liability is to a company or trust, under which any of the following are directors, employees, trustees or beneficiaries: the claimant, his or her partner, a close relative (of the claimant or his or her partner) who resides with the claimant, or a former partner (of the claimant or the claimant's partner).
- Where, before the liability was created, the claimant was a non-dependant of someone who resided and continues to reside in the dwelling (see paras 9.99–9.102 below for an explanation of non-dependants).

Non-commercial agreements

9.24   When deciding whether an agreement is on a commercial basis the authority must have regard to whether the agreed terms are legally enforceable.[20]

9.25   Authorities sometimes argue that an agreement is not commercial where there is a shortfall between the rent and the HB where the landlord has taken no action to enforce the payment of the full rent.

> This issue was considered in the Commissioner's case CH 1076/2002. The commissioner overturned the tribunal decision that the agreement was not commercial, holding that the tribunal had failed to give sufficient weight to the evidence that it was common practice for landlords to accept the amount of rent paid by HB. The commissioner found that there was nothing to suggest that this was not a sensible commercial decision for the landlord to make. Furthermore, the tribunal had attached too much weight to the parties' failure to vary the tenancy agreement formally so as to lower the rent to the amount that HB was paying. The issue should have been assessed in the context of parties who knew and could trust each other.

20 HB Regs 2006 reg 9(2).

9.26　Note that the existence of a tenancy and a liability to pay rent does not depend on there being a written agreement. Housing benefit should not be refused because there is no written agreement provided there is other evidence of the tenancy, e.g. letter from the landlord, rent book or other proof of the amount of rent payable. Furthermore, it is not necessary to draw up a new tenancy agreement when a fixed-term agreement expires: a legally binding statutory tenancy automatically comes into existence. See paras 3.42–3.49 above.

Occupying the dwelling as a home

9.27　The general rule is that a person is entitled to HB only for a dwelling occupied as his or her home.[21] However, there is express provision for temporary absences, for the payment of HB on two properties, and for the payment of HB before moving in.

9.28　As is explained in paras 4.5–4.12, an occupier who is temporarily absent does not necessarily cease to occupy premises as his or her home. Even during an extended absence a person may continue to occupy a dwelling provided:

- he or she intends to return; and
- there is some physical evidence of that intention.

9.29　However, this does not necessarily mean that a person who is absent for an extended period will continue to receive HB.

9.30　Specific provision is made in the regulations for:

- periods of absence when HB will continue to be paid; and
- circumstances in which HB will be paid for two dwellings.

Temporary absence

Up to 13 weeks' absence

9.31　Any claimant temporarily absent from home for any reason, eg for a holiday, or visiting friends and family, may continue to receive HB for a period of up to 13 weeks provided the following conditions are met:[22]

- the claimant intends to return to occupy the dwelling as his or her home;

21　SSCBA 1992 s130(1).
22　HB Regs 2006 reg 7(13).

- it has not been let or sublet during the claimant's absence; and
- the period of absence is unlikely to exceed 13 weeks.

9.32   This does not mean that HB can be paid for the first 13 weeks of an absence likely to exceed 13 weeks. If the absence is likely to exceed 13 weeks no HB is payable. Furthermore, if, during the absence, there is a change of circumstance so that the absence will extend beyond 13 weeks, entitlement ends at that point.

Convicted prisoners

9.33   This rule applies to an absence caused by being imprisoned *after* conviction and sentence for a criminal offence. Again, note that benefit is payable only if the likely absence will not exceed 13 weeks. An assessment must be made of the likely release date. Most prisoners on short-term sentences serve only half the term of imprisonment and may be released earlier under home detention curfew schemes ('tagging') or on temporary licence.

9.34   In contrast, prisoners who are detained on remand, pending trial or sentence, are entitled to receive HB for up to 52 weeks, see below at para 9.37.

Trial period of residential care

9.35   Housing benefit can be paid for up to 13 weeks in respect of a claimant who goes into residential accommodation on a trial basis.[23]

9.36   In such a case the claimant must intend to return to occupy the dwelling as his or her home in the event that the residential accommodation proves not to be suitable. As in all cases of HB paid during a temporary absence, the home must not be let or sublet during the absence.

Up to 52 weeks' absence

9.37   Housing benefit may be paid during an absence of up to 52 weeks to the following claimants:[24]

- a prisoner on remand pending trial or sentence;[25]
- a person on bail who is required to live in an approved bail hostel or an address other than the person's usual home;

23   HB Regs 2006 reg 7(11) and (12).
24   HB Regs 2006 reg 7(16) and (17).
25   If the prisoner is convicted and sentenced to a term of imprisonment his or her entitlement is then dealt with under the 13-week rule, see para 9.33 above. A prisoner who has already received housing benefit for a period of 13 weeks on remand will be entitled to no further housing benefit.

- a person who is in a hospital or similar institution as a patient;
- a person who is, or whose partner or child is, undergoing medical treatment or medically approved[26] convalescence in the UK or abroad, other than in residential accommodation;[27]
- a person who is receiving medically approved care in the UK or abroad, other than in residential accommodation;
- a person who is providing medically approved care to someone else residing in the UK or elsewhere;
- a person who is caring for a child whose parent or guardian is away from home receiving medically approved care or medical treatment;
- a person undertaking an approved training course in the UK or abroad;[28]
- a person who is a student who would be entitled to HB if not absent from home (ie someone studying away from home);
- a person in residential accommodation for respite care; this is different from a person in residential accommodation for a trial period, when the maximum period for which HB can be paid is 13 weeks;
- a person who is away from home because of fear of violence in the home or from a former family member.

9.38　In all cases the following conditions must also be met:

- the claimant intends to return to occupy the dwelling as his or her home;
- it has not been let or sublet during the claimant's absence;
- the period of absence is unlikely to exceed 52 weeks or, in exceptional circumstances, is unlikely to substantially exceed that period.

9.39　Note that although there is provision for benefit to be paid even where the absence is likely to exceed 52 weeks (in exceptional circumstances) the total period for which benefit is paid cannot exceed 52 weeks.

26　'Medically approved' means certified by a medical practitioner: HB Regs 2006 reg 7(18).

27　Residential accommodation means a care home, an independent hospital or an Abbeyfield Home: HB Regs 2006 reg 7(18).

28　See HB Regs 2006 reg 7(18). 'Approved' training courses generally mean courses provided by or approved by a government department. They include courses under various EU initiatives involving periods abroad and courses for occupational, vocational or social rehabilitation skills for disabled persons.

Housing benefit for two homes

9.40   The general rule is that HB can only be paid in respect of one home. However, in certain circumstances HB may be paid on two dwellings, see paras 9.41–9.47 below.[29]

Unavoidable liability for previous home: up to four weeks

9.41   When a person moves into a new home but remains liable to pay for his or her previous home, HB can be paid on both homes for up to four weeks, where the dual liability could not reasonably have been avoided.[30] This commonly occurs when a person is allocated a social tenancy under the local authority's allocations scheme (see chapter 17) and the new tenancy starts before the old tenancy can be ended. See paras 1.61–1.68 regarding the termination of tenancies by tenants.

Delay in moving into new home: up to four weeks[31]

9.42   As HB may only be paid in respect of a home actually occupied, if a person takes on a liability but delays actually moving into a dwelling, HB cannot usually be paid. However, provision is made for a person to be treated as occupying a new home for up to four weeks if the delay was necessary to carry out works to the new home to meet 'disablement needs'.[32]

9.43   In all cases the claim for HB must be made before the person moves into the new home. If refused, a new claim must be made within four weeks of moving to qualify. Payment will not actually be made until the claimant moves into the new home.

---

29 HB Regs 2006 reg 7(6).
30 HB Regs 2006 reg 7(6)(d) and (7).
31 In addition, applicants who do not have a current HB liability who delay in moving into a new home can also claim housing benefit before moving in where the move was delayed pending an application for a social fund or welfare payment necessary to meet needs arising out of the move or in setting up the home. This applies only if other conditions are also met. Also, where the person's liability starts at a time when he or she was a patient or in residential accommodation.
32 In *Mahmoudi v Lewisham LBC and Secretary of State for Work and Pensions* [2014] EWCA Civ 284, 6 February 2014, the Court of Appeal held that this provision was not limited to adaptations of a physical nature and could extend to cleaning and redecorating where this was necessary to meet the 'disablement needs' of a man with a kidney condition who needed clean surroundings to avoid infection.

Fleeing violence (intending to return home): up to 52 weeks

9.44   Where a person remains absent because of a fear of violence in the home or from a former family member, HB may be paid on two homes for up to 52 weeks where it is considered reasonable to do so.[33] This entitlement depends on the victim having a continuing intention to return to occupy the home.

Fleeing violence (not intending to return home): up to four weeks

9.45   In addition, benefit may be paid on two homes for up to four weeks even where the victim does not have an intention to return to the home he or she has left.[34]

Accommodation in two dwellings: indefinitely

9.46   Where, because of the number of people in the household, a housing authority has accommodated the household in two separate dwellings, HB will be paid on both dwellings.[35]

Couple including an eligible student: indefinitely

9.47   Where a student who is eligible for HB (see above at para 9.19) is part of a couple, benefit may be paid on two homes if it is unavoidable that they should occupy two separate dwellings and it is reasonable to pay HB on both.[36] The same rule applies if he or she is on an approved training course (see above para 9.37).

Maximum housing benefit

9.48   In all cases the amount of HB paid cannot exceed the 'maximum housing benefit'.[37]

The private sector

9.49   Until recently the maximum HB limit applied only in relation to private sector tenancies (and a small number of social tenancies where

33   HB Regs 2006 reg 7(6)(a).
34   HB Regs 2006 reg 7(10).
35   HB Regs 2006 reg 7(6)(c).
36   HB Regs 2006 reg 7(6)(b).
37   SSCBA 1992 s130(4) and HB Regs 2006 regs 12(3)(a) and 13.

the rent was deemed to be unreasonably high). The amount of HB payable was restricted if the accommodation was more extensive than needed by the particular claimant and/or was let at a higher rent than deemed reasonable. Various different methods of assessing the maximum HB have been applied over the years but the current system, introduced in April 2008, is the Local Housing Allowance (LHA). The LHA system applies to most private sector tenancies. The LHA is a flat rate allowance payable for categories of properties determined by reference to the number of bedrooms the claimant is entitled to. LHAs are set for each 'broad rental market area' by rent officers. So, instead of an individual assessment of a household's needs, a potential claimant can see how many bedrooms they are entitled to by reference to the individuals in their household, and then check the maximum LHA for a property of that size, in the relevant area. In addition payment of HB can be restricted by the benefit cap.

The social sector

9.50   Since April 2013, maximum HB limits also apply to tenants of registered providers of social housing. This is because of the various 'welfare reform' measures, including the 'bedroom tax' and the 'benefit cap'. In the social sector, the assessment focuses not on high rents (since rents in the social sector are generally set at affordable levels) but on under-occupation (the bedroom tax) or overall benefit levels (the benefit cap). In either case, the effect may be to reduce the level of HB to less than the net rent payable.[38]

Local housing allowances

9.51   This section focuses on the setting of the LHAs. The assessment of the claimant's requirements in terms of the number of bedrooms (the 'size assessment') is dealt with below at para 9.54, since it is the same as that applied in relation to the bedroom tax.

9.52   LHAs apply to claims made on or after 7 April 2008 and to existing claimants who move to a new property on or after 7 April 2008.

---

38 The term 'net rent' is used in this section to denote the part of the rent that would usually be deemed 'eligible' rent and would exclude non-eligible charges, such as water rates etc (see paras 9.13–9.14 above). The term 'eligible rent' is avoided since this is tied up with the assessment of the maximum housing benefit.

9.53   The LHA scheme applies only to private sector tenancies. It does not apply to:[39]

- tenancies where the landlord is a local authority;[40]
- tenancies where the landlord is a registered provider of social housing;
- exempt accommodation (principally shelters and supported accommodation, see para 9.67 and footnote 51 below);
- excluded tenancies, which includes regulated tenancies (to which the fair rent scheme applies);
- houseboats, caravans, mobile homes, hostels and tenancies where a substantial amount of the rent is attributable to board and attendance.

The LHA cap

9.54   LHAs are based on the area in which the claimant lives and the size of the property. However, there is a cap applied nationally limiting the maximum HBs. The caps, for April 2015–16 are as follows:[41]

Size of accommodation	Maximum HB
One bedroom (either shared or exclusive use)	£260.64 pw
Two bedrooms	£302.33 pw
Three bedrooms	£354.46 pw
Four bedrooms and above	£417.02 pw

The number of bedrooms a household needs is determined by the 'size test' below, at paras 9.68–9.69 below, and is the same as for the bedroom tax. Larger properties are capped at the four bedroom rate regardless of the actual number of bedrooms in the property.

The area

9.55   The areas for which rents are calculated are based on 'broad market rental areas'(BRMA). The LHA rates are based on the rent at the 30th

---

39   HB Regs 2006 reg 13C.
40   The scheme applies only to cases in which a rent allowance may be awarded. Local authority tenants receive a rebate and not a rent allowance.
41   Rent Officers (HB and UC Functions) (LHA Amendments) Order 2014 SI No 3126.

percentile (the highest of rents in the cheapest 30 per cent of all rents in the BRMA).[42] Until 1 April 2011, LHAs were based on the median rents (ie the middle of the range).

9.56   A BRMA consists of two or more areas of residential accommodation in which the claimant could reasonably be expected to live, having regard to facilities and for health, education, recreation, banking and shopping, and taking account of public and private transport to and from facilities and services.[43]

Under 35s – the shared accommodation rate

9.57   For single, childless claimants under the age of 35 the LHA is based on the cost of a shared room: the 'shared accommodation rate'. This will vary according to locality but will usually be less than the LHA for a one-bedroom property. Until January 2012 the shared accommodation rate only applied to single applicants under the age of 25. A claimant in receipt of HB prior to January 2012, who has had no break in the claim and who remains in the same accommodation will continue to receive benefit on this basis. So, a person aged over 25 but under 35 who has self-contained accommodation may be well advised to remain in that accommodation since any move will result in the shared accommodation rate applying.

Exceptions

9.58   The following are exceptions to the shared accommodation rate and can receive the LHA for a self-contained one-bedroom property:

- care leavers under the age of 22;[44]
- claimants who are severely disabled (in receipt of severe disablement benefit);

AND

- those aged over 25 who are:
  - homeless people who had spent at least three months in a hostel as defined in the regulations and have accepted resettlement support. The three-month period does not have to be

---

42   The formula is set out in article 2 of the Rent Officers (HB and UC Functions) (LHA Amendment) Order 2013 SI No 2978.

43   See *R on the application of Heffernan v Rent Service* [2008] UKHL 58, 30 July 2008.

44   'Care leaver' is defined in reg 2(1) of the HB Regs 2006 and includes someone 'formerly provided with accommodation under section 20 of the Children Act 1989'. See para 19.13.

continuous, or in a single hostel, or immediately before the HB claim is made.

- ex-offenders who pose a risk of serious harm to the public and are subject to Multi Agency Public Protection Arrangements (MAPPA).

Payment of the local housing allowance

9.59 Under the LHA scheme payment is made to the claimant unless one of the following applies:[45]

- the authority considers the claimant is likely to have difficulty in managing his or her financial affairs;
- the authority considers that it is improbable that the claimant will pay his or her rent;
- payment was previously made directly to the landlord because of rent arrears;
- the authority considers that the payment will help the tenant retain or secure their tenancy.

9.60 Payment must be made to the landlord if:

- there are 8 weeks' arrears, and
- deductions are being made from social security benefits to pay arrears directly to the landlord.

9.61 While considering whether to make payment direct to the landlord direct payments may be made for up to eight weeks.

9.62 Decisions about direct payments can be appealed, by either the tenant or the landlord.

Information about local housing allowances

9.63 LHAs are published at the end of each month to apply the following month. They can be checked online through each local authority's website or through 'LHA-direct' which is part of the Rent Service website.

9.64 The LHA payable to a particular claimant will not be reviewed until 12 months after the claim is made unless there is a relevant change of circumstances.

---

45 Prior to LHAs a claimant could elect that HB be paid direct to a non-local authority landlord.

Transitional arrangements

9.65   The method of assessing HB for private sector rents changed in 1996 and in 2008 (when the LHA was introduced). Complex transitional arrangements apply so that some private tenants who have been in occupation of the same property and in continuous receipt of HB since before 1 January 1996 or before 7 April 2008 will continue to have their 'maximum rent' assessed according to the scheme in force at the time.

The bedroom tax[46]

9.66   This controversial measure came into force in April 2013[47] and operates as a deduction to the HB of a tenant deemed to be under-occupying social housing. It depends on an assessment of the number of bedrooms needed by a household. For tenants assessed as having one spare bedroom, HB is reduced by 14 per cent of the net rent. For a tenant deemed to have two or more spare bedrooms, the deduction is 25 per cent of the net rent. The permitted number of bedrooms is the same as under the LHA scheme.

9.67   The following are exempt from the bedroom tax:[48]

- pensioners[49] – the deduction only applies to claimants of working age;
- those occupying shared ownership properties;
- those occupying 'non-mainstream' accommodation, eg houseboats, caravans and mobile homes;
- people living in certain kinds of temporary accommodation provided to homeless people;[50]

---

46   Known, officially as the 'spare room subsidy'.

47   See, the Housing Benefit (Amendment) Regulations 2012 SI No 3040. The HB Regulations were further amended by the Housing Benefit and Universal Credit (Size Criteria) (Miscellaneous Amendment) Regulations 2013 SI No 2828.

48   See HB Regs 2006 reg A13.

49   Any claimant over the qualifying age for state pension credit or with a partner over that age is exempt.

50   Specifically, this exception is where the accommodation includes board or is in a hotel, guest house, lodging house, or similar, or is provided under a private sub-leasing arrangement. This includes most temporary accommodation provided other than by way of assured tenancies in the private sector or non-secure tenancies of self-contained local authority accommodation.

- 'exempt' supported accommodation and women's refuges;[51]
- housing association tenancies granted prior to 15 January 1989 (which are subject to the 'fair rent' regime under Part VI of the Rent Act 1977, see para 4.187).

The size criteria/bedroom assessment

9.68　The test is now the same for the LHA scheme and for housing benefit claimants living in social housing.

9.69　It provides that one bedroom is permitted for each of the following persons in the household. Each person must be included in the first category applicable, in the order stated:

- a couple;[52]
- a person over the age of 16 (including a lodger);
- a child who cannot share a bedroom [because of a disability];[53]
- two children of the same sex [for these purposes children are defined as those under the age of 16 years];
- two children under the age of 10;
- any other child.

Additional bedrooms/special provisions

9.70　In addition, an additional bedroom is permitted in the following cases:

- where the claimant or the claimant's partner needs overnight care and a bedroom is available/used for an overnight carer;
- where the claimant or the claimant's partner is an approved foster carer between placements;[54]

51　This means accommodation provided by a local authority, housing association, registered charity or voluntary organisation in which care, support or supervision is also provided and refuges for people fleeing domestic violence. See para 4, Sch 3 to the HB and Council Tax (Consequential Provisions) Regulations 2006 SI No 217 and reg 2 of the HB and Universal Credit (Supported Accommodation) (Amendment) Regulations 2014 SI No 771. This includes most, but not all, 'supported accommodation' such as group homes, hostels, refuges, sheltered housing, supported living complexes and adapted housing for the disabled.

52　This is defined in Part VII of the SSCBA 1992, and means people who are married or civil partners and members of the same household or who are living together as if they were a married couple or in a civil partnership.

53　The children must be in receipt of the middle or higher rates of the DLA care component.

54　When a foster child is part of the household they are assessed as any other child. This provision means that the bedroom tax will not apply when there is

- where a child/step child is in the armed forces away on operations, provided they were residing with the claimant before joining and intend to resume occupying as their home when they return.

Disability needs not specifically addressed

9.71   It should be noted that there is no provision for an extra room in the following situations:

- when a night time carer is needed for a child;
- when a couple cannot share a room because one of them is disabled;
- when a person occupies accommodation specifically adapted for their needs such that they will find it difficult/impossible to move to a smaller property.[55]

9.72   Note that the term 'bedroom' is not defined. Indeed the Guidance, (issued prior to the new regulations coming into force) states: 'We will not be defining what we mean by a bedroom in legislation and there is no definition of a minimum bedroom size set out in regulations. It will be up to the landlord to accurately describe the property in line with the actual rent charged.'[56] There have been numerous tribunal decisions about what constitutes a bedroom. The landlord's definition of the number of bedrooms in the property is not decisive and several decisions have held that a room cannot be classed as a bedroom on the grounds that it is too small and/or has never been used as a bedroom. Summaries of a many of these decisions can be found on the Nearly Legal housing law blog: http://nearlylegal.co.uk/blog.

9.73   The government has increased the funding to local authorities for discretionary housing payments (DHPs) specifically to address some of these issues. The DHP system is dealt with below at paras 9.80–9.86.

---

no foster child in the household, for up to 52 weeks from the last placement (or for up to 52 weeks after receiving initial approval from the local authority).

55   This issue was specifically recognised in the July 2012 guidance which stated: 'it may not be practical or cost effective for these people to move to different accommodation or they may have no other option for making up the shortfall in rent.'

56   Para 12, Circular, HB/CTB A4/2012, July 2012.

The benefit cap

9.74 The benefit cap is another key policy under the government's welfare reform programme.[57] It operates so as to reduce the total package of prescribed benefits to a set figure for working-age claimants. This is set on a national basis, and differentiates only between single claimants and others. No account is taken of the number of children in the household. The necessary deduction is applied to the HB claim so does not affect those who do not receive HB (or Universal Credit).

9.75 The current caps are: £350 per week for a single claimant and £500 for all others. The prescribed benefits include: child benefit, child tax credit and HB. The stated aim of the provision is to encourage non-working households to seek work. So, state pension and retirement pension are not prescribed benefits.

9.76 Furthermore, the cap does not apply where the claimant or partner is entitled to working tax credit. The effect of this is that the following will be exempt from the cap:

- a single parent or disabled person working at least 16 hours a week;
- a couple with children working at least 24 hours per week (one of whom must be working at least 16 hours per week);
- someone who was recently in work, as above, for a 39-week period.

9.77 Furthermore, the following benefits are not prescribed benefits:[58]

- employment and support allowance (ESA) which includes a support component;
- a personal independent payment (PIP);
- industrial injuries benefit;
- attendance allowance;
- a war pension;
- disability living allowance (DLA);
- an armed forces independence payment.

9.78 Furthermore, receipt of DHPs, council tax support and social fund payments are not included in the income to which the cap applies.

9.79 For obvious reasons the cap has a much more significant effect in areas where rents are high and for claimants with children, particularly single parents who will find it more difficult to obtain work. The

---

57 The provisions are set out in the Welfare Reform Act (WRA) 2012 and the Benefit Cap (Housing Benefit) Regulations 2012 (Ben Cap Regs) SI No 2994.

58 Ben Cap Regs reg 75(c)(2).

cap has been challenged on the basis that it discriminates against women, who are more likely to be adversely affected: *R (SG & Others) v Secretary of State for Work and Pensions.*[59] The Supreme Court rejected the challenge: the discriminatory effect of the legislation was justified by the legitimate aims of the measures. See below at para 9.88.

Discretionary housing payments

9.80   Discretionary housing payments (DHPs) are not strictly HB.[60] They are, as indicated, discretionary and can be awarded to a person who receives HB where the local housing authority is satisfied that the person needs additional help with housing costs. The budget for DHPs is cash-limited. DHPs can be paid to enable a person to meet a shortfall between the contractual rent and HB but can only be paid for a period when the person is in receipt of HB. They have historically been applied by local authorities for short periods to assist tenants with short-term problems to resolve those problems without getting into debt or risking the loss of their home. However, the DHP fund was increased by the government when introducing the welfare reform programme and the guidance suggests that they should be used to mitigate the impact of the measures. DHPs are becoming a much more important part of the funding of housing costs by local authorities and, as is clear from the cases at paras 9.87–9.90 below, may have to be awarded to provide long-term funding to avoid the otherwise discriminatory nature of the welfare reform measures.

9.81   The most recent Guidance Manual, issued in April 2014,[61] states that '... in most cases a claimant will need to demonstrate that they are unable to meet housing costs from their available income or that they have a shortfall as a result of the welfare reforms.'[62] Before an award can be made the authority must be satisfied that the claimant is entitled to HB (or Universal Credit including a housing element towards rent) and requires further financial assistance with housing costs.

59 [2015] UKSC 16, 18 March 2015. The Supreme Court heard the case in May 2014.
60 See Discretionary Financial Assistance Regulations 2001 SI No 1167.
61 The Guidance Manuals are available online from the DWP website.
62 Para 2.0.

Shortfalls in rent

9.82　The types of shortfall that can be covered, includes, but is not limited to:[63]

- reductions in HB or UC where:
  - the benefit cap has been applied;
  - the bedroom tax has been applied; or
  - the LHA has been restricted;
- rent officer restrictions on maximum rent (including the application of the shared room rate);
- the application of non-dependant deductions (see below);
- rent shortfalls to prevent homelessness while alternative options are explored;
- reductions due to income tapers (see below at para 9.95).

Because DHPs are discretionary there is no right of appeal to a tribunal if refused. The only challenge will be by way of an internal review/appeal (if offered) and ultimately by judicial review, see paras 2.4–2.25.

Other types of payment

9.83　DHPs can also be used for rent deposits or rent in advance or to cover rent liability on two homes, eg when a person is fleeing domestic violence.

9.84　DHPs cannot be awarded to cover any of the following:[64]

- ineligible services charges;
- water rates;
- certain sanctions, reductions and suspension of benefits;
- repayment of rent arrears;
- shortfalls arising because of the recovery of previous overpayments;
- shortfalls between council tax support and council tax liability.

Length of payment

9.85　DHPs are usually awarded to meet housing costs in the short term. However, the April 2014 guidance suggests that it may be appropriate for local authorities to make 'long-term or indefinite' awards pending a change in circumstance where the payment is to meet a shortfall due

---

63　Para 2.3.
64　2001 SI No 1167 reg 3 sets out the full list of excluded payments.

to meet the housing costs caused by the impact of the welfare reform measures on disabled people. The examples given of those affected by the bedroom tax are: a disabled claimant in significantly adapted accommodation, claimants who have a medical condition making it difficult to share a bedroom and disabled children who cannot share (but who do not meet the DLA requirement, see above at para 9.69).

9.86   Despite this, DHPs remain at the discretion of local authorities and the funding is limited. If an authority has spent its allocation for the year, it cannot make further DHP awards. Furthermore, although the government has made much of the extra funding, this has only been allocated for the year 2014/15. The guidance refers to this as being 'to give Local Authorities the confidence to make long-term awards where appropriate.'[65] The government appears to view the extra funding as a short-term measure to enable local authorities to deal with the transitional effects of the welfare reform provisions, particularly on disabled people. However, the courts have made findings as to the lawfulness of the welfare reform measure which depend upon the existence of the DHP scheme and the possibility of long-term DHP payments.[66] In those cases the government has argued that DHPs are part of the overall benefit scheme and that this justifies the discriminatory effects of the measures, see below at para 9.88. This may mean that the government is forced to continue to provide additional funding for DHPs in the long term.

Challenges to the welfare reform measures in housing benefit

9.87   There have been a number of judicial review challenges to the welfare reforms, most of which have focused on the discriminatory effect of the rules and the application of Article 14 of the ECHR. Article 14 prohibits discrimination when rights under the convention are engaged, see paras 2.63–2.67.

> *Burnip v Birmingham CC and Secretary of State for Work and Pensions, Trengrove v Walsall MC and Secretary of State for Work and Pensions*

---

65 Para 5.0.
66 See *Burnip v Birmingham CC, R (MA & Others) v Secretary of State for Work and Pensions, R(SG) v Secretary of State for Work and Pensions* and *Rutherford v Secretary of State for Work and Pensions & Pembrokeshire County Council*, all summarised below at paras 9.87–9.88..

and *Gorry v Wiltshire Council and Secretary of State for Work and Pensions*[67] were challenges to the changes to the LHA rules which applied 'size criteria' based on the number of bedrooms needed by a claimant. These rules were similar to those initially proposed under the 'bedroom tax' and made no allowance for an extra bedroom where a disabled adult needed an overnight carer. This was the issue for *Burnip* and *Trengrove*. The *Gorry* case was about the failure of the rules to make any provision for children unable to share a room because of a disability. The Court of Appeal upheld all three appeals finding that the new rules did discriminate against disabled people on the grounds of disability. Furthermore, the government could not establish objective and reasonable justification for the discrimination. The Court considered the government's case that the scheme (HB and DHPs) had to be considered as a whole but rejected the argument that DHPs were an appropriate way of dealing with the issue: DHPs were discretionary, for limited periods and paid from a cash-limited fund, whereas the needs of disabled people was for long- term accommodation, particularly if the accommodation was adapted. The Court of Appeal made a declaration that the new rules constituted unlawful discrimination against disabled people.

9.88 Following *Burnip* the LHA rules were amended to provide for an additional room where the claimant or the claimant's partner needed a room for an overnight carer and, later, for situations where disabled children could not share a room, see above at para 9.69. In *Burnip* the availability of DHPs to make up the shortfalls between rent and HB was specifically considered but in each case, although DHPs had been awarded, these had been partial and had not covered the whole shortfall for the whole period.

R (MA and others) v Secretary of State for Work and Pensions[68] was a challenge by five claimants to the bedroom tax on the grounds of disability discrimination under article 14. One of the claimants was part of a couple who could not share a bedroom because of her disability (she needed a separate, adapted bed and space for carers and a wheelchair and there was no space for an additional bed in the room). Another claimant was occupying accommodation that

---

67 [2012] EWCA Civ 629, 15 May 2012.
68 [2014] EWCA Civ 13, 21 February 2014.

had been specifically adapted and to move would be impractical and expensive (if indeed possible). Neither of these situations were catered for under the size criteria. The Court of Appeal found that there was discrimination. However, the Court held that the government had succeeded in justifying the discrimination. The Court took into account the government's additional funding of the DHP scheme, specifically to assist with such cases, and also the fact that these specific types of situations had been debated in Parliament when the new rules were introduced. The Court accepted the government's argument that the DHP system was a more appropriate way of dealing with disabled people with a need for extra rooms, or who could not move. Taking account of the scheme as a whole, both the HB system and the DHP scheme, the discrimination was justified.

R (SG) v Secretary of State for Work and Pensions[69] was a challenge to the benefit cap on the basis that it discriminated against women who were more likely to be single parents. The Supreme Court held by a majority of 3 to 2 that the benefit cap was lawful. It did discriminate, albeit indirectly, against women. This being the case the government had to justify the measure. The policy reasons for introducing the cap were to limit the extent to which non-working families were publicly funded, to motivate people to work and to reduce public expenditure. These were legitimate aims and no credible means had been put forward as to how these aims might have been achieved without impacting more women than men. Since women headed most of the households at which the aims were directed, a disparity between the number of men and women affected was inevitable.

9.89   Effectively, the outcome of the decision in *MA* is that disabled claimants whose benefit is reduced because of the bedroom tax should apply to the local authority for a DHP. Despite the increased funding for 2014/15 the fundamental characteristics of the scheme remain: it is discretionary, awards are time limited and the fund is 'cash-limited' so that if a local authority spends its allocation it will have no further funds from which to pay awards. Furthermore, HB is reimbursed

69 [2015] UKSC 16, 18 March 2015.

in full by central government (in almost all cases) and DHPs are not. The Court of Appeal in *MA* identified this as a factor that would mean local authorities would exercise more 'financial discipline'. It will also provide a strong incentive for awards to be refused.

> *Rutherford v Secretary of State for Work and Pensions and Pembrokeshire County Council*[70] was a judicial review by claimants penalised by the bedroom tax whose circumstances were not catered for under the regulations: the child in the household needed overnight care. They argued that the case was different from *MA* in that this was a small, distinct category for which an exception could have been made under the regulations. The claim was dismissed, the court pointing to the fact that the DHP guidance specifically referred to DHPs being used to fund a shortfall for disabled claimants subject to the bedroom tax. In this case, DHPs had been awarded to date and it was found that 'there is at present adequate assurance that the Claimants will continue to benefit from awards of DHPs to plug the gap that would otherwise exist. It the scheme or other circumstances were to change materially, different considerations might apply; but they do not apply now.'[71]

9.90   This suggests that where local authorities cannot guarantee long-term payment of DHPs, the application of the new rules will be unlawful. Given that the funding from central government has only been increased for the financial year 2014/15 and that the scheme remains discretionary and cash limited, it is likely that there will be many more challenges. At the time of writing, in *Rutherford* an application for permission to appeal to the Court of Appeal is pending.

How decisions are challenged

9.91   As is illustrated by the cases described above, challenges to the lawfulness of the rules themselves are brought by judicial review. Similarly, a challenge to a refusal to award a DHP would have to be brought by judicial review since there is no statutory appeal for such decisions. However, where the dispute is about how the rules are applied by the authority (eg a challenge to a decision as to how many bedrooms a property has or whether a member of the household is living in the

---

70 [2014] EWHC 1613, 30 May 2014.
71 Stuart-Smith J, at [54].

property) this would be brought by way of an appeal to the First-tier Tribunal.

9.92   There have been numerous appeals on such issues in the First-tier Tribunal and on appeal to the Upper Tribunal. A comprehensive description of these cases can be found on the Nearly Legal housing law blog: http://nearlylegal.co.uk/blog.

Assessment of income and capital

9.93   Subject to the rules regarding the maximum amount of HB described above in paras 9.48–9.73, the amount of housing paid also depends on an assessment of the claimant's income and capital.

9.94   Claimants who receive income support (IS), income-based job-seeker's allowance (JSA), income-related Employment and Support Allowance (ESA) or the guarantee credit of pension credit are entitled to maximum HB. This may be less than the net rent payable where the maximum HB is less than the contractual rent (see paras 9.48–9.73 above), or the benefit is subject to 'non-dependant deductions' (see para 9.99 below).

9.95   For other claimants, an assessment is made which depends on the claimant's 'applicable amount'. The applicable amount depends on the age of the claimant, the number and age of any dependants and whether the claimant or a member of the household has any special needs. The claimant's weekly income, less the applicable amount equals 'excess income'. If this is zero or less than zero the person is entitled to the maximum HB. If it is greater than zero, the amount of HB payable will be the maximum HB less 65 per cent of the weekly excess income. Obviously, if the excess income is above a certain level no HB will be payable. Certain income is disregarded, including child benefit, disability living allowance, attendance allowance, mobility allowance, war widows' pension and a proportion of war disablement pension. The 'disregards' depend on whether the claimant is single, a lone parent or part of a couple.

9.96   If a working-age claimant has savings (including investments) of £16,000 or more, no HB is payable. Savings below this level but more than £6,000 may mean that the claimant does not receive full HB as a notional income from the capital is applied. Different rules apply for those over the age of 60.

9.97   Many local authority websites include a self-assessment facility so potential claimants can assess own their entitlement.

Shared accommodation – assessment of liability

9.98 Where accommodation is shared, for example, by joint tenants (other than couples), the liability is apportioned between the occupiers.[72] This is the case even though legally each tenant is liable for the whole of the rent (see para 1.51). If there is only one tenant liable to pay the rent, a deduction may be made for other occupiers as 'non-dependant deductions', see below, paras 9.99–9.102.

Non-dependant deductions

9.99 'Non-dependants' are people who normally reside with a claimant, other than dependent children and partners. Because they are expected to contribute to the rent, a deduction is made from the claimant's HB for each non-dependant in the household. The amount of the deduction depends on the age and the income of the non-dependant. 'Non-dependants' include:[73]

- any member of the claimant's family (apart from one who is part of the claimant's family for benefit purposes, for example, a dependent child);
- a carer.

9.100 For certain non-dependants no deduction is made. The most common examples are:[74]

- those under the age of 18;
- those under the age of 25 who are in receipt of IS, income-based JSA or the assessment phase of income-related ESA;[75]
- those in receipt of pension credit;[76]
- full-time students;[77]
- any person who resides with a claimant where the claimant or partner is registered blind or in receipt of attendance allowance or the care component of disability living allowance;[78]
- foster children.

---

72 This is not the case if the LHA scheme applies, see paras 9.51–9.53 above.
73 HB Regs 2006 reg 3.
74 Note that rent paid by lodgers is taken into account when assessing the claimant's income, rather than being applied as a non-dependant deduction.
75 HB Regs 2006 reg 74(8).
76 HB Regs 2006 reg 74(1).
77 HB Regs 2006 reg 74(7)(c).
78 HB Regs 2006 reg 74(6).

9.101   Where a non-dependant deduction is made, if the non-dependant is in 'remunerative work' this is based on the person's weekly gross income and is applied on a sliding scale, currently ranging from £14.55 per week to £93.80 per week (for the year 2015/16 but this usually increases when benefit rates change). If the non-dependant is not in remunerative work, the deduction is £14.55 per week regardless of income. Remunerative work means paid employment for not less than 16 hours a week.[79] The lowest deduction (£14.55) is made for each non-dependant aged 25 or over who is in receipt of income support, income-based JSA and 'main phase' ESA.

9.102   It is the claimant's responsibility to submit evidence of the income of a non-dependant. Where no such evidence is submitted, local authorities often apply the maximum deduction (as was recommended in earlier DWP guidance). However, this approach was successfully challenged in a Commissioner's appeal: it was held the authority should have made an assessment based on the evidence it did have (ie, the likely income of a 19-year-old shop worker).[80] The guidance now provides that if no, or inadequate, information about the non-dependant's gross income is provided, the highest deduction should only be made after considering all the relevant facts.

Housing benefit applications and payments

9.103   Although the HB scheme is a national scheme each local authority has its own application forms. A claim should be made to the local authority as soon as possible so that no benefit is lost. Claims may also be made via Jobcentre Plus when a claim is made for income support, jobseeker's allowance, pension credit or employment and support allowance.

9.104   In addition to completing an application form, the claimant must provide further information and evidence. This will be indicated on the form or the authority may subsequently request it (it must be reasonably required to determine entitlement). This will usually include, as a minimum, proof of identity, rental liability, residence, capital and income, plus any documents necessary to establish immigration status, if relevant.

9.105   The authority is only obliged to process the claim when all this information and evidence has been submitted.

79 HB Regs 2006 reg 6.
80 See CH/48/2006.

9.106   Authorities often request further information and evidence following receipt of a claim. The general rule is that this must be provided within one month of the request, or a longer period if the authority considers this reasonable. If the information is not provided within the specified time period the claim may be assessed as being made at a date later than the date the application form was delivered to the authority. This will mean a loss of benefit and the accrual of rent arrears. In such a case, a person may make an application for backdated HB (see para 9.111 below).

9.107   Disputes as to whether information and evidence has been provided are common and claimants should always obtain and keep receipts for information delivered to local authority offices.

Delays

9.108 Following receipt of the written application form together with all supporting evidence, the local authority must make a decision within 14 days or as soon as reasonably practicable thereafter.[81] The authority should notify the claimant of its determination within 14 days or as soon as reasonably practicable.

Payments on account

9.109 Where the landlord is not the local authority, if it is impracticable for a decision to be made within 14 days, the authority *must* make a payment on account of entitlement.[82] This duty arises only if the delay in making a decision is not caused by the claimant's failure, without reasonable excuse, to provide information or evidence. The amount of the payment will be the amount the authority considers reasonable having regard to the information that is available. Usually, authorities will pay a percentage of the anticipated entitlement.

9.110   Authorities routinely ignore this provision, often resulting in substantial arrears of rent arising at the start of the tenancy. Legal action may be taken in the county court to enforce the duty to make interim payments on account. In practice, the threat of a claim based on breach of the statutory duty often results either in a payment on account being made or the claimant's entitlement being assessed.

81 HB Regs 2006 reg 89(2).
82 HB Regs 2006 reg 93(1).

Backdating housing benefit

9.111   Claims for HB can be backdated for up to six months if there is good cause for the late claim.

9.112   If a claimant has reached the qualifying age for state pension credit and is not (and his or her partner is not) on income support or income-based jobseeker's allowance, benefit can be backdated for up to three months without good cause provided there was continuous entitlement to HB during the relevant period.[83] This should be applied automatically by the authority, ie does not have to be claimed.

9.113   Note that there is no time limit for making claims and no need to consider backdating for claims from people who have a daily rent liability and live in:

- a hostel, or
- accommodation provided by local authorities, outside the Housing Revenue Account (HRA), under
  - their statutory duties to the homeless, or
  - the short-term leased scheme.[84]

9.114   For other claimants there must be continuous good cause for the failure to claim and the claimant must ask for it to be backdated.[85]

9.115   In deciding whether a claimant has shown good cause for not claiming earlier, the authority must be satisfied that the reason for not claiming earlier is such that any reasonable person of that age, health and experience would probably not have claimed earlier in the same way as the claimant. The burden of proving good cause rests on the claimant but the authority must examine all the relevant facts in each case.

9.116   Annex A to the Adjudication Officers' Guide (AOG) contains a useful summary of the situations in which good cause should be accepted, based on Commissioners' decisions. Although the AOG is no longer current the annex is attached to the current DWP Guidance Manual (see para 9.3 above).

Overpayments of housing benefit

9.117   Where a person receives HB that he or she was not entitled to, this is an overpayment and will be recoverable unless:

- it was the result of an official error; and
- the claimant did not materially contribute to the error; and

---

83   HB(PC) Regs 2006 reg 64(1).
84   See HB Guidance Manual, A2, para 2.510.
85   HB Regs 2006 reg 83(12).

- he or she could not reasonably have realised that he or she was being overpaid.

9.118   This definition of a recoverable overpayment means that most over-payments are recoverable. However, overpayment decisions are contentious and the DWP website contains guidance (HB/CTB Over-payments Guide) in 10 parts, which runs to more than 240 pages.

Notification

9.119   The authority must notify a claimant that he or she has been overpaid and that the overpayment is recoverable. The notification should also inform the claimant of the right of appeal and must:[86]

- state that there is a recoverable overpayment;
- give the reason why there is a recoverable overpayment;
- state the amount of the recoverable overpayment;
- explain how the amount has been calculated;
- indicate the benefit weeks to which the recoverable overpayment relates.

9.120   In addition:

- if recovery is to be made by deduction from future HB this must be stated and, if so, the amount of the deduction;
- if recovery is to be made from the landlord, the notice must iden-tify the person on whose behalf the recoverable overpayment was made and the person (ie another tenant) from whose claim deduc-tion will be made.

Underlying entitlement

9.121   An overpayment may occur when a person's situation changes, for example, when he or she moves from one type of benefit to another, or commences employment. If the authority is not notified at the time, an overpayment will occur. However, it may be the case that the claimant would have continued to be entitled to housing benefit. In all such cases the local authority should calculate the claimant's 'underlying entitlement' and deduct from the overpayment any HB that he or she was entitled to.[87]

9.122   If the authority needs more information or evidence to calculate the underlying entitlement it must request this from the claimant. The claimant need not make an application for underlying entitlement to

---

86 HB Regs 2006 Sch 9 para 15.
87 HB Regs 2006 reg 104.

be assessed. However, if the claimant fails to respond to a request for information within one month, the full amount of the overpayment will be recoverable and the claimant should receive notification of this.

Recovery of overpayments

By deduction from future benefit

9.123   An authority can recover a previous overpayment by making deductions from a claimant's future benefit.[88] The maximum weekly deduction, calculated as a percentage of a claimant's personal allowance, is, for the year 2015/16, £11.10 per week (£18.50 if the overpayment is due to fraud) plus 50 per cent of any income disregarded for benefit purposes. However, authorities may reduce the weekly deductions where this is causing hardship.

9.124   Advisers should always request a deduction in the rate of recovery where a claimant on means-tested benefit is in rent arrears. If the maximum deduction continues, the claimant will be expected (by the landlord or by the court) to pay at least £3.70 per week towards the arrears as well as to make up the shortfall of HB, this could result in a weekly payment of £14.80 (on 2015/16 rates) in addition to water rates and any service charges. Most claimants will be unable to maintain the payments resulting in breaches of any agreement or conditions imposed by the court.

As a 'lump sum' from the tenant

9.125   An authority cannot suspend the payment of HB until the whole overpayment is recovered. Nor can a housing authority which is also the tenant's landlord recover an overpayment by entering the sum as arrears on the rent account. However, where there is a delay in assessing a new/renewed claim, an authority may recover any outstanding overpayment from a lump sum that is due for a past period. This will place a claimant in arrears. For example, a claimant may have an outstanding overpayment in the sum of £2,000. Following a delay in assessing a renewed claim, the authority may decide that a credit of £1,000 is due in respect of the period between the making of the claim and the assessment. The authority may set off the £1,000 against the amount outstanding so that although weekly HB payments commence, the lump sum of £1,000 is not paid. The result

88 HB Regs 2006 reg 102.

is that the tenant is in rent arrears of £1,000 and the balance of the outstanding overpayment is reduced to £1,000.

9.126   The authority can make a claim to a county court for a money judgment, see chapter 22.

From the landlord

9.127   Where payment was made to the landlord the authority may recover the overpayment from the landlord.[89] If the authority does this the landlord is entitled to treat the rent as unpaid.[90]

Challenging decisions

Decisions

9.128   A claimant is entitled to notification of a decision in writing[91] and the notification must include certain information, including:[92]

- the right to request a written statement of reasons; and
- the right to apply for a revision and the right to appeal against the decision, the time limits and way to do so.

9.129   Particular kinds of decision (for example, where a decision is made that a recoverable overpayment has been made – see para 9.119 above) require particular information to be given.

Time limits

9.130   The time limit for appealing against a decision is one calendar month. However, a claimant may request a written statement of reasons for a decision. If the reasons are provided within one month, the one-month period is extended by 14 days. If the reasons are provided outside the one-month period, the appeal must be made within 14 days of the reasons being provided. The tribunal has the power to extend the time limit but not beyond 13 months after date of the decision being appealed.

---

89 HB Regs 2006 reg 101. An exception is where the overpayment was caused by a misrepresentation or failure to disclose a material fact. If so, the overpayment is only recoverable from the person responsible, if different from the person to whom payment was made.

90 HB Regs 2006 reg 95(2), see para 7.28 above.

91 HB Regs 2006 reg 90.

92 HB Regs 2006 Sch 9.

Revisions

9.131   In response to a request for reasons or an indication that the claimant wishes to appeal, an authority may reconsider its decision. If the authority accepts that the decision was wrong it can revise the decision. A revised decision takes effect from the date the decision was first made. An example would be an error in the calculation of the claimant's income.

9.132   A claimant who believes the authority has made an error may request a reconsideration. However, a claimant should also indicate an intention to appeal as a request for a reconsideration does not extend or suspend the time limit for appealing.

Supersession

9.133   Where the claimant's representations indicate a change of circumstances, a decision may be superseded. An example would be a change in income or a change to the make-up of the household. Supersession takes effect from the date of the change of circumstance (or, in fact, the first Monday following notification of the change of circumstance).

9.134   If an authority supersedes a decision, the claimant can still appeal against the original decision on the basis that it was wrong at the time.

Appeals

9.135   Some decisions may not be appealed. These include decisions by the rent officer about the level of the local housing allowance and decisions to suspend the payment of HB.

9.136   Where there is a right of appeal, any person affected by the decision may appeal, including the landlord. If the authority is not willing to revise the decision the appeal will be referred to Social Security and Child Support Tribunal, which is part of the First-tier Tribunal.

9.137   Appeals are usually dealt with at a hearing but may be determined without a hearing if both parties agree. Advice about welfare benefits is now outside the scope of legal aid, so no legally aided help will be available to assist with a HB issue or appeal.

9.138   An appeal against a decision of the First-tier Tribunal is made to the Upper Tribunal (Administrative Appeals Chamber). As the issue concerns welfare benefits, legal aid will not not available, unless by way of exceptional case funding, see para 22.170.

CHAPTER 10

Disrepair and housing conditions – action by occupiers

continued

continued

Key points

- An occupier can take two types of legal action to address disrepair and poor housing conditions: a civil action in the county court and a criminal action in the magistrates' court.
- Most civil actions rely on contractual rights under a tenancy agreement.
- In all short-term tenancies a landlord has a legal obligation to keep in repair the structure and exterior and the installations for gas, electricity, sanitation and heating. This applies whether or not the tenancy agreement is in writing. The landlord cannot avoid this obligation.
- Usually a landlord will not be in breach of the obligation until the tenant has given notice of the necessary repairs and a reasonable time has elapsed.
- If a landlord is in breach of the repairing obligation a county court can award compensation and order the landlord to carry out the necessary works of repair.
- In most tenancies there is no legal requirement on a landlord that premises let as dwellings are fit for human habitation. A tenant cannot therefore take civil legal action against a landlord because premises are unfit unless this is caused by disrepair.
- The general rule is that a tenant can only take civil action against a landlord if there is 'disrepair' as opposed to poor housing conditions caused by bad design or insufficient amenities.
- Where poor housing conditions are caused by bad design and/ or lack of amenities, an occupier may be able to bring a criminal prosecution.
- An occupier with a social landlord may also make a formal complaint about a landlord's failure to carry out repairs and refer to an Ombudsman if the landlord does not resolve the problem.
- Although it is inadvisable for a tenant to withhold rent because of disrepair, damages for disrepair may be set off against arrears of rent and may provide a defence to a claim for possession.

Introduction

10.1   Many people who live in rented accommodation are unhappy with their living conditions. They may want more suitable and healthy accommodation provided by a social landlord. Unfortunately, the shortage of affordable accommodation is such that even those in great need may wait for many years to be offered more appropriate accommodation. Advisers will need to be familiar with the transfer and allocation policies of local authorities and other social landlords to advise realistically about the prospects of obtaining better accommodation. Chapter 17 deals with local authorities' duties to operate housing allocation and transfer systems.

10.2   This chapter examines the legal action occupiers can take to obtain repairs or improvements to their homes. The following options are available to an occupier:

- a civil claim in the county court for compensation and an order for works of repair;
- a criminal action in the magistrates' court for an abatement order and compensation;
- a formal complaint to a social landlord;
- using the rent to pay for repairs.

Occupier's status

10.3   Before advising anyone about the best course of action consideration must be given to the occupier's status. Most private tenants have assured shorthold tenancies which give no more than six months' security. A private landlord may respond to a complaint or threat of legal action by applying for a possession order so clients need to be made aware of this possibility.

10.4   In addition, for local authority tenants it may be necessary to check whether a suspended possession order has been made in the past. If so, this could mean that for a relevant period, they were not actually tenants but 'tolerated trespassers'. The Housing and Regeneration Act 2008 restored secure tenancies automatically, but only from 20 May 2009 (see para 6.150). If the tenant wishes to claim damages for breach of any period prior to that date, an application must be made to the court so that the tenancy is treated as continuing (see para 10.93 below).[1]

---

1   This will be relevant for claims issued prior to 20 May 2015 since the claim will be limited to the previous six years. But note that different rules apply if the claim is brought as a counterclaim, see paras 10.180–10.182.

Actions in the county court

10.5   A county court claim will usually be based on:[2]

- breach of contract (see paras 10.6–10.96); and/or
- a claim in tort (see paras 10.97–10.117).

Breach of contract

The repairing covenant

10.6   A claim for breach of contract relies on the landlord's repairing covenant. This means the landlord's legal obligation to repair the premises. The covenant may be set out expressly in the tenancy agreement and/or or implied by statute or by common law.

Express terms of the tenancy agreement

10.7   A tenancy agreement is a legal contract and the obligations on the landlord and tenant are legally binding. A written tenancy agreement may contain express terms setting out the landlord's and the tenant's respective obligations for repairs. There is a minimum obligation on the landlord that cannot be overridden by the express terms (see below, paras 10.9–10.25). But the tenancy agreement may set out more extensive obligations on the landlord, and advisers should always obtain a copy of the tenancy agreement. Tenancy agreements used by private landlords often say little or nothing about the landlord's repairing obligations while those issued by social landlords usually set out the landlord's obligations. In more recent standard tenancy agreements issued by social landlords the express repairing obligation tends to mirror the minimum legal standard. However, older tenancy agreements often contain more generous repairing covenants.

> In *Welsh v Greenwich LBC*[3] the landlord's obligation was to keep the premises 'in good condition and repair' which was held to include liability for severe condensation. This would not normally fall within the landlord's repairing obligations.

2 See para 22.8 for an explanation of 'causes of action'.
3 (2001) 33 HLR 438, CA.

In *Long v Southwark LBC*⁴ the landlord covenanted 'to take reasonable steps to keep the estate and common parts clean and tidy'. The tenant brought a claim against the landlords because of inadequate arrangements for collecting rubbish on the estate.

The Court of Appeal held that a failure to supervise the performance of outside contractors engaged to collect rubbish amounted to a failure to take reasonable steps and the landlords were in breach of the tenancy agreement.

Variation of tenancy agreement

10.8   Local authorities are able to vary the terms of a tenancy agreement provided they follow the proper procedure (see para 3.150). Advisers should therefore check to see whether the original tenancy agreement has been varied.

Section 11: landlord's implied repairing obligation

10.9   Section 11 of the Landlord and Tenant Act (LTA) 1985 implies into every tenancy agreement granted for a period of seven years or less an obligation on the landlord to carry out certain repairs. In this chapter this is referred to as 'section 11'. Disrepair claims in the county court are often referred to as 'section 11 claims'.

Section 11 – the dwelling-house

10.10   In relation to the premises let to the tenant, section 11 provides that there is an implied covenant on the landlord:

(a) to keep in repair the structure and exterior of the dwelling-house (including drains, gutters and external pipes);

(b) to keep in repair and proper working order the installations in the dwelling-house for the supply of water, gas and electricity and for sanitation (including basins, sinks, baths and sanitary conveniences but not other fixtures, fittings and appliances for making use of the supply of water, gas or electricity); and

(c) to keep in repair and proper working order the installations in the dwelling-house for space heating and heating water.

4 [2002] EWCA Civ 403.

Section 11 – the building

10.11 For tenancies that began on or after 15 January 1989 the covenant extends to other parts of the building in which the dwelling-house is situated, provided that the building is also owned by the landlord. In such a case the Landlord and Tenant Act (LTA) 1985 s11(1A) provides that the landlord must also keep in repair the structure and exterior of the building. Furthermore, he or she must keep in repair and proper working order any installation that serves the dwelling, directly or indirectly, provided that it is part of the building that the landlord owns or it is in the landlord's control.

10.12 The wider duty applies only if the disrepair affects the tenant's enjoyment of his or her own dwelling or of the common parts.[5]

When section 11 doesn't apply

10.13 LTA 1985 s11 is implied into almost all tenancy agreements.[6] It is implied into a weekly or monthly periodic agreement, even if the tenant has lived in the accommodation for seven years or more.

10.14 Section 11 is not implied if:[7]

- the tenancy began before 24 October 1961; or
- the tenancy is for a fixed term of seven years or more.

Section 11 is unavoidable

10.15 Landlords cannot avoid LTA 1985 s11 by providing in the tenancy agreement that the repairing obligations fall on the tenant or that section 11 is excluded. Any attempt to contract out of the section 11 duty is void.[8] A term in the tenancy agreement that limits or restricts the landlord's obligation under section 11 is valid only if authorised by a county court. The court can do this only if the parties agree and the court considers that it is reasonable.[9]

10.16 Furthermore, terms that seek to make the landlord's repairing obligation dependent on the tenant complying with the tenancy agreement or to prevent a tenant from setting off damages for disrepair against rent arrears may be held to be unfair and unenforceable.[10]

---

5 LTA 1985 s11(1B).
6 This includes tenancy agreements that are not in writing.
7 LTA 1985 s13(1).
8 LTA 1985 s12(1).
9 LTA 1985 s12(1)(b).
10 See para 4.181, Unfair Terms in Consumer Contracts Regulations 1999 SI No 2083; *Cody v Philps,* January 2005 *Legal Action* 28, 4 November 2004, see para 4.171.

What does section 11 cover?

Keep in repair the structure and exterior

10.17   'Keep in repair' has been interpreted by the courts to mean 'put and keep in repair'.[11] It is no defence for a landlord to argue that the item was in disrepair when the tenancy started.

10.18   The 'structure and exterior of the dwelling-house' does not mean 'the entire dwelling-house, or the entire constructed building' but 'consists of those elements of the overall dwelling-house which give it its essential appearance, stability and shape'. This is to be contrasted with 'the many and various ways in which the dwelling-house will be fitted out, equipped, decorated and generally made to be habitable'. It is not limited to:

> ... those aspects of the dwelling-house which are load bearing ... but ... to be part of the structure of the dwelling-house a particular element must be a material or significant element in the overall construction.[12]

10.19   It includes:

- drains, gutters and external pipes (section 11 expressly states this);
- all outside parts of the dwelling;[13]
- the external walls;[14]
- partition walls between the dwelling and another house or flat;[15]
- partition walls within the flat;[16]
- internal plaster applied to walls and ceilings;[17]
- the roof (including skylights); however, if the dwelling is a flat, only if it is a top floor flat and the ceiling and roof are part of the same unit;[18]
- external joinery;

---

11 *Saner v Bilton* (1878) 7 Ch D 815.
12 *Irvine v Moran* (1990) 24 HLR 1, QB.
13 *Campden Hill Towers Ltd v Gardner* (1976) 13 HLR 64, CA.
14 *Campden Hill Towers Ltd v Gardner* (1976) 13 HLR 64, CA.
15 *Green v Eales* (1841) 2 QB 225.
16 *Campden Hill Towers Ltd v Gardner* (1976) 13 HLR 64, CA.
17 *Grand v Gill* [2011] EWCA Civ 554, 19 May 2011.
18 *Douglas-Scott v Scorgie* (1984) 13 HLR 97, CA. If disrepair to the roof of a building is causing damage to a flat within the building the tenant could rely on section 11(1A) under which the landlord is obliged to keep in repair the structure and exterior of the building. This is only possible if the landlord owns the building and the tenancy started on or after 15 January 1989. If the tenancy commenced before this date an action in nuisance may be possible, see below, paras 10.116–10.117.

- external doors;
- windows, including glass, sashes and necessary window furniture;[19]
- paths and steps that are part of the immediate access to the dwelling.[20]

10.20 The following are not part of the structure and exterior:

- internal doors;
- internal glazing;
- internal joinery such as skirting boards and architraves;[21]
- floor coverings.

The installations

10.21 The landlord's obligation is to keep the installations 'in repair and proper working order'. If there is a defective installation in the dwelling when the tenancy starts the landlord must put it in a state of repair and proper working order. Furthermore, it is no defence if an installation is not in working order because of a design defect.[22]

10.22 'Installations' include:

- basins, sinks, baths and toilets;
- radiators;
- gas fires;
- fitted electric fires or heaters (including storage heaters) but not moveable plug-in electric heaters;
- boilers within the premises;
- water tanks within the premises;
- water and gas pipes and electrical wiring;
- under-floor heating vents.

10.23 It does not include fixtures and fittings for sanitation apart from basins, sinks, baths and toilets. This means that installations such as showers or bidets will not be the landlord's responsibility unless specified in the tenancy agreement.

10.24 However, if there is no installation (eg no central heating system or hot water boiler) there is no obligation on the landlord to provide one. However, tenants may ask the local authority to take action against a landlord to improve the premises by installing some facility

---

19 *Irvine v Moran* (1990) 24 HLR 1.
20 *Brown v Liverpool Corporation* [1969] 3 All ER 1345, CA.
21 *Irvine v Moran* (1990) 24 HLR 1.
22 *Liverpool CC v Irwin* (1976) 13 HLR 38, HL.

if it is necessary to make the accommodation free from hazards (see paras 11.17–11.53).

10.25   In addition a landlord must comply with the Gas Safety (Installation and Use) Regulations 1998 (see para 11.87).

Landlord's right of access

10.26   Landlord and Tenant Act 1985 s11(6) provides that there is an implied covenant on a tenant to allow the landlord (or someone authorised in writing by the landlord) to enter to inspect the premises. The right is to enter at reasonable times of the day and on giving 24 hours' notice in writing.

10.27   In addition to section 11 the landlord can rely on the following provisions to gain access:

- At common law a landlord who has a duty to keep premises in repair has a right to enter premises to carry out the works.[23]
- Under the Rent Act 1977 ss3(2) and 148 statutory tenants and protected tenants have a duty to give access to a landlord to carry out repairs.
- Housing Act 1988 s16 provides that it is an implied term of every assured tenancy that the tenant shall give access to a landlord to carry out repairs.

10.28   Almost all written tenancy agreements will include an express obligation on the tenant to give access to the landlord to inspect or carry out works.

When is the landlord in breach of section 11?

10.29   Before action can be taken in the county court the landlord must be in breach of the contractual repairing obligations. The tenant must therefore prove:

- that there is disrepair that falls within the landlord's repairing covenant;
- that the landlord knows about the disrepair (the position is different if the disrepair is outside the dwelling, see below, para 10.58);
- that the landlord has failed to carry out repairs within a reasonable time;

---

23 *Saner v Bilton* (1878) 7 Ch D 815.

- if damages are claimed, that the tenant has suffered some inconvenience or loss.

10.30 Each of these aspects of a claim is considered below.

Disrepair

10.31 There must be 'disrepair'. This means that part of the dwelling is in a worse condition than it was at some earlier time as opposed to lacking some amenity or being of defective design.[24]

10.32 The disrepair must be because of a failure by the landlord to carry out repairs for which he or she is responsible under the tenancy agreement.

Defective installations or absent installations

10.33 As indicated above at para 10.24, the fact that accommodation is in poor condition because of the absence of an installation does not mean that the property is in disrepair. Under the terms of the tenancy agreement a landlord can be forced to repair a defective installation but not to install something not present in the dwelling when the tenancy started.

Disrepair or design defect?

10.34 Poor housing conditions such as damp and cold may be caused by disrepair or by the design of the dwelling, or sometimes a combination of both. In some local authority accommodation condensation dampness is common. This is frequently caused by poor design: inadequate insulation, poor ventilation and insufficient heating. This is not disrepair.

> In *Quick v Taff Ely Borough Council*[25] the tenant occupied a house on an estate constructed in the 1970s. There was severe condensation such that the house was virtually unfit for habitation in winter. The cause of the condensation was a combination of the following factors: cold bridging due to lack of insulation, sweating from the windows and inadequate heating. The condensation had caused extensive damage to the tenant's belongings. The county court

---

24 *Post Office v Aquarius Properties* [1987] 1 All ER 1055; *Quick v Taff Ely BC* [1986] QB 809.
25 (1985) 18 HLR 66.

> judge awarded damages and, in accordance with the tenant's expert evidence, ordered the landlords to replace the windows and install insulation to alleviate the high levels of condensation. The Court of Appeal upheld the local authority's appeal: the damage to property was not caused by a breach of the repairing obligation because the dampness was caused by a design defect not disrepair.

10.35　The question of whether a problem is caused by a design defect or by disrepair is closely related to the issue of whether the landlord's repairing obligation can extend to remedying a design defect.

Repair or improvement?

10.36　A tenant cannot bring a civil action to force a landlord to remedy a design defect. However, if the tenant can show that there is disrepair, the landlord's repairing obligation may extend to remedying the design defect that caused the disrepair. Whether, in a particular case, a landlord's repairing obligation will extend to taking action to remedy a design defect will depend upon the following factors:

- whether the works are to the whole or substantially the whole of the structure or only a subsidiary part;
- whether the effect of the works will be to produce a building of a wholly different character than that which had been let; and
- the cost of the work in relation to the previous value of the building and the effect of the works on the value and lifespan of the building.

> These criteria were set out in *McDougal v Easington DC*.[26] The premises were stripped back to the original framework with new front and rear elevations, windows, doors and roof installed. The cost of the works exceeded £10,000, increased the value of the premises from £10,000 to £18,000 and extended the expected life of the premises by about 30 per cent. The works were held not to constitute works of repair.

10.37　Below are some examples of cases where the courts have found that the landlord's repairing obligation extended to remedying a design defect.

26　(1989) 21 HLR 310, CA.

In *Ravenseft Properties Ltd v Davstone Holdings Ltd*[27] a block of flats
was clad in stone on a concrete frame. Because of a design fault the
construction lacked any expansion joints which caused the stone
cladding to fall away from time to time. Without the inclusion of
expansion joints this would continue to happen so that the only
way to reinstate the cladding would be by also providing expansion
joints. It was argued that this amounted to remedying an inherent
defect and was outside the repairing covenant.

The court rejected this, holding that it is always a question of
fact and degree whether works constitute works of repair or
improvement. The works fell within the repairing covenant.

Elmcroft Developments Ltd v Tankersley-Sawyer[28] concerned premises
that suffered from rising damp caused by the fact that the slate
damp-proof course (DPC) was ineffective as it was below ground
level. The county court judge held that the necessary remedial work
included: the installation of a horizontal DPC by silicone injection;
the formation by silicone injection of vertical barriers where the
front and external walls met the dividing walls; plus re-plastering
and redecoration.

The Court of Appeal rejected the landlord's appeal. Following
Ravenseft, it was a question of fact and degree whether the remedial
works fell within a repairing covenant. The works were works of repair.

In *Stent v Monmouth District Council*[29] there was a design defect in
the premises: the concrete step outside was at the same level as the
floor inside the entrance hall. This caused water ingress beneath
the door which, in turn, caused the door to warp and eventually to
rot. After carrying out patchwork repairs several times a new door
was fitted by the council but this did not remedy the design defect.
Several years later a self-sealing aluminium door was fitted in
accordance with the recommendations of the tenant's surveyor.

The Court of Appeal decided that the tenant was entitled to
damages because of the council's failure to carry out appropriate
remedial works sooner. It was held that where there was no

27 [1980] QB 12.
28 (1984) 15 HLR 63. See also *Uddin v Islington LBC*, CA, 10 March 2015
    (AC9401696).
29 (1987) 19 HLR 269, CA.

disrepair (as in *Quick*, see para 10.34) there was no obligation
on the landlord to remedy design defects. However, where there
was a defect that the landlord was obliged to repair, 'on a true
construction of the covenant to repair there is required to be done,
not only the making [good] of the immediate occasion of disrepair,
but also, if this is what a sensible, practical man would do, the
elimination of the cause of that disrepair through the making good
of an inherent design defect at least where the making good of that
defect does not involve a substantial rebuilding of the whole'.[30]

10.38 These cases can be contrasted with *Quick v Taff Ely* (see para 10.34):
the landlords had an obligation to repair and the issue was the extent
of works necessary to comply with that obligation. In *Quick* the tenant had not argued that the works were necessary to remedy disrepair but rather to alleviate the effects of the condensation and it was
held that 'there must be disrepair before any question arises as to
whether it would be reasonable to remedy a design fault when doing
the repair'.[31]

Dampness

10.39 The fact that premises are damp does not necessarily mean that a
landlord is in breach of the repairing obligation. It is for the tenant to identify the cause of the dampness. Unless it is obvious (eg a
leaking roof or rotten windows) expert evidence will be needed. As
is clear from the cases referred to above (paras 10.34–10.37), if the
cause of the dampness is a design defect this is not disrepair and the
landlord has no obligation under section 11 to prevent the premises
being damp. This has been held to be the case where the dampness
was caused by condensation due to inadequate heating and thermal
insulation (see *Quick* above at para 10.34).

In *Post Office v Aquarius Properties*[32] the basement of the premises
was ankle deep in water whenever the water table rose because of a
design defect. However, this caused no damage to the structure.
    The Court of Appeal held that there was no obligation under the
covenant to remedy the defect.

30 The President, Sir John Arnold, at 285.
31 (1985) 18 HLR 66, Lawton LJ at 77.
32 [1987] 1 All ER 1055.

10.40   If dampness caused by a design defect results in damage to the structure of the premises (which includes damage to wall and ceiling plaster) there will be an obligation to carry out repairs. This obligation may include remedying the design defect depending on the nature of the defect and the cost of remedial works (see the cases discussed at para 10.37).

10.41   Clearly, if dampness is caused by disrepair (such as defective windows or leaking roof) then the landlord will be liable if he or she has failed to carry out repairs within a reasonable period of time.

10.42   As in any civil claim it is for the claimant to prove the case on the balance of probabilities.

> In *Southwark LBC v McIntosh*[33] an award of general damages of £7,500 was made to a tenant whose flat was damp and whose claim against the council alleged a breach of the repairing covenant.
>
> The council's appeal succeeded: the tenant had failed to establish that the dampness was caused by a breach of the covenant or that the dampness had caused damage to the structure and exterior. All that the tenant had pleaded was the *existence* of dampness which was insufficient to establish that the landlords were in breach.

10.43   This does not mean that there is nothing a tenant can do about damp conditions where there is no actual disrepair. The premises may be prejudicial to health so that a prosecution under the Environmental Protection Act 1990 can be brought against the landlord. Also, the dampness may constitute a 'hazard' under the Housing Health and Safety Rating System (HHSRS). This would give the local authority the right to serve an improvement notice on the landlord. These options are discussed below in paras 10.217–10.242 and in paras 11.17–11.62.

Common disputes

Kitchen units

10.44   Kitchen units and work surfaces are not covered by section 11 – they are not part of the structure and exterior and are not installations. It is therefore the tenant's responsibility to repair or replace broken or worn out parts, unless the tenancy agreement provides otherwise.

---

33 [2002] 08 EG 164.

10.45   It should be noted, however, that in the social rented sector works have been or are being carried out in many homes to improve properties in order to bring them up to the 'Decent Homes' standard (see para 11.84). In most cases this includes installing new kitchens and bathrooms. If a new kitchen is fitted by the landlord the work must be carried out to a reasonable standard and any problems caused by poor workmanship or defective fittings will be the landlord's responsibility. However, future repairs needed because of 'fair wear and tear' will not be the landlord's responsibility unless the tenancy agreement expressly states that the landlord is responsible.

Broken windows and other 'accidental' damage

10.46   Window panes are covered by LTA 1985 s11. However, many social landlords will not agree to repair window panes without evidence that the damage was not caused by the tenant or his or her family or visitors. Alternatively, the landlord may agree to replace the pane but re-charge the repairs to the tenant (see para 10.50 below).

10.47   A landlord is not legally responsible for repairing damage caused by the tenant: LTA 1985 s11(2)(a) provides that a landlord is not required to carry out works or repairs for which the tenant is liable by virtue of the duty to use the premises in a 'tenant-like manner'. The duty to use the premises in a tenant-like manner includes a duty not to cause damage to the premises deliberately or carelessly, see below, para 10.91.

10.48   Some landlords have a policy that they will repair broken window panes provided the tenant can provide a crime reference number as evidence that the damage was caused by someone outside the premises and was reported to the police as a crime.

10.49   Sometimes there may be a dispute about the evidence available regarding the cause of the damage. If unexplained damage has been caused within the premises it is reasonable for the landlord to hold that the tenant is responsible.

10.50   A landlord may carry out repairs for which the tenant is legally responsible and then charge the cost of the repairs to the tenant. Most public sector tenancy agreements include a term permitting the landlord to do this. It is common for a landlord to enter the charge as arrears of rent on the rent account. If the landlord then seeks possession on the basis of rent arrears, this can be challenged. The correct way for the landlord to recover the cost of repairs is by sending to the tenant an invoice and seeking a money judgment in the county court if the invoice is not paid.

Tenant's improvements and tenant's fixtures

10.51 Tenants may carry out works of improvement or install fittings that become 'fixtures'. A fixture is something that becomes part of the premises. This would include laminate flooring, shower fittings, fitted cupboards and fitted shelving. Most tenancy agreements require the tenant to obtain the landlord's consent to carry out such works. A tenant who fails to obtain consent is in breach of the tenancy agreement and this can provide a ground for possession. However, the ground is a discretionary one and a possession order will be made only if it is reasonable to do so. A tenant who has carried out improvements without the landlord's consent can seek consent retrospectively and consent must not be unreasonably withheld.[34]

10.52 Installations and improvements made by the tenant without consent will not fall within the landlord's repairing obligation. Furthermore, most public sector tenancy agreements expressly state that the landlord is not responsible for repairs and improvements carried out by the tenant.

10.53 Under landlord and tenant law, a tenant's fixtures become part of the premises and should be left in the premises when the tenant leaves. However, many tenancy agreements for social housing provide that a tenant must remove fixtures and fittings and put the premises back into their original state before leaving. This will override the usual rule.

Knowledge/notice of disrepair

Disrepair within the dwelling

10.54 A landlord is only in breach of section 11 if he or she has had notice of the disrepair and has failed to carry out effective repairs within a reasonable time.[35]

10.55 There is no requirement that the tenant gives notice in a particular way and the landlord may be put on notice by events other than a direct complaint by the tenant. For example:

- a local authority inspection that is communicated to the landlord;[36]
- a visit by an agent or employee of the landlord such as a rent

---

34 HA 1985 s97(3)
35 *O'Brien & Another v Robinson* [1973] 1 All ER 583; *McGreal v Wake* (1984) 13 HLR 107.
36 *McGreal v Wake* (1984) 13 HLR 107.

collector, environmental health officer or housing officer, provided the disrepair is visible;[37]

- a report prepared by a rent officer that is sent to the landlord;
- a valuer's report prepared in respect of a right-to-buy application sent to the chief executive's office.[38]

10.56   A tenancy agreement may provide that notice of disrepair must be given in a particular form or within a particular period. However, this does not mean that the tenant cannot prove that the landlord is in breach where notice is given in a different way.[39] Oral notice is sufficient although obviously more difficult to prove than written notice.

10.57   It is not necessary for the tenant to identify the cause of any problem or specify each defect. It is sufficient that the landlord is made aware that something may need to be investigated.[40]

Disrepair in the building in which the dwelling is situated

10.58   Where the disrepair is in the building rather than within the dwelling itself the landlord is liable as soon as the disrepair occurs regardless of notice.

In *British Telecommunications plc v Sun Life Assurance Society plc*[41] the landlords argued that liability for damages could only start after a reasonable period had elapsed from the date the defect became apparent.

The Court of Appeal rejected this: the general rule where a landlord had to keep premises in repair was that the landlord was liable as soon as the premises fell into disrepair. It was an exception to this general rule that in relation to disrepair inside the premises let liability only arose after notice had been given and the landlords had had a reasonable opportunity to carry out the repairs.

So, in *Passley v Wandsworth LBC*[42] the council was held liable when pipes in the roof of a block of flats burst causing damage to the

---

37 *Dinefwr BC v Jones* (1987) 19 HLR 445.
38 *Dinefwr BC v Jones* (1987) 19 HLR 445.
39 *Dinefwr BC v Jones* (1987) 19 HLR 445. Furthermore, such a term may contravene the Unfair Terms in Consumer Contracts Regulations 1999 SI No 2083 and be unenforceable, see para 4.163.
40 *Griffin v Pillet* [1926] 1 KB 17.
41 [1995] 4 All ER 44, CA.
42 (1986) 30 HLR 165, CA.

> belongings of the tenant in the top flat. This was despite the fact
> that neither the tenant nor the landlord had been aware that the
> pipes were in disrepair prior to the flood.

10.59 The reason for this distinction is that a landlord can inspect the exterior and common parts of the building at any time. In contrast, a tenant has exclusive possession of the premises let so the landlord must be given notice of disrepair within the premises.

10.60 This does not mean that a tenant need not report defects in the building to the landlord. A tenant who knows about disrepair to the building and fails to inform the landlord may have any damages reduced on the basis that he or she failed to 'mitigate' loss (see para 10.67 below).

Long leases

10.61 The situation is different for long-leaseholders because the landlord may have a duty to consult all of the leaseholders in the building before carrying out works. In such a case the duty to repair will be set out in the lease and LTA 1985 s11 will not apply as the lease will be for more than seven years.[43]

> In *Earle v Charalambous*[44] the disrepair was in a building let to
> various long-leaseholders. In a claim for damages for breach of the
> landlord's repairing obligation the parties had proceeded on the
> basis that the starting point for liability was the date of notice.
>   The Court of Appeal held that, following notice by the tenant,
> the landlord was entitled to a further reasonable period to carry out
> the works and commented that the *British Telecommunications* case
> (see para 10.58) was about a commercial lease and was not decided
> in the context of the modern statutory and contractual framework
> concerning residential leases. A landlord's repairing obligation in
> respect of a long residential lease was linked to the leaseholder's
> obligations to pay service charges and subject to a duty to consult
> the leaseholders about major works. The court suggested that the
> rule set out in *British Telecommunications v Sun Life* case may have
> to be modified to take account of modern residential long leases.

43 LTA 1987. See chapter 5.
44 [2006] EWCA Civ 1090.

Failure to carry out repairs within a reasonable time

10.62   What is a reasonable time will depend on the effect of the disrepair and the extent of the necessary repairs. A landlord may be in breach if he or she fails to repair a leaking pipe within a number of hours but a timescale of several months may be reasonable if the works are extensive, for example, fitting a new roof. Where extensive works will take a long time to complete, a landlord may be expected to carry out patchwork repairs to minimise inconvenience in the interim.

10.63   Social landlords sometimes publish expected response times for certain kinds of repairs and these may provide a good starting point in deciding what would be a reasonable time. However, these are set by the landlords themselves and the court may find a landlord liable even when the repairs were carried out within the target time. A surveyor will be able to comment on what is a reasonable time to repair a particular defect.

10.64   There may be a dispute about whether a landlord has carried out repairs within a reasonable time when ineffective works have been done and the problem has recurred. This is common when the defects concern central heating systems. Tenants often complain that the system keeps breaking down and that the landlord carries out works so that the system functions only for a short time before breaking down again. Whether and at what point a landlord must accept that the whole system or boiler needs to be replaced will normally be a matter for expert evidence. If this is in dispute it may be necessary to obtain expert evidence from a heating engineer rather than a general surveyor.

Tenant's inconvenience or loss

10.65   If a tenant is claiming damages it must be established that he or she has, as a consequence of the landlord's breach, suffered some inconvenience or loss.

10.66   Damages are not limited to quantifiable loss, such as the cost of replacing damaged furniture or belongings or paying for alternative accommodation. Damages may also be awarded to compensate for the tenant's loss of the enjoyment of the accommodation and for such things as injury to health. The way such damages are assessed is explained below at 10.152–10.156.

Mitigating loss

10.67   A tenant has a duty to 'mitigate' (or minimise) his or her losses. For example if water is leaking into the premises the tenant would be expected to place a bucket to catch the falling water rather than to allow it to damage carpets.

Giving access to the landlord and workmen

10.68   Landlords sometimes argue that they are not in breach of the repairing obligation because the tenant has not given access. If it is proved that access has been unreasonably refused it may be held that the landlord is not in breach or damages may be reduced on the basis that the tenant has delayed completion of the works (and thereby failed to mitigate his or her loss). Disputes often arise in relation to access. Advisers must make sure the tenant is aware of the obligation to give access. The tenant should also be advised to keep records of the dates and times access is requested and whether the tenant was at home when it is alleged that access has not been given. Sometimes landlords allege a failure to give access when an unscheduled attendance was made and the tenant was not at home. The duty to give access under section 11 is conditional upon the landlord giving written notice 24 hours in advance. However, once works have been agreed, a tenant will be expected to act reasonably in giving access to the landlord's workmen and contractors. If a court takes the view that the tenant has failed to act reasonably, damages could be reduced on the basis of the tenant's failure to mitigate his or her loss.

10.69   If reasonable access *is* being refused a landlord can obtain an injunction to gain access and any legal costs incurred will be set off against any damages subsequently awarded to the tenant.

Disturbance during works

10.70   In every tenancy agreement it is implied that a landlord will allow the tenant 'quiet enjoyment' of the premises. The covenant is breached if a landlord 'does anything which substantially interferes with the tenant's title to or possession of the ... premises or with his ordinary and lawful enjoyment of the demised premises. The interference need not be direct or physical'.[45] The carrying out of works of repair may cause some unavoidable interference with the tenant's enjoyment of his or her home but the landlord has a duty to minimise the

---

45   *Southwark LBC v Tanner* [2001] 1 AC 1, Lord Millett at 23.

interference: a landlord should take 'all reasonable precautions' to avoid disturbing the tenant but need not take 'all possible' precautions.[46] Where a landlord fails to take all reasonable precautions, the tenant may be awarded additional damages for breach of the covenant of quiet enjoyment. Alternatively, the damages recovered in the disrepair claim may be higher to reflect the additional distress and inconvenience.

Alternative accommodation during works

10.71   A common issue when extensive works of repair are to be carried out is whether it is necessary for the tenant to vacate the premises and, if so, who will arrange for alternative accommodation to be provided.

10.72   Whether it is necessary for the tenant to vacate will depend on the nature and extent of the works and whether it is possible to carry out the works so as to minimise inconvenience without disproportionately increasing the cost of the work. Experts should be asked to comment on whether works can reasonably be expected to be carried out with the tenant in occupation.

10.73   If it is necessary for the tenant to give vacant possession to enable the works to be completed, the court can make an order to this effect.[47] In practice, it is often the tenant who maintains that it will be necessary to move into alternative accommodation while the landlord proposes to carry out extensive work with the tenant in occupation. The dispute often occurs because of the expense to the landlord of providing alternative accommodation.

10.74   In fact, there is no legal obligation on a landlord to arrange alternative accommodation for a tenant even if vacant possession is clearly necessary. However, if the landlord is in breach of the repairing obligation and vacant possession is needed, the tenant can include in the claim for damages the cost of the alternative accommodation. In practice, social landlords will usually arrange alternative accommodation if satisfied it is necessary.

In *McGreal v Wake*[48] the court held that, although it would have been possible to remain in occupation during the works, it was reasonable for the tenant to choose to move into temporary accommodation as this meant that the works could be carried

---

46   *Goldmile Properties v Lechouritis* [2003] EWCA Civ 49.
47   See *English Churches Housing Group v Shine* [2004] EWCA Civ 434.
48   (1984) 13 HLR 107.

out more quickly and more cheaply. On that basis the cost of the temporary accommodation could be recovered by the tenant as part of her damages for the landlord's breach of covenant.

10.75 If a landlord is refusing to provide alternative accommodation and the tenant cannot afford to obtain it and claim reimbursement later from the landlord, the tenant may make an application to the court for an interim payment of damages. To obtain an interim payment, the claim must be commenced and the court must be satisfied that if the claim went to trial the tenant would obtain judgment for a substantial amount of money from the landlord.[49]

10.76 Where works are being carried out by a private landlord in compliance with a local authority notice (see chapter 11), the local authority may agree to provide the alternative accommodation for which the landlord must pay.

Redecorating following works

10.77 A landlord is responsible for 'making good' decorations following repair works. Disputes often arise about the extent of this duty.

In *Vukelic v Hammersmith & Fulham LBC*[50] damage was caused to the tenant's restaurant due to the landlord's nuisance. The landlord argued that, following repair works, the obligation was to redecorate only the immediate areas in which repairs had been carried out. The court held that:

... the decoration should be undertaken utilising good quality materials and a good standard of workmanship. It is not ... demonstrating a good standard of workmanship to hang a couple of strips of non-matching wallpaper on a wall where the other paper would not otherwise need replacement, or to patch a hole in wallpaper caused by removal of a light switch by sticking a random piece of non-matching wallpaper over the hole. It makes no difference ... that the non-matching wallpaper and the original wallpaper is then painted the same colour if the non-matching wallpaper remains ... obtrusive.[51]

49 CPR 25.7, see chapter 22.
50 [2003] EWHC 188 (TCC).
51 HHJ Richard Seymour QC at 102.

Other implied contractual terms

Fitness for habitation

10.78   There is no general term implied into tenancy agreements that a property let as a dwelling must be fit for habitation.[52] If a property is unfit for habitation the local authority has the power, or in some cases a duty, to take action against the landlord (see chapter 11). However, the fact that there is no contractual term as to fitness means that a tenant cannot bring legal proceedings against the landlord on the ground that the premises let are unfit for human habitation.

10.79   There are, in fact, two situations in which a term as to fitness for habitation is implied but both are extremely limited. These are furnished dwellings (para 10.80) and premises let at a low rent (paras 10.81–10.82).

Furnished dwellings

10.80   In relation to lettings of furnished houses and flats, common law implies a contractual term that they are fit for habitation at the date of letting. The term relates to initial fitness only.[53]

Premises let at low rent

10.81   Section 8 of the Landlord and Tenant Act 1985 implies into lettings at a low rent a contractual term that the premises are fit for habitation at the date of the letting and that they will be kept fit for habitation by the landlord throughout the tenancy.

10.82   The current limit was set in 1957 and has remained unchanged: for lettings starting on or after 1 April 1965, the term is implied only where the rent is less than £80 per annum (£1.54 per week!) in Greater London and £52 per annum elsewhere. It would be surprising if there were a single tenancy to which this implied term applies. Moreover, any tenancy at such a low rent would fall outside all the schemes of statutory protection and the tenant would have no long-term rights.[54]

---

52 The Law Commission recommended that a fitness term should be implied into tenancy agreements in its report *Landlord and Tenant: Responsibility for the State and Condition of a Property*, report no 238, published in 1996. This report has not yet been implemented.

53 *Smith v Marrable* (1843) 11 M&W 5; *Wilson v Finch Hatton* (1877) 2 Ex D 336.

54 See chapter 3.

Unfit premises and human rights

10.83 In *Lee v Leeds City Council and Ratcliffe and Others v Sandwell MBC*[55] the tenant argued that the effect of the Human Rights Act 1998 was that a local authority landlord had a duty to ensure that her home was fit for habitation. The argument was rejected by the Court of Appeal but the court did accept that there may be cases in which the state of the premises is such as to establish a breach of human rights.

Maintaining common parts and facilities

10.84 Where a landlord retains control of facilities that are essential or necessary to the tenant, the landlord is under a contractual obligation to maintain those facilities so that they remain available for the use of the tenant. This will include communal stairs, lifts and door entry systems.[56]

10.85 A repairing obligation may also be implied into the tenancy agreement if necessary to give the agreement 'business efficacy', ie to make it workable. Such a term will only be implied when 'necessary', not because it appears fair or desirable.

In *Barrett v Lounova*[57] the tenancy was granted in 1941 so section 11 did not apply. The only term relating to repairs provided that the tenant was responsible for internal repairs. The exterior of the premises fell into substantial disrepair causing water penetration and damage to the internal plaster and timbers.

The Court of Appeal held that the only way to make the tenancy agreement 'workable' was to imply a repairing obligation on the landlord in respect of the exterior of the premises.

Landlord's covenant of quiet enjoyment

10.86 This has been referred to above at para 10.70 in relation to the way in which repair works are carried out. It is also discussed below at para 10.143 in relation to inadequate sound insulation.

---

55 [2002] EWCA Civ 6.

56 *Liverpool Corporation v Irwin* [1977] AC 239. This is in addition to LTA 1985 s11(1A) which applies only to tenancies commencing on or after 15 January 1989, see para 10.11 above.

57 (1988) 20 HLR 584.

10.87   A landlord's breach of a repairing obligation may also constitute a breach of the covenant of quiet enjoyment. This was held to be the case in *Gordon v Selico Ltd*[58] where the failure to observe a covenant regarding the building in which the flat was situated caused water penetration and extensive dry rot in the leased flat. However, the covenant cannot create an obligation to repair where none exists by virtue of the express or implied terms of the tenancy agreement.

Non-derogation from grant

10.88   It is also implied into every tenancy agreement that a landlord shall not 'derogate from the grant' of the tenancy. This is an obligation on the landlord not to do anything in relation to premises he or she retains control of that will interfere with the tenancy. This obligation is closely related to the covenant of quiet enjoyment.

10.89   As is the case with the covenant for quiet enjoyment the covenant does not create new repairing obligations.

10.90   It is more likely that a landlord will be found to be in breach of the covenant of quiet enjoyment and/or non-derogation from grant by virtue of the way works are carried out than because of a failure to carry out works.

Using the premises in a tenant-like manner

10.91   A tenant has an obligation to use the premises in a 'tenant-like manner' which means 'taking proper care of the place'. This includes mending lights and fuses, clearing minor blockages in the sink, and doing 'the little jobs about the place which a reasonable tenant would do'. It also means that a tenant must not damage the premises wilfully or negligently. However, it does not extend to carrying out works where premises fall into disrepair through fair wear and tear or carrying out the necessary regular maintenance to ensure the premises do not fall into disrepair.[59]

10.92   See above (paras 10.46–10.50) in relation to broken windows.

58   (1986) 18 HLR 219.
59   *Warren v Keen* [1954] 1 QB 15.

The limits of contractual claims

Tolerated trespassers and replacement tenancies

10.93   Where a claim includes damages for a period prior to 20 May 2009 it may be necessary to make an application for an order that the court treat the tenancy as a 'continuing tenancy'. This will be the case if, prior to 20 May 2009, a suspended possession order had been made against a secure tenant (thereby making the former secure tenant a 'tolerated trespasser').

10.94   This is because the 'replacement tenancies' that automatically came into place for tolerated trespassers on 20 May 2009[60] are deemed for these purposes to have commenced on that date. So, from the date of the possession order to 20 May 2009, there will have been no tenancy and no right to contractual damages.

10.95   This will only affect claims issued prior to 20 May 2015 (as the six-year limitation period will go back to 20 May 2009). But it will continue to be relevant for counterclaims made in possession proceedings because the six year period is calculated from the date the claim is made, not the date the counterclaim is brought, see paras 10.180–10.186.

Only parties to the contract can sue

10.96   The general rule is that only a party to a contract can take action to enforce the contract or claim damages for a breach of the contract. This rule is called 'privity of contract'. This means that a civil claim for breach of the repairing obligation can only be brought by the tenant or tenants. However, a tenant can include a claim for damages for the inconvenience and loss suffered by his or her family because the benefit of the contract is for the whole family.[61]

Tort

10.97   A tort is a civil wrong which does not depend on a contractual relationship. The law recognises that certain situations create a 'duty of care': one party owes the other a duty to take reasonable care to ensure that he or she does not suffer injury or damage by reason of some act or omission. A breach of the duty gives the injured party the right to seek damages in the civil courts. The relationship of landlord

60 Under the Housing and Regneration Act 2008, see para 6.150.
61 *Jackson v Horizon Holidays* [1975] 3 All ER 92, CA.

and tenant does not, of itself, create a duty of care. What this means is that, at common law, a landlord may let to a tenant a property that is unsafe, unfit for habitation or in a poor state of repair. The landlord does not commit a tort by doing so. The tenant's rights relating to the state of the premises are contractual: they are found in the express terms of the tenancy agreement or implied by LTA 1985 s11. Nevertheless, there are some situations in which a duty of care *is* placed on a landlord.

10.98   Some torts have developed through case-law and are called 'common law' torts, others are set out in legislation and are called 'statutory' torts. In a disrepair claim the common law torts of nuisance and negligence may be relevant. Also, the Defective Premises Act (DPA) 1972 and the Occupiers' Liability Act 1957 set out statutory duties of care that may be owed in relation to residential premises. Some of the statutory duties set out in those Acts reflect common law duties previously recognised by the courts.

10.99   An action in tort is usually only possible *after* a person has suffered some injury or damage to belongings. In most disrepair claims the tenant will rely on both breach of the contract *and* a breach of a duty of care, sometimes arising out of the same facts.

The builder's duty: DPA 1972 s1 and common law

10.100   Section 1 of the Defective Premises Act 1972 places a duty on those who carry out work in connection with the provision of a dwelling. This includes building or converting premises. The duty is to do the work in a workmanlike or professional manner; to use proper materials; and to ensure that the dwelling is fit for human habitation when completed. The duty is owed to the person for whom the dwelling was provided and to anybody who later acquires an interest, including future tenants. It applies to all work commenced after 1 January 1974.[62]

10.101   Dwellings covered by the National House Building Council (NHBC) warranty scheme are excluded from DPA 1972.[63] Most new dwellings in the private sector are covered by the NHBC scheme.

10.102   A social landlord that builds or converts a building for letting therefore owes a duty of care to the initial tenant and subsequent

---

62   For an example of a successful claim under DPA 1972 s1, see *Bole v Huntsbuild Ltd* [2009] EWCA Civ 1146, 20 October 2009. The Court of Appeal upheld the finding that the premises were unfit for habitation by reason of inadequate foundations causing widespread cracking due to 'heave'.

63   DPA 1972 s2.

tenants. Any injury or damage suffered as a result of any breach of the duty under DPA 1972 s1 will create a liability.

10.103   In addition to DPA 1972, there is a common law duty on a person who builds or designs a dwelling to use reasonable skill and care and a landlord also has a common law duty to exercise a reasonable degree of care and skill when undertaking works of repair or improvement.[64]

> In *Rimmer v Liverpool CC*[65] the tenant injured himself on a glass pane in an internal wall. It was held that, although landlords of unfurnished dwellings did not owe any general duty of care to tenants, a landlord who also designed and built the dwelling did owe a duty of care to anyone who might reasonably be expected to be affected by faults in the design or construction of the premises. The authority was held to have been negligent and liable to pay damages.

Duty to maintain or repair: DPA 1972 s4

10.104 Section 4(1) of the DPA 1972 provides that where premises are let on a tenancy under which the landlord has an obligation to repair or maintain the premises:

> ... the landlord owes to all persons who might reasonably be expected to be affected by defects in the state of the premises a duty to take such care as is reasonable in all the circumstances to see that they are reasonably safe from personal injury or from damage to their property caused by a relevant defect.

10.105 A landlord who has a *right* to enter to carry out any kind of maintenance or repair is treated as if he or she were under an *obligation* to maintain or repair.[66]

10.106   The duty is owed 'if the landlord knows ... or if he ought in all the circumstances to have known of the relevant defect'.[67] The duty therefore exists independently of actual notice being given to the landlord.

---

64 *Ball v London CC* [1949] 2 KB 159 and *Billings (AC) & Sons v Riden* [1957] 3 All ER 1.

65 [1984] 1 All ER 930. The premises were built before 1974 so DPA 1972 was not relevant.

66 DPA 1972 s4(4).

67 DPA 1972 s4(2).

10.107   The landlord cannot restrict or exclude liability. Any provision in the tenancy agreement attempting to do so, will be void.[68]

Relevant defects

10.108   The 'section 4 duty' under DPA 1972 depends on there being a 'relevant defect'. A relevant defect is one that arises or continues because of the landlord's failure to carry out repairs or maintenance (whether it is a duty or only a right to repair or maintain). It covers items of repair or maintenance even where notice has not been given.[69]

10.109   The definition of relevant defect is therefore tied to the definition of disrepair – it does not extend to a defect that arises from something other than the landlord's obligation or right to carry out 'repairs'. It does not include design defects or defects that arise because of the tenant's failure to carry out any obligation under the tenancy.[70] However, the duty under DPA 1972 s4 is wider than the contractual repairing obligation in the following ways:

- the landlord may be liable for defects that affect not only the tenant but also other occupiers and visitors to the property;
- the landlord may be liable for a defect that has not been reported if the landlord 'ought' to have known of the defect; and
- the defect may arise from disrepair that the landlord is not obliged to remedy but that he or she has a right to remedy.

10.110   The following cases illustrate the way in which liability under DPA 1972 s4 is more extensive than the landlord's contractual repairing obligation.

> In *Clarke v Taff Ely BC*[71] the sister of one of the joint tenants was helping them to decorate. She suffered an injury when the leg of a table on which she was standing went through the floorboards. No complaint had been made to the council about the floorboards but it was known that the area was damp and that there was no ventilation under the floorboards.
>
> It was held that the council was liable for the injury suffered: arrangements should have been made for regular inspections and the tenant's sister was someone who 'might reasonably be expected to be affected by defects' in the premises.

68   DPA 1972 s6(3).
69   DPA 1972 s4(3).
70   DPA 1972 s4(4).
71   (1984) 10 HLR 44.

In *Smith v Bradford MDC*[72] a tenant had built a patio outside the dwelling. A subsequent tenant complained to the council that it was dangerous and later suffered an injury when he fell from the patio onto a grassed area several feet below.

The Court of Appeal held that the council was liable: the patio was part of the 'premises' and the council had a right to enter and repair it and were therefore liable.

10.111   However, DPA 1972 s4 does not extend to an obligation to make safe; the duty arises only in relation to defects, ie disrepair.

In *Alker v Collingwood Housing Association*[73] the tenant injured her hand on a glass panel to the entrance door of her home. The panel was not constructed of safety glass but ordinary annealed glass. It was likely that, at the time of construction, the door complied with the relevant building regulations but it has been accepted since at least 1963 that the use of annealed glass in doors presents a safety hazard. The tenancy agreement set out the landlord's repairing obligations, including the term: 'We must keep your home in good condition'.

The Court of Appeal held that the landlords were not liable because the unsafe glass panel was not a 'relevant defect': it was not in need of repair or maintenance. Even the duty to keep the premises in good condition did not encompass a duty to put them in safe condition.[74]

Duty to visitors: Occupiers' Liability Act 1957 and common law

10.112 The Occupiers' Liability Act 1957 provides that the occupier of premises owes a common duty of care to visitors. A landlord who lets premises but retains control of the common parts, such as stairs, paths and other means of access, is the occupier for the purposes of the Act. The landlord therefore owes a duty to all visitors 'to take such

72 (1982) 4 HLR 86.
73 [2007] EWCA Civ 343, 7 February 2007.
74 Note that the difference in *Rimmer v Liverpool CC*, see para10.103 above, was that the landlords were liable under s1 as the designers/builders of the premises.

care as in all the circumstances of the case is reasonable to see that the visitor will be reasonably safe in using the premises'.

10.113 There is also a common law duty of care owed by the occupier of premises to visitors. Again, this duty is on a landlord in relation to the common parts that remain in his or her control.[75]

Common law negligence

10.114 In addition to the specific duties of care set out above in paras 10.100– 10.112, the common law also recognises a general duty not to cause injury or damage because of careless or negligent behaviour.

10.115 The tort of negligence is committed when a person with a duty of care to another, breaches the duty, thereby causing loss or harm. A duty of care can exist if it is reasonably foreseeable that a person's act or omission may cause harm to another. Some relationships are accepted as creating a duty of care but the relationship of landlord and tenant is not such a relationship. So, when letting premises, at common law a landlord does not owe to a tenant a duty of care: the premises may be unfit or dangerous when let without the landlord being liable. However, this does not mean that a landlord is immune from liability for acts or omissions during the course of the letting. An example would be where the landlord fits a dangerous installation[76] or carries out repair works in a negligent way.

Common law nuisance

10.116 Nuisance is some act or state of affairs in one set of premises which amounts to unlawful interference with another person's use or enjoyment of neighbouring premises.[77] Where the condition of common parts retained by the landlord is affecting the tenant's enjoyment of the premises let an action may be brought in nuisance. This would cover, for example, a leaking pipe from a communal boiler which is causing dampness in the tenant's premises. For a tenancy granted on or after 15 January 1989 the tenant can rely on the extension of LTA 1985 s11 to the common parts. For other tenancies, the tenant could rely on the law of nuisance.

10.117 Note that the definition of 'statutory nuisance' is different. This is explained at paras 10.223–10.228 below.

75 *Dunster v Hollis* [1918] 2 KB 795; *Cockburn v Smith* [1924] 2 KB 119.
76 See *Ball v London CC*, referred to above at para 10.103.
77 *Read v Lyons & Co Ltd* [1945] KB 216.

Infestations

10.118 Tenants may complain of infestations of vermin. Cockroach and ant infestations frequently occur in local authority estates of a certain design. Infestation in itself is not disrepair and the landlord's repairing obligation will not usually extend to preventing or abating infestation within a dwelling. Although infested premises will usually be unfit for human habitation, there is no implied term in most tenancy agreements that the premises are fit for habitation.

10.119   There are two situations in which the landlord may be held liable for an infestation under the repairing covenant:

- if the tenancy agreement contains an express term such as that the landlord will keep the premises 'in good or habitable state', this may be interpreted as including an obligation to prevent infestations; and
- if there is disrepair that is causing or contributing to the infestation, such as holes in the floors or skirting boards.

10.120 In some circumstances it may be possible to use the law of nuisance and/or negligence to force a landlord to take action to prevent infestations and to claim damages for a failure to do so.

In *Sharpe v Manchester MDC*[78] the tenant of a local authority flat suffered from a cockroach infestation. It was likely that the cockroaches came through the service ducts which remained in the control of the authority, although other flats were unaffected. The authority carried out ineffective works to eliminate the infestation over a two-year period.

The Court of Appeal held that the council was liable in nuisance and was also negligent as it had failed to treat the service ducts and the other spaces in the walls and floors and had used a discredited insecticide.

However, in *Habinteg Housing Association v James*[79] there was no liability on the landlord for an infestation of cockroaches even where several tenants on the estate suffered from similar problems. There was no evidence that the infestation emanated from property occupied by the landlord. Although, following service of a statutory

78 (1977) 5 HLR 71.
79 (1994) 27 HLR 299.

notice by the local authority, an effective block treatment had been carried out to abate the nuisance, there had been no negligence in failing to carry out a block treatment earlier; the association did not have the power to carry out a block treatment in the absence of the local authority notice.

10.121   Where premises are suffering from an infestation and the landlord cannot be held responsible, complaint may be made to the local authority. Local housing authorities have powers and duties in relation to premises that are prejudicial to health or contain health hazards (see chapter 11). If the landlord is the local authority, while it may not be responsible as a landlord, most authorities have pest control departments which will carry out treatments to eradicate infestations. Most charge for such services although in some cases tenants of the authority are not charged. Alternatively, private companies offer pest control services.

In the county court case of *Dolan v Sefton MBC*[80] the tenant brought a claim in nuisance and negligence for three years of severe cockroach infestation following which she abandoned the premises. After two days of evidence the council agreed to pay £16,000 in damages and to abandon a claim for rent arrears of £2,500. Personal injury claims in respect of the claimant's two children were also settled. Each had suffered insect bites that became infected and developed a disease causing rashes, swollen joints and abdominal pains for a year. The court approved awards of £2,000 per child.

Water penetration from neighbouring properties

10.122   Tenants of flats may suffer from water penetration from neighbouring flats, usually those above. Landlords often deny responsibility, maintaining that the tenant must take up the issue with the tenant above. Liability depends on whether the water penetration causes 'disrepair' to the tenant's premises and the reason for the water penetration.

80   July 2001 *Legal Action* 27.

Disrepair caused by flooding

10.123 Where a flood from a neighbouring property causes damage to the structure of the tenant's premises (for example, collapsed ceiling) the tenant's landlord has an obligation to repair, regardless of the cause of the water penetration.

10.124 However, unless the landlord is responsible for the flood, there will be no liability for any damage caused to the tenant's belongings or to compensate for any inconvenience caused by the flood. The landlord is only responsible for damage and inconvenience which results from the landlord's breach, ie failing to carry out repairs within a reasonable period of being notified.[81]

10.125 If the flood was caused by the neighbour's misconduct or carelessness (eg a badly fitted washing machine, or a bath left to overflow) action could be taken against the neighbour in nuisance or negligence. The landlord could claim damages from the neighbour for the cost of the repairs and the tenant could also make a claim against the neighbour for compensation for inconvenience and damage to belongings.

Sustained water penetration

10.126 Where there is a problem of less severe but enduring water penetration, liability for repairs also depends on whether the water penetration causes damage to the structure.

10.127 Where there is damage to the ceiling or wall plaster, the landlord will be responsible for repairing the damage.

> In *Grand v Gill*[82] the Court of Appeal held that the judgment in *Irvine v Moran*[83] had been correct in describing the structure and exterior as consisting of 'those elements of the overall dwelling-house which give it its essential appearance, stability and shape', but was wrong to hold that internal plasterwork was not part of the structure but more in the nature of a decorative finish. Rather,
>
> > In the days when lath and plaster ceiling and internal partition walls were more common than now, the plaster was … an essential part of the creation and shaping of the ceiling or partition wall, which serve to give a dwelling-house its essential

---

81 See *Hyde Southbank Homes v Oronsay and Obadiara*, December 2005 *Legal Action* 28, 18 February 2005.

82 [2011] EWCA Civ 554, 19 May 2011.

83 (1990) 24 HLR 1, QB, see para 10.18.

> appearance and shape ... plasterwork generally, including
> that applied to external walls, [is] ordinarily in the nature of a
> smooth constructional finish to walls and ceilings, to which the
> decoration can then be applied, rather than a decorative finish in
> itself.[84]

However, if the only damage is to the tenant's belongings, the landlord will not be liable unless the water penetration is caused by disrepair (eg leaking service pipes).

10.128   If sustained water penetration is caused by the neighbour's conduct, although the landlord will have an obligation to repair any consequent damage to the structure, the tenant will have to take direct action against the neighbour to prevent ongoing problems. A tenant may bring a county court action in nuisance and/or negligence to obtain an injunction against the neighbour. Alternatively, he or she may bring a criminal prosecution against the neighbour based on statutory nuisance, described below at paras 10.221–10.242.

Neigbouring tenants with same landlord

10.129 A tenant may want the landlord to take action against another tenant where there is sustained water penetration or repeated floods. If the problem is caused by the other tenant's misconduct or carelessness the landlord can take possession proceedings against him or her under the nuisance ground. However, one tenant cannot take legal action to force the landlord to take action against another tenant guilty of nuisance.[85] Furthermore, the landlord cannot be held liable for nuisance committed by tenants because nuisance is based on the occupation of land and where there is a tenancy, the tenants and not the landlords are the occupiers.

10.130   The situation is different if the nuisance is coming from land occupied by the landlord (such as the common parts) and the nuisance is not being caused by other tenants but by trespassers.

---

84 Rimer LJ at [25].

85 *O'Leary v Islington LBC* (1983) 9 HLR 83, CA. The situation may be different if the tenancy agreement contains a term stating that the landlord will take action to prevent nuisance by other tenants.

In *Octavia Hill Housing Trust v Brumby*[86] the tenant complained of nuisance caused by people sitting directly outside her living room on a paved area that was part of the common parts. The landlords applied to strike out the claim relying on cases which found that a landlord could not be held liable for nuisance caused by its tenants, including *Southwark v Mills*.[87]

The court dismissed the landlord's application to strike out the claim. The House of Lords has previously held that an occupier of land can be liable for nuisance committed by someone else if they have 'continued or adopted' the nuisance. This requires that they know of the nuisance and have failed to take reasonable steps to bring it to an end (*Sedleigh-Denfield v O'Callaghan*[88]). The cases relied on by the landlord were about nuisance caused by tenants who were the occupiers. In this case the landlords were the occupiers of the common parts so could be liable if the evidence supported them having continued or adopted the nuisance.

10.131 If the tenants share a social landlord, a complaint may be made if the landlord declines to take action against the neighbour. Social landlords must publish their polices on nuisance and anti-social behaviour, see para 10.137 below.[89]

Disrepair in the neighbour's flat

10.132 It may be that the cause of the water penetration is disrepair in the neighbour's flat. If this is the case and the landlord is notified of the need for repair, or asked to inspect but takes no effective action, the landlord may be liable not only for the repairs to the affected flat but also for loss, inconvenience and damage to the tenant's belongings. It is no defence for the landlord to argue that access cannot be obtained to the premises above. If access is refused, the landlord can apply for an injunction to force the tenant to give access.

10.133 As disputes about access often delay matters being resolved, tenants should try to maintain an amicable relationship with the neighbour where possible. If the neighbour agrees to allow the tenant access to inspect, the cause of the water penetration will be identified more quickly.

---

86 [2010] EWHC 1793 (QB), 15 July 2010.
87 [1999] 4 All ER 449, see para 10.143 below.
88 [1940] AC 880.
89 HA 1996 s218A, as amended by Anti-social Behaviour Act (ASBA) 2003 s12.

Noise nuisance/sound insulation problems

10.134   The intrusion of noise from other tenants is also a common problem in flats. The cause may be particularly noisy neighbours or inadequate sound insulation between the flats. Sometimes this is difficult to determine or the problem may be a combination of both. Sensitivity to noise varies from one person to another and tenants who have suffered from noise penetration for some time may become hyper-aware of the sound of their neighbours.

10.135   There are two types of sound transmission: airborne sound and impact sound. Inadequate sound insulation between properties can mean that ordinary footsteps sound like stamping and that the bass notes of amplified music are heard in another property. This can lead tenants to believe, incorrectly, that the problem is excessively noisy neighbours. If other household sounds, such as telephones ringing, toilets flushing, light switches etc, are also heard, this suggests a sound insulation problem.

10.136   It may be necessary to obtain an expert report on the cause of the problem. This will require the co-operation of the neighbour so it is important to avoid bad feeling if possible.

Noisy neighbours

10.137   If the problem is caused by the behaviour of neighbours who are also tenants of the same landlord complaint may be made to the landlord. Local authorities and other registered providers must publish their policies on 'anti-social behaviour'. This should set out the steps a landlord will take on receipt of a complaint, including the timescale for action.[90] The landlord may serve notice of seeking possession and take steps to evict the tenant. Sometimes the service of notice will be sufficient to stop the behaviour. In most cases, it is advisable for tenants first to make the neighbours aware of the way their behaviour is disturbing them to see if the problem can be resolved amicably.

10.138   Tenants who complain in the hope that their neighbours will be evicted should be aware that the landlords may decide not pursue a possession claim. The complaining tenant cannot force the landlord to do so (see para 10.129 above). If possession proceedings *are* issued, the complaining tenant will usually be required to give evidence by way of a statement and/or in person at a possession hearing.

90   HA 1996 s218A, as amended by ASBA 2003 s12.

10.139 Alternatively, or in addition, complaint can be made to the local authority's environmental health team. Some authorities operate mobile noise patrols and may visit the neighbouring property to measure the noise and to advise the occupier about reducing the noise. The authority can also serve a notice requiring the occupier to 'abate' the nuisance and can prosecute if the notice is not complied with.[91]

Action against the neighbour

10.140 An occupier may bring a civil claim against a neighbour relying on the common law tort of nuisance. The court can award damages and an injunction to restrain future nuisance.

10.141 In addition, an occupier could bring a private prosecution in the magistrates' court under the Environmental Protection Act 1990, seeking an order that the neighbour abate the nuisance (see para 10.233 below).

Action against the landlord for inadequate sound insulation

10.142 Current building regulations require minimum levels of sound insulation in newly built dwellings or conversions. However, the regulations do not have retrospective effect and, before 1976 for new dwelling and 1985 for conversions, there were no specific requirements for builders to meet designated standards for sound insulation.[92] Many dwellings and conversions therefore have little or no sound insulation.

10.143 As noted above (paras 10.78–10.83), in respect of most tenancies there is no implied term that premises are fit for habitation. A landlord therefore has no contractual obligation to ensure that premises are properly insulated against sound transmission from outside.

> In *Southwark LBC v Mills and Camden LBC v Baxter*[93] the tenants relied on the covenant of quiet enjoyment[94] and the tort of nuisance in claims brought against their respective landlords. Both tenants occupied local authority flats, one in a purpose-built block and the other in a converted house. They complained that the absence of

91 Under the Environmental Protection Act 1990, discussed below at paras 10.221–10.248 and 11.5–11.10.

92 The minimum standards for the construction of buildings are set out in the Building Acts and Regulations. Local authorities are responsible for ensuring that the minimum standards are met.

93 [1999] 4 All ER 449.

94 Despite the term, the covenant is not specifically about noise but about the tenant's right to use the premises without interference by the landlord.

sound insulation meant that they were disturbed by the ordinary household noise made by their neighbours. Both wanted their landlords to carry out works to remedy the situation.

The House of Lords held that the landlords had no obligation to install sound insulation. There was no breach of the covenant of quiet enjoyment: the covenant can only be breached by the landlord doing something to interfere substantially with the tenant's quiet enjoyment *after* the grant of the lease, not by reason of the state of the premises at the commencement of the tenancy and thereafter. With regard to nuisance, it is possible for a landlord to be liable for nuisance caused by his or her tenant if the landlord authorises or permits the nuisance. However, the nuisance complained of was caused by the other tenants using their premises in the ordinary way. Such use is not capable of being an actionable nuisance.

10.144 There is therefore no way for a tenant to bring a civil action against a landlord to compel the landlord to install sound insulation.

10.145 Furthermore, the Environmental Protection Act 1990 cannot be used to achieve the same end.[95]

Remedies in county court proceedings

10.146 The above paragraphs (10.6–10.145) describe the possible 'causes of action' in a civil claim for disrepair. In practice, in most disrepair claims the same set of facts may establish several different causes of action.

10.147 The cause of action is the legal basis for the tenant's claim. The remedy is what the tenant is asking the court to order.

10.148 In most disrepair claims the tenant will be seeking:

• damages (compensation); and
• an order for works.

10.149 The vast majority of claims are settled before a final hearing; the parties agree what works will be carried out and how much compensation will be paid. The Disrepair Protocol, described at para 10.188 below, may result in works being started soon after the landlord receives the initial protocol letter. This can mean that when the claim is issued the tenant is seeking damages only because all of the works

95 See *R (Vella) v Lambeth LBC* [2005] EWHC 2473 (Admin) at para 10.232 below.

have been completed. If damages are agreed there will be no need for litigation.

10.150   Even though most claims are settled without a final hearing advisers should be familiar with the powers of the court and the level of damages a court would be likely to award.

10.151   In disrepair claims there are usually two kinds of damages awarded:

- *general damages*: these are quantified by the court to compensate the tenant for the inconvenience and loss of enjoyment caused by the disrepair; and
- *special damages*: these are damages capable of precise quantification.

General damages

10.152   Where a landlord has breached the contract and/or a duty of care towards a tenant the purpose of damages is to place the tenant in the position he or she would have been in had the landlord not breached those legal obligations, as far as it is possible for a financial award to do so.

Assessing by loss of value

10.153   In many of the early cases a tenant's damages were assessed on the basis of 'loss of value' or 'diminution of value' to the tenant. These cases mostly concerned tenancies that had a commercial value to the tenant: the tenant had a long lease and was entitled to sublet or assign the lease. In such cases the assessment of damages is straightforward: the difference between the value of the lease with the property in its present condition and its value had the property been kept in repair. This may be assessed by obtaining expert valuation evidence. Such an approach is not appropriate when assessing damages for a tenant who remains in occupation while the property is in disrepair. Furthermore, for most periodic tenants, as opposed to long-leaseholders, the tenancy does not have a commercial value – it cannot be sublet or sold.

In *Calabar Properties Ltd v Stitcher*[96] the Court of Appeal considered the way in which damages should be assessed when a tenant remains in occupation of a property in disrepair.

96 (1983) 11 HLR 20, CA.

The court held:

1) 'The object of awarding damages against a landlord for breach of his covenant to repair is not to punish the landlord but, so far as money can, to restore the tenant to the position he would have been in had there been no breach'.

2) Where a tenant remains in occupation it is 'wholly artificial' to award damages on the basis of the loss in market value.

3) In such a case valuation evidence is unnecessary.

4) When a tenant remains in occupation the damages should 'include the cost of the redecoration, a sum to compensate for the discomfort, loss of enjoyment and health involved in living in the damp and deteriorating flat and any reasonable sum spent on providing alternative accommodation after the flat became uninhabitable'.[97]

Global awards and assessing by reference to rent

10.154   Although 'diminution of value' is not an appropriate way to assess damages for a tenant in occupation, one approach adopted by the courts has been to assess damages by reference to the rent paid by the tenant. For example, if one third of a property has been affected by disrepair it may be appropriate to assess damages on the basis of a rebate of one-third of the rent for the relevant period. However, this approach sometimes leads to an award that is inadequate to compensate a particular tenant for the 'discomfort, loss of enjoyment and health' caused by the landlord's breach. Courts may therefore adopt an alternative approach of making a 'global' award of damages to cover such loss.

In *Wallace v Manchester CC*[98] the tenant argued that the court was bound to assess damages on both bases: diminution of value/rent rebate *plus* an award for discomfort and inconvenience.

The Court of Appeal rejected this argument holding that 'diminution of value' and 'discomfort' were alternative ways of expressing the same concept for a tenant who remains in occupation: damages for the 'loss of comfort and convenience which results from living in a property which was not in the state of repair it ought to have been if the landlord had performed his

97 Griffiths LJ at 34 and 36.
98 (1998) 30 HLR 1111, CA.

obligation'. A court may assess damages on one basis or the other, or by a combination of the two. The Court of Appeal recommended that where damages are assessed on a global basis it is advisable to cross-check the assessment by reference to the rent payable for the period of disrepair. This will avoid over- or under-assessment 'through failure to give proper consideration to the period of the landlord's breach of obligation or the nature of the property'.[99] The court also held that when assessing damages by reference to the rent payable the fact that most or all of the rent is actually paid by housing benefit is irrelevant.

In *English Churches Housing Group v Shine*[100] the Court of Appeal overturned a global award of £19,000 for a seven-year period and substituted an award of £8,000. The original award exceeded the total amount of rent payable over the relevant period. The judge had failed to cross-refer the global award with the rent payable and had failed to give reasons for the award. It was held that 'the basic rule of thumb [is] that – all other things being equal – the maximum award for damages in the case such as the present should be the rental value of the premises'.[101] The court, however, recognised that there will be cases in which an award in excess of the rent payable will be justified but held that in such a case clear reasons need to be given.

Amount of general damages

10.155   In *Wallace* (para 10.154) the appeal was argued on the basis that there was an 'informal tariff' for damages for discomfort and inconvenience. The Court of Appeal did not decide the issue but did consider the damages awarded on the assumption that there was such a 'tariff' ranging from £1,000 per year at the bottom of the tariff to £2,750 per year at the top, the case being decided in 1998. Given inflation this would translate, in 2014, as a range of between approximately £1,580 and £4,300 per year. For information about the levels of damages awarded by county courts (or agreed between the parties to litigation) advisers should refer to the 'Disrepair roundup' published in *Legal Action* on a regular basis.

99 (1998) 30 HLR 1111, CA, Morritt LJ at 1121.
100 [2004] EWCA Civ 434.
101 [2004] EWCA Civ 434, Wall LJ at [109].

10.156   In addition to damages levels being increased to reflect inflation, for all civil claims in which general damages are awarded after 1 April 2013 any award should be increased by 10 per cent.[102]

Special damages

10.157   Special damages are damages that can be precisely calculated by the claimant. If possible, the parties should agree the amounts. A defendant may agree the quantification of special damages while maintaining that he or she is not liable for the loss. In a disrepair claim examples of special damages would be the value of damaged belongings, the cost of alternative accommodation, the cost of extra heating to dry out damp premises or while central heating systems were not functioning, and any other item of expenditure caused by the landlord's breach.

10.158   The calculation of special damages should be included as a schedule in the particulars of claim if possible. Sometimes special damages are ongoing and it will be necessary to serve a schedule of special damages at a later date.

Damaged belongings

10.159   Where disrepair causes damp conditions damage is often caused to items of furniture, carpets and clothing. Details of the damage caused and the amount claimed must be included in a special damages schedule. The disrepair pre-action protocol contains a template for a Special Damages schedule for damaged items. This can be downloaded from the CPR website: www.justice.gov.uk/courts/procedure-rules/civil/protocol/prot_hou.

10.160   It is important that the amounts claimed are realistic and not exaggerated. Landlords will sometimes indicate that they will only offer compensation for items where there is proof of purchase such as receipts or bank statements. Tenants on low incomes often do not have such documentation as many goods are purchased with cash at

---

102 *Simmons v Castle* [2012] EWCA Civ 1039, 10 October 2012. This was recommended as part of the 'Jackson reforms'. Under the reforms success fees charged by lawyers acting under a conditional fee agreement (CFA) and the cost of ATE insurance are no longer recoverable as costs from opponents. To compensate claimants, damages awards are increased by 10 per cent. This applies to all civil claims save those in which a CFA was entered into prior to 1 April 2013 (in such cases success fees and ATE premiums can still be recovered from opponents). The Court of Appeal has made clear however that the 10 per cent uplift applies to all civil claims, not just those funded by CFAs.

markets or second-hand shops. There is no reason why the courts will not award compensation on the basis of the tenant's oral evidence or witness statement provided the amounts claimed are reasonable.

10.161   If an item can be repaired or professionally cleaned then the tenant will only recover the cost of this and not replacement value.

10.162   There is often a dispute about whether items were so badly damaged that they needed to be disposed of. Tenants should keep damaged belongings for a reasonable period to allow the landlord to inspect. Furthermore, photographs should be taken before damaged goods are disposed of.

Valuing damaged belongings

10.163 When something has been damaged beyond repair the damages awarded should enable the tenant to replace the item. If a tenant chooses to replace the damaged item with something better the damages awarded will not be for the full amount of the replacement item but will be discounted to take account of the fact that the tenant is getting something better than that which was damaged. This is referred to as 'betterment'. However, if the tenant has no choice but to purchase something that, incidentally, is better than the original item there should be no discount. Furthermore, if the landlord is maintaining that there should be a discount for betterment, the landlord must establish this.

> In *Lagden v O'Connor*[103] the House of Lords held:
>
> It is for the defendant who seeks a deduction from expenditure in mitigation on the ground of betterment to make out his case for doing so. It is not enough that an element of betterment can be identified. It has to be shown that the claimant had a choice, and that he would have been able to mitigate his loss at less cost. The wrongdoer is not entitled to demand of the injured party that he incur a loss, bear a burden or make unreasonable sacrifices in the mitigation of his damages.[104]

10.164 In terms of damages for disrepair, this may mean, for example, that there would be no discount for replacing a fitted carpet with a new fitted carpet even though the existing carpet was a few years old.

---

103 [2003] UKHL 64, 4 December 2003.
104 [2003] UKHL 64, Lord Hope at 34.

However, where it is possible and reasonable to purchase second-hand items, only the second-hand cost would be awarded.[105]

Orders for works

Interim injunction

10.165　A tenant may apply for an injunction to compel a landlord to carry out urgent repairs before the final hearing. However, interim injunctions (unlike final orders for works) are discretionary remedies. They are to be granted only in exceptional circumstances.

> In *Parker v Camden*[106] a number of tenants took action against the local authority because they were without heating and hot water as a result of a strike of boiler workers employed by the council. They sought a mandatory injunction on an urgent basis to compel the council to restore the heating and hot water systems. The council admitted the breach but offered to provide electric heaters and undertake to reduce heating charges at a future date. It argued that to bring in external contractors would risk escalating the industrial dispute.
>
> 　The Court of Appeal held that mandatory interlocutory injunctions should be granted only in 'the most exceptional circumstances' but that this was such a case in that there was 'an undoubted breach of covenant giving rise to actual and immediate major discomfort and inconvenience and to a real risk of damage to health flowing from the admitted breach'.[107]

10.166　To succeed in obtaining an interim ('interlocutory') injunction, a tenant will need to have an expert report identifying those repairs that require urgent attention and the remedial works necessary. The application must be supported by evidence in the form of a witness statement from the tenant and a copy of the expert report. Three clear days' notice must be given to the landlord (this does not include the date notice is given or the date of the hearing).[108] In a case of exceptional urgency an application may be heard without three clear days'

105　It may be argued that it is reasonable to purchase a second-hand table but not more personal items such as a beds, bedding or clothing.
106　(1985) 17 HLR 380, CA.
107　Browne Willkinson LJ at 389.
108　CPR 23.7(1)(b).

notice but in all cases the landlord should be notified and invited to put forward proposals to deal with the urgent issues.

Final order for works

10.167   Unless all outstanding works have been completed when the claim is heard, part of the final order will be that the landlord carries out specified works within a specified time. If they are works the landlord is contractually obliged to carry out the order is an order of specific performance. Otherwise the order will be a mandatory injunction. An injunction is a discretionary remedy which means that it may be refused because of the tenant's conduct. An order for specific performance is not discretionary: Landlord and Tenant Act 1985 s17.

10.168   The terms of the order must be sufficiently clear for the defendant to know exactly what must be done and by what time.[109]

10.169   It is usual for a schedule of works to be drawn up by the expert or experts with a deadline for completion and some mechanism for ensuring that the works are completed satisfactorily (for example, confirmation by the tenant's surveyor). This agreed schedule will be attached to a consent order. Such an order is known as a 'Tomlin Order': see appendix to chapter 22 for a precedent. A consent order must be signed by the parties or their representatives and sent to the court for approval. Once approved and sealed by the court it is sent to the parties. Alternatively, at a hearing the landlord may give to the court an undertaking to carry out works set out in an agreed schedule by an agreed time.

Enforcement of orders

10.170   A court order is legally binding. However, the court does not take action to enforce the orders it makes unless the claimant makes further application. Social landlords usually comply with orders although there may be some delay before they do so. For tenants of private landlords it is often necessary to make further application to the court after the order has been made.

Money judgments

10.171   The various methods of enforcing money judgments are set out in CPR Parts 70–85, summarised at para 22.113 below.

---

109 *Morris v Redland Bricks Ltd* [1970] AC 652.

10.172   It is essential *before* starting a claim for damages against a private landlord to know whether it is going to be possible to enforce the order. A Land Registry search may be carried out to establish who owns the premises let and/or the landlord's home address, if known.[110] Such a search will reveal whether the premises are mortgaged.

Orders for works

10.173   An injunction or order of specific performance will require that the landlord carry out certain works by a specified time. If the order is not complied with it may be enforced by an application to commit the landlord to prison for contempt of court.[111]

10.174   An application can be made for committal only if the order contains a penal notice. This is a notice addressed to the respondent warning him or her that disobedience with the order is a contempt of court punishable by imprisonment. A penal notice can be attached when the order is made or approved by the court. If the order does not contain a penal notice, a further application must be made for a penal notice to be attached to the order.

10.175   In all cases the order must be personally served on the respondent. In the case of a local authority landlord the order will usually be served on the director of housing or the chief executive and in the case of a registered provider on a director or other senior officer.

10.176   An application for committal will be listed for a hearing before a circuit judge. The respondent must be personally served with the application notice and notice of the hearing date. Unsurprisingly, when an application for a penal notice or committal is made, the landlord will usually ensure that the works are completed. The court may make a suspended order for committal providing that, if the works are not completed by a certain time, the landlord, or the named officer employed by the landlord, will be liable to imprisonment.

10.177   An undertaking given by a landlord may also be enforced by committal proceedings, provided again that a penal notice has been attached.[112]

10.178   If the works and the timescale have been agreed between the parties and set out in a schedule to a consent order (a Tomlin Order) the proceedings must be restored and the court asked to make an order against the defendant with penal notice attached.

110 See para 4.139 above.
111 The procedure is set out in the old County Court Rules (CCR) Order 29.
112 CCR Order 29 rule 1A.

Appointment of receivers

10.179 The court also has the power to appoint a receiver who can receive rents and arrange for works to be completed in compliance with any order.[113]

Time limits for county court claims

10.180 The ordinary time limits for bringing civil claims are set out in the Limitation Act 1980. The general rule for claims in contract and tort is that they must be brought within six years. In a disrepair claim where the breach is ongoing this means that any damages can only be awarded for a period starting six years before the claim is issued. The time limit is 12 years if the agreement is a deed, which includes long leases.

10.181 However, if the claim is brought as a counterclaim (eg in possession proceedings) the counterclaim is treated as being commenced on the date the claim was commenced so the period for which damages could be claimed would be six years prior to the claim for possession being issued.[114]

10.182 In respect of a contractual claim, the time limit begins at the date of the breach (not necessarily the date the premises first fell into disrepair, see para 10.54 above). In respect of a claim in tort, the time limit runs from the date of the damage or injury, even though the negligence or unlawful act may have occurred years earlier.

10.183 Personal injury claims must be brought within three years. Where a disrepair claim includes a claim for personal injury (for example, a claim that ill health has been caused by the housing conditions) the three-year time limit applies to the whole claim. Before issuing a disrepair claim including a claim for personal injury both the personal injury and the disrepair protocols should be followed. In practice, disrepair claims often make reference to the effect of the disrepair on the claimant's health without being treated by the courts as personal injury claims. Advisers should, however, be aware that including a claim for personal injury may result in the period for which damages are awarded being limited to three years rather than the usual six years.[115]

---

113 CPR 69, see para 22.126. In addition, under the Commonhold and Leasehold Reform Act 2002, leaseholders have a right to manage, see para 5.64.

114 Limitation Act 1980 s35.

115 For example in *Vukelic v Hammersmith & Fulham LBC* (see para 10.77 above) the claimant included a claim for injury to health, namely depression and

10.184   Where a claim is for injury to the health of a child a separate action should be brought in the name of the child. A litigation friend must be appointed to represent the child (see para 7.207). As time limits do not begin to run until a child reaches adulthood, a claim can be brought up to the child's 21st birthday.

10.185   The limitation of actions is a defence that must be pleaded by the defendant. If the defence fails to refer to the limitation period there will be no limit to the period for which damages can be awarded. However, the courts will usually be willing to allow a late amendment to permit the defendant to rely on the limitation defence.

10.186   The Limitation Act 1980 permits the usual time limits to be extended by the court in certain situations, for example where the claimant was under a disability, or where there has been fraud or concealment.

Procedural issues

10.187   Advisers must be aware of the way claims are dealt with under the Civil Procedure Rules before advising a person about the most appropriate course of action. Most importantly, the Pre-Action Protocol must usually be followed before proceedings are issued. Furthermore, the value of the claim will determine how the court will deal with it and will affect how the case can be funded.

The Disrepair Protocol

10.188   The Pre-Action Protocol for Housing Disrepair ('Disrepair Protocol') applies to all civil claims arising from the condition of residential premises. The protocol can be found online as part of the Civil Procedure Rules: www.justice.gov.uk/courts/procedure-rules. The Protocol includes precedent letters for use by advisers or litigants in person. If a claim proceeds to litigation, the court will expect all parties to have complied with the protocol as far as possible. The court has the power to order parties who have unreasonably failed to comply with the protocol to pay costs or be subject to other sanctions.

---

anxiety. The conditions complained of had existed for many years. The court limited the period for which any damages could be claimed to three years prior to issue even though ultimately the claimant was not awarded damages for personal injury. Had the claimant omitted the reference to injury to health she would have been entitled to claim for a six-year period.

10.189 The protocol does not apply to Environmental Protection Act 1990 prosecutions (see para 10.221 below) or to disrepair claims brought under CPR Part 20 (counterclaims).

10.190 The protocol is intended to encourage the exchange of information between parties at an early stage and to encourage the settlement of claims prior to issue.

10.191 The specific aims of the protocol are:

- to avoid unnecessary litigation;
- to promote the speedy and appropriate carrying out of any repairs which are the landlord's responsibility;
- to ensure that tenants receive any compensation to which they are entitled as speedily as possible;
- to promote good pre-litigation practice, including the early exchange of information and to give guidance about the instruction of experts; and
- to keep the costs of resolving disputes down.

10.192 The steps set out in the protocol include the following (paras 10.193– 10.202).

Letter to landlords

10.193 The tenant must send to the landlord a letter setting out the nature of the potential claim. If the claim needs further investigation this letter will be an 'early notification letter'. If not, it will be a 'letter of claim'. Precedents for both are included in the protocol. Certain information must be included in the initial letter (whether an early notification letter or a letter of claim), including:

- the tenant's name, address and telephone number;
- details of the defects;
- details of previous notice given to the landlord;
- proposed single joint expert;
- proposed letter of instruction to expert;
- disclosure of relevant documents in the tenant's possession.

10.194 The letter should request disclosure from the landlord of relevant documents including the tenancy agreement and records of complaints and works carried out.

10.195 If the initial letter is a letter of claim it should also include the following information:

- the effect of the defects on the tenant; and
- details of special damages.

Landlord's response

10.196 The landlord should respond within 20 working days and should:

- give the disclosure requested; and
- respond to the tenant's proposal for an expert indicating whether a single joint expert is agreed or, if not agreed, whether the landlord agrees to a joint inspection.

10.197 If the letter is a letter of claim the landlord's response should also indicate:

- whether liability is admitted;
- any points of dispute;
- a full schedule of intended works with timescale for completion;
- any offer of compensation; and
- any offer of costs.

10.198 This may be done either 20 days after receipt of the letter of claim or 20 days after receipt of an expert report or schedule of works.

Failure to respond

10.199 If no response is received to an early notification letter, a letter of claim should be sent. If no response is received to a letter of claim, proceedings may be issued.

Cases of urgency/preserving evidence

10.200 It is specifically stated that the protocol does not prevent a tenant from instructing an expert at an earlier stage if it is considered necessary because of urgency or to preserve evidence.

Alternative dispute resolution

10.201 The protocol provides that the parties should consider whether some form of alternative dispute resolution (ADR) procedure would be more suitable than litigation and, if so, should endeavour to agree the form of ADR.

Experts

10.202 Expert evidence is essential in most disrepair claims. The written evidence of a surveyor,[116] in the form of an inspection report, will usually be necessary to:

- describe the defects in the premises;

116 Depending on the nature of the defect(s), reports may also be needed by other experts, such as heating engineers or damp-proof specialists.

- express an opinion on which are the landlord's responsibility under the tenancy agreement;
- comment on the severity of each defect;
- specify the works necessary to remedy the defect;
- give an estimate of the cost of the necessary works; and
- express an opinion on the likely timescale for the completion of the works.

10.203 Before the Disrepair Protocol was introduced the parties would usually instruct separate experts, with social landlords often using in-house surveyors. The protocol recommends the use of a single joint expert (SJE). If the parties can agree on which SJE to use they will jointly instruct the SJE, whose duty is to the court rather than to the parties. In disrepair claims against social landlords it is common for the landlord to refuse to agree the proposed SJEs put forward by the tenant's advisers and either to maintain that it is not necessary to instruct an expert at all or to put forward one of their own employed surveyors as the proposed SJE. As landlords must usually prepare a schedule of works anyway they often send their own surveyors to inspect and continue to use them as their expert. Despite the protocol, therefore, it is common in disrepair cases for each party to instruct their own expert witness. In all cases attempts should be made to ensure that there is a joint inspection by the experts and that the experts clarify precisely what is agreed. The courts will sometimes order the experts to provide a statement of issues specifying precisely what is agreed and what is disputed. If fundamental issues, such as the cause of dampness, cannot be agreed it will be necessary for the parties to seek the court's permission to call the experts to give oral evidence. It must be remembered that in every case the claimant has the burden of proving the case.

> In *McIntosh v Southwark LBC*[117] and *Ball and Ball v Plymouth City Council*[118] the claimants and the defendants each relied on written expert evidence which was in conflict. In both cases the tenants failed to satisfy the court, on balance of probabilities, that the dampness was caused by the landlord's failure to carry out repairs and the claims were dismissed.

---

117 [2001] All ER (D) 133 (Nov) and see para 10.42 above.
118 [2004] EWHC 134 (QB).

10.204   As is the general rule in county court litigation, if the tenant is successful in bringing a claim, the court should order that the landlord pays the tenant's legal costs. Sometimes landlords carry out works following receipt of the pre-action protocol letter, leaving only the amount of damages to be resolved. In such a case, even if the damages are less than £10,000, the landlord should pay the tenant's pre-allocation costs.[119]

Track allocation

10.205   A defended claim will be allocated to one of the three tracks which are:[120]

- the small claims track;
- the fast track; and
- the multi-track.

10.206   The main criteria in track allocation is the financial value of the claim. In respect of money claims, the small claims track is for claims of less than £10,000, the fast track for claims of between £10,000 and £25,000 and the multi-track for claims of more than £25,000. For the purpose of track allocation the claimant must, when completing the claim form, estimate the amount of damages he or she expects to recover. However, factors other than the value of the claim are also taken into account and a claim will not generally be allocated to the fast track if it is likely to take more than one day to resolve and there is disputed expert evidence.

10.207   For disrepair claims where the only claim is for damages the small claims limit of £10,000 applies: claims for less than this amount will be allocated to the small claims track on receipt of the defence. However, if a claim includes an application for an order for works it will be allocated to the small claims track only if *both*:

- the estimated damages are less than £1,000; and
- the estimated cost of the works is less than £1,000.

10.208   So if either is expected to exceed £1,000 the claim should be allocated to the fast track or the multi-track.

10.209   An expert should always be asked to give an opinion on the estimated cost of the works so that the claim can be allocated appropriately.

---

119 See *Birmingham CC v Lee* [2008] EWCA Civ 891, 30 July 2008.
120 See CPR Parts 27, 28 and 29.

10.210   The other factors that should be taken into account in allocating claims are:

- the complexity of fact, law or evidence;
- the number of parties or the importance of the case to people who are not parties;
- the amount of oral evidence that will be required; and
- the views and circumstances of the parties.

10.211 In practice, the allocation is usually done on the basis of the estimated damages and/or cost of works and any more subtle arguments may have to be made on an application to re-allocate to a different track.

10.212   The court can make an order for works in a claim allocated to the small claims track: *Joyce v Liverpool City Council*.[121]

Public funding

10.213 Until April 2013, legal aid was available both for the preliminary work and the issuing of civil proceedings for claims in disrepair. However, legal aid is now only available 'in relation to the removal or reduction of a serious risk of harm to the health or safety of the individual or a relevant member of the individual's family … where the risk arises from a deficiency in the individual's [rented] home'. The aim of providing legal aid must be 'with a view to securing that the [landlord] makes arrangements to remove or reduce the risk'.[122]

10.214   This means (1) only if the conditions are such as to pose a serious risk of harm to the health or safety of the occupiers will legal aid be available and (2) only for the steps necessary to remove or reduce the risk. Many cases where premises are in substantial disrepair will satisfy this test: it is well established that damp conditions cause and excacerbate such conditions as asthma and other respiratory conditions, particularly in children. However, it may be that expert evidence will be needed from a doctor or environmental health officer before legal aid will be granted.

10.215   Most disrepair claims are to obtain damages and an order that the landlord carries out the necessary works. If, after the claim is issued, the landlord carries out sufficient work to remove any serious risk of harm to the health or safety of the occupiers, legal aid will cease to be available. To continue the claim for damages and/or to have further

---

121 (1995) 27 HLR 548, CA.
122 LASPO 2012 Sch 1 para 35.

repairs carried out the tenant will have to represent themselves or obtain representation under some other sort of funding arrangement, such as a conditional fee agreement, see below at para 10.217 (or pro bono).

Other funding

10.216   Clients should always be asked to provide a copy of their home insurance policies, which sometimes cover legal advice and representation.

10.217   Conditional fee agreements (CFAs) can be used to fund disrepair claims. CFAs provide that if the claim is successful the claimant's legal fees will be paid by the defendant; if the claim fails the claimant's lawyers will not be paid for their services. Where a claim is allocated to the small claims track the usual rule is that the successful party cannot recover their legal costs from the opponent (only certain out-of-pocket expenses, including the court fee, see para 22.101). So, a claim for damages only will only be feasible on a CFA if the damages are likely to exceed £10,000.

10.218   As well as paying their own laywers, a further consideration for claimants is the risk of being unsuccessful and being ordered to pay the defendant's legal costs (see paras 22.119–22.137). To guard against this risk it is possible to obtain insurance which covers the payment of fees such as court fees and expert reports and that also will meet the defendant's costs if the claim fails. This is called After the Event (ATE) insurance. Obviously, the availability and cost of such insurance polices will depend on the strength of the case.

10.219   A solicitor may indeminify the client against the risk of a costs order, effectively agreeing to be liable for the opponent's costs if the claim is unsuccessful.

> In *Sibthorpe and Danri Morris v Southwark LBC*,[123] the local authority sought to challenge such an agreement on the basis that it was 'champerty' (an arrangement under which the legal representatives have a financial interest in the outcome of litigation, which is unlawful).
>
> The Court of Appeal rejected this: the lawyers would lose out if the claim failed but would not gain anything other than the payment of their fees if the claim succeeded.

123 [2011] EWCA Civ 25, 25 January 2011.

Summary of funding options for civil claim

10.220 The options are as follows:

- Legal aid if an order for works is needed to remove a serious risk of harm to the health or safety of the occupier and/or family. Legal aid will only cover the work necessary to remove the risk.
- CFA for a claim which includes an order for works provided either the damages or the likely cost of the works will be more than £1,000.
- CFA for a damages only claim where likely damages will be more than £1,000.

Actions in the magistrates' court

Environmental Protection Act 1990

10.221 The Environmental Protection Act (EPA) 1990 concerns dwellings and public nuisances that may affect health. The EPA 1990 replaced the Public Health Act 1936, which in turn had replaced earlier legislation introduced to address concern about outbreaks of cholera and typhus. The temporary 'Act of 1846' provided 'For the speedy removal of certain nuisances'. Prosecution could follow a certificate of two doctors 'of the filthy and unwholesome condition of any dwelling-house or other building, or of the accumulation of any offensive or noxious matter, refuse, dung, or offal, or of the existence of any foul or offensive drain, privy, or cesspool' and that 'the same is likely to be prejudicial to the health' of the occupiers or neighbours. The concept of dwellings that are 'prejudicial to health' remains central in the 1990 Act.

10.222 Under EPA 1990 local authorities have the power to ensure that nuisances are 'abated' to prevent prejudice to health. This is done by service of an abatement notice on the person responsible; if the notice is not complied with, the authority may then prosecute the person. However, sometimes the buildings that constitute a nuisance are owned or controlled by local authorities. To enable action to be taken against local authorities, the Act provides a procedure for a private individual to bring a prosecution to abate a nuisance. The procedure is set out in EPA 1990 s82. Although it has mainly been used against local authority landlords by their tenants a 'section 82 prosecution' may be brought against any landlord.

Statutory nuisance

10.223　A prosecution under EPA 1990 depends on there being a statutory nuisance as defined in section 79. This includes 'any premises in such a state as to be prejudicial to health or a nuisance'.[124] Section 79 lists a number of 'matters' that may constitute a statutory nuisance. The definition is not confined to dwellings and may include such things as smoke, fumes and noise.

Prejudicial to health

10.224　Prejudicial to health means 'injurious, or likely to cause injury, to health'.[125] Premises are prejudicial to health if they are in such a state as would cause a well person to become ill or the health of a sick person to deteriorate further. 'Health' has been interpreted broadly to include physical and mental health and well-being.[126]

10.225　The burden is on the complainant (usually the tenant) to prove beyond reasonable doubt that the state of the premises is likely to cause ill health. It is not necessary that the state of the premises has actually caused ill health, only that it is likely to do so. Usually medical evidence of the effect or likely effect of the premises on the health of the occupants will be needed. However, in some cases it may be sufficient to rely on the expert evidence of an environmental health officer (EHO).

10.226　In some circumstances prejudice to health is well established, such as premises severely affected by dampness and mould growth. In most cases an EHO report will be essential anyway to prove the case beyond reasonable doubt and because the court will need expert opinion on the works necessary to abate the nuisance.

Or a nuisance

10.227　The term 'nuisance' in EPA 1990 s79 has been interpreted restrictively to mean either:[127]

- a public nuisance at common law: this requires that the comfort or quality of life of the general public, or of a class of persons, is adversely affected; or

---

124　EPA 1990 s79(1)(a).
125　EPA 1990 s79(7).
126　*Malton Board of Health v Malton Manure Company Ltd* (1879) 4 Ex D 302.
127　*National Coal Board v Thorne* [1976] 1 WLR 543.

- a private nuisance at common law: this means something that causes substantial interference with the use and enjoyment of neighbouring property.

10.228 If it is the conditions *within* the property that are affecting the occupiers of the property there will not be such a nuisance. In most cases therefore in prosecutions of landlords it is the 'prejudice to health' limb of the condition that is relied upon.

When are premises prejudicial to health?

Dampness and mould growth

10.229 Many successful prosecutions have been brought in relation to buildings that are badly designed and prone to condensation and mould growth; the kind of property described in *Quick v Taff Ely*.[128] There is considerable evidence that such conditions may cause injury to health by exacerbating asthma and other respiratory conditions.

Likelihood of accident and unhygienic layout

10.230 In *R v Bristol CC ex p Everett*[129] the Court of Appeal held that an offence under EPA 1990 is not committed where the design of the premises is dangerous and likely to cause accidental injury. 'Prejudicial to health' means a risk of disease or illness and does not extend to the danger of accidental physical injury.

Similarly, in *Oakley v Birmingham City Council*[130] the House of Lords held that the 'unhygienic layout of premises' is not a statutory nuisance. In *Oakley* the only WC was located next to the kitchen. There was no hand basin or room to install one. The court accepted that there was a risk of cross-infection because it was necessary, after using the WC, for the tenant and her family to either wash their hands in the kitchen sink or to cross the kitchen to get to the bathroom. However, by a majority of 3:2 it was decided that the implications of holding that a landlord must carry out works to re-arrange the layout were such, in terms of the expenditure of public funds, that this was a decision for Parliament and not the courts.

128 (1985) 18 HLR 66, see para 10.34 above.
129 (1999) HLR 1102, CA.
130 (2000) 33 HLR 283, HL.

10.231   The kind of 'hazards' that were the cause of complaint in both *Everett* and *Oakley* may now be dealt with by a local authority under the Housing Act 2004, see chapter 11.

Lack of sound insulation

10.232   Premises that lack sound insulation so that the occupant is disturbed by the noise of his or her neighbours are not in such a state as to be prejudicial to health or a nuisance.

> In *R (Vella) v London Borough of Lambeth*[131] a tenant of a social landlord was disturbed by noise from the flat above and the communal stairs caused by a lack of sound insulation. He requested that the local authority serve an abatement notice on his landlords to force them to carry out works of sound insulation. There was evidence that the tenant suffered from depression and that the 'noise pollution' he experienced was a 'significant perpetuating factor' in his depressive illness. The local authority refused to serve an abatement notice and the tenant sought judicial review of that decision.
>
> The court, following *Everett* and *Oakley* (above, para 10.230), held that EPA 1990 and the previous legislation are 'sanitary statutes' and that 'there can be no room for holding that a lack of sound insulation sufficient to comply with current standards renders premises in such a state as to be prejudicial to health'.[132] The earlier cases of *Southwark LBC v Ince*[133] and *Network HA v Westminster*,[134] were held to have been wrongly decided in light of the judgments in *Everett* and *Oakley*.

Noisy neighbours

10.233   EPA 1990 s79(1)(g) specifically provides that 'noise emitted from premises so as to be prejudicial to health or a nuisance' is a statutory nuisance. This, however, is distinct from noise pollution caused by the state of the premises. Section 79(1)(g) can be used against a person who is making excessive noise. As this is a private nuisance at common law (see para 10.227 above) it is not necessary to prove

131 [2005] EWHC 2473 (Admin), 14 November 2005.
132 [2005] EWHC 2473 (Admin), Poole J at [69].
133 (1989) 21 HLR 505.
134 (1995) 27 HLR 189.

prejudice to health. This is one option for a person who is suffering from disturbance by a noisy neighbour. The prosecution is brought against the neighbour and the court can make an abatement order requiring the neighbour to stop making the noise. Alternatively, the local authority can be asked to prosecute (see chapter 11).

Parties to the proceedings

The complainant

10.234 Proceedings can be brought by 'any person aggrieved by the statutory nuisance'.[135] This will usually be the occupier of the premises if the complaint is about the state of premises.

The defendant

10.235 Where the statutory nuisance arises from any defect of a structural character, proceedings must be brought against the owner of the premises.[136]

10.236 If the statutory nuisance is noise caused by a neighbour, he or she will be the defendant.

Procedure

Notice of intended prosecution

10.237 Before proceedings under EPA 1990 s82 can be started, the tenant must give written notice of the intended prosecution to the intended defendant.[137] There is no prescribed form for such notice but it must state the nature of the statutory nuisance and its effect on the occupants. It is not necessary to specify the works required to remedy the nuisance.[138] If an expert report has been obtained it should be attached to the notice. If the complaint is about the state of the premises, the notice must give the defendant at least 21 days to respond; if it is about excessive noise, at least three days' notice must be given.

10.238 If the action is against a local authority, notice must be served on the chief clerk or chief executive and, if posted, must be sent to the registered or principal office, unless the authority have specified a different address at which notices must be served.[139] In *Leeds v*

---

135 EPA 1990 s82(1).

136 EPA 1990 s82(4)(b).

137 EPA 1990 s82(6).

138 *East Staffs BC v Fairless* [1998] EGCS 140.

139 EPA 1990 s160(4)–(5).

Islington LBC[140] notice was served on the senior estate manager of the local housing office. The proceedings were dismissed on the basis that notice had not properly been given.

Starting the prosecution

10.239   The action is a criminal prosecution, initiated by 'laying a complaint or information' in the local magistrates' court. There is no prescribed form but the complainant must describe the offence in ordinary language and give the necessary particulars to provide reasonable information about the nature of the charge.[141] Following the complaint being sent to the court, the court will issue a summons with a hearing date and send this to the defendant. It is good practice for the claimant to send a further copy to the defendant in case of any dispute about receipt.

Hearings

10.240   At the first hearing the defendant will usually be asked to enter a plea of guilty or not guilty to the charge of failing to abate a statutory nuisance. Sometimes the defendant may seek an adjournment with the intention of carrying out the necessary works to abate the nuisance. If works are completed before the final hearing there will be no conviction. It is the court's decision whether to grant an adjournment but the wishes of the parties will be relevant. The complainant may be willing to adjourn if this means that the works will be carried out quickly. However, if the nuisance is abated before a guilty plea is entered or before a trial, the court will have no power to award compensation.

10.241   If a plea of not guilty is entered, the court will list the case for a trial to take place at a later date. At the trial the court will hear evidence from both parties and decide whether the complainant has proved the case beyond reasonable doubt. Any expert witness must be available to give oral evidence.

10.242   If the defendant pleads guilty it will not be necessary to call evidence to prove the offence. In practice a schedule of works with timetable will usually be agreed between the parties for the court to endorse. Evidence may be given to enable the court to assess the appropriate fine or compensation.

---

140 [1998] Env LR 655; [1998] EGCS 15.
141 See Magistrates' Courts Act 1980 s1 and the Criminal Procedure Rules 2005 Part 7.

Court's powers

Order for works

10.243 If the court is satisfied that a statutory nuisance exists at the date of the hearing it must make an order requiring the defendant to abate the nuisance. The abatement order must set out in detail the works to be carried out and the time limit. The court will usually adopt a schedule prepared by the environmental health officer acting on the complainant's behalf or agreed between the parties. If, at the date of the hearing, the nuisance has abated but the court is satisfied that recurrence is likely it can make an order requiring works within a specified time to prevent recurrence. In either case, a conviction will be entered against the defendant.

10.244   The court may order the defendant to do whatever is necessary to abate the nuisance.

> In *Birmingham DC v Kelly*[142] the order required the authority to install central heating. The council's appeal was dismissed: the order was made not because the absence of central heating was prejudicial to health but because mould growth was present and was likely to cause health problems and food poisoning. The installation of central heating was a way to remove the threat to health created by the mould growth. The court was entitled to make such an order even though the effect was to require the landlord to improve the premises.

Fines and compensation

10.245 The court can impose a fine and can also order the defendant to pay compensation to the complainant. The compensation is for 'any personal injury, loss or damage' resulting from the offence.[143] The action is a summary prosecution which means that it must be brought within six months of the offence. A failure to abate a statutory nuisance will usually be a continuing failure so this does not prevent someone bringing a prosecution even if the problem started more than six months ago. However, the court cannot award compensation for losses occurring earlier than six months before the complaint was laid. Furthermore, the offence is only committed if a nuisance is not

142 (1985) 17 HLR 572.
143 Powers of the Criminal Courts (Sentencing) Act 2000 s130(1).

abated within 21 days of notice being given. Therefore compensation can only be for the period starting 21 days after the notice was served.[144] This will usually be a period of weeks or months (up to a maximum of six months before the proceedings commenced), so the level of compensation will be limited. The maximum compensation the courts can award is £5,000 and the maximum fine is also £5,000.

10.246   Compensation or fines can only be ordered if there is a conviction. If the nuisance is abated, and not likely to recur before the final hearing (or guilty plea) there will be no conviction.

Costs

10.247   Where a court is satisfied that the statutory nuisance existed when the information was laid then, even if it has been abated by the time of the hearing, the court *must* order the defendant to pay the complainant's fair and reasonable legal costs.[145]

Enforcement

10.248   A failure without reasonable excuse to comply with any requirement of a nuisance order within the time limit specified is a further offence.[146] A further prosecution may be brought for the non-compliance. On conviction, a further fine may be imposed and, if the nuisance remains unabated, the court can impose, in addition, a daily fine continuing until such time as the order is fully complied with.

Funding an EPA 1990 action

10.249   Legal aid has never been available for representation in private prosecutions. Under the Legal Help scheme advice and assistance to prepare for the issue of proceedings is available on the same basis as for civil claims: only where there is a 'serious risk of harm to the health or safety' of the individual or a member of their family. This should include most cases where the conditions are such as to be prejudicial to health.

10.250   A solicitor can represent a client in an EPA 1990 prosecution under a conditional fee agreement (CFA) (see para 10.217 above).[147]

---

144 *R v Liverpool Crown Court ex p Cooke* (1997) 29 HLR 249.
145 EPA 1990 s82(12).
146 EPA 1990 s82(8).
147 Courts and Legal Services Act 1990 s58(a), as amended by Access to Justice Act 1999 s27(1).

However, it can be difficult to find solicitors willing to do so. Also, expert evidence is almost always necessary to succeed in a prosecution and the fees of any expert required to attend at court will need to be paid (though they may subsequently be recovered as part of the costs).

Costs orders against the complainant

10.251 Unlike civil proceedings, when the usual order is that the unsuccessful party must pay the legal costs of the successful party, a complainant can be ordered to pay the costs of the defendant only if he or she required proceedings to be issued or continued improperly.[148]

Formal complaint/landlords' internal procedures

10.252 This section examines how a tenant may use a landlord's internal procedures to get repairs carried out and compensation paid. This is generally possible only if the landlord is a social landlord.

Voluntary compensation schemes

10.253 Many local authorities and registered providers operate internal procedures for compensating their tenants for disrepair, particularly the loss of heating and hot water caused by the failure of block systems. Such a scheme will usually be for the payment of compensation on a daily or weekly basis after a minimum period during which the tenant has been without services. The levels of compensation tend to be low, some schemes only reimbursing charges actually paid by the tenant to the landlord as part of an inclusive rent.

Statutory 'right to repair' scheme

10.254 In addition, for secure tenants there is a statutory 'right to repair' scheme.[149]

10.255 The scheme is convoluted and of limited application. It applies only to 'qualifying repairs' which are specified in a schedule. Each type of repair has a prescribed period during which the repair should

---

148 See Prosecution of Offences Act 1985 ss16–19, and *Bentley-Thomas v Winkfield PC* [2013] EWHC 356, 5 February 2013.
149 Secure Tenants of Local Housing Authorities (Right to Repair) Regulations 1994 SI No 133.

be completed. These are essentially minor repairs that, in the opinion of the landlord, will not cost more than £250 to carry out. The process is triggered by the tenant giving notice of the necessary repair, following which the landlord must, if satisfied that the repair is a qualifying repair, issue a repair notice to a contractor.

10.256   If the work is not then carried out within the prescribed period, the tenant may require the landlord to appoint a different contractor. If still not completed within the prescribed period, the tenant is entitled to compensation of £10 plus £2 per day, up to a maximum of £50 for any one repair.

10.257   The disadvantages of the scheme are:

- the onus is on the tenant to serve the appropriate notices on the landlord;
- the scheme depends on the landlord accepting that the repair is a qualifying repair;
- the prescribed period may be suspended by the landlord if there are exceptional circumstances beyond the landlord's control;
- only relatively minor repairs are covered;
- the level of compensation is extremely low.

Formal complaint and Ombudsman complaint

10.258   Complaints procedure and the relevant Ombudsman schemes are described in paras 2.93–2.100.

10.259   Complaints about repairs make up a significant proportion of all Ombudsman complaints. The Housing Ombudsman's annual report for 2011/2012 shows that 46 per cent of all complaints were about repairs, while for the Local Government Ombudsman 32 per cent of housing complaints were about repairs.

10.260   Most complaints are resolved or abandoned prior to an investigation by the Ombudsman. In a disrepair claim resolution may mean that outstanding works are carried out but no compensation offered. If compensation is offered or recommended by the Ombudsman it will usually be much less than the amount a court would award.

10.261   The Ombudsman can recommend that the authority or association make a contribution to any legal costs incurred by the complainant but has expressed the view that legal representation is unnecessary in pursuing complaints to the Ombudsman and such recommendations are rare.

Rent and disrepair

10.262 There are three different situations to consider regarding unpaid rent:

- a tenant may withhold rent and use the money to pay for repairs;
- a tenant may withhold rent in protest to try to force a landlord to carry out repairs;
- a tenant whose landlord is in breach of the repairing obligation may be in arrears of rent for reasons unconnected with the disrepair.

Applying rent to pay for repairs

10.263 There is a common law right to use money due as rent to pay for repairs.[150] However, a tenant must follow the following steps:

- Give the landlord notice of the need for repair in writing.
- If, after a reasonable period has elapsed, the repairs have still not been done, write again telling the landlord of the intention to arrange the repairs and to deduct the cost from the rent.
- Obtain estimates for the cost of the work from at least two reputable contractors and write again enclosing copies of the estimates, and giving the landlord a deadline to carry out the work, failing which the tenant will arrange for the works to be done and deduct the cost from the rent.
- If there is no response from the landlord, arrange for the work to be done by the contractor who submitted the lowest estimate, obtaining receipts showing the extent of the work.
- Send to the landlord a copy of the receipts and explain exactly how the rent deductions will be made, or have been made, so as to cover the cost of the work.

10.264 This remedy depends on the tenant being able to pay the contractor at the time of carrying out the work and recouping the money from future rent payments or from rent previously withheld. It is therefore unlikely to be available to a tenant with a limited income where the repair works are extensive. Furthermore, a tenant in receipt of housing benefit may not be in control of the payment of rent as benefit may be paid direct to the landlord. Housing benefit for local authority tenants is made by way of a rent rebate.

---

150 *Lee-Parker v Izzett* [1971] 1 WLR 1688.

Withholding rent/'rent strike'

10.265 A tenant may simply withhold rent to try to force the landlord to carry out works or as a protest for the landlord's breach. While it is true that landlords who are receiving rent may have little incentive to carry out expensive works of repair, this is a dangerous tactic. Tenants on a low income who withhold rent often find it difficult not to use the money for ordinary household expenses. A tenant in rent arrears risks the landlord issuing possession proceedings. If the tenant is an assured tenant the mandatory ground (HA 1988 Ground 8) is made out if there is at least eight weeks' arrears, see appendix to chapter 7. Although the tenant can bring a counterclaim in the possession proceedings, the court has a discretion to order that the disrepair claim be heard separately (see para 7.43).

10.266   If the tenant is an assured shorthold tenant the landlord is entitled to possession as of right and any counterclaim in disrepair will be irrelevant.

Set off against rent

10.267 A tenant sued for arrears of rent may have a defence of 'set off': a tenant is entitled to set off any damages awarded against the arrears of rent. The defence exists even when the damages have yet to be assessed. See paras 7.41–7.43.

10.268   It is often the case that advisers are consulted only after rent arrears have built up, at the point when the tenant receives a notice of possession or a possession summons. Even if there appears to be a strong claim for damages for disrepair the tenant should be advised to pay current rent plus a regular payment towards the arrears, pending a final hearing. This is to guard against the risk that the arrears may exceed any damages awarded. If the ground for possession is a discretionary the regular payments towards the arrears will help persuade the judge that it is not reasonable to make a possession order even if the arrears do exceed damages.

CHAPTER 11

Disrepair and housing conditions – action by local authorities

continued

Key points

- Local authorities have a power and in some cases a duty to take action against landlords of premises that pose a risk to the health and safety of the occupants. However, such action cannot be taken against a local authority as landlord.
- Local authorities can prosecute landlords for failing to abate a statutory nuisance, which may include the state of premises.
- Local authorities can force landlords to carry out improvements to premises that contain 'hazards' – risks to the health and safety of the occupants.
- Local authorities can also prohibit landlords from letting certain buildings for residential use and can make orders that buildings are demolished or that whole areas are cleared.
- The 'Decent Homes' programme aimed to ensure that all social housing met the 'Decent Homes' standard by 2010. This target was not met and the 'backlog' programme is now being managed by the Homes and Communities Agency.
- If a local authority fails to take action against a private landlord following a tenant's complaint, the authority's internal complaints scheme may be used and complaint may be made to the Ombudsman.
- In some circumstances a person may judicially review a local authority's decision or failure to take action.

Introduction

11.1 A local housing authority has a range of powers and duties to deal with the condition of dwellings in its area. They are set out in different statutes:

- the Environmental Protection Act (EPA) 1990 – power to deal with 'statutory nuisances';
- the Building Act (BA) 1984 – emergency procedure for dealing with 'statutory nuisances' in dangerous buildings; and
- the Housing Act (HA) 1985 and the Housing Act 2004 – power to deal with 'hazards' in dwellings and houses in multiple occupation (HMOs).

11.2 Although an authority may act on its own initiative, usually action is prompted by a complaint to the authority. A person making a complaint need not identify the powers they want the authority to exercise but must describe the conditions about which they are concerned. Local authorities are often slow to respond to complaints so it is best to put the complaint in writing with sufficient information to enable the authority to prioritise the complaint. Alternatively, if made by telephone, a note should be kept of the date of the call and the name of the officer spoken to.

11.3 Complaint will usually be made to the authority's Environmental Health Department but some authorities have other teams such as Housing Standards and specific teams dealing with HMOs.

11.4 The Acts and the powers given to local authorities are summarised below.

Environmental Protection Act 1990

11.5 The Environmental Protection Act 1990 is described at para 10.217 in relation to private prosecutions. Under the Act it is the duty of every local authority to inspect its area from time to time to detect any statutory nuisances which ought to be dealt with. However, local authority action under EPA 1990 is usually instigated by a complaint from an occupier or concerned individual. Where a complaint of a statutory nuisance is made to an authority by someone living within its area, the authority is under a duty 'to take such steps as are reasonably practicable to investigate the complaint'.[1]

11.6 The procedure is different from action taken by a tenant under EPA 1990 s82 and is set out in section 80. If the authority is satisfied that a statutory nuisance exists or is likely to recur, the authority must serve an abatement notice on the person responsible for the nuisance.[2] The notice must do the following:[3]

- require that the nuisance be abated or prevented from recurring;
- if works are required to abate the nuisance, specify the works;[4]
- specify the time limit for compliance; and
- indicate the time limit for appealing against the order (21 days).

11.7 A person served with an abatement notice must carry out the works specified or appeal to the magistrates' court within 21 days of service of the notice.

1 EPA 1990 s79(1).
2 EPA 1990 s80(1).
3 EPA 1990 s80.
4 *Kirklees MBC v Field* (1997) 30 HLR 869.

11.8   If the person does not appeal and does not comply with the notice without reasonable excuse, he or she is guilty of an offence. A landlord convicted of the offence is liable to a fine of up to £5,000, plus a further fine of £500 for each further day of non-compliance.

11.9   Whether or not the authority prosecutes the owner, the authority can itself do the work necessary to abate the nuisance and seek reimbursement from the owner or from the person served with the abatement notice. In practice, local authorities are very reluctant to carry out works because obtaining reimbursement is difficult.

11.10   It should be noted that the authority has a duty to take reasonable steps to investigate and, if satisfied that a statutory nuisance exists, a duty to serve a notice.[5] Where an authority fails or refuses to act on a complaint or, having inspected, declines to serve a notice, an application may be made for judicial review to obtain a mandatory order against the authority. Alternatively, a formal complaint may be made and, if not resolved satisfactorily, the complaint may be referred to the Local Government Ombudsman (see paras 2.93–2.100).

Building Act 1984: emergency procedure

11.11   A speedier procedure which local authorities can use in urgent cases is found in BA 1984 s76. This provides that, where a local authority is satisfied that a statutory nuisance exists and that following the standard procedure under the Environmental Protection Act 1990 would cause unnecessary delay, it may serve notice on the landlord stating its intention to do the remedial works and specifying the defects which it proposes to remedy.

11.12   Nine days after service, the authority may carry out the work and recover its expenses from the person on whom the notice was served. However, this cannot be done if, within seven days of the notice, the landlord serves a counter-notice on the authority stating that he or she intends to remedy the defects. The authority can then take no further action unless:[6]

- the landlord fails to start remedial works within a reasonable time; or
- having started them, the landlord proceeds unreasonably slowly or makes no progress at all.

---

5   EPA 1990 s80(1).
6   BA 1984 s76(3).

Housing Acts 1985 and 2004

11.13   Since the mid-19th century local authorities have had the power to enforce improvements to dwellings and to demolish slums and build new dwellings. These powers are now contained in the Housing Acts 1985 and 2004. Under these Acts local authorities have a range of options when dealing with dwellings in poor condition. These include serving notice on an owner to improve a dwelling, carrying out works in default, prohibiting the use of a building as a dwelling, demolishing individual buildings or providing that whole areas be cleared of dwellings.

11.14   The Housing Act 1985 (HA 1985) was, until April 2006, the statute which set out these powers. The key concept was 'fitness for habitation'. If premises were unfit by reason of specific matters[7] the local authority could serve notice on the landlord to carry out the necessary works to make the dwelling fit for habitation. The fitness standard has now been replaced by the Housing Health and Safety Rating System (HHSRS)[8] introduced by the Housing Act 2004 (HA 2004). The new system is based on identifying 'hazards' in dwellings and is described below at paras 11.17–11.62.

11.15   In addition to the powers relating to unfit premises, HA 1985 also gave local authorities special powers in relation to houses in multiple occupation (HMOs) and overcrowded premises. The HA 2004 has replaced the provisions of HA 1985 in relation to HMOs but the powers relating to overcrowding are still found in the HA 1985.

11.16   Although the assessment process and enforcement action to improve dwellings is now governed by the HA 2004, the local authority powers to make demolition orders and declare clearance areas are still to be found in the HA 1985, as amended by HA 2004.

---

7   These matters were set out in HA 1985 s604 and concerned: structural stability, serious disrepair, damp that is prejudicial to health, adequacy of lighting, heating and ventilation, adequacy of supply of 'wholesome' water and facilities for the preparation and cooking of food (including a sink with hot and cold water), suitably located WC, baths, showers and wash-hand basins with hot and cold water, and effective drainage.

8   HA 2004 Part 1 and the Housing Health and Safety Rating System (England) Regulations 2005 SI No 3208 and Housing Health and Safety Rating System (Wales) Regulations 2006 SI No 1702 (HHSRS Regs).

Housing Act 2004 – hazardous dwellings

11.17   The fitness standard, as the trigger for local authority action, has been replaced by the concept of hazards in residential premises. A hazard is a risk of harm to the health or safety of an actual or potential occupier of a dwelling or HMO that arises from a deficiency in the dwelling or HMO or any building or land in the vicinity. The deficiency may arise because of the construction of the building, or because of a failure to maintain or repair.[9]

11.18   A prescriptive system of assessment is set out in the Housing Act 2004, the HHSRS Regulations 2005 and Guidance. The assessment should result in a determination as to whether there are in the premises serious hazards ('Category 1' hazards) and/or less serious hazards ('Category 2' hazards). Authorities have a duty to take enforcement action in relation to Category 1 hazards and a power to do so in relation to Category 2 hazards.

Triggering an assessment

11.19   Local authorities are required to keep housing conditions in their area under review.[10] However, in practice it will usually be necessary for the occupier to request that the local authority carry out an inspection. Local authorities are sometimes slow to respond to such requests or give them low priority so that there may be a considerable delay before an inspection is arranged.

Official complaints

11.20   If an authority receives an 'official complaint' which indicates that a Category 1 or 2 hazard may exist, an inspection must be made by a 'proper officer'.[11] An official complaint means one made by a Justice of the Peace with local jurisdiction or by the parish or community council. An occupier whose request for a local authority inspection is ignored should therefore arrange for an official complaint to be submitted on his or her behalf. This will place the authority under a duty to inspect.

11.21   If, following an official complaint, an authority refuses or fails to inspect, a claim for judicial review can be brought for a mandatory

---

9   HA 2004 s2(1).
10   HA 2004 s3.
11   HA 2004 s4.

order forcing the authority to inspect and comply with its duties under HA 2004.

11.22   Alternatively, a complaint may be made under the authority's complaints procedure. Ultimately, complaint may be made to the Ombudsman if the authority does not resolve the complaint satisfactorily (see paras 2.96–2.100).

Assessing hazards

11.23   The inspection must be carried out in accordance with the HHSRS Regulations and Guidance[12] and, if the officer is of the opinion that a Category 1 or 2 hazard exists, a report in writing must be made to the authority. Authorities must consider any report made to them as soon as possible and must take the most appropriate action in relation to the hazard. See below, paras 11.30–11.36.

11.24   The HHSRS Regulations set out the assessment process. There are two stages: first, an assessment of the likelihood of an occupier suffering any harm as a result of the hazard; then, an assessment of the range of probable harmful outcomes. The two factors are combined using a standard method and expressed as a numerical score. There are prescribed bands applicable to the range of numerical scores: where a hazard falls within bands A, B or C the hazard is a Category 1 hazard. Where it falls within any other band it is a Category 2 hazard.

11.25   The assessment must record the presence of all hazards. Whether they are classed as Category 1 or Category 2 will determine the action the local authority must or may take. A record of the inspection must be prepared and kept either in written or electronic form.[13]

11.26   The HHSRS Regulations list the 'matters and circumstances' that may give rise to a hazard and set out the classes of harm that may occur. The classes of harm are set out in four bands: Classes I to IV.

11.27   By way of example, the first two matters and circumstances listed are:

- damp and mould growth – exposure to house dust mites, damp, mould or fungal growths; and
- excess cold – exposure to low temperatures.

11.28   In the list of classes of harm, regular severe pneumonia is included under Class I, with cardio-respiratory disease, asthma and non-

---

12 The *Housing Health and Safety Ratings System – Operating Guidance,* published in February 2006, is available on the www.gov.uk website.

13 HHSRS Regs 2005 reg 5.

malignant respiratory diseases under Class II and occasional mild pneumonia and regular serious coughs or colds under Class IV.

11.29　The likelihood of the class of harm arising as a result of the matter described, combined with the severity of the class of harm will result in a numerical assessment of the hazard such that it can be classified as Category 1 or Category 2.

Action following the assessment

11.30　If a local authority discovers a Category 1 hazard it has a duty to take the most appropriate enforcement action. Where a Category 2 hazard exists the authority has a power to take enforcement action.

11.31　The action available to local authorities is:

- serving an improvement notice (see paras 11.37–11.40);
- making a prohibition order (see paras 11.41–11.47);
- serving a hazard awareness notice (see paras 11.56–11.57);
- making a demolition order (see paras 11.58–11.60); or
- declaring the area to be a clearance area (see paras 11.61–11.62).

11.32　In addition, in cases of imminent risk from a Category 1 hazard, an authority may:

- take emergency remedial action; or
- make an emergency prohibition order.

11.33　In deciding which course of action to take, authorities must have regard to the Enforcement Guidance issued in February 2006.[14]

11.34　If only one course of action is possible, the authority must take that action. If more than one course of action is possible, it must decide which is the most appropriate. More than one form of action cannot be taken at the same time but if the chosen action does not prove satisfactory the authority may take another course of action in the list.[15]

11.35　Although the authority may have a duty to act it is for the authority to decide which course of action to take. If the chosen course is to serve a hazard awareness notice, this merely warns the occupier of the existence of the hazard.

11.36　When the authority has decided on one of the above courses of action it must prepare a statement of the reasons for its decision. The statement of reasons must be served on every person on whom the relevant notice or order is served.

14　The Enforcement Guidance is also available on the www.gov.uk website.
15　HA 2004 s5(3)–(5).

Improvement notices

11.37   An improvement notice requires the person on whom it is served to take specified remedial action in respect of the hazard or hazards concerned.[16] Where a Category 1 hazard exists, the remedial action must, as a minimum, be sufficient to ensure that the hazard ceases to be a Category 1 hazard but may extend beyond such action.[17] The notice must give certain information about the hazard, specify the remedial action required and give a date when the action must start and be completed. It must also inform the recipient of the right of appeal and the time limit for bringing an appeal, which is 21 days.

11.38   As is clear from the name, the works that a landlord can be forced to carry out may be works to improve as well as works to repair the premises. An example might be the installation of central heating or the fitting of a handrail on a steep stair.

11.39   The notice may provide for its operation to be suspended until a time or event specified in the notice.[18] This could be the time when certain kinds of occupier move in or out of the premises.

11.40   If the notice is complied with the local authority must revoke it. If the notice specifies more than one hazard, the authority must revoke the part of the notice that concerns the hazard or hazards that have been remedied. The authority may vary the remainder of the notice.[19]

Prohibition orders

11.41   A prohibition order prohibits the use of premises for specified purposes, for example, use as a dwelling or HMO.[20]

11.42   A prohibition order must also specify the hazard concerned and the action the authority considers would result in revocation of the order.[21] The order must also inform the recipient of the time limit for appealing, which is 28 days.

11.43   Prohibition orders may also be suspended until a time or event specified in the order. For example, if the order prohibits the use of the building as a dwelling, its operation may be suspended until the current occupiers have vacated. The effect of such an order would be

16   HA 2004 s11(2).
17   HA 2004 s11(5).
18   HA 2004 s14(1) and (2).
19   HA 2004 s16.
20   HA 2004 s20(3).
21   HA 2004 s22(2)(e).

to then prohibit future use of the premises as a dwelling until works had been carried out to remove the hazard or hazards.

11.44 The prohibition order must be revoked when the hazard specified in the notice has been removed.

Tenants' loss of security

11.45 If a prohibition order is made, and its operation is not suspended, any tenants and/or licensees may be evicted by the landlord. The security of tenure enjoyed by statutory and assured tenants is effectively removed by the making of such an order.[22]

11.46 The Enforcement Guidance requires the authority to 'consider the availability of local accommodation for re-housing any displaced occupants' when considering the making of a prohibition order[23] and states that 'the authority may consider offering temporary or permanent alternative accommodation to the tenant to assist in progressing remedial works'.[24] If the tenant loses his or her home because of the order there is a limited re-housing duty on the authority, see para 11.66 below.

11.47 Authorities will generally avoid making outright prohibition orders whenever possible and, in a case where remedial works cannot be carried out with the tenants in occupation, may opt to serve a suspended prohibition order or a hazard awareness notice.

Access

11.48 It may be that the works can be carried out with the tenants in occupation. In such a case, if access is not given, the magistrates' court has the power to order an occupier to permit the owner or manager of the premises to carry out any action necessary and expedient for the purpose of complying with an improvement notice or a prohibition order.[25]

Emergency cases

11.49 If a local authority is satisfied that a Category 1 hazard exists on any residential premises and that 'the hazard involves an imminent risk

22 Section 33 provides that nothing in the Rent Act 1977, Housing Act 1988 and the Rent (Agriculture) Act 1976 prevents a landlord from obtaining possession if necessary to comply with the order.
23 Enforcement Guidance para 6.23.
24 Enforcement Guidance para 6.21.
25 HA 2004 s5(2).

of serious harm to the health or safety of any of the occupiers' it can take emergency remedial action or make an emergency prohibition order.

11.50   Emergency remedial action means 'such remedial action in respect of the hazard concerned as the authority consider immediately necessary in order to remove the imminent risk of serious harm'.[26]

11.51   If emergency remedial action is decided on as the most appropriate course of action, the local authority has an immediate right of access and the notice regarding the remedial action must be served on the occupiers. Notice may be served by being fixed to a conspicuous part of the premises or building.[27] Notice must also be served on the owner or manager within seven days of starting emergency remedial action. This notice must identify the hazard, the works that are to be carried out and must give information about the right of appeal.

11.52   The local authority may recoup the cost of taking emergency remedial action from the owner or manager.

11.53   An emergency prohibition order is an alternative to carrying out emergency remedial action. An emergency prohibition order also has immediate effect.[28] The order must be served on the day it is made.

Appeals

11.54   The person on whom a notice of improvement or a prohibition order is served has a right to appeal. The time limit for appealing is 21 days for an improvement notice and 28 days for a prohibition order. Appeals against emergency remedial action or an emergency prohibition order must be brought within 28 days. Appeals are to the Residential Property Tribunal.

Sanctions

11.55   Failure to comply with an improvement notice or prohibition order is an offence punishable by a fine of up to £5,000.[29] For a prohibition order, a further fine of £20 per day can be imposed for each day following the conviction that the defendant uses or permits the premises to be used in contravention of the order.

---

26 HA 2004 s40.
27 HA 2004 s40(6).
28 HA 2004 s43.
29 HA 2004 ss30 and 33.

Hazard awareness notices

11.56   A hazard awareness notice is a notice advising the person on whom it is served of the existence of a Category 1 or Category 2 hazard.[30] It must specify the nature of the hazard and give details of any remedial action the authority consider would be practicable and appropriate. However, the notice does not require that such action is taken.

11.57   There is no appeal against a hazard awareness notice.

Demolition orders

11.58   A demolition order may be made only if there is a Category 1 hazard and the building is not a listed building. In deciding whether to make a demolition order, the authority must take into account the availability of local accommodation for re-housing the displaced occupants, the demand for and the sustainability of the accommodation if the hazard was remedied, the prospective use of the cleared site, and the impact on the local environment.[31]

11.59   A demolition order may be substituted by a prohibition order if proposals are submitted to use the premises other than for human habitation.

11.60   An appeal lies to the Residential Property Tribunal and must be exercised by 'an aggrieved person' within 21 days.

Clearance areas

11.61   An authority can declare an area a clearance area if it is satisfied that each of the residential buildings in the area contains a Category 1 hazard or that the buildings are dangerous or harmful to the health and safety of inhabitants because of the arrangement of the buildings.[32] The declaration of a clearance area means that all the buildings in the area will be demolished. It will be part of the authority's proposals for the wider neighbourhood of which the area forms part. Such a declaration will only be made after extensive consultation with all owners and occupiers and the authority must be satisfied that alternative accommodation can be provided for the displaced occupiers.

11.62   Such action may be taken in conjunction with the declaration of a renewal area under the Local Government and Housing Act 1989.

---

30   HA 2004 ss28 and 29.
31   HA 1985 s265, as amended by HA 2004, and Enforcement Guidance para 6.44.
32   HA 1985 s289, as amended by HA 2004, and Enforcement Guidance para 6.48.

Compensation and re-housing

11.63   Whenever a house is demolished as a result of a demolition order or slum clearance, displaced occupiers are entitled to compensation. Displaced owner-occupiers are entitled to a 'home loss' payment depending on the value of the property. Currently the maximum payment is £49,000.[33]

11.64   Tenants who are permanently displaced are entitled to a home loss payment currently set at £4,900. To qualify, the tenants must have occupied the property as their only or principal home for at least 12 months prior to eviction.

11.65   Although local authorities will not make prohibition orders or demolition orders in relation to their own properties, they may decide to demolish properties or redevelop areas. In such cases possession can be gained under Grounds 10 or 10A (see appendix to chapter 7) which require the landlord to make suitable alternative accommodation available for the tenant.

11.66   For tenants of other landlords who lose their homes as a result of a prohibition order, demolition order or clearance order, the local authority has a duty to ensure that some form of alternative accommodation is available. The Land Compensation Act 1973 provides that wherever

> ... suitable alternative residential accommodation on reasonable terms is not otherwise available to that person, then ... it shall be the duty of the relevant authority to secure that he will be provided with such other accommodation.

However, this duty has been interpreted by the courts as requiring the authority to do no more than to act reasonably and to do its best, as soon as practicable, to provide the person with other accommodation. The authority is not required to give the person priority over other people on the waiting list.[34] Temporary accommodation will be sufficient pending permanent accommodation becoming available.[35] Many local authorities award a certain level of priority under their allocation schemes to those forced to move because of demolition and redevelopment schemes (see chapter 17).

---

33 Land Compensation Act 1973 s30; Home Loss Payments (Prescribed Amounts) (England) Regulations 2014 SI No 1966. The prescribed amounts are usually increased on a regular basis. The current limits apply where the date of displacement is on or after 1 October 2014.

34 *R v Bristol Corporation ex p Hendy* [1974] 1 All ER 1047.

35 *R v East Hertfordshire DC ex p Smith* (1990) 23 HLR 26, CA.

Houses in multiple occupation

11.67   HMOs are buildings in which more than one household lives, sharing facilities. The Housing Act 2004 introduced a new system of regulation for HMOs.

11.68   The following are defined as HMOs:[36]

- a house or flat which is let to three or more tenants who form two or more households and who share a kitchen, bathroom or toilet;
- a house converted into bed-sits or other forms of non-self-contained accommodation which is let to three or more tenants who form two or more households;
- a house converted into one or more flats which are not wholly self-contained (ie, do not contain within the flat a kitchen, bathroom and toilet) and which is occupied by three or more tenants who form two or more households;
- a building converted entirely into self-contained flats if the conversion did not meet the standards of the Building Regulations 1991[37] and more than one-third of the flats are let on short-term tenancies.

11.69   In order to be an HMO the property must be used by the occupiers as their only or main residence[38] and must be used solely or mainly as residential accommodation.

11.70   A single household means members of the same family, which includes spouses, unmarried couples (including same-sex couples) and blood relatives.[39]

Mandatory licensing

11.71   Larger HMOs are subject to mandatory licensing operated by the local authority. These are HMOs which:

- have five or more occupants;
- comprise two or more households; and
- are situated in a dwelling that has three or more habitable storeys.

---

36 HA 2004 ss254–260. The Localism Act 2011 exempts fully mutual co-operatives from the HMO requirements.
37 Building Regulations 1991 SI No 2768.
38 This includes students occupying while undertaking a full-time course of education and those occupying a building as a refuge: HA 2004 s259(2).
39 HA 2004 s258.

11.72   Application must be made to the local authority for a licence and before granting a licence the authority must be satisfied that:

- the HMO is reasonably suitable for occupation for the number of people allowed under the licence;
- the proposed licence holder is a fit and proper person and the most appropriate person to hold the licence;
- the proposed manager, if there is one, is a fit and proper person;
- the proposed management arrangements are satisfactory and the manager(s) competent;
- the financial structures for the management are suitable.

11.73   An appeal against the refusal of a licence is to a residential property tribunal and should be made within 28 days.

Penalties for failing to apply for a licence

Fines

11.74   If a landlord fails to apply for a licence he or she commits an offence and can be fined up to £20,000.[40]

Rent repayment orders

11.75   Furthermore, a tenant living in a property that should have been licensed but was not can apply to a Residential Property Tribunal to re-claim rent paid during the unlicensed period, for a maximum period of 12 months and the local authority can reclaim the total amount of housing benefit paid during the unlicensed period.[41]

Restriction on possession proceedings

11.76   No section 21 notice may be given in relation to a shorthold tenancy of the whole or part of an unlicenced house so long as it remains unlicenced. An assured shorthold tenant would therefore have a defence against a claim for possession (see para 7.2).[42]

Selective registration

11.77   In addition to the mandatory scheme, Housing Act 2004 allows local authorities to operate local registration and licensing schemes for HMOs that do not fall within the mandatory scheme.

---

40 HA 2004 s95.
41 HA 2004 s73.
42 HA 2004 s98.

Overcrowding

11.78 The mandatory licensing provisions for HMOs give local authorities the power to specify the number of people permitted to live in a property. It is an offence to permit more people than the maximum specified and the offence carries a fine of up to £20,000.

11.79 Overcrowding is also relevant to the hazard rating process. One of the 'matters and circumstances' that may give rise to a potential hazard is 'a lack of adequate space for living and sleeping'. Depending on the number of occupants and the likely consequences in relation to the health and safety of the occupants overcrowding may therefore create a Category 1 or Category 2 hazard in any dwelling.

Statutory overcrowding

11.80 The Housing Act 1985 still sets out the statutory test for overcrowding.[43] The provision is often misunderstood. The statutory overcrowding test is the basis for local authority powers to prevent overcrowding in private sector dwellings. Overcrowding was first recognised in legislation in the Nuisance Removal Act of 1855. The concern was about the moral as well as the health consequences of overcrowding, hence a statutory definition that focuses on preventing people of opposite sex (other than couples) being required to share a sleeping room.

11.81 There are two alternative tests to determine whether a dwelling is statutorily overcrowded: the room standard and the space standard.[44] Under the room standard, a household is overcrowded whenever two persons of the opposite sex must share a sleeping room. However, in applying the room standard, children under the age of ten are not considered at all. Under the space standard the number of people in the household is compared with either the number of sleeping rooms or the floor area of those rooms. In applying the space standard, children under the age of ten count as half a person and children under the age of one are not considered at all. Whichever standard is applied, living rooms are considered to be rooms in which people can sleep.

11.82 An occupier or landlord may be prosecuted for causing premises to be statutorily overcrowded but no offence is committed if the overcrowding is caused by children in the household reaching the age of ten. In practice, many overcrowded households are living in

---

43 HA 2004 makes provision for this test to be amended by regulations but there are no firm plans to do this at present.
44 HA 1985 ss325 and 326.

dwellings owned by local authorities and have become overcrowded because of the natural growth of their families.[45]

11.83   Many occupiers who live in overcrowded accommodation believe that if they are statutorily overcrowded they must be entitled to be transferred or allocated social housing. Unfortunately, this is not the case. Most allocation and transfer schemes give some priority to over-crowded households but this will not guarantee an offer of more suitable accommodation. Furthermore, statutory overcrowding does not mean that the occupiers will necessarily qualify as homeless; it is one factor an authority must take into account when deciding whether it is reasonable for the occupier to remain in occupation. See *Harouki v Kensington & Chelsea RLBC*[46] at para 14.43.

Decent Homes Standard

11.84   In the green paper *Quality and Choice: A Decent Home for All*, published in July 2000, the government set out targets in relation to the quality of social housing. The green paper defined a 'decent home' as 'one which is wind and weather tight, warm and has modern facilities'. The two targets set by the government were:

- to reduce by one-third the number of dwellings in the social rented sector which fall below the standard by 2004; and
- to have all social rented homes meet the standard by 2010.

11.85   The Decent Homes Standard is based around four components. To comply with the Standard a dwelling should:

- be free from Category 1 hazards;
- be in a reasonable state of repair;
- have reasonably modern facilities (in particular kitchens and bathrooms); and
- offer a reasonable degree of thermal comfort, which means having efficient heating, insulation and ventilation.

11.86   Both targets were missed. The Homes and Communities Agency is now responsible for the backlog Decent Homes programme and estimated that 92 per cent of homes in the social sector satisfied the Decent Homes Standard by the end of 2010. The target for all social rented homes meeting the standard was put back to 2015.

---

45   The offence can also be committed by a local authority but the consent of the Attorney-General is needed for an authority to be prosecuted.
46   [2007] EWCA Civ 1000.

Gas Safety Regulations

11.87   Under the Gas Safety (Installation and Use) Regulations 1998[47] land-lords are legally responsible for making sure that any gas appliances, gas piping and flues are well maintained and safe.[48] The landlord must ensure that an annual gas safety check is carried out by a registered gas engineer.[49] A landlord who fails to do so commits a criminal offence.

11.88   The regulations are enforced by the Health and Safety Executive (HSE) whose website is www.hse.gov.uk. This gives information about the local HSE offices to which complaint may be made. Alternatively, the matter can be reported to the local authority who may take action under the HA 2004, see above, paras 11.17–11.36.

11.89   The duty is owed by any landlord of a short-term tenancy, for example, a tenancy for a period of seven years or less, and to residential licences. It does not apply to long leases.

New provisions: preventing retaliatory evictions

11.90   The Deregulation Act (DA) 2015 makes provisions to prevent 'retaliatory evictions', ie landlords seeking to evict assured shorthold tenants who complain about the conditions of the property let. Initially it applies only to tenancies that began on or after 26 March 2015 but after three years it will apply to all assured shorthold tenancies, including those that started prior to this date.

11.91   The provisions operate so as to make a section 21 possession notice 'invalid' if served after a tenant has made a complaint about the conditions in the property if the landlord fails to provide an adequate response. However, for there to be a prohibition on the service of a notice the tenant must follow up a complaint to the landlord with a complaint to the local housing authority and the authority must act on the complaint.

11.92   For the section 21 notice to be invalid, all of the following requirements will have to be met:

---

47 SI No 2451.
48 Reg 36.
49 Reg 36(3). The register is now kept by Gas Safe who replaced CORGI. Gas Safe is the national watchdog for gas safety. All registered gas engineers must carry photo ID bearing their registration number. This can be checked on the Gas Safe website at www.gassaferegister.co.uk.

- the tenant, before the section 21 notice was given, made a complaint in writing (subject to certain exemptions set out below) 'regarding the condition of the dwelling-house at the time'; and
- the landlord did not provide a response or an 'adequate response' within 14 days of the day the complaint being 'given', or the landlord served a section 21 notice following the complaint; and
- the tenant then made a complaint to the local housing authority about the same or substantially the same thing; and
- the local authority served a 'relevant notice' (under the Housing Act (HA) 2004, see below at para 11.99) in relation to the property in response to the complaint; and
- in a case where the section 21 notice was given after the tenant's complaint to the relevant local authority, the s21 notice must have been given before the service of the relevant notice.

11.93   An 'adequate response' means a response in writing providing a description of the action the landlord intends to take and setting out a reasonable timescale within which the action will be taken.

11.94   If the tenant doesn't have a postal or e-mail address for the landlord the necessary conditions will be met where the tenant 'made reasonable efforts to contact the landlord to complain about the conditions in the dwelling-house but was unable to do so.'

11.95   Furthermore, it is provided that if the conditions set out at para 11.92 above mean that a section 21 notice becomes 'invalid' at a later date (ie after it has been served) 'the court must strike out proceedings for an order for possession'. However, the court may not set aside a possession order on the grounds that a relevant notice was served after the order was made.

11.96   So, the provisions will apply where a landlord fails to provide an adequate response to the tenant's complaint and further complaint is made to the local authority, which then serves a relevant notice. However, it would appear that they will not apply where the landlord provides an adequate response but fails to take the action set out in the response.

11.97   Where the provisions do apply, if the relevant notice is served before a possession order is made the proceedings must be struck out but if notice is served after the possession order the court must not, on that ground, set aside the possession order. So, in such a case the tenant must persuade the local authority to serve the relevant notice prior to the making of a possession order.

11.98   Where a relevant notice has been served the landlord is effectively prevented from serving a section 21 notice for a period of six months from the date of service of the relevant notice.[50] The aim is presumably to prevent the landlord from evicting the tenant for a period which should be long enough for the landlord to be forced to carry out the necessary improvement works. However, after this period (six months) there is nothing to prevent the landlord from evicting the tenant even if the landlord's motivation is 'retaliation' and/or even if the landlord has still not carried out the necessary works.

11.99   A 'relevant notice' is a notice served under

- section 11 or section 12 of the HA 2004 (improvement notices relating to Category 1 and Category 2 hazards), see paras 11.37–11.40; or
- section 40(7) of the HA 2004 (emergency remedial action), see paras 11.49–11.53.

11.100   The provisions do not make a section 21 notice invalid where the relevant notice has been wholly revoked (where the notice was served in error), quashed under para 15, schedule 1 of HA 2004 (by a tribunal on the landlord's appeal), where the authority has reversed its decision to serve a notice or where the authority suspend the notice, see below at para 11.103.

11.101   The complaint and the relevant notice may relate to common parts of the building in which the dwelling-house is situated but only if the landlord has a controlling interest in those parts and the conditions affect the tenant's enjoyment of the dwelling-house or common parts that the tenant is entitled to use (eg, a shared access).

11.102   The provisions do not apply in the following situations:

- the conditions giving rise to the service of the relevant notice is due to a breach by the tenant of the implied (or express) obligation to use the premises in a tenant-like manner;
- the property is 'genuinely on the market for sale' when the section 21 notice is given;[51]
- the property is subject to a mortgage granted before the beginning of the tenancy and the lender requires possession in order to sell with vacant possession pursuant to a power of sale under the mortgage;
- the landlord is a private registered provider of social housing.

---

50 Or, if the notice is suspended, from the date of the end of the suspension.
51 A property is not genuinely on the market where the landlord proposes to sell to an associated person, a business partner or a person associated to a business partner of the landlord. These terms are defined in the DA 2015 and in s178 of the HA 1996.

11.103 The provisions are new and yet to be tested but their effect may be limited by the following:

- A landlord only has to provide an 'adequate response' which includes setting out proposed works and a timetable. However, there is no sanction if the landlord then does nothing to carry out the works.
- A landlord who serves a section 21 notice at the earliest opportunity (which will be four months after the tenancy commenced, see para 6.57) may circumvent the provisions if the notice is served prior to the tenant's complaint. However, the landlord must act on the notice within six months or will have to serve a new notice that will be caught by the provisions (see para 6.57).
- The making of a possession order is only prevented if, before the order is made, the local authority has served a relevant notice. Local authorities already struggle to comply with their statutory obligations under the HA 2004 and the expected funding cuts from 2015 onwards will exacerbate the situation. Furthermore, environmental health officers will usually seek a landlord's agreement to carry out works to avoid the need to serve a formal notice and/or will suspend notices where the landlord indicates a willingness to undertake improvements works. Suspension of the notice will mean that the provisions no longer apply.

Further provisions regarding section 21 notices

11.104 The DA 2015 also makes provision for further 'prescribed requirements' to be introduced by way of statutory instrument, breach of which would prevent a landlord from serving a section 21 notice. These must relate to the condition of the dwelling-house or the common parts, the health and safety of the occupiers or the energy performance of the dwelling-house.

Relationship breakdown

continued

Key points

- Being married or in a civil partnership gives a person the right to occupy the shared home and to pay the rent or mortgage. These are known as 'home rights'.
- Where accommodation is shared the court can make orders to regulate rights of occupation. An 'occupation order' may give a person a right to occupy and/or prevent a person otherwise entitled to occupy accommodation from exercising a right to occupy.
- To protect a person from violence or harassment a 'non-molestation order' may be made against any 'associated person'. Associated persons are not confined to those who are or have been a 'couple'. It includes relatives and other people who share accommodation.
- It is a criminal offence to breach a non-molestation order without reasonable excuse.
- Non-molestation orders and occupation orders are for limited periods to protect a person or child until a long-term housing solution is achieved.
- If the shared home is rented and the parties are married, civil partners or cohabitants the court can transfer the tenancy from one party to the other.
- Where property is owned by one or both parties the court may transfer ownership or order a sale only if the parties are married or in a civil partnership.
- A person who is not a legal owner may be able to establish a beneficial interest by having contributed to the purchase of a property.
- Where the parties have children the court can transfer a tenancy or ownership for the benefit of the children.

Introduction

12.1 This chapter deals with some of the housing issues that arise when a relationship breaks down. Where the parties are in dispute about finance, property and/or children it may be necessary to consult a specialist family lawyer. However, legal aid is no longer available for such issues, unless the person applying has been the victim of domestic violence or there are concerns about child abuse.

This chapter provides an overview of the following issues:

Immediate/short-term issues:
- protection from domestic violence;
- establishing rights of occupation;
- homeless applications.

Long-term solutions – property adjustment:
- transfer of tenancies;
- owner-occupied accommodation.

Immediate/short-term issues

Protection from domestic violence

12.2   Someone facing violence within or around the home may do one or more of the following:
- apply to the local authority as a homeless person (see paras 12.3–12.4);
- obtain emergency shelter in a refuge or with friends or family (see paras 12.5–12.8);
- apply to the court for an injunction (a non-molestation order) and/or for an order excluding the perpetrator from the home (an occupation order), see paras 12.9–12.68.

Homeless applications

12.3   A person is homeless if it is probable that continuing to occupy their accommodation will lead to violence against him or her or a member of the household. Violence is defined as 'violence from another person; or threats of violence from another person which are likely to be carried out'.[1] This 'includes physical violence, threatening or intimidating behaviour and any other form of abuse which, directly or indirectly, may give rise to the risk of harm'.[2]

12.4   A local authority only has a duty to house applicants who have priority need. This includes pregnant women, those with dependent children and those considered vulnerable as a result of having become homeless because of violence, see paras 14.51–14.54.

---

1 Housing Act (HA) 1996 s177, see para 14.146.
2 *Yemshaw v Hounslow LBC* [2011] UKSC 3, 26 January 2011, see paras 14.32–14.38.

12.5   Some applicants will want temporary accommodation only until they can take other steps, such as applying for an injunction, an occupation order and/or a property adjustment order. Some applicants, however, may wish to be permanently accommodated away from the home in which they suffered domestic violence. A person should not be found intentionally homeless because he or she does not wish to seek an injunction and return home, see paras 14.34–14.36.

Women's refuges

12.6   A local authority may discharge its immediate duty to secure emergency accommodation by securing a place in a refuge. It is also possible to contact the National Domestic Violence Helpline directly to find a place in a refuge.[3]

12.7   Refuge places are generally available only to people who have the funds to pay for the accommodation or who can claim housing benefit. Victims of violence who are subject to immigration control may not be entitled to claim benefits or apply as homeless, see paras 20.6–20.48. Their only option may be to seek help from social services if they have children or have community care needs, see chapters 18 and 19.

12.8   Women's Aid and Refuge offer refuge only to female victims of domestic violence. Information about support available to male victims of domestic violence may be obtained by contacting Supportline at www.supportline.org.uk and Respect at www.respect.uk.net, which focuses on the causes of domestic violence and offers a telephone advice service to male victims of domestic violence: www. mensadviceline.org.uk.

Non-molestation orders

12.9   The courts' powers to make injunctions to protect the victims of domestic violence are found in the Family Law Act (FLA) 1996 Part IV. The injunction is known as a non-molestation order, which means an order that:[4]

- prohibits a person from molesting an 'associated person'; and/or
- prohibits a person from molesting a 'relevant child'.

---

3   Womens' Aid and Refuge jointly operate the National Domestic Violence Helpline: Tel 0808 200 0247. The Respect telephone advice line for male victims is 0808 801 0327.
4   FLA 1996 s42.

What is molestation?

12.10   The term is not defined in legislation. It covers actual or threatened violence but also includes behaviour that may be considered to be 'pestering'.[5] It has been held to include 'any conduct which can properly be regarded as such a degree of harassment as to call for the intervention of the court'.[6] The following are examples of behaviour that amounts to molestation:

- a man, who had previously been violent, repeatedly calling on his ex-wife at her home and workplace, making a 'perfect nuisance of himself', knowing that his behaviour was frightening to his ex-wife;[7]
- a man giving his wife notes that were upsetting and intercepting her journey to the railway station;[8]
- a man rifling through a woman's handbag.[9]

Associated person

12.11   A person is associated with another person if:[10]

- they are or have been married to each other;
- they are or have been civil partners;
- they are cohabitants or former cohabitants ie a couple who live together as husband and wife or (if of the same sex) as if they were civil partners;
- they live or have lived in the same household, otherwise than merely because one of them is the other's employee, tenant, lodger or boarder;
- they are relatives;[11]
- they have agreed to marry each other;
- they have entered into a civil partnership agreement, ie an agreement to become civil partners;[12]

---

5   *Vaughan v Vaughan* [1973] 3 All ER 449.
6   *Horner v Horner* [1982] Fam 90, Ormrod LJ at 93.
7   *Vaughan v Vaughan* [1973] 3 All ER 449.
8   *Horner v Horner* [1982] Fam 90.
9   *Spencer v Camacho* (1983) 4 FLR 662.
10   FLA 1996 s62(3).
11   Relatives are defined in FLA 1996 s63(1).
12   This is defined in the Civil Partnership Act 2004 s73. Orders in relation to those who have agreed to marry or agreed to be civil partners can only be made within three years of the termination of the agreement: s42(4)–(4ZA).

- they 'have or have had an intimate personal relationship with each other which is or was of significant duration';[13]
- in relation to any child, they are both parents of the child or have or have had parental responsibility for the child;
- in relation to an adopted child, one person is the natural parent or grandparent and the other is either the child or any adoptive parent or prospective adoptive parent;
- they are parties to the same family proceedings (not the proceedings under FLA 1996 Part IV).[14]

Relevant child

12.12 In addition, the court has a general power to make an order in relation to 'any relevant child'. A 'relevant child' means:

- any child who is living with either party;
- any child in relation to whom an order is in question in the proceedings;[15] and
- any other child whose interests the court considers relevant.[16]

12.13 A relevant child therefore includes any child the court considers needs protection.

12.14 A child may apply for an order but the permission of the court is required if the child is under the age of 16. The court will give permission only if satisfied the child has sufficient understanding to make the proposed application.[17]

When will the court make an order?

12.15 In deciding whether to make an order the court must have regard to 'all the circumstances including the need to secure the health, safety and well-being' of the applicant and any relevant child.[18]

12.16 As a general rule, the courts are reluctant to grant civil injunctions against anyone who is mentally ill because the person may not

---

13 FLA 1996 s62(3)(ea).
14 This would include a party to adoption proceedings, such as the natural father.
15 The proceedings may be under the Adoption Act 1976, Adoption and Children Act 2002 or Children Act 1989.
16 FLA 1996 s62(2).
17 FLA 1996 s43.
18 FLA 1996 s42(5).

be capable of complying with the order and the order may not be enforceable by way of committal.[19]

12.17   It is common practice where the respondent attends the hearing for the court to accept an undertaking instead of making an injunction. An undertaking should not be accepted in a case where the respondent has used or threatened violence against the applicant or a child. In such a case the court should make a non-molestation order, breach of which is a criminal offence, see para 12.21 below.[20]

Urgent cases – orders without notice

12.18   Under FLA 1996 s5 the court may make an order before the respondent has been given notice of the proceedings. In deciding whether to do so, the court must consider all of the circumstances including:

- a risk of significant harm[21] to the applicant or a relevant child if the order is not made immediately;
- whether it is likely that the applicant will be deterred or prevented from pursuing the application if an order is not made immediately; and
- whether there is reason to believe that the respondent is aware of the proceedings but deliberately evading service and that the applicant or a relevant child will be seriously prejudiced by any delay in arranging service of the papers.

12.19   If an order is made without notice to the respondent, he or she must be given an opportunity to make representations at a full hearing. The practice of the courts when making a without notice order is either to list the application for a full hearing at a later date, or to give the respondent the right to apply for a full hearing.

Scope of a non-molestation order

12.20   The order may prohibit molestation in general, prohibit particular acts of molestation, or both. It may be for a specified period or until further order.[22]

19 *Wookey v Wookey* [1991] 3 WLR 135.
20 FLA 1996 s46(3A).
21 'Harm' is defined in FLA 1996 s63. In relation to an adult it means ill treatment or the impairment of physical or mental health and, in relation to a child it means ill treatment or the impairment of physical or mental health or development.
22 FLA 1996 s42(6)–(7).

Sanctions for breach of non-molestation order

12.21 Since 1 July 2007 it has been a criminal offence to breach a non-molestation order without reasonable excuse.[23] The offence can only be committed at a time when the respondent is aware of the existence of the order. The maximum punishment is up to five years' imprisonment and/or a fine, if dealt with by a Crown Court. If the magistrates' court deals with the case, the maximum punishment is up to 12 months' imprisonment and/or a fine not exceeding £5,000.

12.22 In consequence of the new criminal offence, the court can no longer attach a power of arrest to a non-molestation order. This is in contrast to occupation orders in respect of which the court can still attach power of arrest, see para 12.67 below.

12.23 It is still possible for a person who breaches a non-molestation order to be committed to prison for contempt of court, see paras 10.173 and 22.116. However, a person cannot be convicted of the criminal offence of breaching a non-molestation order *and* punished for contempt of court.[24] However, if the act which constituted the breach was a criminal offence, the perpetrator can be convicted of the criminal offence, in addition to being punished for contempt.

Protection from Harassment Act 1997

12.24 A victim may also apply for an injunction under the Protection from Harassment Act (PHA) 1997 or make a complaint to the police who can prosecute a person guilty of harassment. See paras 8.101–8.114 for a summary of the provisions of the PHA 1997.

Occupation orders

12.25 In addition to or instead of a non-molestation order an application may be made for an occupation order under the Family Law Act (FLA) 1996. An occupation order may grant a person a right to occupy and may prevent another person from interfering with such a right. It may also suspend another person's rights of occupation or even exclude the person from the area where the home is. The purpose of an occupation order is to provide short-term protection where there

---

23 FLA 1996 s42A was inserted by the Domestic Violence, Crime and Victims Act 2004 s1.

24 FLA 1996 s42A(3) and (4).

has been violence or where one of the parties, or children living in the home, is likely to suffer harm without the court's intervention.

12.26   Occupation orders are always for a temporary period pending a more long-term arrangement being agreed or ordered by a court.

12.27   The courts' powers under the FLA 1996 depend on the parties' existing rights of occupation. A person may have a right to occupy under the general law, for example, because he or she is a tenant or owner or under FLA 1996 by virtue of marriage to or civil partnership with the tenant or owner. These rights of occupation are summarised below, paras 12.28–12.64.

Rights to occupy under the general law

Joint tenancy/jointly owned property

12.28   Where accommodation is let to two joint tenants or is jointly owned both are entitled to occupy the whole of the accommodation, see paras 1.49–1.52. Other than by applying for an order under the FLA 1996, one joint tenant or owner cannot exclude the other.

12.29   However, one joint tenant can terminate a joint tenancy without the consent of the other (see para 1.64). This may be done in order to frustrate a future application for a transfer into the sole name of one of the joint tenants (see below para 12.87). It is also sometimes encouraged by local authority landlords that also have a duty to accommodate the victim of domestic violence. The notice to quit determines the tenancy and the authority can then seek a possession order.

12.30   If seeking to procure a notice to quit, an authority must consider the remaining occupier's right to respect for his or her home under the European Convention on Human Rights and whether such a course of action is necessary and proportionate.[25]

Sole tenancy/sole ownership

12.31   Where one party is the sole tenant or sole owner of a property and the parties are not married or in a civil partnership that person's cohabitant does not have a right to occupy. He or she has a licence (permission) to occupy given by the sole tenant or owner. Because they share the accommodation the tenant or owner may give the other reasonable notice to leave (see para 1.122). What is reasonable notice

---

25   See *McCann v UK*, App No 19009/04, 13 May 2008, ECtHR. See paras 7.128 and 7.146–7.159. See also *Sims v Dacorum BC* [2014] UKSC 63, 12 November 2014.

depends on the circumstances. If there has been violence or unreasonable behaviour, very short or immediate notice may be considered reasonable. The notice need not be in writing.

12.32 After the period of notice has expired, the tenant or owner can exclude the cohabitant by changing the locks. However, the use of force to evict a person who is inside the home is a criminal offence under the Criminal Law Act 1977 (see para 8.38).

12.33 Where a cohabitant refuses to leave, a sole tenant or owner may apply for a possession order and use the court bailiffs to evict, even though under landlord and tenant law this is not necessary. See chapter 6 for an explanation of the procedure for possession claims and chapter 22 for a general description of civil proceedings.

12.34 In theory, a person who has been excluded and believes that he or she was not given reasonable notice can apply to a court for an injunction ordering the other party to give reasonable notice before excluding. In practice, a court is unlikely to make an order that forces two people to live together, even for a short period, after the relationship has broken down.

Rights to occupy under FLA 1996 – home rights

12.35 The right of a spouse to occupy the 'matrimonial home' is well established and such rights were previously called 'matrimonial home rights'. Since the Civil Partnership Act 2004 these rights have been renamed 'home rights': a person has a legal right to occupy accommodation that is solely owned or rented by his or her spouse or civil partner, provided it is or has been their shared home during the marriage or civil partnership.[26]

12.36 Home rights are set out in FLA 1996 s30. The following points should be noted:

- Home rights only exist in relation to accommodation which is, has in the past been, or was intended to be, a matrimonial home or a civil partnership home.[27]
- Home rights can exist in relation to a dwelling-house, which includes a building or part of a building, a caravan, house-boat or any structure occupied as a dwelling.[28]

---

26 FLA 1996 s30. The provisions are not limited to rights of occupation under tenancies. Section 30(1)(b) also refers to 'any enactment giving ... the right to remain in occupation'.

27 FLA 1996 s30(7).

28 FLA 1996 s63(1).

- If the spouse or civil partner claiming home rights is in actual occupation, the right exists independently of the court. However, if the person is not in actual occupation, he or she must apply for the permission of the court to gain the right to enter and occupy.[29]
- The right of occupation ends when the marriage or civil partnership ends, unless extended by court order.[30]

12.37   In relation to tenancies, the occupation of a spouse or civil partner satisfies any residence condition necessary for the tenant to have long-term security.[31]

12.38   A spouse or civil partner exercising a home right is entitled to pay rent or mortgage payments, and any payment or offer of payment is as good as if made by the tenant or borrower.[32] Housing benefit can be awarded if necessary to enable the person to continue living in the home (see para 9.15).

12.39   Where accommodation is owner-occupied, home rights can be registered as a charge with the Land Registry.[33] This would protect the right in the event that the sole owner tried to sell the property.

Applying for an occupation order

12.40   Different provisions apply depending on the status of the applicant and whether he or she has a right to occupy.

FLA 1996 s33: applicant entitled to occupy

12.41   Most applications are made under FLA 1996 s33, which applies when the applicant has a right to occupy, whether under the general law or by virtue of a home right under FLA 1996, see para 12.35 above.

---

29 FLA 1996 s30(2).
30 FLA 1996 s30(8)(a).
31 FLA 1996 s30(4). See paras 4.2–4.11 for an explanation of the issues arising in relation to tenants' residence conditions.
32 FLA 1996 s30(3). This means, for example, that if a landlord refuses a payment from the spouse or civil partner, there would be a defence to a possession claim based on rent arrears.
33 FLA 1996 s31.

The court's powers under FLA 1996 s33

12.42 The court may make an order to:[34]

- enforce the right of occupation against the other person (the respondent);
- require the respondent to permit the applicant to enter and remain in the home;
- regulate the occupation of the home by either or both parties;
- prohibit, suspend or restrict the rights of a respondent who is ordinarily entitled to occupy under landlord and tenant law;
- restrict or terminate a right of occupation the respondent has under FLA 1996 s30 (home rights);
- require the respondent to leave the home or part of it;
- exclude the respondent from a defined area where the home is.

In practice the courts will usually make orders to restrict a right of occupation where there has been violence or threats of violence.

12.43 The court may also make orders declaring that a person has a right of occupation by virtue of the general law or under FLA 1996 s30, where this is in dispute. Such orders simply state the entitlement and do not restrict the exercise of any right of occupation.

Criteria for making orders under FLA 1996 s33

12.44 When deciding whether to make an order and in what terms the main issue is 'the balance of harm' test, see below. However, the court must have regard to all of the circumstances, including:[35]

- the housing needs and housing resources of each of the parties and any relevant child;
- the financial resources of each of the parties;
- the likely effect of any order, or refusal to make an order, on the health, safety or well-being of the parties and any relevant child; and
- the conduct of the parties in relation to each other and otherwise.

12.45 See para 12.12 above for the definition of 'relevant child'.

34 FLA 1996 s33(3).
35 FLA 1996 s30(6).

The balance of harm test

12.46   The court *must* make an order if it appears that the applicant or any relevant child is likely to suffer significant harm if an order is not made which is greater than the harm the respondent or any child is likely to suffer if an order *is* made.[36]

12.47   When considering an occupation order and applying the balance of harm test the court will take account of whether an applicant or respondent is likely to be owed a homeless duty.

> In *B v B*[37] a woman left her husband because of his violence. She took their 2-year-old daughter leaving him and his 6-year-old son from a previous relationship in occupation of their home. She was placed in temporary accommodation by the local authority and applied for an occupation order. An order was made ordering the husband to vacate with his son.
>
> The Court of Appeal allowed his appeal. The authority was likely to find that he was intentionally homeless and that no housing duty was owed. The likely harm to the son would therefore be greater to that caused to the wife and daughter who would be housed by the local authority.

12.48   When considering an occupation order a central issue will be which party is likely to have primary responsibility for any children in the future. An application for an occupation order can be made at the same time as an application for a residence order under the Children Act 1989.[38]

12.49   Where the court is making a declaratory order relating to entitlement rather than restricting the exercise of a right of occupation, the balance of harm test need not be applied.

How long does the order last?

12.50   Occupation orders are for limited duration. An order must be for a specified period, until a specified event or until further order.[39]

---

36   FLA 1996 s33(7). See para 12.18, note 21 for definition of harm.
37   [1999] 1 FLR 715, CA.
38   FLA 1996 s39(2).
39   FLA 1996 s33(10).

12.51 The court may make an order that home rights extend beyond the death of the spouse or civil partner, or the end of the marriage or civil partnership.[40]

FLA 1996 s35: applicant (former spouse or civil partner) not entitled to occupy

12.52 An application for an occupation order may be made by a former spouse or former civil partner who has no existing right of occupation.[41] This would be the case when a marriage or civil partnership has ended, thereby terminating any home rights previously enjoyed (under FLA 1996 s30). An order may only be made in respect of a dwelling which was or was intended to be the matrimonial or civil partnership home. The application will be against the former spouse or civil partner.

12.53 If an order is made it must:

- if the applicant is in occupation, give the applicant the right not to be evicted or excluded from the home and prohibit the respondent from doing so;
- if the applicant is not in occupation, give the applicant the right to enter into and occupy the home and require the respondent to permit the exercise of the right.

12.54 An order may also restrict the respondent's rights of occupation, as under FLA 1996 s33 (see para 12.42 above).

12.55 When considering an application for occupation rights under FLA 1996 s35 the court must apply the criteria set out at para 12.44 above but in addition the court must consider the following:

- the length of time that has elapsed since the parties ceased to live together;
- the length of time that has elapsed since the marriage or civil partnership ended;[42] and
- the existence of any pending proceedings for property transfer or relating to the legal or beneficial ownership of the home, see para 12.96 below.[43]

12.56 If the court is considering an order that restricts the respondent's occupation rights, the court need not take account of the additional

---

40 FLA 1996 s30(5).
41 FLA 1996 s35.
42 FLA 1996 s35(6)(f).
43 FLA 1996 s35(6)(g). Such applications may be pending under the Matrimonial Causes Act 1973, Civil Partnership Act 2004 or Children Act 1989.

considerations set out above (para 12.55), save for the time since the parties lived together. However, the balance of harm test must be applied, see para 12.46 above.

12.57   An order under FLA 1996 s35 may not be made for a period longer than six months, but or more application to extend the period for a further six months may be made.

FLA 1996 s36: applicant (cohabitant or former cohabitant) not entitled to occupy

12.58   A cohabitant who has no right of occupation may apply under FLA 1996 s36 for an occupation order. An order may only be made in respect of a dwelling in which the parties cohabit or at any time cohabited or intended to cohabit. The application will be against the other cohabitant or former cohabitant.

12.59   If an order is made it must:

- if the applicant is in occupation, give the applicant the right not to be evicted or excluded from the home and prohibit the respondent from doing so;
- if the applicant is not in occupation, give the applicant the right to enter into and occupy the home and require the respondent to permit the exercise of the right.

12.60   An order may also restrict the respondent's rights of occupation.

12.61   When considering an application for occupation rights under FLA 1996 s36 the court must apply the criteria set out at para 12.44 above but in addition the court must consider the following:

- the nature of the parties' relationship and in particular the level of commitment involved in it;
- the length of time during which they cohabited;
- whether there are or have been any children of the relationship, or children for whom both parties have or have had parental responsibility;
- the length of time that has elapsed since the parties ceased to live together; and
- the existence of any pending proceedings for financial provision under the Children Act 1989 or relating to the legal or beneficial ownership of the property, see para 12.96 below.

12.62   If the court is considering an order that restricts the respondent's occupation rights, the court need not take account of the additional considerations set out above at para 12.61 but the balance of harm test must be applied (see para 12.46 above). However, under FLA

1996 s36 there is no presumption that an order should be made, as there is when the court is considering making an order under FLA 1996 ss33 or 35.

12.63 An order under section 36 may not be made for a period longer than six months, but one application to extend the period for a further six months may be made.

Occupation orders under other circumstances

12.64 Under FLA 1996 s34 an occupation order can be made in relation to premises where the respondent's interest has passed to someone else. Under FLA 1996 s37 an order may be made where neither party is entitled to occupy the premises where the parties have been married or civil partners. Under FLA 1996 s38 an order may be made in respect of cohabitants where neither has a right to occupy.

Ancillary provisions

12.65 When making an occupation order the court may also make orders that:[44]

- either party is responsible for repairs and maintenance, the payment of rent, mortgage payments or other outgoings;
- a party occupying the home makes payments to the other;
- either party has possession or use of furniture or other contents; and
- either party takes reasonable steps to keep the home and any furniture or contents safe.

Cases of urgency

12.66 An occupation order may also be made at a hearing of which the respondent has not been given notice if the court considers it just and convenient to do so. The same criteria apply when considering making such an order as when considering a non-molestation order, see para 12.18. However, the court should only make an occupation order without notice in an exceptional case. In *Moat Housing Group-South Ltd v Harris and Hartless*,[45] which concerned anti-social behaviour injunctions, the Court of Appeal commented that 'as a matter of principle no order should be made in civil or family proceedings

44 FLA 1996 s40(1).
45 [2005] EWCA Civ 287, 16 March 2005. See para 7.98 above.

without notice to the other side unless there is a very good reason for departing from the general rule that notice must be given'.

Enforcement

12.67   The court can attach a power of arrest to an occupation order and *must* do so in cases where there has been actual or threatened violence, and in cases where the court is not satisfied that the applicant or any child will be adequately protected without one. However, if the order is made without notice the court may attach a power of arrest only if it appears that the respondent has used or threatened violence against the applicant or a relevant child and there is a risk of significant harm to the applicant or child attributable to the respondent if a power of arrest is not attached immediately.

12.68   Where a power of arrest is attached this means that the police can arrest the perpetrator and bring him or her before the civil courts to be punished for contempt of court. Otherwise, the applicant must make an application for committal, see paras 10.73 and 22.116. Breach of an occupation order, unlike breach of a non-molestation order, is not a criminal offence.

Long-term solutions

Property adjustment: courts' powers

12.69   Under FLA 1996 when a marriage, civil partnership or cohabiting relationship breaks down the court can make an order transferring a tenancy from one party to another, or from joint names into sole names.

12.70   In addition, under the Matrimonial Causes Act (MCA) 1973[46] and the Civil Partnership Act (CPA) 2004[47] a court can transfer ownership of property from one party to the other on divorce or termination of a civil partnership.[48] Alternatively the court can order that a property is sold and the proceeds of sale divided between the parties.

12.71   Under the Children Act (CA) 1989 the court can order one party to transfer property to a child or to another adult for the benefit of the child.[49]

46 MCA 1973 s24.
47 CPA 2004 Sch 5.
48 Such orders can also be made on judicial separation (married partners) or when a separation order is made (civil partners). This is where the partners are formally separated but the marriage or civil partnership has not ended.
49 CA 1989 Sch 1 para 1.

12.72 In addition, where a property is legally owned by one person, a party who made a contribution to the purchase may have a 'beneficial interest'. If this cannot be agreed between the parties an application may be made to a court. This is not the same as property adjustment: it is asking the court to make a declaration about the existing ownership of the property in accordance with the principles of the law of trusts. In the same proceedings the court can be asked to make an order for the sale of the property and the division of the proceeds of sale. A brief summary of the relevant principles is set out at paras 12.96–12.103 below.

Transfer of tenancies

12.73 Under the FLA 1996, on divorce, termination of a civil partnership[50] or if cohabitants cease to cohabit, the following tenancies may be transferred from one party to the other or from joint names into sole names:

- a secure tenancy;
- an introductory tenancy;
- a flexible tenancy;
- an assured tenancy;
- an assured agricultural occupancy;
- a protected tenancy;
- a statutory tenancy;
- a statutory tenancy under the Rent (Agriculture) Act 1976.

12.74 The following are not capable of being transferred:

- any licence;
- a demoted tenancy;
- a family intervention tenancy.

12.75 See chapter 3 for an explanation of the types of tenancy listed above.

12.76 The court can only make an order in relation to a dwelling-house which was a home shared by the parties.[51]

12.77 A landlord must be notified of a pending application.[52]

---

50 Again, such orders may also be made when a decree of judicial separation or a separation order is made.
51 FLA 1996 Sch 7 para 4.
52 FLA 1996 Sch 7 para 14(1).

How does the transfer happen?

12.78   Under the Family Law Act 1996 the court order has the effect of transferring the interest. The tenancy vests in the party at the date specified in the order.

12.79   Under the Matrimonial Causes Act 1973, Children Act 1989 and Civil Partnership Act (CPA) 2004 the court can order one party to assign the tenancy to the other. If such an order is made, the tenancy is only transferred when the actual assignment takes effect. This must be done by a properly executed deed entered into by both parties, see paras 4.56–4.57.[53]

12.80   If the tenancy agreement prohibits assignment, the fact that it is a court that ordered the assignment does not mean that it is not in breach of the tenancy agreement. An assignment in breach of the tenancy agreement will give the landlord a ground for possession but the ground is discretionary and the circumstances in which the transfer took place will be relevant.

When will the court transfer a tenancy?

12.81   The court must apply certain criteria when deciding whether to transfer a tenancy. These are set out in the relevant Acts.

12.82   Under FLA 1996, where the transfer is on the termination of a marriage or civil partnership, the criteria are:[54]

- the circumstances in which the tenancy was granted;
- the housing needs and housing resources of each of the parties and of any relevant child;
- the financial resources of each of the parties;
- the likely effect of any order, or refusal to make an order, on the health, safety or well-being of the parties and any relevant child;
- the suitability of the parties as tenants.

12.83   If parties are cohabitants the court must also have regard to:

- the nature of the parties' relationship and in particular the level of commitment involved in it;
- the length of time during which they cohabited;
- whether there are or have been any children of the relationship, or children for whom both parties have or have had parental responsibility;

53 FLA 1996 Sch 7 para 5.
54 FLA 1996 Sch 7 paras 8(2)–(4), 9 and 10. See para 4.33 above for a description of the different rights of succession.

- the length of time that has elapsed since the parties ceased to live together.

Effect of a transfer

12.84   When a tenancy is transferred, whether by a court order or by assignment, the new tenant takes the tenancy subject to any limits or restrictions on the tenancy. If the tenancy was a tenancy by succession, the new tenant will be treated as if he or she is a tenant by succession.[55] A flexible tenancy is for a fixed period of terms and the new tenant will only have the right to occupy for the remainder of the term, though the landlord may agree to grant a further tenancy at the end of the term, see paras 3.151–3.159.

12.85   The court can order that one party pays compensation to the other for the loss of the tenancy[56] and can also make orders setting out the respective liabilities of the parties, for example, ordering one party to pay rent arrears pre-dating the transfer.[57]

Protecting home rights and/or safeguarding future transfer

Tenants' residence conditions

12.86   Where the tenant is out of occupation but his or her spouse or civil partner remains in occupation this fulfils any residence condition under the tenancy agreement, see above at paras 12.37 and 4.14. However, this applies only as long as the marriage or civil partnership subsists. It is essential therefore that the tenancy is transferred before the divorce is made absolute or the civil partnership terminated. Otherwise the landlord may terminate the tenancy and evict the occupier on the basis that the tenancy has ceased to be statutorily protected.

Preventing dispositions that would frustrate a transfer

12.87   As indicated above (para 12.39), a spouse or civil partner can protect home rights in relation to owner-occupied accommodation by registering a charge at the Land Registry. Furthermore, the court can prevent a party from making a 'disposition' intended to defeat an

55 FLA 1996 Sch 7 para 10.
56 FLA 1996 Sch 7 para 11.
57 MCA 1973 s37(2) and CPA 2004 Sch 5 para 74.

application for a property adjustment order. If the disposition has already been made it can be set aside.[58]

12.88   A home right in relation to a tenancy cannot be registered. In most cases it will not be possible to 'sell' or transfer the tenancy to another person to avoid an application for a transfer to an ex-partner. However, the tenant can terminate the tenancy in order to defeat such an application. A sole tenant can do this by either surrendering the tenancy or by serving notice to quit.[59] A joint tenant can serve notice to quit to end a periodic joint tenancy, regardless of the wishes of the other joint tenant, see para 1.64.

12.89   A surrender is a disposition of property and could be prevented by the court or set aside where the parties are or have been married or in a civil partnership. However, a notice to quit is not a disposition and where a joint tenant serves notice to quit in order to prevent a future application for a transfer of the tenancy into the other tenant's sole name the court does not have the power to set the notice aside.[60]

12.90   A joint tenant can apply for an injunction to prevent the other party from serving notice to quit. This was suggested by the Court of Appeal in *Bater v Greenwich LBC*.[61] However, it is unclear whether an order prohibiting service of a notice to quit would render a notice served in breach of the order ineffective. The point is undecided but it may be that while serving notice would be contempt of court the notice would nevertheless determine the joint tenancy.[62]

Assignment by agreement

12.91   Where the parties are in agreement that the tenancy should be transferred into the sole name of one person the tenancy may be assigned. However, in most cases assignment will be prohibited and an assignment in breach of the tenancy agreement will give the landlord a ground for possession. The landlord's consent should always be sought. If the landlord does not object to the proposed transfer, the landlord may, instead of consenting to an assignment, agree to a surrender and then grant a new tenancy to the party remaining in the home. Some social landlords have policies under which an offer of alternative accommodation will be made to the departing tenant

58   *Sanctuary Housing Association v Campbell* (2000) 32 HLR 100, CA.
59   See paras 1.61–1.77.
60   *Newlon Housing Association v Al-Sulaiman* (1998) 30 HLR 1132, HL.
61   [1999] 4 All ER 944.
62   *Harrow LBC v Johnstone* (1997) 29 HLR 475, HL.

on relationship breakdown. However, such policies are increasingly rare; more commonly a tenant who voluntarily leaves the home following the breakdown of a relationship will be left with the possibility of a homeless application, applying through the local authority's housing waiting list or finding private rented accommodation. See paras 14.60–14.70 below for an explanation of the homeless duty when the care of children is to be shared by two parents living in different places.

12.92 If the landlord will not agree to an assignment, an application may be made for an order under the FLA 1996 to transfer the tenancy. The landlord will have an opportunity to make representations as to why the tenancy should not be transferred.

12.93 Under the Housing Act 1985 a secure tenant can assign to a person who would be qualified to succeed to the tenancy, see para 4.78. This would include a spouse or civil partner or a cohabitant who has lived with the tenant for at least one year and still does so immediately before the date of the assignment. However, such an assignment would prevent a future succession so a transfer under FLA 1996 may be preferred.

Owner-occupied accommodation

12.94 Under the Matrimonial Causes Act 1973 and the Civil Partnership Act 2004 the court may transfer the ownership of property from one party to the other or may order the sale of property and the division of the proceeds of sale. An order for sale may be postponed until a future date, for example when children reach a certain age. Such orders will usually be made as part of a package of financial provision and the assistance of a specialist family lawyer should be sought to negotiate and make the necessary applications.[63]

12.95 The court has no power to make such orders in relation to cohabitants unless there are children of the family, in which case an application can be made under the Children Act 1989 for the benefit of the children.

---

63 However, legal aid is no longer available for family cases involving disputes between separating couples about children and financial provision, in the absence of domestic violence or risk of abuse to a child.

Beneficial ownership

12.96   Where property is held in the sole name of one party, another party may nevertheless have a 'beneficial' interest. This arises under the law of trust, see para 1.139.

12.97   An express trust may be created by deed setting out the terms of the trust.

12.98   In addition, a person who has contributed to the purchase of a property may be able to establish that an implied trust has arisen even though the parties did not expressly agree that the property was to be held on trust.

12.99   Where the parties intended that the interest would be shared this is known as a 'constructive trust' and indirect as well as direct contributions may be taken into account, such as payment of household expenses.

12.100   Where there is no common intention that the interest would be shared this is known as a 'resulting trust'. In such a case only direct contributions to the purchase will be taken into account. This would include paying part of the deposit or the mortgage payments.

12.101   If the parties are in dispute about whether there is a trust or the extent of their respective shares it will be necessary to apply to the court for a declaration. The court can also order that the property be sold and the proceeds of sale (the 'equity') divided between the parties in the proportions determined by the court. See para 1.141.

12.102   Where a party is seeking to establish a beneficial interest, specialist advice should be sought. If the parties are able to reach agreement about the existence of a trust and their respective interests the costs of legal proceedings will be avoided. If not, the legal costs incurred may have the effect of reducing the value of one or both parties' interests.

12.103   Note that a spouse or civil partner who is a beneficial owner but not a legal owner is treated as having a right of occupation by virtue of FLA 1996 (as opposed to by virtue of the beneficial interest). Such a home right can be registered as a charge to prevent sale until resolution of any dispute about the beneficial ownership.[64]

---

64   FLA 1996 s30(9).

CHAPTER 13

Homelessness applications, inquiries and miscellaneous duties

continued

Key points

- A local authority should accept a homeless application and make formal inquiries if it has *reason to believe* a person *may be* homeless and eligible (an immigration test).
- If the authority also has *reason to believe* the person *may be* in priority need, interim accommodation must be provided until inquiries are complete and a decision made.
- 'Homeless Prevention' strategies often result in people being discouraged from making homeless applications and encouraged to find privately rented accommodation. A homeless person is entitled to pursue a homeless application and to insist on a formal written decision from the authority as to what housing duty, if any, is owed to him or her.
- The interim accommodation provided pending inquiry must be suitable but, because it is for a very temporary period, what is deemed suitable may be of a low standard.
- A failure or refusal to accept a homeless application or to provide suitable interim accommodation pending a decision can be challenged by an application for judicial review.
- An applicant who has had a negative decision may apply again to the same authority but the authority need not investigate an application based on the same facts. It is for the applicant to demonstrate that the application is not on the same facts.

Introduction

13.1   This chapter provides an overview of the law on homelessness, and examines the following issues:

- applications;
- interim accommodation pending decision;
- the local authority duty to make inquiries;
- repeat applications;
- miscellaneous duties.

13.2   Some homeless people are entitled to be provided with accommodation by a local housing authority. Local authority duties to homeless people are set out in the Housing Act (HA)1996 Part VII; some of the detail of the duty is found in statutory instruments. Additionally, local authorities must have regard to the *Homelessness Code of*

Guidance for Local Authorities. Since 1997 there has been a clear distinction between a local authority's duty to accommodate homeless applicants and the way it allocates permanent accommodation. The law on allocations is dealt found in HA 1996 Part VI and is explained in chapter 17.

Reference materials

13.3 The main reference materials when dealing with homeless applications are:

Housing Act 1996 Part VII	Sets out: the legal tests applied to decide whether a housing duty is owed; the nature of the housing duties; and the way decisions are challenged.
Homelessness (Suitability of Accommodation) Order 1996[1] 'Suitability Order 1996'	Sets out: matters to be taken into account when assessing suitability with particular reference to affordability.
Homelessness Act 2002	Amended the HA 1996 and added some general duties to prepare and review homelessness strategies.
Homelessness (Priority Need for Accommodation) (England) Order 2002[2] 'The priority need order'	Sets out additional categories of people with priority need.
Homelessness (Suitability of Accommodation) (England) Order 2003[3] 'Suitability Order 2003'	Provides that B&B accommodation is not suitable for families and pregnant women (unless nothing else available and then for no longer than six weeks).
Allocation of Housing and Homelessness (Eligibility) (England) Regulations 2006[4]	Sets out the classes of people from abroad who are and are not eligible for homeless assistance. These regulations have been amended many times.

1 SI No 3204.
2 SI No 2051.
3 SI No 3326.
4 SI No 1294. For issues of eligibility other statutes and regulations are also relevant: see para 20.5.

Homelessness Code of Guidance [4 September 2006] 'The 2006 Code of Guidance'	A summary of the law and good practice. Local authorities must 'have regard' to the code.[5]
Supplementary Guidance on Intentional Homelessness [August 2009] 'The 2009 Supplementary Guidance'	Supplements the 2006 Code of Guidance – deals with how authorities should treat homeless applicants with mortgage difficulties.
Statutory Guidance on the provision of accommodation for 16- and 17-year-olds [April 2010]	Sets out the arrangements housing and social services departments should make for homeless 16- and 17-year-olds.
Localism Act 2011	Amends HA 1996 mainly by permitting housing authorities to end the homelessness accommodation duty by way of a 'private rented sector offer'.
Homelessness (Suitability of Accommodation) (England) Order 2012[6] 'Suitability Order 2012'	Sets out: relevant matters when assessing suitability with reference to location, particularly out of borough placements; and when private rented sector offers will not be suitable.
Supplementary Guidance on the Changes made by the Localism Act and the 'Suitability Order 2012' 'The 2012 Supplementary Guidance'	Supplements the 2006 Code of Guidance with particular reference to private rented sector offers and location in relation to suitability.

5 All the relevant Codes and Guidance can be downloaded from the website of the Department for Communities and Local Government at: www.communities.gov.uk.
6 SI No 2601

Case-law	The courts frequently decide disputes between applicants and local authorities. Decisions of the Court of Appeal and above are binding. County Courts generally follow the decisions of the High Court. Previous decisions will be reflected in the Code of Guidance. However, many cases are about procedural irregularity rather than the merits of the decision itself.

13.4　A duty to provide accommodation specifically for homeless people was first introduced by the Housing (Homeless Persons) Act 1977. Previously, local authorities had various powers and duties to provide temporary accommodation in emergencies.

13.5　The basic structure and legal 'tests' central to the homelessness duty have changed little since 1977: the authority must investigate an application to satisfy itself of certain matters relating to the applicant's circumstances and the cause of the homelessness. The outcome of the authority's investigations will determine what duty, if any, is owed. This may range from simply providing advice and assistance to securing suitable accommodation for the applicant and his or her family. In some cases the authority's duty will be limited to providing a written decision giving reasons why no substantive duty is owed.

The 'full housing duty'

13.6　What has changed most significantly since 1977 is the nature of the 'full housing duty'. Prior to HA 1996, a successful homeless applicant would usually be offered a long-term tenancy by the authority or another social landlord. HA 1996 was introduced because most long-term social housing was being allocated to the 'statutory homeless' while others in great housing need waited for many years on council waiting lists. HA 1996 provides that the full housing duty to homeless applicants is a duty to provide temporary accommodation only; the person's need for permanent accommodation is assessed in the same way as waiting list applicants. All allocation schemes must comply with the provisions of HA 1996 Part VI, which specifies the groups to whom 'reasonable preference' must be given. Homeless people are a group that must be given 'reasonable preference', but local authorities have considerable discretion as to the relative levels of priority given. 'Reasonable preference' may not necessarily result in an offer of permanent accommodation under Part VI, see paras 17.31–17.32.

13.7 The Localism Act 2011 made further changes by permitting local authorities to bring the homelessness duty to and end by way of a 'private rented sector offer' (see para 16.28).

Homelessness prevention

13.8 The number of people applying and being accepted as homeless and owed a housing duty (acceptances) increased every year between 1997 and 2001. At the same time, families accommodated by authorities were spending longer periods in temporary accommodation before securing a permanent home. The government began to promote 'homelessness prevention' strategies following the publication of its report: *More than a roof – a report into tackling homelessness* in March 2003. Many local authorities adopted measures to encourage homeless or potentially homeless applicants to find accommodation in the private sector by offering rent guarantee or deposit schemes and by liaising with private landlords to encourage lettings. However, some adopted procedures that discouraged or even prevented people from pursuing homeless applications – such practices are commonly known as 'gatekeeping'. The government's homelessness statistics[7] show that the numbers of those accepted for the full housing duty by local authorities rose to an all time high of 135,000 in 2003 before falling to 41,800 in 2010. Since then the numbers have increased again and 53,000 were recorded in 2013.

13.9 These figures are based on local authority returns, which indicate only those applications recorded by the authority. What is not recorded is the number of homeless people who approach an authority but whose approach is not recorded as a formal application. Ways of assisting those faced with 'gatekeeping' are discussed below at paras 13.30–13.35.

13.10 The problem of 'inappropriate gatekeeping' is identified in the Local Government Ombudsman report published in July 2011: *Homelessness: How councils can ensure justice for homeless people*. The report summarises complaints upheld against local authorities that have failed to act lawfully in relation to those homeless or threatened with homelessness. The report can be downloaded from: www.lgo.org.uk.

---

7 Available from the website of the Department for Communities and Local Government: www.communities.gov.uk.

Summary of the homelessness tests and duties

13.11   A housing authority must be satisfied of certain matters (referred to here as the 'homelessness tests') before deciding whether a housing duty is owed. The tests are dealt with in chapter 14. They are summarised here because they are essential to understanding the process of homeless applications and the nature of the duty that may be owed.

13.12   The full housing duty will be owed if, after inquiry, the authority is satisfied of the following matters:

- the applicant is *homeless;*
- the applicant is *eligible for assistance* (an immigration test);
- the applicant has a *priority need;*
- the applicant is not *intentionally homeless.*

13.13   Although the full housing duty will be owed, it may be that the duty is not owed by the authority that investigated the application. At this point the authority *may* consider:

- whether the applicant can be referred to another authority to be housed by the other authority.

13.14   These tests must be applied in the correct order because the homelessness duties depend on the outcome of each test. If an applicant 'fails' one test, it may be unnecessary to go on to determine other matters. A summary of the tests and the duties owed is as follows.

The test	The duty
Is the applicant eligible?[8] Yes: Apply the next test	No: Decision letter only.
Is the applicant homeless? Yes: Apply the next test	No: Decision letter only.[9]
Is the applicant in priority need? Yes: Apply the next test	No: Decision letter and housing advice and assistance addressing the applicant's needs.[10]

8   An authority may inquire first into homelessness or eligibility. In either case, if the answer is negative, the authority's duty is limited to issuing a decision letter giving reasons.

9   An applicant who is found not eligible or not homeless is entitled to use the advice and information services authorities must provide or fund locally but there is no specific duty to advise and assist the particular applicant.

10   An authority has the power to accommodate non-priority need applicants, but only if they are not intentionally homeless.

The test	The duty
Is the applicant intentionally homeless? No: Apply the next test	Yes: Decision letter and housing advice and assistance addressing the applicant's needs plus accommodation for a 'reasonable' period.
Can the applicant be referred elsewhere?	No: Full housing duty owed. Yes: Full housing duty owed by another authority. Duty to accommodate temporarily continues until referral is accepted or any dispute resolved.

Making an application

13.15   In theory it should be easy to make a homeless application: no particular form of application is prescribed and an authority has a duty
to make formal inquiries if they 'have reason to believe' a person
'may be' homeless and eligible. However, the opposite is often the
case and the most difficult part of the process can be persuading
the authority to accept an application in the first place. Those who
approach an authority for help may be told:

- 'you can't apply here as you have no local connection';
- 'you aren't homeless if you had somewhere to sleep last night';
- 'you have no priority need, so we can't help you';
- 'you were previously evicted for rent arrears or anti-social behaviour, so you will be found intentionally homeless';
- 'here is an application form for the housing waiting list';
- 'we can't see you until next week/month';
- 'we will make an appointment with the private sector team who
  can help you to find somewhere to live'.

13.16   In many cases the approach is not recorded or is recorded as a simple
housing inquiry. It is unlawful and amounts to maladministration
for an authority to refuse to accept a homeless application for such
reasons.[11] However, it is often difficult to prove that the authority had

11 See the Ombudsman special report referred to at para 13.10 above. Also,
the report of the complaint against Thurrock Council: 05/ A/09461: three
approaches were made by a woman who was clearly homeless and in
priority need. No proper inquiries were undertaken or decision made. The

evidence sufficient to trigger the duty to commence inquiries under HA 1996 Part VII. Advisers may therefore find it useful to ensure that a letter is sent or taken by the applicant summarising the situation and making clear that the person wishes to make an application under Part VII. See the appendix to this chapter for an example of such a letter.

The law on applications and the duty to make inquiries

13.17   HA 1996 ss183 and 184 provide that:

> ... where a person applies to a local housing authority for accommodation, or for assistance in obtaining accommodation, and the authority have reason to believe that he is or may be homeless or threatened with homelessness ... they shall make such enquiries as are necessary to satisfy themselves – whether he is eligible for assistance, and if so, whether any duty, and if so, what duty, is owed to him under [HA 1996 Part VII].

13.18   The duty to make inquiries under HA 1996 Part VII should therefore be triggered not only when a person specifically indicates a wish to make a homeless application, but whenever a person seeks help with housing, provided the authority has *reason to believe* that the applicant *may be* homeless or threatened with homelessness.[12]

13.19   Authorities must also ensure that emergency assistance is available to applicants out of office hours. This may be by arrangement with social services or sometimes the local police, who may arrange emergency accommodation until a formal application can be taken.[13]

13.20   A refusal to accept an application may be challenged by judicial review. See paras 2.4–2.39.

Restrictions on who can apply

13.21   Under HA 1996 Part VII there is no restriction on who can make an application. However, the courts have considered arguments that local authorities are not bound to accept applications from the following:

- people in the UK unlawfully;

Ombudsman found injustice caused by maladministration and recommended compensation of £2,250. See also the report into a complaint against Hammersmith & Fulham LBC, 09001262, published in January 2010.

12   See 2006 Code of Guidance, paras 6.2 and 6.5 and *Bury MBC v Gibbons* [2010] EWCA Civ 327, 26 March 2010.
13   2006 Code of Guidance, para 6.8.

- dependent children; and
- people lacking mental capacity.

13.22　In *R on the application of Westminster v Castelli and Tristan-Garcia*[14] the Court of Appeal held that an authority was not bound to accept an application from a person in the UK unlawfully. Now the eligibility test excludes such people from assistance. However, an applicant found to be ineligible still has the right to a decision letter giving reasons and can challenge the decision by statutory review and, if appropriate, by county court appeal.

13.23　Applications by two children, each aged four, were considered by the House of Lords in *R v Oldham ex p Garlick* and *R v Bexley LBC ex p Bentum*.[15] The applications were submitted on behalf of the children because the parents had been found intentionally homeless. The House of Lords held that the authorities owed no duty. However, this was not because an applicant must be an adult but it was held that dependent children had no priority need in their own right: it was presumed that they were cared for by adults and it was the adults with whom they lived who had priority need.

13.24　While the House of Lords in *R v Oldham ex p Garlick and R v Bexley LBC ex p Bentum* held that the homeless duty was intended for those who could decide whether or not to accept an offer of accommodation, and not for dependent children, it was acknowledged that the situation would be different where the children had left home and ceased to be dependent. Subsequently, the Priority Need Order came into force which specifically provides that certain 16- and 17-year-olds have priority need, although in most cases the duty to accommodate will fall on social service, see paras 14.101–14.107 and 19.37–19.39.

In *R v Tower Hamlets ex p Begum*[16] an application was submitted on behalf of a profoundly disabled adult whose parents had been found intentionally homeless.

The House of Lords held that an authority was entitled to refuse an application from someone who lacked the capacity to make the application herself, to instruct an agent to do so or to respond to an offer and understand the responsibilities of being a tenant.

14　(1996) 28 HLR 607, CA.

15　[1993] AC 509; (1993) 25 HLR 319, HL. The case was recently followed by the High Court in *R (MT) v Oxofrd City Council* [2015] 6 March 2015. The court rejected the argument that such an approach, in relation to a disabled person, was incompatible with ECHR.

16　[1993] AC 509; (1993) 25 HLR 319, HL.

Again, if such a person was in need of accommodation, social services would owe a duty, but this may not extend to the whole family.[17]

Multiple applications

13.25 It is possible for a person to apply to more than one authority at the same time. The 2006 Homelessness Code, at para 6.7, suggests that authorities should agree which authority will take responsibility for making inquiries. In reality, most authorities will indicate that only one application can be pursued and that an application will be closed unless the other is withdrawn. This approach may be challenged, although it is difficult to see any benefit to pursuing more than one application simultaneously.

13.26 The issues that arise when an application is made following a negative decision, or where an authority has discharged its duty are dealt with below at paras 13.59–13.76.

Accommodation pending inquiries

13.27 An authority should accept an application if it has 'reason to believe' that a person 'may be' homeless and eligible. It must then go on to make full inquiries to 'satisfy' itself of the necessary matters to decide what duty, if any, is owed. In most cases, the necessary inquiries will take several days at least, more often weeks or months. The 2006 Homelessness Code recommends that inquiries be completed within 33 working days.[18] However, where the authority is seeking information from third parties they may take longer. In most cases authorities will have a duty to provide 'interim accommodation' until they have completed their inquiries. This duty is referred to as the 'section 188 duty'.

Accommodation duty: HA 1996 s188

13.28 Housing Act 1996 s188(1) provides:

> If the local housing authority have reason to believe that an applicant may be homeless, eligible for assistance and have a priority need, they shall secure that accommodation is available for his occupation pending a decision on the duty (if any) owed to him under [Part VII].

17 National Assistance Act 1948 s21 See paras 18.14–18.16.
18 2006 Code of Guidance, para 6.16.

13.29   The key features of the section 188 duty are:

- the duty to provide interim accommodation is triggered by a low level of 'evidence': whenever the authority have reason to believe the applicant may be homeless, eligible and in priority need: s188(1);
- the duty arises immediately and there is no 'reasonable period' for a local authority to find accommodation;
- the duty arises irrespective of any possible referral to another local authority: s188(2);
- the duty ends when the applicant is notified of a decision: s188(3);
- the authority has a discretion to provide interim accommodation pending a review of a negative decision: s188(3);
- the accommodation must be provided for the applicant and the family members he or she normally lives with, and for anyone who might reasonably be expected to live with the applicant: s176;
- the accommodation must be suitable: s206;
- if the authority decides that no housing duty is owed, the applicants may be evicted from the interim accommodation without a court order, see para 8.18;
- if the applicant is being evicted from a 'private rented sector offer' (see paras 16.28–16.36) within two years the interim accommodation duty arises even if the person has no priority need: s188(1A).

Common issues in relation to interim accommodation

Avoiding the section 188 duty

13.30   The Act is clear: applicants with apparent priority need should not remain homeless pending a decision. However, the cost of providing interim accommodation is such that many authorities seek to avoid doing so. This is often done in one of the following ways.

Refusing to admit that a homeless application was made

13.31   This can be challenged by ensuring that the local authority has sufficient evidence such that the duty to inquire and to provide interim accommodation arises, ie reason to believe that the person may be homeless, eligible and in priority need. A letter summarising the person's situation should be sufficient (see appendix to this chapter).

Arguing that there is no evidence that the person is homeless or in priority need

13.32　If the authority is saying that it has satisfied itself of these issues, a decision letter should be requested. If the authority is unable to provide a decision letter, or indicates that its inquiries are not complete, this itself indicates that the interim duty to accommodate is owed.

13.33　　An example of a letter to a local authority regarding the section 188 duty is in the appendix to this chapter.

13.34　　In both cases, if the authority maintains its refusal to provide interim accommodation, a claim for judicial review can be made.

Cursory inquiries for 'non-priority need' applicants

13.35　Where an authority is of the view that an applicant is unlikely to be found to have a priority need, they may purport to reach a decision without carrying out full inquiries. This approach is illustrated in the recent case of *IA*:

> In *R (IA) v Westminster CC*[19] the claimant was a refugee who had been imprisoned in Iran and subjected to mental and physical torture in 2005. He lived alone in Westminster in private rented accommodation. Because of the changes to Local Housing Allowance payments his housing benefit was to be capped and his landlord informed him that he would be evicted because of this. He visited the council's Housing Options Service office on 8 November 2012 to enquire about possible homeless assistance. He was told that he would be unlikely to have a priority need for accommodation and therefore there would be no duty to rehouse him. He was offered no further assistance save for an information pack explaining the options for someone in his position.
>
> In anticipation of his imminent homelessness he went to see his GP and a medical report was provided describing his depression and panic attacks, insomnia and back and leg pains and listed his current medication.
>
> He received a possession notice to take effect on 4 April 2013 and on 7 March 2013 he visited the same office he had previously visited to make a homeless application. He was immediately given an interview which took approximately one hour. The interviewer

19　[2013] EWHC 1273, 20 May 2013. The case is about interim relief and permission to appeal so ordinarily would not be a binding authority but the court gave a direction that because of the 'importance and topicality' of the case, it could be cited as an authority.

took a copy of the medical report and asked a number of questions. At the end of the interview she printed off, signed and handed to him a written decision under section 184 of HA 1996. She had typed up the letter during the interview. The claimant said that she had not interrupted the interview at any time to speak to anyone else by telephone or by leaving the room. The decision was that the claimant did not have a priority need. He requested a review through a solicitor and the council was asked to provide interim accommodation pending review.

The council refused to exercise its discretion to provide interim accommodation and a claim for judicial review was started. An urgent 'without notice' order was made that the council provide interim accommodation. A hearing took place to consider an extension of the interim accommodation and permission to bring the claim for judicial review. The judicial review challenged: the purported section 184 decision on the basis that it was neither a section 184 decision or a lawful decision; the failure to comply with the section 188(1) duty to accommodate pending a lawful section 184 decision; and, the decision not to secure interim accommodation pending review.

The court found that the council had started and completed its enquiries into the homeless application within an hour or so of the claimant arriving at the office, the inquiries consisted of no more than a face-to-face interview with the housing caseworker during which she typed out the non-standard parts of the decision letter. She did not, or at least did not appear to the claimant to, communicate with anyone else during the interview. She had a copy of the claimant's GP's letter medical report which she referred to in her decision. The decision letter that she printed out and handed to the claimant at the conclusion of the interview was based on what the claimant has told her during the interview and the brief contents of the GP's report. However, it also stated 'We sought advice from our in-house medical adviser regarding your health problems. She told us that you do not appear to be on any combination of medications that we would normally associate with someone who has a severe or unstable mental health issue ... She noted that you have long-standing depression. This suggests that the depression is manageable and would continue to be manageable if you were to become homeless.'

The judicial review pre-action protocol letter had been answered by the Housing Options Service Manager on the same day, 12 April

2013. In response to the claim that the council had failed to take into consideration new information, particularly in relation to suicidal feelings it was stated:

'In particular you refer to your client mentioning to your firm that he is feeling suicidal. In our letter dated 5 April 2013 we attributed these thoughts to the circumstances rather than his mental health. As stated in your letter we are in agreement that [IA] has mental health issues, but there is no evidence to suggest that his mental illness is the cause of his present thoughts regarding harm. No definitive evidence has been presented to support the idea that [IA's] thoughts of harm are attributed to mental illness.'

The court held that: 'Given that the [GP] report attributed [his difficulties in coping] directly to his long-term depression, panic attacks, low moods, insomnia, chronic back pain and leg pains which affected his mobility and that he had suffered torture in his home country as recently as 2005 prior to his arrival as an asylum-seeker in England, it seems irrational and, indeed, perverse for the defendant to conclude that there was no reason to believe that the claimant was vulnerable and in priority need and to screen him out of the section 184 inquiries that it had otherwise had a duty to undertake. It follows that the claimant has a highly arguable case demonstrating that no section 184 enquiry was ever conducted and that, conversely, the inquiry was screened out by the adverse screening decision taken on 7 March 2013.'[20]

In relation to the refusal of interim accommodation pending review, additional information had been provided by the claimant's solicitors relating to a possible deterioration of his mental health, his inability to cope with homelessness and the fact that he had received news from his home country that five of his friends had been sentenced to death. Further details were also provided as to his loneliness, his lack of any support and the debilitating nature and effects of the depression, physical disabilities, insomnia and other similar factors.

The judge held: 'None of this additional information had been assessed by appropriate inquiries and the most distressing of these details were dismissed in somewhat cavalier and speculative fashion by the Team Leader and, subsequently, by the Housing Options Service Manager. It followed that, in the light of the original apparently flawed section 184 decision, the *Pereira* decision taken

20 HHJ Anthony Thornton at [26]–[27].

by the defendant in refusing the claimant interim accommodation pending a review of his case was highly arguably flawed since it made no assessment of the merits of the claimant's case that he was vulnerable on mental health and other grounds, it failed to take account of the caseworker's failure to make any enquiries when reaching the section 188 [sic] decision, it did not assess or inquire into the new material submitted by the claimant's solicitors and it overlooked or dismissed peremptorily the claimant's personal circumstances.'[21]

Suitability of interim accommodation

13.36 Interim accommodation must be suitable and it is expressly provided that to be suitable, accommodation must be affordable.[22]

13.37 It is for the local authority to decide what is suitable and the temporary nature of the accommodation will be relevant: accommodation that is suitable for short-term occupation may not be suitable in the longer term. The limited resources of an authority may mean that accommodation secured for short-term occupation may of a low standard. However, there is a 'bottom line', below which the accommodation could not be said to be suitable, however constrained resources are: see *R on the application of Sacupima v Newham LBC*.[23]

13.38 Any challenge to the suitability of interim accommodation must be brought by way of judicial review. Given the pressure on resources the courts are reluctant to interfere with local authority decisions as to the suitability of s188 accommodation. Set out below are a number of cases in which the issue has been considered.

Location

In *R (Sacupima) v Newham LBC*[24] a decision to provide section 188 accommodation in the Great Yarmouth area to a family settled in Newham was quashed. The authority had failed to have regard to the effect on the children's schooling and the employment of other family members.

---

21 HHJ Anthony Thornton [33].
22 Homelessness (Suitability of Accommodation) Order 1996 SI No 3204. Also, when assessing suitability the authority must have regard to the law on slum clearance, overcrowding and houses in multiple occupation: HA 1996 s210.
23 (2000) 33 HLR 1, CA, see para 13.37.
24 (2000) 33 HLR 1, CA.

In *R (Yumsak) v Enfield LBC*[25] the court upheld the challenge to an offer of section 188 accommodation. The applicant was a single parent who had lived as an asylum-seeker in Enfield for seven years with her three children in accommodation provided by social services. After being granted leave to remain in the UK, she applied as homeless and was provided with bed & breakfast accommodation in Birmingham. She contended that the accommodation was unsuitable as she suffered from epilepsy, had no friends or family in Birmingham and her children's schooling would be disrupted. Furthermore, the children's father was based in London and was keen to maintain contact with the children. The court held that there was an interference with the applicant's rights under ECHR article 8 and the authority had failed to provide any evidence to demonstrate that no other accommodation was available or to justify the interference.

As noted at para 16.57, London authorities in particular are now using out of borough accommodation regularly and in *TN v City of Westminster*,[26] see para 16.58, accommodation was offered to a family with five children in Bletchley, some 50 miles from their previous home. The Supreme Court upheld the challenge: the accommodation was not suitable because of the location. The judgment giving reasons is pending at the time of writing.

Split accommodation

In *R v Ealing LBC ex p Surdonja*[27] the authority made an offer of section 188 accommodation to a family comprising a couple and their three young children. The accommodation was at two separate addresses less than a mile apart. The court held that the accommodation was not suitable: section 176 requires that accommodation must be available for the applicant and those family members who normally live with the applicant.[28]

---

25   [2002] EWHC 280 (Admin).

26   3 UKSC 2014/0275, hearing: 17 March 2015.

27   (1998) 31 HLR 686.

28   But see *Sharif v Camden* [2013] UKSC 10, 20 February 2013, at para 14.12: accommodation need not be in a single unit. Accommodation provided in two flats in the same corridor of a hostel was held to be accommodation available to the whole family.

Size

In *R (Flash) v Southwark LBC*[29] the applicant challenged the suitability of a one-bedroom flat provided for her and her grandson on the ground that it was too small. The court held that the offer was suitable: the grandson could sleep in the living room.

Bed & breakfast accommodation

13.39   Bed & breakfast (B&B) accommodation is commonly used as interim accommodation. However, the 2006 Code of Guidance para 7.6 provides:

> Housing authorities should avoid using Bed & Breakfast (B&B) accommodation wherever possible. Where B&B accommodation has been used in an emergency situation, applicants should be moved to more suitable accommodation as soon as possible. The Homelessness (Suitability of Accommodation) (England) Order 2003 provides that B&B accommodation is not suitable accommodation for families with children and households that include a pregnant woman unless there is no alternative accommodation available and then only for a maximum of six weeks.

13.40   The 2006 Code of Guidance and the April 2010 Guidance issued by the Department for Children, Schools and Families[30] both state that bed and breakfast accommodation is not appropriate for homeless 16- and 17-year-olds.

13.41   Despite this guidance the government's homelessness statistics showed that on 30 June 2014 there were 2,130 families with children in bed and breakfast accommodation with 30 per cent having been there for longer than six weeks. And, on the same date there were 60 cases in which 16- and 17-year-olds were in bed and breakfast accommodation.

Refusal of offers made under section 188

13.42   The nature of the interim duty means that an applicant rarely has the opportunity to view accommodation or take advice if he or she believes it to be unsuitable. An applicant may be sent to the accommodation late in the evening and it may be some distance away. An

---

29 [2004] EWHC 717 (Admin).
30 Statutory Guidance on the provision of accommodation for 16- and 17-year-olds.

applicant may fail to get to the accommodation or refuse the offer. Alternatively, an applicant may move into the accommodation but be evicted because of his or her conduct.

13.43   In such a situation two issues arise:

- whether the authority has any further duty to make interim accommodation available; and
- the authority's duty to continue its inquiries into the homeless application.

Continuation of the section 188 duty

13.44   If an applicant has refused an offer of interim accommodation, a decision must be made as to whether the decision on suitability can be challenged. As indicated, accommodation may be suitable for very short-term occupation but not suitable in the longer term. Because of this, successful challenges to the suitability of interim accommodation are rare. Applicants may be best advised to tell the authority that, having taken advice, they now wish to accept the accommodation. The section 188 duty is not like the full housing duty: there is no express provision that the duty ends because of a failure to accept an offer. It may be argued that the applicant misunderstood the nature of the offer or did not intend to refuse it. An authority that adopts a rigid approach, maintaining that the duty has ended because of the failure to take up the offer may be challenged by way of judicial review.

13.45   Where an applicant is evicted from interim accommodation because of his or her behaviour, an authority may indicate that it has no further section 188 duty. There is no authoritative case-law on this issue but the Court of Appeal has considered it in relation to accommodation offered under the National Assistance Act (NAA) 1948 s21.[31]

In *R v Kensington and Chelsea RLBC ex p Kujtim*[32] an asylum-seeker was provided with hotel accommodation by the authority under NAA 1948. He was evicted from two hotels because of his behaviour.

The Court of Appeal held that the duty under NAA 1948 s21 was a continuing duty: once a person had been assessed as needing accommodation, the authority was under a duty to provide it.

31 See para 18.15 for an explanation of the duties under NAA 1948.
32 (1999) 32 HLR 579.

However:

... if an applicant assessed as in need of ... accommodation [under section 21] either unreasonably refuses to accept the accommodation provided, or if, following its provision, by his conduct he manifests a persistent and unequivocal refusal to observe the reasonable requirements of the local authority in relation to the occupation of such accommodation then the local authority is entitled to treat its duty as discharged and to refuse to provide further accommodation. That will remain the position unless or until, upon some subsequent application, the applicant can satisfy the local authority that his needs remain such as to justify provision of ... accommodation and that there is no longer reason to think that he will persist in his refusal to observe the reasonable requirements of the local authority in respect of the provision of such accommodation.[33]

13.46 Note that the court held that the section 21 duty was discharged by a 'persistent and unequivocal refusal to observe reasonable requirements' but that the duty may be revived if the applicant can satisfy the authority that he or she will no longer persist in the behaviour complained of.

Continuation of the duty to inquire into homeless application

13.47 Even if an applicant refuses section 188 accommodation unequivocally, this does not mean the authority can treat the homeless application as withdrawn or closed. The authority must still complete its inquiries and issue a decision. However, a refusal of section 188 accommodation may have an adverse effect on the outcome of the inquiries, for example, if an applicant chooses to remain in accommodation which he or she was previously told to leave or which it is argued is unreasonable for continued occupation.

13.48 However, some authorities encourage applicants to remain in their current accommodation by accepting a 'homeless at home' application. In such cases advisers must ensure that the authority proceeds to make a decision on the housing duty and, if a duty is owed, makes an offer of suitable accommodation without delay.[34]

33 Potter LJ at 593.
34 See, however, *Birmingham CC v Ali* [2009] UKHL 36, see para 16.44 below.

Homeless inquiries

13.49   The triggering of the duty to inquire is dealt with above (paras 13.17–13.20). To decide what, if any, housing duty is owed, the authority must satisfy itself that the relevant tests are met: homelessness, eligibility, priority need and unintentional homelessness. As a general rule, it is the local authority that must make the decision and it cannot be delegated to another person or body. An authority can, however, ask for assistance from another body in the discharge of its functions.[35] Furthermore, it is now possible for an authority to contract out almost all of its functions under HA 1996 Parts VI and VII.[36]

Extent of the inquiries

13.50   The burden is on the authority to make appropriate inquiries to obtain the relevant information. An applicant is not required to prove his or her case, but must co-operate with the authority's inquiries.[37] This will mean agreeing to the authority contacting third parties for information and providing information when required.

13.51   The inquiries should be rigorous, but an authority need not conduct 'CID type' inquiries.[38]

13.52   An authority is not under an obligation to make all necessary inquiries to determine the truth, but can be challenged if it fails to make an inquiry that no reasonable authority could fail to regard as necessary.

> In *R v Nottingham CC ex p Costello*[39] the applicants had left accommodation that was adapted for their disabled son, alleging that it was unsuitable because they were dissatisfied with the modifications. Also, Mr Costello alleged that the property was troubled by a poltergeist. Social services had indicated that Mr Costello blamed his wife for the visitations and believed that they

---

35 See HA 1996 s213; *R v West Dorset HA ex p Gerrard* (1994) 27 HLR 150, QBD and *R v Hertsmere BC ex p Woolgar* (1995) 27 HLR 703, QBD.

36 Local Authorities (Contracting Out of Allocation of Housing and Homelessness Functions) Order 1996 SI No 3205.

37 See 2006 Code of Guidance, para 6.15, and *R v Woodspring DC ex p Walters* (1984) 16 HLR 73, QBD. This point was re-iterated in the case of *R (IA) v Westminster CC* [2013] EWHC 1273, 20 May 2013, see para 13.35 above.

38 *Lally v Kensington and Chelsea RLBC* (1980) *Times* 27 March, QBD.

39 (1989) 21 HLR 301, QBD.

would occur wherever she was present. He denied having said this. The applicants challenged the decision that they were intentionally homeless on the ground that the authority had failed to make adequate inquiries of Mr Costello regarding his beliefs about the poltergeist.

This was rejected, the court holding that:

> The duty to make necessary enquiries is not a duty to make all enquiries in fact necessary before the truth is ascertained. A council which makes numerous enquiries can, in my judgment, only be attacked for failing to make one more, if it fails to make an enquiry which no reasonable council could have failed to regard as necessary.[40]

13.53   Nevertheless, if it is found that an authority has carried out inadequate inquiries, its decision will be unlawful (see para 2.11).

13.54   An alleged failure to inquire into relevant matters may be corrected during the review process. The general rule is that any complaint about inadequacy of inquiries must be raised at the review stage and an applicant may be prevented from arguing at an appeal matters which were not put to the authority on review.

In *Cramp v Hastings BC* and *Phillips v Camden LBC*[41] the applicants challenged decisions that they were not in priority need. In the county court appeals they argued that the decisions were flawed because of failures to make sufficient inquiries. However, this point had not been made in the representations submitted as part of the reviews. The Court of Appeal held that it was not appropriate to interfere with the local authorities' decisions that the applicants were not in priority need:

> Given the full-scale nature of the review, a court whose powers are limited to considering points of law should now be even more hesitant [than before the right of review was introduced] if the applicant's ground of appeal relates to a matter which the reviewing officer was never invited to consider, and which was not an obvious matter he should have considered.[42]

---

40 Schiemann J at 309.
41 [2005] EWCA Civ 1005, 29 July 2005.
42 [2005] EWCA Civ 1005, Brooke LJ at [14].

13.55   However, there are exceptions to this general rule. For example, in *R (Pieretti) v Enfield LBC*[43] the Court of Appeal held that where an authority had breached its disability equality duty when making inquiries about the cause of homelessness, the fact that this argument was not raised in the review did not prevent it being a ground of appeal in the County Court. See para 2.90 for details of the case. Similarly, an authority has a clear, freestanding duty to take into account the issue of affordability when assessing the suitability of accommodation; the County Court may still take account of a failure to do so even if the issue was not raised in the review.[44]

Fairness

13.56   The inquiries must be carried out fairly and interviews conducted in a sympathetic way, but this does not preclude asking searching questions in appropriate cases.[45]

13.57   Where an authority intends to take account of information adverse to the applicant, it should give the applicant the opportunity to comment on the information.[46] An authority cannot take account of information obtained in confidence if it is not able to disclose it to the applicant and obtain the applicant's comments.[47]

13.58   If, following inquiries, the authority is undecided, the issue should be resolved in favour of the applicant.[48]

Repeat applications

13.59   Often, following a negative decision, or where a housing duty has ended, the applicant remains homeless. Several issues arise: the circumstances in which an applicant can apply again to the same authority; whether another member of the household can make an application; and whether an application can be made to a different authority.

---

43   [2010] EWCA Civ 1104, 12 October 2010.

44   See *Odunsi v Brent LBC* [1999] CLY 3063, Willesdon County Court, 25 February 1999.

45   *R v Tower Hamlets LBC ex p Khatun* (1994) 27 HLR 465, CA.

46   *R v Tower Hamlets LBC ex p Rouf* (1989) 21 HLR 294.

47   *R v Poole BC ex p Cooper* (1994) 27 HLR 605, QBD.

48   *R v North Devon DC ex p Lewis* [1981] 1 WLR 328, QBD and *R v Thurrock BC ex p Williams* (1981) 1 HLR 129, QBD.

Same applicant applying to same authority

13.60 If the applicant was found to be not homeless, not eligible or not in priority need, it may be that there is a change of circumstances which means that a fresh application may be made. For example, a person may be evicted from accommodation, having previously argued that it was not reasonable to occupy the accommodation; a woman found to have no priority need on health grounds may become pregnant; a previously ineligible person may be granted leave to remain in the UK. Clearly, in such cases a fresh application can be made.

13.61 The issue will be less clear where the change of circumstances is one of degree: a person found not to be in priority need may claim that a medical condition has worsened or that he or she has obtained a new medical report. A person found not to be homeless on the basis of the condition of accommodation may claim that the conditions have deteriorated. An example of such a case is *Gardiner v Haringey LBC*,[49] at para 13.66 below.

13.62 The issue also arises when the authority has found that an applicant is intentionally homeless or decided that the HA 1996 section 193 duty has come to an end because an offer of suitable accommodation has been refused.

13.63 The combined effect of HA 1996 ss183 and 184 and s193(9) suggest that there is nothing to prevent such a person from making a further application to the authority, which will be bound to carry out full inquiries and offer interim accommodation pending a decision. Not surprisingly, the issue has been considered by the courts on a number of occasions.

13.64 The question is whether the authority is required, in every case, to go through the whole statutory inquiry process. Alternatively, is there a 'threshold test' which the authority can apply before deciding whether it is under a duty to undertake full inquiries? If so, what is the threshold test?

In *R v Harrow LBC ex p Fahia*[50] the court considered a second application made by a woman previously found to be intentionally homeless by the same authority. Since the first decision, she had remained in the accommodation previously provided as interim accommodation, successfully applying for housing benefit to be paid. After 12 months she was evicted and made a fresh application

49 [2009] EWHC 2699 (Admin), 30 October 2009.
50 [1998] 1 WLR 1396; (1998) 30 HLR 1124, HL.

to the authority. The authority declined to accept the application on the basis that she had not had settled accommodation since the decision. Following a number of previously decided cases, it maintained that a fresh application would only be considered if there had been a 'material change of circumstances' or some new relevant fact had come to light.

The House of Lords held that this was the wrong approach. Where a person has been found intentionally homeless, he or she cannot make a further application 'based on exactly the same facts as [the] earlier application' but such cases are 'very special cases' where it can be said that there is no application before the authority.[51] Harrow LBC had argued that it was entitled to make 'non-statutory inquires' before deciding whether it was under a duty to take a fresh application. This was rejected: there is no such short-cut available to the authority. Unless the application was based on exactly the same facts, the authority was bound to make inquiries under HA 1996 s184 and to provide interim accommodation under section 188 until a decision was made.

13.65   *Fahia* suggested that there *was* a threshold test: whether the application was based on exactly the same facts as the previous application. Having specifically excluded the possibility of 'non-statutory' inquiries, however, this left open the question of how an authority could decide whether the application was based on the same facts without making some inquiry.

13.66   This issue was considered by the Court of Appeal in *Rikha Begum v Tower Hamlets LBC*.[52]

In *Rikha Begum* the applicant had rejected a suitable offer of accommodation made under Part VII. She returned to live with her parents. Subsequently, two of her brothers, one a heroin addict, also moved in. After almost two years she applied to the authority again. The authority declined to accept her application on the basis that there was no material change in her circumstances since the authority had discharged its duty on the previous application.

Following *Fahia*, the court held that the authority had applied the wrong test: there was no requirement that the applicant demonstrate a material change of circumstances. Rather, an

---

51 Lord Browne-Wilkinson at 1402D–E.
52 [2005] EWCA Civ 340.

authority may only treat a fresh application as 'no application at all' if it is based on exactly the same facts as the previous application. The court went on to consider how an authority should determine the issue, setting out the following principles:

- in deciding whether an application is based on the same facts, the authority must compare the facts at the date of the subsequent application with the facts known at the date of the previous determination (ie the section 184 decision or decision on review, not at the date of the application);
- it is the applicant's responsibility to identify which facts make the application different from those at the date of the previous determination;
- if no new facts are revealed or if the facts are, to the authority's knowledge, not new or are fanciful or trivial, the authority should reject the application;
- if the new facts are not within the authority's knowledge and are not, in light of the information known to them, fanciful or trivial, the authority must accept a new application;
- it is not open to the authority to investigate the accuracy of the new facts before deciding whether to accept a new application.

This test was applied in *Gardiner v Haringey LBC*.[53] The applicant, who was a British national, had been found not to be homeless because she had accommodation in Colombia. She contended that it was not reasonable for her to occupy the accommodation in Colombia because her daughter was severely disabled and needed special educational provision available in the UK but not in Colombia. While the council accepted that the provision in the UK was better than that in Colombia it did not accept that this meant it was not reasonable for the family to live in the accommodation in Colombia. The applicant was unsuccessful in the review and county court appeal and had applied for permission to appeal further to the Court of Appeal. Having obtained new medical reports on the progress the girl had made since receiving the special educational provision in the UK, a fresh application was made. The council refused to investigate the fresh application, claiming it was based on the same facts as the previous application.

---

53 [2009] EWHC 2699 (Admin), 30 October 2009.

> The applicant's judicial review of the decision was successful. The court held that it was not enough that the council had already made a decision that the provision in Colombia was inferior to that in the UK:
>
> ... the extent of the difference and the impact of that difference upon [the child] would be important factual matters in determining the question of reasonableness [to occupy the Colombia property] ... I am unable to accept the Council's submission that they did not need to look beyond whether Colombian facilities were better or worse than those available here.[54]

13.67   Note that whether an application is accepted and investigated is distinct from the question of whether any duty will be owed. In *Rikha Begum* it was specifically suggested that the likely outcome of the application would be a decision that no housing duty was owed.

Applications by other household members

13.68   Where a decision has been made that no duty is owed to an applicant, can another member of the household make an application in his or her name? This will depend on the reason for the decision that no duty is owed.

13.69   If the issue is intentional homelessness, another member of the household may apply to the authority. The authority cannot refuse to accept the application on the basis of the previous decision: each individual is entitled to individual consideration. The authority may, however, decide that the applicant is also intentionally homeless, having acquiesced in the decision or behaviour that caused the homelessness, see para 14.145.

13.70   The Court of Appeal held in *R v Camden LBC ex p Hersi*[55] that an adult daughter who had been unaware of her mother's refusal of an offer could not re-apply on behalf of the household. At best she could apply for housing as a single person. However, in that case the daughter had no priority need because the children in the household were not dependent on her. Had she had a priority need in her own right the outcome is likely to have been different.

---

54   [2009] EWHC 2699 (Admin), at [22].
55   (2001) 33 HLR 52, QBD.

Applying to another authority

13.71 There is nothing to prevent a person refused assistance by one authority from applying to a different authority. The outcome will depend on two things:

- whether the applicant can be referred, under the local connection provisions, back to the first authority; and
- the reason why no duty is owed by the first authority.

No local connection referral possible

13.72 If the applicant has been refused because he or she failed one of the substantive tests, the second authority cannot simply adopt the findings of the first authority.[56] It must make its own decision. Usually, however, the second authority will obtain information from the first authority and is likely to make the same decision. While carrying out the inquiries, interim accommodation must be provided if there is reason to believe the applicant is homeless, eligible and has priority need.

13.73 If the applicant is homeless because the HA 1996 section 193 duty owed by the first authority has ended, the second authority must consider the application, but, given the circumstances in which the duty ends, it is likely that the second authority will have no housing duty: if the person has refused an offer of accommodation or been evicted from the section 193 accommodation he or she is likely to be found to be intentionally homeless by the second authority.

13.74 If the authority makes a different decision from the first authority on a substantive issue (for example, priority need or intentional homelessness), the second authority may owe the full housing duty.

Local connection referral possible

13.75 Again, if the applicant was refused assistance by the first authority because of failing one of the substantive tests, the second authority must consider the application and make its own decision. An authority that knows that the full housing duty will be owed by a different authority may be less rigorous in its inquiries. The second authority may find the person to be in priority need or not intentionally homeless even though the first authority had decided otherwise. Unless the first authority can challenge the decision by way of judicial review, it

---

56 *R v Newham LBC ex p Khan and Hussain* (2000) 33 HLR 29, QBD.

will be under a duty to accept a referral and will owe the full housing duty.[57]

13.76   However, if a section 193 duty owed by the first authority has ended (for example, because of the refusal of an offer) the first authority can refuse to accept the full housing duty following a local connection referral on the basis that it has already discharged its duty to the applicant. In that instance, a duty will be owed by neither authority.

Miscellaneous duties

Duties to particular applicants

Threatened homelessness

13.77   Local authorities also have duties to those who are 'threatened with homelessness'. A person is threatened with homelessness if he or she is likely to become homeless within 28 days.[58]

13.78   If the authority is satisfied that a person is eligible, has a priority need and is not threatened with homelessness intentionally, the duty is to 'take reasonable steps to secure that accommodation does not cease to be available for [the applicant's] occupation'.[59]

13.79   If the authority is not satisfied that the applicant has a priority need, or is satisfied that the applicant is threatened with homelessness intentionally, the duty is to provide the applicant with advice and assistance in any attempts he or she makes to secure that the accommodation does not cease to be available. Alternatively, it may refer the applicant to another agency for such advice and assistance.[60]

13.80   In practice, local authorities rarely make full inquiries or issue decision letters at the stage when a person is threatened with homelessness. Assistance will usually be given by the authority's housing advisory services or by voluntary agencies acting in cooperation with the authority. Strictly, the duty does not arise unless homelessness is likely within 28 days. However, where there is a chance of avoiding homelessness, for example by negotiating with a landlord or helping to resolve housing benefit problems, any effective homeless prevention service will offer assistance at an early stage.

---

57 See *R v Newham LBC ex p Tower Hamlets LBC* [1992] 2 All ER 767, see para 14.328.

58 HA 1996 s175(4).

59 HA 1996 s195(2).

60 HA 1996 s195(5).

13.81   The duty is most relevant when a person is certain to become homeless but the date of actual eviction is not imminent. In such cases most authorities will advise a person to return nearer to or on the date of eviction. The specific duty to begin the inquiry process in relation to a particular applicant does not arise until the date of anticipated homelessness is within 28 days. Within the 28-day period, steps should be taken by the authority to identify suitable accommodation.[61]

13.82   However, if the person is being evicted from accommodation provided under s193 as a 'private rented sector offer' within two years (see paras 16.28–16.36) the position is different. In such a case when the person receives a valid section 21 notice, he or she must be treated as threatened with homelessness from the date the notice is issued and as homeless from the date the notice expires.[62]

13.83   Local authorities also have general duties regarding the provision of advice and assistance (see para 13.88) and in relation to the prevention of homelessness and those services will be available to an applicant even if a specific duty has not yet arisen.

Protection of property

13.84   A local authority has a duty in relation to the property of a homeless applicant, where the authority:

> ... have reason to believe that –
> (a) there is a danger of loss of, or damage to, any personal property of an applicant by reason of his inability to protect it or deal with it, and
> (b) no other suitable arrangements have been or are being made.[63]

13.85   The duty is to 'take reasonable steps to prevent the loss of the property or mitigate damage to it'.[64] The authority may make 'reasonable charges' and may specify conditions regarding the disposal of the property, for example if charges are not paid or the belongings are not collected.[65] In most cases when an applicant is in receipt of means-tested benefit, no charge or minimal charges will be made. However, the full cost of the storage of belongings may be charged to an applicant with sufficient means to pay.

---

61 *R v Newham LBC ex p Khan and Hussain* (2000) 33 HLR 29, QBD.
62 HA 1996 s195A(2) and (4) and paras 37–39 of the 2012 Supplementary Guidance. See para 16.35.
63 HA 1996 s211(1).
64 HA 1996 s211(2).
65 HA 1996 s211(4).

Liaison with social services – children

13.86   Where a local authority has reason to believe that an eligible applicant whose household includes a dependent child may be intentionally homeless, or threatened with homelessness intentionally, it must
ask the applicant for consent to refer the case to the relevant social
services department. If consent is given, the case must be referred to
the social services department to consider exercising its powers and
duties under the Children Act (CA) 1989.[66]

13.87   Local authorities may give financial assistance to such a family
under CA 1989 s17 to help them to secure private sector accommodation. However, such assistance is discretionary and many authorities
will instead offer assistance by way of taking the children into care.
See chapter 19 and particularly paras 19.9–19.12 for an explanation
of social services' duties under CA 1989.

Advice and assistance

13.88   Local authorities have a specific duty to provide advice and assistance
to applicants who are not in priority need and to those found intentionally homeless. In both cases the advice and assistance must be
tailored to the needs of the applicant:[67]

- the authority must provide the applicant with advice and assistance in any attempts he or she makes to find accommodation (or
  must ensure that others do so);
- the applicant's housing needs must be addressed before advice
  and assistance is given; and
- the advice and assistance must include information about the
  likely availability of types of accommodation appropriate to the
  person's housing needs (including in particular, the location and
  sources of such types of accommodation).

13.89   Note that under HA 1996 s192(3) an authority has a *power* to secure
accommodation for a person found not to have a priority need. For
someone found to be intentionally homeless there is a duty to provide
temporary accommodation for a reasonable period (see para 16.14).

---

66 HA 1996 s213A.
67 HA 1996 ss190 and 192.

General duties

Advice and information

13.90   Every local authority must ensure that advice and information about homelessness and the prevention of homelessness is available free of charge in their district.[68] An authority may also fund voluntary organisations to provide services to prevent or alleviate homelessness.

Homelessness strategies

13.91   The Homelessness Act 2002 placed on all local housing authorities a duty to formulate and publish a 'homelessness strategy' at least every five years. However, this obligation does not apply to local authorities rated excellent or three or four star authorities under the best value auditing regime established under the Local Government Act 2003.[69]

13.92   The published document must set out the authority's strategy for:[70]

- preventing homelessness;
- ensuring that sufficient accommodation is available for the homeless in the district; and
- securing the satisfactory provision of support for the homeless in the district.

13.93   In exercising its functions (including those under HA 1996 Part VII) the authority must take its homelessness strategy into account.[71]

13.94   Often, an authority's strategy is expressed in expansive terms, in contrast to the restrictive application of HA 1996 Part VII by the authority's homeless persons' department. Being familiar with the authority's strategy may assist in challenging decisions.

> In *R (Omatoyo) v City of Westminster*[72] the applicant was a man with a history of homelessness, drug and substance abuse, offending and prison. He was found not to be in priority need and refused interim accommodation pending review. The council's homelessness strategy indicated that it aimed to reduce the

---

68   HA 1996 s179(1).
69   See Local Authorities' Plans and Strategies (Disapplication) (England) (Amendment) Orders 2005 SI No 157 and 2009 SI No 714.
70   Homelessness Act 2002 s3.
71   Homelessness Act 2002 s1(5).
72   [2006] EWHC 2572 (Admin), 21 September 2006.

numbers of rough sleepers in the district and that it had a target of ensuring that all offenders released on licence were assisted to access appropriate accommodation. Mr Omatoyo applied for permission to bring judicial review proceedings to challenge the decision not to provide interim accommodation.

At the hearing, the court was required to consider the merits of the decision subject to review. One of the factors the judge considered relevant to the lawfulness of the decision was that the authority had failed to take account of its own homelessness strategy. Permission to bring the claim was granted.

13.95   Failing to follow its own policies without good reason will usually make a public body's decision unlawful. Advisers should be aware of all policies and strategies local authorities publish which may impact upon the homelessness duties. For example, in addition to those mentioned in paragraph 13.96 below, authorities must also publish their strategies for tackling anti-social behaviour[73] and their policy for implementing the various equality duties.[74] In addition, they may have adopted policies for dealing with rent arrears and for supporting vulnerable people, see paras 7.170–7.174.

13.96   When formulating or modifying its homelessness strategy an authority must have regard to its current allocation scheme, its current tenancy strategy (under Localism Act 2011 s150) and, in London, the current London housing strategy.[75]

73 Anti-social Behaviour Act 2003 s12.
74 Equality Act 2010 s153 and the Equalities Act 2010 (Specific Duties) Regulations 2011 SI No 2260.
75 Localism Act 2011 s153.

APPENDIX

Homeless application letter

Letter to local authority – homeless applications and interim accommodation

Dear Sir/Madam, Re: Mrs A

We are advising the above named who has made a homeless application to your authority.

[Set out some details about application/dealings with the council]

Mrs A is a British national who has lived in the UK all her life. She is therefore eligible for assistance.

Mrs A is homeless, having been told to leave her sister's accommodation.

Mrs A is pregnant and has a dependent child, aged two years. She is clearly in priority need.

Mrs A first approached your authority on [date] and informed you that she had been asked to leave her sister's accommodation as it is overcrowded. She was advised by an officer at reception that her sister was required to give her written notice. Her sister then gave her seven days' written notice and she returned to your offices on expiry of the notice. She was then advised that she could not be seen until the following week. She was forced to return to her sister's home and her sister reluctantly agreed that she could stay until her appointment with the homeless persons unit.

At the appointment a homeless application form was completed but Mrs A was told that she must remain at her sister's home until a decision had been made. Our client's sister indicated that our client could stay for only two further days.

When our client returned to your offices two days later she was told that the authority did not accept that she was homeless. When we telephoned your office we were told that your authority was of the view that our client could continue to reside with her sister but that any decision must be approved by the manager, who was currently on leave.

[Set out the law]

As your authority is aware, under section 188 of the Housing Act 1996 if you have *reason to believe* that an applicant *may be* homeless you have a duty to carry out inquiries under Part VII of the Act. Further, if you have *reason to believe* that an applicant *may be* eligible and in priority need you have a duty to provide interim accommodation until a decision is notified to our client.

If you are still carrying out inquiries then the duty is to provide interim accommodation until our client is notified of your decision.

If you have concluded your inquiries then our client is entitled to be notified in writing of the decision.

[What you want them to do and by when]

Can you please confirm by close of business today that interim accommodation will be provided to Mrs A until you notify her of your decision on her application. Alternatively, please can you forward to us the decision letter made pursuant to section 184. We enclose our client's signed authority for you to send this to us.

If we do not hear from you by [time and date] we can only assume that you are refusing to provide interim accommodation and/or to issue a decision letter.

We will then advise our client to commence judicial review proceedings/ refer our client to our legal team/a solicitor with a view to a claim for judicial review.

Yours faithfully

Adviser

Advice Agency

[If this letter is being sent by solicitors or an agency able to to provide legal representation the letter should be in the form of a judicial review protocol letter – see chapter 18, appendix 2 for the template. This means that proceedings can be issued immediately if the issue is not resolved by the deadline.]

The homelessness tests

continued

Key points

- A local authority must secure accommodation for homeless people only if satisfied of the matters set out below.

The person is eligible

- Certain people from abroad are 'ineligible'. This includes people who do not have leave to be in the UK or who have leave that is limited. It also includes European nationals with no 'right to reside' in the UK and some people, including British nationals, who are not habitually resident in the UK. If a person is ineligible no housing duty will be owed.

The person is homeless

- A person can be homeless if he or she has accommodation but it is not reasonable to continue to live in it.
- It is not reasonable to live in accommodation if violence is probable.

The person has priority need

- There are several categories of priority need. If a homeless person does not have priority need there is no duty to provide accommodation only a duty to give advice and assistance to help the person find accommodation. Some categories of priority need depend on a finding that a person is 'vulnerable'. Such decisions usually depend on the strength of expert evidence about a person's physical or mental health.

The person is not intentionally homeless

- If a person has caused his or her homelessness by something done or not done deliberately, he or she will usually be intentionally homeless. There are several elements to the test and each element must be addressed. An authority must identify the deliberate act or omission that caused the homelessness.

The person may be referred to another authority

- If a person applies to a local authority where he or she has no local connection, that authority may refer the person to another authority to be housed. This should only be done after all the inquiries have been completed and it has been decided that a housing duty is owed.

- This chapter deals in detail with the homelessness tests save for the 'eligibility test' which is dealt with in chapter 20. The tests are set out in Part VII of the Housing Act 1996.

Eligibility

14.1 In homelessness law 'eligibility' has a specific meaning: it is a test that excludes certain people from abroad from homeless assistance. Similar rules apply to exclude largely the same groups of people from housing allocations and from housing benefit. Chapter 20 describes in detail how the eligibility test works in relation to homelessness, housing allocations and housing benefit entitlement.

14.2 The eligibility test was first introduced in the Housing Act 1996 and is a 'threshold' test: if not met, no further inquiry is necessary and no substantive duties will be owed under Part VII. However, if an authority decides that a person is not eligible for homelessness assistance a 'section 184 decision letter' must be provided setting out the reasons for the decision. In some instances, particularly in relation to EU nationals, the test is complex and local authorities often misunderstand the law. An authority cannot refuse to accept an application from a person from abroad. Sufficient inquiries must be carried out and, in an appropriate case, the decision can be challenged by way of review and county court appeal.

Homelessness

14.3 The homelessness test, like the eligibility test, can be described as a 'threshold' test: if the authority is not satisfied that a person is homeless, no duty is owed under HA 1996 Part VII.

14.4 To be homeless does not necessarily mean to be without any form of accommodation. A person is also homeless under Part VII if he or she has accommodation but living in it puts the person at risk of violence, or if the nature of the accommodation is such that it is not reasonable to continue to live there.

Definition of homelessness

14.5   The Housing Act 1996 s175 defines 'homelessness' as follows:

(1) A person is homeless if he has no accommodation available for his occupation, in the United Kingdom or elsewhere, which:

(a) he is entitled to occupy by virtue of an interest in it or by virtue of an order of a court,

(b) he has an express or implied licence to occupy, or

(c) he occupies as a residence by virtue of any enactment or rule of law giving him the right to remain in occupation or restricting the right of another person to recover possession.

(2) A person is also homeless if he has accommodation but:

(a) he cannot secure entry to it, or

(b) it consists of a moveable structure, vehicle or vessel designed or adapted for human habitation and there is no place where he is entitled or permitted both to place it and to reside in it.

(3) A person shall not be treated as having accommodation unless it is accommodation which it would be reasonable for him to continue to occupy.

14.6   The Housing Act 1996 s177 refers to the risk of violence. It provides:

(1) It is not reasonable for a person to continue to occupy accommodation if it is probable that this will lead to domestic violence or other violence against him, or against:

(a) a person who normally resides with him as a member of his family, or

(b) any other person who might reasonably be expected to reside with him.

For this purpose 'violence', means violence from another person; or threats of violence from another person which are likely to be carried out; and violence is 'domestic violence' if it is from a person who is associated with the victim.

14.7   Broadly therefore there are three possible ways in which a person may be homeless:

- *No accommodation* The person has no accommodation in which he or she is permitted or has a legal right to reside. See paras 14.15–14.30.

- *Accommodation but not reasonable to occupy* The person may have accommodation but it is not reasonable to occupy it.[1] This may be because of the risk of violence or for other reasons. See paras 14.31–14.46.

---

1 Although the term used is 'continue to occupy', it is not necessary that the person has previously occupied: *Waltham Forest LBC v Maloba* [2007] EWCA Civ 1281, 4 December 2007. See para 14.28 below.

- *Accommodation but excluded from occupation* The person may have a legal right to occupy accommodation but be physically excluded from it; or the accommodation may be a mobile home and the person has no pitch or mooring for it. See paras 14.47–14.49.

14.8   The legislation and case-law in respect of each of these categories is examined below.

Meaning of 'available' accommodation

14.9   In every case, accommodation must be available for a person to occupy together with his or her family or household. A central aim of the homelessness legislation has always been to keep families together. HA 1996 s176 applies in relation to any reference in Part VII to 'accommodation' and provides:

> Accommodation shall be regarded as available for a person's occupation only if it is available for occupation by him together with:
> (a) any other person who normally resides with him as a member of his family, or
> (b) any other person who might reasonably be expected to reside with him.

14.10   Section 176 applies not only to the definition of homelessness but also to the definition of intentional homelessness and to the accommodation provided by an authority when discharging its housing duties.

14.11   Family members are not defined, but the 2006 Code of Guidance provides that 'the phrase 'member of the family' will include those with close blood or marital relationships and cohabiting partners (including same sex partners)'.[2]

14.12   Although 'accommodation' must be available to the whole 'household' this does not mean that the household must be accommodated in a single unit of accommodation.

> In *Sharif v Camden LBC*[3] the council sought to discharge its duty to a family by making available two self-contained flats on the same floor of a building but a short distance apart. One was offered for occupation by the applicant and her sister and the other by her father. The family argued that this did not satisfy the section 176 definition of 'accommodation'. However, the Supreme Court dismissed the challenge: section 176 does not require a single

---

2   2006 Homelessness Code para 8.5.
3   [2013] UKSC 10, 20 February 2013.

unit of accommodation. On the facts, the family were able to live together in practical terms.

Who might reasonably be expected to live with the applicant?

14.13   Family members who normally live with a person *must* be regarded as part of that person's household. However, it is for the authority to decide in respect of other people whether it is reasonable to expect them to reside with the person. This could include partners who have not previously lived together or other family members who do not normally live together but wish to do so. It may also include people who are not family members and the 2006 Homelessness Code suggests that this group 'might include a companion for an elderly or disabled person, or children who are being fostered by the applicant or a member of his or her family'.[4]

14.14   The family members who normally live with a person and anyone else who might reasonably be expected to live with a person are referred to in this chapter as 'the household'.

Having no accommodation

What constitutes 'accommodation'?

14.15   The mere fact that a person's right to occupy accommodation is only temporary does not mean that the person is homeless. However, he or she must occupy 'a place which can fairly be described as accommodation'.[5] The following has been held not to be 'accommodation':

- a night shelter where a bed was provided on a nightly basis and the occupant was not allowed to remain indoors during the day;[6]
- a prison cell occupied by someone eligible for release on licence.[7]

14.16   This issue overlaps with the question of whether it is reasonable to occupy accommodation which is dealt with below, paras 14.31–14.46. A woman in a women's refuge remains 'homeless' for the purposes

---

4 Homelessness Code para 8.5.
5 *R v Brent LBC ex p Awua* (1996) 27 HLR 453 at 459.
6 *R v Waveney DC ex p Bowers* (1983) 4 HLR 118, CA.
7 *R on the application of B v Southwark LBC* [2004] HLR 3, QBD.

of section 175 as it is not reasonable for her to remain in the accommodation for anything other than a short period.[8]

What is a right or permission to occupy accommodation?

14.17   Housing Act 1996 s175 refers to entitlement to occupy by virtue of an interest or by virtue of a court order. A tenant or owner-occupier has an interest in a property. A person may occupy by virtue of a court order where a family court has made an order that he or she may occupy a former matrimonial home despite not being the tenant or owner.

14.18   Section 175 also refers to having an express or implied licence to occupy. This would include a person granted permission to share premises as a lodger or family members who live in the family home.

14.19   A person may also occupy a home because of 'any enactment or rule of law' giving the person the right to remain in occupation or restricting 'the right of another person to take possession'.[9] This would include a statutory tenant who no longer has a contractual tenancy (see para 3.90) and also a person whose right to occupy has ended but who has not yet been evicted by court bailiff, where this is required, see paras 8.10–8.15.

Practical issues

Possession proceedings – when does the occupier become homeless?

14.20   As is described in chapter 6, when a landlord seeks possession, there are several stages before the tenant is actually evicted. In most cases the tenant has the right to remain in occupation until the date on which a warrant is actually executed by court bailiffs. See paras 8.10–8.15.

In *R v Newham LBC ex p Sacupima*[10] the Court of Appeal considered the issue of exactly when someone subject to a possession order becomes homeless. The applicant had an assured shorthold tenancy and occupied the accommodation with her five children. Her landlord obtained a possession order and she approached the local authority for help. She was advised to await the bailiff's warrant and to return on the day of the eviction with her children and

---

8   *Birmingham CC v Ali, Moran v Manchester CC* [2009] UKHL 36, 1 July 2009.
9   HA 1996 s175(1)(c), see para 14.5 above.
10   (2001) 33 HLR 1, CA.

belongings. The claim was principally to challenge the suitability of the interim accommodation but Ms Sacupima also argued that the authority's duty to provide interim accommodation under HA 1996 s188 had arisen as soon as the possession order was made, as this ended her legal right to occupy the accommodation.

The Court of Appeal held that this was not the case: she became homeless only when evicted by the bailiffs. Until that date there was a restriction on the landlord's right to take possession.

So, in such a case the person is not yet homeless because, under HA 1996 s175(1)c), there is a restriction on the right of the landlord to recover possession. However, there are two other issues: whether it is reasonable for the person to remain in occupation pending an inevitable eviction and the duty the local authority has to those threatened with homelessness, see below at para 14.49.

14.21   In practice, most local authorities will advise people against whom a possession order has been made to return when they have received notice of the eviction, or, in some cases, on the day of the eviction itself. However, an authority should always consider whether it is reasonable for the occupier to remain in occupation pending eviction. Indeed this issue may arise at an earlier point when the occupier receives a possession notice, particularly where the occupier has no defence to a possession claim.

14.22   The 2006 Homelessness Code of Guidance sets out the approach an authority should take to applicants who have received notice of possession proceedings:

Para 8.32: Each case must be decided on its facts, so **housing authorities should not adopt a general policy of accepting – or refusing to accept – applicants as homeless or threatened with homelessness when they are threatened with eviction but a court has not yet made an order for possession or issued a warrant of execution.** In any case where a housing authority decides that it would be reasonable for an applicant to continue to occupy their accommodation after a valid notice has expired – and therefore decides that he or she is not yet homeless or threatened with homelessness – that decision will need to be based on sound reasons which should be made clear to the applicant in writing ...

The Secretary of State considers that where a person applies for accommodation or assistance in obtaining accommodation, and:
(a) the person is an assured shorthold tenant who has received proper notice in accordance with section 21 of the Housing Act 1988;

(b) the housing authority is satisfied that the landlord intends to seek possession; and
(c) there would be no defence to an application for a possession order;
– then it is unlikely to be reasonable for the applicant to continue to occupy the accommodation beyond the date given in the section 21 notice, unless the housing authority is taking steps to persuade the landlord to withdraw the notice or allow the tenant to continue to occupy the accommodation for a reasonable period to provide an opportunity for alternative accommodation to be found.

14.23   In practice authorities rarely issue a formal decision at this stage, but the 2006 Homelessness Code is clear: an authority should consider whether it is reasonable for such a person to remain in occupation pending eviction and, if it decides that it is, a reasoned decision should be given in writing. This will be a decision that the person is not homeless and carries a right of review.

14.24   An authority may lawfully depart from the Codes of Guidance if there is good reason to do so. Many authorities will justify their decision on the grounds of the expense of interim accommodation and the fact that the time people spend in interim accommodation can be reduced by remaining in their own home as long as possible. However, this will only be a valid justification if the authority is actively dealing with the application prior to eviction rather than just advising people not to approach them until the day of eviction. Advisers may wish to press the authority for a written determination at an early stage, addressing the issue of whether it is reasonable for the occupier to remain in occupation. When forced to explain the decision in writing, the authority may concede the issue and offer interim accommodation prior to the actual eviction.

Re-applications under section 195A

14.25   Note that the situation is different if the person applying is being evicted from accommodation provided under s193 as a 'private rented sector offer' within two years, see para 16.35. In such a case when an applicant is served with a valid section 21 notice, he or she must be treated as threatened with homelessness from the date the notice is issued and as homeless from the date the notice expires.[11]

---

11   HA 1996 s195A(2) and (4) and paras 37–39 of the 2012 Supplementary Guidance.

The cost of possession proceedings

14.26 When the County Court makes a possession order, the occupier will usually be ordered to pay the landlord's legal costs. However, in civil proceedings a party may apply to join another party (a third party) to the proceedings and to seek an order that the third party pays the costs of the claimant, the defendant or both (see para 22.149). It is therefore possible to ask the court to join the local authority and order it to pay the costs of the landlord on the basis that the tenant has been forced, by the authority, to remain in occupation. However, if an application is unsuccessful, this will increase the total costs of the proceedings and the occupier would usually be ordered to pay the costs of the landlord and the local authority.

14.27 An alternative would be to make a formal complaint to the authority and ask for reimbursement of the costs of the possession claim. If not agreed, further complaint may be made to the Local Government Ombudsman. However, the Ombudsman would have to find that there was maladministration in order to recommend compensation.[12]

Accommodation available anywhere in the world

14.28 If an applicant has accommodation anywhere in the world, he or she may not be homeless. The accommodation must, however, be available to the applicant and his or her household, and it must be reasonable to live in the accommodation.

In *Nipa Begum v Tower Hamlets LBC*[13] the local authority decided the applicant was not homeless because accommodation was available to her in Bangladesh. Ms Begum was a 21-year-old British national, born in Bangladesh. She had lived in the UK from the age of 13 or 14, but at the age of 17 had married in Bangladesh before returning to the UK. Later she stayed in Bangladesh with her husband at his father's home for 12 months. Shortly after returning to the UK, she gave birth to a son and then travelled to Bangladesh with her son, again staying in her husband's father's house. After a short while her son became ill and she returned to the UK. Her husband remained in Bangladesh awaiting entry clearance to join her in the UK. After a short stay with relatives in London she was asked to leave and applied to the authority as homeless. The authority

12 See para 2.96 above.
13 (1999) 32 HLR 445, CA.

decided that she was not homeless because her father-in-law's accommodation in Bangladesh was available to her and was reasonable to occupy. She requested a review, arguing that she could not afford to live in Bangladesh permanently, but acknowledging that it was Bengali tradition for a married couple to live with the husband's family, that she could continue to live in the house and that her husband's family were supporting him financially. The review decision confirmed the original decision. A county court appeal was lodged and the court quashed the decision holding, among other things, that the authority had failed to consider the issue of whether Ms Begum could afford to travel to the accommodation. The authority appealed.

The Court of Appeal upheld the authority's appeal, holding that:

Financial inability to travel is only one of many possible reasons why it may not be reasonable for an applicant to return to occupy overseas accommodation. In addition to factors concerning the legal availability, suitability and affordability of the accommodation, others may be, for example, connected with family or other personal problems, ill health, immigration restrictions, physical security and many others. In the absence of an indication of a particular difficulty or difficulties of that sort it is not, in my view, an authority's duty to take an applicant through a check list to negative all possible obstacles to his or her return to the overseas property.[14]

In *Waltham Forest LBC v Maloba*[15] the applicant was from Uganda but had lived in the UK for many years and become a British citizen. He met his wife on a visit to Uganda and they married and lived for two years in an annex to the family home. After his father's death other family members moved into the house and Mr Maloba and his wife and child returned to the UK and applied as homeless. The local authority found that he was not homeless and argued that it did not have to consider whether it was reasonable for the family to live in the accommodation in Uganda; it was sufficient that it was available. The court quashed the decision and the authority appealed.

14   (1999) 32 HLR 445, CA, Auld LJ at 458.
15   [2007] EWCA Civ 1281, 4 December 2007.

The Court of Appeal held that 'continue to occupy' did not mean that reasonableness was only relevant if the person was still in occupation. To find that a person was not homeless an authority must be satisfied not only that accommodation was available, but also that it was reasonable for the person to reside in it. The authority also argued that if it had to consider reasonableness, the only relevant factors were the size, structural quality and amenities of the accommodation. The Court of Appeal rejected this: the authority had erred in failing to consider whether it was reasonable for Mr Maloba to relocate to Uganda, having lived in the UK for many years and becoming a British citizen.

14.29   As is clear from *Nipa Begum*, it is essential to explain to an authority any reasons why it would not be reasonable to occupy accommodation. However, the authority must consider, in all cases, the affordability of the accommodation (see para 14.42 below).

Matrimonial/civil partnership home

14.30   A person who is married or in a civil partnership has a right to occupy accommodation owned or rented by the spouse or civil partner, provided that it has been the matrimonial or civil partnership home. This right lasts until the marriage or civil partnership ends. Where the relationship has broken down, the authority will consider whether it is reasonable for the person to continue to occupy the shared accommodation. An authority may decide that it is, in spite of the fact that the couple no longer wish to be in partnership. Relevant factors will be the size of the accommodation and the nature of the relationship. However, if continued occupation means that a person would be at risk of domestic violence, he or she should be accepted as homeless (see below, paras 14.32–14.38).

Not reasonable to continue to occupy

14.31   There are two distinct parts to this category of homelessness: (1) where it is not reasonable to occupy because of the risk of violence; and (2) where it is not reasonable to occupy for other reasons. If violence is probable, an authority *must* find the applicant to be homeless. If considering reasons other than the risk of violence, the authority has a wide discretion and can take account of housing needs in its own area.

Probability of violence

14.32   Housing Act 1996 s177 provides that 'it is not reasonable for a person to continue to occupy accommodation if it is probable that this will lead to violence against him or her, or a member of the household'. Violence is defined as 'violence from another person; or threats of violence from another person which are likely to be carried out'.

What is violence?

14.33   The term 'violence' is not restricted to physical violence or the threat of physical violence, whether it is 'domestic violence' or 'other violence':

> In *Yemshaw v Hounslow LBC*[16] the applicant had left her husband claiming that, although he had not physically assaulted her or threatened to assault her, his behaviour towards her and the children was abusive: he shouted at her in front of the children, refused to give her money for housekeeping and she was afraid that if she confronted him he would hit her or take the children from her. The Supreme Court held that that violence 'includes physical violence, threatening or intimidating behaviour and any other form of abuse which, directly or indirectly, may give rise to the risk of harm'.[17]

> The Court of Appeal, in *Hussain v Waltham Forest LBC*,[18] confirmed that this extended definition of violence was not confined to domestic violence. The applicant had suffered from a sustained period of serious and targeted racial abuse from the son of a neighbour and applied as homeless on the basis that it was not reasonable to remain in occupation of her home. The Court of Appeal held that in relation to 'other violence' (from someone not associated with the applicant) this covered 'not only physical violence (actual or threatened) but other threatening or intimidating behaviour or abuse, if of such seriousness that it may give rise to psychological harm'. The term 'psychological harm' was not a formal requirement under section 177(1) and should not be applied in a technical or medical sense. But 'It connotes something more

16   [2011] UKSC 3, 26 January 2011.
17   Lady Hale at [28]. See also the Homelessness Code of Guidance at para 8.21.
18   [2015] EWCA Civ 14, 20 January 2015.

than transient upset or distress. Psychological harm will often shade into, or overlap with, a diagnosed psychiatric injury or illness, such as depression; but that need not always be so.'[19]

14.34   A local authority must make a finding of fact: whether violence is probable if the person remains in occupation. The authority cannot refuse assistance or find a person not homeless because there are other remedies available for his or her protection. If the authority concludes that violence is probable, it must find the person to be homeless.

In *Bond v Leicester CC*[20] the applicant had fled two properties because of domestic violence from the father of her two young children. She was re-housed by a housing association, but again suffered violence from the same man. He began to visit her at the new premises and would refuse to leave when asked. On one occasion he assaulted her and she began to refuse to allow him into the property; he continued to visit, shouting and throwing stones at the windows. Ms Bond left and fled to London. After staying in a refuge, she returned to Leicester and alternated between her mother's address and a friend's. She then applied to the council. At that stage the housing association property was still available and the authority decided that it was reasonable for her to return there and that she was not homeless. The authority noted that, although she had a long history of fleeing harassment from the perpetrator, she had 'never taken any preventative measures to address this matter', referring to the possibilities of contacting the police or other bodies in relation to the 'alleged harassment'. She was advised to 'take action to address the alleged harassment'. She requested a review. The housing association property was then repossessed and the review decision was that Ms Bond was, by then, homeless, but homeless intentionally. The review letter accepted that she had been the subject of domestic violence for some considerable time, but stated that she 'should have taken action under the criminal/civil law to prevent [the perpetrator] from coming near her' or her property. The letter went on to detail the various actions Ms Bond could or should have taken and stated that 'she became homeless intentionally as she failed to take these measures and as a consequence of her failure, she ceased to occupy

19   Underhill LJ at [31] and [32].
20   [2002] HLR 6, CA.

> accommodation which was available for her occupation and would
> have been reasonable for her to continue to occupy'.
>   The Court of Appeal held that when considering whether a
> person is homeless or intentionally homeless: 'The only test is
> what is probable. This ... is a pure question of fact, devoid of value
> judgments about what an applicant should or should not do'.[21]
> The decision was varied to the effect that Ms Bond was not
> intentionally homeless.

14.35   The Homelessness Code reflects the decision in *Bond v Leicester CC*:
'An assessment must be based on the facts of the case and devoid of
any value judgments about what an applicant should or should not
do, or should or should not have done, to mitigate the risk of any violence (for example, seek police help or apply for an injunction against
the perpetrator)'.[22]

14.36   Nevertheless, an authority may legitimately advise an applicant
of the measures that may be taken to provide protection or increase
security in the home. The 2006 Homelessness Code recommends
that authorities should consider the option of improving the security
of the applicant's home, which may enable him or her to continue
to live there safely and thereby prevent homelessness. However, it
is a matter for the applicant whether to accept such assistance or to
pursue the application for homeless assistance.

Evidence of violence

14.37   It is not necessary to show a history of violence. The question is
whether it is probable that continued occupation would lead to violence, which includes the threat of violence from someone likely to
carry out the threat. Local authorities sometimes suggest that certain
kinds of evidence are necessary before they can accept a homeless
application from someone alleging violence: eg police reports, doctors' letters or court orders. While it is lawful for the authority to
request supporting evidence to complete its enquiries, it is unlawful
to refuse assistance on the basis that an applicant cannot provide
the evidence requested. The availability of evidence is relevant to
the determination of whether violence is probable. An authority is
entitled to conclude that, on the available evidence, violence is not

---

21 [2002] HLR 6, CA, Hale LJ at 25–26.
22 Homelessness Code para 8.22.

probable, but if it is rejecting the applicant's account this must be made clear to the applicant and reasons given.

Refuges

14.38 A woman who flees violence and obtains a place in a women's refuge remains homeless: a refuge is 'a temporary haven'.[23] However, despite this, and the fact that women fleeing violence rarely have any choice as to the location of the placement, the Court of Appeal recently held that residence in a refuge counts as 'residence of choice' for the purpose of local connection,[24] see para 14.170 below.

Unreasonable to occupy for other reasons

14.39 If the issue is whether someone is homeless because it is not reasonable to occupy accommodation for reasons other than the risk of violence, an authority has a wide discretion. There is no restriction on the nature of the factors that may make it unreasonable to occupy accommodation, but paras 8.29–8.34 of the 2006 Code of Guidance draw attention to the following factors:

- affordability;
- physical characteristics;
- type of accommodation;
- people fleeing harassment;
- the fact that a person has been given notice to leave (see paras 14.20–14.24 above).

14.40 When considering the issue, an authority may take account of the general housing need locally. HA 1996 s177(2) provides:

> In determining whether it would be, or would have been, reasonable for a person to continue to occupy accommodation, regard may be had to the general circumstances prevailing in relation to housing in the district of the local housing authority to whom he has applied for accommodation or for assistance in obtaining accommodation.

14.41 This means that in an area of great need, where many people are living in dwellings that are overcrowded and/or in substantial disrepair, it will be difficult to satisfy the authority that it is not reasonable to continue to occupy on the basis of the condition of the accommodation.

---

23 *Birmingham CC v Ali, Moran v Manchester CC* [2009] UKHL 36, 1 July 2009, Lady Hale at [65].
24 *London Borough of Wandsworth v NJ* [2013] EWCA Civ 1373, 7 November 2013.

Affordability

14.42   Affordability must be considered in all cases even if not directly raised by the applicant. The Homelessness (Suitability of Accommodation) Order 1996[25] specifies that an authority must take into account the financial resources available to the applicant, the cost of the accommodation, any maintenance payments made in respect of a former spouse or children, and the applicant's reasonable living expenses. If a property is not affordable, an authority must find the applicant to be homeless. But it is for the authority to decide what are reasonable living expenses.[26] Most authorities will consider a property to be affordable if, after discharging all necessary outgoings, including rent or mortgage payments, a person is left with a disposable income equivalent to the level of income support. If arguing that a property is unaffordable, it will usually be necessary to prepare a detailed financial statement. The issue usually arises in relation to intentional homelessness: for a person to be intentionally homeless the home lost or given up must have been affordable. The issue has been considered recently in a number of cases, discussed at paras 14.143–14.144 below.

Overcrowding

14.43   Overcrowding is a factor that may mean that it is not reasonable to remain in occupation of accommodation. Paragraph 11.80 above explains 'statutory overcrowding' – a legal measure of overcrowding that can lead to prosecution of owners or occupiers. The test for statutory overcrowding is very high, but even a household that meets the test is not necessarily homeless.

> In *Harouki v Kensington and Chelsea RLBC*[27] a family of six occupied a small three-bedroom flat in contravention of the 'space standard' under HA 1985 s326. The Court of Appeal upheld the authority' decision that the applicant was not homeless. Despite the fact that the occupation constituted a criminal offence, the authority was entitled to find that it was reasonable for the family to remain in occupation and await an allocation under HA 1996 Part VI.[28]

25 SI No 3204.
26 See *R v Brent ex p Baruwa* (1997) 29 HLR 915, CA.
27 [2007] EWCA Civ 1000, 4 July 2007.
28 However, in *Elrify v Westminster CC* [2007] EWCA Civ 632, the local authority's decision that the family were not homeless was held to be flawed as it had applied the overcrowding standard incorrectly. The authority was ordered to reconsider its decision.

Challenging decisions

14.44   It is very difficult to challenge decisions under this provision. Strong supporting evidence will be needed, such as medical reports, environmental health reports and recommendations from social services. Even then, the final decision is one for the housing authority. If an authority has considered all the relevant issues and decided that it is reasonable to continue to occupy, the only possible challenge will be that the decision is irrational, ie a decision no reasonable authority could reach (see para 2.15).

14.45   However, local authorities have powers and duties in relation to the condition of private sector accommodation, described in chapter 11. Even where a person wants to pursue a homeless application rather than remain in occupation, it may assist to report the premises to the appropriate department of the authority. This may result in enforcement action that compels a private landlord to carry out works. Alternatively, it may result in the landlord terminating the tenancy and claiming possession.

14.46   Whether it is better to make a homeless application or to pursue an allocation via the 'waiting list' depends on the priority given to those in unsatisfactory housing conditions in the particular authority's allocations scheme. A successful homeless application may result in more suitable accommodation being provided temporarily, but may also mean waiting longer for suitable permanent accommodation.

Excluded from occupation

Illegal eviction

14.47   A person who has been unlawfully evicted retains a legal right to occupy, but is homeless under HA 1996 s175(2)(a). Such a person should be entitled to a court order to gain re-entry. In such a case, if the person is in priority need, a local authority should provide temporary accommodation for as long as it takes to obtain and enforce an injunction. However, there may be reasons why someone does not want to seek re-entry, eg fear of the landlord, having limited rights of occupation, being unable to obtain legal aid or find a solicitor to assist. An authority may say that someone who does not enforce his or her rights through the courts will be found intentionally homeless. In making such a decision an authority must be satisfied that it would have been reasonable to take the necessary steps to resume occupation, taking account of the reasons for not doing so. See chapter 8 for an explanation of illegal eviction.

Mobile homes

14.48   A caravan or houseboat is capable of being 'accommodation' so that an occupant may not be homeless. However, this is the case only if there is somewhere the person can keep the mobile home and live in it. The fact that a site or mooring is only temporary will not of itself mean that the person is homeless.[29]

Being threatened with homelessness

14.49   A person is threatened with homelessness if it is likely that he or she will become homeless (applying the definition described above) within 28 days: HA 1996 s175(4). In such a case, the authority's duty is to 'take reasonable steps to secure that accommodation does not cease to be available for [the applicant's] occupation',[30] see paras 13.77–13.83.

Priority need

14.50   No housing duty will be owed unless an applicant has a 'priority need'. A person who is homeless, eligible but does not have priority need is entitled to advice and assistance only. However, there is a *power* to provide accommodation to non-priority need applicants: HA 1996 s192(3).

Categories of priority need

14.51   There are several categories of priority need. Some are easily established on the facts, others depend on a judgment by an authority, eg whether something is 'reasonable' or whether a person is 'vulnerable'.

Priority need categories under HA 1996 s189(1)

14.52   The Housing Act 1996 s189(1) provides:

The following have a priority need for accommodation:
(a) a pregnant woman or a person with whom she resides or might reasonably be expected to reside;
(b) a person with whom dependent children reside or might reasonably be expected to reside;

29   Homelessness Code of Guidance para 8.17.
30   HA 1996 s195(2).

(c) a person who is vulnerable as a result of old age, mental illness or handicap or physical disability or other special reason, or with whom such a person resides or might reasonably be expected to reside;

(d) a person who is homeless or threatened with homelessness as a result of an emergency such as flood, fire or other disaster.

14.53 Under the Housing Act 1996 s189(2) further categories of priority need may be added by the Secretary of State and by the Welsh National Assembly. In both cases regulations have been made, adding the following additional classes of priority need: 16- and 17-year-olds, care leavers under the age of 21, and additional classes of vulnerability. The substance of the English and Welsh regulations differs. Only the English regulations are dealt with in this book.

14.54 In England the following further categories added by regulations have applied since 31 July 2002:[31]

- children aged 16 or 17 (provided they are not owed certain accommodation duties by social services under the Children Act 1989);
- 18- to 20-year-old 'care leavers' (provided they are not students to whom social services owe a duty to provide out-of-term accommodation);
- a person who is vulnerable as a result of:
  - being a care leaver who is 21 or older,
  - having been in the armed forces,
  - having been in custody, or
  - having become homeless because of violence.

14.55 Each category of priority need is examined below in paras 14.56–14.109.

Pregnancy

14.56 This should be a relatively straightforward category. No 'minimum period' of pregnancy is required. However, disputes often arise at the point of application about the evidence of pregnancy.

Interim duty to accommodate

14.57 This arises if the authority 'has reason to believe' that a woman 'may' be pregnant (as well as homeless and eligible).[32] If a woman

---

31 Homeless Persons (Priority Need for Accommodation) (England) Order 2002 SI No 2051.
32 HA 1996 s188, see paras 13.28–13.29.

approaches an authority in an emergency late in the day or out of hours, she may have no supporting evidence of her pregnancy. In such a situation, her explanation of why she believes she is pregnant should be sufficient until she can obtain a doctor's letter. However, it is common for authorities to refuse interim accommodation until supporting evidence is provided. This is unlawful, but in practice it may be simpler and quicker to obtain a doctor's letter than to challenge the authority by way of judicial review.

Inquiries/full decision

14.58   As in all cases, the burden is on an authority to satisfy itself of the relevant matters. An applicant will usually be requested to provide documentary evidence such as doctor's letters, pre-natal appointment cards, copies of scans or letters stating the expected date of delivery. If an applicant fails to provide such evidence, an authority may decide that it is 'not satisfied' that she is pregnant.

14.59   It is unlawful to delay making a decision in case the pregnancy does not go to full term.[33] Furthermore, once a decision has been made that a housing duty is owed, the duty does not end if the applicant is no longer in priority need (see paras 16.18–16.22).

Dependent children

14.60   There are three possible questions the authority must decide:
- is the child dependent on the applicant?
- does the child reside with the applicant?
- if not, is the applicant someone with whom the children 'might reasonably be expected to reside'?

Dependence

14.61   The term 'dependent children' is not defined. The courts have held that a 16-year-old who was in receipt of a training allowance was not dependent on his father, but indicated that the concept of dependence was not confined to financial dependence: *R v Kensington and Chelsea RLBC ex p Amarfio*.[34]

14.62   The 2006 Homelessness Code para 10.7 states that authorities:

---

33   *R v Ealing LBC ex p Sidhu* (1982) 2 HLR 45, QBD: it is unlawful for an authority to defer a decision in case there is a change of circumstance in the future. This is discussed below at para 14.106 in relation to priority need based on age.
34   (1995) 27 HLR 543, CA.

... may wish to treat as dependent all children under 16, and all children aged 16–18 who are in, or are about to begin, full-time education or training or who for other reasons are unable to support themselves and who live at home.

14.63 The children need not be the natural children of the applicant, but there must be 'some form of parent/child relationship'.[35] Where a man whose wife was under the age of 18 made an application on the basis that she was a dependent child, the court upheld the authority's decision that he was not in priority need: *Hackney LBC v Ekinci*.[36]

14.64 The child must be dependent in some way on the applicant, but need not be 'wholly and exclusively' dependent on the applicant.[37]

In *R v Westminster CC ex p Bishop*[38] the applicant had two children. When he and their mother separated it was agreed that the children would live with him for part of each week and that during holidays they would divide their time equally. The mother received child benefit for both children. He applied for homeless assistance from the council. The authority decided that he was not in priority need because it was not satisfied that the children were dependent children who resided with him. The reasons were that the children were adequately housed with their mother and they were not dependent on him because the mother received child benefit for them and the applicant did not have the financial means to support them.

His application for judicial review was dismissed: it was necessary that a child should be dependent at least in part on an applicant, and it was for the authority to decide the issue. The authority had taken account of relevant facts and was entitled to reach that conclusion.

Residing with the applicant

14.65 There must be some degree of permanence or regularity in the residence, as opposed to a temporary or limited arrangement.

14.66 Where parents are separated, it is possible for children to reside with both parents, but an authority may find, as a matter of fact, that

35 Homelessness Code para 10.8.
36 [2001] EWCA Civ 776, 24 May 2001.
37 *R v Lambeth LBC ex p Vagliviello* (1990) 22 HLR 392, CA.
38 (1997) 29 HLR 546, QBD.

children do not reside with the parent with whom they spend less time.

> In *R v Port Talbot BC ex p McCarthy*[39] the parents were separating. They agreed that their child would stay with Mrs McCarthy for four nights each week and with Mr McCarthy for three. The authority decided that he was not in priority need and that the arrangement was one of 'staying access' rather than residence. The court upheld the decision.

14.67   In the following case, the decision was quashed because the authority had failed to apply the correct test.

> In *R v Leeds ex p Collier*[40] the parents had separated and the father applied for housing, indicating that the children stayed with him for part of each week. The authority found that he had no priority need on the basis that the children's mother had 'greater residency responsibility for the children'. The court held that the council's decision was 'fatally flawed' as it had applied an incorrect test.

14.68   Where children are residing with an applicant in interim accommodation pending a decision, an authority cannot simply disregard this state of affairs when applying the test.

> In *Oxford CC v Bull*[41] the applicant's three children stayed with their mother in the three-bedroom council property when the couple separated. Mr Bull left the family home and rented a single room in a shared house. Subsequently, the children, unhappy about their mother's new relationship, decided they wanted to live with their father and moved in with him which caused his landlord to serve notice to quit. He applied as homeless and was accommodated on an interim basis with the children pending inquiries. During this period the children lived with Mr Bull but also spent time staying with their mother. He was found not to be in priority need on the basis that the children did not live with him; the period in interim accommodation was not taken into account. He was also found to

---

39   (1990) 23 HLR 207, CA.
40   June 1998 *Legal Action* 14, QBD.
41   [2011] EWCA Civ 609, 18 May 2011.

be intentionally homeless because his decision to take the children into his home led to his eviction. The decisions were upheld on review but Mr Bull succeeded in his county court appeal.

The authority appealed to the Court of Appeal which held that it was wrong to disregard the time spent in interim accommodation. In accordance with the House of Lords' decision in *Mohamed v Hammersmith & Fulham LBC*[42] the relevant time for deciding the issue was the date of the review and at that date the children clearly resided with Mr Bull. However, the Court of Appeal upheld the appeal in relation to intentional homelessness. By inviting the children to live with him he had deliberately done something that led to the loss of his accommodation.

Reasonable to reside with the applicant

14.69   Where a separated parent does not have accommodation and is therefore unable to have the children residing with him or her, the authority must be satisfied of two things: first, that the children are dependent in some way on the non-resident parent and, second, that the person is someone with whom they might reasonably be expected to reside. The courts have considered this in the following cases.

In *R v Kingswood BC ex p Smith-Morse*[43] the applicant's son lived with him for part of the week following his divorce. The authority found that he had no priority need as the child's 'main residence' was with the mother. The decision was quashed: the authority should have gone on to consider whether the child might reasonably be expected to reside with the applicant in the future.

However, in *R v Westminster CC ex p Bishop* (para 14.64 above), the fact that the children were adequately housed with the mother and that the father could not support them financially was held to justify a decision that they were not dependent on him.

14.70   Where a family court has made an order that separating parents should have 'joint residence', whether by consent, or after a contested hearing, this does not determine the issue of whether it is reasonable

---

42 [2001] UKHL 57, see para 14.324 below.
43 (1994) *Times* 8 December.

to expect the children to reside with both parents for the purpose of priority need.

> In *Holmes-Moorhouse v Richmond upon Thames LBC*[44] the House of Lords considered a case in which a joint residence order had been made by a family court in respect of the couple's three children.
>   The court held (1) a joint residence order made by the family court does not determine the issue of whether it is reasonable for the children to live with both parents, in separate accommodation; (2) it was not unlawful for the housing authority to consider the scarcity of accommodation when deciding whether it would be reasonable for the children to live with the both parents; (3) the family courts should not make joint residence orders unless it appears reasonably likely that both parties will have accommodation in which the children can reside and should not make such orders to place pressure on the housing authority to allocate accommodation in a particular way.

Children in the care of the local authority

14.71   The local authority's duty to consider whether it is reasonable to expect children to reside with an applicant is to avoid a 'Catch-22 situation', ie applicants who cannot live with their children for lack of accommodation being refused housing because they do not live with their children. Although the decision about reasonableness is a judgment for the housing authority, where social services wish the children to return to their parents, this should determine the issue. The 2006 Homelessness Code states that in such a case 'liaison with the social services authority will be essential'.[45]

Vulnerability

14.72   Several categories of priority need depend on the local authority being satisfied that a person is vulnerable because of some personal characteristic or circumstance. The term 'vulnerable' is not defined in HA 1996, but it has been considered by the courts on many occasions.

---

44   [2009] UKHL 7, 4 February 2009.
45   2006 Homelessness Code para 10.11.

14.73   In *R v Waveney DC ex p Bowers*[46] it was held that the term means 'less able to fend for oneself so that injury or detriment will result when a less vulnerable man will be able to cope without harmful effects'. Subsequent cases suggested that to be vulnerable two tests must be met: first, that the person is less able to obtain suitable accommodation than the ordinary person and, second, if suitable accommodation is not found, the person will suffer more than most. However, the Court of Appeal in *R v Camden LBC ex p Pereira*[47] held that this approach was wrong.

In *Pereira* the applicant was a former drug addict. He was accommodated on an interim basis while the authority investigated his application. There was psychiatric evidence that if he became homeless he would be under immense psychological stress that would adversely affect his efforts at rehabilitation. The authority applied the two-part test suggested by previous case-law and found Mr Pereira not to be vulnerable; the council's medical officer found that he had an ability to find accommodation and was therefore no less able to fend for himself than other people.

The Court of Appeal held that this was the wrong approach. The authority should have asked whether the applicant was, when homeless, less able to fend for himself than an ordinary homeless person so that injury or detriment to him would have resulted when a less vulnerable man would be able to cope without harmful effect. There is a single composite test that is about the applicant's ability to cope with being homeless. A particular inability of a person to obtain housing for himself may be an aspect of his inability as a homeless person to fend for himself.

14.74   The 2006 Code of Guidance reflects the *Pereira* test in setting out the approach an authority should take in deciding whether a person is vulnerable:[48]

> 10.13 It is a matter of judgement whether the applicant's circumstances make him or her vulnerable. When determining whether an applicant in any of the [relevant] categories ... is vulnerable, the local authority should consider whether, when homeless, the applicant would be less able to fend for him/herself than an ordinary homeless person so that he or she would suffer injury or detriment, in

46 (1983) 4 HLR 118, CA, Waller LJ at 122.
47 (1999) 31 HLR 317.
48 Homelessness Code paras 10.13–10.14.

circumstances where a less vulnerable person would be able to cope without harmful effects.

10.14 ... The assessment of an applicant's ability to cope is a composite one taking into account all of the circumstances. The applicant's vulnerability must be assessed on the basis that he or she is or will become homeless, and not on his or her ability to fend for him or herself while still housed.

The non-vulnerable homeless person

14.75   The applicant's ability to cope with homelessness is compared with that of the non-vulnerable homeless person. The Court of Appeal has confirmed that this means the 'ordinary homeless person' and not the ordinary person (who may become homeless), see below at para 14.76. It has been observed that this is 'a legal test which itself makes the dubious assumption that homelessness is something fit people can always cope with'.[49] Clearly, any person is likely to suffer injury or detriment if 'street homeless'. The issue is whether, because of one or more of the specified reasons, the particular applicant would suffer more than the non-vulnerable homeless person.

Recent developments

14.76   The vulnerability test has been considered by the Court of Appeal in three recent cases (*Johnson*, *Hotak* and *Kanu*, summarised below), all of which were heard on appeal by the Supreme Court in December 2014. At the time of writing, judgment is pending.

- *Johnson v Solihull MBC*[50] concerned a homeless applicant with a history of drug abuse, criminal offending and imprisonment. The local authority decided that such personal circumstances were not uncommon in the homeless population and that the *Pereira* test required a comparison with 'the ordinary homeless person'. Applying that test, Mr Johnson was not less able to fend for himself so as to make him vulnerable.
- In the case of *Hotak v Southwark LBC*,[51] the applicant was a refugee with learning difficulties who also suffered depression and PTSD. He relied on his brother for day-to-day support. They had been living together in a flat belonging to a friend but had to leave because of overcrowding. The council decided that, were it

---

49   *Shala v Birmingham CC* [2007] EWCA Civ 624, 27 June 2007, Sedley LJ at [24].
50   [2013] EWCA Civ 752, 6 June 2013
51   [2013] EWCA Civ 515, 15 May 2013.

> - not for the support of his brother, Mr Hotak would be accepted as vulnerable. However, taking into account the fact that the brother's support would continue if Mr Hotak was homeless, and applying the *Pereira* test, they concluded that he was not vulnerable.
> - In *Kanu v Southwark LBC*[52] the same local authority applied that approach to a man who received support from his wife and adult son. He suffered from physical and mental health problems but was also found to be not vulnerable, on the basis of the support he would continue to receive from his family when homeless. In addition, in this case, it was argued that the local authority had failed to comply with the public sector equality duty (PSED) in relation to Mr Kanu's disability. The Court of Appeal concluded that the PSED added nothing since the local authority had to decide whether the applicant was vulnerable as a result of factors, specifically including disability.

14.77   The Supreme Court heard argument over three days to determine the following issues:

- Does the vulnerability test require a 'comparator'? And, if so, is the proper comparator the 'ordinary homeless person' or the ordinary person who becomes homeless?
- Can a local authority take account of the personal support offered by family and friends when deciding if a person is less likely to be able to fend for themselves when homeless?
- Does the PSED add anything to the process a local authority must undertake when deciding if an applicant is vulnerable because of disability?

14.78   This is the first time the issue of vulnerability has been considered by the Supreme Court/House of Lords and it is possible that the *Pereira* test will be revised or modified. Judgment is expected in early 2015.

Challenging vulnerability decisions

14.79   It is for the authority to weigh up the relevant factors in deciding whether someone is vulnerable. If all relevant issues have been taken into account, the decision can only be challenged on the grounds

52 [2014] EWCA Civ 1085, 29 July 2014.

that it is irrational or perverse[53] (see paras 2.15–2.17). Some common errors in decisions on vulnerability are:

- Considering the person's physical or mental health at a time when interim accommodation is being provided. The question is whether the person would suffer injury or detriment *when homeless*.
- Considering potential categories of vulnerability, including 'other special reason', in isolation. An authority must consider whether, as a result of a combination of all of the relevant factors, the person is vulnerable. It must make a composite assessment.
- Delegating decision-making to a medical expert. The decision must be taken by the housing authority, not a medical adviser. An authority should take into account a medical adviser's opinion, but it is not for the medical adviser to decide whether an applicant is in priority need.[54]

Extent of necessary inquiries

14.80   In cases of vulnerability it is often argued that the authority made insufficient inquiry. But it is not enough to show that the authority could have made more inquiries; it must be established that the inquiries the authority failed to make are those that no reasonable authority could have failed to regard as necessary.

14.81   In *Cramp v Hastings BC* and *Phillips v Camden LBC*[55] (see para 13.54) the Court of Appeal held that the County Court had been wrong to quash decisions on the basis of insufficient inquiry into potential vulnerability. At the review stage no representations had been made that further inquiry was necessary and:

> The duty to decide what inquiries are necessary rests on [the review officer], and her decision will be a lawful decision unless no reasonable council could have reached the same decision on the available material.[56]

---

53 This has been held to be the case in a number of Court of Appeal decisions, and in the House of Lords in the case of *Runa Begum* [2003] UKHL 5, 13 February 2003. However, the issue of the level of scrutiny to be applied in cases involving assessments of vulnerability was raised in the *Johnson, Hotak* and *Kanu* appeals, see para 14.76 above, so the Supreme Court may re-visit this issue.

54 *R v Lambeth LBC ex p Carroll* (1987) 20 HLR 142, QBD, and *Osmani v Camden* [2004] EWCA Civ 1706, 16 December 2004, at para 14.83.

55 [2005] EWCA Civ 1005, 29 July 2005.

56 [2005] EWCA Civ 1005, Brooke LJ at [68].

14.82   However, it has also been observed by the courts that in certain cases, what is at stake for the applicant is such that the authority's duty to inquire may be set at a high level.

In *Khelassi v Brent LBC*[57] the authority was considering an application by a man suffering from depression. A psychiatrist had expressed concern about the risk of suicide. The authority, without offering reasons, preferred the opinion of a general practitioner whose opinion was that the man was not vulnerable. At the applicant's appeal the county court judge stated:

I agree ... that the local authority's duty is to make such inquiries as are necessary ... I further agree ... that the decision as to what inquiries are necessary is primarily a question for the decision-maker, not for the court. What is necessary will depend on what is at stake. Where a significant risk of suicide is in issue a great deal is at stake.

The decision was quashed and the Court of Appeal endorsed the county court decision when refusing the authority permission to appeal.

Decisions to be made by local authority not court

14.83   In all cases the starting point is that local authorities, not the courts, have the decision-making responsibility. This has been emphasised in cases about priority need decisions which, the House of Lords has held, is about making judgments about competing demands and the allocation of scarce resources.[58]

In *Osmani v Camden LBC*[59] the applicant's doctor confirmed that he was suffering from depression and post-traumatic stress disorder, that this made it difficult for him to find secure accommodation and that leaving him without secure accommodation would put his mental health at risk. However, the authority found that he was not vulnerable.

The Court of Appeal dismissed the applicant's appeal: the council had applied the correct test and reached a decision that was not

57 [2006] EWCA Civ 1825.
58 See *Holmes-Moorhouse* at para 14.70 above.
59 [2004] EWCA Civ 1706, 16 December 2004.

> perverse; the issue of vulnerability is not exclusively or even
> necessarily a medical question:
>
> > Given that each authority is charged with local application of
> > a national scheme of priorities but against its own burden of
> > homeless persons and finite resources, such decisions are often
> > likely to be highly judgmental. In the context of balancing the
> > priorities of such persons a local housing authority is likely to be
> > better placed in most instances for making such a judgment.[60]

Role of medical evidence

14.84   Vulnerability as a result of 'mental illness or handicap or physical disability' means a person has priority need. To establish this, medical evidence of the degree or impact of the illness or disability be usually be needed. If the authority decides that medical evidence is necessary, it is the authority's responsibility to obtain it. Most authorities will require an applicant to complete a medical questionnaire, which may then be referred to a medical adviser employed by the authority. Alternatively, the authority may send a questionnaire to the applicant's GP with the decision on vulnerability being based on the questionnaire plus a medical adviser's opinion on the contents of the questionnaire: the nature of any illness or disability and the treatment received.

14.85   The 2006 Homelessness Code para 10.16 provides that, where there is doubt about the extent of vulnerability, authorities 'may' consider seeking a clinical opinion, but stresses that the final decision is for the authority to make.

14.86   In practice, authorities may avoid seeking an independent clinical opinion because of the cost. Those representing applicants under the Legal Help scheme may be able to obtain an independent report paid for by the Legal Aid Agency provided the 'sufficient benefit test' is met (see para 22.158 below).

14.87   If experts are instructed to offer opinions it is essential that they are asked to give relevant information, namely:

- a description of the person's health problems/disability;
- an opinion as to how the person would be able to cope if homeless, in light of the health problems/disability; and

---

60 [2004] EWCA Civ 1706, Auld LJ at [38].

- an opinion as to the likely effect on the person of being homeless; in particular, whether the person would suffer greater 'injury or detriment' when homeless, than the average person, by reason of his or her health problems/disability.

Contested medical reports

14.88 Several reported cases have concerned applicants with medical reports suggesting vulnerability, where the authority's medical adviser's opinion is that the person's condition is not severe enough to establish vulnerability.[61] Some of the principles established in those cases are as follows:

- Where the potential vulnerability arises from a mental health problem, an opinion more expert than that of a GP may be needed.
- The opinion of a medical adviser who merely considers another expert's report and advises the authority on its content does not have the same weight as the opinion of an expert who has actually examined the patient. It is a valid role, but must be distinguished from the role of an expert who has examined the patient or who has personal knowledge of the patient.
- Where the authority relies on the opinion of a medical adviser on the content of a report, it should make this clear in the decision letter. Where the opinion of the medical adviser differs from that of the other expert, the authority should indicate why it prefers the view of one over the other.
- Where the authority obtains an opinion that raises new issues or contentious points, the applicant should normally be given a chance to comment on the opinion, in the interests of fairness. However, if the advice is merely directed to helping the authority assess the weight of evidence on matters already fully in play, there is no automatic obligation to disclose it. There is no 'absolute rule of natural justice that an applicant must have the last word in every case'.[62]
- If there is a difference of opinion between the medical adviser and the applicant's expert, the medical adviser could be asked to examine the patient or to contact the applicant's expert to resolve the difference of opinion.

---

61 See *Hall v Wandsworth LBC; Carter v Wandsworth LBC* [2004] EWCA Civ 1740, 17 December 2002; *Bellouti v Wandsworth LBC* [2005] EWCA Civ 602, 20 May 2005; *Khelassi v Brent* LBC [2006] EWCA Civ 1825 and *Shala v Birmingham CC* [2007] EWCA Civ 624, 27 June 2007.

62 *Bellouti v Wandsworth LBC* [2005] EWCA Civ 602, Jonathan Parker at [62].

- The way medical evidence is treated by the authority goes to the duty of inquiry and the interim accommodation duty. See *R (IA) v Westminster CC*[63] at para 13.35 for an example of a particularly cynical approach to the medical evidence provided at an initial interview, which was condemned by the court.

14.89   The nature of the *Pereira* test and the court's reluctance to interfere with local authority decision-making on vulnerability makes it hard to challenge decisions even where applicants suffer from conditions that would clearly render them 'vulnerable' in the ordinary sense of the word. In relation to depression, it has been held that any homeless person is likely to suffer depression and that continued homelessness is likely to exacerbate depression.[64] So to establish vulnerability, evidence will be needed that, in the particular case, homelessness will cause or exacerbate an applicant's depression to a very significant extent. Even in such a case, an authority may respond that, in their judgment, the level of depression, risk of suicide etc is not significantly greater than that which the 'ordinary homeless person' would suffer. It is hoped that the Supreme Court revise the *Pereira* test in their judgment on the *Johnson, Hotak* and *Kanu* appeals, see above at para 14.76.

Vulnerability because of old age

14.90   Authorities must not apply rigid age criteria, either by accepting all applicants over a certain age or by rejecting those below a certain age; an applicant is only in priority need if 'vulnerable as a result of old age'.[65]

Other special reasons

14.91   There is no restriction on the nature of the 'other reasons' that may make a person vulnerable.

14.92   The 2006 Homelessness Code provides:[66]

The legislation envisages that vulnerability can arise because of factors that are not expressly provided for in statute. Each application

---

63   [2013] EWHC 1273, 20 May 2013. The case is about interim relief and permission to appeal so ordinarily would not be a binding authority but the court gave a direction that because of the 'importance and topicality' of the case, it could be cited as an authority.

64   See *R on the application of Yeter v Enfield LBC* [2002] EWHC 2185 (Admin) at [16].

65   Homelessness Code para 10.15.

66   Homelessness Code para 10.30.

must be considered in the light of the facts and circumstances of the case. Moreover, other special reasons giving rise to vulnerabiity are not restricted to the physical or mental characteristics of a person. Where applicants have a need for support but have no family or friends on whom they can depend they may be vulnerable as a result of an other special reason.

14.93 In practice, it is difficult to establish vulnerability in cases where a combination of factors is relied on, particularly when drug and alcohol addiction are amongst those factors.

> The Court of Appeal dismissed the applicants' appeals in *Simms v Islington LBC*[67] and *Mangion v Lewisham LBC*.[68] Mr Simms had a history of crack cocaine and cannabis addiction, had suffered family bereavements, had asthma, depression and anxiety and suffered panic attacks. Ms Mangion had an alcohol addiction and suffered back problems and moderate depression. In both cases the authority had correctly applied the *Pereira* test and the court held that the detailed letters, read as a whole, did not give grounds for the decisions to be quashed.

The additional categories of priority need

14.94 The English Priority Need Order 2002[69] added new categories of potential vulnerability and two new categories of priority need not dependent on vulnerability, see para 14.54 above.

Institutional background

14.95 A person who is vulnerable as a result of being a care leaver (aged 21 or above), having been in the armed forces or in custody, or having become homeless because of violence is in priority need.

14.96 Common to all those with an institutional background the following factors are identified in the 2006 Homelessness Code as relevant to assessing vulnerability:

- the length of time the person was in care, in prison or in the armed forces;

---

67 [2008] EWCA Civ 1083, 16 August 2008.
68 [2008] EWCA Civ 1642, 11 December 2008.
69 The Welsh Priority Need Order differs and is not dealt with in this book.

- the length of time since the person was in care, in prison or in the armed forces and whether they have been able to obtain and/or maintain accommodation during that period; and
- whether the person has existing support networks, particularly by way of family, friends or mentors.

Fleeing violence

14.97   In relation to those who have left accommodation because of violence, the 2006 Homelessness Code also provides that the authority may wish to take account of:[70]

(i)   the nature of the violence or threats of violence (there may have been a single but significant incident or a number of incidents over an extended period of time which have had a cumulative effect);

(ii) the impact and likely effects of the violence or threats of violence on the applicant's current and future well being;

(iii) whether the applicant has any existing support networks, particularly by way of family or friends.

14.98   The Code further states:[71]

In cases involving violence, the safety of the applicant and ensuring confidentiality must be of paramount concern. It is not only domestic violence that is relevant, but all forms of violence, including racially motivated violence or threats of violence likely to be carried out. Inquiries of the perpetrators of violence should not be made. In assessing whether it is likely that threats of violence are likely to be carried out, a housing authority should only take into account the probability of violence, and not actions which the applicant could take (such as injunctions against the perpetrators).

Children and care leavers

14.99   In addition to the new classes of vulnerability the Priority Need Order added two other categories of priority need:

- children aged 16 or 17; and
- young people aged 18 to 20 who are 'care leavers'.

In both cases the housing duties under HA 1996 and the social services duties under the Children Act (CA) 1989 overlap. However, in 2009 the House of Lords made clear that the primary duty for homeless 16- and 17-year-olds lies with social services; only in exceptional

---

70 Homelessness Code para 10.29.
71 Homelessness Code para 10.28.

cases will the duty under HA 1996 Part VII arise, see paras 14.102 below and 19.38.

14.100 The relevant accommodation duties under the Children Act 1989 are explained in detail at paras 19.6–19.36.

Children aged 16 and 17

14.101 Any child aged 16 or 17 is in priority need unless a duty to accommodate is owed by social services. This means that the young person will not be in priority need:

- where social services owe a duty to accommodate him or her as a 'child in need' under CA 1989 s20; or
- where he or she is a 'relevant child' under the Children (Leaving Care) Act 2000 (Leaving Care Act), ie where if the child has previously been in the care of the authority for at least 13 weeks, ending after the age of 16 (see paras 19.22–19.23).

14.102 In *R (G) v Southwark LBC*[72] the House of Lords held that the primary duty for homeless 16- and 17-year-olds is the duty under CA 1989 s20. This case and the way the s20 duty operates is described in detail in paras 19.13–19.15.

14.103 Therefore the circumstances in which the homelessness duty is likely to arise will be exceptional. In *R (G) v Southwark LBC* the court referred to examples such as a 16- or 17-year-old who has accommodation but is temporarily unable to occupy and has the resources to pay for hotel accommodation or who simply needs help in getting to the accommodation. So, in almost all cases, a homeless 16- or 17-year-old will be a child in need by virtue of being homeless and will require accommodation, and so the social services authority will owe a duty under CA 1989 s20. However, the section 20 duty cannot be forced on an unwilling child and a child may make an informed decision that he or she does not wish to be provided with accommodation by social services. In such a case the child must be advised of the support available if he or she were accommodated under section 20. This includes help with education and training and ongoing support up to the age of 21, or possibly 24 if in full-time education, see para 19.23. Additionally, many local authorities give high priority in their allocations schemes for 'care leavers' and those previously accommodated under section 20 will, on reaching the age of 18, be care leavers.

---

72 [2009] UKHL 26, 26 May 2009. See para 19.38.

14.104   Social services and housing departments must operate joint working practices or protocols. Statutory guidance was issued in April 2010 by the Department for Children, Schools and Families and the Department for Communities and Local Government.[73] This provides that if the homeless child approaches housing services interim accommodation should be provided but that 'housing services should make an immediate referral to children's services for an assessment.'[74]

14.105   The guidance reflects the previous judgments of the House of Lords and states:

> It is essential that services for homeless 16- and 17-year-olds are underpinned by written joint protocols which set out clear, practical arrangements for providing services that are centered on young people and their families and prevent young people from being passed from pillar to post.[75]

Local authorities should be asked for a copy of their protocol: a failure to follow its protocol (or to even have a protocol) may mean the decisions it takes are unlawful, see paras 2.8–2.25.

Delays in decision-making

14.106   Clearly, since both priority need and Children Act 1989 duties depend on the child's age, applications must be made in sufficient time to enable a decision to be made before the child turns 18. In most homeless applications a final decision is not made immediately on presentation and the general rule is that decisions are made on the basis of the circumstances at the date of the decision, whether this is an initial decision or a decision on review.[76] However, an authority cannot take advantage of this general rule to refuse assistance to an applicant who was in priority need by virtue of age when he or she applied to the authority.

> In *Akilah Robinson v Hammersmith and Fulham LBC*[77] the court held that an authority had acted unlawfully in postponing a decision on priority need, where the young person had turned 18 by the time the decision was taken. Ms Robinson was told to leave the family home

---

73 *Provision of accommodation for 16 and 17 year old young people who may be homeless and/or require accommodation*, available from www.communities.gov. uk/publications/housing/homelesssixteenseventeen.

74 Guidance para 2.11.

75 Guidance para 5.2.

76 *Mohamed v Hammersmith & Fullham LBC* [2001] UKHL 57, see para 14.177.

77 [2006] EWCA Civ 1122.

by her mother and applied to the authority for homelessness assistance. Initially she was told that it would take 28 days for her case to be investigated and that, as she would be 18 within 28 days, there was no point in continuing with the application. However, having taken advice, she approached the authority again the following day and was placed in interim accommodation. The authority referred her case for mediation in accordance with the 2006 Homelessness Code. The homelessness decision was postponed until after the mediation. The mediation failed and the authority then made its decision that, as she was now 18, Ms Robinson was not in priority need. The review officer upheld the decision on the basis that the decision-maker had been correct to refer the case to mediation.

The Court of Appeal held that the authority had acted unlawfully in postponing a decision. It was clear when Ms Robinson first applied that she was homeless unintentionally and, as she was under the age of 18, was in priority need. The fact that inquiries normally take a certain time does not mean that a person who will become 18 within that time is not in priority need.

Furthermore, if, on review, the decision had been found to be unlawful, the review officer should have ensured that Ms Robinson had the rights she would have had if the decision had been lawful.

Nevertheless, there are cases in which it may take a reasonable period of time for the necessary inquiries to be made and the applicant may turn 18 before the inquiries are complete. In such a case the authority is entitled to take the decision by reference to the facts as they exist at the date of the decision.

14.107   It is now clear that in such a case the applicant should be referred to social services for an assessment under the Children Act 1989. Again, it is important to ensure that there is no delay in carrying out an assessment and particularly in providing accommodation. A child accommodated under CA 1989 s20 for *any* period of time between the ages of 16 and 18 will be in automatic priority need as a care-leaver after the age of 18, but before turning 21, see para 14.108 below. And, if the child is accommodated for at least 13 weeks before turning 18, he or she will be entitled to ongoing support under the Leaving Care Act, see paras 19.23–19.33.

Care leavers aged 18–20

14.108   A care leaver under the age of 21 is in priority need, regardless of vulnerability. The person must have been in care after reaching the age of 16 but while under the age of 18. This means having been 'looked after, accommodated or fostered'.[78] However, 'relevant students' are excluded. These are students to whom social services owe a duty under the Leaving Care Act, which includes a duty to provide out-of-term accommodation, see para 19.33. It does not, as some authorities assert, include all care leavers who happen to be students.

14.109   An authority may deny that a child was accommodated under s20 and assert that instead assistance was given under CA 1989 s17, see paras 19.40–19.42. The label the authority gives is not determinative and advisers should seek further information. A copy of the young person's social services file should be requested under the Data Protection Act 1998 (see para 2.102). Even if the assistance was described throughout as 'section 17' it may be possible to establish that, as a matter of law, the authority was acting under the section 20 duty on the basis that the section 20 conditions were met and accommodation was provided, see paras 19.40–19.42.

Emergency or disaster

14.110   Someone made homeless because of an emergency such as a flood, fire or other disaster is treated as having a priority need regardless of personal circumstances.[79]

14.111   The event that makes the person homeless must be both an emergency and a disaster. Homelessness resulting from an unlawful eviction does not come within this category.[80] The sudden disappearance of a mobile home, however, was accepted as an emergency akin to flood or fire as: 'It involved the sudden and wholly unexpected loss of [his] home in circumstances wholly outside his control by the loss of the structure in which he made his home'.[81]

---

78   This is defined in CA 1989 s24.
79   This is a category of priority need that reflects the original provisions of the National Assistance Act 1948 – local authorities owed a duty to provide emergency accommodation to people made homeless in such circumstances.
80   *R v Bristol CC ex p Bradic* (1995) 27 HLR 584, CA.
81   *Higgs v Brighton & Hove CC* [2004] HLR 9, Kay LJ at [20].

Household members

14.112 It should be noted that most of the 'old' priority need categories provide that anyone with whom such a person resides or might reasonably be expected to reside also has a priority need. The exception is a person made homeless as a result of flood, fire or other disaster. However, none of the new categories of priority need extend to household members.

14.113 Nevertheless, if a duty is accepted, accommodation must be made available for the applicant:

... together with:

(a) any other person who normally resides with him as a member of his family, or

(b) any other person who might reasonably be expected to reside with him.[82]

In *R (Ogbeni) v Tower Hamlets LBC*[83] permission was granted for a claim for judicial review to challenge the authority's decision that this did not apply in relation to a 17-year-old who had priority need by virtue of his age. He had been living with his aunt but both became homeless when she lost her tenancy. Had she applied, she would have been found intentionally homeless. The court rejected the council's argument that it was implicit that this category of priority need related only to single applicants.

Intentional homelessness

14.114 Being 'intentionally homeless' does not mean intending to become homeless. It means that a person's homelessness was caused by something he or she did (or did not do) deliberately. Where a person is found to be intentionally homeless the local authority's duty is limited; it must provide advice and assistance and accommodation for a 'reasonable period' to give the person an opportunity to find his or her own accommodation.

14.115 The definition of intentional homelessness is set out in HA 1996 s191:

(1) A person becomes homeless intentionally if he deliberately does or fails to do anything in consequence of which he ceases to occupy

---

82 HA 1996 s176.
83 [2008] EWHC 2444 (Admin), 8 August 2008.

accommodation which is available for his occupation and which it would have been reasonable for him to continue to occupy.

(2) ... an act or omission in good faith on the part of a person who was unaware of any relevant fact shall not be treated as deliberate.

14.116   In addition, since 1996 there has been an additional limb to the test of intentional homelessness: 'contrived homelessness'. This is dealt with below at para 14.163.

14.117   There are several elements to the definition. In all cases, the following questions must be asked:

- Which accommodation did the person cease to occupy, thereby causing the homelessness?
- Was that accommodation available to the applicant, ie available for the occupation of the applicant *and* his or her household?
- Would it have been reasonable for the applicant to continue to occupy the accommodation?
- What was the act or omission in consequence of which he or she ceased to occupy?
- Was the act or omission deliberate?
- If apparently deliberate, was it an act or omission made in good faith in ignorance of a relevant fact?

It is useful to examine each of these questions separately.

Which accommodation did the person cease to occupy, thereby becoming homeless?

Ceasing to occupy

14.118   Note that to be intentionally homeless a person must *cease to occupy* accommodation.[84] A failure to take up accommodation does not, in most cases, make a person intentionally homeless. An apparent exception to this is when an offer of suitable accommodation is refused (whether under HA 1996 Part VI or Part VII). In such a case, the person can be said to have ceased to occupy the interim or temporary accommodation provided by the authority in consequence of refusing the offer.[85]

14.119   This situation must be distinguished from that of a person who, when homeless, declines to take up accommodation that becomes available to him or her.

---

84   *R v Westminster CC ex p De Souza* (1997) 29 HLR 649, QBD.
85   *R v East Hertfordshire DC ex p Hunt* (1986) 28 HLR 51, QBD.

14.120   Under homeless prevention strategies (see para 13.8 above) many authorities offer to those who present as homeless help to obtain private sector accommodation. Applicants may prefer to take a tenancy in the private sector than pursue a homeless application. However, an authority should not advise a person that refusing an offer of accommodation from a private landlord (made under a homeless prevention or homeless options scheme) will render them intentionally homeless. A person can only be intentionally homeless if he or she *ceases to occupy* accommodation *as a result of* his or her act or omission. A person who is already homeless or threatened with homelessness cannot be found intentionally homeless for refusing to accept assistance to take up a private sector tenancy.

14.121   However, where a local authority is seeking to discharge a housing duty under HA 1996 Part VII by using private sector accommodation the situation is different. A local authority may use private sector accommodation to provide temporary accommodation under section 193, or may make a 'private rented sector offer' to end its housing duty under section 193, see para 16.28. In such a case the authority must write to the applicant explaining the consequences of a refusal and giving information about the right to seek a review of the suitability of the accommodation. Paras 16.70–16.73 explain the different situations in which private sector accommodation is used by local authorities under HA 1996 Part VII.

Which accommodation?

14.122 It may be that the loss of the most recent accommodation is not the cause of the person's homelessness.

> In *Dyson v Kerrier*[86] the applicant voluntarily gave up a council tenancy and took an unprotected 'out of season' holiday let. When she was required to leave the unprotected tenancy she applied to the local authority as homeless. The authority found that she was intentionally homeless; her homelessness had been caused by the deliberate act of giving up her council tenancy.
>
> The court upheld the council's decision. The cause of the applicant's homelessness was not the loss of the unprotected tenancy but the previous deliberate act of giving up the council tenancy.

86 [1980] 3 All ER 313, CA.

14.123   *Dyson v Kerrier* was decided in 1980 and subsequently the courts developed the concept of 'settled accommodation'[87] and applied it in the following ways:

- when considering intentional homelessness an authority would ignore any non-settled accommodation;
- a person who did not have settled accommodation was defined as homeless; and
- it was understood that accommodation provided by an authority under the homeless duty must be settled accommodation.

14.124   In 1995 the House of Lords held that this was the wrong approach. In *R v Brent LBC ex p Awua*[88] it was held that the concept of settled accommodation was only relevant to intentional homelessness and only then in the *Dyson v Kerrier* type of situation: to ensure that a person who is intentionally homeless, following the loss of permanent accommodation, does not cease to be intentionally homeless by obtaining non-settled accommodation which later ceases to be available. What this means is:

- A person who has non-settled accommodation is not homeless provided it is reasonable to continue to occupy the accommodation.
- The duty to secure accommodation does not necessarily mean securing accommodation that is settled.
- In relation to intentional homelessness, non-settled accommodation is ignored only if the person lost that accommodation unintentionally. Then the authority can look back to the accommodation previously occupied. However, a person may be intentionally homeless from non-settled accommodation.

14.125   Given the development of the case-law advisers must be cautious of reported cases regarding settled accommodation decided before *Awua* in 1995.

What is settled accommodation?

14.126   The term 'settled' means something more than merely temporary: 'What amounts to a 'settled residence', is a question of fact and degree depending on the circumstances of each individual case'.[89] An assured shorthold tenancy is capable of being settled accommodation but is not necessarily so, depending on the circumstances.

---

87   *Din v Wandsworth LBC* (1982) 1 HLR 73, HL.
88   (1995) 27 HLR 453, HL.
89   Ackner LJ in *Din v Wandsworth LBC*, CA, 23 June 1981 (unreported).

In *Knight v Vale Royal BC*[90] the applicant had been found intentionally homeless by the authority. She then obtained a six-month assured shorthold tenancy. She was informed by the landlord at the outset that he would require the property back after six months. After she was evicted the authority again found her to be intentionally homeless on the basis that there was still a causal link between her previous loss of accommodation and her homelessness. She argued that she had had settled accommodation which had broken the chain of causation. In the Court of Appeal she argued that because the assured shorthold tenancy was the most commonly available form of tenure in the private sector such a tenancy must necessarily be settled accommodation.

The court rejected this, holding:

In our judgment the occupation by a tenant of accommodation let on a six months' assured shorthold tenancy is capable of constituting settled accommodation for the purposes of breaking a chain of causation from past intentional homelessness ... What we cannot accept is that the occupation by a tenant of accommodation let on a six months' assured shorthold tenancy is, as a matter of law, always sufficient to constitute settled accommodation. The question remains one of fact and degree to be determined by the local authority in the circumstances of a particular case.[91]

Ms Knight's appeal was dismissed.

But, see *Moran v Manchester CC*,[92] para 14.133 below, in which it was held that a woman evicted from a refuge was not intentionally homeless on the ground that it was not reasonable to occupy such accommodation indefinitely.

14.127 While the parties' intentions are relevant in deciding whether accommodation is settled, the test is not entirely subjective; an authority may find that accommodation was not settled even if the applicant's stated intention was to remain in the accommodation permanently.[93] Other factors, such as the level of security and the suitability of the accommodation, will also be taken into account.

90 166 [2003] EWCA Civ 1258, 31 July 2003.
91 [2003] EWCA Civ 1258, Sir Martin Nourse at [24]–[25].
92 [2009] UKHL 36, 1 July 2009.
93 *R v Purbeck DC ex p Cadney* (1985) 17 HLR 534, QBD.

Examining the accommodation history

14.128   What this means is that, in deciding the cause of homelessness, a local authority can look back through an applicant's history of previous accommodation until it finds either settled accommodation which was not lost intentionally or accommodation, settled or not, from which the applicant was intentionally homeless. In the first case the finding would be that the person is not intentionally homeless and in the second case that he or she is intentionally homeless.

14.129   This is also referred to as 'breaking the chain of causation': in most cases a person who is intentionally homeless will only cease to be intentionally homeless (ie break the chain of causation) by obtaining settled accommodation. If this is later lost unintentionally, so that the person becomes homeless again, this homelessness will no longer be 'intentional'. However, it is possible for other events to 'break the chain' or, in other words, to be the true cause of the present homelessness. An example is a person suffering domestic violence or relationship breakdown. See para 14.154 below.

Was the accommodation available for the applicant and his or her household?

14.130   The authority must be satisfied that the accommodation was available for the applicant to occupy together with any other person who normally resides with the applicant as a member of his or her family, or any other person who might reasonably be expected to reside with him or her.[94]

14.131   Which family members normally live with the applicant is a question of fact. However, in relation to other people, it is for the authority to decide whether it is *reasonable* to expect a person to live with the applicant.[95] It is not necessary for the person to have previously lived with the applicant, see para 14.9 above.

Would it have been reasonable for the applicant to continue to occupy that accommodation?

14.132   The test is the same as when considering whether a person is homeless. If the authority is satisfied that violence would have been probable if the person had remained in occupation it *cannot* find the

---

94   HA 1996 s176. See *R v Hillingdon LBC ex p Islam* (1981) 1 HLR 107, HL.
95   See *R v Barking & Dagenham LBC ex p Okuneye* (1995) 22 HLR 174, QBD.

person to be intentionally homeless. The fact that the person could have taken other steps to protect him or herself is irrelevant: *Bond v Leicester CC*, para 14.34 above.

14.133   While it is possible to be intentionally homeless by losing non-settled accommodation, a place in a women's refuge is not accommodation that it would be reasonable to continue to occupy indefinitely. In *Moran v Manchester CC*[96] it was held that a woman living in a refuge remains homeless and therefore cannot be intentionally homeless by virtue of eviction from the refuge.

14.134   If the applicant contends that it would not have been reasonable to remain for a reason other than the probability of violence, the issue is one for the authority to decide. In making the decision, it can take account of housing conditions in the local area.[97]

14.135   The question is not whether it was reasonable to leave but whether it would have been reasonable to remain.[98] This is judged on the basis of the facts at the time the accommodation ceased to be available, not at the date of the application. So, the fact that accommodation would inevitably have been lost in the future does not prevent a person from being found intentionally homeless if he or she decided to leave at a time when it would have been reasonable to remain.[99] Furthermore, it will not assist an applicant who leaves accommodation when it would have been reasonable to remain that a subsequent change in circumstances would have made it unreasonable or impossible to continue to occupy. In *Haile v Waltham Forest LBC*[100]a woman left a bedsit in which only single occupancy was allowed. She was found intentionally homeless but argued the decision was wrong because by the date of the decision she had given birth to a daughter and so could not have remained in the bedsit. The Court of Appeal confirmed the approach in *Din* is correct: section 190(1) uses the phrase 'is homeless', 'is eligible for assistance' and 'became homeless intentionally'. The deliberate switch from the present to the past tense indicated that the local authority has to investigate the historic cause of the applicant's homelessness, but to consider all other issues by reference to the present state of affairs.

14.136   A person may have acted reasonably in giving up accommodation but may be intentionally homeless if it would also have been

96   [2009] UKHL 36, 1 July 2009.
97   HA 1996 s177(2), see paras 14.39–14.46 above.
98   *R v Hammersmith and Fulham LBC ex p Duro-Rama* (1983) 9 HLR 71.
99   *Din v Wandsworth LBC* (1981) 1 HLR 73, HL.
100   [2014] EWCA Civ 792, 13 June 2014.

reasonable to remain in occupation. However, the reasons why a person left accommodation will be relevant if considering whether a person was acting in good faith, in ignorance of a relevant fact (see paras 14.157–14.162).

What was the act or omission in consequence of which he or she ceased to occupy?

14.137 The authority must identify what the applicant is alleged to have done or failed to do and be satisfied that this act or omission caused the homelessness. It is possible for there to be more than one cause of homelessness: see *Noel & Ferguson v London Borough of Hillingdon*[101] below at para 14.142. Note also that a person who did not make the relevant decision may have acquiesced in the decision, see below at para 14.145.

Causation/foreseeability

14.138 Where the law provides that one thing must cause another, or that an outcome must be a consequence of an act or event, this is referred to as 'causation'. Related to this is the concept of 'foreseeability': for a person to be deemed to have caused a certain event by his or her action, the consequence of the action must be, to a certain degree, foreseeable.

14.139   For an act or omission to be the cause of a person's homelessness this must be a reasonably foreseeable consequence of the act or omission. The courts have considered this issue in the following cases.

Tenant's imprisonment

14.140   In *R v Hounslow LBC ex p R*[102] the applicant was convicted of several offences of indecent assault and sentenced to seven years' imprisonment. He surrendered his tenancy while in prison as he could not maintain the rent payments. On his release he applied as homeless, but was found to be intentionally homeless: the offences were deliberate acts and the surrender of the tenancy was the 'direct and reasonable' result of the acts. His judicial review of the decision was dismissed. The court held that:

101 [2013] EWCA Civ 1602, 21 November 2013.
102 (1997) 29 HLR 939, QBD.

... the question to be asked is whether his ceasing to occupy the accommodation would reasonably have been regarded at the time as the likely consequence of the deliberate conduct. It is an objective, not a subjective test.[103]

The same test was approved and applied by the Court of Appeal in *Stewart v Lambeth LBC*.[104] Mr Stewart was a tenant of the authority, but a suspended possession order had been made on the basis of rent arrears. He was sentenced to five years' imprisonment for drugs offences and made an arrangement that while he was in prison his sister would maintain his tenancy and pay the rent. No rent was received and a warrant was executed. He found this out after the event. When he applied as homeless following his release on licence, he was found intentionally homeless. He argued that the cause of his homelessness was not his imprisonment, but the failure by his sister to make rent payments.

The Court of Appeal rejected this: 'the chain of events that ultimately led to Mr Stewart's eviction began with the supply of heroin in respect of which he was duly convicted'.[105] The fact that arrangements could have been, or were, made to avoid the eviction were irrelevant, especially as the arrangements made were ineffectual. The finding of intentional homelessness was upheld.

Rent/mortgage arrears

14.141   As is stressed in the 2009 Supplementary Guidence where rent or mortgage payments are unaffordable, the failure to pay will not be deliberate. However, a person may be intentionally homeless because of a decision to enter into an unaffordable arrangement.

In *R v Barnet LBC ex p Rughooputh*[106] an applicant was evicted following mortgage possession proceedings, having entered into a mortgage that she could not afford. She had claimed that she earned £18,000 a year, but was in fact unemployed. The council

103 (1997) 29 HLR 939, Stephen Richards J at 947.
104 [2002] EWCA Civ 753, 26 April 2002.
105 [2002] EWCA Civ 753, Longmore LJ at [20].
106 (1993) 25 HLR 607.

decided that she was intentionally homeless. The deliberate act causing the homelessness was not the failure to make the mortgage payments, but entering into the mortgage agreement. The Court of Appeal upheld the council's decision.

14.142   The same principles apply in relation to rented accommodation.

In *Noel & Ferguson v LB Hillingdon*[107] a man was found intentionally homeless having failed to pay the rent for a tenancy where his housing benefit entitlement was less than the relatively high rent. The Court of Appeal dismissed his appeal against the decision that he was intentionally homeless. There were two causes to his homelessness: both the taking on of a tenancy at an unaffordable rent and failing to pay the rent when he was receiving housing benefit and/or failing to apply for higher levels of housing benefit during periods when his income fell.

Affordability

14.143   Perhaps unsurprisingly given the recent economic climate and the restrictions in the levels of housing benefit, the Court of Appeal has recently considered intentional homelessness and affordability of accommodation in a number of cases:

In *Carthew v Exeter CC*[108] the applicant was a sole tenant of the council and purchased the property under 'right to buy' jointly with her partner who had recently moved in. Following the breakdown of the relationship he moved out and she agreed to sell her interest to him, but remained in occupation with the children. Later they decided to give the relationship another go and he moved back in. However, the relationship again broke down and she and the children left and applied as homeless. She was found intentionally homeless but the Court of Appeal upheld her appeal on the basis that the council had failed to consider whether she could have afforded to live in the property alone at the point at which she agreed to transfer her interest to him.

107 [2013] EWCA Civ 1602, 21 November 2013.
108 [2012] EWCA Civ 1913, 4 December 2012.

In *Birmingham CC v Balog*[109] the applicant initially claimed to have left a privately rented flat because of its condition and because he was told to leave by the landlord. The issue of whether it was affordable was also raised, but at a late stage. The authority accepted that for periods there had been a shortfall between the rent and the housing benefit he received when unemployed but held that he could have reduced his outgoings to ensure the rent was paid. The county court upheld Mr Balog's appeal holding that the council had failed to have regard to the Code of Guidance or to consider whether meeting the shortfall would have meant that the family income fell below the level of income-based JSA. The Court of Appeal upheld the council's appeal, holding that the review officer had conducted a careful and considered examination and should not be criticised for not including an express reference to the relevant Code of Guidance. This would be to subject the decision to the kind of nit-picking analysis criticised by Lord Neuberger in the *Holmes-Moorhouse* case.[110]

Huzrat v London Borough of Hounslow[111] concerned a single parent of two children aged one and two, renting in the private sector. She also had a shortfall between the rent and the housing benefit paid. The council found that the shortfall could have been paid had she reduced her 'non-essential' expenditure, including 'pocket money' for the children of £80 per month. The Court of Appeal dismissed her appeal: the authority were entitled to reach this conclusion and the local authority's duty to treat the interests of the children as a primary consideration (under section 11 of the Children Act 2004) did not change the way that section 191 applied when deciding if someone was intentionally homeless.

However, in *R (Farah) v London Borough of Hillingdon*[112] the Court of Appeal upheld an appeal by a disabled single parent who faced a shortfall between the rent and the housing benefit. She had submitted a detailed income and expenditure form. The authority

---

109 [2013] EWCA Civ 1582, 12 December 2013.
110 Kitchin LJ at [51].
111 [2013] EWCA Civ 1865, 21 November 2013.
112 [2014] EWCA Civ 359, 26 March 2014.

had decided that some items of expenditure were not essential but having removed those items there was still a shortfall. They concluded that 'some items of your weekly expenditure are exaggerated' and that she had failed to give adequate priority to the payment of the rent and was therefore intentionally homeless. The Court of Appeal held that the failure to explain which items of expenditure were considered excessive or exaggerated meant that the decision was flawed:

> ... I accept, of course, that it is neither realistic nor necessary to expect already burdened local authorities to identify each and every paragraph of the guidance they have taken into account or provide an over-detailed set of reasons reaching their financial conclusions. Cases like *Birmingham CC v Balog* ... show that this is not necessary. ... In some cases it will be enough to say that the housing authority concluded that the amount spent on a particular form of expenditure was excessive or unnecessary without going into further detail or qualification. In other cases, where the tenant has produced and relied on a justification for the expenditure under review, a more detailed explanation of the reasons for rejecting those arguments may be required.[113]

14.144   These cases illustrate the importance of preparing a detailed income and expenditure statement. It is not enough simply to assert that a person on benefits such as income-based JSA or income support cannot pay a shortfall so as to make the property unaffordable. Full details should be given so that the authority will have to identify precisely what items of expenditure are unnecessary or should have been reduced. Furthermore, as a family's income often changes frequently, particularly for those in insecure and low paid employment, a person must ensure that they submit up-dated claims for housing benefit when necessary.

Acquiescence

14.145   The act or omission must be that of the applicant. Authorities often treat applications by couples or families as 'joint' applications but there is no provision under the Act for doing so. An authority may be required to consider each applicant individually where it is the act or omission of one person that caused the homelessness. However,

113 Patten LJ at [31].

a party who acquiesced in (ie, passively accepted) the act or omission of another may also be found homeless intentionally. An authority is entitled to assume that members of a family were party to the conduct of one member, unless there is evidence to the contrary.[114]

In *R v North Devon DC ex p Lewis*[115] a man who gave up his employment and therefore lost his tied accommodation was found to be intentionally homeless. His wife then applied and the authority found she was also intentionally homeless on the basis that she had acquiesced in her husband's decision to give up his job. Her application for judicial review was dismissed, Woolf J holding:

... the fact that the [Housing] Act requires consideration of the family unit as a whole indicates that it would be perfectly proper in the ordinary case for the housing authority to look at the family as a whole and assume, in the absence of material which indicates to the contrary, where the conduct of one member of the family was such that he should be regarded as having become homeless intentionally, that was conduct to which the other members of the family were party.

So, for example, where the husband is a tenant and gives notice in circumstances where he is properly to be regarded as having become homeless intentionally, the wife, even though she was not the tenant and she did not give the notice, can be regarded in the same way. In normal circumstances this would be treated as a joint decision. If, however, at the end of the day because of material put before the housing authority by the wife, the housing authority is not satisfied that she was a party to the decision, it would have to regard her as not having become homeless intentionally.

14.146 The reasoning in *Lewis* has been approved in a number of subsequent cases.

14.147 The correct approach therefore is that:

- each family member is entitled to individual consideration;
- an authority may assume that the members of a family agree to the decision of one family member;
- but there may be evidence that this is not the case.

---

114 *R v Tower Hamlets LBC ex p Khatun* (1993) 27 HLR 344, CA, see para 14.294.
115 [1981] 1 WLR 328, QBD.

14.148　So, where a person claims that they did not acquiesce in another's decision that person has the burden of providing evidence of this.

14.149　The courts have upheld decisions that a family member has acquiesced in the act or omission causing the homelessness in the following cases:

> In *R v Swansea CC ex p John*[116] the applicant was the sole tenant of a council property. A possession order was made because of nuisance and annoyance caused by the tenant's long-term partner, who was her lodger. The court found that the tenant had acquiesced, in as much as she could have terminated his right to occupy, but failed to do so.

> *R v East Hertfordshire DC ex p Bannon*[117] concerned an application made by the ex-partner of a man whose anti-social behaviour had led to both being evicted. The decision that she was intentionally homeless, having either been a party to his behaviour or done nothing to prevent it, was upheld.

14.150　The same approach is applied when a family is evicted because of a failure to pay rent:

> In *R v Ealing LBC ex p Salmons*[118] a couple were evicted for rent arrears of some £12,000. Both maintained that the husband had been unaware of the arrears and that he had provided his wife with the money to pay the rent but she had not done so. The authority held that it was inconceivable that he was unaware of the arrears or the threat of eviction and that he had acquiesced in the non-payment of the rent.
>
> The court dismissed the claim for judicial review of the decision: the authority had made sufficient enquiries and was entitled to conclude that the applicant had known about or at least turned a blind eye to the arrears.

116 (1982) 9 HLR 58, QBD.
117 (1986) 18 HLR 515, QBD.
118 (1990) 23 HLR 272, QBD.

14.151　However, simply being aware of arrears may not be sufficient to establish that there was acquiescence.

> In *R v East Northamptonshire DC ex p Spruce*[119] a couple were evicted because of substantial rent arrears. The evidence was that Mrs Spruce had become aware of the arrears only at a late stage.
>
> The court quashed the decision that she was intentionally homeless: it was not enough that she was aware of the arrears; the authority had failed to make sufficient inquiries into whether or not she had acquiesced in the failure to pay the rent.

14.152　Even where an applicant has had no part in a decision leading to the loss of accommodation, if he or she is content to leave such decisions to someone else, an authority may find there has been acquiescence.

> In *R v Tower Hamlets LBC ex p Khatun*[120] a man gave up accommodation with his brother when his wife was about to give birth to their third child. They subsequently applied as homeless and his wife argued that her husband had not consulted her about the decision and that she had not wanted to leave, but that her husband had told her that if she wanted them to remain together she must follow him. She was nevertheless found to be intentionally homeless.
>
> Her claim for judicial review was refused and her appeal dismissed by the Court of Appeal: if a wife is content to leave decisions about where the family lives to her husband, then a decision in which she co-operates may be regarded as a decision in which she had joined, unless there is some reason for holding that she did not do so.

Breaking the chain of causation

14.153　Once a person has been found intentionally homeless, the question arises: when, in the future, might he or she no longer be homeless intentionally? In other words, when might the chain of causation be broken?

119　(1988) 20 HLR 508, QBD.
120　(1993) 27 HLR 344, CA.

14.154   It will usually be necessary for a person found intentionally homeless to obtain settled accommodation in order to 'break the chain'.
However, it is possible for some other event to do so: for example, a
person who subsequently becomes homeless as the result of domestic violence or a relationship breakdown.[121] See paras 13.59–13.76 for
a summary of the position relating to future applications following a
negative decision.

Was the act or omission deliberate?

14.155   It is not the case that the person must have deliberately become
homeless or deliberately given up accommodation. The requirement
is that the act or omission *leading to* the homelessness was deliberate
in the ordinary sense of the word.

14.156   A person suffering from mental health problems may act in a way
that cannot be said to be deliberate. This will depend on the nature
of the mental illness and an opinion of a psychiatrist will usually
be needed. However, someone may be in priority need by reason of
mental illness but still capable of deliberate acts or omissions.[122]

Was the act or omission made in good faith in ignorance of a relevant fact?

14.157   This provision is to ensure that a person who gives up accommodation honestly but mistakenly believing that circumstances are such
that he or she will have accommodation elsewhere is not found intentionally homeless. The fact of which the person is ignorant must, of
course, be relevant to the person's housing.

14.158   A person may give up accommodation to move to another area or
country in order to work there. In such a case the courts have distinguished between 'mere aspiration' and belief in specific employment
or housing opportunities.

> In *Aw-Aden v Birmingham CC*[123] the applicant, a well-qualified
> scientist, came from Belgium to the UK to seek work. He was
> unable to find work and when his family joined him in Birmingham
> the accommodation he was staying in became overcrowded and

---

121 See for example: *R v Camden LBC ex p Aranda* (1998) 30 HLR 76, CA and *R v
      Basingstoke and Deane BC ex p Bassett* (1983) 10 HLR 125, QBD.
122 See *R v Wirral MBC ex p Bell* (1995) 27 HLR 234, QBD.
123 [2005] EWCA Civ 1834, 7 December 2005.

> he applied as homeless. He was found intentionally homeless for giving up his accommodation in Belgium. He submitted that he had not acted deliberately, having been ignorant of his true prospects of finding employment and therefore his ability to afford to pay for accommodation privately.
>
> The Court of Appeal dismissed his appeal, approving the approach of the court in *Obeid*[124] in which it was said:
>
> > ... an applicant's appreciation of the prospects of future housing or future employment can be treated as 'awareness of a relevant fact' for the purposes of this subsection, provided it is sufficiently specific (that is related to specific employment or specific housing opportunities) and provided it is based on some genuine investigation and not mere 'aspiration'.

14.159 In all cases, the person must have acted in good faith. The question is not whether the person acted reasonably although this may be relevant when assessing good faith. It is possible to be guilty of 'honest blundering and carelessness' but still be acting in good faith.[125] As the 2009 Supplementary Guidance states, at para 9:

> Intentionality does not depend on whether applicants have behaved wisely or prudently or reasonably. Where an applicant's failure to seek help may have been foolish, imprudent or even unreasonable, this would not necessarily mean his or her conduct was not in good faith.

14.160 Ignorance of the law or the legal consequences of an act or omission should be disregarded when considering whether an act or omission is deliberate.[126] So, a person who claims that he or she did not know that abandoning premises or failing to pay the rent would lead to the loss of a tenancy. However, a belief that premises were still available to a person who had been out of the UK for a long period was held to constitute ignorance of a relevant fact.[127]

14.161 It can be hard to distinguish between ignorance of the law and ignorance of fact: ignorance about entitlement to housing benefit has been held to constitute ignorance of a fact, as has ignorance of the

---

124 *R v Westminster CC ex p Obeid* (1996) 29 HLR 389, QBD, Carnwath J at 398.

125 *R v Hammersmith & Fulham LBC ex p Lusi* (1991) 23 HLR 260, QBD.

126 See *R v Eastleigh BC ex p Beattie (No 2)* (1984) 17 HLR 168, QBD and *R v Croydon LBC ex p Toth* (1988) 20 HLR 576, CA.

127 *R v Tower Hamlets LBC ex p Rouf* (1991) 23 HLR 460, QBD.

fact that a tenant did not have to leave accommodation until a court order was obtained.[128]

In *Ugiagbe v Southwark LBC*[129] the applicant had a one-year assured shorthold tenancy agreement expiring on 27 May 2007. On 16 April 2007 the landlord wrote to her stating that he could not extend the agreement and asking her to leave by 31 May 2007. She sought advice from the council's One Stop Shop where she was told that she should go to the Homeless Persons Unit (HPU), that they would place her in temporary accommodation and that, if she had friends or relations who could store her belongings, they could be left with them. Not wanting to be treated as homeless, she did not go to the HPU but instead tried to secure accommodation by bidding through the allocations scheme and by asking her landlord for more time. The landlord agreed for a short period but in November 2007 he told her that he needed the property back and asked her to leave. Believing that she had to go, she left the premises. It was common ground that had she followed the advice and attended the HPU she would have been advised that she did not have to leave until ordered by the court to do so.

The Court of Appeal held that her ignorance of the fact that she could not be made to leave without a court order meant that she was unaware of a relevant fact. On the issue of whether she was acting in good faith, the council found that this was wilful ignorance as she had deliberately chosen not to seek advice. The court rejected this:

Her failure to go to the HPU for help could be said to have been foolish or imprudent. But neither of those would be sufficient to put her conduct into the category of not being in good faith, nor would it even if she were regarded as having been unreasonable ... She was not turning a blind eye to that which she knew she would be told, and did not want to know. On the contrary, she had been led to think that she would be treated as within the scope of the homeless duty, and wanted to avoid that if she possibly could. Foolish or not, her subjective motivation seems to me to be the opposite of bad faith.[130]

---

128 R v Westminster ex p Moozary-Oraky (1994) 26 HLR 213, QBD.
129 [2009] EWCA Civ 31, 10 February 2009.
130 [2009] EWCA Civ 31, Lloyd LJ at [26] and [28].

14.162 When considering intentionality in a case when there is evidence that the applicant may have a disability, the authority may be under a duty to be proactive in investigating the extent of the disability and whether it may be relevant to the issue of any 'deliberate' act or omission: *Pieretti v Enfield LBC*.[131]

Contrived homelessness

14.163 An additional definition of intentional homeless was introduced by the Housing Act 1996. Section 191(3) provides that:

A person shall be treated as becoming homeless intentionally if:
(a) he enters into an arrangement under which he is required to cease to occupy accommodation which it would have been reasonable for him to continue to occupy, and
(b) the purpose of the arrangement is to enable him to become entitled to assistance under this Part, and there is no other good reason why he is homeless.

14.164 This is to prevent collusion to take advantage of the homelessness duty. The 2006 Homelessness Code refers to the possibility of parents and children taking advantage of the automatic priority need given to homeless 16- and 17-year-olds, ie a parent and child agreeing that the parent gives notice to leave so the child can make a homeless application. However, it may be difficult to obtain evidence of such an agreement and the authority must 'be satisfied that collusion exists, and must not rely on hearsay or unfounded suspicions'.[132] Furthermore, there must be 'no other good reason' for the person's homelessness. Examples of good reasons are identified as overcrowding or obvious relationship breakdown.

Referral to another authority

14.165 A homeless person may apply for assistance to any local authority, regardless of whether he or she has ever lived in that authority's area. The authority to which the application is made has the duty to carry out the inquiries. However, if the authority decides that a housing duty is owed it *may* consider whether the person can be referred to another authority for the actual provision of housing. A referral

---

131 [2010] EWCA Civ 1104, 12 October 2010. See para 2.90 for a summary of the case.
132 See para 11.28, 2006 Homelessness Code of Guidance.

should be considered only if and when the authority is satisfied that the applicant is eligible, homeless, in priority need and not intentionally homeless.[133] However, it is common for authorities to consider the issue on first presentation. An authority may advise an applicant that the duty to provide housing will probably rest with a different authority, but it is unlawful to refuse to accept an application because the applicant appears to have no local connection.

Local referral conditions

14.166   The conditions for a referral are set out in HA 1996 s198. A referral can be made in the following situations:

- **No local connection**: where there is no local connection with the authority making the referral.
- **Out of borough homelessness placement**: where the applicant is applying within two years of accepting a 'private rented sector offer' arranged by another authority; or, where the applicant was accommodated in the area within the last five years by another authority, acting under a homeless duty.

Local connection referral

14.167   An authority can refer a case to another authority if the following conditions are satisfied:

- neither the applicant nor any person who might reasonably be expected to live with the applicant has a local connection with the district of the authority to which the application was made; *and*
- the applicant or any person who might reasonably be expected to live with the applicant does have a local connection with the other district; *and*
- there is no risk of violence in the other district, see below at para 14.179 for the definition of violence.

14.168   A referral cannot be made because an applicant has a stronger connection with another authority. Only if there is *no* local connection with the referring authority can a referral be made.

---

133   HA 1996 ss184(1)–(2) and 198(1).

What is a local connection?

14.169 HA 1996 s199(1) provides that:

A person has a local connection with the district of a local housing authority if he has a connection with it:
(a) because he is, or in the past was, normally resident there, and that residence is or was of his own choice,
(b) because he is employed there,
(c) because of family associations, or
(d) because of special circumstances.

Residence of choice

14.170 Residence must be residence of choice. Section 199(3) expressly provides that residence is not of choice where it is because of detention 'under the authority of an Act of Parliament' (this would include imprisonment, whether on remand or after conviction, immigration detention and detention under the Mental Health Act 1983.

In *Wandsworth LBC v NJ*[134] the applicant had travelled to London having fled domestic violence in Leicester. A place was found for her in a refuge in Lambeth, which she accepted. After six months, she applied as homeless to Wandsworth because she had friends there and wanted her daughter to attend a school there. She argued that she did not have a local connection in Lambeth since her residence there was not 'of choice'. The Court of Appeal held that she did have a local connection: she had chosen to come to London and accept the offer of the place in the refuge and this was therefore accommodation of choice. (In fact the decision was quashed because new information had come to light that her ex-partner had been seen in the Lambeth area, see para 15.34).

Armed forces

14.171 Prior to 1 December 2008 those serving in the armed forces could not establish local connection in an area, either by residence or employment. The Housing and Regeneration Act 2008 repealed those provisions. Note also that local authorities cannot exclude from their allocations schemes most of those who have recently served in the armed forces on the grounds that they do not have a local connection,[135] see para 17.36.

134 [2013] EWCA Civ 1373, 7 November 2013.
135 Allocation of Housing (Qualification Criteria for Armed Forces) (England) Regulations 2012 SI No 1869 reg 3.

Former asylum-seekers

14.172   Residence by asylum-seekers accommodated by the Home Office have a local connection in the area where they were accommodated (at any time, for any period), despite this not being of their own choice: s198(6). However, if they are subsequently accommodated in a different local authority area by the Home Office that authority will have the responsibility, ie they cannot use the local connection provisions to refer the person to the authority where they were previously dispersed: s198(7)(a).[136]

14.173   Note that an asylum-seeker or family member may gain a local connection by obtaining employment in an area or may have a local connection by virtue of family association. In such a case referral to the dispersal area will not be possible. Similarly, after a period of residence in the area local connection will be established. As in all cases, a referral can only be made if there is *no* local connection with the authority to which the application is made.

The local authority agreement

14.174   Local authorities have devised an agreement to avoid disputes: the Local Authority Association Joint Local Connection Agreement.[137] This sets out a working definition of how local connection is established. It provides:[138]

- 'Normal residence' should be accepted if the person has lived in the area for six months during the previous 12 months or no less than three of the previous five years.
- 'Family associations' normally arise where an applicant or a member of the household has parents, adult children or brothers or sisters currently living in the area who have been resident for at least five years, and the applicant indicates a wish to be near them.

---

136   This covers only those dispersed in England and Wales. If the person was dispersed in Scotland, where the HA 1996 does not apply, the situation is different. If the former asylum-seeker has no local connection with any authority in Scotland, England or Wales, no duty under HA 1996 s193 arises. An authority has power to provide accommodation for a reasonable period to enable the applicant to find accommodation in the private sector and to provide advice and assistance. See, the Asylum and Immigration (Treatment of Claimants) Act 2004 s11(2)–(3).

137   See A Arden, E Orme and T Vanhegan, *Homelessness and allocations*, 8th edition, LAG, 2010.

138   Paragraph 3.5 of the Local Authority Agreement.

- A referral should not be made on the basis of family association if the person objects.
- Employment should not be of a casual nature.

14.175   The Agreement is not law and an applicant may establish a local connection even if the Local Connection Agreement tests are not met.

> In *R v Southwark LBC ex p Hughes*[139] a woman moved to Southwark to set up a permanent home with a man by whom she became pregnant. The relationship ended because of domestic violence and she applied as homeless. The authority's decision to refer her to another authority on the basis that she had resided in Southwark for less than six months was quashed: the authority had failed to make proper inquiry into whether she had gained a local connection by virtue of ordinary residence or other special reason.

14.176   However, it is for the local authority to decide, on the evidence, whether a person has a local connection. While the Local Connection Agreement must not be applied rigidly, an authority is entitled to take account of it as a guideline.

> In *Betts v Eastleigh BC*[140] an applicant and his family had moved to Eastleigh to take up employment. The employment ended and he was forced to leave his private sector accommodation. The family had lived in the area for less than six months but intended to settle in the area. Eastleigh found that the full housing duty was owed, but referred him to the local authority where the family had previously resided. Both authorities agreed that the referral was properly made but the applicant sought judicial review, arguing that the family was normally resident in the area of Eastleigh and that the authority had erred in applying the Local Connection Agreement criteria too rigidly.
>   The challenge was successful in the Court of Appeal but the House of Lords upheld the authority's appeal. It is for the local authority to decide whether an applicant has a local connection because of normal residence. The decision must be made by reference to the facts of each individual case, but an authority may operate a policy or establish guidelines provided it does not close its mind to the particular facts of the individual case. On the facts of the case the authority had made a lawful decision.

139   (1998) 30 HLR 1082, QBD.
140   *Re Betts* [1983] 2 AC 613, HL.

Relevant date for establishing local connection

14.177 The general rule in relation to homeless decisions is that the person's circumstances are assessed as at the date of the decision, not the date of the application. This means that an applicant may not have local connection by way of normal residence at the date of application but may establish such a connection by the time the final decision is made.

> In *Mohamed v Hammersmith and Fulham LBC*[141] the applicant applied to the authority after living in the borough for about three months. He and his family were placed in interim accommodation and a decision made that they would be referred to another authority. He argued that he had acquired a local connection because of the time the family had spent in interim accommodation awaiting a decision.
>
> The House of Lords held that the relevant time for deciding on local connection was the date of the decision, whether the original decision or the decision on review. Furthermore, time spent in interim accommodation could, in appropriate circumstances, amount to 'normal residence' for the purpose of establishing a local connection.

Referral of someone owed the section 195A duty

14.178 As is explained in chapter 16, the 'full housing duty' under HA 1996 Part VII can now be ended by a local authority arranging a 'private rented sector offer', see para 16.28. If the accommodation comes to an end within two years, the person may re-apply and a housing duty may be owed even if there is no longer any priority need (the section 195A duty). If the private rented sector offer is outside the first authority's district and the person applies to the authority in whose district they now live, that authority may refer the person back to the first authority, provided there is no risk of violence in that area.

Risk of violence

14.179 For local connection referrals and for referrals of those owed the section 195A duty, no referral may be made if either:

141 [2001] UKHL 57, 1 November 2001.

1) the applicant or any person who might reasonably be expected to live with the applicant would run the risk of domestic violence in the other district, or

2) the applicant or any person who might reasonably be expected to live with the applicant has suffered violence (other than domestic violence) in the other district and it is probable that the return to that district will lead to further violence of a similar kind.[142]

14.180 Note that the similar provision under HA 1996 s198(4), which permits a referral where a person has been accommodated out of borough within the last five years, has no similar provision in relation to the risk of violence. The referral can be made and it will be the responsibility of the receiving authority to ensure that any accommodation offered is suitable, which it would not be if in an area where the applicant was at risk of violence.

Disputes between authorities

14.181 The authority proposing to refer the applicant must notify the applicant and the other authority at the same time, giving reasons why it is considered that the local referral conditions are met.[143] The applicant may request a review and, if unsuccessful, may appeal to the County Court. As between the two authorities, any issue about whether the local referral conditions are met should be decided by agreement or, in the absence of agreement, by arbitration.

14.182 The procedure is set out in the Homelessness (Decisions on Referrals) Order 1998.[144] The Local Government Association operates an independent panel to resolve such disputes.

14.183 Where the authorities are in dispute about the referral, the applicant should be kept in temporary accommodation by the referring authority until the dispute is resolved. It is unlawful for the referring authority simply to terminate interim accommodation on the basis that it believes the referral conditions are met. The applicant must continue to be accommodated until either the referral is accepted or the dispute resolved. If the referral is ultimately accepted, the referring authority may claim reimbursement from the receiving authority

---

142 HA 1996 ss198(2), (2ZA) and (2A). Violence is defined in the same way as under HA 1996 s177. Note that the Court of Appeal has confirmed that the term 'violence' extends beyond physical violence, see para 14.33 above.

143 HA 1996 s184(4).

144 SI No 1578.

for the cost of interim accommodation pending the resolution of the dispute.

Challenging the decision that a housing duty is owed

14.184   A referral can only be considered after it has been decided that a housing duty is owed. A local authority, aware it will be referring an applicant to another authority, may be tempted to apply the relevant tests less rigorously than usual. In such a case, the authority to which the referral is made may challenge the decision by way of judicial review if the decision is flawed on recognised public law grounds.

> In *R v Newham LBC ex p Tower Hamlets LBC*[145] Newham decided that a housing duty was owed. It then referred the case to Tower Hamlets, where the applicant had a local connection. He had previously been found intentionally homeless by Tower Hamlets whereas Newham had found him not intentionally homeless. In reaching that decision, Newham had taken account of housing conditions in the area of Newham. Tower Hamlets challenged the decision, arguing that Newham had erred in law in considering housing conditions in its own area rather than in the area of Tower Hamlets.
>
> The Court of Appeal agreed and quashed Newham's decision that a housing duty was owed.

14.185   Note that in such a case the receiving authority must have the decision quashed by a court on public law grounds. A dispute about whether the housing duty is owed cannot be resolved through the arbitration procedure.[146] Unless the decision is quashed by a court, the receiving authority is bound to accept the referral if the referral conditions are met.

Challenging a decision not to refer

14.186   The decision to refer an applicant to another authority is discretionary: there is no right to be referred or to review a decision not to refer.

---

145   (1991) 23 HLR 62, CA.
146   *R v Slough ex p Ealing LBC* [1981] 1 All ER 601.

In *Hackney LBC v Sareen*[147] a homeless family applied to Hackney but indicated they would like to be housed in another part of London because of family and friends who lived there. Hackney decided that a housing duty was owed. The decision letter made no reference to referral but stated that the applicant had a right to a review of the decision. The applicant requested a review of the decision not to refer the case to the area where he wished to be housed, stating that he had no local connection with Hackney, but did have connections with the other local authority. Hackney responded that he had no right to a statutory review of the decision, but agreed to reconsider the issue. It then confirmed the decision not to refer. A county court appeal was lodged and was successful.

However, the Court of Appeal upheld Hackney's appeal, holding that the decision to refer was discretionary and that: (1) there was no duty to investigate local connection, only a power to do so; (2) there was no right to a statutory review of a decision not to refer; (3) there was therefore no right to a county court appeal in relation to such a decision; and (4) although an 'extra statutory' reconsideration could be challenged if there were grounds, this would not be by way of county court appeal, but by judicial review. Put simply: 'If an applicant wants to be housed in another local authority housing area, he should apply there'.[148]

---

147 [2003] EWCA Civ 351, 19 March 2003.
148 Auld LJ at [28].

Homeless decisions, reviews and appeals

continued

15.63   Accommodation pending appeal

Appendix: Request for review

Key points

- A local authority must give a written decision to a homeless applicant.
- The written decision must give reasons for any adverse finding.
- An applicant can request a review of the decision and must do so within 21 days of notification.
- An authority may agree to conduct a review even if the request is made outside the 21-day time limit.
- The review should be completed by the authority within eight weeks and must be carried out by someone not involved in the original decision.
- The parties can agree in writing to extend the time limit for completion of the review.
- An authority has a power but not a duty to provide interim accommodation pending a review.
- The review decision must also be notified in writing, with reasons, to the applicant.
- An applicant may appeal to the County Court against a negative review decision on a point of law. This covers all of the matters that can be challenged by judicial review.
- The appeal must be lodged at court within 21 days of notification of the review decision.
- The court may allow an out of time appeal in certain circumstances.
- An authority has a power but not a duty to provide interim accommodation pending the appeal.
- If the authority refuses interim accommodation pending review the applicant may judicially review the decision.
- If the authority refuses interim accommodation pending appeal the applicant may appeal to the County Court.

Notification of the decision

15.1   When its inquiries are complete, a local authority must notify the applicant of its decision.[1] The decision letter is often referred to as a 'section 184 decision'. It must be in writing and inform the applicant of:

- the decision, with reasons for any issue decided against the applicant's interests;
- the right to request a review of the decision; and
- the time within which the request must be made, which is 21 days from the date of notification.

Reasons

15.2   The reasons must explain why the decision has been made. It is not enough simply to recite the legal tests, list all the matters taken into consideration and state the conclusion (for an example of such an approach see *R v Newham ex p Lumley*,[2] at para 16.9). The Court of Appeal has held that:[3]

> ... where ... an authority is required to give reasons for its decision, it is required to give reasons which are proper, adequate and intelligible and enable the person affected to know why they have won or lost. That said, the law gives decision-makers a certain latitude in how they express themselves and will recognise that not all those taking decisions will find it easy to express themselves with judicial exactitude.

15.3   A decision may be flawed solely because of a failure to give reasons or sufficient reasons. However, the review process enables local authorities to correct such a deficiency. In such a case, the applicant must be given the opportunity to make further representations before the final review decision. See below, paras 15.33–15.40.

Matters arising after the decision

15.4   After the decision has been made, in the absence of fraud or a mistake of fact, an authority has no power to make further inquiries or

---

1   Housing Act (HA) 1996 s184(3).
2   (2003) HLR 111, CA.
3   *R v Brent LBC ex p Baruwa* (1997) 29 HLR 915, Schiemann LJ at 920. For an example of a case in which inadequate reasons meant the decision was quashed, see: *R (Farah) v LB Hillingdon* [2014] EWCA Civ 359, 26 March 2014, at para 14.143.

re-open the decision unless the applicant seeks a review or makes a fresh application.

> In *R v Lambeth LBC ex p Miah*[4] a housing duty was accepted and the applicant was granted a non-secure tenancy. The authority, having evidence that the applicant was not living in the accommodation but was subletting it, issued a second decision letter stating that the applicant was not homeless.
>
> The court held that the authority had no power to make further inquiries following the decision: there was no application to be investigated. In such a situation, however, a local authority may consider itself discharged from its obligation to continue to provide accommodation. If the authority believed the applicant was abusing the temporary accommodation, the correct course of action would have been to determine the occupation agreement.

15.5 This decision pre-dates the HA 1996 and the position is now clearer: s193 sets out the specific circumstances in which the duty to accommodate ends. This includes becoming homeless intentionally from the accommodation provided or ceasing to occupy it.

Fraud/false information

15.6 The situation is different where there has been fraud or the information given to the authority is untrue.

> In *R v Dacorum BC ex p Walsh*[5] an applicant was found to be homeless and not intentionally homeless, having reported a threat of an eviction by her landlord. Subsequently the authority conducted further inquiries and concluded that she had pretended to be locked out of her home and her claim to be threatened with eviction was false. A second decision was made stating that she was intentionally homeless.
>
> The applicant's claim for judicial review was dismissed: it was absurd to suggest that the Housing Act made it impossible to do what the authority had done.

---

4 (1994) 27 HLR 21, QBD.
5 (1991) 24 HLR 401.

Re-opening an application wrongly decided

15.7   Where an application was decided against the applicant, an authority may re-open the application after receiving new information.[6] However, where the applicant wishes the authority to consider new information, the proper course of action is to seek a review and to submit the new information in support of the review.[7]

15.8   An authority is also entitled to re-open an application where its decision was based on a fundamental mistake of fact.

> In *Porteous v West Dorset DC*[8] the applicant had a secure tenancy of a local authority property in London. She moved to Germany in 2002, believing the tenancy had been transferred into her sister's name. In fact it had not been transferred and remained in the applicant's sole name. On her return from Germany she applied to the authority as homeless. The authority's inquiries did not reveal that the tenancy remained in her sole name and a decision was made that she was eligible, homeless, in priority need and not intentionally homeless and was therefore owed a housing duty. A few weeks after the decision was made, the London authority contacted West Dorset DC and informed them that Ms Porteous was still the tenant of the property and that it remained available for her occupation. A second decision was then made stating that she was not homeless because she had a right to reside in the London property and it was reasonable for her to do so. Ms Porteous applied for a review. Although a notice to quit was served in respect of the London property, the landlord authority indicated that it would await the outcome of the review before commencing possession proceedings. The review decision confirmed the decision that Ms Porteous was not homeless. She appealed to the county court. At the hearing of the appeal, evidence was submitted that the London property remained available for her occupation. Her appeal was dismissed; the judge held that the authority had been entitled to re-consider its original decision and that the London property was available to Ms Porteous.
>
> The Court of Appeal dismissed her appeal: an authority was entitled to revisit and change a decision if the decision resulted from a fundamental mistake of fact, even where there was no bad faith on the part of either party.

6 *R v Hambleton DC ex p Geoghan* [1985] JPL 394, QBD.
7 *Demetri v Westminster CC* (2000) 32 HLR 470, CA.
8 [2004] HLR 30, 4 March 2004.

The statutory review

15.9　Before the HA 1996 the only way to challenge a homeless decision was by judicial review. The HA 1996 introduced a statutory right to an internal review and a county court appeal on a point of law for most substantive homeless decisions. Judicial review remains available for decisions that do not carry the right of review.

15.10　　The way reviews must be conducted is set out in regulations: the Allocation of Housing and Homelessness (Review Procedures) Regulations 1999 ('the Review Regs 1999').⁹

Decisions with a right of review

15.11　Under HA 1996 s202 an applicant has a right to a review of a decision that he or she:¹⁰

- is not eligible;
- is not homeless or threatened with homelessness;
- is not in priority need;
- is intentionally homeless;
- is to be referred to another authority.

15.12　There is also a right to a review of any decision about:

- the suitability of accommodation offered following the acceptance of a housing duty – the temporary accommodation duty;
- the suitability of accommodation offered under HA 1996 Part VI (because a refusal may end the duty to provide temporary accommodation);
- whether the duty to accommodate has come to an end.

Decisions with no right of review

15.13　There is no right of review in relation to:

- a refusal to accept a homeless application;
- a refusal to provide interim accommodation pending a decision;
- the suitability of interim accommodation pending decision;

9　SI No 71.
10　HA 1996 s202 refers specifically to decisions about eligibility, local referral and suitability. In relation to the other matters it refers to any decision as to what duty (if any) is owed under ss190–193, 195 and 196. The duties owed under these sections depend on the decisions regarding the substantive issues of homelessness, priority need and intentional homelessness.

- a decision not to provide interim accommodation pending a statutory review and/or appeal to the County Court;
- decisions about the protection of an applicant's belongings;
- a refusal to review a decision which has already been reviewed;
- a refusal to extend the time limits within which a review should have been requested.

15.14   Decisions about these issues may be challenged by judicial review, with the exception of decisions about interim accommodation pending a county court appeal: such decisions are challenged by way of a further county court appeal (see para 15.63 below).

Time limits

Requesting the review

15.15   The request for the review must be made within 21 days of the 'day on which [the applicant] is notified'.[11] The time limit runs from the receipt of the letter, not the date of the letter. If the letter is not received by the applicant, or there is no address where it can be sent, it can be treated as having been given to the applicant if it is made available for collection at the authority's office for a reasonable period.[12]

15.16   It is only the *request* for the review that must be made within 21 days. Representations and any new evidence can be submitted later. In most cases, the way the decision was made will be relevant and advisers should always request a copy of the homeless file at the same time as requesting a review, indicating that further representations may follow. A standard letter requesting a review is included in the appendix to this chapter. At the same time it may be necessary to request an extension of interim accommodation pending review. This is dealt with in chapter 16 and a model letter is included in the appendix to chapter 16.

Completing the review

15.17   Following a request for a review, the authority should complete the review in accordance with the procedure set out in regulations and within a specified time, currently eight weeks from the day the

---

11   HA 1996 s202(3).
12   HA 1996 s184(6).

request is made. This time limit may be extended by written agreement between the parties.[13]

Out of time reviews

15.18 An authority has a discretion to extend the time for requesting a review and must exercise this discretion in a lawful way. This means that the decision must not be made in bad faith or capriciously for improper motives. Furthermore, it must not be limited to rigidly defined situations because that would involve an unlawful fetter on the discretionary power given by the Housing Act 1996[14] (see para 2.11).

15.19 In most cases the authority will consider both the reasons for the delay and the potential merits of the review when exercising its discretion. However, the discretion is very wide and it is not necessary in all cases to consider the merits of the review.[15] Notwithstanding this, there may be some cases where a failure to consider the merits of a review would be 'obvious perversity' if, on the face of it, the review was bound to succeed.[16]

Conduct of the review

15.20 The following rules are laid down in the Review Regs 1999:

- after receiving a review request the authority must notify the applicant:
  - of the right to make written representations, and
  - what the authority's review procedure is;
- the authority must then carry out the review, considering any representations made;
- if the person conducting the review is an officer (as opposed to a member or person independent of the authority) he or she must be someone who was not involved in the original decision and who is senior to the officer who made the original decision;
- if the reviewer considers that there is a deficiency or irregularity in the decision or the way it was made, but is still minded to make an adverse decision, the reviewer must notify the applicant:

---

13 Review Regs 1999 reg 9(1)–(2). The time limits are different if the review concerns a disputed local referral. In such a case the time limit may be ten or 12 weeks, depending on the nature of the decision: reg 9(1)(b)–(c).
14 *R (C) v Lewisham LBC* [2003] EWCA Civ 927, 4 July 2003.
15 *R (C) v Lewisham LBC* [2003] EWCA Civ 927, 4 July 2003.
16 *R (Radhia Slaiman) v Richmond upon Thames LBC* [2006] EWHC 329 (Admin), 9 February 2006.

- that the reviewer is so minded and the reasons why, and
- that the applicant has the right to make oral and/or written representations (in person or by a representative).

Scope of the review

15.21   The review is not limited to a consideration of whether the original decision was correct. The reviewer must take account of any representations made in support of the review and must make a decision based on all of the information and evidence available at the date of the review.[17] The review decision may decide an issue against the applicant even if this issue was decided in the applicant's favour in the initial decision.

> In *Temur v London Borough of Hackney*[18] the applicant had left the matrimonial home due to alleged violence. Her daughter remained with her husband and his family. She was found to be not in priority need in February 2012 and requested a review of the decision on the basis that it was expected that the child would come to live with her. In March 2012 Ms Temur took a tenancy of a bed-sit and in July 2012 an interim shared residence order was made, following which the child lived mostly with her, staying with her father on some weekends. The council made its review decision in August 2012: it found that she was not homeless because she now had accommodation. The authority agreed to re-consider the decision taking into account representations about the suitability of the accommodation. However, in February 2013 the decision was again confirmed (the authority having followed regulation 8(2) and invited further representations). Her County Court appeal was dismissed and she appealed to the Court of Appeal, arguing that the review officer did not have the power to substitute an adverse decision on different grounds. The appeal was dismissed: there is nothing in the regulations preventing a reviewing officer from making a decision less favourable than the original decision or from substituting an adverse decision on different grounds.

17 The previous regulations (Allocation of Housing and Homelessness (Review Procedures and Amendment) Regulations 1996) stated: 'The authority shall – ... carry out the review on the basis of the facts known to them at the date of the review.' The 1999 regulations do not state this, only that the reviewer should consider any representations made.
18 [2014] EWCA Civ 877, 26 June 2014.

Submissions

15.22 When making submissions in support of a review, it is important to identify the alleged flaws in the original decision. If not, it may not be possible to rely on these flaws in any subsequent county court appeal.

15.23 In *Nipa Begum*[19] (see para 14.28 above) the court refused to quash a decision even though the authority had failed to consider whether the applicant could afford to travel to Bangladesh to occupy accommodation there, because the issue had not been raised in the review process.

15.24 Similarly, in *Cramp v Hastings BC*[20] (see para 13.54 above) the court upheld the council's appeal against the quashing of a decision for failure to make adequate inquiries. The inquiries the applicants alleged should have been made had not been mentioned in their review submissions.

15.25 There are, however, certain issues that an authority must address, regardless of the review submissions. The affordability of accommodation must always be considered when deciding whether it is or would have been reasonable to occupy.[21] Furthermore, a failure to comply with the public sector equality duty (see para 2.86) when making a decision may make the decision unlawful even if the issue was not raised in the review.[22]

New information/evidence

15.26 Where vulnerability is the issue, it is common that further medical evidence is submitted as part of the review. While this may be the most effective way to challenge a decision, the applicant's advisers may not be able to pay for expert evidence.[23] In such a case, the submission should still be made that further medical evidence is needed. If the authority declines to obtain such evidence the County Court may uphold a challenge based on inadequate inquiry.

15.27 Where a local authority does obtain new medical evidence or advice it will usually have to disclose it to the applicant in the interests of fairness and invite his or her comments. However, if the

19 (1999) 32 HLR 445, CA.
20 [2005] EWCA Civ 1005.
21 Homelessness (Suitability of Accommodation) Order 1996 SI No 3204. See paras 14.42 and 14.143.
22 See *Pieretti v Enfield LBC* [2010] EWCA Civ 1104, 12 October 2010, at para 2.90.
23 The fee for further medical evidence may be covered by the Legal Help scheme, see para 22.158.

advice relates to issues of which the applicant is fully aware this may not be necessary.[24]

Relevant date for decision

15.28   The requirement to consider the information and evidence at the date of the review means that the review decision must take account of any change of circumstances since the original decision. This can work either for or against the interests of the applicant, see *Temur* at para 15.21 above.

15.29   This benefitted the applicant in a case where he had no local connection when he applied as homeless, but had established one by the time of the final decision: *Mohamed v Hammersmith and Fulham LBC*[25] (see para 14.177).

> The same principle was applied in *Sahardid v Camden LBC*.[26] The review was about the suitability of an offer of accommodation. The offer had been made in accordance with the council's policy to offer a single parent with a child under the age of five years a one-bedroom dwelling. The review decision was taken three days after the child's fifth birthday and the Court of Appeal held that the decision was flawed because it had failed to take account of the fact that the applicant was entitled, under the council's policy, to accommodation with two bedrooms.

15.30   An exception to this rule may apply when the decision is about the priority need of an applicant aged 16 or 17. This priority need is automatically lost when the young person reaches the age of 18. An authority cannot take advantage of an unlawful decision made at a time when the applicant was under 18 by finding, at the date of the review, that the young person is no longer in priority need, because of turning 18: *Akilah Robinson v Hammersmith & Fulham LBC*.[27]

---

24 See *Hall v Wandsworth LBC; Carter v Wandsworth LBC* [2004] EWCA Civ 1740, 17 December 2002 and *Bellouti v Wandsworth LBC* [2005] EWCA Civ 602, 20 May 2005.

25 [2001] UKHL 57.

26 [2004] EWCA Civ 1485, 26 October 2004.

27 [2006] EWCA Civ 1122, see para 14.106.

Independence of reviewing officer

15.31 The review may be conducted by a panel of members or may be con-tracted out to an independent person.[28] Most commonly it is done by an officer. In this case, he or she must be senior to the original deci-sion-maker and must not have been involved in the original decision. However, a reviewing officer may be assisted in making inquiries by the junior officer who made the original decision.[29]

15.32 In some cases there will be more than one review. An authority may accept that a review decision was flawed and agree to carry out a further review. Also, in most successful county court appeals the review decision will be quashed, with the result that the authority must carry out a further review. It is not unlawful for a subsequent review to be carried out by the same officer who carried out the first review.[30] However, as in all local authority decision-making, actual bias would make the decision unlawful (see paras 2.20–2.21).

Deficient or Irregular decision: regulation 8(2)

15.33 Regulation 8(2) of the Review Regs 1999 applies where the reviewer decides that there was a 'deficiency or irregularity' in the original deci-sion or the manner in which it was made, but is nevertheless minded to make a decision which is against the interests of the applicant on one or more issues. Regulation 8(2) provides that the applicant must be notified that the reviewer is so minded and that the applicant, or someone acting on the applicant's behalf, 'may make representations to the reviewer orally or in writing or both orally and in writing'.

Regulation 8(2): what is a 'deficiency or irregularity'?

15.34 In *Hall v Wandsworth LBC*[31] the Court of Appeal held that the word 'deficiency' does not have any particular legal connotation. It simply means 'something lacking' which is 'of sufficient importance to the fairness of the procedure to justify an extra procedural safeguard'. Therefore

> ... the reviewing officer should treat reg 8(2) as applicable, not mere-ly when he finds some significant legal or procedural error in the

---

28 Local Authorities (Contracting Out of Allocation of Housing and Homelessness Functions) Order 1996 SI No 3205; *De-Winter Heald, Al-Jarah, Ahmad & Kidane v Brent LBC* [2009] EWCA Civ 930, 20 August 2009.

29 *Butler v Fareham BC*, May 2001 *Legal Action* 24, CA.

30 *Feld v Barnet LBC; Ali Pour v Westminster CC* [2004] EWCA Civ 1307, 18 October 2004.

31 [2004] EWCA Civ 1740, 17 December 2002.

decision, but whenever (looking at the matter broadly and untechnically) he considers that an important aspect of the case was either not addressed, or not addressed adequately, by the original decision-maker ...[32]

The original decision can be rendered 'deficient' by virtue of events that happen after the date of the original decision.

> In *Wandsworth LBC v NJ*[33] the applicant's challenge to the decision on local connection failed (see para 14.170). She had fled domestic violence and following the original decision she put forward fresh evidence that her ex-partner had been seen in the Lambeth area. Her appeal was upheld because of a failure to apply regulation 8(2): although the reviewing officer did take account of the fresh evidence she should have followed regulation 8(2) and given the applicant the opportunity to make further representations before making the review decision.

> In *Mohamoud v Birmingham CC*[34] the Court of Appeal found that Regulation 8(2) applied where there had been nothing wrong with the information given to the applicant about a 'final offer' of accommodation made to the applicant. She had explained that she had refused the offer due to confusion about the number of offers she would receive. The review officer should have sent a 'minded to' letter and given her the opportunity to make further representations. See para 16.67.

Regulation 8(2): the procedural rights that follow

15.35   Regulation 8(2) requires that the applicant is informed of the fact that the reviewer is 'minded' to make a decision against the applicant, and why, and that further representations may be made, orally and/or in writing.

15.36   The right to an 'oral hearing', means having the opportunity to make 'face-to-face' representations and an authority cannot

---

32 Carnwath LJ at [29] and [3].
33 [2013] EWCA Civ 1373, 7 November 2013.
34 [2014] EWCA Civ 227, 7 March 2014.

limit the right to making representations by telephone. However, it does not mean having a 'hearing' with witnesses or conducting cross-examination.[35]

15.37 So, once the reviewing officer has identified a deficiency or irregularity he or she must send a 'minded to' letter to the applicant, explaining the reasons for the provisional view and giving the applicant the opportunity to make further representations. The reviewing officer does not have a discretion as to whether to offer the right of review on the basis that further representations will make no difference; that would mean that 'the reviewing officer has the power to decide, in effect, that nothing the applicant can say will cause him to change his mind on the issue which he has found against the applicant'.[36]

> In *Lambeth LBC v Johnston*[37] the Court of Appeal held that the applicant's right under regulation 8(2) is 'a valuable procedural right' in all such cases. It 'is not a discretionary option that the reviewing officer can apply or disapply depending on whether he or she considered that giving a "minded to find" notice would be of material benefit to the applicant' or where it was considered the applicant had already made representations on the relevant issues.

Notification and reasons

15.38 The review decision must be given in writing. If it is not received, it is treated as having been given if it is made available at the authority's office for a reasonable period for collection: s203(8).

---

35 *Makisi v Birmingham CC, Yosief v Birmingham CC, Nagi v Birmingham CC* [2011] EWCA Civ 355, 31 March 2011.

36 *Mitu v Camden LBC* [2011] EWCA Civ 1249, 1 November 2011, Lewison LJ at [28]. However, where the deficiency does not result in any prejudice to the applicant, the courts may refuse to intervene. In *Ibrahim v Wandsworth LBC* [2013] EWCA Civ 20, 30 January 2013, the decision letter to someone found intentionally homeless failed to inform her of the duty to provide accommodation for a reasonable period. However, the authority did in fact provide interim accommodation throughout the review, the county court appeal and appeal in the Court of Appeal. The Court of Appeal dismissed the appeal.

37 *Lambeth LBC v Johnston* [2008] EWCA Civ 690, 19 June 2008.

15.39   If the original decision is confirmed, reasons must be given.[38] Furthermore, the applicant must be informed of the right to appeal to the County Court on a point of law and the time limit for bringing such an appeal, which is 21 days from the date of notification: s203(5). If reasons are not given or if the applicant is not informed of the right to appeal to the County Court, the notice of the decision is treated as not having been given: s203(6). This means that any deadline for appealing to the County Court does not apply until proper notice is given.

15.40   As is the case for the HA 1996 s184 decision, the period for appealing runs from the date of notification (ie receipt of the letter), not the date endorsed on the letter or the date it was posted. Notice can be given to the applicant's representatives where they have made representations on the applicant's behalf and the applicant has authorised the local authority to deal with them.

In *Dharmaraj v Hounslow LBC*[39] the review decision had been faxed to the applicant's solicitors and stated that: 'Any application for appeal must be made within 21 days of the date of the letter.'

The Court of Appeal rejected the argument that the review decision must be sent personally to the applicant: his solicitors had made representations in support of the review and the applicant had signed an authorisation to correspond with them about it. Furthermore, the letter was not defective for failing to state that the 21-day period runs from the date of notification: in this case, since the letter was sent by fax, that was the same as the date of notification. The court suggested that even where such a letter was received a few days later so that the review letter had misinformed the applicant about the deadline for the appeal by 'a couple of days', this would not necessarily make the review letter defective. However, if this contributed to the applicant missing the 21-day deadline, the court would almost certainly allow a late appeal.

38 HA 1996 s203(4). There is no right to be given reasons where the review succeeds and the decision is withdrawn: *Akhtar v Birmingham* [2011] EWCA Civ 383, 12 April 2011, see para 16.68.
39 [2011] EWCA Civ 312, 24 January 2011.

Outcome of the review

15.41 The best outcome for the applicant will be an acceptance of the full housing duty. Often, however, the review decision will be that the s184 decision should be withdrawn and further inquiry carried out. If this is the outcome, the authority will have a duty to provide interim accommodation pending further decision (provided there is reason to believe the applicant may be homeless, eligible and in priority need).

15.42 If the review decision confirms an adverse section 184 decision, the applicant may appeal to the County Court.

Appeals to the County Court

15.43 Section 204 of the HA 1996 provides that:

> ... if an applicant who has requested a review under section 202:
> (1) is dissatisfied with the decision on the review, or
> (2) is not notified of the decision on the review within the time pre-scribed ...
> he may appeal to the county court on any point of law arising from the decision or, as the case may be, the original decision.

Time limits

15.44 An appeal must be brought within 21 days of the applicant being notified of the review decision. If the appeal is being brought to challenge the original decision (because of a failure to carry out the review within the statutory period) it must be brought within 21 days of the date on which the applicant should have received notification (in most cases this means 11 weeks from the original notification under s184).[40]

15.45 Where the 21 days ends on a day when the court is closed, an appeal may be lodged on the next working day.[41]

Out of time appeals

15.46 The court may give permission for an appeal to be brought out of time only if satisfied that there was a good reason for the failure to bring

---

40 HA 1996 s204(2).
41 *Adan v Brent LBC* (1999) 32 HLR 848, CA.

the appeal in time and for any delay in applying for permission.[42] It is also possible to apply, *within* the 21-day period, for permission to lodge the appeal out of time. If it is possible to make such an application, it is probably safer instead to draft and lodge the appeal notice itself as the detailed grounds can be lodged by way of a skeleton argument later.

15.47   To give permission for a late appeal, the court must be satisfied there is a good reason for the delay. If not, permission must be refused and the court should not consider the merits of the appeal.[43]

Procedure on appeals

15.48   There is no requirement to be legally represented but in most cases the applicant will need to instruct solicitors to advise whether there is a point of law arising from the decision and to draft notice of appeal or instruct a barrister to do so. Legal aid is available, depending on the applicant's means and the likelihood of success. It is important that someone seeking to challenge a review decision is referred to solicitors without delay. The solicitor will usually need to send a 'letter before claim' to the authority and consider the response before legal aid will be granted. Most solicitors will then instruct a barrister to draft the appeal notice.

15.49   The procedure is set out in Part 52 of the Civil Procedure Rules (CPR) and the appeal notice is form N161. Part 52 and form N161 are available online, along with guidance notes. Chapter 22 contains a general explanation of county court procedure. In most cases the form N161 will be drafted by a solicitor or barrister, as the legal grounds on which it is argued the decision is unlawful must be identified. A skeleton argument summarising the legal principles and case-law relied on should be either included in the appeal notice or filed within 14 days. The forms and procedure are confusing because they are designed primarily for appeals against court decisions not local authority decisions.

15.50   The hearing of an appeal will usually consist of purely legal argument about the lawfulness of the decision. Oral evidence is not given and it is unusual even for witness statements to be needed. If the appellant (the homeless applicant) is legally represented, he or she is not strictly required to attend the hearing. However, it is good

---

42 HA 1996 s204(2A).
43 *Short v Birmingham CC* [2004] EWHC 2112 (QB), 10 September 2004.

practice to do so because proposals may be put forward to resolve the appeal on which his or her instructions will be needed.

Reconsidering a review decision

15.51 There is nothing to prevent an authority reconsidering a decision made on review.[44] Indeed an authority will often respond to a letter indicating an intention to appeal by offering to reconsider the decision. However, if this is agreed between the parties, the authority must confirm that it is withdrawing its previous review decision and that the reconsidered decision will be the review decision for the purposes of any appeal. If the authority does not agree, any appeal must be lodged within 21 days of the notification of the initial review decision.

> In *Demetri v Westminster CC*[45] the authority's decision on review was notified in the correct form to the applicant, including information about the right to appeal to the county court within 21 days. The applicant's advisers discovered that certain documents had not been sent to the review officer and the council agreed to consider its review decision further in light of these documents. Two months later the council indicated that it had considered the documents, but would not change its review decision. An appeal was lodged in the county court but was struck out on the grounds that it had been lodged out of time. The applicant's appeal to the Court of Appeal was dismissed.

15.52 *Demetri* was decided at a time when the County Court had no power to extend the time for an appeal. However, advisers should always ensure that the authority confirms that the first review decision is withdrawn pending reconsideration. In *Demetri* the court indicated that where an applicant is unrepresented the authority must make it clear if the time for a county court appeal is not being extended.

Appealing the original section 184 decision

15.53 Where a review is requested but the authority fails to carry out the review within the time limit, the applicant has two choices: a county

---

44 *R v Westminster CC ex p Ellioua* (1998) 31 HLR 440, CA.
45 (2000) 32 HLR 470, CA.

court appeal against the original decision or judicial review to force the authority to carry out the review. Often it will be sufficient to invite the authority to agree an extension of time to complete the review. Such agreement must be confirmed in writing. Where the applicant wishes to submit new information or make submissions, it is better for a review to be conducted than to appeal against the original decision. Appeals are limited to considering the lawfulness of the decision at the time it was made. If the appeal is successful the likely outcome is the quashing of the decision so that the authority must make a fresh section 184 decision. Furthermore, there is nothing to prevent an authority from notifying the applicant of the decision on review after a county court appeal has been commenced. The appellant would then need to amend the appeal grounds or (if the review decision is positive or unchallengeable) to withdraw the appeal. In such a case the local authority should be ordered to pay the costs of the appeal.

What is a point of law?

15.54   A 'point of law' is not limited to matters of legal interpretation, but embraces all of the matters usually challenged by way of judicial review, including irrationality and inadequacy of reasons.[46]

15.55   Broadly, the main types of judicial review challenge have been categorised under the following heads:[47]

- illegality;
- irrationality; and
- procedural impropriety.

15.56   In addition, a failure to give reasons, or adequate reasons, may in itself make a decision unlawful. Breaches of statutory duties such as under the Equality Act 2010 would also make a decision unlawful.

15.57   The grounds for judicial review are examined in more detail in paras 2.8–2.25. All of the grounds that may be used in judicial review proceedings may be argued as points of law in a homeless appeal. In *Tachie v Welwyn Hatfield BC*[48] it was confirmed that this includes an 'ultra vires' argument, ie that the authority did not have the power to do what it did, in this case to contract out all of its homelessness functions. However the appeal was dismissed on the basis that the

---

46 *Nipa Begum v Tower Hamlets LBC* (1999) 32 HLR 445, CA, para 14.28.
47 *CCSU v Minister for Civil Service* [1985] AC 374, HL.
48 [2013] EWHC 3972, 13 December 2013.

authority was entitled to contract out its functions to a company owned and controlled by the local authority.

The powers of the County Court

15.58 It is not for the court to reach its own decision on the facts. The court is exercising a supervisory function, as in judicial review; it is limited to considering the lawfulness of the authority's decision. The court may:[49]

- confirm a decision;
- quash a decision; or
- vary a decision.

15.59 If an appeal is successful, the most common order is the quashing of the review decision. This means that the authority must conduct a fresh review. Of course this can mean that after a successful appeal the authority then makes another negative review decision. Indeed, it sometimes happens that an authority makes several review decisions in relation to the same applicant.

15.60 When a court is asked to vary a decision, the question is whether there is any real prospect that the authority, acting rationally and with the benefit of further inquiry, might be satisfied that the issue could be decided in an adverse way.[50] If so, the decision should be quashed, rather than varied.

> In *Ekwuru v Westminster*[51] the Court of Appeal considered an appeal against a county court decision not to vary a decision that the appellant was intentionally homeless. The authority had already agreed twice to its decisions being quashed, following successful appeals by Mr Ekwuru. On the third occasion it again indicated that it would submit to the decision being quashed and carry out what would be a fourth review. Mr Ekwuru argued that the court should vary the decision. The county court declined to do so on the basis that such a decision would involve a hearing of the original facts. Mr Ekwuru appealed to the Court of Appeal, and the appeal was heard almost four years after he had applied as homeless.
>
> It was held that there was no realistic possibility that the further inquiries the authority proposed would produce more information

49 HA 1996 s204(3).
50 *R (Deugi) v Tower Hamlets LBC* [2006] EWCA Civ 159, 7 March 2006.
51 [2003] EWCA Civ 1293, 31 July 2003.

than was available at the date of the third review. On the basis of the material before the authority at that time, it could not lawfully have come to the conclusion that Mr Ekwuru was intentionally homeless and the court varied the decision to one that he was not intentionally homeless.

In contrast, *P v Ealing LBC*[52] concerned a complex factual situation in which the applicant alleged that she had been unable to occupy a property because she had been raped by a neighbour. The authority failed to consider all of the evidence and decided that she was intentionally homeless (implicitly rejecting her allegation). The county court varied the decision to one that she was not intentionally homeless. However, the authority succeeded in its appeal. The appropriate order was to remit the matter to the local authority. It could not be said that there was no real prospect that the local authority, acting rationally, might find that the alleged rape had not taken place.[53]

Time limit for further review

15.61   HA 1996 provides no time limit for a further review following the quashing or withdrawal of a previous review decision. If the review is to be carried out following a county court appeal, the court may be asked to set a time limit for the further review decision. If the review is withdrawn by agreement, a time limit should be agreed.

15.62   In all cases it should be stipulated that the applicant be provided with interim accommodation pending any further review decision.

Accommodation pending appeal

15.63   An authority has a discretion to provide interim accommodation pending an appeal. If this is refused, an applicant may bring a second appeal in the County Court, under HA 1996 s204A, to challenge the refusal. Interim accommodation pending review or appeal is discussed in paras 16.4–16.13.

---

52 [2013] EWCA Civ 1579, 5 November 2013
53 Similarly, in *Hussain v Waltham Forest LBC* [2015] EWCA Civ 14, 20 January 2015, the Court of Appeal remitted the case to the local authority where the wrong test had been applied in relation to the risk of violence, see para 14.33.

APPENDIX

Request for review

Dear Sir/Madam,

Re: Mrs A – section 184 decision dated

We are advising Mrs A with regard to her homeless application. Mrs A requests a review of the above decision.

Please provide to us a copy of the complete homelessness file under the Data Protection Act 1998. We enclose a cheque in the sum of £10 together with our client's signed authority.

We intend to make representations in support of the review following receipt of the file. We would therefore be grateful if this could be provided as a matter of urgency.

Yours faithfully,

Adviser

Advice Agency

Homelessness: accommodation duties

continued

Key points

- There are several different stages at which an authority may provide accommodation to a homeless applicant: pending an initial decision; pending a review of a decision; pending an appeal of a decision; and, under the 'full housing' duty.
- An authority *must* provide interim accommodation pending a decision if it has reason to believe the applicant may be homeless, eligible and in priority need.
- An authority *may* provide interim accommodation pending review or appeal.
- Interim accommodation must be suitable but the temporary nature of the accommodation means the standard may be low.
- All accommodation provided under HA 1996 Part VII must be available to the applicant and the family members who normally live with the applicant, plus any other person who might reasonably be expected to live with the applicant.
- The suitability of accommodation can be challenged but the way it is challenged depends on the stage at which the accommodation is offered.
- An applicant can accept accommodation offered under the full housing duty and still challenge the suitability by way of review and county court appeal.
- If an applicant refuses accommodation offered under the full housing duty and a challenge to suitability fails, the authority will owe no housing duty.
- One way the full housing duty can now be ended is by the making of a private rented sector offer.
- Long-term social housing is only obtained through an authority's allocations scheme.

Introduction

16.1   An authority may have a duty or a power to provide accommodation for the applicant at different stages in the homeless application process. These stages are as follows:

Temporary accommodation:
- interim accommodation pending decision;
- interim accommodation pending review;
- interim accommodation pending appeal;
- temporary accommodation for a person found intentionally homeless.

The 'full housing duty':
- accommodation provided under Housing Act (HA) 1996 s193.

Permanent accommodation:
- the allocation of permanent social housing.

16.2   The principles involved at each stage vary, as do the ways of challenging decisions. Chapter 13 deals with the interim accommodation duty pending decision. This chapter deals with interim accommodation pending review and appeal, the accommodation duty owed to those found intentionally homeless and the 'full housing duty' under HA 1996 s193. The allocation of permanent accommodation is dealt with in chapter 17.

Temporary accommodation duties

Accommodation pending decision

16.3   This is dealt with in detail in paras 13.26–13.46. The main features of the duty to provide interim accommodation pending a decision are:

- the duty is triggered whenever the authority has reason to believe the applicant may be eligible, homeless and in priority need;
- the accommodation must be suitable and it must be made available to the applicant and his or her household;
- the duty ends when a decision is made on the homeless application;
- challenging a failure to provide accommodation or the suitability of the accommodation is by way of judicial review.

Accommodation pending review

16.4   The *duty* to provide interim accommodation ends if a negative decision is made. If the applicant seeks a review, the authority has a *power*
to continue to provide interim accommodation pending the review
decision.

16.5   The authority does not have to consider whether to provide or
extend interim accommodation pending review unless requested to
do so.[1]

16.6   A refusal to provide interim accommodation pending review is
challenged by way of judicial review.

16.7   The principles an authority must apply when deciding whether
or not to provide interim accommodation were set out in *R v Camden
LBC ex p Mohammed*.[2]

In *Mohammed* the authority operated a policy of providing interim
accommodation only in exceptional circumstances. The evidence
was that the proportion of successful reviews was small.

The Court of Appeal held that it is not unlawful to operate
such a policy and that an authority must balance the objective of
maintaining fairness between homeless persons to whom they have
decided no duty is owed, with proper consideration of the possibility
that the applicant may be right and may therefore be deprived of an
entitlement. In carrying out the balancing exercise certain matters
will always require consideration:

- the merits of the case – that is, the merits of the case that the
  decision is flawed, not the merits of the case on the facts, once
  all necessary inquiries have been made;[3]
- whether there is new material, information or argument which
  should be considered and which could have a real effect on the
  decision under review; and
- the personal circumstances of the applicant and the
  consequences of a refusal to provide interim accommodation.

1 *R v Newham LBC ex p Lumley* (2003) 33 HLR 111, 28 January 2000.
2 (1997) 30 HLR 315, CA.
3 See the comments of Brooke LJ in *Lumley* (2003) 33 HLR 111, CA (see para
   16.9 below) at [52] and [54]. This distinction is important: in many cases the
   quality of the initial decision-making is poor, with cursory inquiries being
   made and letters issued in a pro forma manner. The conclusion may be the
   same following full inquiries, but the applicant is entitled to a lawful decision
   made in accordance with HA 1996 and properly explained.

The applicant claimed to have left her home because of domestic violence from her husband. The authority had taken account of inconsistencies in her account of his conduct. The authority did not give her the opportunity to explain the inconsistencies, but decided that accommodation was available to her and that therefore she was not homeless.

The court decided that the merits of the challenge to the initial decision were such that the original decision was tainted with unfairness; the authority had been wrong to refuse to provide interim accommodation pending review.

16.8   These criteria should be addressed when requesting interim accommodation. Because such requests usually have to be made on an urgent basis, it is useful to have a template to use when making such a request. An example of such a request is contained in the appendix to this chapter.

16.9   Local authorities often cite *R v Brighton and Hove Council ex p Nacion*[4] to support the argument that, if the authority has considered all material factors, successful judicial review applications will be exceptional. *Nacion* concerned a refusal to provide interim accommodation *after* a review decision and pending a county court appeal.[5] In *Nacion* the court did refer to the fact that the provision of accommodation pending appeal *and review* was entirely within the discretion of the local authority. However, an original decision is more likely to be flawed than a decision made following a review. On the other hand, a local authority that has extended accommodation pending review will usually agree a further extension until appeal.

In *R v Newham LBC ex p Lumley*,[6] the applicant suffered from depression and had been homeless for some time. A medical report was sent to the authority referring to the risk of suicide if he remained homeless. The authority's medical officer considered the doctor's report and indicated, without giving reasons, that he did not consider the applicant to be vulnerable.

It was conceded that the decision letter simply recited the terms of HA 1996 s189 (the priority need categories) 'parrot-fashion'

4   (1999) 31 HLR 1095.
5   This was at a time when judicial review was the only way to challenge a refusal to accommodate pending appeal.
6   (2003) 33 HLR 111, CA.

and gave no substantive explanation for the decision that the applicant was not in priority need. The court held that the authority had failed in its duty to carry out proper inquiries into the applicant's psychiatric history. In relation to the provision of interim accommodation pending review, the authority

... had clearly not yet made a lawful decision, because of the shortcomings which [were conceded]. Justice therefore demanded that it should continue to provide him with temporary accommodation until it did.[7]

In *R (F) v Westminster CC*[8] the court refused permission for a claim challenging a refusal to provide accommodation pending review of a local connection referral. The referral had been accepted by Cardiff Council but the applicant had put forward reasons why she did not want to live in Cardiff. The court held that the council had properly applied the 'Mohammed criteria' and that the decision not to accommodate pending review was lawful. Furthermore, an interim injunction had been obtained without the court being told that Cardiff was willing to accommodate the applicant immediately. The injunction was discharged and the court ordered the legal representatives to 'show cause' why they should not pay the costs wasted by the non-disclosure, see para 22.150.

In contrast, in *R (IA) v Westminster CC,*[9] the court was scathing about the council's cursory initial inquiries and the 'cavalier' dismissal of new information provided to support the request for interim accommodation pending review and extended the order granted on a without notice application. See para 13.35 for a full summary of the case.

7 (2003) 33 HLR 111, CA, Brooke LJ at [55].
8 [2012] EWCH 1357 (Admin), 21 March 2012.
9 [2013] EWHC 1273, 20 May 2013.

Accommodation pending appeal

16.10   An authority also has a power to provide interim accommodation pending a county court appeal: HA 1996 s204(4). Prior to the Homelessness Act 2002 the only way to challenge a refusal to do so was by way of judicial review (as in *Nacion*, see para 16.9 above). Now such challenges are brought by way of a county court appeal.

16.11   The Housing Act 1996 s204A(2) provides that, where an applicant has a right to a county court appeal against a homeless decision, the applicant may also appeal against a decision not to provide accommodation up to the date of appeal.

16.12   The court may order the authority to secure that accommodation is available until the determination of the main appeal, or an earlier time, as specified, and must confirm or quash the decision not to provide interim accommodation. The court cannot order the authority to provide interim accommodation beyond the final determination of the homeless appeal.[10]

16.13   Under section 204A the County Court may only order an authority to provide interim accommodation if satisfied that a failure to do so would 'substantially prejudice the applicant's ability to pursue the main appeal'.[11] The most compelling argument will be where, without interim accommodation, the appellant will be 'street homeless' pending the appeal, so that his or her solicitors may find it impossible to obtain instructions to pursue the appeal.

16.14   In the case of *R (ZH and CN) v Newham LBC and Lewisham LBC*,[12] see para 8.18, the Supreme Court stated that one way a person facing eviction from interim accommodation might challenge the proportionality of the eviction would be by way of a s204A appeal. This is puzzling given the restrictive terms of the County Court's powers s204A, and the fact that it only has jurisdiction where there is a pending appeal against a substantive homelessness decision. It seems likely that most 'proportionality' challenges will continue to be brought by way of judicial review.

---

10 HA 1996 s204A(6)(b).
11 HA 1996 s204A(6)(a).
12 [2014] UKSC 62, 12 November 2014, Lord Hodge at [71]. In this case it was decided that those in interim accommodation had no protection from eviction: local authorities and private landlords can evict without obtaining possession orders.

Temporary accommodation for the intentionally homeless

16.15   If an applicant is found to be eligible, homeless and in priority need, but intentionally homeless, HA 1996 s190(2) provides that an authority must:

(a) secure that accommodation is made available for his occupation for such period as they consider will give him a reasonable opportunity of securing accommodation for his occupation; and

(b) provide him with advice and such assistance as they consider appropriate in the circumstances in any attempts he may make to secure that accommodation becomes available for his occupation.

16.16   In determining what is a reasonable period the authority must consider an applicant's individual circumstances and should not operate a blanket policy as to the period of temporary accommodation offered in all cases.[13]

The Court of Appeal considered the nature of this duty in *R on the application of Conville v Richmond upon Thames LBC*.[14] The decision that the applicant was intentionally homeless was made in February 2005 and she was told she could remain in the interim accommodation for a further 28 days. She was subsequently granted a number of extensions until 8 June 2005. She made genuine but unsuccessful attempts to find her own accommodation. Her efforts were hampered by the fact that she could not afford the deposit and advance rent required by most private landlords. She could not borrow the money and was ineligible for the council's rent deposit scheme. In deciding on the period that was reasonable, the authority had taken into account the applicant's circumstances, the authority's limited resources and the needs of other homeless applicants.

The Court of Appeal held that the authority should not have taken account of its resources, but should have assessed what was a reasonable period

... by reference to the particular needs and circumstances of the applicant. It should have regard to the possibilities open to the applicant ... If the applicant is not making reasonable efforts to pursue the possibilities open to him, that will be a strong indication that he should not be given more time.[15]

13   *Lally v RLBC Kensington and Chelsea* (1980) *Times* 27 March.
14   [2006] EWCA Civ 718, 8 June 2006.
15   [2006] EWCA Civ 718, Pill LJ at [38].

However, giving a person a reasonable opportunity to find accommodation does not mean a period sufficient to ensure that the person will necessarily succeed.

What amounts to a reasonable opportunity will depend on the particular circumstances but it is an assessment the authority are capable of making without converting it into a duty to meet the appellant's needs. In this statutory context, a distinction is maintainable between giving a reasonable opportunity and giving such opportunity as will succeed in obtaining accommodation.[16]

Advice and assistance for the intentionally homeless

16.17   In addition to providing accommodation for a reasonable period, the authority must also provide (or ensure the applicant is provided with) advice and assistance in any attempt made to secure accommodation. Before providing the advice and assistance the applicant's housing needs must be assessed and the advice and assistance must include information about the likely availability in the district of the types of accommodation appropriate to the applicant's housing needs (including, in particular, the location and sources of such types of accommodation).[17]

The full housing duty – HA 1996 s193

16.18   The 'full housing duty' under HA 1996 s193 arises where the local authority is satisfied that the applicant is homeless, eligible for assistance and has a priority need. Unless a referral to another authority is possible, the local authority must 'secure that accommodation is available for occupation by the applicant': HA 1996 s193(2). This is known as 'the full housing duty'. The authority remains subject to the duty until it ceases in one of the ways specified in section 193.[18]

---

16 [2006] EWCA Civ 718, Pill LJ at [40].
17 HA 1996 s190(2)(b), (4) and (5).
18 HA 1996 s193(3).

Recent changes: the 'private rented sector offer'

16.19 The Localism Act 2011 introduced a fundamental change to the 'full housing duty' by providing that the duty can be brought to an end by the making of a 'private rented sector offer', which satisfies certain conditions. It is important to distinguish between a private rented sector offer that ends the housing duty and a situation in which the local authority use the private sector in order to discharge its continuing housing duty.

16.20 It has always been possible for a local authority to discharge the full housing duty by arranging for accommodation to be provided by a private landlord.[19] However, while such accommodation may be temporary the housing duty is a continuing one (ending only in specified circumstances). So, where a local authority is discharging its accommodation duty by arrangement with a private landlord, there may be circumstances when an applicant would have to leave the private sector accommodation. However, the local authority's housing duty continues and alternative accommodation has to be made available by the authority. The 'private rented sector offer' is different: the acceptance of the offer brings the accommodation duty to an end.[20]

16.21 Note that for most homeless applicants authorities have the *option* of using 'private rented sector offers' to end the duty. However, for applicants with certain immigration status ('restricted persons') authorities **must**, where reasonably practicable, end the duty by way of a 'private rented sector offer', see paras 20.174–20.178.

The ending of the full housing duty

16.22 In summary, the full housing duty ceases if the applicant:

- refuses suitable accommodation offered under Part VII;
- ceases to be eligible for assistance (ie a change of immigration status);
- becomes homeless intentionally from the Part VII accommodation;
- accepts an offer of accommodation under Part VI (an allocation);
- accepts an offer of an assured tenancy (other than an assured shorthold tenancy) from a private landlord;

---

19 HA 1996 s206.
20 There is an important distinction between the term 'discharge' and 'end' in relation to the s193 housing duty. The duty can be discharged in a number of ways but discharging the duty does not mean that the duty has ended.

- voluntarily ceases to occupy as his or her only or principal home the accommodation made available for his occupation;
- refuses a final offer made under Part VI (having been advised of the consequences of refusal);
- accepts or refuses a private rented sector offer, having been informed in writing of certain specified matters.

Refusals of Part VII or Part VI offers are dealt with below at para 16.37 below.

Ceasing to be eligible

16.23   Eligibility is dealt with in detail in chapter 20. A person's immigration status may change such that they are no longer eligible, eg time limited leave may expire with no application being submitted to extend or vary the leave. If this happens, the section 193 housing duty will end.

Becoming homeless intentionally

16.24   If a person is evicted from the accommodation provided under s193(2) because of a failure to pay rent or anti-social behaviour, he or she is likely to be found to be intentionally homeless. If so, the duty ends. The definition of intentional homelessness is found in HA 1996 s191 (see paras 14.114–14.162). For the section 193 duty to end, all the elements of the intentional homelessness test must be met; a policy that the duty will end in relation to any person evicted because of rent arrears or complaints of nuisance would be unlawful.

Ceasing to occupy as only or principal home

16.25   Again, this has a specific meaning and an authority cannot conclude that the duty has ended simply because a person has been absent from accommodation for a period. Where a person is occupying hostel accommodation, the accommodation provider may simply terminate the licence on the basis of a short absence, or a failure to sign a register. This is not sufficient to end the section 193 duty unless the test for intentional homelessness is met or there is evidence that the person no longer occupies as his or her only or principal home. See paras 4.5–4.7 for an explanation of the law on 'only or principal home'.

Accepting a Part VI offer or an assured tenancy from a private landlord

16.26 The aim of most homeless applicants is to achieve a Part VI offer. Clearly the s193 housing duty will end if long-term social housing is offered and accepted. However, problems often arise when an applicant disputes the suitability of the Part VI offer, see below at paras 16.48–16.69.

16.27 Assured tenancies (as opposed to assured shorthold tenancies) are so rarely offered by private landlords that this would be a very unusual way for the housing duty to end.

Private rented sector offers[21]

16.28 Provided a private rented sector offer satisfies the following conditions, the acceptance or refusal of the offer will bring the housing duty to an end.

The conditions

16.29 A private rented sector offer is, for these purposes:[22]

- an offer of an assured shorthold tenancy for a fixed period of at least 12 months;
- made by a private landlord to the applicant;
- with the approval of the authority and pursuant to arrangements made by the authority with a view to bringing the s193 duty to an end.

In addition, the authority must be satisfied that the offer is suitable for the applicant.

Suitability

16.30 In addition to the statutory conditions set out in HA s193, article 3 of the Homelessness (Suitability of Accommodation) (England) Order 2012[23] provides that a private rented sector offer will not be suitable where the authority is 'of the view' that:

- the accommodation is not in a reasonable physical condition; or

---

21 Where the full housing duty was accepted prior to 9 November 2012 local authorities do not have the option of ending the duty by way of a private rented sector offer, other than for 'restricted cases'.

22 HA 1996 s193(7AC) and (7AF).

23 2012 SI No 2601.

- any electrical equipment provided does not meet the relevant safety regulations; or
- the landlord has not taken reasonable fire safety precautions or carbon monoxide poisoning prevention measures; or
- the landlord is not a fit and proper person to act in the capacity of landlord.

In deciding whether the landlord is a fit and proper person the authority must have regard to whether he or she has ever committed any acts of fraud or other dishonesty, violence or use of illegal drugs or sexual offences requiring notification, practiced unlawful discrimination, contravened any law relating to housing or acted otherwise in accordance with any code of practice for the management of an HMO (under section 233 of the Housing Act 2004, see paras 11.67–11.79).

16.31   Furthermore, the accommodation will not be suitable if any of the following apply:

- the accommodation is in an unlicensed HMO (whether subject to mandatory or additional licencing, see paras 11.71 and 11.77);
- the accommodation does not have a valid energy performance certificate;
- the accommodation does not have a current gas safety record under the Gas Safety (Installation and Use) Regulations 1998; or
- the landlord has not provided to the authority a written tenancy agreement which the authority considers adequate.

16.32   Although the first set of conditions are based on the authority's 'view' the precise requirements of the 'fit and proper person' test, make clear that the authority will be required to carry out detailed inquiry about both the landlord and the property/properties proposed to be used for the purposes of a private sector offer. For these reasons it seems that, to date, few local authorities have used such offers to end the housing duty.[24]

16.33   Specific guidance has been issued on the changes: Supplementary Guidance on the homelessness changes in the Localism Act 2011 and on the Homelessness (Suitability of Accommodation) (England) Order 2012.

16.34   Acceptance or refusal of a private rented sector offer brings the authority's housing duty to an end. The applicant must be informed in writing of the possible consequences of refusal or acceptance of

---

24 The most recent quarterly statistics for England for April–June 2014 record 20 cases of 're-applications' under s195A.

the offer, of the right to request a review of the suitability of the offer and of the re-application duty under Housing Act s195A.[25]

The re-application duty: s195A

16.35 Since the private rented sector offer need only be for a 12-month period it is of course possible that the applicant will have to leave through no fault of their own on expiry of the initial fixed term. Where this happens and the person re-applies within two years of accepting the offer, s195A applies. This provides that:

- A person served with a valid notice under section 21 of the Housing Act 1988 (see para 6.47) shall be treated as homeless from the date the notice expires and as 'threatened with homelessness' from the date the notice is given.
- If the authority is satisfied that the person is homeless and eligible, and is not homelessness intentionally, the housing duty under HA 1996 s193(2) applies regardless of whether the person has a priority need.

16.36 Note that the re-application must be made within two years of accepting the private rented sector offer to benefit from s195A. Any application after this date will require a fresh homeless application and no housing duty will arise unless priority need is established. HA 1996 s188 is also amended so that where s195A applies, the interim accommodation duty arises regardless of priority need, see para 13.29.

Refusal of Part VI and Part VII offers

16.37 Disputes often arise about whether the s193 housing duty has come to an end where an applicant has refused an offer arguing that the accommodation was unsuitable. The issue of 'suitability' is dealt with below at paras 16.48–16.68. Certain procedural safeguards are provided to ensure that applicants are aware of the consequences of refusing an offer.

16.38 A Part VI offer must be made in writing and must state that it is a 'final offer'. The applicant must also be informed of the possible consequences of refusal or acceptance and of the right to request a review of the suitability of the accommodation.[26] The authority must be satisfied that the offer is suitable and that the applicant does not

---

25 HA 1996 s193(7AB).
26 HA 1996 s193(7) and (7A).

have contractual or other obligations that cannot be brought to an end prior to taking up the offer.[27]

16.39   Where a Part VII offer is made, the applicant must also be informed of the possible consequences of refusal or acceptance, and the right to request a review of the suitability of the accommodation.

16.40   See below at paras 16.67–16.68 for a summary of recent cases on the issue of suitability of offers.

When does the duty arise?

16.41   Usually an applicant will be residing in interim accommodation when a decision is made that the full housing duty is owed. An authority may propose that the applicant remain in the same accommodation pursuant to the HA 1996 s193 duty. If so, the applicant must be informed that the accommodation currently occupied is considered suitable, that there is a right to seek a review of its suitability, and state the time limit for requesting a review. Sometimes this information is included in the section 184 decision letter. If the applicant does not agree that the accommodation is suitable for occupation in the immediate future, a review must be requested within 21 days.

16.42   More commonly, the interim accommodation will be unsuitable for long-term occupation. Clearly, in most cases, some time will elapse before the authority can identify and make available accommodation suitable for longer-term occupation. However, disputes may arise where there is significant delay in providing suitable accommodation.

16.43   In some cases an authority may acknowledge that the accommodation being provided is not suitable, but maintain that no suitable accommodation is currently available.

Delays in providing suitable accommodation

16.44   The following cases illustrate the courts' approach to the issue of delay.

---

27   HA 1996 s193(7F) and (8). This is a change to the position prior to 9 November 2012. Previously the authority had to be satisfied that the accommodation offered was suitable *and* that it was reasonable for the applicant to accept the offer. The courts had interpreted these as separate requirements with the second condition being focused on the circumstances of the particular applicant, see *Ravichandran v Lewisham LBC* [2001] EWCA Civ 755. There is now no requirement to consider whether it is reasonable to accept the offer.

In *R v Southwark LBC ex p Anderson*[28] the HA 1996 s193 duty was accepted in May 1997. The authority agreed to discharge its duty by providing four-bed accommodation. However, to speed the process the applicants agreed to take three-bed accommodation, in or out of the borough. Three offers were made, but withdrawn because they were unsuitable. A fourth offer was the subject of an internal review. The applicants sought judicial review of the council's failure to secure accommodation between May 1997 and February 1999.

The application was dismissed. It was held that 'there is no time limit within which the housing authority is obliged under the statute to comply with a duty to secure available accommodation for those who fall within s193'. On the evidence the council was trying to secure suitable accommodation but was hampered by the lack of available stock; it was in the process of complying with its duty and was not in breach of its obligations.

In *R v Merton LBC ex p Sembi*[29] the applicant was disabled. The council accepted a section 193 duty and decided that her needs would be best met by specially adapted long-term accommodation. In the meantime, she was given a place in a home for the elderly and terminally ill. The applicant sought judicial review of the delay in securing more appropriate accommodation.

Her application was dismissed. The suitability of the current accommodation could be challenged by way of a review and county court appeal. With regard to the delay, the reasoning of *Anderson* was followed. The authority was not in breach of the duty, but was in the process of complying.

In *R v Newham LBC ex p Begum and Ali*[30] it was held that any suggestion in *Anderson* and *Sembi* that an authority had a 'reasonable period' to comply with the HA 1996 s193 duty was incorrect. The applicants comprised a family including six children, another young relative and an elderly disabled relative who was a wheelchair-user. On application they were provided with bed &

28 (1998) 32 HLR 96, QBD.
29 (1999) 32 HLR 439, QBD.
30 (1999) 32 HLR 808, QBD.

breakfast accommodation outside the borough. This was conceded to be unsuitable. Following acceptance of the full duty, the family was placed in a four-bedroom privately leased house which was also unsuitable as it was not adapted for wheelchair use. The applicants sought judicial review to require the council to discharge its duty by providing suitable accommodation. The council relied on *Anderson* and *Sembi*, arguing there was no time limit for the provision of s193 accommodation and that provided it was using its best endeavours it could not be criticised. Alternatively, the HA 1996 was to be read as giving a reasonable period for a council to find suitable accommodation, and they could not achieve the impossible: providing suitable accommodation if none was available.

The claim was successful. It was held that HA 1996 s193 (and ss188, 190 and 200) required that the council secure suitable accommodation as soon as the duty to accommodate arose. The performance of those duties could not be deferred and any suggestion in *Anderson* and *Sembi* that that was the case was based on an erroneous approach to HA 1996 Part VII.

However, the 'safeguards' for a council in such a case were threefold: (1) the test of suitability was flexible – what could be provided might not be ideal, but might be suitable if intended for the very short-term; (2) a premature application to the court would be refused; and (3) if the court was satisfied that performance was really impossible, relief might be refused.

In this case the council had not considered using its own stock, but had only considered 'temporary' accommodation such as privately leased premises and bed and breakfast hotels. The council was ordered to provide suitable accommodation within 28 days.

In *Birmingham CC v Ali*[31] the House of Lords considered the issue of the suitability of accommodation under HA 1996 s193 and the duty to applicants found to be homeless because it was not reasonable for them to continue to occupy grossly overcrowded accommodation. The authority had accepted the applicants as homeless on this basis but then indicated that they should remain in the accommodation until suitable permanent accommodation became available.

---

31 [2009] UKHL 36. In the Court of Appeal the case was known as *R on the application of Aweys v Birmingham CC.*

The House of Lords held that when considering homelessness under HA 1996 s175(3) and intentional homelessness under s191(1) it was necessary to look to the future as well as to the present: it may not be reasonable for a person to occupy accommodation indefinitely but it may be reasonable for them to continue to do so in the short term. Thus it was not unlawful for Birmingham to discharge their accommodation duty under section 193(2) by allowing the family to remain in the same accommodation in the short term. Despite it being unreasonable for the family to occupy the accommodation indefinitely, the accommodation could be suitable for the purposes of the section 193(2) duty. However, it would not be lawful for an authority to leave a family in the accommodation indefinitely and it was inevitable that there would come a time when the accommodation could no longer be described as suitable.

16.45   So, what may be suitable for short-term occupation may become unsuitable for an extended period of occupation (even if the applicant's circumstances do not change). Although the issue was not made clear in *Birmingham CC v Ali*, it seems that any challenge to suitability on the basis that the time has come so as to render the accommodation unsuitable should be brought by way of a request for a review of suitability and county court appeal rather than judicial review. However, some caution must be exercised since the HA 1996 s193 duty will end where alternative suitable accommodation is offered and refused.

In *Muse v Brent LBC*[32] a housing duty was accepted and Mrs Muse was placed in social housing, under an assured shorthold tenancy, under section 193(2). At the time she had one child. After her third child was born her landlords wrote to the local authority stating that she was overcrowded. Her solicitors also wrote to the authority asking that she be reallocated to a higher band within the allocations policy, and also transferred to more suitable housing or (confusingly) to be accommodated as a homeless person, whichever would be sooner.
   The housing authority made an offer of alternative temporary accommodation but Mrs Muse declined to move on the basis that it was unsuitable and she preferred to stay in her overcrowded

32 [2008] EWCA Civ 1447, 19 December 2008.

accommodation. The property was re-offered and the offer letter stated that if she failed to take the accommodation the authority would conclude that it had discharged its duty to her. The letter stated: 'This means that any temporary accommodation that you are currently occupying will be terminated and your homeless application will be closed. If you are already in temporary accommodation managed by a housing association, the council will instruct the association to obtain a court order for possession.' Her solicitors responded that their client was already bidding for properties and that: 'She is not obliged to accept an alternative temporary accommodation if she does not wish to do so.' The authority then sent a further letter to Mrs Muse extending the deadline for accepting the accommodation and warning her that if she did not accept it the authority would conclude that it had discharged its statutory duty towards her. After the deadline expired the authority wrote to Mrs Muse stating that it considered that the housing duty was now discharged and that it would instruct her housing association landlords to commence eviction proceedings. A review of the decision was then requested on the grounds that the s193(2) duty did not apply to Mrs Muse and that the property offered was unsuitable. The review officer rejected both arguments and upheld the decision that the offer was suitable and that the s193 duty had ended. The county court upheld Mrs Muse's appeal and the authority appealed to the Court of Appeal.

The appeal was allowed. The Court of Appeal held that the authority was obliged to, and did, offer alternative suitable accommodation. It complied with that duty and, pursuant to s193(5), the offer was on terms that its duty would end if Mrs Muse declined to accept the alternative accommodation.

16.46   Where an authority maintains that accommodation is suitable then a review should be requested. However, if the authority accepts that the current accommodation is not suitable but is not using its best endeavours to find suitable accommodation, or is limiting the type of accommodation that may be used (eg only considering private sector accommodation), a claim for judicial review may be appropriate. First, the authority should be asked to disclose the steps it is taking to find suitable accommodation. Often, this results in more suitable accommodation being located. However, if the authority is making all reasonable endeavours but is hampered by the lack of suitable accommodation, a court may refuse to make an order. This is more likely to be the case where the applicant needs accommodation of an unusual size or type.

16.47 Most authorities use private landlords to discharge the section 193 housing duty (as distinct from ending the duty by way of the new 'private rented sector offer'). Complaints about the conditions and lack of repair are common. If a tenancy has been granted, the occupier will have the right to have certain repairs carried out by the landlord: see chapter 10.[33] However, in many cases the occupier communicates not with the landlord directly, but with the authority's temporary accommodation section or with a social landlord who is managing the property. The occupier may want alternative accommodation rather than have repairs carried out. In such a case the making of a formal complaint and, ultimately, an Ombudsman complaint may be effective.

An Ombudsman complaint was made against Hackney LBC[34] about a seven-year delay in making accommodation available to a homeless applicant. The housing duty had been accepted in 1992 and a succession of private sector leased properties were made available until 1999, when the applicant was nominated to a housing trust for permanent accommodation. A complaint was made of maladministration for (1) the delay in securing permanent accommodation, and (2) the poor quality of the temporary accommodation.

The Ombudsman found that in 1993 an offer of permanent accommodation had been made, but had been sent to an old address and had not come to the applicant's attention. This resulted in the applicant remaining in temporary accommodation for six years longer than necessary. Furthermore, because of mistakes by the council's agents (a housing association), the quality of the temporary accommodation had been unsatisfactory and for three years the family had lived in accommodation deemed 'prejudicial to health' by the council's environmental health department. The Ombudsman recommended compensation of £6,000.

33 If the tenancy agreement is between the private landlord and the applicant, the applicant's rights will be against the private landlord. However, the private landlord may have leased the property to the local authority, which will then be the applicant's landlord.

34 98/A/1857, reported in November 1999 *Legal Action* 17.

Suitability

16.48   It is for the authority to decide what is suitable but it must have regard to certain statutory factors:

- the legislation on slum clearance, overcrowding and houses in multiple occupation (HMOs);[35]
- the particular circumstances of the applicant and his or her family, including any medical and physical needs or social considerations such as the risk of racial harassment or domestic violence, access to and stability in schools, and access to other facilities;[36]
- the affordability of the accommodation, in particular, the financial resources available to that person, the cost of the accommodation and his or her other reasonable living expenses;[37]
- for 'private rented sector offers' additional criteria apply to the suitability assessment, see para 16.29 above

Housing standards

16.49   The 2006 Code of Guidance provides:

> **The Secretary of State recommends that when determining the suitability of accommodation secured under the homelessness legislation, local authorities should, as a minimum, ensure that all accommodation is free of Category 1 hazards.** In the case of an out-of-district placement it is the responsibility of the placing authority to ensure that accommodation is free of Category 1 hazards.[38]

Particular circumstances of the applicant

16.50   A homeless applicant has little choice over the type or location of accommodation offered under HA 1996 s193. While an authority must take account of the needs of the applicant's household, it is difficult to challenge decisions as to suitability unless the applicant has particular needs that have been ignored.

> In *R v Brent LBC ex p Omar*[39] the applicant was offered accommodation in a basement flat on an estate. She was a refugee and has suffered imprisonment and abuse in Somalia. She rejected

---

35   HA 1996 s210.
36   2006 Homelessness Code paras 17.5–17.6.
37   Homelessness (Suitability of Accommodation) Order 1996 SI No 3204.
38   2006 Homelessness Code para 17.15. See paras 11.17–11.44 for an explanation of the Hazard rating system.
39   (1991) 23 HLR 446, QBD.

the offer, indicating that the premises were reminiscent of the conditions of her imprisonment and that she would rather commit suicide than live there. The authority maintained that the offer was suitable because there were no pure medical grounds or other social grounds why it should not be accepted.

The applicant's judicial review claim was upheld. In addition to the matters referred to in the statute, an authority must also have regard to the particular circumstances of the applicant and her family. This was an exceptional case in which no reasonable housing authority, properly directing itself, could conclude that the property was suitable for the applicant.

Location

16.51   Location is relevant to suitability. It is referred to in the 2006 Homelessness Code, the Homelessness (Suitability of Accommodation) (England) Order 2012 and in the 2012 Supplementary Guidance.

16.52   The pressure on accommodation in London means that London authorities are increasingly using accommodation outside of their own areas, and often in parts of the country far from London. This is specifically dealt with in the 2012 Supplementary Guidance and below at para 16.58.

16.53   Para 17.41 of the 2006 Code of Guidance refers to the need to take account of family members in paid employment and to minimise disruption to the education of young people, particularly at critical points, such as when they are close to taking GCSE examinations. Most applicants wish to be accommodated in the locality where they are settled, and where their family and friends live. However, given the shortage of available accommodation, very strong reasons will be needed to challenge suitability on the grounds of location.

In *Abdullah v Westminster CC*[40] the applicant rejected accommodation because it was too far from her family and friends who helped her to care for her children. The county court upheld her first appeal: the review officer had failed to take sufficient account of her need to be near family and friends. Following reconsideration the review officer again found the property to be suitable. On a second county court appeal the decision was upheld.

40 [2007] EWCA Civ 1566, 21 June 2007.

> The Court of Appeal dismissed the applicant's appeal. The review officer had relied on advice and information received from social services to the effect that the property was suitable. The medical officer had indicated that it would be advantageous for the applicant to be near family and friends, but not that she would be unable to cope without it. There was sufficient material for the review officer to reach the decision and no grounds to appeal against the county court's refusal to interfere.

Out of area placements

16.54   The Housing Act 1996 s208 provides that:

> So far as reasonably practicable a local housing authority shall in discharging their housing functions under this Part secure that accommodation is available for the occupation of the applicant in their district.

16.55   An authority's starting point should be to locate accommodation within its own area. However, it is not unlawful to operate a policy under which some out of borough accommodation is used, provided it is suitable for the particular applicant. In deciding whether it is reasonably practicable to secure accommodation within the borough, the authority may take into account the cost of providing the accommodation.

> In *R (Calgin) v Enfield LBC*[41] the court held that the authority's policy of using accommodation in Birmingham and Luton to house a small proportion of homeless applicants was lawful. Furthermore, when deciding what was 'reasonably practicable' the issue of the authority's resources and the comparative cost of providing accommodation within and outside the borough were relevant. In the circumstances the accommodation in Birmingham was suitable, having regard to the needs of the family and their links in the borough of Enfield.

16.56   However, as in all cases, the accommodation must be suitable for the particular applicant. A challenge to the same authority was successful in *R (Yumsak) v Enfield LBC*,[42] see para 13.38. The applicant

41   [2005] EWHC 1716 (Admin), 29 July 2005.
42   [2002] EWHC 280 (Admin), 5 February 2002.

had a number of strong reasons to remain in the area where she had lived for seven years and the authority had failed to justify the breach of her rights under article 8 of the European Convention on Human Rights that would be involved in her being accommodated in Birmingham.

16.57 These cases were decided some time ago. More recently, the cost of accommodation in London has increased so much that London authorities are using out of borough accommodation routinely.[43] The most recent government homelessness statistics record that 24 per cent of those in temporary accommodation were in another authority's district. Of these, the vast majority (93 per cent) were placed by London authorities.

16.58 Although HA 1996 s208 has not been repealed, the 2012 Supplementary Guidance anticipates that authorities may be forced to accommodate outside their borough:

> 47. Where it is not possible to secure accommodation within district and an authority has secured accommodation outside their district, the authority is required to take account of the distance of that accommodation from the distance of the authority. Where accommodation which is otherwise suitable and affordable is available nearer to the authority's district than the accommodation which it has secured, the accommodation which it has secured is not likely to be suitable unless the authority has a justifiable reason or the applicant has specified a preference.

> 48. Generally, where possible, authorities should try to secure accommodation that is as close as possible to where an applicant was previously living. Securing accommodation for an applicant in a different location can cause difficulties for some applicants. Local authorities are required to take into account the significance of any disruption with specific regard to employment, caring responsibilities or education of the applicant or members of their household. Where possible the authority should seek to retain established links with schools, doctors, social workers and other key services and support.

In *TN v Westminster CC*[44] a woman and her five children lived in a four bedroom house in Westminster until November 2012 when it became unaffordable because of reductions in the Local Housing

---

43 Moreover, the changes to the Local Housing Allowance and the introduction of the 'benefit cap' means that the accommodation in London and the South East is often unaffordable to anyone reliant on housing benefit, see paras 9.66 and 9.74.

44 UKSC 2014/0275.

Allowance, see para 9.51. The authority offered a five bedroom property more than 50 miles away. Although the Court of Appeal found in favour of the local authority, the Supreme Court recently the applicant's appeal, holding that the accommodation was unsuitable. At the time of writing, the Supreme Court's judgment, setting out the reasons for upholding the tenant's appeal, is pending.

Affordability

16.59   An authority must in all cases consider whether accommodation is affordable for the applicant. The Homelessness (Suitability of Accommodation) Order 1996[45] requires a local authority to take account of the income and necessary outgoings as well as the reasonable living expenses of a household when deciding if accommodation is affordable to a particular applicant.[46] Para 17.40 of the 2006 Code of Guidance suggests that if, after taking these into account, the 'residual income' would be less than that of a household reliant on income support or income-based jobseeker's allowance, a property is unaffordable. See para 14.143 for a summary of recent cases where an authority has assessed affordability in this way.

16.60   It is common for the amount of housing benefit awarded to a private tenant to be less than the full amount of the rent. Where an authority discharges its duty by arranging for the offer of a private tenancy, it may use its powers to top up payments of housing benefit so that the landlord receives the full rent.[47]

Reviews of suitability

16.61   The consequences of refusing a suitable offer (made under Part VI or Part VII) are that no further housing duty will be owed; the household will be evicted from any Part VII accommodation currently occupied and the housing authority will have no further duty to accommodate. In addition, any priority on the waiting list given by virtue of being homeless or accommodated under Part VII will be lost. Since it is possible to accept an offer and at the same time request a review of

---

45   SI No 3204.
46   The Order prescribes the income and outgoings that must be taken into account.
47   See 2006 Homelessness Code para 16.20.

the suitability of the accommodation,[48] this is almost always the best course of action. If the suitability challenge fails, at least the household will have some accommodation.

16.62 However, sometimes a person seeks advice only after refusing the offer. In such cases, care should be taken to ensure that the authority has complied with the procedural requirements described above. If not, the authority may be persuaded to 're-offer' the accommodation, or, if no longer available, to make an alternative offer. Even if there is no procedural irregularity the authority should be asked if it will give the applicant the opportunity to accept the offer if the accommodation is still available.

16.63 If an applicant refuses accommodation and seeks a review of suitability, the authority is not obliged to keep the accommodation available pending the outcome of the review.[49]

16.64 Challenges to the suitability of accommodation offered under HA 1996 s193 (or under Part VI) rarely succeed. When advising on the merits of a challenge to suitability, it must be remembered that it is for the local authority to decide whether the offer is suitable. The courts are very reluctant to interfere with decisions about suitability and if an authority has taken into account all relevant information, it may be impossible to challenge the decision unless there is some obvious procedural unfairness, see para 16.67 below.

16.65 HA 1996 s193 prescribes the information that must be given to an applicant in relation to offers made under s193 or under Part VI, and is detailed above at paras 16.37–16.39. See below at para 16.67 for cases where the applicant has argued that the information given was inadequate.

16.66 Although most authorities will allow a person to view a property and give a short time for a decision on accepting it, there is no requirement to permit a viewing before the applicant has to sign for a tenancy offered under s193. See *Newham LBC v Khatun, Zeb, Iqbal & the OFT*[50] in which the Court of Appeal held that it is for the authority to decide whether the accommodation is suitable and, if the applicant disagrees, a review of suitability can be requested.

16.67 It may happen that an applicant indicates to the authority, before taking advice, that he or she will not accept the accommodation. If, following advice, the person agrees to accept the offer while seeking a review of suitability, urgent steps must be taken to contact the

---

48 HA 1996 s202(1A).
49 *Osseily v Westminster CC* [2007] EWCA Civ 1108, 5 October 2007.
50 [2004] EWCA Civ 55, 24 February 2004.

authority to see if the property is still available. If it has not been let to someone else, an authority may allow the person to accept the offer.

In *Maswaku v Westminster CC*[51] the applicant refused an offer made under s193 because it was too far away from her college and from her children's schools; in both cases the journey by public transport was much longer. The offer letter had stated that by offering a suitable temporary home, the council had discharged its duty and if the offer was refused she would have to find her own accommodation unless she successfully challenged the decision. Her review and county court appeal were unsuccessful. In the Court of Appeal she argued that she should have been informed of all the specific consequences of a refusal, namely that she would be evicted from her current home, that her homelessness application would be cancelled, that there would be no obligation on the council to secure any further homelessness accommodation, that she could make a fresh application but may be found intentionally homeless, and that she could remain on the waiting list but would lose her priority status. The Court of Appeal dismissed her appeal holding that the information she had been given was sufficient to satisfy the requirements of section 193.

In contrast, in the case of *Mohamoud v Birmingham CC*[52] the applicant succeeded in a challenge based on regulation 8(2) of the Allocation of Housing (Review Procedures) Regulations 1999 (see para 15.33) and her misunderstanding of the number of offers she would receive. Clear written information had been given stating that the offer being made was a 'final offer' under Part VI and that she was entitled to only one offer. However, the applicant's first language was not English and she claimed that friends had advised her that she would receive three offers. A letter about the bidding scheme made reference to being able to bid for 'a maximum of three properties in each weekly advertising cycle' which she understood to support her friends' advice. At the review stage this was explained by her advisers and they indicated that, now that she understood the process, she would accept the offer. The Court of Appeal upheld her appeal: although the review officer was entitled to be sceptical about

51 [2012] EWCA Civ 669, 18 May 2012.
52 [2014] EWCA Civ 227, 7 March 2014.

her explanation about why she had refused the offer, she was not in a position to reject it out of hand. She should have accepted that in light of the explanation there was a deficiency in the original decision and given the applicant an opportunity to make representations about her reasons for refusing the offer before making a final decision. The decision was therefore quashed. However, it was pointed out that this did not mean that a further offer would necessarily be made, only that a 'minded to find' notice should have been served enabling the applicant to make further representations. The merits of the review were a matter for the reviewing officer.

16.68   There is no requirement to give reasons as to why an authority has decided that a particular property is suitable. The local authority must take account of the needs and preferences of an individual applicant but the pressure on accommodation may mean that they are not all met. If an applicant believes that an offer has been made in error the authority should be asked for clarification of the reasons for making the offer.

In *Akhtar v Birmingham CC*[53] an applicant had succeeded in a review of the suitability of an offer and the offer was withdrawn with no explanation given. She had objected to the offer on the basis of the size and location of the accommodation. When a second offer was made in the same location, she refused it and argued that it could not be suitable since the authority had agreed that the previous offer was unsuitable. On this review the council confirmed that the previous review had found the earlier offer to be unsuitable not because of the location but because it was too small. A 'minded to' letter was issued and further representations made. The review upheld the decision as to suitability, as did the county court. The Court of Appeal dismissed her further appeal holding that the facts of the case did not give rise to a duty on the authority to give reasons at the time as to why the previous review had been successful.

53   [2011] EWCA Civ 383, 15 February 2011.

> The same approach was followed in *Khan v Solihull MBC.*[54] The
> applicant had indicated that she could not live in a particular area
> because of a fear of violence in that area. The council did not accept
> that there was such a risk. When an offer was made in that area,
> the applicant refused it claiming that because she had informed the
> council about her fears of living in the area she believed the offer
> had been made in error. The Court of Appeal held that the council
> had no duty to explain why it had made the offer. The offer letter
> had expressly stated 'if you are not sure of your position, it is very
> important that you ask your housing advisor or homelessness offer
> before making any hasty decisions.' In such a case, the onus was on
> the applicant to seek an explanation rather than on the council to
> give reasons for its decision.

Change of circumstances

16.69   Section 193 accommodation may be occupied for many years. During
that time the applicant's circumstances may change. If the change
is such as to make the accommodation unsuitable, a request for a
review of the suitability can be made. A local authority has a duty
to conduct a statutory review on request.[55] If the review decision is
unfavourable, a county court appeal may be brought. Note however
that a refusal of an offer of suitable alternative accommodation will
bring the section 193 duty to an end, see: *Muse v Brent LBC* at para
16.45 above.

Use of the private sector under HA 1996 Parts VI and VII – a summary

16.70   Most local authorities use private landlords to assist in the discharge
of their various housing duties under HA 1996 Part VII. The standard form of occupation agreement in the private sector is the assured
shorthold tenancy (AST) and there are several different situations
in which a homeless applicant may be offered an assured shorthold
tenancy in the private sector. These are summarised below at paras
16.71–16.73.

---

54 [2014] EWCA Civ 41, 28 January 2014.
55 *R on the application of Zaher v City of Westminster* [2003] EWHC 101 (Admin),
28 January 2003.

Homeless prevention/gate-keeping

16.71 Potential homeless applicants may be offered help to obtain an AST from a private landlord by way of preventing homelessness (see para 13.8). If the tenancy is accepted, no homeless application is recorded and no ongoing duty is owed by the authority.[56] An applicant may decline this help and pursue a homeless application.

Discharge of section 193 duty – continuing duty

16.72 The 'full housing duty' may be discharged by the authority making an arrangement with another person to secure that suitable accommodation becomes available, ie an offer of an AST. Accepting the offer means the applicant continues to be owed the s193 duty and retains priority under the allocations scheme. Refusing the offer means that the authority's duty under HA 1996 s193 ends, see above at para 16.22. Should the tenancy end through no fault of the applicant the authority will have to secure alternative accommodation.

'Private rented sector offer' – end of section 193 duty

16.73 An offer of an AST for a minimum of 12 months that complies with the requirement set out above at paras 16.29–16.31 (including the checks on the property and the landlord passing a 'fit and proper' person test) will end the duty. Refusing or accepting a suitable offer means that the housing duty ends. If the offer is accepted, special provision is made for 're-application' within two years, see para 16.35. The offer letter must set out that the offer is a 'private rented sector offer' and that it will bring the housing duty to an end, see para 16.22 above.

Fresh applications

16.74 Housing Act 1996 s193(9) provides:

> A person who ceases to be owed the [section 193] duty ... may make a fresh application to the authority for accommodation or assistance in obtaining accommodation.

16.75 An authority may decide that no duty is owed, but cannot simply refuse to accept an application on the basis that the section 193 duty has ended following a previous application. See paras 13.59–13.67.

---

56 See *Hanton-Rhouila v Westminster Council* [2010] EWCA Civ 1334, 24 November 2010.

APPENDIX

Request for review and interim accommodation

Dear Sir/Madam,

Re: Mrs A – section 184 Decision dated

We are advising Mrs A with regard to her homeless application.

[Request for review]

Mrs A requests a review of the above decision.

[Request for interim accommodation to be extended]

We ask you to confirm that our client will continue to be provided with interim accommodation pending the outcome of the review. It is our view that our client satisfies the test set out in the case of *R v Camden LBC ex p Mohammed* (30 HLR 315, CA):

The merits of the case

[what is wrong with the decision]

New information or argument

[anything likely to change the decision, including medical evidence not yet obtained]

The applicant's personal circumstances

[whether any alternative accommodation, likely effect of being homeless on applicant, children etc]

[Deadline for reply]

Our client has been informed that she must leave the accommodation currently provided on ... In order that we may advise our client about possible judicial review proceedings we would ask you to communicate your decision regarding interim accommodation no later than 4 pm on ... If the decision is that interim accommodation will not be provided pending review please give reasons.

[Data Protection request]

Please provide to us a copy of the complete homelessness file under the Data Protection Act 1998. We enclose a cheque in the sum of £10 together with our client's signed authority.

We intend to make further representations in support of the review following receipt of the file. We would therefore be grateful if this could be provided as a matter of urgency.

Yours faithfully,

Adviser

Advice Agency

Allocation of social housing

continued

Key points

- All new allocations of social housing must be made through the local housing authority's 'allocations scheme'.
- Authorities must publish their allocations scheme and a summary must be available free of charge.
- Certain assistance must be given free of charge to people in the district who want to apply and may have difficulties, eg language and literacy.
- People who are ineligible for immigration reasons cannot be allocated social housing so will not be accepted on the 'waiting list'
- Local authorities now have more say over who can go on the waiting list: who is 'qualified' under their particular scheme
- Authorities have a wide discretion as to the kind of allocation scheme they operate but must give 'reasonable preference' to certain people.
- 'Reasonable preference' does not mean absolute preference.
- There is a right of review for decisions about eligibility and qualification for the 'waiting list'. There is also a right of review about the facts taken into consideration in making an allocation decision. There is no county court appeal but decisions may be challenged by judicial review.
- A scheme itself may be unlawful if it is not in accordance with the principles set out in the Housing Act 1996 Part VI. This can only be established by judicial review.
- Legal aid is no longer available for advice about allocations but is available for judicial review claims.

Introduction

17.1 In most parts of the UK there is a severe shortage of affordable rented accommodation. Since 1989 private tenancies have been at market rents and usually offer no more than six months' security. This means that for many households the only way to obtain a secure home at an affordable rent is to be allocated social housing, ie accommodation let by local authorities and other social landlords (private registered providers of social housing). However, the supply of social housing has decreased significantly in recent years. The

Barker report, published in March 2004, estimated that the supply of social and affordable homes would need to increase by 17,000 units per year for the next ten years to meet the anticipated need for social housing.[1] This did not happen and in 2010 local authorities recorded almost 1.8 million households (estimated at approximately 5 million people) on council housing waiting lists. This figure increased to 1.83 million on 1 April 2012 but was down to 1.69 million on 1 April 2013.[2] The figures for 2014 are likely to be considerably reduced, not because of any increase in the numbers of people housed in suitable accommodation but because of changes to the allocation system: local authorities can now refuse access to the waiting lists for those who do not 'qualify' under a particular local authority's policy.

17.2   Nevertheless, it is still the case that many people on the housing waiting lists will never be allocated social housing and others will wait for many years. People often seek advice about the fact that they have been waiting for a long time without receiving an offer. In most cases there is little an adviser can do to assist.

17.3   In April 2013 legal advice about the allocation of accommodation was taken out of the scope of legal aid. Legal aid remains available for judicial review claims, including challenges to the lawfulness of allocations policies or the treatment of individual applications.

17.4   Common issues that arise relate to:

- decisions that a person is not eligible for an allocation because of their immigration status;
- decisions that a person does not qualify under a particular scheme;
- decisions to defer or suspend an application;
- decisions about whether the correct level of priority has been given under the authority's policy;
- the lawfulness of a particular allocations policy, ie whether it complies with HA 1996 Part VI or other statutory duties such as under the Equality Act 2010.

17.5   Before examining these issues, this chapter sets out the way HA 1996 Part VI governs allocation schemes.

---

1   Kate Barker, *Review of housing supply, delivering stability: securing our future housing needs*, March 2004. The report can be downloaded from: www.hm-treasury.gov.uk.

2   See www.gov.uk/government/statistics/local-authority-housing-statistics-for-england-2012-to-2013.

Housing Act 1996 Part VI

17.6 The Housing Act Parts VI and VII were designed to address the perceived problem that the stock of social housing was being allocated only to those classed as 'statutorily homeless'. Prior to the HA 1996, a successful homeless application usually resulted in an offer of long-term social housing. The shortage of social housing together with the increasing numbers of homeless applicants meant that in some areas almost all of the stock was allocated to the homeless while those in unsuitable accommodation waited for decades on the housing waiting list.

17.7 Part VII sets out the homeless duty: instead of granting long-term social tenancies to homeless applicants, the duty is to provide only temporary accommodation. Homeless applicants temporarily accommodated by housing authorities are considered for an allocation in the same way as others in housing need. The fact that a homelessness duty is owed will give the person some priority ('reasonable preference') on the allocation scheme, but reasonable preference is also given to those occupying unsuitable accommodation. The aim of Part VI was to create 'a single route into social housing'.[3]

17.8 Whenever a local housing authority is allocating accommodation it must comply with HA 1996 Part VI.[4] However, while Part VI sets certain principles that must be followed, local authorities retain a broad discretion as to how they frame their allocation policies; subject to the provisions of Part VI 'a local housing authority may allocate housing accommodation in such manner as they consider appropriate'.[5] However, once it has devised its allocation scheme, an authority can only allocate in accordance with the scheme. Part VI sets out the principles that must be followed when framing the policy.

17.9 Authorities must have regard to the relevant codes of guidance.[6] The current codes are:

- Allocation of accommodation: guidance for local housing authorities in England (June 2012).
- Providing social housing for local people (December 2013).[7]

---

3 Hansard (HC), Standing Committee G, 16th Sitting, col 614, 12 March 1996, Minister for Local Government, Housing and Urban Regeneration.
4 HA 1996 s159(1).
5 HA 1996 s159(7).
6 HA 1996 s169.
7 These codes reflect the changes introduced by the Localism Act 2011 which gave local authorities more power to frame their allocation policies in accordance with local priorities. The previous codes published in November

The codes of guidance are not law but reflect the government's understanding of the law and make recommendations for good practice. As with all statutory guidance, an authority may depart from the code if there is good reason to do so.

Allocations governed by Part VI

17.10   An allocation is defined as:[8]

- Selecting someone to be a secure or introductory tenant of accommodation held by the local authority. This includes notifying an existing (non-secure) tenant or licensee that he or she is to become a secure tenant of the same premises.
- Nominating someone to be a secure or introductory tenant of accommodation held by a different authority.
- Nominating someone to be an assured tenant of accommodation held by another social landlord (a 'private registered provider of social housing').
- Most transfers at the tenant's request, see below at para 17.12.

Allocations not governed by Part VI

17.11   The following are not 'allocations' for the purpose of HA 1996 Part VI:[9]

- a succession to a secure or introductory tenancy;[10]
- an assignment of a secure or introductory tenancy by mutual exchange;
- an assignment of a secure or introductory tenancy to someone who would have been entitled to succeed to the tenancy;
- a transfer of a secure or introductory tenancy pursuant to a court order made in matrimonial proceedings or on relationship breakdown;[11]
- an introductory tenancy becoming secure.

2002 (the main Code), August 2008 (Choice Based Lettings) and December 2009 (Fair and Flexible) no longer apply.

8   HA 1996 s159(2).

9   HA 1996 s160.

10   See para 4.33 above.

11   This includes orders made under Matrimonial Causes Act 1973 s24, Matrimonial and Family Proceedings Act 1984 s17(1), Children Act 1989 Sch 1 and Civil Partnership Act 2004 Schs 5 and 7. See chapter 12.

Transfers

17.12 Transfers are when a tenant is offered alternative social housing either by their own landlord or by another social landlord. This may be at the tenant's request or on the initiative of the landlord. Many tenants seek transfers to larger accommodation as their families grow or may seek a more suitable property or one in a different area. As a result of the 'bedroom tax', see para 9.66, increasing numbers of people will be seeking smaller accommodation. Part VI does apply to transfers where the tenant applies for the transfer and qualifies for 'reasonable preference'.[12] This means that a social tenant who is in unsuitable accommodation and wants to move must have their needs assessed in the same way as those occupying private accommodation. In contrast, transfers instigated by the authority are not governed by Part VI. This would include, for example, decants for major works.

Dealing with applications

17.13 A housing authority must ensure that:[13]

- advice and information is available free of charge to people in the district who want to apply for an allocation;
- any necessary assistance in making such an application is available free of charge to those people in the district likely to have difficulty making an application without assistance;
- the fact that a person has applied is not divulged to any other member of the public without his or her consent; and
- any applicant is informed of his or her right to request information about the application, how the application is likely to be treated, whether he or she is likely to be given reasonable preference and whether appropriate housing is likely to be made available and when that is likely to happen.

17.14 An authority cannot refuse to make a decision on an application or simply advise a person that he or she cannot make an application. Although authorities have wide powers to decide who qualifies for their register, if an authority decides that an applicant is ineligible (because of being a person from abroad) or is not a qualifying person (under the particular scheme) the authority must notify the applicant

---

12 HA 1996 s159 (4A)–(4B).
13 HA 1996 s166.

of their decision and the grounds for it.[14] The notice must be given in writing and carries a right of review.[15]

An applicant's duty

17.15 An applicant for an allocation must give correct information to the authority in support of the application and may commit an offence if false information is given or if information is withheld.

17.16 Under HA 1996 s171 an offence is committed if, in connection with an application under Part VI, a person:

- knowingly or recklessly makes a statement which is false in a material particular; or
- knowingly withholds information which the authority has reasonably required.

17.17 The offence can be committed by any person, not just the applicant, and is punishable by a fine of up to £5,000.

17.18 In addition, where an assured or secure tenancy is granted because of a false statement made by the tenant or someone acting on his or her behalf, the landlord has a ground for possession and may seek to evict the tenant if this comes to light after the tenancy has been granted, see appendix to chapter 7.

Eligibility and qualification for allocations

17.19 A person who is not 'eligible' by reason of immigration status cannot be allocated social housing.[16] In addition, each local authority can decide who is a 'qualifying person' in relation to their particular allocations scheme.

Eligibility

17.20 Eligibility for housing allocations is explained in chapter 20. A person who is ineligible cannot be allocated accommodation and cannot be granted a joint tenancy of social accommodation with a person who is eligible.

---

14 HA 1996 s160ZA(9)
15 HA 1996 s160ZA(10). However, if it is not received by the applicant it is treated as having been given if it is made available at the authority's office for collection for a reasonable period.
16 HA 1996 s160ZA.

17.21   However, this does not prevent an ineligible person who is already a social tenant from being allocated accommodation by way of a transfer.[17]

17.22   Where an eligible person's household includes an ineligible person, the ineligible person need not be disregarded but a local authority may decide that ineligible adults who have lived independently should not be considered part of the household, see para 20.180.[18]

Qualifying persons

17.23   Local authorities may decide who can qualify to go onto their allocation scheme/waiting list.[19] However, regulations may prescribe that certain persons must be treated as qualifying persons and others may not be.[20] Regulations may also prescribe criteria that cannot be used in deciding what classes of persons are qualifying. Furthermore, as the Code of Guidance makes clear, local authorities must observe their other statutory duties eg under the Equality Act 2010. Criteria that are directly or indirectly discriminatory will be unlawful.

Decisions about eligibility and qualifying persons

17.24   If an authority decides that an applicant is ineligible for an allocation or is not a qualifying person, it must notify the applicant in writing of the decision and the grounds for the decision.[21] The applicant has the right to request a review of the decision.[22]

---

17   HA 1996 s160ZA(5).
18   See *R (Kimvono) v Tower Hamlets LBC* (CO/3579/2000), 5 December 2000 and *Ariemuguvbe v Islington LBC* [2009] EWCA Civ 1308, 21 October 2009.
19   Prior to the amendments made by the Localism Act 2011 only 'unacceptable behaviour' could be used as a criterion to prevent a person from being allocated social housing. The Localism Act 2011 permits local authorities to decide who is or is not qualifying based on much broader criteria.
20   To date the only regulations made are to prevent local authorities excluding armed services personnel on the grounds of local connection, see para 17.36.
21   HA 1996 s160ZA(9).
22   HA 1996 s166(9)(c).

Allocation schemes

17.25   The Housing Act 1996 s166A(1) provides that:

> Every local authority must have a scheme (their 'allocation scheme') for determining priorities, and as to the procedure to be followed, in allocating housing accommodation.

> For this purpose 'procedure' includes all aspects of the allocation process, including the persons or descriptions of persons by whom decisions are to be taken.

17.26   The authority must not allocate accommodation except in accordance with its allocation scheme.[23]

17.27   The scheme must include a statement of the authority's policy on offering applicants a choice of accommodation, or the opportunity to express preferences.[24] Note that this does not mean that the scheme must offer choice or the opportunity to express a preference: only that the scheme must state what the authority's policy is.

The reasonable preference categories

17.28   The scheme *must* be framed so as to secure that reasonable preference is given to the following classes:[25]

a) people who are homeless within the meaning of HA 1996 Part VII – this includes non-priority need applicants to whom no duty is owed;[26]

b) people who are owed a duty by an authority under HA 1996 s190(2) (intentionally homeless but in priority need), s193(2) (the full housing duty) or s195(2) (duty to those threatened with homelessness) or those accommodated under s192(3) (discretion to accommodate non-priority need homeless applicants);

c) people occupying insanitary or overcrowded housing or otherwise living in unsatisfactory housing conditions;

d) people who need to move on medical or welfare grounds, including grounds relating to a disability; and

---

23   HA 1996 s166A(14).
24   HA 1996 s166A(2).
25   HA 1996 s166A(3).
26   However, if a person would not be homeless or owed these homelessness duties, but for a 'restricted person', they are to be disregarded (HA 1996 166A(4)), see para 20.174.

e) people who need to move to a particular locality in the district where a failure to meet that need would cause hardship to themselves or others.

Additional preference for those in urgent housing need

17.29 Furthermore, the scheme must be framed so as to give 'additional preference' to those in the reasonable preference categories above, who have urgent housing needs and who are or have been serving in the armed forces, see below at para 17.34. For those who do not fall into this category but are in urgent housing need, additional preference may be given.[27] Note that in all cases the person must fall into one or more of the reasonable preference categories.

'Relative' preference

17.30 A scheme may make provision for deciding on the relative priority of people in the reasonable preference (and possible additional preference) groups. In doing so the following factors may to be taken into account:[28]

a) the financial resources available to the applicant to meet his or her housing costs;

b) any behaviour of a person (or a member of the household) affecting his or her suitability to be a tenant;

c) any local connection (as defined under HA 1996 Part VII, see para 14.167) the person has with the authority.

So, for example, a local authority may give higher priority to those on a low income who are working and/or have local connection over others.

What is 'reasonable preference'?

17.31 Reasonable preference does not mean absolute preference; it has been defined as giving an applicant a 'reasonable head start'.[29] Authorities do not have to give equal priority to each category but must give reasonable preference and ensure that the scheme does not result in a situation where one of the reasonable preference categories is effectively given no priority at all.

27 HA 1996 s166A(3).
28 HA 1996 s166A(5)
29 *R v Wolverhampton MBC ex p Watters* (1997) 29 HLR 931, Leggatt LJ at 936.

In *R (Jakimaviciute) v Hammersmith and Fulham LBC*[30] the new
allocation scheme introduced by the local authority was challenged
by judicial review. The scheme provided that homeless applicants
placed in long-term suitable temporary accommodation under the
homelessness duty could not normally qualify to register under the
scheme. The Court of Appeal held that the scheme was unlawful
since it effectively excluded a class of persons who were to be given
reasonable preference: 'on the natural interpretation of the statutory
provisions the setting of the qualification criteria is subject to the
reasonable preference duty'.[31] However, the scheme operated so
that a sub-group within a reasonable preference category were given
no priority at all but were simply excluded from qualification under
the scheme: 'This amounts to an attempted redefinition of the
statutory class or, putting the point another way, to an attempt to
thwart the statutory scheme.'[32]

However, this does not mean that local authorities cannot use their
power to decide who qualifies for their scheme in a way that does
in fact exclude people with reasonable preference. As the Court of
Appeal went on to say in *Jakimaviciute*: 'It is permissible to adopt a
rule excluding individual applicants by reference to factors of general
application, such as lack of local connection or being in rent arrears,
but it is not permissible to cut down the statutory class in the way
that [the scheme] attempts to do'.[33]

17.32   'Preference' should not be confused with the prospect of being
successful in obtaining accommodation: it is possible that a person
with reasonable preference may never be allocated accommodation
under HA 1996 Part VI.

In *R (Mei Ling Lin) v Barnet LBC*[34] the authority's scheme gave extra
points to homeless applicants in temporary accommodation, but
these were insufficient to enable them to bid successfully for an
allocation. It was only when the temporary accommodation was
coming to an end (often as long as ten years after the applicant was
given the accommodation) that sufficient points were given to

30 [2014] EWCA Civ 1438, 21 October 2014.
31 Richards LJ, at [31]
32 Richards LJ at [45].
33 Richards LJ at [45]
34 [2007] EWCA Civ 132, 22 February 2007.

enable an applicant to bid successfully. One of the grounds of challenge was that the policy failed to give adequate priority to homeless applicants.

The Court of Appeal rejected the argument, stating that:

Preference should not be confused with prospects of success. Prospects of success depend on many factors, of which the most material is the fact that the demand for accommodation greatly exceeds the supply. It is quite possible for a lawful scheme to give reasonable preference to a person within section 167(2) and for that person never to be allocated Part VI housing. Such a person is entitled to no more than a reasonable preference.[35]

Localism Act 2011 changes

17.33　The most significant change introduced by the Localism Act 2011 is that local authorities have the power to decide who qualifies to go onto their allocation register. As authorities have introduced new schemes, with their own qualifying conditions, large numbers of people have been removed from local authority housing registers. The evidence of Hammersmith & Fulham in *Jakimaviciute*, see above at para 17.31, was that in March 2013 there were 11,077 households on the register of which 49 per cent had no identified housing need. By introducing the new scheme, the numbers were reduced to 831 households by April 2014 (although the Court of Appeal held that having removed a large proportion of a reasonable preference category was unlawful). The majority were removed because they had no 'qualifying need' (5,551) or did not meet the council's residence condition (3,701).

Armed service personnel

Additional preference

17.34　Part VI has been amended to ensure that additional preference is given to 'armed service personnel' who have urgent housing needs.[36]

35　[2007] EWCA Civ 132, Dyson LJ at [25].
36　HA 1996 s166A(3), as amended by the Housing Act (Additional Preference for Armed Forces) (England) Regulations 2012 SI No 2989 which came into force on 30 November 2012.

17.35   For the purposes of the additional preference, this applies only to a person who falls into one or more of the existing reasonable preference categories:

- a person who is serving or has served in the regular armed forces: to qualify for the additional preference he or she must be suffering from a serious injury, illness or disability attributable wholly or partly to that service;
- a person who has recently ceased or will cease to be entitled to reside in Ministry of Defence accommodation following the death of a spouse or civil partner who was serving in the regular forces and whose death was attributable, in whole or in part, to that service; and
- a person who is serving or has served in the reserve forces who is suffering from a serious injury, illness or disability attributable wholly or in part to that service.

Local connection rules cannot exclude

17.36   Regulations made under HA 1996 s160ZA(8)(b) provide that armed services personnel cannot be excluded from a scheme on the basis that they do not have a local connection with the authority to which they apply.[37] Armed services personnel, as defined above, who apply within five years of leaving the services, cannot be excluded from a local authority register on the grounds of having no local connection with that authority. To benefit from this provision it is not necessary for the person serving, or previously serving in the regular armed forces to be suffering from a serious injury, illness or disability attributable wholly or partly that that service (those conditions are only necessary to qualify for the additional preference).

How allocations schemes work

Points schemes

17.37   Before 2000, most housing authorities operated 'points-based' schemes. These generally operated by giving a certain number of points/level of priority to each applicant, based on an assessment of the household's housing needs (usually based on similar criteria to those set out in the reasonable preference categories). In addition,

---

37 Allocation of Housing (Qualification Criteria for Armed Forces) (England) Regulations 2012 SI No 1869.

'waiting time' points would usually be awarded. Those with the highest number of points when a suitable property became available would be offered that property.

17.38 There were several problems with such schemes: (1) new applicants coming on to the scheme may be awarded more points than existing applicants who had been waiting for a long time; (2) as needs change, frequent re-assessment was needed; (3) Although such schemes usually allowed an applicant to express some preference as to area and type of accommodation, the decision on whether to offer a particular property was usually made by the authority. This often meant that a significant proportion of offers were refused, often with the consequence that further offers would not be made for a period of time, if at all.

Choice-based lettings

17.39 The Housing Green Paper, *Quality and Choice: A Decent Home for All*, published in April 2000, recommended that authorities adopt choice-based lettings schemes. It was suggested that a scheme could operate at its simplest level on the basis of three 'bands' of applicants:

- those with an urgent need for social housing;
- those in non-urgent need of social housing; and
- those with no particular need for social housing.

17.40 Within the bands, priority could be determined on the basis of waiting time. However, it was recognised

... that in areas of high demand the number of households within the urgent category would be significant and that authorities in such areas may introduce additional bands to differentiate between demand priorities. However, the principle of giving priority according to the time spent in housing need remains valid.[38]

17.41 The changes introduced by the Localism Act 2011 mean that there is now no requirement for authorities to accept onto their register people with no particular need for social housing, ie those who would fall into the lowest of the three bands.

Choice-based lettings and 'direct offers'

17.42 Some authorities operate choice-based lettings schemes but with exceptions, permitting 'direct offers' to be made to certain applicants.

38 *Quality and Choice: A Decent Home for All* para 9.23.

These may be used where someone urgently needs to be moved, such that it is not practicable to use the bidding scheme (as in the case of *Ahmad* below). In addition, many authorities use them to ensure that people accommodated in temporary accommodation as homeless applicants do not effectively opt to remain in the temporary accommodation rather than bid for permanent accommodation. In *R (Tout a Tout) v Haringey LBC*[39] the court dismissed challenges brought by two homeless applicants to the council's 'auto-bid' system under which they were deemed to have bid for a property to which their points entitled them to bid, if, after a certain period, they had not secured a property through the choice-based lettings scheme. The scheme gave the applicants a reasonable opportunity to bid before the auto-bid scheme commenced and they had the opportunity to challenge the suitability of the offer under Part VII, see paras 16.37–16.40.

Giving priority to those in greatest need

17.43 In a series of cases, both before and after choice-based lettings became the norm, allocations policies were challenged for failing to assess cumulative need, in other words, for failing to operate a system of allocations that gave greatest priority to those in greatest housing need.[40] A number of choice-based lettings policies that operated on the basis of the broad bands recommended in the green paper were held to be unlawful for failing to give priority *within* the bands to those in greatest need.

17.44 However, these cases were overruled by the House of Lords in *R (Ahmad) v Newham LBC*[41]

> In *Ahmad* the challenge was to an allocations policy that operated a choice-based lettings scheme under which applicants were placed in one of three categories: 'Priority Homeseekers' (households containing at least one person who satisfied one or more of the reasonable preference criteria); 'Tenants Seeking a Transfer (council tenants not within the Priority Homeseekers category who wanted to move); and 'Homeseekers' (who fell into neither of the other two categories). 75 per cent of properties were let through the choice-

39 [2012] EWHC 873, 3 April 2012.
40 See: *R v Islington LBC ex p Reilly and Mannix* (1998) 31 HLR 651; *R v Tower Hamlets LBC v Uddin* (1999) 32 HLR 391; *Lambeth LBC v A and Lambeth LBC v Lindsay* [2002] EWCA Civ 1084, 23 July 2002; and *R (Cali, Abdi and Hassan) v Waltham Forest LBC* [2006] EWHC 302 (Admin), 24 February 2006.
41 [2009] UKHL 14, 4 March 2009.

based lettings scheme with the other 25 per cent being let as 'Direct Offers'. The Direct Offers lettings were to applicants who would be Priority Homeseekers but who had especially pressing needs for rehousing. The criteria for this group were very stringent. For example, under the Direct Offers scheme was a category for 'multiple needs' which depended on three family members having a certain level of need.

Mr Ahmad's family of six lived in very overcrowded accommodation and his daughter was severely disabled. Mr Ahmad also suffered from depression and one of the other children had behavioural problems. Under the Direct Offers scheme, they did not pass the threshold and no additional priority was given. This meant that they were in the Priority Homeseekers band of the choice-based lettings scheme. Within that band priority was given to those who had been on the waiting list the longest.

The Court of Appeal held that the scheme was unlawful for failing to give preference to those with cumulative need over others in the same band. It also held that the authority's policy of allocating 5 per cent of choice-based lettings to ordinary transfer applicants in the same band was unlawful for failing to give reasonable preference to those in housing need, as required under HA 1996 s167.

The House of Lords, however, upheld the council's appeal:

Identifying the individual households in greatest need could only be done though some sort of points-based system and experience has shown that these too may be open to attack, either on the ground that they are too rigid and therefore unduly fetter the council's discretion or on the ground that the particular distribution of points is for some reason irrational ... Furthermore, relative needs may change over time, so that if the council were really to be assessing the relative needs of individual households, it would have to hold regular reviews of every household on the waiting list in order to identify those in greatest need as vacancies arose ... the question is how broad the brush can be ... it is not irrational to have a policy which gives priority to some tightly defined groups in really urgent need and ranks the rest of the 'reasonable preference' groups by how long they have been waiting ... Section 167(6) makes it clear that, subject to the express provisions, it is for the council to decide on what principles the scheme is to be framed.[42]

42 [2009] UKHL 14, Baroness Hale at [15] and [16].

> Furthermore, a 5 per cent 'quota' for transfer applicants was not unlawful:
>
> ... section 167(2) only requires that these groups be given a 'reasonable preference'. Still less does it require that an individual household in one of those groups should be given absolute priority over an individual household which wishes to transfer.[43]

17.45   Shortly after the decision in *Ahmad*, a challenge to using local connection to give greater priority was also dismissed.

> In *R (Van Boolen) v Barking & Dagenham LBC*,[44] the council's policy provided that where two applicants were in the same needs band, priority would be given to those with a local connection over those without. It held that it was not 'remotely arguable' that such a policy was irrational. The court also rejected the argument that the policy was unlawful for failing to state in the published policy that the authority had a discretion where a person had a need to move that was sufficiently compelling as to require an exception to be made to the general policy on local connection. The claim was dismissed.

17.46   Since these cases were decided the Localism Act 2011 has amended Part VI to give local authorities greater power over who qualifies for an allocation. Local authorities can not only give higher priority to a person with a local connection but can now operate a scheme under which those with no local connection will not qualify to go on the register at all.

Right to information and reviews

General information

17.47   Authorities must publish a summary of their allocation scheme and provide a copy free of charge to any member of the public on request.[45]

17.48   The scheme itself must be available for inspection at the principal office of the authority and a copy provided on request to any member

---

43 [2009] UKHL 14, Baroness Hale at [18].
44 [2009] EWHC 2196 (Admin), 31 July 2009.
45 HA 1996 s168(1).

of the public, on payment of a reasonable fee.[46] Most authorities now publish the summary and/or the full allocation policy on their websites.

17.49 When making any alterations to the scheme reflecting major changes of policy the authority must take reasonable steps to bring the effect of the changes to the attention of those likely to be affected, within a reasonable period of time.[47]

Particular information

17.50 An authority's allocation scheme must also ensure that an applicant has the right to the following information, on request:[48]

- general information so as to be able to assess how his or her application is likely to be treated;
- whether he or she is likely to be given preference under the scheme;
- whether it is likely that appropriate accommodation will be made available; and, if so, the timescale; and
- the facts that have been taken into account (or are likely to be taken into account) in considering whether to allocate accommodation to him or her.

17.51 Furthermore, if an authority decides that an applicant is ineligible for an allocation or is not a qualifying person they must notify the applicant in writing of the decision and the grounds for it.

Reviews

17.52 There is a right to request a review of any of the following:[49]

- a decision that a person is ineligible;
- a decision that a person is not a qualifying person;
- a decision about the facts of the person's case which have been taken into account in considering whether to allocate accommodation.

Note that in the third category above a request will usually need to be made for information about the relevant facts whereas in the first two categories the authority must notify the applicant in writing with grounds for the decision.

---

46 HA 1996 s168(2).
47 HA 1996 s168(3).
48 HA 1996 s166A(9)(a)–(b).
49 HA 1996 s166A(9)(c).

17.53   These are the only decisions which carry the right of review. If an applicant believes that he or she has been given insufficient priority, unless this is effectively a decision about the facts of the case, there is no right of review. Furthermore, there is no right of review where the applicant is seeking to challenge the lawfulness of the policy itself.

17.54   When HA 1996 first came into force regulations provided for the procedure to be followed in conducting both homeless and alloca-tion reviews. The current regulations no longer apply to allocation reviews. Nevertheless, an authority must follow a fair procedure and this should be described in the published scheme.

17.55   Unlike homelessness decisions, there is no right of appeal to the County Court following the internal review. Judicial review will there-fore be the only way to challenge a decision confirmed on review, as well as any decision that does not carry the right of review. However, as with all public decision-making, an authority may reconsider a decision and advisers will usually invite an authority to do so before beginning a claim for judicial review.

17.56   In summary, the ways to challenge allocation decisions is as follows:

- Decision that person is not eligible (immigration status): right of review, then judicial review.
- Decision that person is not qualifying (authority's own rules): right of review, then judicial review.
- Decision based on incorrect facts (eg number of children in the household, size of the home, a failure to record disability or a medical condition): right of review, then judicial review.
- Decision (based on correct facts) that household entitled to a low level of priority: no review, only judicial review.
- Policy itself is unlawful (eg because it is discriminatory or fails to comply with Part VI): judicial review.

Common issues for advisers

17.57   In practice, the most common complaint is that an applicant has been waiting for a long time but no offers have been made. This may prove to be a less common complaint now that local authorities can refuse to place those not in reasonable preference categories on the allocations register. However, there may in turn be more complaints about decisions that a person is not qualified to go on the housing register.

Has the applicant been given the correct number of points or placed in the correct band?

17.58 Although there is no right of review about the level of priority given, there is a right of review about the facts that the authority has taken into account in making its decision. Therefore, to advise a person about whether their needs have been properly assessed, it will usually be necessary to obtain further information from the authority. In addition to the right to information under the Data Protection Act 1998 an applicant has a right to specific information pursuant to section 167(4A) (see para 17.50 above).

17.59   An example of a pro forma letter requesting relevant information is contained in the appendix to this chapter.

17.60   If the facts taken into account are correct and the level of priority awarded is in accordance with the policy, no action can be taken on a client's behalf unless the policy itself is unlawful. Moreover, even if a policy is declared to be unlawful or a re-assessment ordered, this will not necessarily result in an offer of accommodation to a particular applicant. The court cannot order an authority to make an offer, only to operate a lawful scheme and to allocate in accordance with such a scheme.

17.61   Where medical assessment is at issue, an applicant may find it useful to obtain his or her own medical report and to request a re-assessment of any medical priority. As is the case for priority need, any request for a medical report should set out clearly the relevant criteria under the allocation scheme and ask the expert to express an opinion directed to the relevant issues.

Challenging the lawfulness of the policy itself

17.62 Judicial review is available to challenge not only a specific decision, but also the authority's adoption of a particular scheme. Paragraphs 2.4–2.25 explain the general principles of administrative decision-making. This chapter highlights some of the principles established by case-law regarding the lawfulness of allocation policies. However, in light of the House of Lords ruling in *Ahmad*, para 17.44 above, successful challenges to allocations policies will be rare. As Baroness Hale stated:

> ... it is for the local authority to provide an allocation scheme according to its Part VI duty, and the merits as to who, how and when priority should be afforded is a matter for the local authority subject to its special duties. Judges must be particularly slow in entering the

politically sensitive area of allocations policy by over-broad use of the doctrine of irrationality. A particular scheme cannot be castigated as irrational simply because it is not a familiar one to the court or is not considered to be the perfect solution to a difficult, if not impossible, question to resolve.[50]

17.63   Furthermore, legal aid is no longer available for advice and assistance about transfers and allocations. So, even though judicial review remains within scope, no legal aid funding will be available for the preliminary steps usually necessary in advising a person about their rights.

17.64   The basic principles local authorities must abide by when determining and operating its allocations policy are set out below. Note that most of the cases referred to were decided prior to *Ahmad*, though they do reflect general principles of administrative law.

Allocations must be in accordance with the policy

17.65   Section 166A(14) provides that an authority cannot allocate accommodation except in accordance with its allocation scheme, which must be publicly available. There are two aspects to this:

- an authority cannot make decisions in accordance with policies or practices that are not clearly indicated in the allocation scheme; and
- an authority cannot 'earmark' a vacant property for a particular applicant prior to allocation through the scheme.

17.66   The following case illustrates the first point:

In *Gallacher v Stirling Council*[51] the authority operated a policy of only considering homeless applicants for low-demand, high-turnover housing, but this policy did not appear in the published housing allocations scheme.

A homeless person offered such accommodation brought a claim for judicial review to challenge the policy and was successful. It was held that the policy was invalid in so far as it rendered inapplicable to homeless applicants the provisions of its allocations policy and applied special rules to such applicants. Furthermore, any decision

---

50   [2009] UKHL 14, 4 March 2009, Baroness Hale, endorsing the words of the first instance judge, at [22].
51   May 2001 *Legal Action* 22. See also *R (Faraah) v Southwark LBC* [2008] EWCA Civ 807, 11 July 2008.

made in accordance with a policy that was unpublished would be invalid. To treat as valid an unpublished rule or a decision made on the basis of such a rule would destroy the value of requiring the publication of allocations schemes.

17.67 With regard to the second point in para 17.65, it is very common that applicants become aware of a vacant property which they believe would be suitable and which they wish to be allocated to them. Authorities will rarely accede to such a request and, under HA 1996 Part VI, such an allocation may be unlawful.

In *Amirun Begum and Nashima Begum v Tower Hamlets LBC*[52] the claimants had applied as homeless and were placed in temporary accommodation, consisting of two neighbouring houses sublet by the authority to a social landlord. The household comprised 14 individuals, several of whom had special needs. Wheelchair-adapted accommodation was required. The authority conceded that the accommodation provided was unsuitable. There was a proposal that the two houses should be adapted to comprise a single home. A judicial review claim was commenced, seeking, among other things, an order that the authority nominate the family for the allocation of specific accommodation, ie the same two houses, following refurbishment and adaptation.

It was conceded at the hearing that the court could not make such an order, and the judge stated:

I am satisfied that only in exceptional circumstances, if at all, may a local authority lawfully earmark a property for a particular applicant on its waiting list before that property is allocated. It must apply its policy, and exercise any residual discretion, when it allocates the accommodation in question, not before. There is otherwise a risk that when the accommodation is allocated, there will be someone who has priority according to the allocation scheme over the person for whom the property has been earmarked.[53]

17.68 Similarly, those in unlawful occupation of council accommodation may argue that the authority would owe a homeless duty if they were

52 [2002] EWHC 633 (Admin), 30 April 2002.
53 [2002] EWHC 633 (Admin), Stanley Burnton at [29].

evicted and that they should therefore be allowed to remain in occupation and be granted a secure tenancy. This may arise, for example, where a tenant dies and a family member is not entitled to succeed to the tenancy. Unless the authority has a policy to grant 'non-statutory succession' (see para 4.53) an authority would be acting unlawfully if it sought to grant a secure tenancy to such a person outside of its allocation scheme.

17.69   In *Thurrock BC v West*,[54] see para 7.164, such an argument formed the basis of an 'article 8' defence to a claim for possession against a man with no right to succeed to a property. The Court of Appeal rejected the defence and the judge was criticised for not dismissing it at an early stage. In contrast, in *Leicester CC v Shearer*,[55] a family who occupied accommodation to which they could not succeed established that the conduct of the local authority was unlawful, see para 7.171. The local authority had told the family that a direct let of the accommodation was impossible, which was not correct. They later defended their decision not to consider a direct let on the basis that the family had failed to provide the necessary information to enable an allocation to be made. The Court of Appeal held this conduct was unlawful.

The scheme must sufficiently explain the way accommodation is allocated

17.70   This is closely related to the above principle. Allocations must be in accordance with the published policy and the published policy must describe, in sufficient detail, how the policy operates. This includes the criteria on which priority is assessed.

In *R (Mei Ling Lin) v Barnet LBC* (see para 17.40), it was held to be unlawful in failing to make sufficiently clear the way in which extra points were awarded to homeless applicants when their temporary accommodation was coming to an end.

17.71   However, provided a decision is properly explained, it is not necessary to set out in the allocation policy in prescriptive detail how priority is awarded. In *R (Van Boolen) v Barking and Dagenham LBC*,[56] (para 17.44 above) the court held that the council's policy was not

---

54 [2012] EWCA Civ 1435, 8 November 2012.
55 [2013] EWCA Civ 1467, 19 November 2013.
56 [2009] EWHC 2196 (Admin), 31 July 2009.

unlawful for failing to state in the allocation scheme that it had a discretion to make exceptions to a policy which gave greater priority to applicants with local connection.

Deferrals and suspensions

17.72 Long before HA 1996 Part VI came into force, the courts had considered the deferring or suspending of applications by local authorities. Many authorities suspend active consideration of applications because of such factors as rent arrears or a previous refusal of an offer of accommodation. The courts have held that such policies are not unlawful, provided they are not so rigidly applied as to fetter the discretion of the authority.

R v Wolverhampton MBC ex p Watters[57] concerned an authority's policy regarding waiting list applications by those in rent arrears. The applicant had been a council tenant, but had been evicted because of rent arrears in excess of £2,300. The council's policy was that applicants with more than two weeks' rent arrears would not be eligible for council accommodation unless (a) they had a social or medical need award of 60 points in one single category; (b) they had made substantial efforts to reduce the arrears; or (c) there were other exceptional circumstances. The applicant fell into three of the statutory groups to whom reasonable preference was to be given and argued that the council's policy was unlawful because its effect was that she was accorded no preference at all.

The court dismissed her application: the policy was not so inflexible as to be a fetter on the council's discretion. Furthermore, the council was required only to give reasonable and not absolute preference to certain groups and this meant that the authority was entitled 'to consider any other relevant fact including the extent to and circumstances in which the applicants have failed to pay due rent or have otherwise been in breach of the obligations of the existing or earlier tenancies. Such considerations are not excluded from the selection process.'[58]

17.73 The issue has also been considered in relation to allocations governed by HA 1996 Part VI.

57 (1997) 29 HLR 931, QBD.
58 (1997) 29 HLR 931, Judge LJ at 938.

In *R v Westminster CC ex p Nadhum Hussain*[59] the authority's policy was to suspend applicants from the waiting list for two years if they unreasonably refused an offer. The authority's social services department had carried out an assessment and referred to the need for an additional room to enable a carer to stay from time to time. The assessment also stated that 'Mr Hussain needs separate sleeping and living rooms to be able to store specialist equipment for that room'. An offer was made of a ground floor bed-sit and the authority made no reference to the social services assessment. When the applicant refused the offer, he was suspended from the waiting list.

The court held that, as the policy to suspend applicants did not allow for exceptions in most cases, it was therefore an unreasonable fetter on the discretion of the authority. The decision was also flawed as no mention had been made of the social services' assessment (see para 17.82 below).

17.74   The change in the courts' approach following *Ahmad* is illustrated by a more recent consideration of the issue:

In *R (O) v Newham LBC Lettings Agency*[60] the applicant was the victim of domestic violence and therefore qualified for the council's additional preference group as being in need of emergency rehousing. However, the council's policy also provided that those with 'any property related debt' would be given less priority than other applicants. The applicant owed more than £3,000 from temporary accommodation occupied as a homeless applicant. In one of the letters to the applicant it was stated that 'Newham operates a 'no debt' policy' and that until the matter was resolved satisfactorily she would receive no offers of accommodation. The council maintained that it always considered exercising discretion in exceptional circumstances but that because the applicant had made no attempts to reduce the debt or even enter into an agreement to do so, it was not minded to exercise that discretion.

The court held that, despite the fact that some of the council's letters suggested the restriction of the exercise of discretion by a rule, taken as a whole, the council's correspondence and its stated position, 'describe a rational exercise of the discretion vested in the

59   (1998) 31 HLR 645.
60   [2010] EWHC 368 (Admin), 27 January 2010.

council with reference, as the decision letter also makes clear, to the whole file'.[61] The council's decision was not unlawful.

Exercising discretion

17.75   Where a local authority has a discretion to make certain decisions, a policy that is rigidly applied may be unlawful on the basis that it fetters the discretion of the authority.

17.76   As is illustrated in *Nadhum Hussain* (see para 17.73 above), a policy that suspends or defers applications in certain circumstances may be unlawful if it fails to provide for exceptions to be made.

However, in the case of *Mehdi Babakandi v Westminster CC*[62] the court dismissed a challenge brought on a number of grounds, including that the scheme was flawed because it automatically debarred tenants with rent arrears from bidding for properties. The scheme did give the council a discretion to allow someone with rent arrears to bid and the court held that it was not unlawful for failing to set out the criteria for the 'exceptional circumstances' in which the discretion would be exercised.

Fairness

17.77   As in all administrative decision-making, the process of decision-making must be 'fair' and comply with the rules of 'natural justice'. The rules of natural justice are embodied in a duty to act fairly and the extent of that duty varies according to the circumstances, see para 2.20. It is a fundamental principle of fair decision-making that a person should be given notice of adverse information and the opportunity to comment on any such information.

17.78   In many allocation cases an applicant will submit medical reports and the authority may take its own medical advice on reports sent by the applicant or obtain information and opinions directly from those treating the applicant. In such cases, where significant information is obtained by the authority, there will be a duty to disclose this to the applicant and invite him or her to comment on the information.

---

61   [2010] EWHC 368 (Admin), Lord Carlile of Berriew QC at [30].
62   [2011] EWHC 1756, 6 July 2011.

However, there is no duty to give the applicant the last word in every case.[63]

> In *Amirun Begum and Nashima Begum v Tower Hamlets LBC*[64] (see para 17.67 above) information sent to the authority by the applicant's GP was inconsistent with that provided by the applicant. The information from the GP had been taken into account by the authority without offering the applicant the opportunity to comment.
>
> It was held that: 'The information provided by the claimants' general practitioner is significant, and has materially affected [the defendant's] conclusions. It follows that the defendant may not lawfully finally decide whether any particular accommodation is suitable for the claimants without taking into account their responses, now in evidence, to their general practitioner's letters'.[65]

17.79   Part of the duty of fairness also requires that a decision is taken by a person who is impartial. Most allocations decisions will be taken by officers who are employed to do so and whose impartiality will not be questioned.[66] However, some authorities may use elected members as part of an appeal or review process. Previous regulations provided that no elected member may take part in any decision-making in relation to allocations if either the accommodation is in his or her ward or the person concerned lives in that ward.[67]

Giving reasons

17.80   There is no general duty on local authorities to give reasons for all the decisions they make. However, HA 1996 Part VI requires that reasons are given when a decision is made:

---

63   *Bellouti v London Borough of Wandsworth* [2005] EWCA Civ 602, 20 May 2005, Jonathan Parker LJ at [62]. This case concerned the assessment of priority need under HA 1996 Part VII but similar principles apply when medical evidence is at issue in an assessment of an application for an allocation. See paras 14.84–14.88.
64   [2002] EWHC 633 (Admin), 30 April 2002.
65   [2002] EWHC 633 (Admin), Stanley Burnton J at [35].
66   Applicants may complain that an officer they have dealt with is 'biased'. However, it is extremely difficult to establish bias in such cases, see para 2.21.
67   Allocation of Housing (Procedure) Regulations 1997 SI No 483 reg 3. However, those regulations were made under HA 1996 s165 which has since been repealed.

- that a person is ineligible (on the grounds of being a person from abroad or because of unacceptable behaviour); or
- that a person does not qualify to go on the register.

17.81 Where an authority is required to give reasons for a decision, the reasons must be 'proper, adequate and intelligible and enable the person affected to know why they have won or lost'.[68]

17.82 In addition to these statutory requirements, in respect of specific decisions, there may be situations in which the circumstances call for reasons to be given, even when there is no express duty to give reasons.

In *R v Westminster CC ex p Nadhum Hussain*[69] (see para 17.73 above) it was held that the authority could lawfully have decided not to follow the recommendation of the social services department if it had identified reasons for declining to do so. However, the decision letters had ignored the assessment altogether and the authority had therefore failed to provide adequate reasons for the offer of a bed-sitting room rather than a flat with a bedroom and separate living room, as recommended by social services. This was a further reason for holding the decision unlawful.

The future for allocations challenges

17.83 In light of the *Ahmad* decision (see para 17.44 above), the changes made by the Localism Act 2011 and the removal of legal aid, challenges both to the lawfulness of allocations schemes and in relation to individual decisions are likely to be less common.

17.84 In *R (Jakimaviciute) v Hammersmith & Fulham LBC*,[70] however, an allocations policy was found to be unlawful for excluding a sub-class of persons from within a reasonable preference category, see above at para 17.31. Although housing authorities have a wide discretion as to who can qualify for an allocation, that discretion must be applied lawfully and within the parameters of the provisions of Part VI. A scheme that excludes people for illegitimate reasons and/or that may impact adversely on a protected group under the Equality Act 2010, without justification, may be unlawful. In the case of *R (Winder) v*

---

68 *R v Brent ex p Baruwa* (1997) 29 HLR 915 at 929.
69 (1998) 31 HLR 645.
70 [2014] EWCA Civ 1438, 21 October 2014.

Sandwell MBC[71] a local authority's scheme for administering the new council tax relief was held to be unlawful as it introduced criteria unrelated to financial need (a two-year residence requirement). Furthermore, there was no evidence that the authority had had any regard to its public sector equality duty under section 149 of the Equality Act 2010, see para 2.86.

APPENDIX

Letter requesting information about allocation decision

Dear Sir/Madam,

Re: *[name of client/DOB/current address]*

We are advising [client] who has applied to your authority for an allocation of accommodation.

In order that we may advise him/her as to the way in which the application is being dealt with can you please provide the following information:

- A copy of our client's application form, any relevant documents submitted in support and a summary of the relevant facts that have been taken into account in considering his/her application.
- A breakdown of the number of points allocated/the priority category into which our client has been placed.
- Whether any medical priority has been awarded to our client and, if so, a breakdown of the way the points have been awarded/explanation of the way in which the priority has been assessed.
- How likely it is that accommodation will be made available to our client, and when this is likely to happen.

This request is made pursuant to our client's right to information under s166A of the Housing Act 1996. Our client's signed authority is enclosed and we look forward to receiving the information requested.

[Please treat this request as also being made pursuant to the Data Protection Act 1998. A cheque in the sum of £10 is enclosed.]

Yours faithfully,

[Adviser]

Notes
- Advisers may prefer to give to clients a draft letter addressed to the authority from the client.
- The letter will need to be adapted depending on whether the authority has a system of points or banding and how medical priority is assessed.
- The advantage of also making reference to the Data Protection Act is that there is a statutory time limit for the provision of the information. Also an applicant is entitled to all relevant data held, not just the information specified in section 167. An authority may decline to provide

some documents under section 167 because the section refers only to information about the facts that have been taken into account. If the request is made under the Data Protection Act a fee of £10 is usually required by the authority before it will comply with such requests – see para 2.102.

CHAPTER 18

Community care: accommodation duties to adults

continued

Key points

- Community care law is mostly about the needs of adults for 'care' due to disability and ill health. However, in some situations care services may extend to the provision of accommodation.
- Currently, the law about the assessment of needs and the provision of services is set out in several different statutes. The Care Act 2014 consolidates the law but most of the Act is not in force at the time of writing.
- Presently, and under the Care Act 2014, social services authorities' duties to those in need of care and support may extend to the provision of residential accommodation.
- Case-law has established that under the current accommodation duty (under the National Assistance Act 1948) ordinary accommodation may be provided if this is necessary to ensure that a need for care and attention is met.
- Before any community care service is provided a person's needs must be assessed by the local authority. A refusal or failure to assess may be challenged by judicial review.
- If, following an assessment, an authority decides a person needs accommodation this may become an enforceable duty.
- For some patients discharged from detention in a psychiatric facility there is a duty to provide aftercare services which may include accommodation and financial support. This is a joint social services and health authority duty.
- In cases of urgent need there may be a duty to provide interim services, including accommodation, until an assessment is complete. A refusal to provide interim services may also be challenged by judicial review.
- Local authority social services departments must operate a formal complaints procedure for both adults and children.

Introduction

18.1   The main ways of obtaining accommodation from a local authority are under the Housing Act 1996: by applying for an allocation of housing under Part VI, or by making a homeless application under Part VII. These housing duties are described in detail in chapters 13 to 17. In addition, a local authority may have a duty to provide accommodation to a person in need of community care services. In practice, it is usually people unable to obtain accommodation under the Housing Act 1996 who seek accommodation under community care law.

18.2   This chapter deals with the main accommodation duties for adults under community care law. The Care Act (CA) 2014 consolidates the powers and duties for adults presently found in a number of different statutes. Some of the CA 2014 is not in force at the time of writing so references for both old and new legislation are given throughout this chapter. Chapter 19 deals with social services accommodation duties to children and chapter 20 with the immigration restrictions on community care services. Chapter 21 deals with improvements or adaptation of existing accommodation which may be facilitated under community care law.

18.3   This chapter covers the following:

- possible accommodation duties to adults under community care law;
- the duty to assess adults' needs;
- judicial review and complaints.

Sources of community care law

18.4   In May 2011 the Law Commission published its *Adult Social Care Report* (LC 326) which described the legislative position in this way: 'The legal framework for the provision of adult social care services dates back to 1948, and consists of a complex and confusing patchwork of legislation.' The report recommended the simplification of the system for assessment, eligibility and provision of all adult social care services. The result is the Care Act (CA) 2014. At the time of writing most of the CA 2014 is not in force. It is expected to come into force during 2015. In October 2014 the government issued statutory guidance: 'Care and Support Statutory Guidance'. This is more than 500 pages long and can be downloaded from www.gov.uk.

Legislation

18.5 Below is a summary of the key community care statutes applying prior to the relevant provisions of the CA 2014 coming into force:[1]

Statute	Provision
National Health Service and Community Care Act (NHSCCA) 1990	Defines community care services and sets out framework for assessment and provision of services.
National Assistance Act (NAA) 1948	Local authority duty to provide residential accommodation to adults in need of care and attention not otherwise available.
Health Services and Public Health Act (HSPHA) 1968 s45	Local authority discretion to make arrangements 'for promoting the welfare of old people'. This may include assisting a person to find lodgings.
Mental Health Act (MHA) 1983 s117	Duty to provide 'after care' services following release from detention under MHA 1983. Joint duty on local social services authority and the health authority. This may include accommodation.
Chronically Sick and Disabled Persons Act (CSDPA) 1970 s2.	Mainly about the provision of adaptations and services in the home for disabled people.

Directions and guidance

18.6 Local authorities must follow statutory guidance and directions issued by the Secretary of State for Health.[2]

Directions

18.7 Directions are mandatory and authorities must act in accordance with them. An example is the *Secretary of State's Approvals and Directions under section 21(1) of the National Assistance Act 1948* (LAC(93)10),

---

1 Note that all of these statutes, apart from the Mental Health Act 1983, will be repealed by the Care Act 2014.
2 Local Authority Social Services Act (LASSA) 1970 s7.

see para 18.14. Directions and Guidance are usually referred by the year of issue and the number. LAC stands for 'Local Authority Circular' and this was the tenth circular issued in 1993.

Guidance

18.8   Formal guidance issued under LASSA 1970 s7 is usually referred to as 'policy guidance' or 'statutory guidance' and will state that it is issued under section 7. Such guidance should be followed by local authorities but an authority has 'liberty to deviate from it where the local authority judges on admissible grounds that there is good reason to do so, but without freedom to take a substantially different course'.[3]

18.9   Additionally, general or practice guidance is issued by the Department of Health. Local authorities should have regard to such guidance but are not bound to follow it. Failure to have regard to relevant guidance may provide grounds for challenge. But an authority will not be acting unlawfully if it can show that it has taken the guidance into consideration but decided, for a legitimate reason, not to follow it.

What are community care services?

Present position

18.10   NHSCCA 1990 defines 'community care services' as services that a local authority may provide or arrange to be provided under any of the provisions set out in the table in para 18.5 above (the CSDPA is not mentioned in the NHSCCA 1990 but it does deal with the provision of care services in the home).

18.11   The main community care duties that can lead to the provision of accommodation are found in the NAA 1948 s21 and MHA 1983 s117.

Care Act 2014

18.12   Section 8 of the CA 2014 gives 'examples of what may be provided to meet needs under sections 18–20'. These include: 'accommodation in a care home or in premises of some other type' and 'goods and

---

3 *R v Islington LBC ex p Rixon* (1997–98) 1 CCLR 119, 15 March 1996, Sedley J at 123.

facilities'. The needs may be met by a local authority providing a service, by arranging for someone else to provide a service, or by making direct payments.

18.13 So, clearly there remains the possibility of the provision of accommodation or help to pay for accommodation under the CA 2014.

National Assistance Act 1948

18.14 NAA 1948 was part of the post-war package of social welfare legislation. Originally provided for both adults and children in need of care and attention and introduced the system of mainstream social security benefits ('national assistance'). Part III of the Act dealt with accommodation and included a duty to provide temporary accommodation for people made homeless in unforeseen circumstances. The provisions for children are now contained in the Children Act 1989 and social security benefits are governed by different statutes and regulations. The duty to provide accommodation to homeless people was removed from Part III when the Housing (Homeless Persons) Act 1977 came into force. What remains of Part III contains the main accommodation duty to adults in need of care and attention and remains a 'safety net' for those unable to gain access to mainstream accommodation. It has been described as 'the last refuge for the destitute'.[4]

NAA 1948 s21: the accommodation duty

18.15 Under section 21, local authorities have a duty to provide: 'residential accommodation for persons who are aged 18 or over who by reason of age, illness, disability or any other circumstances are in need of care and attention which is not otherwise available to them.'[5]

18.16 Also, local authorities *may* 'make arrangements to provide residential accommodation for expectant and nursing mothers who are in need of care and attention which is not otherwise available to them'.[6] So, this is a power not a duty to provide accommodation. It is not limited to those over the age of 18.

---

4 See *R v Wandsworth LBC ex p O* and *R v Leicester CC ex p Bhikha* (2000) 3 CCLR 237, CA, 26 February 2000. See also para 20.13.

5 NAA 1948 s21(1)(a) and *Secretary of State's Approvals and Directions under section 21(1) of the National Assistance Act 1948* (LAC(93)10).

6 NAA 1948 s21(1)(aa).

Nature of the section 21 duty

18.17　Since 1996 the courts have considered the duty under NAA 1948 s21 in a number of cases. This has mainly been in consequence of the legislation restricting the rights of migrants to benefits and access to mainstream housing. This created a large group of destitute adults who sought help from local authorities. Other people unable to obtain appropriate housing under HA 1996 have also relied on NAA 1948 to obtain accommodation. This has created a significant volume of case-law about the nature of the section 21 duty, which is summarised below at paras 18.18–18.25. See also paras 20.189–20.213 which explain how the law has developed in relation to immigrants.

Provision of ordinary housing

18.18　There is no requirement that the residential accommodation provided by the authority must be institutional accommodation in which other services are also provided. Under NAA 1948 s21 ordinary accommodation may be provided along with food or vouchers for food. This was established in one of the early cases in which asylum-seekers excluded from mainstream housing sought help from local authorities.

> In *R v Newham LBC ex p Medical Foundation for the Care of Victims of Torture*[7] the local authority accepted a duty under NAA 1948 s21 to provide accommodation to the applicants but argued that the duty was to provide residential accommodation together with board and other services as part of a package. The authority offered accommodation in a hotel in Eastbourne on the grounds that this would enable it to provide the package of services required under NAA 1948.
>
> The court rejected the authority's argument, holding that the services additional to accommodation need not be provided 'in' the accommodation. Furthermore, statutory guidance required an authority, as far as possible, to preserve or restore normal living. It is therefore lawful for an authority to provide ordinary accommodation suitable to the needs of the applicants. Other services may be provided from outside the accommodation.

7　(1998) 30 HLR 955. The case concerned destitute asylum-seekers before NAA 1948 was amended to exclude those whose need arose solely because of destitution, see para 20.205.

Need for care and attention

18.19 While the need may be met by providing ordinary accommodation rather than a package of care, a section 21 duty will arise only if there is an unmet need for care and attention, as opposed to a need for housing or for more appropriate housing.

> In *R (Wahid) v Tower Hamlets LBC*[8] the applicant suffered from schizophrenia. He and his wife lived with their eight children, aged between 28 and 9, in a two-bedroom flat. The applicant's wife was his carer and intended to continue to care for him but the family contended that his mental health was likely to deteriorate because of the stress of the overcrowded home. Social services decided that he was not in need of care and attention that was 'not otherwise available'; his needs were being met.
>
> The Court of Appeal dismissed the family's appeal: Tower Hamlets was entitled to conclude that the overcrowding did not create the need for care and attention within NAA 1948 s21. The need for care and attention is a pre-condition to the duty to accommodate under section 21. The fact that a person is in need of ordinary accommodation does not mean that he needs care and attention. The provision of ordinary accommodation is merely one way in which a need for care and attention can be met.

18.20 The situation will be different, however, where the person is excluded from mainstream housing and benefits because of immigration status. In such a case the provision of accommodation may be essential even if family or friends are able to provide the care and attention. See for example *R (Mani) v Lambeth LBC*[9] at para 20.16. However, it is not enough that there is a need for care and attention and that the individual needs accommodation. The care and attention must be of a kind calling for the provision of accommodation: *SL v Westminster CC*[10] discussed in more detail at para 20.211.

8 (2001) 4 CCLR 455, 7 March 2002.
9 [2003] EWCA Civ 836, 9 July 2003.
10 [2013] UKSC 27, 9 May 2013.

The duty is enforceable

18.21   If an authority assesses a person's needs and finds that appropriate accommodation is a need that should be met, this may create an enforceable duty.

18.22   In *R v Kensington and Chelsea ex p Kujtim*[11] the Court of Appeal described the section 21 duty as follows:

> Once a local authority has assessed an applicant's needs as satisfying the criteria laid down in section 21(1)(a), the local authority is under a duty to provide accommodation on a continuing basis so long as the need of the applicant remains as originally assessed.[12]

In *R (Batantu) v Islington LBC*[13] the local authority's social services department assessed a man with mental health and mobility problems. He lived with his wife and four children in a two-bedroom flat on the twelfth floor of a high rise block. The assessment concluded that he needed a ground floor property with enough space to house the rest of the family. Proceedings were issued to force the authority to provide such accommodation and, nine months after the assessment, the court made an order that the authority provide accommodation in accordance with its statement of need. The authority was given three months to identify suitable accommodation, in consultation with the family, and a further three months to make the accommodation available to the family.

18.23   Note that in *Batantu* the social services department prepared a care plan stating that the applicant needed a safe, secure, easily accessible and spacious environment. Having assessed this as a need, the social services department could not just leave the issue to be resolved by the housing department. In contrast, in *Wahid,* the authority decided that the applicant did not have any unmet need for care and attention.

18.24   Whether an enforceable duty to accommodate arises will depend on the precise terms of the needs assessment. In light of cases such as *Batantu,* local authorities will usually ensure that housing needs are addressed in terms of a need for help to obtain appropriate housing and will avoid simply stating that a person has a need for housing or more appropriate housing.

---

11   (1999) 2 CCLR 340, 9 July 1999.
12   (1999) 2 CCLR 340, Potter LJ at 354C.
13   (2001) 4 CCLR 445, QBD.

In *R (Mooney) v Southwark LBC*[14] the claimant was a disabled single parent with three children, including twins, both of whom had special needs. A community care assessment was carried out, as were Children Act 1989 assessments and a carer's assessment on the claimant's eldest child. A number of recommendations were made, including that the twins should have separate bedrooms and that the family should have new accommodation in which the claimant could access to all rooms. Following this, and in accordance with the council's allocations scheme, the social services department made a nomination to the housing department. The nomination was accepted and Ms Mooney was placed in the highest priority band for rehousing under the authority's choice-based lettings scheme. After 11 months the claimant had not obtained a suitable property. This was because of a combination of factors: others in the same band took precedence having being registered before the applicant; not every four-bedroom property was capable of being fitted with a lift; and, the claimant was not willing to accept any area in the borough because she wanted to be near her extended family, who provided support and assistance. The court also found that, even within those constraints, the claimant had been 'overly selective' in the properties she had bid for. The claim for judicial review alleged a continuing failure to make provision for the family's need. A mandatory order was sought, requiring the authority to identify and make available an appropriate property.

The claim was dismissed. Although the assessments undoubtedly identified a need for more suitable accommodation, this did not trigger a duty under NAA 1948 s21. As in *Wahid*, the court held that the assessments did not identify any need for care and attention that was not available other than by the provision of accommodation under section 21. Rather, the assessment concluded that the proper course was for social services to provide additional support and to make a priority nomination under the allocations policy. Furthermore, NAA 1948 s21(8) provides that section 21 cannot authorise or require a local authority to make any provision that was authorised or required to be made by another statute. The fact that suitable accommodation could be provided under HA 1996 prevented an obligation arising under section 21.

14 [2006] EWHC Admin 1912, 6 July 2007.

18.25   Nevertheless, it is still the case that if social services assess a person as having an unmet need for care and attention which requires the provision of accommodation, social services may then have the duty to provide that accommodation. Judicial review proceedings can be brought to enforce the duty. In addition, where there is a delay in providing for the assessed need, damages may be awarded on the ground that the authority's failure has led to a breach of the person's human rights.

> In *R (Bernard) v Enfield LBC*[15] the applicant was a wheelchair-user, living in unadapted accommodation, having previously been found intentionally homeless by the housing department. An assessment by the authority concluded that the family needed assistance to move to suitably adapted property but no steps were taken to make such accommodation available for 20 months. In judicial review proceedings damages were claimed on the grounds that the applicant's rights under article 3 (inhuman and degrading treatment) and article 8 (the right to respect for private and family life) of the ECHR had been breached. For the period in question Mrs Bernard had been unable to access the toilet or keep herself clean without great difficulty. She soiled herself several times each day, was unable to go out of the house or upstairs and relied on her husband to assist her to move about downstairs. She had no privacy because she shared a room with her husband and two youngest children, and the older children had to pass through the room to go upstairs. Her husband's back problem was exacerbated by having to carry her to the bathroom.
>   The court dismissed the claim under article 3 on the basis that the authority had failed to deliver a service rather than subjecting the family to 'treatment'. However, it found that there had been a breach of the claimant's rights under article 8. Damages of £10,000 were agreed.

Immigration status

18.26   Where the person in need of community care services is a 'person subject to immigration control' the duty under NAA 1948 s21 arises only if the person's need for care and attention is not caused solely by destitution. This issue is explained in detail in paras 20.11–20.18.

---

15   [2002] EWHC Admin 2282, 25 October 2002.

The same formulation is adopted in the CA 2014 in relation to the 'need for care and support': see CA 2014 s21.

Mental Health Act 1983

18.27 Mental Health Act 1983 s117(2) provides that:

It shall be the duty of the clinical commissioning group or Local Health Board and of the local social services authority to provide, in co-operation with relevant voluntary agencies, aftercare services for any person to whom this section applies until such time as the Primary Care Trust or Health Authority and the local social services authority are satisfied that the person concerned is no longer in need of such services ...

18.28 The duty applies to patients who have been detained in hospital under one of the following sections of MHA 1983:

- *section 3*: detention for treatment (as opposed to detention for assessment under section 2);
- *section 37*: a 'hospital order' made by order of a criminal court after conviction of an offence committed when the offender was suffering from a 'mental disorder';[16]
- *section 45A*: detention following a direction by the Crown Court that a person suffering from a psychopathic disorder should be detained in a specified hospital (this power is available when sentencing such a person to a term of imprisonment);
- *section 47*: detention of a prisoner serving a sentence who is suffering from a mental disorder;
- *section 48*: detention of a prisoner, imprisoned on remand, a civil prisoner or someone detained under the Immigration Act 1971, who is suffering from a mental disorder.

18.29 Section 117 does not define 'aftercare services' and there is limited guidance on the nature of the duty. It clearly can include the provision of accommodation. The new section 117A[17] allows for someone to express a preference for particular accommodation where a local authority is discharging its section 117 duty by providing or arranging for accommodation. Where the preferred accommodation is more expensive, the person may be charged for some or all of the additional cost.

---

16 Mental disorder means mental illness, psychopathic disorder, severe mental impairment or mental impairment.

17 In force from 1 October 2014.

18.30   In most cases accommodation will be provided by the appropriate housing authority, which (if accommodation is needed) should be involved in the assessment. However, some migrants are unable to access housing in this way and may be able to rely on section 117 to obtain accommodation. The duty under section 117 is one of the few community care duties for which there is no restriction based on immigration status.

> However, in *R (Mwanza) v Greenwich LBC and Bromley LBC*[18] the court refused permission for a judicial review to challenge the refusal to provide accommodation under MHA 1983 s117. The man and his family had no access to housing or benefits because of their immigration status.
>   The court held that 'an aftercare service must ... be a service that is necessary to meet a need arising from a person's mental disorder' and that although it was not the case that ordinary accommodation could never be provided under section 117, 'it is difficult readily to envisage circumstances in which a mere roof over the head would, on the facts of a particular case, be necessary to meet a need arising from a person's mental disorder'.[19]

18.31   The duty arises on discharge and continues until the authorities 'are satisfied that the person concerned is no longer in need of such services'.[20] A person who has been discharged from one of the relevant sections some time ago should receive aftercare services until he or she is assessed as no longer needing such services.

18.32   The section 117 duty applies to only a small proportion of patients who receive in-patient psychiatric care. However, other people with mental health problems may be entitled to services under NAA 1948 if they have an unmet need for care and attention.

18.33   Local authorities can charge for the provision of most community care services, including under NAA 1948, subject to an assessment of means. However, no charge can be made in respect of services provided under section 117,[21] save for the additional costs of providing more expensive accommodation in accordance with the person's preference, under section 117A, see para 18.29 above.

---

18 [2010] EWHC 1462 (Admin), 15 June 2010.
19 [2010] EWHC 1462 (Admin) at [64] and [67].
20 MHA 1983 s117(2), see para 18.26.
21 *R v Manchester CC ex p Stennett and Others* [2002] UKHL 34.

How to obtain community care services

18.34 A duty to provide accommodation will arise only when a person has been assessed as needing accommodation. Under the MHA 1983, the assessment of needs should be carried out before discharge but for other community care services it can be difficult to persuade an authority to carry out an assessment.

Community care assessments

The current position

18.35 Section 47 of the NHSCCA 1990 sets out how a local authority's duty to carry out an assessment of a person's need for community care services arises. Section 47(1) provides:

> ... where it appears to a local authority that any person for whom they may provide or arrange for the provision of community care services may be in need of such services, the authority –
> (a) shall carry out an assessment of his needs for those services; and
> (b) having regard to the results of that assessment, shall then decide whether his needs call for the provision by them of any such services.

18.36 The duty to assess a person's needs should therefore be easily triggered. The authority should not refuse to assess because it anticipates that the person may not actually be eligible to *receive* a service. The duty arises if it *appears* that a person for whom the authority *may* provide a service *may* be in need of services. This is a 'very low threshold test'.[22] In practice many authorities are reluctant to carry out assessments and only do so on threat of complaint or legal action. Additionally, the pressure on staff resources in social services authorities means that there is often significant delay before an assessment is commenced.

18.37   It is often necessary to make the request for an assessment in writing and a precedent letter for such a request is contained in appendix 1 to this chapter.

Assessment procedure

18.38 Section 47 of NHSCCA 1990 requires an authority to carry out a two-stage procedure:

---

22 See *R v Bristol CC ex p Penfold* (1997–98) 1 CCLR 315.

- to assess the apparent needs of the person (the 'presenting needs'); and
- to decide which of them call for the provision of services (the 'eligible needs').

18.39   The authority must have regard to the results of the assessment of need in deciding what services to provide. There is no obligation to meet all presenting needs.

Relevance of resources

18.40   In *R v Gloucestershire CC ex p Barry*[23] the House of Lords considered services provided under NAA 1948 s29 and the Chronically Sick and Disabled Persons Act (CSDPA) 1970.
The court held that an authority could not assess a person as needing a service but decline to provide it because resources were limited. However, in determining which needs called for the provision of a service, an authority was entitled to take account of the availability of resources: 'needs for services cannot sensibly be assessed without having some regard to the cost of providing them.'[24]

18.41   Following the *Barry* case, since 2003 local authorities have been obliged to set 'eligibility criteria' in accordance with the *Fair Access to Care Services 2002 Policy Guidance in England*[25] ('FACS guidance'). The criteria are set with a view to preserving or facilitating independence and are contained in bands based on risk factors. The four bands are graded according to a risk assessment of the likely consequences of failing to provide a service as follows:

- critical;
- substantial;
- moderate; and
- low.

18.42   The FACS guidance requires authorities to estimate the likely need for services and the costs of meeting the needs falling into each band. If the authority's resources are sufficient only to meet critical need

---

23 [1997] 2 All ER 1, 20 March 1997.
24 [1997] AC 584, Lord Nicholls at 604C.
25 LAC(2002)13. This has been superseded by new guidance issued in February 2010 but the new guidance adopts the FACS eligibility bands.

then its eligibility criteria would mean that only critical needs would be met. If the resources were sufficient to meet critical and substantial, then needs assessed as falling into those bands would be met.[26] So, although each authority is obliged to follow the same process in setting its eligibility criteria, different authorities will operate different criteria and some will provide services that others will not.

Care Act 2014

18.43   Under the CA 2014 the assessment duty is in similar terms. CA 2014 s9 provides for a 'needs assessment':

> (1) Where it appears to a local authority that an adult may have needs for care and support, the authority must assess –
> (a) whether the adult does have needs for care and suport, and
> (b) if the adult does, what those needs are.
>
> ....
>
> (3) The duty to carry out a needs assessment applies regardless of the authority's view of –
> (a) the level of the adult's needs for care and support, or
> (b) the level of the adult's financial resources.

Subsections (4) to (6) set out some requirements as to how the needs assessment is to be carried out.

18.44   Eligibility for the provision of services is found in section 13(1) which provides:

> Where a local authority is satisfied on the basis of a needs or carer's assessment that an adult has needs for care and support or that a carer has needs for support, it must determine whether any of the needs meet the eligiblity criteria ...

18.45   If at least some of the needs meet the eligibility criteria the local authority must consider what could be done to meet those needs that do, ascertain whether the person wants those needs met by the local authority, and establish whether the adult is ordinarily resident in the local authority area: s13(3).

Eligibility criteria under Care Act 2014

18.46   Presently, each local authority sets its own 'eligibility criteria' within the parameters set out in the FACS guidance, see above at para 18.41. Under the CA 2014 'the eligibility criteria' are nationally determined. At the time of writing, the relevant regulations are in draft: The Care

---

26 The National Audit Office report *Adult Social Care in England: overview* published in March 2014 reported that 87 per cent of adults live in areas where the local authorities meet only critical and substantial needs.

and Support (Eligibility Criteria) Regulations 2014. An adult will meet the eligibilty criteria if, as a result of needs arising from or related to a physical or mental impairment or illness, they cannot achieve two or more of a list of specified outcomes, and as a consequence there is, or is likely to be, a significant impact on the adult's well-being. The specified outcomes are:

- managing and maintaining nutrition;
- maintaining personal hygiene;
- managing toilet needs;
- being appropriately clothed;
- being able to make use of the adult's home safely;
- maintaining a habitable home environment;
- developing and maintaining family or other personal relationships;
- accessing or engaging in work, training, education or volunteering;
- making use of necessary facilities or services in the local community including public transport, and recreational facilities or services; and
- carrying out any caring responsibilities the adult has for a child.

Form of assessment

18.47   Although there is presently no statutory requirement that the assessment is in writing, local authorities usually complete pro forma documentation and practice guidance recommends that a 'copy of the assessment of needs should normally be shared with the potential service user ... Except where no intervention is deemed necessary, this record will normally be combined with a written care plan'.[27] The FACS policy guidance states that the person should receive a copy of the care plan.[28]

18.48   The CA 2014 provides expressly that the needs assessment and the eligibility assessment must be in writing with copies provided to the person concerned. In relation to the eligibility assessment, section 13(2) provides that 'having made a determination ... the local authority must give the adult concerned a written record of the determination and the reasons for it.'

---

27   *Care Management and Assessment: A Practitioner's Guide*, 1991, Department of Health, para 4.54.
28   FACS guidance LAC(2002)13, para 49.

Cases of emergency

18.49 NHSCCA 1990 s47(5) provides that a local authority may temporarily provide a service without carrying out a prior assessment of needs 'if, in the opinion of the authority, the condition of that person is such that he requires those services as a matter of urgency'. Where services are provided in an emergency, the duty to assess still remains and an assessment should be done as soon as reasonably practicable. Although this is a power rather than a duty, an authority must consider whether or not to exercise the power and, in clear cases of urgent need, the courts will order an authority to make provision pending an assessment.

18.50 The CA 2014 also makes express provision, under section 19(3):

A local authority may meet an adult's needs for care and support which appear to it to be urgent (regardless of whether the adult is ordinarily resident in its area) without having yet –
(a) carried out a needs assessment or a financial assessment, or
(b) made a determination under section 13(1) [the eligibilty assessment].

18.51 The CA 2014 also makes provision for how ordinary residence is to be determined when a person has been living in specified accommodation where care and supoort has been provided, and also for the resolution of disputes between authorities, see ss39–41.

Resolving disputes: judicial review or complaint?

18.52 Social services authorities must operate complaints procedures in accordance with specific regulations. Social services decision-making can also be challenged by way of judicial review. Judicial review is described in more detail in paras 2.4–2.39. This section highlights some of the issues that arise in relation to social services decision-making and explains when decisions might be challenged by judicial review and when the complaints procedure will be appropriate.

18.53 Presently the sources of community care law are complex. But it is clear that local authorities are subject to the following duties:

• a duty to assess an adult who is potentially in need of services;
• as part of the assessment process, a duty to set out the person's needs and to state what services are to be provided, by whom and by when;
• a duty to provide accommodation to adults with an unmet need for care and attention that calls for the provision of accommodation.

Authorities will usually have to first assess the person's needs but in cases of urgency may have to provide interim accommodation while doing so.

18.54   It is the *enforcement* of these duties that has generated a large volume of litigation. In most cases the reason for this is, as Lord Nicholls pointed out in *G, W and A* (see para 19.9), 'the seemingly intractable problem of local authorities' lack of resources'.[29]

Judicial review

18.55   In judicial review, the role of the court is 'supervisory'; a claim for judicial review is not an appeal against a decision. Judicial review is a review of the lawfulness of a decision, action or failure to act in relation to the exercise of a public function.[30]

18.56   The most common reasons for judicial review claims in community care cases are:

- failure or refusal to carry out an assessment;
- delay in carrying out an assessment;
- failure or refusal to provide interim services, (including accommodation) pending full assessment;
- an assessment that is so inadequate as to be unlawful.

18.57   The following are examples of reasons why an assessment may be unlawful:

- *Failing to take account of relevant information/failing to make sufficient inquiries* This could include failing to follow statutory guidance.
- *Unfair procedure* This could include failing to follow an authority's own stated policy or procedure.
- *Error of law* Given the requirement to determine a person's immigration status and to carry out 'human rights assessments' there is an increased risk of errors of law when assessing the needs of migrants (see chapter 20).

18.58   The main advantage of using judicial review is that an application to the court can be made on an urgent basis. An interim order can be obtained at short notice to force an authority to commence an assessment and to provide services on an urgent basis.

---

29 [2003] UKHL 57, 23 October 2003, at [10].
30 Civil Procedure Rules (CPR) 54.1(2)(a).

Alternative dispute resolution

18.59   Before a claim for judicial review is issued parties should consider alternative ways of resolving the dispute.[31]

> In *Cowl v Plymouth CC*[32] the applicant issued a claim for judicial review to challenge the authority's decision to close a residential care home. The authority responded, proposing that the issue be dealt with as a complaint and the proceedings adjourned. The applicants rejected this proposal.
>
> The Court of Appeal held that the courts should not, except for good reason, permit proceedings for judicial review to go ahead if a significant part of the issues between the parties could be resolved outside the litigation process.

18.60   In a case of urgent need, however, the complaints procedure would not be appropriate unless the authority was prepared to offer assistance pending the resolution of the complaint.

Limits of judicial review

18.61   The disadvantage of judicial review is that the court's role is limited. The court is scrutinising the lawfulness of the local authority's decision or conduct, not considering the merits of a decision or making its own decision on the facts. See R *(P, W, F and G) v Essex*[33] summarised at para 19.63.

Judicial review to obtain an assessment

18.62   Judicial review or the threat of judicial review is commonly used to force a local authority to carry out an assessment and to provide interim accommodation pending assessment. A precedent letter requesting an assessment is contained in appendix 1 to this chapter.

18.63   If the authority refuses to assess or fails to respond within the deadline indicated, the next step may be a judicial review protocol letter. A precedent pre-action protocol letter is contained in appendix 2 to this chapter.

---

31 CPR Judicial Review Protocol, para 4.1.
32 [2001] EWCA Civ 1935, 14 December 2001.
33 [2004] EWHC 2027 (Admin), 19 August 2004.

18.64   In urgent cases, especially where a person has already approached the authority for help, it may be appropriate to send a judicial review protocol letter immediately.

Social services complaints

18.65   The limited scope of judicial review and the fact that judicial review is a 'remedy of last resort' means that in the following circumstances a complaint will usually be the most appropriate way of challenging a decision:

- where a person wishes to challenge a particular aspect of service provision, for example, the way services are delivered or the standard of accommodation provided;
- where services are being provided but there was delay in setting up the services (if services are still not being provided judicial review may be more appropriate);
- where the complaint is about the way a person has been treated, for example, rudeness or failure to keep someone informed.

18.66   An authority may decline to deal with a complaint if legal action is pending or is threatened. However, where legal action or the threat of legal action results in an assessment and/or provision of services, this would not preclude a complaint about any delay or the initial refusal to assist.

Statutory complaints procedure

18.67   Local authorities must operate complaints procedures in relation to services to adults and children.[34] The Local Authority Social Services and National Health Service Complaints (England) Regulations 2009[35] set out how complaints about adult social care must be dealt with by social services, NHS bodies and private providers. The 2009 Regulations replaced a three-stage procedure with clear time limits (this was broadly the same as that applying in relation to children's complaints, see para 19.64). There is now a single stage which provides that the complaint must be acknowledged within three working days but the time limit for completing the investigation is six months, and even this is not a strict deadline.

---

34 LASSA 1970 s7B.
35 SI No 309.

Complaints procedure

18.68 'Responsible bodies' (which means local authorities, NHS bodies, primary care providers or independent providers) must have a complaints procedure so as to ensure that:

- complaints are dealt with efficiently;
- complaints are properly investigated;
- complainants are treated with respect and courtesy;
- complainants receive, so far as is reasonably practical:
  - assistance to enable them to understand the procedure in relation to complaints; or
  - advice on where they may obtain such assistance;
- complainants receive a timely and appropriate response;
- complainants are told the outcome of the investigation of their complaint; and
- action is taken if necessary in the light of the outcome of a complaint.

Complaints manager

18.69 A 'responsible person' and a 'complaints manager' must be appointed to ensure compliance with the regulations. For local authorities and NHS bodies the responsible person must be the chief executive officer. The complaints manager may be the same or a different person. The complaints manager may be someone not employed by the authority.

Who may complain

18.70 Usually this will be the service user but it could be someone else affected by the action, omission or decision of the responsible body (eg a carer or relative). Complaint may be made by someone acting on behalf of the complainant if that person has died, is a child or is unable to make the complaint because of physical or mental incapacity. Or, a person may request a representative to act on their behalf. Complaints may be made orally, in writing or electronically.

Time limits

18.71   The stages of the complaints procedure and the time limits for each stage are summarised in the table below:

Making the complaint	Within 12 months of the issue arising or the complainant becoming aware of it. But this does not apply if the body is satisfied that the complainant had good reasons for not making the complaint within 12 months and it is still possible to investigate the complaint effectively and fairly.
Acknowledging the complaint	Not later than three working days after the day the complaint is received. This may be orally or in writing.
Offering to discuss the complaint	When the complaint is acknowledged the body must offer to discuss the complaint (at a time to be agreed with the complainant), how it is to be handled and the likely timescale for investigation and response.
Setting the timescale	If the complainant does not accept the offer of a discussion the responsible body must decide the period for investigation and response and inform the complainant in writing.
Recording the complaint	Before investigating the complaint the body must make a written record of the complaint and provide a copy to the complainant. No specific time limit.
Investigation	The investigation should be completed within six months of receiving the complaint. A longer period may be agreed between the parties before the end of six months. If the responsible body does not comply with this deadline, it must notify the complainant in writing and explain why and must send a response 'as soon as reasonably practicable after the relevant period.'

Report/response	'As soon as reasonably practicable after completing the investigation' the body must send a written response including a report explaining how the complaint has been considered, the conclusion reached and whether any remedial action is proposed or has been taken.
	For local authority and health body complaints, details of the right to take the complaint to the Local Government Ombudsman or Health Services Commissioner must be given.
Conduct of the investigation	The complaint must be investigated in a manner appropriate to resolve it speedily and efficiently and the complainant should be kept informed, as far as reasonably practicable, of the progress of the investigation.
Exceptions	Oral complaints that are resolved to the complainant's satisfaction by the following working day do not have to be recorded or investigated.
Declining to deal with a complaint	Where the body decides that it is not required to consider a complaint (eg a complaint already dealt with or one about matters that occurred more than 12 months ago) it must notify the complainant in writing with reasons for its decision 'as soon as reasonably practicable.' This does not apply to oral complaints that have been resolved. See above.

The regulations also specify certain monitoring and reporting requirements about complaints generally.

18.72   It should be noted that a complaint to the Ombudsman must also be made within 12 months of knowledge of the matters complained of. However, the Ombudsman will not usually consider a complaint unless the authority has been given the opportunity to resolve the complaint. This is subject to exceptions, see para 19.66.

18.73   See paras 2.96–2.100 for further information about Ombudsman complaints.

APPENDIX 1

Letter requesting community care assessment (adult)

To:
Duty Manager
Assessment Team X Local Authority

Dear Sir/Madam,

Re: Mrs A

DOB: 01.01.1968

We are assisting Mrs A who is a failed asylum-seeker from [country]. We are referring her to your authority for an assessment under section 47 of the NHS & Community Care Act 1990.

[Reasons for possible community care services]

Mrs A suffers from depression which her GP describes as 'sometimes severe' (letter attached). She is receiving treatment for post traumatic stress disorder from the ... clinic. The claimant also has mobility problems caused by an historic hip fracture. This injury causes her pain and means that she cannot carry heavy bags and cannot walk far without additional pain and discomfort.

[Detail where she has been staying, why she can no longer stay there, how managing re food/support etc.]

Mrs A's claim for asylum was refused on [date] and her appeal refused on [date]. Mrs A was being supported and accommodated by NASS until [date]. Since then she has been homeless and destitute. For a period of two weeks she was street homeless but on [date] a friend, Mrs D of [address], permitted her to stay in her home for a maximum of two weeks. Mrs A has no financial support but has been provided with food by Mrs D for the past week. Mrs D has informed Mrs A that she must leave her home on [date].

Mrs A attended your offices on [date] seeking help but was advised that no help could be given as she was a failed asylum-seeker.

[Authority's possible duty to provide community care services]

We believe that your authority may be under a duty to provide support and accommodation to Mrs A under section 21 of the National Assistance Act 1948. Section 21 places a duty on a local authority to provide residential accommodation to an adult in need of care and attention because of age, illness, disability or other circumstance. Mrs A is in need of care and attention and her need does not arise solely from destitution.

[What local authority is being asked to do]

Please can you contact us so that the appropriate arrangements can be made for our client to be assessed. [Or, our client is delivering this letter to you. Please inform him/her of when and where he or she should attend for the assessment to be commenced].

[Deadline]

Please notify us/Mrs A no later than 4 pm on [date] of your agreement to carry out an assessment under section 47.

[In cases of urgent need]

Please also confirm that you will make arrangements to provide accommodation and financial support to Mrs A until the assessment has been completed.

[Consequences of failure to reply]

If we do not hear from you by 4 pm on [date] we will assume that your authority is refusing to carry out an assessment and will take appropriate action/refer our client to solicitors with a view to taking legal action against your authority.

Yours faithfully,

APPENDIX 2

Pre-action protocol letter (failure to assess)

Proposed claim for judicial review

To
Director of Social Services X Local Authority
Address

The claimant
Mrs A
Of no fixed abode

Reference details

The claimant's advisers have spoken by telephone to Mr B, the Duty Manager of the assessment team.

The details of the matter being challenged:

(1) The failure/refusal of the defendants to carry out an assessment of the claimant's needs under section 47 of the National Health Service and Community Care Act (NHSCCA) 1990.

(2) The failure/refusal of the defendants to provide interim accommodation and support to the claimant pending an assessment under section 47 of NHSCCA 1990.

The issue

The claimant is a failed asylum-seeker who has been homeless and destitute since ... She has for the past two weeks been staying with a friend at ... but was told she must leave no later than ... as the premises are overcrowded. The claimant has no other friends with whom she can stay when she has to leave this accommodation. The claimant has no means of support.

The claimant suffers from depression which her GP describes as 'sometimes severe' (letter attached). She is receiving treatment for post traumatic stress disorder from the ... clinic. The claimant also has mobility problems caused by an historic hip fracture. This injury causes her pain and means that she cannot carry heavy bags and cannot walk far without additional pain and discomfort.

The claimant has attended the offices of the defendant's social services assessment team on two occasions. The first time was approximately two weeks ago when she was advised that the defendants could not assist her because of her immigration status. The second time was approximately one week ago when the claimant delivered a letter requesting a community care assessment (copy attached). The claimant was advised that she should apply to NASS for assistance.

The claimant's advisers spoke to the defendant's duty manager, Mr B, by telephone yesterday. He stated that the defendants could not assist the claimant as she was a failed asylum-seeker and that she should apply to NASS for section 4 support.

The defendants are acting unlawfully in refusing to conduct an assessment under section 47 of NHSCCA 1990. The claimant is clearly a person who may be in need of community care services that the defendants may provide. In particular, the claimant is in need of accommodation and support under section 21 of the National Assistance Act 1948 as she is destitute and in need of care and attention not otherwise available. Her need does not arise solely from destitution.

The details of the action that the defendant is expected to take

(1) Confirm that it will immediately commence an assessment of the claimant's needs;
(2) Confirm that it will arrange for the claimant to be provided with accommodation and support under section 21 of the National Assistance Act 1948 on an interim basis until the assessment is completed.

The details of the legal advisers, if any, dealing with this claim

CC and Company [address]

The details of any interested parties

There are no interested parties at present

The details of any information sought

If the defendants maintain that they have no duty to assess the claimant a full explanation is required.

The details of any documents that are considered relevant and necessary

The claimant requests a complete copy of her social services file under the Data Protection Act 1998. The claimant's signed authority is enclosed and a cheque in the sum of £10 is enclosed with the hard copy of this letter.

[If an assessment has been conducted request a copy of the assessment]

The address for reply and service of court documents

CC and Company [address]

Proposed reply date

By 4 pm on ... [two days before the claimant is due to be evicted from her current accommodation]

Yours faithfully,

CHAPTER 19

Community care: accommodation duties to children

continued

Key points

Children in need

- The main provisions regarding accommodation for children in need are sections 17 and 20 of the Children Act (CA) 1989.
- The section 17 duty is a 'target duty' owed to children and families generally. It includes a power to provide accommodation, or financial help to obtain accommodation. It does not create an enforceable duty.
- In contrast, the section 20 duty is an enforceable duty to provide accommodation to children in need who require accommodation in specified circumstances.
- The primary duty to accommodate homeless 16- and 17-year-olds is the social services duty under section 20.
- In an emergency the housing authority can provide accommodation but it should immediately make a referral to social services for an assessment.
- Social services and housing authorities/departments must operate joint working agreements to deal with homeless 16- and 17-year-olds.

Children leaving care

- Social services may also have a duty to accommodate care leavers aged 18 to 20 (or, in some cases, up to age 24).
- Care leavers have automatic priority need for housing until they are 21.

Introduction

19.1   This chapter examines:

- accommodation duties to children in need;
- the duty to assess children's needs;
- duties to children leaving care;
- recent cases on the duty under the Children Act 1989 s20.

Local authority duties to children: Children Act 1989

19.2   The Children Act (CA) 1989 consolidated previously fragmented legislation about children. It reformed and simplified child care law, particularly in relation to child protection. One of the central tenets is that children should, as far as possible, be looked after by their families. Part III of the Act deals with 'Local Authority Support for Children and Families' and contains the two key provisions that may result in a local authority providing accommodation for the benefit of a child: sections 17 and 20.

Children in need

19.3   The concept of a 'child in need' is central to the local authority duties set out in CA 1989 Part III.

19.4   Section 17(10) defines a 'child in need' in the following terms:

... a child shall be taken to be in need if:

(a) he is unlikely to achieve or maintain, or to have the opportunity of achieving or maintaining, a reasonable standard of health or development without the provision for him of services by a local authority under this Part;

(b) his health or development is likely to be significantly impaired, or further impaired, without the provision for him of such services; or

(c) he is disabled.

19.5   Section 17(11) provides further definition: a child is 'disabled' if he or she is 'blind, deaf or dumb or suffers from mental disorder of any kind or is substantially and permanently handicapped by illness, injury or congenital deformity or such other disability as may be prescribed'. 'Development' is defined as 'physical, intellectual, emotional, social or behavioural development' and 'health' means 'physical or mental health'.

General duty under CA 1989 s17

19.6   Section 17(1) provides that every local authority has a 'general duty':

(a) to safeguard and promote the welfare of children within their area who are in need; and

(b) so far as is consistent with that duty, to promote the upbringing of such children by their families,

by providing a range and level of services appropriate to those children's needs.

19.7   The services may be provided for the family of the child or any member of the child's family, so long as they are provided with a view to safeguarding or promoting the child's welfare.[1]

19.8   The services may include providing accommodation and giving assistance in kind or in cash.[2]

Accommodating children and parents under section 17

19.9   Since the Children Act 1989 came into force, many local authorities have used section 17 to provide accommodation, or to give financial help to obtain accommodation, to families who were homeless but unable to get accommodation by way of a homeless application or through the allocations scheme. However, after the House of Lords considered the nature of the section 17 duty in 2003, this became less common.

> *R (G) v Barnet LBC, R (W) v Lambeth LBC and R (A) v Lambeth LBC (G, W and A)*[3] concerned three single parents seeking to compel the local authorities to provide accommodation under CA 1989 s17 for themselves and their children. G was excluded from housing and benefits because she was from Holland and was not 'habitually resident' (see para 20.164 above). W had been found intentionally homeless so was not entitled to housing under Housing Act (HA) 1996 Part VII. A had two disabled children and social services had carried out an assessment concluding that 'the family needs re-housing to an appropriate accommodation'.
>
> The House of Lords held, by a majority of 3:2, that section 17(1) does not impose a duty on social services in respect of the needs of a particular child. The duty is a general duty to safeguard and promote the welfare of 'children within their area who are in need' and to promote the upbringing of such children by their families:
>
> > A social services authority which provides a range and level of services appropriate to meet the various needs of children in its area has discharged its duty under section 17(1). This cannot be read as a duty to meet the needs of any particular child. It is sufficient that the authority maintains services for which his particular needs make him eligible.[4]

1   CA 1989 s17(3).
2   CA 1989 17(6).
3   [2003] UKHL 57, 23 October 2003.
4   [2003] UKHL 57, Lord Millett at [109].

19.10   The local authority in *A* and *W* had a general policy of offering to accommodate the children of a family faced with homelessness (ie offering take the children into voluntary care under CA 1989 s20, see below, para 19.13) but not to accommodate parents and children together under section 17. The House of Lords held that operating a general policy in those terms was not unlawful although each case would have to be considered on its merits. An authority will always need to have regard to the right to respect for family life under article 8 of the European Convention on Human Rights (ECHR) when making a decision on a particular case, see para 2.40.

19.11   Recent developments in immigration law have led to the increased use of CA 1989 s17 to provide accommodation and subsistence to families whose immigration status prevents them from receiving any benefits. The *Zambrano* ruling in the European Court of Justice (see para 20.147) means that in some cases the parents of British children, who are not themselves British or EU nationals, have a right to reside in the UK to care for their children. This right comes from EU law and entitles the parent to work but not to benefits or homelessness assistance. Such parents are also 'persons subject to immigration control'. Instead of relying on this EU right they can apply to the Home Office for leave to remain in the UK. However, the current Home Office policy is to grant a type of leave that is subject to the 'no recourse to public funds' condition. This also means that the parent can work but is not entitled to housing benefit or homelessness assistance.

19.12   Unless the parent can obtain work that pays sufficient money for housing costs and subsistence and/or has other means of support, the family will be destitute and the local authority may have little option but to provide accommodation and financial support to the family under CA 1989 s17, sometimes for extended periods. Where the parent has conditional leave to remain he or she can apply to have the 'no recourse' conditions lifted, see paras 20.31–20.34 and 20.164.

Accommodation duty under CA 1989 s20

19.13   Children Act 1989 s20 sets out the duty to provide accommodation for a child who has no parent or guardian or whose parent or guardian is unable to provide suitable accommodation or care. Section 20(1) provides that:

> ... every local authority shall provide accommodation for any child in need within their area who appears to them to require accommodation as a result of:

(a) there being no person who has parental responsibility for him;
(b) his being lost or having been abandoned; or
(c) the person who has been caring for him being prevented (whether or not permanently, and for whatever reason) from providing him with suitable accommodation or care.

Children aged 16 or older

19.14 For children who are 16 years or older a duty to accommodate a child in need arises if the authority considers that the child's welfare is likely to be seriously prejudiced if it does not provide him or her with accommodation.[5]

Consulting the child

19.15 Before providing accommodation under CA 1989 s20 a local authority must:

... so far as is reasonably practicable and consistent with the child's welfare

(a) ascertain the child's wishes regarding the provision of accommodation, and
(b) give due consideration (having regard to his age and understanding) to such wishes of the child as they have been able to ascertain.[6]

The nature of the section 20 accommodation duty is discussed at paras 19.37–19.43 below.

Assessment of children in need

19.16 There is no specific duty to assess potential children in need equivalent to the duty in relation to adults in need of community care services, see para 18.35. However, the Children Act 1989 places on a local authority a duty to take reasonable steps to identify the extent to which there are children in need in its area[7] and makes clear that this will involve assessing the needs of each child found to be in need. More often it will be an approach by the family of the child or a referral from an adviser or other agency that brings the potential 'child in need' to the notice of the authority.

---

5 CA 1989 s20(3).
6 CA 1989 s20(6).
7 CA 1989 Sch 2 paras 1 and 3.

Timescale

19.17　There is no timescale set out in the CA 1989 but the current statutory guidance, *Working Together to Safeguard Children*,[8] which came into force on 15 April 2013, includes a section on 'Timeliness' in relation to child-in-need assessments. It provides the following:

> 55. Within **one working day** of a referral being received, a local authority social worker should make a decision about the type of response that is required and acknowledge receipt to the referrer.
>
> ...
>
> 57. The maximum timeframe for the assessment to conclude, such that it is possible to reach a decision on next steps, should be no longer than 45 working days from the point of referral. If, in discussion with a child and their family and other professionals, an assessment exceeds 45 workings days the social worker should record the reasons for exceeding the time limit.
>
> 58. Whatever the timescale for assessment, where particular needs are identified at any stage of the assessment, social workers should not wait until the assessment reaches a conclusion before commissioning services to support the child and their family. In some cases the needs of the child will mean that a quick assessment will be required.

So, under the new guidance, a decision should be communicated within one day indicating, eg whether a full assessment is to be carried out. The full assessment should be completed within 45 *working* days, ie nine weeks. If services are required urgently, they should be provided pending the conclusion of the assessment. This replaces the previous requirement for an 'initial assessment' (within seven working days) and a 'core assessment' (within 35 working days).

Which authority?

19.18　A dispute may arise about which local authority is responsible for assessing the child in need and for providing the necessary services.

19.19　　Unlike under the National Assistance Act 1948, there is no requirement for a child to be 'ordinarily resident' in the area of a local authority. The authority's duty is to children 'within their area.'

8　This guidance replaces the previous guidance, the *Framework for the Assessment of Children in Need and their Families*. It is available as a download from the gov.uk website. It is policy guidance issued under the Local Authority Social Services Act 1970 s7 and should therefore be complied with unless there are exceptional reasons which justify departure from it: *R v Islington LBC ex p Rixon* (1997–98) 1 CCLR 119.

In R (Stewart) v Wandsworth LBC, Hammersmith and Fulham LBC and Lambeth LBC[9] a dispute arose between three authorities as to which should carry out a child-in-need assessment. Hammersmith and Fulham had temporarily accommodated a woman and her two children in the area of Lambeth, following a homeless application. The children attended school in Wandsworth. The woman was found to be intentionally homeless and she then sought a child-in-need assessment with a view to obtaining accommodation under CA 1989 s17. Each of the three authorities denied that it had a duty to carry out the assessment.

The court held that Hammersmith and Fulham LBC did not have a duty, because the children were not 'within their area'. The fact that the authority had investigated a homeless application did not place it under a duty to carry out a child-in-need assessment. To establish a duty it was both necessary and sufficient for the children to be 'physically present' in an area. Both Wandsworth and Lambeth were under a duty to carry out assessments and were ordered to do so.

'Looked after' children

19.20 A child who is accommodated under CA 1989 s20 is a 'looked after' child. When a child is 'looked after' this means that the local authority is responsible for the child's accommodation and maintenance.[10] It also means that the local authority may have continuing duties to support the young person after the age of 18. Whether or not a child is a 'looked after' child does not depend on the authority deciding that the child needs to be 'looked after' but on whether the conditions under section 20 are met. The cases examining when the section 20 duty arises are discussed at paras 19.37–19.43 below.

9 [2001] EWHC 709 (Admin), 17 September 2001.
10 CA 1989 ss22A and 22B.

Children leaving care

19.21   The Children (Leaving Care) Act 2000 ('Leaving Care Act') sets out the responsibilities of local authorites to certain children previously in their care, up to and beyond the age of 18.[11]

19.22   The leaving care duties apply only to young people who have been 'looked after' children for a specified period of time. This means having been provided with accommodation by social services for a minimum of 13 weeks in total. The period must end after the child reaches the age of 16. It need not be a continuous period but the child must have been in the care of the authority for at least 13 weeks in total after the age of 14 years.[12] Accommodation provided under CA 1989 s17 or under the leaving care duties does not count towards the total.[13] Therefore the duties apply to children accommodated under CA 1989 s20 and to children subject to care orders under the child protection provisions of the Children Act 1989.

19.23   The powers and duties under the Leaving Care Act 2000 apply to 'eligible' children, 'relevant' children and 'former relevant' children. These are defined as follows:

- *Eligible child:* a child aged 16 or 17, who has been looked after for the minimum period, and is still being looked after.[14]
- *Relevant child:* a child aged 16 or 17, not presently being looked after by any local authority, but who has previously been a 'looked after' child for the minimum period.[15]
- *Former relevant child:* someone aged between 18 and 20 who was previously a 'looked after' child for the minimum period. A young person who, at the age of 21, is being supported by the responsible authority with education or training remains a 'former relevant child' until the end of the agreed programme of education or training even if that takes him or her past the age of 21. This 'extension' of duties can last only up to the date of the young

---

11   The Act amended the Children Act 1989 by introducing duties to children who are leaving or have left the care of the authority. Reference should also be made to Care Leavers (England) Regulations 2010 SI No 2571 (Care Leavers Regulations 2010).

12   See CA 1989 s22 and Care Leavers Regs 2010 reg 3(3). Periods of care in pre-planned placements of less than four weeks (ie, respite care) do not count towards the 13-week total.

13   CA 1989 s22(1), as amended by Adoption and Children Act 2002.

14   CA 1989 Sch 2 para 19B.

15   CA 1989 s23A.

person turning 25.[16] The duty to a former relevant child falls on the authority that was the last 'responsible authority'. This means the authority that most recently owed a duty under the leaving care provisions, or, if there is no such authority, the authority in whose care the child was under CA 1989.[17]

Duties to eligible children

19.24 The local authority must appoint a 'personal adviser' and carry out an assessment of the child's needs with a view to deciding what advice, assistance and support should be provided while the child is still looked after and afterwards. Following the assessment of need, a pathway plan must be drawn up.[18] The pathway plan must set out the way the authority proposes to meet the child's needs and must be recorded in writing, see para 19.34 below.[19]

19.25 Where a 'looked after' child is in a foster placement the local authority must decide whether it is appropriate to facilitate a 'staying put' arrangement. This means that the young person remains living with the foster parent after he or she ceases to be 'looked after.' If the local authority decides this is appropriate it has a duty to monitor the arrangement and to provide advice and assistance to support the young person and the foster parent to maintain the arrangement. This could include giving financial support. These duties will continue until the young person reaches the age of 21.[20]

Duties to relevant children

19.26 The authority must take reasonable steps to keep in touch with the child, whether or not he or she is still within its area. The authority must also appoint a personal adviser, carry out an assessment of need and prepare a pathway plan (if not already done). The pathway plan must be kept under regular review.

19.27 In relation to support and accommodation the authority has a duty to safeguard and promote the child's welfare and (unless satisfied that his or her welfare does not require it) support the child by:

---

16 CA 1989 s24B(3).
17 CA 1989 s23C.
18 CA 1989 Sch 2 para 19B.
19 Care Leavers Regs 2010 reg 6(4).
20 See CA 1989 Sch 2 Para 19BA and s23CZA. These provisions were introduced as from May 2014 by the Children and Families Act 2014.

- maintaining the child; and
- providing the child with, or maintaining the child in, suitable accommodation.[21]

19.28 The presumption therefore is that a local authority should provide accommodation and financial support to a 16- or 17-year-old who has previously been a 'looked after' child. The authority must be satisfied that the child's welfare does not require such assistance to avoid the duty.

19.29 If a local authority has lost touch with a relevant child it must consider how to re-establish contact and take reasonable steps to do so. This duty continues until contact is made or the child reaches the age of 18.

Duties to former relevant children

19.30 The authority must take reasonable steps to keep in touch with the young person, whether within its area or not and, if it loses touch, must take reasonable steps to re-establish contact. It must continue the appointment of a personal adviser and continue to keep the pathway plan under regular review.

19.31 In relation to support and accommodation, the authority must give assistance to the young person to the extent that his or her welfare, educational or training needs require it. This may include contributing to living expenses to enable the child to be near employment, training or education. The authority must also give other assistance to the extent that the young person's welfare requires it.[22] This can include actually providing accommodation.[23]

19.32 Any duty to provide assistance with accommodation and living expenses therefore depends on the authority having assessed that the young person's welfare requires such assistance. This question should be addressed in the assessment of need and the pathway plan. A failure to prepare the needs assessment and/or the pathway plan may be challenged by judicial review. A failure to address the issue of accommodation in those documents may also be challenged.

---

21 CA 1989 s23A–23B.
22 CA 1989 s23C.
23 *R (SO) v Barking & Dagenham LBC* [2010] EWCA Civ 1101, (2010) 13 CCLR 591, 12 October 2010.

Accommodation in student vacations

19.33 Where the local authority is satisfied that a former relevant child in full-time further or higher education needs accommodation during a vacation, because the term-time accommodation is not available, there is a duty to provide suitable accommodation during the vacation or to pay the person enough to enable him or her to secure accommodation.[24]

The assessment and pathway plan

19.34 The Care Leavers (England) Regulations 2010 set out in detail the role of the personal adviser and the way the assessment of need and pathway plan should be prepared. The Regulations provide that the pathway plan must, 'set out – (a) the manner in which the responsible authority propose to meet the needs of the relevant or former relevant child, and (b) the date by which, and by whom, any action required to implement any aspect of the pathway plan will be carried out'. Furthermore, 'the pathway plan must be recorded in writing.'[25]

The pathway plan and accommodation

19.35 The Care Leavers (England) Regulations 2010, deal specifically with the issue of accommodation. Regulation 9 defines 'suitable accommodation' in the following terms:

> For the purpose of section 23B(10) 'suitable accommodation' means accommodation –
> (a) which so far as is reasonably practicable is suitable for the relevant child in the light of their needs, including any health needs and any needs arising from any disability,
> (b) in respect of which the responsible authority have satisfied themselves as to the character and suitability of the landlord or other provider, and
> (c) in respect of which the relevant authority have, so far as reasonably practicable, taken into account the relevant child's

---

24 CA 1989 s24B(5).
25 Care Leavers (England) Regulations 2010 SI No 2571 reg 6(3) and 6(4). The regulations make more detailed provision than the previous regulations and were introduced after the case of *R (J) v Caerphilly County Council* [2005] EWHC 586 (Admin), 12 April 2005. In that case the judge held that the pathway plan was 'hopelessly inadequate' and that 'A pathway plan must clearly identify the child's needs, and what is to be done about them by whom and by when. Or, if another aphorism would help, a pathway plan must spell out who does what, where and when.'

    (i) wishes and feelings, and

    (ii) education, training or employment needs.

In assessing suitability the authority must have regard to the matters set out in Schedule 2.

19.36   Schedule 2 refers to: the facilities and services, state of repair, safety, location, support, tenancy status and the financial commitments involved for the relevant child and their affordability. And, in respect of the relevant child: their views about the accommodation, their understanding of their rights and responsibilities in relation to the accommodation, and their understanding of the funding arrangements.

Accommodating 16- and 17-year-olds

19.37   In recent years the courts have frequently considered the nature of the CA 1989 s20 duty. The reasons for this being an important issue are:

- Duties under the Leaving Care Act 2000 apply when a child has been accommodated by social services under CA 1989 s20 but not where assistance has been given under section 17.
- Unaccompanied asylum-seeking children are the responsibility of local authorities under the CA 1989. When accommodated under section 20 they will also, in most cases, be entitled to Leaving Care Act 2000 services after the age of 18.
- Since 2002, homeless 16- and 17-year-olds have had automatic priority need for homeless assistance, except where a duty is owed under CA 1989 s20 by social services. A potential accommodation duty is therefore owed by both social services and housing departments.

Relationship between the Children Act and the Housing Act

19.38   A homeless 16- or 17-year-old has priority need under HA 1996 Part VII unless he or she is owed an accommodation duty under CA 1989 s20 or under the Leaving Care Act 2000 (see para 14.54). So, a homeless child seeking help from a local authority could present to the housing department or the social services department.[26] This raises

---

26 In non-unitary authorities these will be different authorities, not just different departments.

the issue of which department owes the primary duty. If it is social services (as the courts have now made clear), the second issue is when might a homelessness duty arise in relation to a 16- or 17-year-old applicant.

The Supreme Court considered these issues in *R (G) v Southwark LBC*.[27] G was 17 when he was asked to leave home by his mother. After a period of sleeping on friends' sofas and in friends' cars he presented to social services with a letter requesting accommodation. The following day his solicitors wrote to Southwark asking for an assessment under CA 1989 s17 and for accommodation to be provided under section 20. Southwark's assessment was completed just over a week later and their legal department wrote a letter stating: 'Our client department has fully considered your client's needs and reached the decision that Section 20 is not appropriate as [G] has no identified need for social services support, and his needs can be satisfactorily met through the provision of housing and referrals to other support agencies.' The conclusion was: 'Our client department has fulfilled its duty to assess your client and reached the decision that he is not in need of Section 20 accommodation; he simply requires 'help with accommodation'.' G sought judicial review of that decision.

The Court of Appeal (by a majority of 2:1) held that the authority's decision was lawful and G appealed to the Supreme Court. The Supreme Court identified the issue as being whether, when a child of 16 or 17 who had been thrown out of the family home presents himself to social services and asks to be accommodated under CA 1989 s20, it was open to that authority instead to arrange for him to be accommodated by the local housing authority as a homeless person. The answer was that it was not. The lead judgment was by Baroness Hale, who held that section 20(1) entails a series of questions:

(1) whether the applicant is a child; (2) whether the applicant is a child in need; (3) whether the child is within the local authority's area; (4) whether the child appears to the local authority to require accommodation; (5) whether that need is because of one of the reasons set out in section 20; (6) what the child's wishes and feelings are regarding the provision of accommodation; and (7) what consideration (having regard to the child's age and understanding) should be given to those wishes and feelings?

27 [2009] UKHL 26, 20 May 2009.

In this case there was no issue that the applicant was a child and was within the local authority's area. Furthermore, the parties agreed that, because he was homeless, G was a child in need. Nevertheless, the court held, it was possible that a 16- or 17-year-old temporarily without accommodation may not be a child in need, for example, perhaps a child whose home has been temporarily damaged by fire or flood but who can well afford hotel accommodation while it is repaired:

> But it cannot seriously be suggested that a child excluded from home who is 'sofa surfing' in this way, more often sleeping in cars, snatching showers and washing his clothes when he can, is not in need.[28]

As to whether the applicant appeared to require accommodation:

> ... it is quite obvious that a sofa surfing child requires accommodation. But there may be cases where the child does have a home to go to, whether on his own or with family or friends, but needs help in getting there, or getting into it, or in having it made habitable or safe. This is the line between needing 'help with accommodation' (not in itself a technical term) and needing 'accommodation'.[29]

As to whether the reason for requiring accommodation was because 'the person who has been caring for him being prevented from providing him with suitable accommodation or care', Baroness Hale held that this:

> ... has to be given a wide construction, if children are not to suffer for the shortcomings of their parents or carers. It is not disputed that this covers a child who has been excluded from home even though this is the deliberate decision of the parent.

On the issue of the child's wishes and feelings and the consideration that should be given to those wishes and feelings:

> Some have taken the view that this refers only to the child's views about the sort of accommodation he should have, rather than about whether he should be accommodated at all ... This is supported by the opening words, which are 'before providing' rather than 'before deciding whether to provide.
>
> On the other hand ... it is unlikely that Parliament intended that local authorities should be able to oblige a competent 16- or

28 [2009] UKHL 26, Baroness Hale at [28(2)].
29 [2009] UKHL 26, Baroness Hale at [28(4)].

17-year-old to accept a service which he does not want. This is supported by section 20(11), which provides that a child who has reached 16 may agree to be accommodated even if his parent objects or wishes to remove him. It is a service, not a coercive intervention ... It is not an issue in this case, because [he] wanted to be accommodated under section 20. But a homeless 16- or 17-year-old who did not want to be accommodated under section 20 would be another example of a child in priority need under the Homelessness (Priority Need for Accommodation) (England) Order 2002.[30]

It follows, therefore, that every item in the list had been assessed in [his] favour, that the duty had arisen, and that the authority was not entitled to 'side-step' that duty by giving the accommodation a different label.[31]

19.39 So it is now clear that the primary duty to accommodate homeless 16- and 17-year-olds is a social services duty and the duty cannot be 'side-stepped' by referring the child to the housing department for homelessness assistance. Furthermore, in a number of cases the courts have held that, even when social services purported to assist a homeless child by way of some other duty or power, as a matter of law the section 20 duty had arisen.

Establishing the section 20 duty retrospectively

19.40 In *R (S) v Sutton LBC*[32] a 17-year-old who was ready for release from a young offenders institution (YOI) was assisted by social services to make an application to be placed in a hostel. The authority accepted that a CA 1989 s20 duty had arisen immediately before the child was released from the YOI. However, it claimed that the fact that a hostel placement was secured meant that the applicant no longer required accommodation so that it was no longer under a section 20 duty. At the time her solicitors had written to Sutton, complaining that a hostel placement was inappropriate for a child but the authority had claimed (incorrectly) that if it were to accommodate her under section 20 it could only be by way of a foster placement or residential care.

---

30 [2009] UKHL 26, Baroness Hale at [28(6)].
31 [2009] UKHL 26, Baroness Hale at [28(8)].
32 [2007] EWCA Civ 790, 26 July 2007.

> The Court of Appeal held that Sutton 'was seeking to 'side-step'
> its duties under section 20(1) by having [the applicant] declare
> herself homeless ... '.[33] There was no evidence that Sutton had
> offered her the choices of accommodation that she should have
> been offered, nor was there any evidence that it could not have
> placed her in the hostel in under its CA 1989 duties. It was held that
> the applicant was placed by Sutton at the hostel under the section
> 20 duty and that this obligation continued from the time of her
> release. Therefore, having now turned 18, she was entitled to leaving
> care services.

19.41   Establishing retrospectively that an authority was subject to a section
20 duty may benefit the young person in two ways. First, provided
the authority was under the section 20 duty for the requisite 13 weeks
in total (see para 19.21 above) the young person will be entitled to
ongoing support under the Leaving Care Act 2000. Second, if the
young person is homeless after the age of 18 and before the age of
21 he or she will have automatic priority need for housing as a 'care
leaver' (see para 14.99). Note that to establish priority need as a care
leaver it is not necessary to have been accommodated for 13 weeks;
any period in care between the age of 16 and 18 is sufficient.

19.42   However, this is not the case if the child is accommodated by the
housing department and does not come to the attention of social
services.

> In *R (M) v Hammersmith & Fulham LBC*[34] a 17-year-old had
> presented to the housing department following the breakdown
> of her relationship with her mother. She was given interim
> accommodation under HA 1996 s188. There was some dispute
> about exactly where she had lived over the next few months but
> eight months after presenting she was sentenced to four months in
> a young offenders institution and turned 18 while in custody. On her
> release it was argued that she should have been treated as a child
> in need and accommodated under CA 1989 s20 by social services.
> On that basis she would have been entitled to ongoing support as a
> child leaving care.
>   The House of Lords considered the relationship between local

33   [2007] EWCA Civ 790, Hooper LJ at [50].
34   [2008] UKHL 14, 27 February 2008.

authorities' housing duties and social services duties to homeless teenagers:

> ... the statutory guidance given to both housing and social services departments stresses the need for joint protocols for assessing the needs of homeless 16- and 17-year-olds. This is needed, not only to avoid a young person being passed from pillar to post, but also to ensure that the most appropriate agency takes responsibility for her. The 2002 Priority Need Order clearly contemplates that, if the criteria in section 20 ... are met, social services rather than housing should take the long-term responsibility. Such a young person has needs over and above the simple need for a roof over her head and these can better be met by the social services.[35]

> If [as in S v Sutton, above at 19.40] a local authority's social services department provides or assists with accommodation in circumstances where it should have taken action under section 20 it cannot side-step the further obligations that arose under CA 1989. However, this did not mean that the actions of an authority's housing department should be categorised according to what its social services department should have done if the case had been drawn to its attention.

> M's appeal was dismissed.

19.43   So, while it may be appropriate for the homeless persons unit to arrange interim accommodation in an emergency, it should always refer a potential child in need for an assessment by social services and the primary, long-term accommodation duty lies with social services.

Joint protocols – housing and social services

19.44   For many years the statutory guidance has required local authorities to have joint working practices and joint assessment frameworks between housing and social services to avoid children being passed from one agency to another.[36] The need for this was reiterated by the House of Lords in R (M) v Hammersmith & Fulham LBC (above, para 19.42). Following R (G) v Southwark LBC (above, para 19.38), new statutory guidance was published in April 2010: *Provision of*

35 [2008] UKHL 14, Baroness Hale at [31].
36 See the Homelessness Code of Guidance, paras 10.39 and 12.6.

Accommodation for 16- and 17-year-old young people who may be home-less and/or require accommodation ('2010 Guidance on Homeless 16- and 17-year-olds'), see below at para 19.45.

The 2010 guidance on homeless 16- and 17-year-olds – key provisions

19.45   The guidance was issued jointly by the Departments for Children, Schools and Families and for Communities and Local Government and applies to children's services departments and to local housing authorities.[37] The guidance is issued under the Local Authority Social Services Act 1970 s7, which means that it must be followed unless there is a good reason not to. Key provisions include:

The need for a joint working protocol

It is ... essential that services for homeless 16- and 17-year-olds are underpinned by written joint protocols which set out clear, practical arrangements for providing services that are centred on young people and their families and prevent young people from being passed from pillar to post.[38]

The assessment process – social services as lead agency

... children's services should be the lead agency with regard to assessing and meeting the needs of 16 & 17 year olds', and 'An Initial assessment should be carried out involving interviewing the young person and family members and making enquiries with other agencies...the lead agency will be children's services, given their responsibilities for children in need in their areas.[39]

Accommodation will be under CA 1989 s20

There can be no doubt that where a young person requires accommodation as a result of one of the factors set out in section 20(1)(a) to (c) or section 20(3) then that young person will be in need and must be provided with accommodation. As a result of being accommodated the young person will be looked after ...[40]

---

37   This can be downloaded from www.education.gov.uk/publications.
38   Para 5.2. Despite the requirement to operate joint working protocols, in the case of *TG v Lambeth LBC* [2011] EWCA Civ 526, 6 May 2011, the evidence was that authorities were not doing so.
39   Paras 2.13 and 2.28.
40   Paras 2.23, 2.10 and 3.1.

Emergency accommodation and the use of Bed & Breakfast[41]

> Where a 16 or 17 year old seeks help or is referred, and it appears that he or she has nowhere safe to stay the night, then children's services must secure suitable emergency accommodation for them.

and additionally

> This will mean that the young person will become 'looked after' (under section 20(1)) whilst their need for continuing accommodation and support, are further assessed'.

and

> Bed and breakfast accommodation is not suitable for 16 and 17 year olds.

19.46   It is clear then that a local authority cannot avoid the CA 1989 s20 duty simply by asserting or recording that it is or was assisting under section 17. In almost all cases where a child is homeless, the child will be a child in need and will require accommodation rather than assistance with accommodation. There may be highly exceptional situations where a homeless child either is not a child in need or does not require accommodation to be provided but only help in obtaining accommodation (see Baroness Hale's judgment at [28] in *R (G) v Southwark LBC*, above, para 19.38). Also, while an authority may not side-step the duty by 'persuading' a child to agree to receiving section 17 assistance instead of being accommodated under section 20, there may be instances where a 16- or 17-year-old refuses to be assisted by social services, in which case the homelessness duty may apply.

Asylum-seeking children

19.47   The responsibility for unaccompanied asylum-seeking minors (UASC) falls on local social services authorities under the CA 1989. The Immigration and Asylum Act (IAA) 1999 created a system of support for adult asylum-seekers, including families with children: known as 'NASS' support, see paras 20.192–20.196.

19.48   Under IAA 1999 s122 local authorities are prevented from providing housing and financial assistance under CA 1989 s17 to anyone (ie an adult) who is entitled to asylum support. However, UASC remain the responsibility of local authorities.

19.49   In a number of cases shortly after the IAA 1999 and the Leaving Care Act 2000 came into force the courts considered arguments by local authorities that they had accommodated UASC under CA 1989

---

41 See paras 2.16 and 2.10.

s17 and not s20 and that therefore no ongoing duties arose under the Leaving Care Act 2000.[42] The court made clear that it was not open to an authority to 'elect' to use section 17: the duty was owed under section 20 and this meant in most cases the ongoing duties under the Leaving Care Act 2000 also applied.

19.50   One problem is that many children seeking asylum in the UK have no documentary evidence to prove their age. Local authorities, as part of their assessment duty, must decide whether the asylum-seeker is a child. The CA 1989 s20 duty only applies to 'a child in need.' In the case of *R (A) v Croydon*[43] the House of Lords held that the decision as to whether a person is a child is one of fact so that if this is in dispute, ultimately, the court must decide the issue. Such claims will be claims for judicial review of the refusal to offer accommodation under section 20, based on the local authority's decision that the person is not a child. If permission is granted (and a lower threshold is applied than for most judicial review claims) the case will usually be transferred to the Upper Tribunal (Immigration and Asylum Chamber) for a 'fact finding' hearing. A judge will decide on the basis of all oral and documentary evidence how old the child is likely to be and a date of birth will be allocated.

19.51   The Home Office will usually rely on an age assessment by a local authority but the assessment must comply with certain minimum standards of procedural fairness. These were set out in the case of *R (B) v Merton LBC*,[44] and such age assessments are commonly referred to as '*Merton*-compliant assessments'.

Issues about how and when the section 20 duty arises

19.52   Because of the duties that arise if accommodation is provided under CA 1989 s20, and the benefits to the child which may continue into adulthood, applications have been made to the courts for declarations that, in relation to an arrangement made in the past, the section 20 duty applied. Usually, the local authority is arguing that they were acting under some other provision or duty. The issue is particularly relevant in two situations: (1) where a child was cared for not by local

---

42 See *R (Berhe) v Hillingdon LBC* [2003] EWHC 2075, 29 August 2003, and *P, W, F and G*, referred to at para 19.63 below.

43 [2009] UKSC 8, 17 February 2010.

44 [2003] EWHC 1689 (Admin), 14 July 2003.

authority foster parents but by family or friends and (2) where an asylum-seeking child was wrongly assessed as an adult but is subsequently found to be a child.

Children cared for by family or friends and private fostering arrangements

19.53   In relation to the discharge of duties to 'looked after' children, the CA 1989 provides that, if possible, arrangements should be made for the child to live with his or her parents or those with parental responsibility. If this is not possible, the CA 1989 recommends a placement with relatives, friends or other people connected with the child. This is to be given preference over other placements (such as with local authority foster parents or in children's homes) provided such a placement will safeguard and promote the child's welfare.[45] Such carers must be approved as foster parents by the authority and provision is made for an interim approval to facilitate emergency placements.

19.54   Alternatively, informal arrangements may be made for the child to live with family and friends without becoming a 'looked after' child. The Department of Education issued guidance in March 2011: *Family and Friends Care: Statutory Guidance for Local Authorities*. This states that when a placement with family and friends is made, the authority must decide whether the child still requires accommodation under CA 1989 s20 and, if it decides not, the child would cease to be a 'looked after' child.[46]

19.55   Another situation when the duty under CA 1989 s20 does not arise is when the child is privately fostered. This is when the parent or person with parental responsibility arranges for someone else (not a close relative) to care for the child. Local authorities should be informed of such arrangements in their area and have a duty to ensure that the arrangements are satisfactory.[47]

19.56   In cases of both informal 'family and friends' arrangements and private fostering arrangements the child is not a 'looked after' child. This means that the authority is not responsible for the provision of accommodation and maintenance although it may give assistance under CA 1989 s17 if the child is a child in need. Any assistance

---

45   CA 1989 s22C sets out the provisions as to how an authority should provide accommodation and maintenance for 'looked after' children.

46   Paras 2.13 and 2.19. The guidance can be downloaded from the DoE website: www.education.gov.uk/publications.

47   CA 1989 Part IX deals with local authorities' duties to privately fostered children.

needed by the family under CA 1989 s17 would fall to be provided by the authority in whose area the child lives. This may be a different authority than the one involved in making the arrangements. Most importantly the child will not be entitled to support under the Leaving Care Act 2000 after the age of 18.

19.57   There is obvious scope for dispute about whether a child placed by the local authority with a carer other than the parent is in fact a 'looked after' child and this issue has been considered by the courts in a number of cases.

R (D) v Southwark LBC[48] the authority was arguing that either the child had never been in its care but had been privately fostered or that any duty under CA 1989 s20 had ended when they made arrangements for her to live with a family friend. 'S' had lived intermittently with her father since coming to England at the age of 11. Her mother lived in Jamaica. For several periods of time S had lived with ED, a former girlfriend of her father's. At school S alleged that her father had been violent to her and the school contacted Southwark social services who sent a representative to the school and instructed the school not to let the father take S. A meeting at the school was held and S expressed a desire to live with ED. ED was telephoned by Southwark's representative and agreed that S could live with her. The representative then took S to ED's home and later contacted S's mother by telephone who agreed to the arrangement. A dispute arose when ED sought financial assistance from Southwark. Southwark maintained that it had no obligation to assist because it was a private fostering arrangement.

S thrived in the care of ED and just over a year after she went to live with her, ED obtained a residence order, which had the effect of giving ED parental responsibility for S. ED then issued a claim for judicial review seeking a declaration that for the 16-month period before the residence order S was looked after by Southwark under CA 1989 s20. Southwark argued that it had simply facilitated a private fostering arrangement, admitting that if this was so it had failed to comply with its duty to notify the local authority (Lambeth) of the arrangement. Alternatively, it argued that if it had been under

48   [2007] EWCA Civ 182, 7 March 2007. See also *R (A) v Coventry CC* [2009] EWHC 34 (Admin), 22 January 2009 and *SA v A Local Authority* [2011] EWCA Civ 1303, 10 November 2011, which reached the same conclusion as the Court of Appeal in *R (D) v Southwark LBC*.

a duty under section 20, the duty had ended when arrangements were made for S to live with ED. The Court of Appeal held that:

... in some circumstances, a private fostering arrangement might become available in such a way as to permit a local authority, which is on the verge of having to provide accommodation for a child, to 'side-step' that duty by helping to make a private fostering arrangement. However, it will be a question of fact as to whether that happens in any particular case. Usually, a private fostering arrangement will come about as the result of discussions between the proposed foster parent and either the child's parent(s) or a person with parental responsibility. But we accept that there might be occasions when a private arrangement is made without such direct contact. We accept that there might be cases in which the local authority plays a part in bringing about such an arrangement. However, where a local authority takes a major role in making arrangements for a child to be fostered, it is more likely to be concluded that, in doing so, it is exercising its powers and duties as a public authority pursuant to sections 20 and 23. If an authority wishes to play some role in making a private arrangement, it must make the nature of the arrangement plain to those involved. If the authority is facilitating a private arrangement, it must make it plain to the proposed foster parent that he or she must look to the parents or person with parental responsibility for financial support. The authority must explain that any financial assistance from public funds would be entirely a matter for the discretion of the local authority for the area in which the foster parent is living. Only on receipt of such information could the foster parent give informed consent to acceptance of the child under a private fostering agreement.[49]

In this case the local authority had taken a central role in making the arrangements for S to live with ED and 'Those factors are far more consistent with the exercise of statutory power by Southwark than the facilitating of a private arrangement.'[50]

---

49 [2007] EWCA Civ 182, Smith LJ at [49].
50 [2007] EWCA Civ 182, Smith LJ at [50].

Unaccompanied asylum-seeking children and age disputes

19.58   As explained above, local authorities may dispute that an asylum-seeker is a child. If the authority decides he or she is not a child but an adult, the responsibility for providing accommodation and support will fall on the Home Office. It is most likely that the young person will be accommodated in a dispersal area, outside of London and the South East.

19.59   An issue may arise where an authority assesses a person as not being a child, so that no duty under section 20 could possibly arise, but a court subsequently determines the child's age and this means that, at the time of the assessment, he or she was a child. In such a case, can it be said that the local authority should be 'deemed' to have accommodated under section 20 so that the various leaving care duties apply? Alternatively, if the local authority acted fairly but came to the wrong conclusion on age, was it acting unlawfully such that it should be ordered to provide leaving care support?

The issue was considered by the Court of Appeal in *R (GE) v Secretary of State for the Home Department*.[51] The Court rejected the argument that if a child should have been accommodated by an authority under section 20 (because it was subsequently established that they were in fact a child), he or she is entitled to assistance as a former relevant child. 'The statute does not say that someone is a former relevant child if he or she should have been looked after at the relevant time or for the requisite period.'[52] This is consistent with the decision of the House of Lords in *M v Hammersmith & Fulham*,[53] see above at para 19.42. In GE's case, no decision on age had been taken by a court. The Upper Tribunal had decided that this was not necessary since, even on her claimed age, by the time of the hearing the young woman was an adult. The Court of Appeal held that this was the wrong approach and remitted the case back to the Upper Tribunal for age to be assessed. The Court did not therefore decide the issue as to whether an authority would be acting unlawfully in a case where it had failed to accommodate under section 20 in relation to someone it had fairly, but wrongly, assessed as not being a child at the relevant time.

51 [2014] EWCA Civ 1490, 20 November 2014.
52 Christopher Clarke LJ, at [25].
53 [2008] UKHL 14, 27 February 2008.

19.60 Key features of CA 1989 s20 – a summary

- The primary duty to accommodate homeless 16- and 17-year-olds is under CA 1989 s20.
- Social services and housing should operate joint protocols and working practices to ensure that children are assessed quickly under section 20 and are not passed from one department to another.
- If the conditions under section 20 exist, the section 20 duty may arise even if social services deny that they are acting under the section.
- The courts may declare that an authority did, as a matter of law, act under section 20 in the past with the consequence that a young person may be entitled to leaving care services and have priority need as a care leaver.
- If the child does not come to the attention of social services the section 20 duty cannot arise even if the authority was wrong in the way it dealt with the child.
- A child does not have to agree to become a 'looked after' child for the section 20 duty to arise.
- But section 20 is not intended to be coercive and services cannot be forced on an unwilling young person.

Remedies: judicial review or complaint?

19.61   Decisions made by local authorities about services to children may be challenged by judicial review. Also, local authorities must operate a complaints procedure in accordance with the Children Act 1989 Representations Procedure (England) Regulations 2006.[54]

19.62   As a general rule, where the dispute is about the provision of a service, including accommodation, and the service is needed urgently or when the issue is the legal nature of the duty owed by social services, a claim for judicial review will be appropriate. However, the courts will not generally supervise or monitor the way social services discharge their duties; where the dispute is about the detail of service

---

54   SI No 1738 and Guidance issued by the Department for Education and Skills: *Getting the Best from Complaints, Social Care Complaints and Representations for Children, Young People and Others.* The guidance is issued under Local Authorities Social Services Act 1970 s7 and should be followed unless there are exceptional circumstances which justify a variation. The guidance can be downloaded from www.gov.uk.

provision or about such matters as delay, failure to inform or consult, a complaint may be more appropriate.

19.63   Judicial review is a remedy of last resort and the court may refuse permission if it finds that another remedy, including the complaints procedure, should have been used instead. See *R (Cowl) v Plymouth CC*[55] (para 18.59).

In *R (P, W, F and G) v Essex*[56] Munby J considered challenges to a local authority decision to offer accommodation to children under CA 1989 s17 not s20 and stated:

> I am here concerned with an area of decision-making where Parliament has chosen to confer the relevant power on the County Council; not on the court or anyone else. It follows that we are here within the realm of public law, not private law. It likewise follows that the primary decision-maker is the County Council and not the court. The court's function in this type of dispute is essentially one of review – review of the County Council's decision, whatever it may be – rather than of primary decision-making. It is not the function of the court itself to come to a decision on the merits. The court is not concerned to come to its own assessment of what is in these children's best interests. The court is concerned only to review the County Council's decisions, and that is not a review of the merits of the County Council's decisions but a review by reference to public law criteria ... Although I am, in a sense, concerned with the future welfare of very vulnerable children, I am not exercising a 'best interests' or 'welfare' jurisdiction, nor is it any part of my functions to monitor, regulate or police the performance by the County Council of its statutory functions on a continuing basis.[57]

However, in relation to the the nature of the authority's legal duty the judge held that it was not open to a local authority to choose to provide a package of support under CA 1989 s17 if the conditions under s20 were met.

<hr/>

55 [2001] EWCA Civ 1935, 14 December 2001.
56 [2004] EWHC 2027 (Admin), 19 August 2004.
57 [2004] EWHC 2027 (Admin), at [32]–[33].

Statutory complaints procedure

19.64   The complaints procedure for children has three stages, set out below. In contrast to the complaints procedure for adult social care (see para 18.67), there are clear timescales for each stage and the 2nd stage involves an independent investigation.

Stage of complaint	Timescale
Stage 1: Informal resolution by the authority.	Within 10 working days of receiving the complaint, extendable by 10 working days in exceptional circumstances.
If the complainant is not satisfied, he/she can refer to Stage 2.	Within 20 working days.
Stage 2: Formal investigation. Investigation by an independent officer who submits a report to an adjudication officer. The adjudication officer is employed by the authority and responds to the report, indicating which findings are accepted and which rejected, and setting out what action the authority will take.	Deadline: within 25 working days, extendable, in complex cases to a maximum of 65 working days.
If the complainant is not satisfied, he or she can request a Stage 3 review panel.	Within 20 working days. .
Stage 3: Review panel. Consists of three people, two of whom must be independent. The role of the review panel is to consider whether the authority adequately investigated the complaint at Stage 2, not to re-investigate the complaint. The complainant has a right to attend the panel hearing and be accompanied by a representative who as a general rule should not be a lawyer.	The panel should be held within 30 working days. It should notify the complainant of its findings within 5 working days. The authority should notify the complainant of its response within 15 working days of receiving the panel's report.
If the complainant is not satisfied, complaint to Local Goverment Ombudsman.	Within 12 months of becoming aware of subject of complaint.

Local Government Ombudsman

19.65   If the complaint is not resolved satisfactorily by the local authority, complaint may be made to the Local Government Ombudsman (LGO).

19.66   Paragraphs 2.96–2.100 above describe in more detail how the LGO deals with complaints. In relation to complaints by or on behalf of homeless young people it should be noted that the LGO operates a fast track procedure for complaints from children and young persons (this means up to the age of 21, or 25 if the young person is disabled). In addition, where a person is homeless the LGO will accept a complaint even though the complaint has not been investigated by the authority first.

19.67   The LGO website: www.lgo.org.uk contains further information about how complaints are handled and reports on all the investigations it has undertaken.

CHAPTER 20

Migrants: restrictions on access to housing

continued

Key points

People subject to immigration control

- Most people from outside Europe are 'persons subject to immigration control' and need leave to enter or remain in the UK
- People granted 'protection' in the UK (mostly successful asylum-seekers) are granted a form of leave that entitles them to homelessness assistance, allocations of housing and social security benefits, including housing benefit. They will also be entitled to work.
- People who come to the UK to work or study or to join family members are usually granted leave that is conditional. In most cases such people cannot have 'recourse to public funds'. This means that they are not entitled to homelessness assistance, allocations of social housing or social security benefits, including housing benefit. In some cases they may be allowed to work.

European nationals

- European nationals have the right to come to the UK to work and to seek work.
- European nationals who are working must be treated in the same way as British nationals so are entitled to homelessness assistance, allocations of housing and social security benefits, including housing benefit.
- Close family members of European nationals also have the same rights, even if they are not themselves European and would otherwise need leave to enter or remain in the UK.
- European nationals working in the UK may continue to enjoy these rights even during temporary periods when they are not working, and after they have retired.
- European nationals who come to seek work in the UK ('jobseekers') have a 'right to reside' in the UK but are not entitled to homelessness assistance, allocations of housing and housing benefit.
- If European nationals have lived lawfully in the UK for five years they gain a right to reside in the UK permanently.
- The rules on European nationals retaining their rights to reside and the extension of those rights to family members are very complex. They are often subject to legal challenges and change frequently.

Habitual residence test

- This test applies to only some people from abroad and to British nationals. It generally means that if a person's settled residence is not in the UK, they are not entitled to homelessness assistance, allocations of social housing or social security benefits, including housing benefit.

Safety net services – community care duties

- Most asylum-seekers are provided with accommodation and subsistence ('asylum support') by the Home Office.
- If the asylum claim is refused, asylum support ends unless there are dependent children.
- Local authorities are responsible for asylum-seekers and failed asylum-seekers if they have an un-met need for care and attention that calls for the provision of accommodation.
- Local authorities are also responsible for unaccompanied asylum-seeking children.
- There are no restrictions on services provided directly to children related to immigration status.
- The rules excluding (non-asylum-seeker) migrants from housing and benefits can cause destitution. Some destitute migrants may be able to get accommodation from social services authorities, acting under their 'community care' duties. But special legal tests apply in relation to providing services for migrants.

The new 'right to rent' – restrictions on private lettings

- The Immigration Act 2014 restricts the rights of certain migrants to rent private sector accommodation.

Introduction

20.1   Some people from abroad are excluded from most housing rights. These include: homelessness assistance, housing allocations and housing benefit. In homelessness law the term 'eligible' is used: a person who is not eligible means a person who is not entitled to assistance because of their immigration status (or because they are not 'habitually resident' in the UK). In this chapter the term 'eligibility' is also used to refer to entitlement to other rights such as housing allocations and housing benefit, even though different terms may be used in the particular schemes.[1]

20.2   The rules relating to eligibility for homelessness assistance and housing allocations are almost identical. However, eligibility for housing benefit is different in some respects, in that some people excluded from homelessness assistance and housing allocations can receive housing benefit. Where the rules differ, this is highlighted.

20.3   The rules about eligibility are very complex and subject to frequent change. In this chapter it is only possible to set out the key principles of the eligibility tests and to highlight some of the issues that commonly arise.

The eligibility test

20.4   The eligibility test is broadly relevant to the following persons from abroad:

- persons subject to immigration control (PSIC), see paras 20.6–20.48;
- European nationals and their families, see paras 20.49–20.163;
- people who are not 'habitually resident', see paras 20.164–20.173.

Reference materials

20.5   The following is a list of the principal sources of law relating to immigration status and the rights of European nationals, relevant to housing rights.

Statute/Regulations	Main provisions relevant to housing rights
Immigration and European law	
Immigration Act 1971	The main statute regulating entry and stay in the UK for persons subject to immigration control.

---

1 In the housing benefit scheme, certain 'persons from abroad' are treated as being 'not liable' for rent payments: see HB Regs 2006 reg 10. Reg 10 also provides that people without a 'right to reside' will be treated as persons who are not habitually resident; in allocations schemes the term 'eligible' is now used but until 2012 the relevant term was 'qualifying' persons.

Statute/Regulations	Main provisions relevant to housing rights
Immigration and European law	
British Nationality Act 1981	The main statute governing citizenship, nationality and rights of abode in the UK.
Immigration and Asylum Act 1999	Sets out a list of persons subject to immigration control (who cannot claim any benefits). Created a new system of Home Office support for asylum-seekers and amended community care law to restrict accommodation duties to migrants.
Nationality, Immigration and Asylum Act 2002	Sets out a list of people from abroad who cannot receive community care services unless refusal would breach human rights or European treaty rights.
Immigration Act 2014	Limits access to services (including private rented housing), facilities and employment by reference to immigration status.
Immigration Rules	The detailed rules setting out how immigration applications are dealt with and the different types of leave granted.
The Treaty on Functioning of the European Union (TFEU)	The current 'main' treaty governing membership of the European Union. The right to reside in EU member states derives from the TFEU.
Directive 2004/38/EC passed on 29 April 2004. 'Citizenship Directive' or 'Residence Directive'	The EC directive setting out the requirements of member states in relation to EU citizens' rights to reside in other member states.
Immigration (European Economic Area) Regulations 2006 'EEA Regulations 2006'	Sets out in UK law rights of residence for EEA nationals. Should reflect the terms of the Citizenship Directive.

Statute/Regulations	Main provisions relevant to housing rights
Homelessness and the allocation of social housing	
Housing Act 1996 (Part VII) ss184, 185 and 193	Eligibility rules in homelessness.
Housing Act 1996 (Part VI) s160ZA	Eligibility rules in schemes allocating social housing.
Allocation of Housing and Homelessness (Eligibility) (England) Regulations 2006 SI No 1294 'Eligibility Regulations 2006'	Regulations setting out the detail of who is eligible and who is not: Homelessness: regs 5 and 6; Allocations: regs 3 and 4.
Housing benefit	
Housing Benefit Regulations 2006 SI No 213 (HB Regs 2006) reg 10	Sets out which 'persons from abroad' are entitled to receive housing benefit.

Persons subject to immigration control (PSIC)

Who is subject to immigration control?[2]

20.6   Anyone who needs leave (permission) to enter or remain in the UK, whether or not such leave has been granted, is a person subject to immigration control.[3] It is simplest to list those persons who do not need leave to enter or remain. They are:[4]

---

2   Note that the Immigration and Asylum Act 1999 s115 contains its own definition of 'persons subject to immigration control' for the purpose of exclusions from benefits. This definition is also used in community care law, see below at para 20.2000.

3   See HA 1996 s185(2); Asylum and Immigration Act 1996 s13(2); Immigration Act (IA) 1971 s1, and IA 1988 s7(1).

4   In addition, certain diplomatic and military personnel do not require leave to enter or remain in the UK.

- British citizens;
- Commonwealth citizens with 'right of abode';[5]
- nationals of certain European countries who have a right to reside (see below, paras 20.52–20.68);
- Irish nationals.[6]

20.7   Anyone not listed above is subject to immigration control, ie they need leave to enter or remain in the UK. The rules on the types of leave granted can be complex but, subject to some transitional provisions, the following is clear:

- Anyone who needs leave and does not have leave is ineligible.
- Someone with leave that includes the condition that they can have 'no recourse to public funds' is ineligible.

20.8   The rules on housing benefit are slightly different from the rules on homelessness and allocations: in some cases, a person excluded from homelessness assistance and allocations may be able to claim housing benefit. This is explained where relevant in the later parts of this chapter.

The 'no recourse to public funds' condition

20.9   Many types of leave are granted on the basis that the applicant will support him or herself while in the UK (eg people who come as visitors, to take up employment or to study). Such leave will be subject to the 'no recourse' condition.

20.10   The following are 'public funds' under the Immigration Rules:[7]

- income-based jobseeker's allowance;
- income support;

---

5   Right of abode is enjoyed by Commonwealth citizens born before 1 January 1983 who had a parent born in the UK, and women who were Commonwealth citizens before 1 January 1983 and who were married before that date to a man who was born, registered or naturalised in the UK, or who is a Commonwealth citizen with a parent born in the UK. Whether or not a person has a right of abode may be endorsed in the passport. It is also possible to obtain a 'certificate of entitlement' from the Home Office In the absence of such evidence or if there is any uncertainty, a person who believes they may have a right of abode should be referred to a specialist in immigration and nationality law. In immigration law a person claiming a right of abode has the burden of proving the right.

6   See IA 1971 s1(3).

7   The list may change and can be found in paragraph 6 of the Immigration Rules. See also the 'Guidance on Public Funds' which can be found on the www.gov.uk website.

- child tax credit;
- universal credit;
- working tax credit;
- social fund payments;
- child benefit;
- housing benefit;
- council tax benefit;
- council tax reduction;
- state pension credit;
- attendance allowance;
- severe disablement allowance;
- personal independence payment;
- carer's allowance;
- disability living allowance;
- an allocation of local authority housing;
- homelessness assistance.

20.11 Public funds do not include benefits based on national insurance contributions which includes: contribution-based jobseeker's allowance, incapacity benefit, retirement pension, widows benefit and bereavement benefit, guardians allowance and statutory maternity pay.

20.12 NHS treatment does not count as 'public funds' but the NHS has its own rules about 'ordinary residence' and can charge those who are not ordinarily resident for some treatments. Asylum-seekers are not treated as being not ordinarily resident for these purposes; they have the right to NHS services without charge. The following also do not count as 'public funds': legal aid; community care services provided by local authorities;[8] and local authority education schooling.

20.13 The 'no recourse to public funds' condition has long been attached to leave to remain in the UK. However, it was not until 1996 that this actually prevented a person from receiving benefits and housing assistance. Rather, applying for benefits or housing assistance meant that the person was in breach of the leave and this could, in theory, mean the leave being revoked, or not extended.

---

8 However, as is explained at para 20.214, local authorities are precluded from providing certain community care services to some migrants.

Who is subject to immigration control but nevertheless eligible?

20.14　The following are people who are PSIC but eligible for homelessness assistance, housing allocations and housing benefit. The references to Class A – Class F is taken from the Allocation of Housing and Homelessness (Eligibility) (England) Regulations 2006[9] but the same classes are also eligible for housing benefit. Some PSIC who are not eligible for homelessness assistance or housing allocations can claim housing benefit and this is indicated where relevant.

Class A: Refugees

20.15　This means someone recognised as a refugee in the UK who has been granted leave on that basis.[10] The current practice of the Home Office is to grant to refugees leave for a period of five years. The refugee can apply for indefinite leave to remain shortly before the leave expires.

Class B: Exceptional leave to remain with no condition as to public funds

20.16　A person with exceptional leave to remain[11] granted outside the immigration rules is eligible provided the leave is not subject to the 'no recourse to public funds' condition.

20.17　　See below at paras 20.25–20.30 for an explanation of the terms 'exceptional leave to remain' and 'outside the immigration rules'.

Class C: Leave to enter or remain without limitation or condition

20.18　Someone with leave to enter or remain in the UK not subject to any limitation or condition will be eligible provided they are habitually resident, see para 20.164 below.[12] However, this does not usually

---

9　SI No 1294.

10　A refugee is someone who, owing to a well-founded fear of persecution because of race, religion, nationality, membership of a particular social group or political opinion, is outside his or her country of nationality and is unable or unwilling, owing to such fear, to avail him or herself of the protection of that country. This is defined in the Refugee Convention of 1951.

11　In April 2003 the Home Office abandoned the term 'exceptional leave to remain' and instead adopted the term 'leave outside the rules' (LOTR), see para 20.28.

12　The person must be habitually resident in the UK, the Channel Islands, the Isle of Man or the Republic of Ireland.

apply to people with sponsorship agreements, see below at para
20.20. Leave with no limitation or conditions is usually referred to as
'indefinite leave to remain' (ILR).

20.19   See paras 20.25–20.35 below for a brief explanation of the current
Home Office policy in relation to ILR.

Sponsored immigrants (not usually eligible)

20.20 'Sponsored immigrants' are an exception to the general rule that
a person with ILR is eligible. Sponsorship exists when a person is
given leave to enter or remain in the UK on the basis of an undertaking given by someone else (the sponsor) in the UK that he or she will
be responsible for that person's accommodation and maintenance. A
sponsored immigrant is not eligible unless more than five years have
passed (since entry or the undertaking was given, whichever is later)
or the sponsor has died.

Class D: Humanitarian protection

20.21 A person who has been granted humanitarian protection (HP) under
the Immigration Rules is eligible. HP is granted to people who are
not recognised as refugees but who would, if returned, face a real
risk of suffering serious harm. Serious harm consists of: the death
penalty or execution, unlawful killing, torture or inhuman or degrading treatment or punishment, or serious and individual threat to life
by reason of indiscriminate violence in situations of international or
internal armed conflict.[13]

Class F: Resettled Afghan citizens[14]

20.22 'Relevant Afghan citizens' may be granted limited leave to remain
under the government's resettlement package for Afghans who
worked directly for the UK government in dangerous and challenging roles in Afghanistan prior to 4 June 2013. Despite the leave being
limited, they are eligible for homelessness assistance, housing allocations and housing benefit.

---

13 Immigration Rules paras 339C–339D.
14 See paragraph 276BA1 of the Immigration Rules. Such Afghan citizens are
    eligible for both homelessness assistance and housing allocations but are only
    described as 'Class F' in relation to homelessness.

Transitional provision for pre-April 2000 asylum-seekers

20.23 On 3 April 2000 the new system of asylum support came into being so any asylum-seeker who made the claim for asylum on or after that date will be ineligible. However, transitional protection applies for those whose claims were made before 3 April 2000 *if there has still been no initial decision.*[15] Such people are still eligible for homelessness assistance and housing benefit but not for allocations of social housing. They are 'Class E' under the Eligibility Regulations 2006.

20.24 Care must be taken when someone claimed asylum several years ago. A person may be unaware that a negative decision has been made. The Home Office can be contacted to find out what their records indicate. In all cases, if possible, it is best to take advice from an immigration adviser before doing so.

Exceptional leave to remain, discretionary leave and indefinite leave to remain – current Home Office policy

20.25 Home office policy and practice has changed several times since the Eligibility Regulations 2006 were drafted. This section contains a very brief explanation of the changes and the current Home Office policy. Anyone needing advice about an application to the Home Office should consult a specialist immigration adviser. Note, however, since April 2013 legal aid has not been available for most non-asylum immigration advice.

20.26 When the eligibility rules came into force in 2006 Home Office practice was to grant 'exceptional leave to remain' (ELR) to asylum-seekers who were not recognised as refugees but who were accepted as being unable to return to their country of nationality. ELR was granted 'outside the provisions of the Immigration Rules'. When granted to asylum-seekers it would not include the 'no recourse to public funds' condition. ELR could also be granted to enable someone to come to the UK to live with family members. In such cases the ELR would usually be subject to the 'no recourse to public funds' rule since the UK-based family would have had to satisfy the Home Office that they could support the person needing leave.

20.27 On 1 April 2003 the Home Office stopped granting ELR to asylum-seekers. ELR was replaced by Humanitarian Protection and

---

15 It is likely that there are still some claims pre-dating 2000 on which no initial decision has been made. The evidence before the Public Accounts Committee in March 2013 was that at least 29,000 cases dating back to 2007 and earlier remained outstanding, of which a third had had no initial decision.

Discretionary Leave. Humanitarian Protection is granted to those in need of protection who do not qualify for refugee status, see above at para 20.21. In some cases a person may be excluded from humanitarian protection, eg because of war crimes or other serious crimes, or being deemed a threat to national security. Such people could be granted Discretionary Leave, which is also a form of leave 'outside of the immigration rules'.

20.28   At the same time the Home Office announced that the term 'leave outside the rules' (LOTR) was to replace the term 'exceptional leave to remain'. So, the current equivalent of ELR is LOTR and discretionary leave (DL) is such leave – it is granted outside of the provisions of the immigration rules. A person with DL is eligible under Class B of the Eligibility Regulations 2006.

20.29   Discretionary leave was also granted to unaccompanied asylum-seeking children, usually until they were 17.5 years old (this was to enable arrangements to be made for removal when the child turned 18) and to other applicants whose claims were based on the right to family and private life under article 8 ECHR.

20.30   In July 2012 the Home Office changed its policy in relation to claims based on article 8 and in June 2013 changed its policy in relation to unaccompanied asylum-seeking minors. Both are now granted leave under the rules, not outside the rules. This has the effect of fewer people with such leave being eligible. In many cases the leave will be granted subject to the 'no recourse to public funds' condition and such people cannot be eligible.

Article 8 – family life claims

20.31   Since July 2012 claims for leave to remain based on the right to family life have been dealt with under the Immigration Rules – the relevant rules are found in Appendix FM (Family Members). Appendix FM covers: applications from spouses and other partners, claims by children based on the right to family life and claims by parents of children in the UK.

20.32   Instead of exceptional leave or discretionary leave, the type of leave granted is 'limited leave', usually for a period of 30 months. As each period of leave is about to expire a new application must be made, with a fee payable each time. After a certain period a person will be eligible to apply for indefinite leave to remain.

20.33   The general rule is that the leave will be subject to the 'no recourse to public funds' condition, unless the Home Office considers that the condition should not apply. Working is not usually prohibited.

Where there are very strong reasons why the person needs to be in the UK (eg the family would be unable to enjoy family life in another country) and the family will face destitution (eg the single parent of young children who cannot find work that pays enough to support them) the leave may be granted without the condition (or an application may be made to remove the condition).

20.34　There are broadly two types of situations in which limited leave for 'family life' reasons will be granted: (1) where the family is able to meet the minimum income/capital requirements imposed by the Home Office[16] and have adequate accommodation to support the family member; and (2) where the family cannot satisfy these conditions but there are very compelling reasons to grant limited leave for 'family life' reasons. In the first case, the person will be eligible to apply for indefinite leave after five years (ie two grants of limited leave of 30 months). In the second case, the person will only be eligible to apply for indefinite leave after 10 years (ie after four grants of limited leave).

Discretionary leave

20.35　Discretionary leave (DL) granted outside of the Immigration Rules still exists but current Home Office policy is that it will be granted in exceptional cases only. A policy document 'Discretionary Leave' published in June 2013 is available on the Home Office website and sets out the circumstances in which DL may still be used. This includes when a person's article 3 rights may be breached if they are not allowed to remain in the UK while receiving medical treatment[17] and for the victims of trafficking. It may also be used in other cases where there are exceptional circumstances that justify the grant of DL. People granted DL do have access to public funds and are entitled to work. DL will also usually be granted for periods of 30 months, with the right to apply for ILR after a period of continuous

16　Currently a gross annual income of £18,600 plus £3,800 for the first child and £2,400 for each additional child. Alternatively, savings of £16,000 and additional savings of 2.5 times the amount by which the income falls short of the minimum for the household. In *R (MM) v Secretary of State for the Home Department* [2014] EWCA Civ 985, 11 July 2014 the Court of Appeal held that the provisions were proportionate and therefore lawful.

17　Leave will not usually be granted to enable a person to receive medical treatment in the UK but this could cover someone in the final stages of a terminal illness with no prospect of medical care or family support on return such that removal would involve a breach of the persons rights under article 3 of ECHR, see *N (FC) v Secretary of State for the Home Department* [2005] UKHL 31, 5 May 2005.

DL (usually 10 years). However, the case will be 'actively reviewed' at the end of each period and further leave will only be granted if justified. Charges will be made for each application.

The current situation – a summary

20.36   The main categories of eligible people who are subject to immigration control are:

- refugees with five years' leave;
- a person with HP;
- a person with ILR (provided habitually resident);
- a person with DL. (Unless subject to the 'no recourse to public funds' condition. The Home Office policy statement suggests that this condition will not be applied to DL.)

20.37   In addition, a person with 'limited leave' to remain that is not subject to the 'no recourse to public funds' condition is entitled to housing benefit.

20.38   In practice, most people relying on a right to family life, including the parents of British children, will initially be granted '30 months limited leave' subject to the 'no recourse to public funds' condition. Such people are ineligible: they cannot receive homelessness assistance, a housing allocation or housing benefit. They are allowed to work but if they cannot find work to support their families, may be supported by local authorities under Children Act 1989 s17, see para 19.6.

20.39   An application can be made for the condition to be removed if there are 'exceptional circumstances' which, means (under the Home Office guidance):

- the applicant is destitute; or
- there are particularly compelling reasons relating to the welfare of a child of a parent in receipt of a very low income.

20.40   Evidence in support of an application should include letters from anyone who is supporting the person, including a local authority, charity or other organisation, family and/or friends. An explanation must be provided explaining the person's current financial circumstances, any recent change and how the person is maintaining him or herself.

Common issues

Spouses/civil partners and domestic violence

20.41 A person who marries or enters into a civil partnership with a British national or someone settled in the UK will be granted limited leave for an initial period of two years. This will be subject to the 'no recourse to public funds' condition since the leave will have been granted on the basis that the couple will have adequate accommodation and resources without relying on state benefits. If, during this initial period, the person with conditional leave suffers domestic violence and leaves the shared home, he or she will be ineligible. The only possible assistance will be from social services under the Children Act 1989 or, if the person has community care needs, under the National Assistance Act 1948: see chapters 18 and 19 and para 20.25 above.

20.42 The Home Office policy is to grant leave to remain to such victims of domestic violence provided the necessary evidence of the domestic violence exists.[18] However, until the Home Office make a decision the person remains ineligible.

Long-standing residents without documentation

20.43 Some people, particularly from Commonwealth countries, have been in the UK since childhood but have never been granted any form of leave to enter or remain in the UK. Often such people will have a National Insurance number and will have been living and working in the UK for many years. However, unless they have a right of abode (see para 20.6 above) they are subject to immigration control and are therefore ineligible.

20.44 An application can be made to regularise the person's status (usually an application for ILR) but there may be a long delay before a decision is made and during this period the person will remain ineligible.

Leave that expires

20.45 Any person with leave to enter or remain in the UK may apply to extend the period of leave, or to vary the conditions of leave. Provided an application is made before the leave expires the person is treated as continuing to have the same leave subject to the same conditions

18 Immigration Rules, para 289A.

until the Home Office makes a decision.[19] If refused, an appeal can be made from within the UK and the person continues to be treated as having the same leave until the appeal is determined.

20.46   However, if the leave expires before an application is submitted the person becomes an 'over-stayer' and does not have any form of leave pending a decision. Such a person will be ineligible until an extension or variation of leave is granted.

Home Office delays

20.47   In all of the above examples (paras 20.41–20.46), great hardship may be caused by the long delays common when the Home Office is considering applications. Until leave is granted the applicant may face destitution: they will be ineligible for homelessness assistance or any type of social security benefits such as income support and housing benefit. In most cases, they will also be prohibited from working. The new 'right to rent' provisions, described below at para 20.183, will also prevent private landlords from letting residential properties to such people.

20.48   Judicial review can be used to challenge a failure to make a decision within a reasonable time. The person's immigration solicitor or adviser should always be consulted: sometimes a person's right to remain in the UK will be stronger if a decision is made after a longer period of residence.

European nationals

Introduction

20.49   The European Union (EU)[20] is a group of countries that have entered into treaties whereby certain rights are enjoyed by nationals of each member state in other member states. The most significant of these is the right to work and to seek work in another member state. Member nationals exercising EU rights in another European country generally enjoy the same rights as nationals of that country. The UK therefore has an obligation under the EU treaties to ensure that EU nationals exercising treaty rights have access to the UK's social

---

19 Immigration Act 1971 s3C.
20 The European Community was established in 1957 and renamed the European Union in 1993 by the Maastricht Treaty. The terms EC and EU are generally used interchangeably.

welfare provisions. These rights extend to family members of EU nationals, even if the family members are not themselves EU nationals. A non-EU national may have a right to reside in the UK under EU law, as the family member of an EU national. Such a person will also be a person subject to immigration control who, but for the EU rights, would need leave to enter or remain. Many of the reported cases about EU rights and housing concern non-EU nationals who are the family members of EU nationals.

20.50　　One confusing feature of EU law in the UK concerns border controls and documentation. In theory, an EU national who is not exercising rights under the EU treaties is a person subject to immigration control.[21] However, under EU law the UK has an obligation to admit EU nationals on production of a national identity card or passport.[22] Most EU nationals do not have to obtain any documentary evidence or passport stamps to confirm their right to reside in the UK as EU citizens: the right arises by virtue of their activity in the UK. Decisions about eligibility therefore cannot be based on documents or passport stamps; eligibility is established by a person's current or past activity and residence in the UK.

EU law

20.51　　EU law is based on the international treaties entered into by the member states. Directives issued by the European Commission set out the detail the obligations of the member states and the rights of EU nationals within the territory of the EEA. The various treaties and directives are reflected in UK domestic law by way of statutes and statutory instruments. Issues arising between individuals and member states, and between member states, can be resolved in the European Court of Justice (ECJ). Where an issue arises in a UK court on which the EU law is unclear, or where the domestic law conflicts with EU rights, the UK courts can refer the issue to the ECJ for determination. ECJ decisions are binding on all member states.

21　Immigration Act 1988 s7(1).
22　Article 5(1) of the Directive 2004/38/EC ('Citizenship Directive') and EEA Regs 2006 reg 11(1).

Rights to reside: the EU Treaty; the Citizenship Directive and the EEA Regulations

20.52　Currently, the main EU treaty is the Treaty on the Functioning of the European Union (TFEU).[23] Articles 20 to 25 of TFEU contain the provisions relating to 'EU citizenship'.[24] Other key articles are article 18 (non-discrimination) and article 45 (free movement of workers). Article 45 provides that EU nationals are entitled to move freely within the EU for the purpose of finding and undertaking employment and can, in certain circumstances, remain in another EU country after having been employed in that country.

20.53　The Citizenship Directive (2004/38/EC),[25] passed on 29 April 2004, sets out in detail the obligations of member states to facilitate the rights of EU citizens to move and reside freely throughout the EU. The provisions of the Directive are brought into domestic law by the Immigration (European Economic Area) (EEA) Regulations 2006.[26]

20.54　The EEA Regulations 2006 should mirror the provisions of the Citizenship Directive but in some cases the rights in the Regulations are expressed in more restrictive terms. If there is a conflict, the Directive takes precedence.

20.55　An ongoing issue in the UK courts and in the ECJ is whether the Citizenship Directive contains the exhaustive code for free movement rights in the EU. The current government argues that it does but frequently the ECJ have held otherwise, see for example the case of *St Prix v UK*, discussed below at para 20.86.

20.56　The Citizenship Directive applies 'to all Union citizens who move to or reside in a Member State other than that of which they are a national, and to their family members [as defined in the Directive] who accompany or join them'.[27] Importantly, the Directive sets out

---

23　This can be downloaded from: www.consilium.europa.eu/uedocs/cmsUpload/st06655.

24　The Maastricht Treaty introduced the concept of EU citizenship in 1992 and since then there has been a move from the concept of an economic union to a more social and political one.

25　The Citizenship Directive amended and repealed certain previous directives that concerned the rights of free movement and residence throughout the EU. The repealed directives are: 64/221/EEC, 68/360/EEC, 72/194/EEC, 73/148/EEC, 75/34/EEC, 75/35/EEC, 90/364/EEC, 90/365/EEC and 93/96/EEC. EU Regulation No 1612/68 was amended and partly repealed. The Citizenship Directive is also sometimes referred to as the Residence Directive.

26　SI No 1003.

27　Citizenship Directive article 3(1).

the rights of those *who move to or live in another state* within the EU. It does not apply to EU nationals who remain in their own EU state. This is particularly relevant for family members who are non-EU nationals, see paras 20.89–20.103 below.

20.57 The Citizenship Directive and the EEA Regulations set out:

- the conditions governing the exercise of the right of free movement and residence within the EU by EU citizens and their family members;
- how rights of permanent residence in other member states are established; and
- the limits placed on those rights on the grounds of public policy, public security or public health.

The European Economic Area

20.58 The European Economic Area (EEA) comprises the countries that are members of the EU plus four countries that are members of the European Free Trade Association (EFTA), which have free trade agreements with the EU. When new states join the EU there is usually an initial period during which their rights are restricted. This happened in relation to eight of the 10 countries joining the EU in 2004, and also following the accession of Bulgaria and Romania, in January 2007. These restrictions (mainly the requirement to register as a worker) no longer apply but may still be relevant if a person is seeking to establish a right of residence that depends on past periods as a worker.

20.59 In July 2013 Croatia became the 28th member of the EU and currently Croatian nationals also have limited rights and, for example, must usually have a certificate confirming they are registered workers to have a right to reside in the UK. In contrast the nationals of 'full' member states just need to satisfy the definition of 'worker', see below.

20.60 All of the EEA countries are listed below:

Members of the European Union: Austria, Belgium, Bulgaria†, Croatia, Czech Republic*, Cyprus, Denmark, Estonia*, Finland, France, Germany, Greece, Hungary*, Ireland, Italy, Latvia*, Lithuania*, Luxembourg, Malta, Netherlands, Poland*, Portugal, Romania†, Slovakia*, Slovenia*, Spain, Sweden.

'Accession states' are those whose rights are limited during the initial period after joining the EU. Countries marked * are referred to as the 'A8' (Accession 8) countries, which joined in May 2004 and whose rights were limited between 2004 and 2011. Those marked † are referred to as the 'A2' countries, which joined in January 2007 and whose rights were limited between 2007 and 2014. Croatia is currently the only 'accession state'.

Members of the European Free Trade Association (EFTA): Iceland, Liechtenstein, Norway, Switzerland.

EEA nationals and eligibility

20.61　Only EEA nationals with a 'right to reside' in the UK can be eligible (for homelessness assistance, social housing and housing benefit). However, not everyone with a right to reside is eligible.

20.62　　Note that the rights that follow from having a 'right to reside' under EU law, including the rights that extend to family members, are only enjoyed by EEA nationals who are exercising treaty rights. A British person is an EU national but his or her right to reside in the UK is not by virtue of EU law but because of being British. This means that an EU national who has come to the UK may have the right to be joined by a non-EU family member, whereas if the non-EU person was the family member of a UK national (who had never exercised any rights under EU law) he or she would have to apply for leave as a person subject to immigration law.

20.63　　It is important to remember that an EEA national may have more than one right to reside in the UK. For example a student may also be a worker.

20.64　　The following EEA nationals have a right to reside and are eligible:

- a 'worker' (including, in specified circumstances, someone temporarily unable to work);
- a self-employed person;
- a family member of a worker or self-employed person;
- a person with a right to reside permanently in the UK;
- a person in the UK as a result of deportation, expulsion or other compulsory removal from another country to the UK.

Note also that some persons with 'derivative' rights to reside as carers of children with EU rights are eligible, see below at para 20.147.

20.65　　The right to reside as a worker or self-employed person is generally enjoyed only while the person is working or self-employed (the term used in the EEA Regulations 2006 is 'qualified persons'). However, the right may be retained during periods of unemployment and after retirement. Also, in some circumstances family members may retain their rights even after the EEA national has ceased to be a qualified person.

20.66 A permanent right to reside may be established after five years lawful residence and in some other specified circumstances. A person with a permanent right to reside need not be working or self-employed to maintain the right. However, the permanent right of residence may be lost if the person leaves the UK for an extended period.

20.67 The following EEA nationals have a right to reside but are generally not eligible:

- a person with an initial 'three-month' right to reside;
- a jobseeker;
- a student;
- a 'self-sufficient' person;
- a person with a 'derivative' right to reside as under the *'Zambrano'* principle, see below at para 20.147.

20.68 In relation to jobseekers, those who come to the UK seeking work will be ineligible while those who have worked in the UK but are experiencing a period of unemployment may be eligible. See para 20.79 below.

20.69 Each of these categories is dealt with in more detail below.

Workers and self-employed people

20.70 Workers and self-employed EEA nationals have a right to reside in the UK and are eligible for homelessness assistance, housing allocations and housing benefit. Their family members, as defined below, also have the same rights.

What is a 'worker'?

20.71 The decisions of the ECJ on the question of what it is to be a worker indicate the following:

- being a worker means being employed, in the sense of being obliged to provide services for another person in return for money and being subject to the control of the other person as regards the way the work is done;
- there is no minimum period for which the person must have been employed and the employment need not be permanent or full-time;

- the employment must be 'effective and genuine economic activity' and not activity that could be regarded as 'purely marginal and ancillary';
- the fact that the remuneration may be below the minimum wage or insufficient to support the person without the person claiming benefits in addition is irrelevant.[28] However, the level of remuneration may be relevant in relation to entitlement to jobseeker's allowance (JSA) for periods when not working, see para 20.127 below.

What is self-employment?

20.72   TFEU specifically provides that European nationals have a right to 'establish' themselves in another member state for the purpose of being self-employed or running a business. The EEA Regs 2006 do not define 'self-employment' but simply state that a self-employed person means a person who establishes him or herself to pursue activity as a self-employed person in accordance with article 49 of TFEU.[29]

20.73   To establish eligibility evidence of economic activity as a self-employed person will be needed, eg invoices, bank statements and tax returns.

20.74   A self-employed person does not have to be 'self-sufficient'. Those who are self-employed but whose income is limited may be eligible for working tax credit and child tax credit as well as housing benefit and council tax benefit. [30]

20.75   Arguably, self-employment must, like employment, be 'genuine and effective' and more than a 'marginal and ancillary' activity (see para 20.71 above).

20.76   A person temporarily unable to pursue activity as a self-employed person as the result of an illness or accident is still treated as self-

---

28   See Homelessness Code of Guidance Annex 12, para 17. However, low wages, along with other features, such as a short period of employment and whether the work is regular or erratic would support a conclusion that the work was 'marginal' and not 'effective and genuine economic activity'. See also the new 'minimum earnings threshold', at para 20.134 below.

29   EEA Regs 2006 reg 4(1)(b).

30   A2 and A8 nationals were not required to register to have a right to reside as self-employed people. A period of self-employment for at least five years establishes a permanent right to reside but sufficient evidence of being self-employed during the relevant period will be needed. Croatian nationals may presently have a right to reside by virtue of self-employment, for which registration is not required.

employed, see below.[31] Furthermore, a person who is temporarily unable to find work as a self-employed person may continue to be a self-employed person and therefore eligible.[32] Similarly a person who ceases self-employed activity temporarily due to pregnancy does not lose the status. The length of time a person may retain the status of a self-employed person without having remunerative work is a question of degree.

Workers and self-employed people – retaining status when sick or unemployed

20.77 The Citizenship Directive provides that the status of worker or self-employed person is retained if the person:[33]

- is temporarily unable to work as the result of an illness or accident; or
- is unemployed involuntarily, having been employed for more than one year and having registered as a jobseeker with the relevant employment office; or
- is unemployed involuntarily, 'after completing a fixed-term employment contract of less than a year or after having become involuntarily unemployed during the first 12 months and has registered as a jobseeker with the relevant employment office. In this case, the status of worker shall be retained for *no less than six months*'; or
- has embarked on vocational training. In this case the unemployment must be involuntary or the training must be related to the previous employment.

20.78 The EEA Regulations 2006 differ from the Directive. Under the Regulations the retained rights during periods of illness or accident are expressly retained by both workers and self-employed people but in relation to periods of unemployment further conditions are set out.[34]

---

31 EEA Regs 2006 reg 6(3).
32 CIS/340/2010. 'CIS' refers to Commissioners' decisions relating to income support).
33 Citizenship Directive article 7(3).
34 EEA Regs 2006 reg 6(2)

Involuntary unemployment following a period as a worker

20.79   In relation to involuntary unemployment the EEA 2006 Regulations provide that a person retains worker status if unemployed involuntarily, provided he or she::

- has registered as a jobseeker with the relevant employment agency; and
- entered the UK in order to seek work or is present in the UK seeking employment, immediately after enjoying a right to reside as a worker, self-employed person, self-sufficient person or a student (ie not a right to reside as a jobseeker);[35] and
- can provide evidence that he or she is seeking employment and has a genuine chance of being engaged.

20.80   The regulations provide that if the previous employment in the UK was for less than one year, the person cannot retain the status of worker for *longer than six months*.

20.81   The EEA Regulations 2006 were amended in 2012, 2013 and 2014 in relation to the retention of worker status and the status of jobseeker. The purpose of the amendments is to limit the rights of unemployed workers and jobseekers. The premise appears to be that a 'jobseeker' should be able to find work within six months. The regulations state that after this period the evidence required (of seeking employment and having a genuine chance of being engaged) must be 'compelling' to establish the continuing right to reside. However, the Directive provides that where the person has been employed for more than a year worker status is retained indefinitely provided the person is registered as a jobseeker.

20.82   Note that a person whose only right to reside as a jobseeker is not eligible for homelessness assistance, housing allocations or housing benefit but may be entitled to income-based JSA, child tax credit and child benefit, see paras 20.127–20.133 below.

20.83   So, in relation to housing rights, only someone who retains the status of 'worker' is eligible. Under the Directive, a former worker who has been working for less than one year must be entitled to retain the status of worker for at least six months (provided they are actively seeking work and have a genuine chance of being engaged).

---

35 Furthermore, any periods of 'retained worker status' during unemployment is disregarded when assessing whether a person has a right to reside as a jobseeker, see para 20.131 below.

20.84 Furthermore, the Directive makes clear that the self-employed also enjoy the same rights as workers to retain their status during periods of sickness and unemployment.[36]

Pregnancy

20.85 A woman who takes maternity leave during a period of employment remains a worker during the maternity leave, even if it is unpaid.[37] Similarly, a self-employed woman who takes a period of maternity leave continues to be classed as self-employed.[38]

20.86 A worker on maternity leave still has a contract of employment and retains continuity of employment for all purposes. However, the position is different for a woman who stops working or cannot take up work because of pregnancy or child-care responsibilities after the baby is born. UK benefit rules provide that a woman within 11 weeks of the expected date of birth is not required to be available for work or to be actively seeking work, ie she can claim income support instead of income-based jobseekers allowance (JSA). This can be paid to a woman for a period of up to six months, starting 11 weeks before the expected date of the birth and ending 15 weeks after the date on which the pregnancy ends. So, an unemployed woman in receipt of benefit can claim income support for a period of up to six months, before and after the birth of a child. After this period she will usually be required to transfer [back] to JSA, a condition of which is that she must be actively seeking work and available for work. The problem for an EEA national is that during periods of involuntary unemployment she must be registered as a jobseeker and be actively seeking work in order to retain the right to reside. Under the Citizenship Directive the exceptions for temporary incapacity are limited to illness or accident, see above at para 20.77. In a number of UK Social Security cases it was held that a pregnant woman could not retain her worker status since pregnancy was neither illness nor accident.[39] However, the ECJ decision in *St Prix v Secretary of State for Work and Pensions*[40] makes clear that a woman can retain worker status when incapacitated due to pregnancy/childbirth.

36 In relation to the self-employed, the regulations only make reference to retaining the status when inactive due to sickness or accident.

37 CIS/4237/2007.

38 CIS/1042/2008.

39 See: CIS/4010/2006. This does not preclude a woman from retaining the status of worker if she has a pregnancy-related illness which means that she is temporarily incapable of work, see: CIS/731/2007.

40 C-507/12 [2014] PTSR 1448, 19 June 2014.

Ms St Prix was a French national employed in the UK. She gave up work less than three months before the birth of her child, because of the physical constraints of the pregnancy and the immediate aftermath of childbirth. She returned to work three months after the birth, and had remained in the UK throughout. She was refused income support during this period on the grounds that she had lost her right to reside during the period when she was not working. The Supreme Court referred the case to the ECJ for a preliminary ruling on the question of whether a worker who had temporarily given up work because of pregnancy could be considered a worker under article 45 of TFEU and article 7 of the Citizenship Directive.

The ECJ held that such a person did not come within the definition of someone temporarily unable to work as the result of illness, as required by article 7 of the Citizenship Directive. However, the concept of worker under article 45 of TFEU had to be interpreted broadly in order to allow the fundamental right to freedom of movement provided for under TFEU. Therefore, it could not be said (as the UK government had argued) that article 7 of the Citizenship Directive contained an exhaustive list of the circumstances in which a migrant worker no longer in an employment relationship might nevertheless continue to benefit from that status. So, provided the woman returns to work or found another job within a reasonable period after the birth of her child, she should retain the status of worker throughout. However, what is a 'reasonable period' is a matter for domestic courts and they can take account of the specific circumstances of the case and the national rules on the duration of maternity leave.

Worker registration schemes

20.87   The main restrictions on 'accession state' nationals, during the initial period were that (1) to qualify as a 'worker' a person had to register as a worker with an 'authorised employer' and (2) accession state nationals did not enjoy rights of residence as 'jobseekers'.

20.88   For A8 nationals the restrictions ceased to apply on 1 May 2011 and for A2 nationals they ceased to apply on 1 January 2014. It may still be necessary to consider whether an A8 or A2 national was a registered worker at a time prior to the lifting of the restrictions when trying to calculate previous residence to establish a permanent right to reside. The worker registration rules are complex and are not set out here. Croatian nationals are currently subject to similar worker registration requirements and these will continue until July 2018, but may be extended to July 2020. A Croatian national does not have a right to reside as a jobseeker.

General rules: rights of family members of EU nationals

Family members

20.89 The EEA Regulations 2006 define the right to reside by way of the 'qualified person'. Qualified persons and their family members are entitled to reside in the UK while the relevant person remains a qualified person.[41] In addition, provision is made for certain family members to enjoy extended rights of residence in certain circumstances and permanent rights of residence may be acquired after specified periods of residence and/or activity.

Close family members

20.90 The close family members of qualified EEA nationals (other than students) and EEA nationals with a permanent right of residence also have a right to reside. Close family members are defined as:[42]

- a spouse or civil partner;
- children and grandchildren, including those of the spouse or civil partner, provided they are under 21 or dependent on the qualified person or his or her spouse or civil partner; and
- dependent parents and grandparents, including those of the spouse or civil partner.

Extended family members

20.91 The following relatives and members of the household may gain a right to reside as 'extended family members' if they satisfy certain conditions.[43]

---

41 EEA Regs 2006 reg 14(1) and (2).
42 EEA Regs 2006 reg 7 and article 2.2 of the Citizenship Directive.
43 EEA Regs 2006 regs 7(1)(d) and 8(2)–(5) and article 3.2 of the Citizenship Directive.

- *Dependent member of household* This means a relative of an EEA national, his or her spouse or civil partner who is dependent on him or her and is a member of the household.[44]
- *Relatives requiring personal care* This means a relative of an EEA national, his or her spouse or civil partner who 'on serious health grounds' strictly requires the personal care of the EEA national, his or her spouse or civil partner.
- *Relatives who would qualify for ILR* This means a person who is a relative of an EEA national and who, if he or she were applying to join a non-EEA national who was present and settled in the UK, would qualify for indefinite leave to remain on that basis.
- *Co-habitees* This means the same or opposite sex partner of an EEA national who is not a civil partner or spouse and who can prove he or she is in a durable relationship with the EEA national.

Family members – retaining the right of residence

20.92   The general rule is that family members enjoy a right of residence in the UK only so long as the EEA national remains a qualified person and they remain family members of the qualified person.[45] However, there is provision for the family members' rights of residence to continue in the following circumstances:

- on the death or departure from the host state (as opposed to the family home) of the qualified person or person with a permanent right of residence (see para 20.104);
- on divorce or termination of a civil partnership (see para 20.92);
- where children are in education (see para 20.98).

Death or departure of qualified person[46]

20.93   If the EEA national with a right to reside in the UK (as a qualified person or a person with a permanent right of residence) dies or leaves the UK, this does not affect the rights of residence of their family members who are EEA nationals (regardless of how long they lived with the person).[47]

---

44 For dependent relatives, there is a further requirement that they must be residing in a country other than the UK and be dependent on the EEA national and be either accompanying them to the UK or joining them in the UK, or have done so previously and continue to be dependent: reg 8(2)(a)–(b).
45 EEA Regs 2006 reg 14(2).
46 EEA Regs 2006 reg 10(2) and articles 12 and 7 of the Citizenship Directive.
47 Citizenship Directive Article 12(1).

20.94   For non-EEA family members, they can retain rights of residence provided they lived in the UK as family members for at least the year immediately before the death of the EEA citizen and are themselves workers, self-employed or self-sufficient or the family member of such a person. They do not retain these rights if the EEA citizen simply leaves the UK.

20.95   In addition, in certain circumstances a family member of a qualified person who dies may gain a permanent right of residence, on the death or departure (see para 20.119 below).

Termination of marriage or civil partnership[48]

20.96   Where a non-EEA national ceases to be a family member of a qualified person or a person with a permanent right of residence because of the termination of the marriage or civil partnership the right of residence will be retained provided the following conditions are satisfied:

- the person was residing in the UK at the date of termination; *and*
- he or she is a worker, self-employed or self-sufficient person or the family member of such a person; *and*
- one of the following conditions is satisfied:
  - the marriage or civil partnership had lasted for at least three years and the parties had resided in the UK for at least one year of its duration;
  - the former spouse or civil partner has custody of a child of the qualified person or person with a permanent right of residence;
  - the former spouse or civil partner has the right of access to a child (under the age of 18) of the qualified person or person with a permanent right of residence and a court has ordered that it must take place in the UK; or
  - the continued right of residence in the UK is warranted by particularly difficult circumstances, such as the person or another family member having been a victim of domestic violence during the marriage or civil partnership.

20.97   So, in these situations the non-EEA family members enjoy the same rights as EEA nationals: the right to reside in the UK provided they are working, self-employed, self-sufficient.

---

48 EEA Regs 2006 reg 10(5) and articles 13 and 7 of the Citizenship Directive.

Children in education

20.98   Where a qualifying person or person with a permanent right of residence dies or ceases to be a qualified person on ceasing to reside in the UK, any children or grandchildren attending educational courses in the UK retain a right of residence as long as they continue to attend such a course.[49] They must have been attending an educational course immediately before the qualified person died or ceased to be a qualified person.

20.99   In addition, if the person in education is a child, any parent with actual custody also retains a right of residence in the same circumstances.[50]

20.100   Even if the above conditions are not satisfied, the ECJ has held that the parents of children in education in a member state may have rights to reside beyond those set out in the Citizenship Directive.

In *Ibrahim v Harrow* and *Teixeira v Lambeth LBC*[51] the applicants applied for homelessness assistance from the local authorities. Both had dependent children in full-time education. Ms Ibrahim was a Somali national married to a Dutch national. She could not rely on the EEA Regs 2006 reg 10(3) (see para 20.98 above) because her husband had ceased to work (and therefore ceased to be a qualifying person) *before* leaving the UK. Ms Teixeira was Portugese and had worked in the UK intermittently but was not working when her daughter started school. Both argued that the Citizenship Directive was not the sole source of rights of residence and relied on article 12 of Regulation 1612/68 which provides that:

> The children of the national of a Member State who is or has been employed in the territory of another Member State shall be admitted to that State's general educational, apprenticeship and vocational training courses under the same conditions as the nationals of that State, if such children are residing in its territory. Member States shall encourage all efforts to enable such children to attend these courses under the best possible conditions.

The ECJ found in favour of Ms Ibrahim and Ms Teixeira: the children of an EEA national who works, or has worked, in another member state and the parent who is their primary carer have a right

---

49   EEA Regs 2006 reg 10(3) and articles 12 and 7 of the Citizenship Directive.
50   EEA Regs 2006 reg 10(4) and articles 12 and 7 of the Citizenship Directive.
51   C-480/08 and C-310/08.

> of residence by virtue of article 12 of Regulation 1612/68 and that
> right is not conditional on them having sufficient resources and
> comprehensive sickness insurance in that member state.

20.101   This means that an EEA national who has worked in the UK has an
unconditional right to continue to reside in the UK if he or she is the
primary carer of a child in education, so long as the child remains in
education. A non-EEA national enjoys the same rights if he or she
is married to an EEA national who has worked in the UK. Both are
entitled to homelessness assistance, housing allocations and housing benefit.

20.102   In contrast, a '*Zambrano*' right to reside, see below at para 20.147,
is established only if the denial of such a right would force an EEA
citizen to leave the territory of the EEA. And the '*Zambrano*' derivative right to reside does not entitle the person to homelessness assistance, housing allocations or housing benefit.

20.103   These 'derivative' rights to reside, established by the cases of *Ibrahim and Teixeira* and *Zambrano*, are now set out in regulation 15A of
the EEA Regulations 2006, see below at para 20.150.

Permanent rights of residence

20.104   Those who have a right of residence by virtue of working, being self-
employed, self-sufficient or a student retain the right of residence
while they are pursuing the relevant activity (and may continue to be
qualified persons during temporary periods of inactivity). Rights of
permanent residence may also be acquired after a minimum period
as a qualified person.

20.105   The following people may gain a right of permanent residence:

- those who have resided legally in the UK for a continuous period
of five years (see paras 20.107–20.112);
- those who have previously worked in the UK but are now retired
or permanently incapacitated (see paras 20.113–20.118);
- the family members of the above (see paras 20.119–20.120);
- the family members of a deceased worker who was a qualifying
person (see paras 20.93–20.95).

20.106   The EEA Regulations specifically provide that residence in the UK as a result of a 'derivative right of residence' does not constitute residence for the purpose of establishing a permanent right to reside.[52]

Five years' continuous residence

20.107   Article 16 of the Citizenship Directive provides that:

> Union citizens who have resided legally for a continuous period of five years in the host Member State shall have the right of permanent residence there.

20.108   This must be read in conjunction with recital (17) of the preamble to the directive which provides that:

> A right of permanent residence should ... be laid down for all Union citizens and their family members who have resided in the host Member State in compliance with the conditions laid down in this Directive during a continuous period of five years without becoming subject to an expulsion measure.

20.109   The EEA Regulations 2006 provide that an EEA national who has resided in the UK 'in accordance with these Regulations' for a continuous period of five years acquires the right to reside in the UK permanently[53] as does a non-EEA national who has resided in the UK as a family member of an EEA national for the same period 'in accordance with these Regulations'.[54]

20.110   The meaning of 'residing legally' in the directive and whether the regulations are correct in defining this as residence 'in accordance with these Regulations' has been considered in a number of recent cases by the UK courts and by the ECJ.

> In *Lekpo-Bozua v Hackney LBC and Secretary of State for Communities and Local Government*[55] the claimant was a British citizen whose niece was a French national. She had lived with him in the UK since the age of nine and was 16 at the date of his homeless application. Hackney decided that the niece was a 'restricted person' under the amended section 184(7) of the Housing Act 1996 so that the duty to the family was only to provide a private sector tenancy (see paras 20.174–20.178). The decision was challenged on the basis that the

---

52   EEA Regs 2006 reg 15(1A).
53   EEA Regs 2006 reg 15(1)(a).
54   EEA Regs 2006 reg 15(1)(b).
55   [2010] EWCA Civ 909, 29 July 2010.

niece had a permanent right to reside in the UK by virtue of five years' lawful residence.

The Court of Appeal held that, although the niece had been lawfully resident since arriving in the UK, under article 16, residing 'legally' meant 'in compliance with the conditions laid down in this Directive ... The lawful residence contemplated by Article 16 of the Directive is residence which complies with Community law requirements specified in the Directive'.[56]

The Court of Appeal reached the same conclusion in *Okafor v Secretary of State for the Home Department*[57] which concerned the rights of non-EEA family members following the death of the EEA national. The conditions under articles 7 and 12 were not met. The family argued that, as they had resided in the UK for a continuous period of five years, they had acquired permanent rights of residence.

The Court of Appeal rejected this, holding that the right of permanent residence under article 16 was a right acquired by virtue of establishing rights of residence under the directive, not merely by 'residence that is not unlawful for a period of five years'.[58]

20.111 The following periods of residence have been held not to be residence that can count towards the five-year period to establish a permanent right to reside:

- periods spent in prison;[59]
- residence by a person with dual Irish and British nationality: this was because the right to reside was not pursuant to rights under the EU treaty but was by virtue of being British.[60]

---

56 Sir Anthony May, President of the QBD, at [18].
57 [2011] EWCA Civ 499, 20 April 2011.
58 [2011] EWCA Civ 499, Thomas LJ at [33].
59 *HR (Portugal) v Secretary of State for the Home Department* [2009] EWCA Civ 371, 5 May 2009; *Carvalho v Secretary of State for the Home Department and Secretary of State for the Home Department v Omar* [2010] EWCA Civ 1406, 14 December 2010.
60 *McCarthy v Secretary of State for the Home Department* [2008] EWCA Civ 641, 11 June 2008. This was confirmed as correct in the judgment of the ECJ dated 5 May 2011.

However, the ECJ has rejected the argument that periods of lawful residence prior to the Directive coming into force should be disregarded. In *Lassal* and *Dias*,[61] the ECJ held that periods spent as a worker prior to April 2006, when the Directive came into force, could count towards the requisite five-year period of residence.

20.112   In addition to qualifying persons and their family members, family members who have 'retained' rights of residence (see para 20.292 below) also gain a permanent right to reside after five years' continuous residence. Note, however, that the retained rights of residence depend on that person working, being self-employed or being self-sufficient.

Retirement or permanent incapacity

20.113   A worker or self-employed person who has ceased activity, because of retirement or permanent incapacity, will gain a permanent right to reside if the conditions set out below at paras 20.114–20.118 are met.

20.114   If retired, the person must have been employed or self-employed for at least 12 months and have lived in the UK continuously for more than three years. If previously employed, the person must either have reached the age to qualify for a state pension or have taken early retirement. If previously self-employed, the person must have reached the age to qualify for a state pension.[62]

20.115   If permanently incapacitated, either:

- the person must have lived in the UK continuously for more than two years before the termination; *or*
- the incapacity must have been caused by an accident at work or an occupational disease that entitles him or her to an occupational pension paid in full or part by a UK institution.[63]

20.116   In both cases, the necessary period of residence or activity must have been immediately before termination of employment or self-employment.

---

61   *Secretary of State for Work and Pensions v Lassal* C-192/09, 25 May 2010, ECJ; and *Secretary of State for Work and Pensions v Dias* C-325/09, 21 July 2011, ECJ. This is now found in regulation 6 of the EEA Regulations 2006, and was added when the Regulations were amended in 2012.
62   EEA Regs 2006 reg 5(2) and article 17.1(a) of the Citizenship Directive.
63   EEA Regs 2006 reg 5(3) and article 17.1(b) of the Citizenship Directive.

20.117   Note that for EEA nationals who are married to or in a civil partnership with a UK national the requirement for a minimum period of residence or activity does not apply.[64]

20.118   During periods of inactivity a person may still be treated as being employed or self-employed provided it is for reasons not of the person's own making or it is due to illness or accident. Similarly, a worker who is registered as a jobseeker during a period of involuntary unemployment is classed as continuously working for these purposes.[65] Note that for accession state workers (see above at paras 20.87–20.88) periods of unemployment prior to the ending of the accession periods may not count unless other conditions were satisfied: see EEA Regulations 2006, regs 6(2) and 7A(3) and 7B(3).

Permanent right of residence of family members on death of worker or self-employed person

20.119   Where the worker or self-employed person has died before gaining a permanent resident status, a family member gains a right to reside in the UK permanently if the following conditions are met:[66]

- the family member resided with the person immediately before the death; *and,*
- either:
  - the deceased had resided continuously in the UK for at least the two years immediately before the death; or
  - the death was the result of an accident at work or an occupational disease.

20.120   These provisions, under which the family member gains an immediate right to reside permanently, are set out in Article 17.4 of the Directive. In addition, under Article 12.1 EEA nationals with a right of residence as close family members of a Union citizen who dies or leaves the UK will retain their rights of residence. However, in order to acquire a right to reside permanently such a person must satisfy the usual conditions of residing legally in the UK for a continuous period of five years, either as a family member of a qualified person or as a qualified person in their own right (eg as a worker, self-employed person etc).

---

64 EEA Regs 2006 reg 5(6) and article 7.2 of the Citizenship Directive.
65 EEA Regs 2006 reg 5(7) and article 17.1 of the Citizenship Directive.
66 EEA Regs 2006 reg 15(1)(e) and article 17.4 of the Citizenship Directive.

Meaning of 'continuous residence'

20.121 In calculating any period of 'continuous residence' for the purpose of establishing a permanent right to reside, the following are disregarded:[67]

- any periods of absence from the UK that do not exceed six months in total in any year;
- periods of absence for military service; and
- any one absence from the UK not exceeding 12 months for an important reason such as pregnancy and childbirth, serious illness, study or vocational training or an overseas posting.

Losing the permanent right of residence

20.122 Once acquired, the right of permanent residence is only lost through absence from the UK for a period exceeding two consecutive years.[68]

20.123 However, all of the permanent rights of residence are subject to Home Office powers to remove or exclude EEA nationals in specified circumstances. See para 20.115 below.

EU nationals who may have a right to reside but are not eligible

20.124 The following people have a right to reside in the UK under EU law but are not eligible for homelessness assistance or housing allocations. Some are entitled to housing benefit and this is indicated where relevant. They are:

- a person with an initial 'three-month' right to reside;
- some jobseekers;
- a student;
- a 'self-sufficient' person;
- some people with a 'derivative' right to reside (see below at paras 20.147–20.152).

Initial right to reside

20.125 Freedom of movement and the right to work in other member states is fundamental to the EU. The Citizenship Directive and the EEA Regulations 2006[69] provide that EEA nationals and their family

---

67 EEA Regs 2006 reg 3 and article 16.3 of the Citizenship Directive.
68 EEA Regs 2006 reg 15(2) and article 16.4 of the Citizenship Directive.
69 Citizenship Directive preamble, para (10) and EEA Regs 2006 Reg 13.

members, as defined above, have a right of residence for an initial period of three months but that the right may cease if the person becomes an 'unreasonable burden on the social assistance system.'

20.126   Such people may be entitled to some benefits[70] but only if they are, in fact, habitually resident, which is unlikely. They are not entitled to housing benefit, homelessness assistance or social housing.

Jobseekers

20.127   A person whose only right to reside is as a 'jobseeker' is not eligible for homelessness assistance, housing allocations or housing benefit.[71]

20.128   A 'jobseeker' is a person not currently employed but seeking work in another member state. Under the Citizenship Directive jobseekers cannot be expelled 'for as long as the Union citizens can provide evidence that they are continuing to seek employment and that they have a genuine chance of being engaged.'[72] It is important to distinguish between jobseekers who go to another member state to find work but have not yet found it and former workers who are temporarily unemployed, who may retain the status of 'worker', see above at para 20.77.

20.129   A jobseeker is defined in regulation 6 of the EEA Regulations 2006 as a person who:[73]

- entered the UK in order to seek work *or* is present in the UK seeking employment, immediately after enjoying a right to reside as a worker, self-employed person, self-sufficient person or a student;[74] and
- can provide evidence that he or she is seeking employment and has a genuine chance of being engaged.

20.130   So, under the Directive, as long as there is continuing evidence that the person is seeking employment and has a genuine chance of being engaged the status of jobseeker can be retained indefinitely. However, the EEA Regulations 2006 provide that to retain the status of jobseeker for longer than 182 days (26 weeks/six months) the evidence must be 'compelling'. Where a person is absent from the

---

70   Income-based JSA, child benefit and child tax credit.
71   Croatian nationals do not have rights to reside as jobseekers.
72   Citizenship Directive article 14(4)(b).
73   EEA Regs 2006 reg 6(4).
74   Note that this does not include someone whose previous right to remain was as a jobseeker. Also, any period of 'retained' worker status during unemployment is disregarded.

UK for a continuous period of 12 months, the period of 182 days/six months begins again.[75]

20.131   If the person has already had a right to reside as a jobseeker or been unemployed with 'retained worker status' (see above at para 20.77) for at least six months, an absence of less than 12 months will mean that the evidence must be 'compelling' from the start. Furthermore, any period of less than six months (during which the person has previously been a jobseeker/unemployed worker) will be deducted from the six months starting on return.

20.132   The additional requirement that the evidence be 'compelling' in these circumstances is only in the EEA Regulations 2006 and not in the Directive. The DWP guidance gives as an example of 'compelling' evidence, a letter offering a contract of employment. Arguably, the additional requirement is not lawful since its effect is to limit the rights of EEA nationals to seek work in another member state.

20.133   Importantly, if a person's only right to reside is as a jobseeker he or she is not eligible for housing rights. In theory such people are entitled to claim income-based JSA, child benefit and child tax credit (but not housing benefit or income support). However, to be entitled they must, as a matter of fact, be habitually resident in the UK. A recent arrival seeking work in the UK is unlikely to satisfy the habitual residence test, see para 20.164 below.

The 'minimum earnings threshold' (MET)

20.134   In March 2014 a 'minimum earnings threshold' was introduced by the DWP in relation to benefits for jobseekers who were previously working. If, for the three months prior to the claim, the person has been earning at least the level of income at which national insurance contributions are payable (for 2014/15 this is £153 per week) the DWP will accept that this was genuine and effective work. If the earnings were less than this, they will be subject to a 'fuller examination' to determine whether the work was genuine and effective.[76]

20.135   It should be remembered that a person can have more than one right to reside. A jobseeker may have a right to reside by virtue of being a family member of a worker or self-employed person for example.

---

75 There must still be evidence of seeking work and having a genuine chance of being engaged, but it need not be compelling.

76 The DWP guidance suggests only that such people will be subject to a 'fuller examination' but the likelihood is that benefits will simply be refused to those whose previous earnings did not meet the threshold.

Students

20.136 An EEA national who is a student in the UK has a right to reside. However, the term 'student' is strictly defined. A student is someone who:[77]

- is enrolled to follow a course of study at a private or public establishment listed on the Department of Education and Science Register, or an establishment financed from public funds (this may include vocational training); and
- has comprehensive sickness insurance; and
- assures the Home Office, by means of a declaration or something similar, that he or she has sufficient resources not to become a burden on the social assistance system of the UK during the period of residence.

20.137 If the student has family members who will live with him or her in the UK, the assurance given to UKBA must cover the whole family, who must also be covered by comprehensive sickness insurance.[78] The family members of students who enjoy rights of residence are defined more restrictively than for other qualifying persons (see para 20.140 below).

20.138   In contrast to those who are self-sufficient, a student would not cease to be a qualified person by virtue of making an application for social assistance, for example, making a homeless application. However, such an application would mean that the initial assurance given to the Home Office has not been honoured.

Working while studying

20.139 An EEA student who is working as well as studying will also have a right of residence as a worker provided the work is not marginal and ancillary.

Family members of students

20.140 For those whose only right of residence is as a student, the only family members who have a right to reside for longer than for an initial three months are:

- a spouse or civil partner;
- dependent children under the age of 18.[79]

77 EEA Regs 2006 reg 4(1)(d) and Citizenship Directive article 7.1(c).
78 EEA Regs 2006 reg 4(3) and Citizenship Directive article 7.1(c).
79 In all cases the children and grandchildren must be the direct descendants of the qualified person or his or her spouse or civil partner. This, however, includes adopted children and stepchildren.

Self-sufficient people

20.141 A self-sufficient person is someone who has:

- sufficient resources not to become a burden on the social assistance system of the UK during the period of residence; and
- comprehensive sickness insurance in the UK.[80]

20.142 Self-sufficient people have a right to reside and are therefore theoretically eligible but the very fact of applying for homeless assistance would usually be evidence that the conditions are not met and that the person is no longer a qualified person. However, the circumstances of the person's homelessness will be relevant. If the difficulty is temporary or caused by an emergency such as a flood or fire, it may be argued that the emergency assistance required does not necessarily mean that the person has become a burden on the social assistance system.

20.143 Note that, in contrast to workers and the self-employed, there is no specific provision that a person in temporary difficulty should continue to be regarded as self-sufficient.

20.144 The Homelessness Code of Guidance[81] suggests that where an applicant was previously self-sufficient, guidance should be sought from the Home Office.

20.145 The resources of the whole family must be sufficient to ensure that none become a burden on the social assistance scheme and the necessary comprehensive sickness insurance must cover all of the family members.[82]

20.146 When calculating whether a family has sufficient resources the resources will be deemed sufficient if they are more than the maximum level to qualify for social assistance (ie above the income limit for eligibility for receipt of income support).[83]

'Derivative' rights to reside

20.147 As indicated above, at para 20.51, domestic laws sometimes fail to reflect EU rights and EU citizens can rely on rights under the main EU Treaty to challenge such provisions. The *Zambrano* case, which

---

80 EEA Regs 2006 reg 4(1)(c). The requirement to have comprehensive sickness insurance is not a formality but an essential condition: *FK (Kenya) v Secretary of State for the Home Department* [2010] EWCA Civ 1302.

81 Annex 12 para 34.

82 EEA Regs 2006 reg 4(2). However, if the family members are themselves EEA nationals they may be qualified persons in their own right.

83 EEA Regs 2006 reg 4(4) and article 8.4 of the Citizenship Directive.

led to the recognition of 'derivative' rights, is a good example of such a case.

Ruiz Zambrano v ONEM[84] concerned a challenge by a Colombian national living in Belgium to a decision refusing him a work permit and/or unemployment benefit. Mr Zambrano had resided in Belgium with his wife since 1999. They had been refused asylum though it was accepted that they could not be sent back to Colombia because of the civil war. They had three children, the second and third being Belgian citizens.

The ECJ held that the Citizenship Directive did not apply because it applied only to EU citizens who move to or reside in a member state other than that of which they are a national. The children, who were EU nationals, had never left Belgium. The ECJ held that article 20 of TFEU prevents national measures that have the effect of depriving EU citizens of the genuine enjoyment of the substance of their rights as EU citizens. In this case:

> A refusal to grant a right of residence to a third country national with dependent minor children in the Member State where those children are nationals and reside, and also a refusal to grant such a person a work permit, has such an effect. ... This is because it must be assumed that [a refusal to grant a right of residence] would lead to a situation where those children, citizens of the Union, would have to leave the territory of the Union in order to accompany their parents. Similarly, if a work permit were not granted to such a person, he would risk not having sufficient resources to provide for himself and his family, which would also result in the children, citizens of the Union, having to leave the territory of the Union.[85]

20.148 So, the case of *Zambrano* means that a non-EEA national parent of a child who is an EEA national may have a right to reside in order to care for the child. This applies when otherwise the outcome would be that the parent/s, and with them the EEA national children, would be forced to leave the territory of the EEA, eg because of destitution and/or a prohibition on working.

---

84 ECJ, Case C-34/09, 8 March 2011 (ONEM is the Belgian National Employment Office).
85 ECJ, Case C-34/09, at [43] and [44].

20.149   Since *Zambrano* the EEA Regulations 2006 have been amended and the new Regulation 15A sets out the 'Derivative Rights of Residence' as established by the ECJ in *Zambrano* and also *Ibrahim* and *Teixeira*, see above at para 20.100. These are set out in regulation 15A. Some derivative rights of residence entitle a person to homelessness assistance, housing allocations and housing benefit but the *Zambrano* right does not, see below.

Derivative rights to reside: regulation 15A

20.150   The following may obtain a 'derivative right of residence' if the necessary conditions are met:

15A(2) Primary carer of an EEA national
The primary carer of an EEA national under the age of 18 provided the child is residing in the UK as a 'self-sufficient' person (ie not someone qualified to reside in the UK on other grounds, eg worker, self-employed etc) and would be unable to remain in the UK if the primary carer was required to leave.

15A(3) Child of an EEA national in education
The person must have an EEA national parent and must have been residing in the UK at a time when the EEA national parent was residing in the UK as a worker; he or she must be in education in the UK and have been in education in the UK at a time when the EEA national parent was in the UK.

15A(4) Primary carer of EEA national in education
The person must be the primary carer of a person satisfying the conditions in 15A(3) who would be unable to continue to be educated in the UK if the primary carer were required to leave.

15A(4A) Primary carer of British citizen
The person must be the primary carer of a British citizen, and the British citizen must be residing in the UK and would be unable to continue to reside in the UK or in another EEA state if the primary carer was required to leave the UK.

15A(5) Child whose primary carer is non-EU national without leave
The person must be a child whose primary carer has a right to reside under 15A(2) or 15A(4) but who does not have leave to enter or remain in the UK and requiring the child to leave would prevent the primary carer from residing in the UK.

20.151   'Primary carer' means someone who is a direct relative or legal guardian and either has primary responsibility for the care or shares the responsibility with someone who does not have an EEA right to reside, right of abode or ILR (ie someone with no right to remain in the UK so that the issue will be considered on the basis that both carers would have to leave the UK if the derivative right to reside were not established).

20.152   Derivative rights to reside will not be established in certain circumstances where the person's rights are limited on the grounds of public policy, public security, public health or where decisions have been taken about abuse of rights under the Regulations.

'*Zambrano*' rights

20.153   The derivative rights under regulation 15A(4A) (the primary carer of a British citizen) reflect the '*Zambrano*' right to reside. A person whose only right to reside is under this provision is not eligible for homelessness assistance, housing allocations or housing benefit.[86] Furthermore, the courts have interpreted the conditions establishing such a right in strict terms:

> The Court of Appeal considered the *Zambrano* 'right to reside' in the case of *R (Harrison) v Secretary of State for the Home Department*[87] in relation to a threatened deportation of a non-EU family member. The Court held that the right was only established where the EU citizen would be forced to leave the EU and not where the EU citizen's continued residence would be adversely affected or their quality of life diminished by the non-EU national being forced to leave the UK.

> In the case of *R (HC) v Secretary of State for Work and Pensions*[88] a challenge was brought on the basis that the way the domestic law had been amended discriminated against a non-EU national who had a dependent EU national child. The challenge was to the relevant law in relation to social security benefits, child benefit and homelessness assistance. The claimant was an Egyptian national who had married a UK national with whom she had two children both of whom were British nationals. She was the victim of domestic violence and left the shared home. She and the

---

86 See regs 4 and 6 of the Eligibility Regs 2006 and reg 10 of the Housing Benefit Regs 2006.

87 [2012] EWCA Civ 1736, 21 December 2012.

88 [2015] EWCA Civ 49, 10 February 2015.

children were accommodated by and provided with subsistence by the local authority under the CA 1989 s17. She argued that the law excluding her from benefits and homelessness assistance unlawfully discriminated against her and the children on grounds of nationality. Her claim was dismissed: as a general rule 'third country' nationals were not entitled to claim social security benefits. She did not have rights analogous to those of EEA nationals who were working or self-employed, only a derivative right to remain in the UK as long as her children needed her. The Court of Appeal dismissed her appeal.

Harrison was also applied in the case of *Hines v Lambeth LBC*[89] in which a non-EU national with a five-year-old British son was refused homelessness assistance. The local authority decided that she was not eligible because she was a person subject to immigration control. She argued that she had a right to reside under the EEA Regulations 2006 but this was rejected: if she was forced to leave the UK because of being refused assistance, this would not necessarily force the child to leave the UK. The child could live with his father. The issue was not what was in the best interests of the child but only whether the derivative right to reside was established. Applying *Harrison*, this was only the case if transferring the care to the other parent would so seriously impair the children's quality and standard of life that he would be forced to leave the UK.

20.154   In the UK, the most common situation will be where a non-EEA national is the mother of a child whose father is either a British national or someone with settled status in the UK. In such a case, the child will be a British national. The primary carer's right of residence arises because the child is an EEA national and would be deprived of the benefits of EEA citizenship if forced to leave the EEA. Note that this is different from the situation of a primary carer of someone in education, where the rights arise because of the principle that a child who has moved to another member state with an EEA parent (exercising the right to work) should be entitled to complete their education in that member state. In such a case the child and the carer are eligible for homelessness assistance, housing allocations and housing benefit.

89 [2014] EWCA Civ 660, 20 May 2014.

Exclusion and removal

20.155 EEA citizens may be removed if it is justified on the grounds of public policy, public security or public health. The decision-making framework in relation to the powers of removal gives enhanced protection depending on the length of residence enjoyed by the person concerned. So, a person with a permanent right to reside can be removed only if there are 'serious grounds of public policy or public security' and a person who has resided in the UK for a continuous period of at least 10 years can only be removed if there are 'imperative grounds of public security'.[90] Most decisions to remove are taken in relation to those who have served prison sentences in the UK. Long periods in prison will not usually count towards any relevant residence period. This does not, however, mean that someone who has enjoyed long residence before serving a prison sentence must start again in establishing a period of continuous residence to establish a permanent right to reside under the Citizenship Directive.[91]

Documents and evidence of status

20.156 EEA nationals must be admitted freely to the UK[92] and are not required to have any form of documentation, such as a residence permit or passport stamp confirming a right to enter or to reside in the UK.

20.157 Non-EEA nationals whose right to reside is as family members of EEA nationals will need documentary evidence: a family permit, residence card or permanent residence card.

20.158 Any other EEA national or family member who has a right to reside *may* apply for registration or a residence card from the Home Office but this is not necessary in order to establish a right to reside. Such documents will be issued free of charge.

20.159 In all cases when asserting eligibility by way of an EEA right to reside in the UK it will be necessary to provide documentary evidence of status. This could include, for example, contracts of employment, wage slips, tax returns, bank statements, marriage or civil

---

90 See EEA Regs 2006 reg 21 and article 28 of the Citizenship Directive.

91 See EEA Regs 2006 regs 19 and 20 and *HR (Portugal) v Secretary of State for the Home Department* [2009] EWCA Civ 371, 5 May 2009 and *Carvalho v Secretary of State for the Home Department and Secretary of State for the Home Department v Omar* [2010] EWCA Civ 1406, 14 December 2010.

92 EEA Regs 2006 reg 11(1). But accession state nationals (currently only Croatians) will need a certificate to confirm they are registered workers.

partnership certificates etc. However, in relation to homelessness assistance, obtaining documentary evidence is part of the inquiry process. It is not a prerequisite before the inquiry process can begin or before interim accommodation can be provided (see chapter 13).

'Zambrano' rights of residence or limited leave?

20.160   As explained above at para 20.147, a non-EEA national may have a derivative right of residence under the *Zambrano* principle. However, this type of right to reside does not entitle the person to homelessness assistance, housing allocations or mainstream benefits, including housing benefit, child benefit and child tax credits. It does entitle the person to work in the UK.

20.161   The changes to Home Office policy on leave for people relying on rights under article 8 of ECHR, described above at paras 20.31–20.40, generally means that if leave is granted, it will be limited leave that entitles the person to work but which is subject to the 'no recourse to public funds' condition.

20.162   So, non-EEA nationals who are the parents of British children may be able to rely on a right to reside under the EEA Regulations 2006 or may apply for leave to remain in the UK under the 'family members' policy, described above at para 20.31.

20.163   The advantage of an application for leave is that the Home Office may be persuaded not to apply the 'no recourse' condition, or to remove it. This will entitle the person to mainstream benefits, including housing benefit. However, currently the fee for the application is £550 (subject to waiver in cases of destitution) and a fresh application will be needed every 30 months with a fee payable each time and each application will be considered on its merits. But, once a person has had four grants of leave without any break (ie 10 years' continuous residence) he or she will be entitled to apply for indefinite leave (ILR) to remain in the UK. In contrast, a person relying on rights under the EEA Regs 2006 will always be excluded from benefits and will not automatically become eligible to apply for ILR. Furthermore, the *Zambrano* right to reside will only be established if the alternative would be that the children would be forced to leave the EEA.

The habitual residence test

20.164   When first introduced in 1996, the habitual residence test ('HRT') was designed to exclude European nationals not ordinarily resident in the UK who would otherwise have been eligible for homelessness assistance and benefits immediately on arrival. The test had to be applied equally to British and European nationals otherwise it would have breached EU law by discriminating on the basis of nationality. Between 1996 and 2004 any EEA national who was habitually resident was eligible for homelessness assistance. Furthermore, the test did not apply to EEA nationals exercising treaty rights.

Who must satisfy the habitual residence test?

20.165 The following must be habitually resident in order to be eligible:

- persons who are subject to immigration control but who have indefinite leave to remain in the UK;
- British nationals;
- EEA nationals whose right to reside is by virtue of being self-sufficient (see para 20.141 above);
- EEA nationals with a permanent right to reside by virtue of five years' residence (see para 20.107).

20.166 For those persons who are subject to immigration control but eligible, only those with ILR or the leave granted under the 'Afghan' former employees policy (see above at para 20.22) are required to be habitually resident.

Who is exempt from the habitual residence test?

PSIC

20.167 Refugees and those with HP or DL granted outside the immigration rules do not have to satisfy the habitual residence test.

EEA nationals

20.168 The Eligibility Regs 2006[93] expressly provide that the following people shall not be treated as ineligible by virtue of not being habitually resident:[94]

- EEA nationals who are workers, self-employed or registered accession state workers (currently only Croatians), and their family members;

---

93 Allocation of Housing and Homelessness (Eligibility) (England) (Amendment) Regulations 2009 SI No 358.
94 Eligibility Regs 2006 reg 6(2).

- EEA nationals with a right to reside permanently in the UK by virtue of EEA Regs 2006 reg 15(1)(c), (d) or (e) (workers and self-employed people who are retired or permanently incapacitated and their family members);
- people in the UK as a result of deportation, expulsion or other removal by compulsion of law from another country to the UK.

What is the habitual residence test?

20.169   To satisfy the test a person must be habitually resident in the UK, the Channel Islands, the Isle of Man or the Republic of Ireland: all of which comprise the 'common travel area' (CTA).

20.170   Legislation provides no definition of the term 'habitual residence' but it has been considered by the courts in a number of cases. Usually, a person must show that he or she has taken up residence and lived for a period in the CTA.[95] However, the situation is different for someone who has previously been habitually resident and is returning to resume habitual residence previously established. He or she should not fail the habitual residence test solely on the ground of not living in the CTA long enough.[96]

20.171   There is no minimum period that establishes habitual residence. The central question is where a person's 'centre of interest' is. This will involve considering the person's home, family ties, social connections and employment. Someone who has lived in the UK for only a few months may nevertheless have established his or her centre of interest in the UK. Another person may have been in the UK for longer but his or her centre of interest may be elsewhere, eg someone who retains a home elsewhere and whose family is in another country. The test is not simply about how long a person has been present in the UK but about whether he or she is resident for a settled purpose.

20.172   Annex 10 of the Homelessness Code of Guidance sets out a useful summary of the application of the test.

The habitual residence test and benefits

20.173   Some EEA nationals who are ineligible for homelessness assistance and housing allocations are entitled to some benefits: income-based JSA, child benefit and child tax credit but not income support or housing benefit. But, only those who are habitually resident are entitled.

95   *Nessa v The Chief Adjudication Officer* [1999] 1 WLR 1937, HL.
96   *Swaddling v Adjudication Officer* (ECJ) [1999] ECR I-1090, EC.

The DWP generally interprets this as meaning that the person must have been in the UK for a minimum of three months before they can be entitled.

Eligibility: members of the household

Homelessness

Restricted persons and restricted cases

20.174 When originally enacted, HA 1996 s185(4) provided that any ineligible person was to be disregarded when deciding whether an eligible person was homeless or in priority need. In *R (Morris) v Westminster City Council*[97] the Court of Appeal considered the case of a British citizen whose infant daughter was subject to immigration control. Section 185(4) compelled the authority to disregard the daughter with the effect that Mrs Morris had no priority need. The Court of Appeal made a declaration that HA 1996 s185(4) was incompatible with the ECHR: it discriminated on the grounds of nationality and could not be justified.

20.175　In response the government amended HA 1996 ss184, 185 and 193.[98] The current position is that 'persons from abroad ... not eligible for housing assistance' are no longer disregarded if the applicant is a British citizen or eligible EEA national. Instead, where the decision on homelessness or priority need depends on a person who is not eligible (because they are subject to immigration control and either have no leave to enter or remain in the UK or have leave that is subject to the 'no recourse to public funds' condition), the ineligible person is a 'restricted person' and the case is a 'restricted case'. In the same situation where the applicant is a PSIC but nevertheless eligible (eg a person with indefinite leave to remain), an ineligible family member is still disregarded.

20.176　So, the situation is as follows:

- *Ineligible applicant*: no homelessness duty so issue does not arise.
- *British or eligible EEA applicant*: if homelessness or priority need decision depends on a household member who is a PSIC with no leave or conditional leave, this will be a restricted case.

---

97 [2005] EWCA Civ 1184, 14 October 2005, see paras 2.75–2.77.
98 In fact in *Bah v UK* App no 56328/07, 27 September 2011, the ECtHR found that the original provisions did not breach articles 8 and 14: the 'discrimination was justified'. However, s185 had already been amended.

- *Eligible PSIC applicant*: if homelessness or priority need decision depends on a household member who is a PSIC with no leave or conditional leave, that person is disregarded so the applicant will be found not homeless or not in priority need.

Restricted cases: the housing duty

20.177   Any housing duty under s193 HA 1996 in relation to a restricted case must be ended by way of a 'private rented sector offer' if reasonably practicable. In contrast, for a non-restricted case the ending of the duty by way of a private rented sector offer is optional. See para 16.28 for details of the requirements of a 'private rented sector offer.'

20.178   Note that these rules apply only in relation to homelessness and priority need: if the applicant is homeless and in priority need for other reasons, and the full housing duty is owed, account will be taken of the ineligible members of the household when deciding what accommodation is suitable for the household. However, an authority may decide that certain ineligible family members should not be included as part of the 'household' when allocating accommodation, see below at para 20.180.[99]

Allocations

20.179   A person who is ineligible cannot be allocated accommodation under HA 1996 Part VI and cannot be granted a joint tenancy with a person who is eligible. However, this does not prevent an ineligible person who is already a social tenant from being allocated accommodation by way of a transfer.[100]

20.180   HA 1996 Part VI does not require a housing authority to disregard ineligible members of the household when deciding on the type of accommodation to allocate, but the authority may determine what the 'household' comprises.

> In *R (Kimvono) v Tower Hamlets LBC*,[101] the applicant was eligible but his 13-year-old daughter was not. The local authority decided that for the purposes of an allocation, she could not be included in the application and that the size of property to be allocated

---

99   But the fact that some members of the household are ineligible will be relevant when deciding on the size of the accommodation that is offered, see *Ariemuguvbe v Islington LBC* [2009] EWCA Civ 1308, 21 October 2009.

100   HA 1996 s160ZA(5) .

101   CO/3579/2000, 5 December 2000.

would be on the basis that she was not part of the household. This was held to be unlawful: there was nothing in Part VI that entitled the authority to disregard the daughter and the court rejected the authority's argument that they had a discretion to exclude her from consideration.

Ariemuguvbe v Islington LBC[102] concerned a family comprising a mother, five adult children and three grandchildren, all under the age of two. The local authority offered accommodation under Part VI for the applicant and her grandchildren stating that the adult children were not part of her household and, as they were all subject to immigration control, it was appropriate to disregard them when assessing the suitability of accommodation to be offered under HA 1996 Part VI. The court held that HA 1996 Part VI did not require a local authority to disregard members of a household because they were ineligible. However, 'the Council was entitled to interpret 'household' by reference to its ordinary, everyday usage. It was up to them to decide whether these five adult children were members of the claimant's household. They decided that these adult children ought not to be taken into account as part of the household, given their ages and also given their precarious immigration status.'[103] The claim was dismissed and the Court of Appeal dismissed Ms Ariemuguvbe's appeal.

Housing benefit

20.181 Only a person who is eligible can claim housing benefit. The Housing Benefit Regulations 2006 provide that a person who is not eligible is treated as being 'not liable' for rent or other payments, ie he or she cannot receive housing benefit.

20.182 The amount of housing benefit payable depends on an assessment of the number of bedrooms a household needs, see paras 9.54 and 9.69. This depends on the number of people in the household. Ineligible members of the household are not disregarded.

---

102 [2009] EWHC 470, 24 February 2009; [2009] EWCA Civ 1308, 21 October 2009.
103 Cranston J at [14] in the original decision.

The right to rent

20.183   The 'right to rent' provisions introduced by the Immigration Act 2014 set out three classes of persons: those with an unlimited right to rent; those with a time-limited right to rent; and those with no right to rent.

Unlimited right to rent

20.184   Two groups have an unlimited right to rent: (1) British citizens, EEA citizens and Swiss nationals; and (2) people with a right of abode in the UK, with ILR or with leave to remain in the UK with no time limit.

Time-limited right to rent

20.185   This category covers anyone with leave to enter or remain for a limited period of time; or qualifying family members of EEA nationals with enforceable right to reside under the EEA Regs 2006.

20.186   This does not include anyone who is a British citizens, EEA citizens or Swiss national (who have an unlimited right to rent). Anyone in this category will need to provide documentary evidence to a landlord and the landlord has an obligation to carry out follow up checks.

No right to rent

20.187   Any PSIC who does not have leave to be in the UK has no right to rent. However, a person whose leave to remain would normally not entitle them to rent may be given permission to rent by the Home Office.

20.188   The Home Office issued the *Code of Practice on illegal immigrants and private rent accommodation* in October 2014 (available from the Home Office website). At the time of writing the right to rent scheme is being piloted in the West Midlands and is expected to be rolled out nationally from April 2015.

The 'safety net' provisions: community care services for ineligible migrants

20.189   The restrictions on access to housing and benefits described above, together with prohibitions on employment means that many migrants face destitution in the UK. This includes significant numbers of people waiting decisions from the Home Office on applications for leave to remain.

20.190　Destitute migrants, including asylum-seekers and failed asylum-seekers, have turned to local authorities for help under the safety net provisions of community care law described in chapters 18 and 19. This led to significant developments in the scope of community care duties, particularly relating to the provision of accommodation. However, two statutes were introduced to restrict community care duties to certain migrants:

- the Immigration and Asylum Act (IAA) 1999; and
- the Nationality, Immigration and Asylum Act (NIAA) 2002.

20.191　This section examines these restrictions and the legal tests applied by social services authorities when destitute migrants seek help. A flow chart is included in the appendix to illustrate how the tests should be applied.

Asylum-seekers: history of support arrangements

20.192　Before 1996 asylum-seekers were entitled to homelessness assistance and social security benefits while awaiting a decision on their asylum claims. This access to benefits and housing was restricted by the Asylum and Immigration Act 1996 (most of the relevant provisions are now found in the Immigration and Asylum Act 1999). Many migrants with limited leave to enter or remain in the UK and asylum-seekers who claimed asylum after entering the UK were unable to claim benefits or receive homelessness assistance. This led to destitute asylum-seekers seeking support from local authorities. It was clear that a duty was owed to families with children under the Children Act (CA) 1989. And through litigation it was established that a duty could be owed to childless asylum-seekers who were destitute under the National Assistance Act (NAA) 1948.

R v Hammersmith & Fulham LBC ex p M, R v Lambeth LBC ex p P, R v Westminster CC ex p A and R v Lambeth LBC ex p X ('*M, P, A and X*')[104] concerned four single, healthy asylum-seekers who applied for assistance under NAA 1948 s21. As a result of the Asylum and Immigration Act 1996 they were not entitled to benefits or homelessness assistance because they had applied for asylum after

104　(1997–98) 1 CCLR 85, CA, 17 February 1997.

entering the UK. They argued that because of their destitution they were in need of care and attention not otherwise available to them. The Court of Appeal held that destitute asylum-seekers were 'in need of care and attention' and were therefore eligible for residential accommodation under section 21(1)(a). Furthermore, even if they were not yet in need of care and attention their destitution would lead to an almost certain future need, and it was not necessary for social services to wait for that point before providing assistance.

20.193   Subsequently, from 1996 to 1999 local authorities provided support and accommodation for large numbers of destitute asylum-seekers. Others (who claimed asylum at the port of entry) could get homelessness assistance and social security benefits until their asylum claims were decided.

Asylum support

20.194   One of the central aims of the IAA 1999 was the transfer of responsibility for the support and accommodation of asylum-seekers to the Home Office. The IAA 1999 created the current system of support administered by the Home Office. Originally this was the responsibility the National Asylum Support Service (NASS), a department of the Home Office. NASS was officially disbanded in 2006 but the system of asylum support is still commonly referred to as 'NASS support' or 'section 95' support (to distinguish it from 'section 4' support for failed asylum-seekers, see below at para 20.197). Asylum support usually consists of a package of accommodation and subsistence. It is provided to asylum-seekers and their households, usually in areas outside of London and the South East.

20.195   If the asylum claim is refused this support ends unless there are dependent children in the household, in which case it continues until the family leaves the UK or the children reach the age of 18.[105] Under IAA 1999 s122 local authorities are prevented from providing housing and financial assistance under CA 1989 s17 to anyone who is entitled to asylum support. However, unaccompanied asylum-

---

105   This is subject to a provision contained in the Asylum and Immigration (Treatment of Claimants etc) Act 2004 under which a family can be 'certified' as failing to make sufficient effort to leave the UK. If this happens, asylum support will terminate. As with most decisions regarding asylum support, an appeal lies to the First-tier Tribunal (Asylum Support).

seeking children remain the responsibility of local authorities under the Children Act 1989 (see para 19.47).

20.196   The way the IAA 1999 amended the National Assistance Act 1948 was to exclude certain adults 'subject to immigration control' whose need arose solely from destitution.[106] This 'test' has been considered by the courts in several cases, see para 20.206 below.

Failed asylum-seekers: section 4 support

20.197   For asylum-seekers whose claims have been refused and all appeal rights exhausted, the IAA 1999 s4 contains a power to provide accommodation and support pending voluntary return or removal. This is referred to as 'section 4 support' (previously 'hard cases support') and is administered by the Home Office. To qualify, the applicant must in all cases be destitute, or likely to become destitute within 14 days. Most section 4 support is provided outside London. It is available only if the failed asylum-seeker satisfies one of five criteria. These are:[107]

- the person is taking all reasonable steps to leave the UK;
- the person is unable to leave the UK by reason of a physical impediment to travel or for some other medical reason;
- the person is unable to leave the UK because, in the opinion of the Secretary of State, there is currently no viable route of return available;
- the person has an outstanding application for judicial review of a decision in relation to his or her asylum claim; or
- the provision of accommodation is necessary to avoid a breach of the person's human rights.

Asylum support – appeals

20.198   Asylum-seekers and failed asylum-seekers who are refused asylum support or whose support is terminated can appeal to the First-tier Tribunal (Asylum Support). The deadlines for lodging appeals are very short. Assistance can be obtained from the Asylum Support Appeals Project (ASAP) whose website is: www.asaproject.org.

---

106   The same test is applied under the Care Act 2014 to the provision of care and support for destitute migrants. This is expected to come into force in 2015.

107   See IAA 1999 s4 and Immigration and Asylum (Provision of Accommodation to Failed Asylum-seekers) Regulations 2005 SI No 930.

20.199   For both asylum-seekers and failed asylum-seekers, issues may arise as to whether accommodation should be provided by a local authority under its community care duties or by the Home Office under IAA 1999 section 95 or section 4. The courts have held that where accommodation duties arise under the National Assistance Act 1948 and the Leaving Care Act 2000, local authorities cannot take account of the availability of support under IAA 1999 (either under section 95 or section 4). This is because asylum support is a residual form of support, available only to the destitute.[108] Where the person is seeking support from a local authority, any challenge to the authority's decision will be by way of judicial review.

Restrictions on adult community care services to 'persons subject to immigration control'

20.200   IAA 1999 s115(9) defines a 'person subject to immigration control' (PSIC) as a person who is not a national of an EEA state[109] and who:

- requires leave to enter or remain in the UK but does not have it;
- has leave to enter or remain in the UK which is subject to a condition that he or she does not have recourse to public funds;
- has leave to enter or remain in the UK given as a result of a maintenance undertaking; or
- continues to have leave to enter or remain in the United Kingdom only as a result of an appeal against a decision to vary, or to refuse to vary, any limited leave.

Asylum-seekers

20.201   Asylum-seekers are PSICs: they need leave to enter or remain in the UK. 'Temporary admission' is often granted to asylum-seekers pending a decision. Temporary admission is not leave to enter but an alternative to detention. This means that until a decision on the

---

108   See *Westminster CC v NASS* [2002] 1 WLR 2956, HL, 17 October 2002, at para 20.14 above, *R (AW) v Croydon LBC* [2007] EWCA Civ 266, 4 April 2007, at para 20.28, and *R (SO) v Barking & Dagenham LBC* [2011] EWCA Civ 1101, 12 October 2010.

109   The EEA refers to the European Economic Area. For a complete list of EEA countries, see para 20.60 above.

asylum claim is made, an asylum-seeker is in the UK lawfully but is nevertheless a PSIC.[110]

20.202 If the claim for asylum is refused and no leave granted, the legality of the person's presence in the UK will depend on whether the application for asylum was made 'on entry' or 'in country' (after entry) into the UK. An asylum-seeker who claimed asylum after entering the UK unlawfully will be in the UK in breach of immigration law after the claim has been refused and all appeal rights exhausted. This is relevant if the person seeks social services assistance as a 'failed asylum-seeker' (see paras 20.218–20.220 below).

No recourse to public funds

20.203 As explained above at paras 20.31–20.34, most limited leave under the Immigration Rules is granted subject to the condition that the person has no 'recourse to public funds' while in the UK. The condition therefore applies to most forms of leave, other than that given to refugees and those in need of protection.

Maintenance undertakings

20.204 These are generally required when an application is made for a dependent relative (other than spouse and children) to join family members in the UK if the person coming to the UK is being granted indefinite leave to remain (ILR). ILR cannot be conditional on having no recourse to public funds. Therefore the Home Office usually requires that a nominated 'sponsor' offer an undertaking to be responsible for supporting the applicant in the UK for the first five years. This must be a formal written undertaking.

Adult care needs and Persons Subject to Immigration Control

20.205 In relation to a PSIC, as defined in IAA 1999 s115(9), see para 20.200 above, a local authority's duty is restricted. Section 21 of the Care Act (CA) 2014 (not in force at the time of writing) provides that:

> A local authority may not meet the needs for care and support of an adult to whom s115 ... applies and whose needs for care and support have arisen solely –

110 Persons subject to immigration control (as defined under IAA 1999 s115, see para 20.200) are also excluded from social security benefits including housing benefit.

(a) because he or she is destitute, or

(b) because of the physical effects, or anticipated physical effects, of his being destitute.[111]

Need arising solely from destitution: the case-law

20.206 In a number of cases the courts have considered the question of whether the need for 'care and attention' has arisen solely from destitution. All were in relation to the same formulation in the NAA 1948.

> In *R v Wandsworth LBC ex p O* and *R v Leicester CC ex p Bhikha*[112] the claimants were persons subject to immigration control, as defined in IAA 1999 s115. Mrs O had serious mental health problems and Mr B was suffering from cancer. The local authorities argued that they could not provide accommodation under NAA 1948 s21 because the applicants' need arose solely from destitution.
>
> The court rejected this, holding that if an applicant has a need for care and attention made more acute by something other than destitution then a duty arises which is not excluded because of a person's immigration status.

20.207 The test set out in *O* and *Bhikha* was subsequently confirmed by the House of Lords.

> In *Westminster CC v NASS*[113] the applicant was an asylum-seeker who had spinal cancer, used a wheelchair and needed assistance with transfers and with personal care. She lived with her 13-year-old daughter, and needed regular hospital treatment. Westminster contended that NASS should accommodate and provide financial support while the council would provide the necessary community care services.
>
> The House of Lords upheld NASS's argument that Westminster was responsible for providing accommodation and support as well as community care services under NAA 1948 s21. It was held that

---

111 The Care Act 2014 repeats the amended provisions of the NAA 1948 s21(1A). At the time of writing, the NAA 1948 is the source of the accommodation duty for adults, see para 18.14. It was amended by the IAA 1999 so as to restrict the duties to destitute migrants.

112 (2000) 3 CCLR 237, CA.

113 [2002] 1 WLR 2956, HL, 17 October 2002.

Parliament must have intended local authorities to retain responsibility for some asylum-seekers. Lord Hoffmann stated that the Asylum and Immigration Act 1996 created two distinct classes of asylum-seeker, the 'able bodied destitute' and the 'infirm destitute'. The need of the infirm destitute for care and attention arises 'because they are infirm as well as because they are destitute'. It was acknowledged that, if they were not asylum-seekers, section 21 would not be needed because accommodation would be provided under the housing legislation. However NAA 1948 s21(1A) is not stating that the need for *accommodation* must not arise solely due to destitution.

20.208   The test approved in *Westminster v NASS* means that a person who is destitute and who has a need for care and attention may be entitled to accommodation under NAA 1948 even though the level of need is not high.

In *R on the application of Mani v Lambeth LBC*[114] the applicant was also an asylum-seeker. He had a leg abnormality and required some help with housework and heavy shopping. He also had a history of mental health difficulties.

The Court of Appeal confirmed the test set out in *O and Bhikha*, and found that the applicant was entitled to accommodation under NAA 1948 s21. The fact that he would probably not have a need for care and attention if he were not an asylum-seeker (because he would be housed) did not disentitle him. On the contrary, the fact that he is an asylum-seeker means that care and attention 'is not otherwise available' to him. As in *Westminster v NASS* (see para 20.207), this meant that the local authority and not NASS were responsible for providing support and accommodation, under section 21.

20.209   In relation to accommodation under NAA 1948 s21 in all cases there must be a need for 'care and attention', as opposed to a need for accommodation. A person who has no such need but who has a health problem for which NHS treatment is available is not entitled

114 [2003] EWCA Civ 836, 9 July 2003.

to accommodation and support under the National Assistance Act 1948.[115]

> In *R (M) v Slough BC*[116] the House of Lords considered the test in relation to a man who was HIV positive but was taking medication and was physically well. He needed continuing medical treatment and a fridge to store his medication.
>
> The House of Lords held that, on the facts, M's needs did not amount to a need for care and attention. The need for care and attention was more than a need for accommodation. It meant a need to be 'looked after' which meant doing something for the person that the person could not do for him or herself. It did not matter that if the person was housed the care and attention could be provided in the home. There had to be a need for care and attention (ie looking after) as opposed to a need for medical care. Provided that there was such a need the local authority should intervene before the need became worse but the duty under NAA 1948 s21 did not arise if there was no present need for care and attention.

20.210　Following *R (M) v Slough* above, local authorities have sought to refuse accommodation on the basis that an applicant did not have a need for care and attention in the sense of a need to be 'looked after'.[117] The Court of Appeal considered the issue in relation to a blind applicant.

> In *R (Zarzour) v Hillingdon LBC*[118] Mr Zarzour was completely blind. The local authority had assessed him as needing help with shopping and laundry and with travelling safely outside, particularly when in an unfamiliar area. It concluded, however, that this did not constitute a need for care and attention. The authority decided that the applicant's friends could continue to provide the assistance they were currently providing and that accommodation would be

---

115　The equivalent formulation in the Care Act 2014 is 'care and support' (see para 18.43). The Care Act 2014 does not have a separate accommodation duty; accommodation is identified as a service that could be provided. There is no equivalent to the 'not otherwise available' condition but the whole process of assessing and meeting need implies this.

116　[2008] UKHL 52, 30 July 2008.

117　See for example *R (Almeida) v Kensingon & Chelsea RLBC* [2012] EWHC 1082, 27 April 2012, at para 20.226.

118　[2010] EWCA Civ 1529, 17 December 2009.

provided by NASS. On Mr Zarzour's claim for judicial review, the court made a declaration that the authority was under an NAA 1948 s21 duty to accommodate.

The Court of Appeal dismissed Hillingdon's appeal, holding that Hillingdon's own assessment had established that Mr Zarzour had a need for care and attention and, as was clear from *Westminster v NASS*, above para 20.207, NASS support is intended to be 'residual' and would not be available to anyone who was entitled to accommodation under section 21.

20.211 In 2013 the issue was considered by the Supreme Court in relation to a failed asylum-seeker suffering from depression (who had in fact been granted leave to remain by the time of the hearing):

In *R (SL) v Westminster CC*[119] the applicant was a failed asylum-seeker who had been diagnosed as suffering from depression and post-traumatic stress disorder and had received in-patient treatment. The community mental health team assessed him as needing continued support on discharge, including community support from a social worker and referrals for counselling and to a befriending service. The authority decided that this was not a need for care and attention and that it had no duty to provide accommodation.

The Supreme Court approved the way the local authority had applied the NAA 1948 s21. Under section 21 there were three conditions: (1) there had to be a need for 'care and attention' (2) by reason of age, illness, disability or other circumstances, and (3) the care and attention needed must be not available otherwise than by the provision of accommodation. The authority was entitled to decide that (1) and (3) were not satisfied. Care and attention means looking after and is not confined to care and attention that can only be provided in specialist residential accommodation. But something more than monitoring the individual was needed.

The appropriate test was whether there was a need for care and attention of a kind calling for the provision of residential accommodation.

At the relevant time SL was a failed asylum-seeker who was eligible for accommodation from the Home Office but this would be outside of London. The type of 'care and attention' he required could be provided in any place and would be available were he

119 [2013] UKSC 27, 9 May 2013.

> to be dispersed. It is still the case that 'NASS' support is a 'last resort' and should be disregarded when considering whether the conditions under NAA 1948 s21 are met. But the local authority was entitled to conclude that the services it provided were not 'care and attention' under NAA 1948 s21.
>
> The Supreme Court also commented (though this was not part of the decision and so is not binding) that in *O* and *Bhikha* and in *Mani* the Court of Appeal had failed to give proper weight to the requirement of NAA 1948 that there must be a need for care and attention 'not otherwise available'. However, the case of *Mani* was correctly decided on the facts: although there was no special requirement as to nature or location of the accxommodation, the care and attention required were of a kind which could only be provided if there were some residential accommodation in which to do so.

Disabled asylum-seekers with children

20.212　A local authority's duty to provide accommodation and support to a disabled asylum-seeker does not extend to the whole family. But where a parent is entitled to accommodation under NAA 1948 s21, it was held that the local authority must arrange for accommodation for the whole family although the Home Office will be responsible for paying for the children's support and a proportion of the accommodation costs.[120]

20.213　However, where it is the children of an asylum-seeker who are disabled, the responsibility for providing adequate accommodation and financial support falls on the Home Office.[121]

Nationality, Immigration and Asylum Act 2002

20.214　In January 2003 the Nationality, Immigration and Asylum Act (NIAA) 2002 came into force and introduced further restrictions on access to community care services by migrants.

120　See *R on the application of O v Haringey LBC and Secretary of State for the Home Department* [2004] EWCA Civ 535, 4 May 2004.

121　*R on the application of A v NASS and Waltham Forest LBC* [2003] EWCA Civ 1473. See also *R (Refugee Action) v Secretary of State for the Home Department* [2014] EWHC 1033 (Admin), 9 April 2014.

20.215   The Act goes further than the IAA 1999: for five categories of people from abroad a local authority is prohibited from offering a service, except to the extent necessary to avoid a breach of a person's human rights or a person's rights under the European treaties.[122]

Who is excluded from services: 'Schedule 3'

20.216 The list of people is set out in NIAA 2002 Sch 3. They are sometimes therefore referred to as 'Schedule 3 people' and are:

- **Para 4**: people who have refugee status in an EEA state,[123] and their dependants;
- **Para 5**: nationals of EEA states, and their dependants;
- **Para 6**: people who were, but are no longer, asylum-seekers and who have failed to co-operate with removal directions, and their dependants;
- **Para 7**: people in the UK in breach of the immigration laws and who are not asylum-seekers, and their dependants; and
- **Para 8**: asylum-seekers who, because of having a dependent child in the household, are eligible for asylum support but have been certified as having failed, without reasonable excuse, to take reasonable steps to leave the UK voluntarily.[124]

EEA nationals

20.217 Most EEA nationals who are exercising rights under the EU Treaty have a right to reside and are therefore eligible for homelessness assistance, social housing and housing benefit, see paras 20.49–20.182 above. EEA nationals who are not exercising treaty rights are covered by NIAA 2002 Sch 3.

Failed asylum-seekers

20.218 NIAA 2002 Sch 3 para 6 refers to failed asylum-seekers who have failed to co-operate with removal directions. When removal directions are issued a formal notice is served informing the person of the date and time of travel. The notice gives a right of appeal. This should

---

122 NIAA 2002 s54 and Sch 3.

123 For the full list of EEA states, see para 20.60 above.

124 This category was introduced by the Immigration and Asylum (Treatment of Claimants etc) Act 2004 s9. The making of such certificates was piloted in certain areas in 2005 but was not widely implemented thereafter.

not be confused with Home Office letters that state that the person is 'subject to removal'.

20.219   Para 7 deals with people in the UK in breach of immigration law. This includes some failed asylum-seekers.

> In *R (AW) v Croydon LBC* and *R (A, D and Y) v Hackney LBC*[125] the Court of Appeal considered the position of failed asylum-seekers who had made their claims for asylum after entering the UK ('in country'). No removal directions had been set.
>
> The court held that the applicants fell within NIAA 2002 Sch 3 para 7. Prior to making their claims for asylum they were in the UK in breach of immigration law. This was also the position after their claims for asylum were exhausted. The situation is different for a person who claimed asylum 'at port'. A 'port applicant' may be detained or granted 'temporary admission'. Someone who is detained or granted temporary admission is not deemed to have entered the UK and is therefore not in the UK in breach of immigration laws. A failed asylum-seeker who claimed asylum at port only falls within Schedule 3 if removal directions are set and he or she fails to comply with them, or if he or she fails to comply with reporting or other conditions.
>
> The court also decided that failed asylum-seekers awaiting a Home Office decision on a potential fresh claim should be accommodated and supported by the local authority under NAA 1948 s21 if they had a need for care and attention.[126] The court rejected the authority's arguments that they should be accommodated and supported by the Home Office under IAA 1999 s4 (Home Office support for failed asylum-seekers).

20.220   In relation to a failed asylum-seeker it is therefore crucial to know whether the claim for asylum was made 'at port' or 'in country'. The majority of asylum claims are made in country.

---

125 [2007] EWCA Civ 266, 4 April 2007.
126 Since this case was decided the Supreme Court has considered the test under NAA 1948 s21: the need for care and attention must be of a kind calling for the provision of accommodation. See *SL v Westminster*, above at para 20.211.

Which services are excluded

20.221 NIAA 2002 Sch 3 para 1 provides that 'Schedule 3' persons shall not be eligible for support or assistance under the following provisions:

Provision[127]	What kind of services
National Assistance Act 1948 ss21 and 29	Local authority provision of accommodation and other services to those in need of care and attention
Health Services and Public Health Act 1968 s45	Local authority provision for the welfare of the elderly
National Health Service Act 1977 s21 and Sch 8	Local authority provision of services at home to avoid hospital admission
Children Act 1989 ss17, 23C, 24A and 24B	Local authority provision (including accommodation) to adults, including care leavers
Housing Act 1996 ss188(3) and 204(4)	Local authority interim accommodation pending review or appeal in homelessness cases
Local Government Act 2000 s2	Local authority power to spend funds promoting well-being in the local area
Any provision of the Immigration and Asylum Act 1999 or the Nationality, Immigration and Asylum Act 2002	Asylum support. This includes mainstream asylum support and support under section 4 of IAA 1999 (hard cases support)

British citizens and children

20.222 NIAA 2002 Sch 3 does not prevent support or assistance being provided to:

- a British citizen; or
- a child.

---

127 Note that the NAA 1948, the HSPHA and the NHSA will all be repealed by the Care Act 2014, and provisions for care and support, including accommodation are set out in the Care Act 2014, see paras 18.4–18.5.

20.223 The duties and powers in the Children Act 1989 that are excluded are those that may be exercised in relation to adults. NIAA 2002 Sch 3 does not prevent services being provided to a child directly, under CA 1989 s17 or s20.

The test: possible breach of human rights or European treaty rights

20.224 NIAA 2002 Sch 3 para 3 provides that the exercise of a power or duty is not prevented 'if, and to the extent that' it is necessary to avoid a breach of a person's rights under the European Convention on Human Rights (ECHR) or under the European Community treaties.

20.225   The most likely ECHR rights that may be breached by a refusal of assistance are:[128]

- article 3: the right not to be subject to torture, inhuman and/or degrading treatment or punishment;
- article 8: the right to respect for private and family life;
- article 6: the right to a fair and public hearing.

20.226 The European treaties confer the right of free movement to EU nationals in order to exercise such rights as working, seeking work, studying and setting up in business in another member state, see paras 20.49–20.182.

In *R (Almeida) v Kensington and Chelsea RLBC*[129] the claimant challenged a decision by the council that (1) he was not entitled to accommodation under NAA 1948 s21 and (2) that they could not, in any event, provide accommodation because of Schedule 3.

Mr Almeida was a Portugese national who had lived in the UK and Spain for 16 years. He returned to the UK, lawfully, in 2008 to work but he became ill in 2009. At the time of the hearing he was suffering from skin cancer, AIDS and Hepatitis C. He had had frequent hospital admissions and his life expectancy was very limited. When he was faced with homelessness the council carried out an assessment and concluded that he was not entitled to assistance under the NAA 1948 as he did not have a need for 'care and attention' (disregarding his needs for health care, in accordance with the decision in *R(M) v Slough* (see above at para 2.209). The assessment had concluded that he was not 'incapable' of

128 See chapter 2 for an explanation of ECHR rights.
129 [2012] EWHC 1082, 27 April 2012.

performing domestic tasks for himself and that his level of need did not meet the council's eligibility criteria (see para 18.41). Furthermore, they decided that even if he had established a need for care and attention sufficient to trigger the duty under NAA 1948 s21, he was caught by Schedule 3 para 5. The authority could not provide him with accommodation unless the refusal to do so would breach his rights under the ECHR. The social worker carried out a 'human rights' assessment and taking into account the social welfare provisions available in Portugal she concluded that there would be no breach of his rights under articles 3 or 8 if he were to return to Portugal.

Mr Almeida's judicial review claim was successful: the judge held that the council had applied too high a threshold when deciding that he had no need for care and attention. Even disregarding his needs for health care, he clearly passed the threshold and the council was acting irrationally in failing to acknowledge that. The eligibility criteria were not applicable to an assessment under NAA 1948 s21. Furthermore, in relation to Schedule 3 the council's decision that he should return to Portugal, when he was only expected to live for a matter of months and would have no support from family and friends would be 'inhumane treatment'; it would mean an undignified and distressing end to his life. As such the refusal of accommodation and support would breach his rights under both article 3 and article 8 of the ECHR.

Assisting Schedule 3 people to travel

20.227 Local authorities have the power to make travel arrangements and to provide temporary accommodation for *some* Schedule 3 people.[130] Travel arrangements can be made for EEA nationals and their dependants and EEA refugees and their dependants (ie, help to return to the relevant member state). Accommodation may be provided to such people pending travel only if they have dependent children. Accommodation may also be provided to a person who is in the UK in breach of immigration law, provided that he or she has not failed to comply with removal directions. Again this is only possible for those who have dependent children.

---

130 NIAA 2002 Sch 3 paras 8, 9 and 10, and the Withholding and Withdrawal of Support (Travel Assistance and Temporary Accommodation) Regulations 2002 (Travel Regs 2002) SI No 3078.

20.228　　There is no power under the NIAA 2002 and the Travel Regs 2002 to give travel assistance to non-EEA nationals and refugees but in *R (Grant) v Lambeth LBC*,[131] the Court of Appeal held that an authority could do so using its powers under the Local Government Act s2. Section 2 has been repealed by the Localism Act 2011, which provided that local authorities have a 'general power of competence' which would also enable them to do so.

20.229　　There is no power to provide accommodation for any person who has failed to comply with removal directions.

20.230　　Schedule 3 also requires a local authority to inform the Home Office of any person 'in the authority's area' who is or may be a Schedule 3 person.[132]

20.231　　The statutory guidance[133] on the Travel Regs 2002 stresses that only 'temporary short-term accommodation' can be provided 'pending departure from the UK'.[134] In reality, however, many people with outstanding immigration applications wait for years for decisions from the Home Office. During that time they will usually be ineligible and therefore unable to receive homelessness assistance, social housing or housing benefit. They will also be prevented from renting privately by the new right to rent provisions, see para 20.183 above.

20.232　　In *Grant* the court was focusing on the local authority's powers and duties under NIAA 2002 Sch 3 and the Travel Regs 2002. Ms Grant's case was not argued on the basis of the family's rights under article 8 ECHR. In a number of subsequent cases the courts held that, where a person has an outstanding immigration application which relies on article 8, it would be a breach of the person's ECHR rights to refuse support if that would mean that he or she would be forced to leave the UK.

In *R (Binomugisha) v Southwark LBC*[135] the applicant had been in the care of the local authority as an asylum-seeking child. As an adult he suffered mental health problems and the authority therefore had potential duties to provide accommodation both under the Leaving Care Act 2000 and the National Assistance Act 1948. Although his asylum claim had been refused, Mr Binomugishu had a pending

131　[2004] EWCA Civ 1711, 17 June 2004.
132　NIAA 2002 Sch 3 para 14.
133　NIAA 2002 s54 and Sch 3 and the Withholding and Withdrawal of Support (Travel Assistance and Temporary Accommodation) Regulations 2002, Guidance to Local Authorities and Housing Authorities.
134　Guidance (see note 30), para 28.
135　[2006] EWHC 2254 (Admin), 18 September 2006.

application for leave to remain relying on article 8 of ECHR. The authority carried out a 'human rights assessment' to decide whether services should be provided despite him being a 'Schedule 3 person'. Its assessment rejected the opinion of two psychiatrists and concluded that there would be no breach of article 8 if Mr Binomugishu were to return to Uganda.

The court held that it is a task for the immigration authorities and not local authorities to make such decisions and that 'a local authority … should only make its decisions on the basis that a person such as the claimant is free to go back to his own country if an outstanding human rights claim to remain in the UK is manifestly unfounded'.[136] The decision was quashed.

20.233 Furthermore, many claims for leave to remain relying on ECHR article 8 will involve not only the right of the adults who are migrants but the rights of their children who may have lived in the UK for years, often having been born in the UK.

In *R (Clue) v Birmingham CC*[137] the applicant had been in the UK since 2000. She had four children, three of whom had been born in the UK. She applied for indefinite leave to remain under the 'seven-year policy', which at the time was that leave would be granted save in exceptional circumstances, where children had resided in the UK for at least seven years. The Immigration Rules also provided that if the person left the UK before a decision was made his or her application would be treated as withdrawn (although there was a discretion to continue to consider the application). Until the application was determined (which in the event took exactly two years) Ms Clue was in the UK in breach of immigration law and therefore fell within NIAA 2002 Sch 3, para 7. Following the breakdown of her relationship with the father of the three youngest children she applied to Birmingham for support and accommodation. The council refused support under CA 1989 s17 but offered financial assistance for the family to return to Jamaica. Its human rights assessment concluded that because the children were not in contact with their father or his family there would

---

136 [2006] EWHC 2254 (Admin), Andrew Nicol QC at [13]. See also *R on the application of PB v Haringey LBC and Others* [2006] EWHC 2255 (Admin), 18 September 2006.

137 [2010] EWCA Civ 460.

be no breach of their rights under article 8 because they could enjoy family life in Jamaica.

The Court of Appeal held that this was unlawful: 'when applying Schedule 3, a local authority should not consider the merits of an outstanding application for leave to remain. It is required only to be satisfied that the application is not 'obviously hopeless and abusive.''

20.234   So, where a person has an outstanding immigration application that is not 'manifestly unfounded' or 'obviously hopeless and abusive' an authority will usually be bound to provide support and accommodation under one of the community care duties, despite the person falling under Schedule 3. It should also be noted that the independent human rights of children whose parents are in the UK unlawfully have since been given greater prominence: see *ZH (Tanzania) v Secretary of State for the Home Department*,[138] discussed at para 2.61.

20.235   Some non-EEA nationals whose children are British may have rights to remain in the UK in order to care for their children. These rights are limited and usually the parents cannot receive homelessness assistance or mainstream benefits, including housing benefit. As a result many families are being supported by local authorities under CA 1989 s17, see above at paras 20.147–20.152 and 19.6.

138 [2011] UKSC 4, 4 February 2011.

APPENDIX

Adults seeking support and accommodation from social services

Applying tests under Immigration and Asylum Act 1999 (1999 Act) and Nationality, Immigration and Asylum Act 2002 (2002 Act)

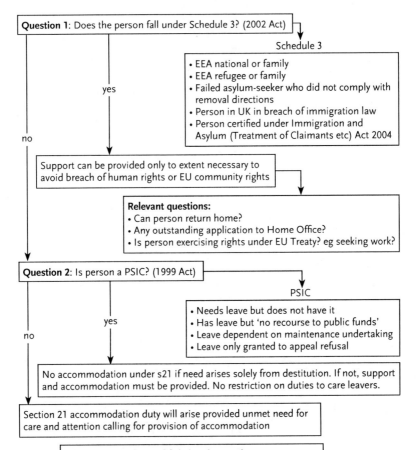

Question 1: Does the person fall under Schedule 3? (2002 Act)

Schedule 3
- EEA national or family
- EEA refugee or family
- Failed asylum-seeker who did not comply with removal directions
- Person in UK in breach of immigration law
- Person certified under Immigration and Asylum (Treatment of Claimants etc) Act 2004

yes

no

Support can be provided only to extent necessary to avoid breach of human rights or EU community rights

Relevant questions:
- Can person return home?
- Any outstanding application to Home Office?
- Is person exercising rights under EU Treaty? eg seeking work?

Question 2: Is person a PSIC? (1999 Act)

PSIC
- Needs leave but does not have it
- Has leave but 'no recourse to public funds'
- Leave dependent on maintenance undertaking
- Leave only granted to appeal refusal

yes

no

No accommodation under s21 if need arises solely from destitution. If not, support and accommodation must be provided. No restriction on duties to care leavers.

Section 21 accommodation duty will arise provided unmet need for care and attention calling for provision of accommodation

NB Asylum-seekers and failed asylum-seekers
Asylum-seekeers do not have leave, so are PSIC
Failed asylum-seekers may be Schedule 3 or PSIC:
- If claimed asylum in-country, will be Schedule 3
- If claimed on entry will be PSIC (unless failed to comply with removal directions, in which case will be Schedule 3)

CHAPTER 21

Housing improvement and adaptation

Key points

- Mandatory grants for home improvements are no longer available. Instead local authorities have a wide discretion as to how assistance is given to improve private sector accommodation. This may include giving grants and loans. Authorities must publish their policies.
- Disabled facilities grants (DFGs) remain mandatory for works costing up to £30,000 in England.
- Discretionary grants may be awarded for costs above this limit.
- Clear statutory provisions, including time limits, apply to local authority decision-making in relation to DFGs. Despite this, many applicants face delays and other difficulties in obtaining grants.
- To qualify for a mandatory grant the works must be for a specified purpose to make the premises more suitable for the disabled person.
- The works must also be 'necessary and appropriate' to achieve the specified purpose and it must be 'reasonable and practicable' to carry out the works in the particular dwelling.
- DFGs are means-tested for adults but not where the disabled occupant is under the age of 19.
- DFGs are administered by local housing authorities.
- Adaptations may also be carried out by social services under the Chronically Sick and Disabled Persons Act 1970.

Housing improvement: grants and assistance

21.1   Until 2002 discretionary and mandatory grants administered by local authorities were available for the improvement of private dwellings. The Regulatory Reform (Housing Assistance) (England & Wales) Order 2002[1] ('2002 Order') replaced the system of discretionary and mandatory grants with a new scheme which gives to local authorities a general power to improve housing.

1   SI No 1860.

21.2   Under the 2002 Order local authorities may, for the purpose of improving living conditions in their area, give financial assistance to enable a person to:[2]

- acquire living accommodation, in or out of the area;
- adapt or improve living accommodation;
- repair living accommodation;
- demolish buildings comprising or including living accommodation; and
- where buildings have been demolished, construct replacement living accommodation.

21.3   The 2002 Order requires every authority to adopt and publish its policy as to how it intends to use these powers for the renewal of the private sector. Most authorities publish their policies on their websites and they are commonly referred to as private sector housing and/or renewal strategies.

Home improvement grants

21.4   A local authority must have a policy about home improvement grants. The policy may be available on the authority's website. If not, a copy should be requested from the authority.

21.5   Under the 2002 Order authorities have a wide discretion as to how to exercise their powers to improve standards in private sector accommodation. It is common for authorities to limit the availability of assistance by providing that grants are available only:

- to vulnerable groups, such as the elderly or disabled;
- for specific works, such as works to improve heating systems and thermal insulation;
- to those on means-tested benefits; and
- to owner-occupiers and not to tenants.

While local authorities have a wide discretion about how much assistance they give to improve and repair private sector homes, they must act lawfully in devising and operating their policies, see paras 2.1–2.25.

---

2 2002 Order art 3(1).

Disabled facilities grants

21.6   The system of grants for disabled adaptations, known as disabled facilities grants (DFGs), is set out in the Housing Grants, Construction and Regeneration Act (HGCRA) 1996 ss19–24.[3] The DFG scheme provides that:

- grants up to a certain level are mandatory provided the necessary conditions are met; and
- decisions and payments must be made within a prescribed time period.

21.7   Despite the clear terms of HGCRA 1996 the administration of DFGs is problematic. This is reflected in the high proportion of Ombudsman complaints about DFGs. This chapter outlines the criteria for DFGs, examines some common problems and describes how decisions may be challenged.

Who can apply for a grant

21.8   An application may be made by:[4]

- an owner (or a person about to become an owner);[5]
- a tenant;[6]
- a licensee;
- an occupier of a houseboat or park home.

Qualifying conditions

21.9   To qualify for a mandatory grant the following conditions must be met (paras 21.10–21.19).

Disabled occupant

21.10 There must be a disabled occupant. This means:[7]

- a person whose sight, hearing or speech is substantially impaired;
- a person who has a mental disorder or impairment of any kind; or

---

3 The Act previously also set out the provisions for home improvement and regeneration grants but those provisions were repealed by the 2002 Order.
4 HGCRA 1996 s19.
5 This includes a landlord applying for the benefit of a disabled tenant.
6 This includes introductory tenants, agricultural occupiers and employees occupying tied accommodation: HGCRA 1996 s9(5).
7 HGCRA 1996 s100.

- a person who is physically substantially disabled by illness, injury or impairment present since birth or otherwise.

21.11 The following are taken as being disabled for the purpose of a DFG:

- any adult for whom social services have made welfare arrangements under section 29(1) of the National Assistance Act (NAA) 1948 or who is registered by the authority as such;[8]
- any child who is, in the opinion of social services, a disabled child as defined in the Children Act (CA) 1989, or who is registered as such.[9]

Only or main home

21.12 The disabled occupant must live in the premises as his or her only or main residence and it must be intended that he or she should do so for at least five years.[10]

Purpose of the works

21.13 The purpose of the works must one or more of the following:[11]

- to facilitate access by the disabled occupant to and from the dwelling or building;
- to make the dwelling or building safe for the disabled occupant and other persons residing with him or her;
- to facilitate access by the disabled occupant to the main family room, or to a bedroom, or to provide such a room;
- to facilitate access by the disabled occupant to a lavatory, a room with a bath or shower or wash-hand basin, or to provide such a room or facilities;
- to facilitate the preparation and cooking of food by the disabled occupant;
- to improve or install a heating system to meet the needs of the disabled occupant;
- to facilitate the use by the disabled occupant of power, light or heat by altering the position of the controls; or
- to facilitate access and movement by the disabled occupant around the dwelling to enable him or her to care for another person who is normally resident and in need of such care.

8 See para 18.14 above.
9 See para 19.4 above.
10 HGCRA 1996 s22(2).
11 HGCRA 1996 s23(1).

21.14　For an applicant to qualify for a mandatory grant the proposed works must be for one of the above purposes. However, a discretionary grant may be awarded to make the dwelling more suitable generally for the disabled occupant.[12]

Need and practicality of works

21.15　The authority must also be satisfied that:[13]

- the proposed works are 'necessary and appropriate' to meet the needs of the disabled occupant; and
- 'it is reasonable and practicable' to carry out the works having regard to the age and condition of the dwelling or building.

21.16　In deciding whether the works are necessary and appropriate the authority must consult social services.[14] Most local authorities will obtain an occupational therapist's report to advise on whether the proposed adaptations will meet the disabled person's needs, increase independence and reduce the requirement for care or support.

21.17　The authority's resources cannot be taken into account in deciding whether the works are necessary or appropriate.[15]

21.18　To decide whether the works are 'reasonable and practicable' the authority will usually rely on an assessment by its own building experts.

21.19　The question of whether the purpose of the works falls into one of the specified categories is separate from the question of whether they are necessary and appropriate to meet the disabled occupant's need.

In *R (B) v Calderdale MBC*[16] the claimant was the father of four children, the eldest of whom (D) was autistic. The family lived in a three-bedroom house owned by a housing association. D shared a bedroom with his younger brother and was uncontrollably aggressive towards him, frightening him while he slept and attacking him when they were in the bedroom together. The claimant applied for a DFG to convert the loft into a separate bedroom for D. The occupational therapy reports obtained suggested that an extra bedroom would be helpful and would enable D to feel safe and to enable his condition to be managed more

12　HGCRA 1996 s23(2).
13　HGCRA 1996 s24(3)(a) and (b).
14　HGCRA 1996 s24(3).
15　*R v Birmingham CC ex p Mohammed* [1999] 1 WLR 33.
16　[2004] EWCA Civ 134, 4 February 2004.

effectively. The authority refused the application, holding that the evidence related to D's behaviour generally rather than the physical layout of the premises or the number of bedrooms. It decided that the works proposed did not fall within the criteria for a mandatory grant and the application was refused. The claimant sought judicial review of the decision.

Initially the application was dismissed: it was held that in deciding whether the purpose of the works was to make 'the dwelling ... safe for the disabled occupant and other persons residing with him' under HGCRA 1996 s23(1)(b), the authority was entitled to take account of the evidence that D's behavioural problems went beyond the issue of the shared bedroom and that his behaviour outside the home had improved. The court held that the decision was within the council's discretion on the basis of the material before it. The claimant appealed.

The Court of Appeal held that the correct approach was to separate the two questions: (1) whether the purpose of the proposed works fell within the criteria for a mandatory grant; and (2) whether the proposed works were necessary and appropriate to meet the needs of the disabled occupant. The council had erred in considering both questions at the same time. On the basis of the facts known to the council the case clearly fell within section 23(1): the purpose of providing a separate bedroom for D was to make the dwelling as safe as was reasonably practicable for D, and, more particularly, for his younger brother. The decision was quashed and it was directed that the council must go on to decide whether a loft conversion was necessary and appropriate to meet D's needs, including the need not to harm his brother. This was a matter for the council's judgment.

The means test

21.20   For disabled adults a financial assessment is carried out to determine eligibility.[17] However, if the disabled occupant is under the age of 19 there is no means test. Certain benefits such as disability living allowance and income support are generally ignored. Savings are taken into account but the first £6,000 is disregarded. The assessment does not take account of actual outgoings but makes standard deductions

---

17 HGCRA 1996 s30.

for items of expenditure, including rent or mortgage payments. The assessment may result in a decision that a contribution is payable. Above a certain level the contribution is 100 per cent.

The maximum grant

21.21　The current maximum mandatory award is £30,000.[18] If a person qualifies for a mandatory grant the authority *must* award a sum up to this amount and has a discretion to award a grant in excess of these limits where the works will cost more than the maximum. The grant may be paid in full on completion or by instalments.[19]

How to apply

21.22　Information on how to apply for a grant should be available on the local authority's website. General information is given on the government website: www.gov.uk/apply-disabled-facilities-grant which provides a link to the relevant part of each local authority's website. Prior to October 2010 there was a prescribed form on which applications were made but each local authority now has its own system for applications. Given the reluctance of many authorities to deal with applications, it can be difficult to make an application and to obtain confirmation that an application has been received. Unless the authority has its own application form, a letter stating clearly that it is an application and accompanied by the relevant documentation should be sufficient. Given the important deadlines that run from the date of the application it will be important to confirm receipt by the authority.

21.23　Applications must be accompanied by the relevant certificates.[20] An owner-occupier who applies must provide an owner's certificate and a tenant who applies must provide a 'tenant's certificate' confirming that it is intended that the disabled occupant will live in the dwelling as his or her only or main residence for at least five years. Unless the authority considers it unreasonable, where a tenant applies, an owner's certificate must also be provided from the landlord confirming his or her interest.

18　Disabled Facilities Grants (Maximum Amounts and Additional Purposes) (England) Order 2008 SI No 1189.
19　HGCRA 1996 s35.
20　HGCRA 1996 ss19 and 22.

Home improvement agencies

21.24   Home improvement agencies (HIAs) assist older and/or disabled homeowners and private sector tenants to remain in their own home, living independently. HIAs advise on improvements and adaptations and help people to apply for grants or loans to carry out works. They also help identify reputable local contractors, oversee works and arrange payments. Many agencies also run schemes to provide handypersons to carry out small repairs or specific schemes to improve safety and security in the home, to improve energy efficiency or make homes suitable for people to return to after a stay in hospital.

21.25   HIAs are usually small, locally based not-for-profit organisations. Some are local authority agencies. Others are independent organisations and are often managed by a housing association or charity.

21.26   'Foundations' is the national co-ordinating body for HIAs in England and provides advice, training and support to HIA staff and managing organisations. A full list of all HIAs in England is contained on the Foundations website: www.foundations.uk.com.

Decisions and time limits

21.27   A local authority must notify an applicant in writing whether the application has been approved or refused as soon as reasonably practicable and, in any event, not later than six months after the date of the application.[21] If the application is approved, the decision letter must specify the works that are eligible for a grant and the amount of grant to be paid. If the application is refused, reasons must be given.[22]

21.28   Delays in dealing with applications are common. If action is to be taken to challenge delay, advisers must ensure that the application has been properly made and supported by the relevant certificates, see para 21.23 above. Authorities 'shall not entertain' an application that is not accompanied by the relevant 'certificates'.[23]

21.29   Payment of the grant should be made no later than 12 months from the date of the application.[24]

---

21   HGCRA 1996 s34(1).
22   HGCRA 1996 s34(4).
23   HGCRA 1996 ss19 and 22.
24   HGCRA 1996 s36.

Common problems

Delays

21.30   Despite the fact that grants are mandatory and that there is a statutory time limit for decision-making, obtaining a DFG is often difficult and delays are common. In practice, it often happens that the delay occurs before a completed application is submitted. The first step in obtaining a DFG will usually to be to request an assessment from social services (see para 18.35). The fact that authorities must carry out a means assessment and must take advice from social services and building experts about the proposed works means that decisions are rarely made within the six-month time limit.

21.31   Research conducted in 2005 by Bristol University revealed that the average delay before an occupational therapist assessment was completed in relation to a DFG was almost 20 weeks.[25] Further delays in the drawing up of plans, the obtaining of planning permission and building regulation approval are also common. The fact that applicants may have to fund part of the cost may also add to the delay if the funds must be raised by the household.

Funding

21.32   Central government funding for DFGs does not meet the full cost to local authorities, which means that many local authorities struggle to find the funding to meet their part of the costs. Furthermore, funding for adaptations for those occupying local authority owned accommodation is not available from the central government grant but must be paid for from the authority's housing budget. Most local authorities therefore do not actively encourage applications.

Limits on maximum grant

21.33   The maximum mandatory grant of £30,000 may be insufficient to pay for substantial adaptations, such as an extension to a dwelling, which may be required for those with the most severe disabilities.

---

25 See *Reviewing the Disabled Facilities Grant Programme*, Bristol University, 2005. See also the more recent report Disabled Facilities Grants in England: a research report, by Astral Advisory in 2013, commissioned by the District Councils Network.

Private sector tenants – lack of security

21.34 Given that most private sector tenants have security of tenure for only the first six months of a tenancy, it will be difficult to establish that the disabled occupier intends to remain in the accommodation for at least five years. Moreover, a private landlord may be unwilling to consent to adaptations. A landlord does, however, have an obligation to make reasonable adjustments to premises, see para 7.196.

Chronically Sick and Disabled Persons Act 1970

21.35 The Chronically Sick and Disabled Persons Act (CSDPA) 1970 lists a range of services that a local social services authority may be under a duty to provide in relation to a disabled person. The duty applies to both disabled adults and children. At the time of writing the CSDPA is in force but will be repealed by the CA 2014, most likely in the early part of 2015.

21.36 For the duty to arise the following conditions must be satisfied:

- the person must be disabled;[26]
- the person must be ordinarily resident in the area of the local authority; and
- the authority must be satisfied that it is necessary to make the arrangements to meet the person's needs.

21.37 Included in the list of services that may be provided under CSDPA 1970 to meet a disabled persons needs is:

> ... the provision of assistance for that person in arranging for the carrying out of any works of adaptation in his home or the provision of any additional facilities designed to secure his greater safety, comfort or convenience.[27]

21.38 Where an assessment of the needs of a disabled adult or child reveals a need for services under CSDPA 1970, the authority is under a duty to provide those services. An authority's duty to carry out assessments is described at paras 18.35 and 19.16.

21.39 A social services authority may discharge the duty to 'assist' a disabled person in arranging for the carrying out of works of adaptation

---

26 This means persons who are blind, deaf or dumb or who suffer from mental disorder of any description or who are substantially and permanently handicapped by illness, injury or congenital deformity. See NAA 1948 s29 and CA 1989 s17(1).

27 CSDPA 1970 s2(1)(e).

by assisting the person to apply for a DFG. However, there may be a delay in the application process, the application may be refused, or the DFG may not cover all of the necessary works. If this is the case, if the social services authority is satisfied that the works are necessary to meet the disabled person's needs, it is under a duty to provide the services. See the Ombudsman complaint summarised at para 21.49 below.

21.40   Minor adaptations that cost less than £1,000 should be provided free of charge.[28] In practice many local authority social services departments provide adaptations themselves if they cost less than £1,000 and provide assistance to apply for a DFG if the cost is likely to exceed this amount.

21.41   If services described in the CSDPA 1970 are provided by an authority for a disabled child, it is not open to the authority to maintain that the services are provided instead under the Children Act 1989.[29] The distinction is important since the courts have held that the duty to provide services under CSDPA 1970 is a specific enforceable duty but that the duty under CA 1989 s17 is a 'target duty': see para 19.9.

Means testing

21.42   There is no provision for local authorities to charge people for services provided under CSDPA 1970. However, it is not possible to avoid the means testing scheme under the DFG system by requesting that adaptations are carried out instead under the CSDPA 1970.

> In *R (Spink) v Wandsworth LBC*[30] it was held by the Court of Appeal that a local authority could decide that it was not satisfied that it was necessary to provide services for a disabled child under the CSDPA 1970 until it had been shown that, having regard to the parent's means, it was not reasonable for the parents to provide them.

21.43   Means testing does not now apply to adaptations for disabled children but the same principle will apply in relation to adaptations for adults.

---

28 See the Community Care (Delayed Discharges etc) Act 2003 s15 and the Community Care (Delayed Discharges etc) Act (Qualifying Services)(England) Regulations 2003 SI No 1196.

29 *R v Bexley LBC ex p B* (2000) 3 CCLR 15, QBD.

30 [2005] EWCA Civ 302, 18 March 2005.

Provision of equipment

21.44 In addition to adaptations, CSDPA 1970 s2 also provides for the provision of 'additional facilities' designed to secure the disabled person's 'greater safety, comfort or convenience'. Such facilities may include handrails, alarm systems and moveable baths.

Challenging decisions

21.45 Local authority decision-making is challenged principally by:

- judicial review proceedings; and
- formal complaints.

21.46 Both courses of action are described in more detail in chapter 2. The merits of judicial review and complaints in relation to social services are discussed at para 18.52.

21.47 One of the main causes of complaint in the administration of DFGs is delay. Some delay may be caused by the need for housing authorities to consult with social services, usually occupational therapists and building experts. Further delays may be caused by the need to obtain planning consent and building regulation approval for major works. However, the lack of funding for DFGs means that many authorities are reluctant to approve applications and several published Ombudsman investigations criticise local authority procedures for dealing with DFGs. However, the complaints procedure is itself very slow, and an application for judicial review may be appropriate where a completed application has been made and the authority is delaying making a decision. Authorities should be reminded of the statutory time limits for decisions and payment and the duty to give reasons if an application is refused.

Judicial review

21.48 A claim for judicial review may be brought against an authority to:

- compel the authority to make a decision;
- give reasons for a negative decision; or
- challenge a refusal to award a grant, where it appears that the authority has applied the law wrongly.[31]

---

31 As in *R (B) v Calderdale MBC*, see para 21.21 above.

Local Government Ombudsman complaints

21.49   The following are examples of successful Ombudsman complaints concerning adaptations.

> *Ombudsman Complaint: 03/A/08718*
> The complaint was about the authority delaying making a decision, referring to possible start dates for works without informing the applicant that the authority might not fund the cost of works above £25,000 and deciding not to exercise its discretion to fund works above the mandatory limit without giving reasons. Following an appeal the authority decided to offer a final grant of £35,000 but this was three years after the applicant first applied for help and by then he had decided he could not afford to pay the non-funded costs and that he would move instead.
>
> The Ombudsman found that there had been maladministration because of the council's failure to advise the applicant about the policy on grants for extensions; to ensure adequate liaison between officers in processing the application; and to record reasons for the decision or to inform the applicant of the reasons.
>
> The Ombudsman recommended that the council should pay compensation of £2,000 because the applicant had spent two years longer than necessary in unsuitable accommodation; a £500 contribution to moving costs; and £150 for the applicant's time and trouble pursuing the complaint.

> *Ombudsman Complaint: 05/C/13157*
> A complaint was made by the husband of a woman who was seriously ill and profoundly disabled about the handling of a DFG application.
>
> The Ombudsman found that the council had delayed in completing a financial assessment; had failed to review the grant section's position that a DFG could not be used to provide or retain a family room (which was wrong in law) and had failed to deal with the conflict between what was thought necessary by both the occupational therapist and the woman's husband, and what the grants section would fund. The council also failed to recognise its duties under CSDPA 1970 s2. As a result, for two years longer than necessary, the woman was confined to bed in the front living room

and was unable to use a special wheelchair provided to relieve her pain and discomfort. She was unable to use a toilet, bath or shower and had to be stri- washed by her carers. She was also unable to sit outside or with her family.

To remedy the injustice, the council agreed to pay £6,605 to the complainant; to establish a mechanism to resolve disputes about the adaptations required to meet a disabled person's needs; to ensure that all relevant officers were aware of the duty under CSDPA 1970 s2; and to produce a report about the lessons to be learnt from the complainant's experience and the changes it would make to its practice and procedures. Alternative accommodation was also identified which would be adapted to meet the woman's needs.

Civil proceedings

continued

Key points

- Most housing disputes are resolved in the civil courts, predominantly the County Court. However, some housing disputes, including disputes about benefits and long leases, are dealt with by tribunals.
- The civil courts deal mainly with disputes between individuals, eg between a landlord and tenant. This includes disrepair and claims for possession.
- The civil courts also deal with challenges to the decisions of public bodies, including local authorities and government departments. Homeless appeals are dealt with by the County Court and many housing decisions by public bodies can be challenged by judicial review in the High Court.
- A single set of procedural rules applies in both the County Court and the High Court: the Civil Procedure Rules (CPR).
- Fees must be paid to the court for starting a claim and at certain stages as the claim progresses.
- Until April 2013 legal aid was available for most housing cases in the civil courts, but not for tribunal cases. Legal aid is now only available for certain types of housing case.
- The general rule in the civil courts is that the losing party will be ordered to pay the legal costs of the winning party. However, legal aid provides a party with 'costs protection' which means that he or she does not usually have to pay the opponent's costs.
- The court controls the amount of legal costs the losing party has to pay to the winning party. In some cases the costs recoverable are fixed or capped.
- After the court makes an order, the successful party may have to take further action to enforce the order.

The civil courts

22.1   The civil courts resolve disputes between individual legal persons (which may include a company or a public body such as a local authority). In contrast, the criminal courts deal mostly with the prosecution by the state of individuals accused of committing criminal offences.

22.2   The civil courts comprise the County Court and the High Court. The civil division of the Court of Appeal hears appeals from the County Court and the High Court. Appendix 1 to this chapter contains a diagram of the relationship between the various civil courts.

22.3   Housing litigation forms a substantial part of the business of the County Court. It includes:

- possession proceedings;
- claims about a landlord's failure to repair premises;
- claims about unlawful eviction and harassment;
- homeless appeals;
- other disputes between landlords and tenants, eg disputes about the rights of secure tenants and the recovery of deposits. The County Court can make declarations, for example, about an occupier's status or the type of tenancy that has been granted if this is in dispute;
- applications for injunctions brought by local authorities and other social landlords to restrain anti-social behaviour.

22.4   Possession claims must usually be made in the County Court. They can be made in any County Court hearing centre. However, if this is not the County Court hearing centre local to the premises the case will be sent to the local hearing centre. It is generally best to make the claim in the local hearing centre to avoid any delay. Most claims for just money must be started in the 'County Court Money Claims Centre' based in Salford.[1]

22.5   High value claims or claims that are complex may be brought in the High Court. Also, the High Court has exclusive jurisdiction for certain kinds of proceedings, including judicial review.

Organisation of the County Court

Judges

22.6   The County Court has two types of judge: district judges and circuit judges. There are also deputy district judges, who are usually lawyers who work part time as judges. District judges deal with most of the housing cases in the County Court, including claims for possession. However, some housing cases can only be dealt with by a circuit judge. These include homeless appeals and most applications for committal for breach of injunctions.[2] Most long trials (more than one day) are

---

1 PO Box 527, Salford, Greater Manchester, M5 0BY.
2 See CPR Part 2, PD.

heard by circuit judges. Circuit judges also deal with most appeals of decisions made by district judges. An appeal from the decision of a deputy district judge can be heard by a district judge.

Court staff

22.7   Much of the work of the County Court is done by the court office staff. This includes issuing claims and bailiffs' warrants, arranging hearings and the drawing up of orders. Most courts have different sections dealing with different stages of litigation, for example, issuing, listing and enforcement. When a claim is issued it is given a court reference number (the 'claim number') which is endorsed on all court documents. This must be quoted in all communications with the court.

Causes of action

22.8   To bring a claim in a civil court a claimant must have a recognised legal claim, known as a 'cause of action'. Furthermore, the claimant must be seeking some 'remedy' that the court is capable of granting, see paras 22.22–22.26.

22.9   Strictly speaking the term 'cause of action' means the facts out of which the right to bring a legal action arises. However, the term is generally used to refer to a claim which is recognised in law as giving a person a right to sue.

22.10   In relation to housing litigation the most relevant causes of action are set out below at paras 22.11–22.21.

Breach of contract

22.11   A party to a contract has a legal right to compel the other party to comply with the contract and/or to be compensated if the contract is breached. The cause of action in such a claim is 'breach of contract'. In housing cases this includes:

- tenants seeking compensation for disrepair and/or an order that a landlord carries out repairs;
- tenants seeking compensation for unlawful eviction and harassment and/or an order that the landlord allows them back into occupation and refrains from further harassment.

22.12   A landlord who claims that a tenant is in breach of the tenancy agreement could also seek compensation and/or an order restraining further breach. However, most landlords will instead claim possession since one of the statutory grounds for possession order is that the tenant has breached the tenancy agreement.

Tort

22.13 Tort means a civil wrong which is independent of a contract. Tort is based on the principle that in certain situations a person has a duty to ensure that his or her actions do not cause harm or loss to another person. Some torts are 'common law' torts, recognised by the courts in previously decided cases. Other torts are 'statutory' torts set out in legislation. The torts which will commonly be alleged in housing cases are:

Common law torts

22.14 Nuisance and negligence are common law torts that often relied on in cases involving harassment, unlawful eviction and disrepair.

Statutory torts

22.15 The Housing Act (HA) 1988 sets out the statutory tort of unlawful eviction for which damages are payable, calculated according to a statutory formula.

22.16 The Protection from Harassment Act 1997 created the statutory tort of harassment where someone is guilty of a course of conduct that causes another person alarm or distress.

22.17 In disrepair claims, the statutory torts set out in the Defective Premises Act 1972 and the Occupiers' Liability Acts 1957 and 1984 may be relevant.

22.18 All of these torts are discussed in more detail in chapters 8 and 10.

Claims for possession

22.19 Claims for possession make up a large part of the work of the County Court. The 'cause of action' is the right to possession, which may be established on the basis that the tenant's right to occupy has ended or because one of the statutory grounds for possession is made out. Claims for possession are dealt with in detail in chapters 6 and 7.

Homelessness appeals

22.20 The jurisdiction of the County Court to hear appeals about homelessness decisions is entirely statutory and is set out in the Housing Act 1996. The provisions are described in chapter 15.

22.21   The court's role in such cases is not the same as in most County Court litigation because homeless decisions are administrative decisions made by a public body. Traditionally such decisions have been scrutinised by the High Court in judicial review proceedings. The volume of judicial reviews about homelessness decision-making during the 1980s and 1990s, however, led to the transfer of such cases to the County Court. Homelessness appeals can only be heard by circuit judges who, in this role, are applying judicial review principles. This means that the court is examining the lawfulness of the decision rather than considering the merits of the decision. The principles of judicial review are explained in more detail in chapter 2.

Remedies

22.22   A remedy is what a person is asking the court to order. This is different from the cause of action, which is the legal basis for the claim, see paras 22.8–22.9 above.

22.23   In a claim based on tort or breach of contract the claimant will usually be seeking one or more of the following remedies:

•   damages (compensation); and/or
•   an injunction (an order that a person does or refrains from doing something) or an order of specific performance (an order that a person must perform the obligations under a contract).

22.24   It is also possible to ask the court to make a declaration of a person's rights, for example, whether or not he or she is a tenant or the nature of the tenancy.

22.25   In a claim for possession, the claimant will be asking the court to make a possession order. This will give the claimant the right to take possession but, unless the defendant gives up possession voluntarily, the order must be enforced by court bailiffs. A social landlord may now also ask the court to make a demotion order in relation to a tenancy. The effect of this is to reduce the tenant's security of tenure, see chapters 6 and 7. If there are arrears of rent a landlord will usually also ask for a money judgment.

22.26   In a homelessness appeal the claimant will be asking the court to make an order quashing (cancelling) the local authority's decision or varying the decision to a positive one.

The parties

22.27 In a civil claim the person bringing the claim is usually called the claimant and the person against whom the claim is brought is the defendant. A defendant may, at the same time as defending a claim, bring a counterclaim against a claimant.

22.28 In some kinds of cases the parties are instead known as the applicant and the respondent, for example, in applications for injunctions and committals.

22.29 In homelessness appeals the parties are referred to as the appellant and the respondent. The same terms are used in any appeal against an order made by a court.

Civil Procedure Rules

22.30 The Civil Procedure Rules 1998 (CPR) set out a code for the conduct of all civil claims and apply in the County Court and in the High Court.[3] The CPR can be accessed online at the Department of Justice website: www.justice.gov.uk. Most of the commonly used forms can be downloaded from the same site.

22.31 Each part of the CPR deals with a specific aspect of procedure or type of claim and contains the relevant rules. Most parts have a practice direction (PD) setting out the more practical requirements.

Pre-action protocols

22.32 The CPR were designed to promote early exchange of information and to encourage the parties to settle disputes so as to avoid litigation. This is reflected in the use of pre-action protocols. These set out the steps the parties should take before proceedings are started in particular kinds of cases. The following pre-action protocols are relevant to housing cases:

- Pre-Action Protocol for Possession Claims based on Rent Arrears;
- Pre-Action Protocol for Possession Claims based on Mortgage Arrears;
- Pre-Action Protocol for Housing Disrepair Claims;
- Pre-Action Protocol for Judicial Review Claims.

3 Previously, different rules applied in the county courts and in the High Court. Very few of these rules are still in force. They are known as the Rules of the Supreme Court (RSC) and the County Court Rules (CCR).

Where a specific protocol does not apply to a case then the more general Practice Direction on Pre-Action Conduct will apply.

22.33   The pre-action protocols for rent and mortgage arrears, disrepair and judicial review are described in chapters 6, 10 and 2 respectively.

The overriding objective

22.35   The CPR were introduced following a comprehensive review of civil procedure conducted by Lord Woolf in 1996. The aims of the review were:

- to improve access to justice and reduce the cost of litigation;
- to reduce the complexity of the rules and modernise terminology; and
- to remove unnecessary distinctions of practice and procedure.

A review of the costs of civil litigation in 2009[4] led to amendments to stress the importance of dealing with cases at proportionate cost.

22.36   These objectives are reflected in CPR 1.1, which is headed 'the overriding objective':

> (1) These rules are a new procedural code with the overrriding objective of enabling the court to deal with cases justly and at proportionate cost.
> (2) Dealing with a case justly and at proportionate cost includes, so far as is practicable:
>   (a) ensuring that the parties are on an equal footing;
>   (b) saving expense;
>   (c) dealing with the case in ways which are proportionate:
>   (i)   to the amount of money involved;
>   (ii) to the importance of the case;
>   (iii) to the complexity of the issues; and
>   (iv) to the financial position of each party;
>   (d) ensuring that it is dealt with expeditiously and fairly; and
>   (e) allotting to it an appropriate share of the court's resources, while taking into account the need to allot resources to other cases; and
>   (f) enforcing compliance with rules, practice directions and orders.

22.37   The CPR also provide that the court must seek to give effect to the overriding objective when exercising its powers and interpreting rules and the parties must help the court to further the overriding objective.

---

4   See: Review of Civil Litigation Costs: Final Report, December 2009, available online from: www.judiciary.gov.uk.

Active case management

22.38 The court has a duty to further the overriding objective by actively managing cases. This includes:[5]

- encouraging the parties to co-operate in the conduct of proceedings;
- identifying issues at an early stage;
- encouraging the parties to use an alternative dispute resolution procedure;
- helping the parties to settle the whole or part of the case;
- dealing with the case without the parties attending court;
- making use of technology; and
- giving directions to ensure that the case proceeds to trial quickly.

22.39 The ability of judges to do this is limited by the fact that judges rarely have the time to exercise any management of cases other than when considering applications made by the parties. However, under the CPR judges do take a more active role in managing cases and are less likely than previously to allow adjournments and extensions of time, even if both parties are in agreement. Judges also take an active part in case management conferences to help clarify the issues and to expedite resolution.

The usual steps in a civil claim

Claims other than possession claims

22.40 Most claims are brought under CPR Part 7 and, if defended, may involve the following stages:

- pre-action correspondence;
- issuing the claim;
- filing a reply/defence;
- track allocation and case management directions;
- parties complying with case management directions;
- off-record negotiations to settle the claim;
- hearing/final order;
- enforcement – if the defendant fails to comply with order.

22.41 CPR Part 8 provides an alternative procedure and is described below at para 22.104.

---

5 CPR 1.4.

Pre-action correspondence

22.42   The CPR encourage early settlement and the narrowing of the issues between the parties. Under the protocols and the Practice Direction on Pre-Action Conduct the parties are expected to act reasonably in exchanging information and documents relevant to the claim and generally try to avoid the need for proceedings to be issued.[6]

22.43   Even before the introduction of the CPR, a party was expected to send a 'letter before claim/action' to the proposed defendant setting out the basis of the claim and inviting the defendant's proposals to settle the claim.

22.44   If a claim is issued without sending a letter before claim and following the relevant protocol or Practice Direction on Pre-Action Conduct, the claimant may be unable to recover costs even if the claim succeeds.

22.45   Under the protocols and Practice Direction, the defendant is obliged to respond to the claimant's pre-action protocol letter, disclosing relevant documents, indicating whether the claim is admitted and, if so, making an offer to settle. Where a defendant fails to comply, the sanction may be that costs are awarded to the claimant on a more generous basis than usual.

Issuing the claim

22.46   To issue a claim, the claimant must draft the relevant papers (usually a claim form and particulars of claim) and send them to the court with enough copies for each defendant together with the fee. The claim is issued when the court endorses the court seal. The papers are then posted by the court to the defendant(s).

Claim form and particulars of claim

22.47   The claim form is a court form (which can be downloaded) and is completed by the claimant.[7] In a simple case, the particulars of claim may be entered on the claim form. In more complicated cases the particulars of claim will be a separate document. The particulars of claim should be a concise statement of the facts on which the claimant relies.[8] Both documents must be endorsed with a 'statement of truth' confirming that the contents are true to the best of the

---

6   PD para 4.1.
7   Under CPR Part 7 this is form N1.
8   CPR Part 16 deals with the content of claims forms and particulars of claim.

claimant's knowledge.[9] The form of the statement of truth signed by a party is:[10]

> I believe that the facts stated in this [claim form/particulars of claim] are true.

22.48 A statement of truth may be signed by a legal representative, in which case the representative must ensure that the party believes the contents to be true and advise him or her of the consequences if this is not the case. Where someone signs a statement of truth without an honest belief that the contents of the document are true, contempt of court proceedings may be brought.[11]

22.49 If the statement of truth is signed by a legal representative the form is:

> The claimant believes that the facts stated in this [claim form/particulars of claim] are true.

22.50 If the particulars of claim are not verified by a statement of truth, it will stand as a summary of the claim but cannot be used as evidence. Furthermore, the court has the power to strike it out.[12] The court could, however, adjourn proceedings to permit a party to verify the document with a statement of truth. If this means that the other party incurs unnecessary costs, the party in default will usually be ordered to pay those costs, regardless of the outcome of the claim, see para 22.150 below.

22.51 The court sends the papers to the defendant with a 'response pack' and notes as to how the defendant should respond.

Fees

22.52 Fees are paid to the court when issuing a claim, and for the hearing. Fees are also payable when making applications to the court. On issue, the fee will depend on the value of the claim. For most applications there is a set fee. Fees are usually increased each year and the most common fees are listed in the leaflet EX50, which can be downloaded from the website: www.justice.gov.uk. A full list of fees can be found in the relevant statutory instrument, a link to which is also on the website. The fees for issuing civil claims were increased by the Civil Proceedings and Family Proceedings Fees (Amendment)

---

9 CPR Part 22 deals with statements of truth.
10 CPR Part 22, PD para 2.1.
11 CPR 32.14.
12 CPR 22.2.

Order 2015[13] which came into force on 9 March 2015. As from that date if the claim is for more than £10,000 the fee is 5 per cent of the value of the claim. This means that the fee for a claim for £20,000 increases from £610 to £1,000 but the fee for a claim for £200,000 increases from £1,315 to £10,000.

Fee exemption

22.53   Claimants on a low income can apply to the court for fee exemption. Most people on 'passporting' benefits will be entitled to fee remission. The fee exemption form (EX150) can be downloaded from the Courts and Tribunals Service website alongside the (currently 31-page) guidance for completing the form. The same form is used to apply for a refund of fees already paid – this must be done within two months.

22.54   Fee exemption does not apply if a party is formally represented by solicitors, ie the solicitors are on the court record as acting for the party. The solicitors pay any court fees. If the party has legal aid these are reimbursed by the Legal Aid Agency (see below at para 22.162).

Filing a reply/defence

22.55   The usual rule is that the defendant has 14 days from the 'date of service' of the particulars of claim to file a defence.[14] However, if the defendant files an acknowledgement of service, the period is extended to 28 days. In most cases the documents will be posted by the court to the defendant and the date of service is deemed to be the second business day after posting. If the documents are delivered to the defendant's address the date of service is, nevertheless, also deemed to be the second business day after delivery.[15]

22.56   The response pack sent to the defendant includes forms for the defendant to complete: admitting the claim, admitting part of the claim or disputing the claim. If the claim is defended it is sufficient to complete the defence form indicating the reasons. However, a defendant may instead file a defence as a separate document. In either case, the defence should deal with each allegation, stating whether it is admitted or denied. If an allegation is denied and the defendant

---

13   SI No 576.
14   'Filing' is when documents are sent or delivered to the court, 'serving' is when they are sent or delivered to another party. A direction to 'file and serve' simply means to send it to the court and the other parties.
15   CPR 6.14.

intends to put forward a different version of events, this should be set out in the defence.[16] If the defence fails to deal with a particular allegation, that allegation will be treated as admitted, unless the defendant has set out the nature of his or her case relevant to the allegation. The form of defence must also be endorsed with a statement of truth and signed by the defendant or the defendant's representative.

22.57   There is no fee for the filing of a defence. However, if the defendant wishes to make a counterclaim a CPR Part 20 claim form must be completed[17] and the same fee will be payable as if it were a claim.

Track allocation

22.58   If the claim is defended the case will be allocated to one of three tracks. On receipt of the defence a court officer will provisionally allocate to the appropriate track. The three tracks are:

- the small claims track;
- the fast track; or
- the multi-track.

22.59   Allocation depends mainly on the value of the claim but other factors such as complexity and the nature of the evidence are also taken into consideration. The small claims track is described in more detail below at paras 22.95–22.103.

Case management directions

22.60   Case management directions set out the steps each party must take before the final hearing. In small claims simple standard case management directions are usually made. For fast track and multi-track cases the parties are expected to agree the appropriate directions and specimen directions for different kinds of cases can be found on the www.justice.gov.uk website. Standard directions for disrepair claims are included.

22.61   Case management directions generally require disclosure by each party of the relevant documents they have (or have had) in their possession and the evidence on which they will rely. This is to encourage the settlement of claims by ensuring that the parties can assess the relative merits of each other's case before the final hearing.

---

16 See CPR 16.5.
17 Form N211.

Disclosure of documents

22.62   Unless the claim is allocated to the small claims track, the parties must disclose *all* relevant documents, including those that are unhelpful to the party's case. Certain documents are excluded from disclosure because they are 'privileged'. This includes documents and correspondence relating to the legal advice given to the party. It also includes documents created for the purpose of the proceedings, eg draft statements and expert reports that the party does not intend to rely on.

Disclosure of evidence relied on

Factual witnesses

22.63   In most cases outside the small track the parties must exchange written statements for all the witnesses they intend to call to give evidence. The statements are a summary of what the witness will say in court. At a final hearing the evidence will usually be given orally by witnesses. However, the parties may agree that certain uncontentious statements can be used as evidence and that the witness need not attend. Also, one party can serve notice on the other party that he or she intends to rely on hearsay evidence.[18] The other party can apply to the court for permission to call the witness so that he or she can be cross-examined. However, if the party on whom the notice is served does not object, the hearsay evidence can be used at the hearing. Hearsay evidence, however, will not have as much weight as direct evidence.

Expert witnesses

22.64   In some cases the parties rely on the opinion of experts such as doctors or surveyors. Expert evidence is different from that of witnesses of fact: expert witnesses' evidence may include a professional opinion. For example, a surveyor may express an opinion about the cause of dampness in a dwelling and a doctor may express an opinion about the effect of dampness on a person's health. The expert's duty is always to the court, not to any party instructing them. The CPR strongly encourage the use of single joint experts (SJEs). This means a single expert instructed by both parties. If, instead, each

---

18   'Hearsay' means second-hand evidence. It includes a written statement if the maker of the statement is not present in court. It also includes one person's evidence about what another person has told him or her, if the evidence is given to prove that what the other person said was true: see Civil Evidence Act 1995 s1(2)(a). See also CPR Part 33.

party instructs a different expert, written reports must be disclosed in advance of the final hearing. The case management directions may order the experts to prepare a joint statement setting out what is agreed and what is at issue. If the experts do not agree on an issue they should attend court to give oral evidence. The use of expert witnesses is discussed in more detail in chapter 10. Expert evidence may be used only if the court gives permission.

Interim applications and hearings

22.65   As the proceedings progress, the parties may be in dispute about procedural issues or may want to apply to the court for remedies available prior to the final hearing (eg injunctions). Examples of procedural disputes would be where one party claims that another party has documents that should be disclosed or where one party wants to use a type of expert evidence and the other party does not agree that it is necessary. An interim remedy would include an application for an interim, or temporary (as opposed to a final) injunction or an application for an interim payment of damages.

22.66   Unless the parties reach agreement such issues will be resolved by one party making an application to the court. The issue will be listed for a short hearing before a district judge (simple hearings can be arranged as telephone conferences). Some applications for interim injunctions have to be made to a circuit judge. Evidence is required in support of any interim application and this will be in the form of written statements or affidavits.

22.67   The party who succeeds in making or resisting an interim application will usually be awarded the costs of the application regardless of the final outcome of the claim (see para 22.125).

Settlement

22.68   One of the central aims of the CPR is to encourage settlement by ensuring that issues are clarified and evidence disclosed early. CPR Part 36 sets out a procedure that can be followed when attempting to settle claims. If this procedure is followed, certain consequences regarding the costs of the proceedings will usually apply automatically.

CPR Part 36 offers

22.69   CPR Part 36 encourages settlement by providing that penalties apply if a party refuses an offer to settle but subsequently fails to obtain a better outcome than under the proposed settlement.

22.70   A Part 36 offer must be made in writing, state that it is made under CPR Part 36, and the period during which, if accepted, the defendant will be liable for the claimant's legal costs. This must be at least 21 days, unless there are fewer than 21 days before the trial.

22.71   Either a defendant or a claimant can make a Part 36 offer. If the offer to settle is accepted within 21 days, this will conclude the matter and the defendant will be liable for all of the claimant's costs (subject to assessment by the court, see para 22.143 below). The offer can be accepted later, but the person who accepts late will pay the other side's costs for the period of delay, unless the parties agree otherwise.

22.72   If a defendant's offer is refused by the claimant and the claimant fails to obtain more in damages at trial (or if a non-monetary remedy is sought, fails to obtain a judgment 'more advantageous'),[19] the defendant will be liable for the claimant's costs up to the end of the period specified in the Part 36 offer (usually 21 days). The claimant will be responsible for the defendant's costs, plus interest, from that date until the claim is decided by the court. As a large proportion of the costs of any case are incurred in preparation for and at trial, the claimant's costs liability may exceed the amount the defendant has to pay in damages and costs.

22.73   If a claimant's offer is refused by the defendant and the claimant goes on to recover the same or more in damages, or obtains a judgment 'at least as advantageous',[20] the defendant will be liable for all of the claimant's costs plus interest. In addition, the court will usually order that the costs are assessed on a basis that is more generous to the claimant and can order that additional interest is paid on any damages and that an extra 10 per cent damages (or costs) are paid.

Settlement outside Part 36

22.74   Offers to settle proceedings may be made outside the Part 36 procedure. A party can make an offer in whatever way he or she chooses but if it is not in accordance with Part 36, the costs consequences

19 CPR 36.14(1)(a).
20 CPR 36.14(1)(b).

referred to above (paras 22.72–22.73) will not automatically apply.[21] The court will nevertheless always take account of the parties' attempts to settle when exercising its discretion in relation to costs.

'Without prejudice' communications

22.75 Whenever a party wishes to communicate an offer to settle a claim, any correspondence setting out or referring to the proposals should be marked 'Without prejudice save as to costs'. This means that the correspondence will not be disclosed to the court until after the claim has been decided; settlement proposals are relevant to the issue of costs only. The most important points in relation to without prejudice communications are:

- Only genuine offers to compromise a claim should be marked 'without prejudice'.
- Offers to compromise may be treated as without prejudice even if not marked as such. However, this would require the agreement of the other party or a decision by the court.
- If a party refers to without prejudice communications at trial the judge may decide that the hearing must be abandoned and heard by a different judge. The party who has revealed the without prejudice communication may be ordered to pay the costs that have been wasted as a result (see para 22.150 below).
- Without prejudice discussions may take place by telephone (or sometimes at court). Both parties must agree that the discussion is on a without prejudice basis.
- Once agreement has been reached, the confirmation of the terms of that agreement should be confirmed in 'open' correspondence (ie not marked 'without prejudice'). Usually the terms of the agreement will be incorporated into a 'consent order' (see para 22.88 and appendix 2 to this chapter).

The hearing/final order

22.76 Unless the parties reach agreement, the claim will be listed for a hearing. The claimant will usually be responsible for preparing a 'trial bundle' which comprises copies of all the relevant documents. The trial bundle will include: the statements of case (ie, claim, defence and any reply or counterclaim); the statements of the witnesses who

---

21 CPR 36.1(2).

will give evidence; expert reports; and all other relevant documents. Copies of the bundle will be provided for the court and the other party or parties. Further copies should be available for the witnesses to refer to when giving evidence. The bundle should be organised chronologically and paginated for ease of reference.

The final hearing

22.77 Despite a move towards the use of written evidence at a final hearing, most evidence will be given orally, ie by witnesses who attend court and answer questions put by the parties' lawyers (or the parties, if unrepresented) and the judge. The format of a formal trial is as follows:

Claimant opens

22.78 This will be a brief summary of the issues and the evidence, including the documents in the trial bundle.

Claimant calls evidence

22.79 All the witnesses (usually starting with the claimant) will be questioned, first by the claimant's lawyer and then by the defendant's lawyer (cross-examination). To save time the witness may be asked to confirm that the witness statement in the trial bundle is true and then questioned only on certain issues by his or her legal representative. The defendant's lawyer must challenge any evidence that is at issue. The claimant's lawyer has the chance to 're-examine' only to clarify anything raised in cross examination. The judge may also ask questions of the witnesses.

Defendant calls evidence

22.80 The defendant's witnesses will be questioned in the same way, starting with questions from the defendant's lawyer.

Defendant closes

22.81 The defendant's lawyer makes a closing speech. This is a summary of the defendant's case and submissions as to why the court should find for the defendant.

Claimant closes

22.82 The claimant's lawyer also makes a closing speech.

Burden and standard of proof

22.83 In civil cases the claimant must prove the case 'on balance of probabilities', which means that the claimant is more likely to be right
than the defendant; this is the 'standard of proof'. The claimant has
the 'burden of proof', ie if the judge cannot decide between the parties, the claim will fail: the claimant will have failed to satisfy the
judge on balance of probabilities.

Decision/order

22.84 In most County Court cases the judge will give judgment immediately, indicating whether the claimant has proved the case and, if
so, assessing the amount of damages and/or deciding the terms of
the order, and dealing with the issue of costs. The judge will also
give reasons for his or her decision. This enables the parties to know
whether there are grounds to appeal the decision. In complex cases
the judge may 'reserve' judgment until a later date.

Rights of audience

22.85 The term 'rights of audience' refers to the right to represent a party
at a hearing. The following people have the right to represent a party
in County Court proceedings:

- qualified solicitors and barristers;
- in local authority possession proceedings before a district judge:
  any person authorised by the local authority;[22]
- authorised employees of housing management organisations in
  relation to certain proceedings brought on behalf of local housing authorities before a district judge (possession claims on nuisance grounds, demotion claims and certain anti-social behaviour
  claims) and possession;[23]
- solicitors' employees only at a hearing 'in chambers' (the judge's
  room): in practice this means small claims hearings and interim
  procedural hearings. It does not include possession proceedings
  even though these are usually now heard in private;[24]

22 County Courts Act 1984 s60.
23 County Courts Act 1984 s60A, inserted by Legal Services Act 2007 s191.
24 Prior to the CPR there was a distinction between hearings in chambers and
hearings in open court. Under the CPR the distinction is between hearings in
private and hearings in public. However, the rules regarding rights of audience
still refer to hearings in chambers: Courts and Legal Services Act 1990
s27(1)(e).

- legal executives[25] who have the same rights of audience as any person employed by a solicitor but, in addition, may appear in open court on unopposed applications for adjournments and applications for consent orders;
- authorised employees of a company that is party to the proceedings;[26]
- 'lay representatives' in small claims proceedings.

22.86   If a party wants any other person to represent him or her at a hearing, the court must first give permission.[27] This will usually be granted on a case-by-case basis. However, in possession proceedings some courts will effectively grant permission to all those assisting in duty advice schemes or employed by certain local housing associations.

McKenzie friends

22.87   Litigants in person are entitled to have help in court. This includes someone taking notes and (quietly) making suggestions and giving advice but not actually speaking for the party.[28] If the court refuses to allow a non-legally qualified person to represent a party at a hearing, he or she could assist in this role instead. Practice guidance issued in 2010 sets out what McKenzie friends can and cannot do in the civil and family courts. McKenzie friends are not entitled to act as advocates for (although judges may allow this) or to conduct litigation (eg sign court documents on behalf of a party). It also sets out the circumstances in which a court may refuse to allow a party to use a McKenzie friend and the procedure the court must follow. The guidance can be downloaded from: www.judiciary.gov. uk/publications/mckenzie-friends.

---

25   Legal executives are regulated by the Chartered Institute of Legal Executives (CILEX), which is a body authorised to grant limited rights of audience to its members.

26   CPR 39.6. A company employee needs the court's permission to represent the company but permission should be given by the court unless there is some 'particular and sufficient reason why it should be withheld': CPR Part 39 PD para 5.3.

27   The court has a broad discretion to do so under the Courts and Legal Services Act 1990 s27(2)(c).

28   The term 'McKenzie friend' does not denote any particular legal status. The term was coined following *McKenzie v McKenzie* [1970] 3 WLR 472 when the Court of Appeal ruled that it was in the interests of justice to allow an unrepresented party to have assistance from another person during a hearing. See also *R v Leicester City Justices ex p Barrow* [1991] 3 WLR 368.

Consent orders

22.88 The vast majority of defended claims are settled by the parties before a final hearing. If settlement is achieved after the claim has been issued the terms of the settlement will usually be incorporated into a 'consent order', which is then submitted to the court for approval. When the court approves the order, it will be stamped with the court seal and is enforceable in the same way as if the order had been made by a judge following a hearing. Where the terms of agreement are complex, the consent order will usually provide for a stay of proceedings on terms set out in a schedule. Either party has the right to apply to the court if the other party does not comply with the agreed terms. This is known as a 'Tomlin Order' and an example is at appendix 2 to this chapter.

Undefended claims

22.89 If a defendant fails to respond to the claim by filing a defence, the claimant can ask the court to enter 'judgment in default'. A default judgment can be enforced against a defendant in the same way as an order made by a judge. CPR Part 12 sets out the rules for default judgments. A default judgment cannot be made in a possession claim.

22.90 The procedure differs according to whether the claim is for a fixed amount of money, for an amount of money to be decided by the court and/or whether some other remedy such as an injunction or order for works is sought.

Claim for fixed amount

22.91 After the time for filing a defence has expired the claimant can apply for judgment by completing form N225[29] and sending it to the court with a fee. A court officer will draw up the judgment and will send it to the parties.

Claim for amount to be assessed by the court

22.92 This will be the case where the claim is for damages that have to be assessed by the court, for example, for disrepair or unlawful eviction and harassment. In such a case the claimant applies for judgment to be entered against the defendant with damages to be assessed by the

29 Or form N205A but this is not available online.

court at a later hearing. This can be done by completing form N227.[30] If judgment is entered this means that the defendant is liable to pay some damages but can attend the hearing to make representations about the amount (known as 'quantum'). He or she cannot argue about liability unless the default judgment is set aside.

Claim for non-money remedy

22.93   A hearing is also necessary where a claimant is asking the court to grant an injunction or an order for specific performance of a contract. Such claims are usually in addition to claims for damages. In this case, an application for judgment in default must be made under CPR Part 23.[31] Part 23 requires the applicant to complete an application notice (form N244). The application is for two things: for judgment on liability to be entered immediately, without notice to the defendant, and for a hearing to be listed so that the court can assess the amount of damages and whether to grant the non-monetary remedy. The defendant will be notified of the hearing and may attend and make representations.

Possession claims

22.94   The procedure described above (paras 22.89–22.93) applies to most claims for money and other remedies such as injunctions, but not claims for possession. Most claims for possession are dealt with as follows:

- *Ordinary possession claims* A hearing is listed when the claim is issued and there is no procedure for obtaining judgment by default. A defendant can attend the hearing and argue against the making of a possession order.
- *Accelerated possession claims* The accelerated procedure is available to a landlord seeking a possession order against an assured shorthold tenant where there is a written tenancy agreement. A possession order can be made without a hearing if the judge decides that the claim is established on the papers.

Both procedures are described in detail in chapter 6.

---

30   Again, there is an alternative form: N205B, not available online.
31   CPR 12.4(2). Part 23 concerns any sort of application made within proceedings.

Small claims

22.95 There is no separate 'small claims court' within the civil system. Rather, defended claims below a certain value are allocated to the small claims track. This determines the type of case management directions that will be given and the way the final hearing will be conducted. CPR Part 27 contains the rules about the conduct of small claims.

22.96 Note that if no defence is filed the claim is not allocated to track and the rules regarding default judgments described above (paras 22.89–22.93) apply.

Allocation to the small claims track[32]

22.97 The criteria for allocation are not limited to financial value but this is the main factor. The following claims will usually be allocated to the small claims track:

- money claims for up to £10,000;
- personal injury claims for up to £1,000;
- housing disrepair claims in which an order for works is sought, where the expected damages are not more than £1,000 *and* the estimated cost of works is not more than £1,000.

22.98 It is possible for claims above these values to be allocated to the small claims track.

22.99 However, the following provisions apply to housing cases:

- claims in respect of harassment or unlawful eviction brought by a tenant against a landlord will not be allocated to the small claims track;[33]
- disputed claims for possession and demotion of tenancies are not generally considered suitable for the small claims track.[34]

Features of small claims cases

22.100 The main features of cases allocated to the small claims track are:

- only very limited legal costs can be recovered by the successful party;
- public funding will not usually be granted for representation;

---

32 CPR Part 26 sets out the criteria for allocation.
33 CPR 26.7(4).
34 CPR Part 26 PD, para 8.1(c).

- simple case management directions will be made – these are usually limited to exchanging copies of the documents each party relies on;
- the hearing will usually be held in the judge's private room and will be informal;
- lay representatives have a right of audience provided the party is present at the hearing.[35]

Costs in small claims

22.101 The general rule is that legal costs incurred by a party in taking or defending a small claim cannot be recovered from the other party.

22.102   Only the following costs are recoverable in small claims:[36]

- court fees;
- any expenses incurred by a witness (including the successful party) in attending the hearing, including travel expenses and loss of earnings (up to a maximum of £90 per person per day);
- if a claim for an injunction or specific performance is made, legal costs of up to £260;
- expert witness fees, up to a maximum of £750.[37]

22.103 Also, in all cases, further costs may be awarded if a party behaves unreasonably.[38]

CPR Part 8 procedure

22.104 Most civil claims are brought under CPR Part 7, which is the procedure described above at paras 22.40–22.93. However, Part 8 provides an alternative procedure which should be used either:[39]

- where the court's decision is sought on a question which is unlikely to involve a substantial dispute of fact; or
- where the CPR require or permit the use of Part 8 for a specific type of claim.

22.105 The claims that *must* be brought under Part 8 are listed in the Practice Direction to Part 8, para 10.4 and Part 56. Tenancy deposit claims

---

35 Lay Representatives (Rights of Audience) Order 1992 SI No 1966 art 2.
36 CPR 27.14(2) and the PD para 7.
37 These are the current 'caps' set out in CPR PD 27, para 7.3 and may be increased in future.
38 CPR 27.14(2)(g).
39 CPR 8.1(2) and (5).

under HA 2004 s214 (see paras 4.142–4.170) must be brought under Part 8.

22.106　PD to Part 8, para 3 lists the claims that *may* be brought under Part 8. These include an application for the court's approval of a claim settled on behalf of a child or a protected person.[40]

22.107　The main features of the Part 8 procedure are:

- The claim is commenced by completing a claim form[41] with written evidence attached: it is not necessary to file particulars of claim.
- The defendant is not required to file a defence but must file an acknowledgment of service,[42] also with written evidence. If the defendant does not do so he or she may attend the hearing but can only take part if the court gives permission.
- There is no default procedure – the matter is usually listed for a hearing but may be dealt with by a judge without a hearing.
- A party may not use written evidence at the hearing unless it was served on the other party with the claim form or acknowledgement of service.
- The evidence at any hearing will mainly be written evidence but the court may order that oral evidence be given.
- At the hearing the court may decide the matter or give case management directions.
- The court may, at any stage, direct that the case proceed as if it had not been issued under CPR Part 8, and give directions for future conduct.

Enforcement

22.108　This section deals with the enforcement of money judgments and injunctions. The enforcement of possession orders is dealt with in chapter 6.

40　See CPR Part 21. A protected party is a person who lacks capacity, see para 7.202. Children and protected parties must have another person acting on their behalf: a 'litigation friend'. A settlement reached before issue must be approved by a court.

41　Form N208.

42　Form N210.

Money judgments

22.109 A successful claim for damages or the repayment of a debt will result in the court making an order that the defendant ('the judgment debtor') pays to the claimant ('the judgment creditor') a sum of money ('the judgment debt') within a specified period. Unless the order states otherwise, payment should be made within 14 days.[43] The money is paid directly to the judgment creditor and not to the court.

22.110 Judgment debts are normally recorded in the Register of Judgments, Orders and Fines.[44] If the debt is paid within one month of the order the registration can be cancelled. If the debt is paid after one month the judgment will be recorded as satisfied. Applications for either cancellation or satisfaction are made by the judgment debtor to the court where the order was made and a fee is payable.

22.111 Apart from entering the judgment in the register, the court takes no further action after making the order. If the judgment debtor fails to pay, further action to enforce the judgment must be taken by the judgment creditor. The different types of enforcement action are described below.

22.112 In all cases a further court fee must be paid. Fee exemption is available for those on a limited income (see para 22.53). If a fee is paid and the enforcement action is successful the fee will be added to the judgment debt and must be paid by the judgment debtor.

Main methods of enforcing money judgments

22.113 The main methods of enforcing money judgments are shown in the following table.[45]

---

43 CPR 40.11.

44 The register is administered by a not-for-profit company: The Registry Trust Ltd. Searches of the register can be carried out online at its website: www. trustonline.org.uk.

45 References to CCR are to the County Court Rules and RSC to the Rules of the Supreme Court. These are rules retained from the old procedural codes which relate to proceedings in the county courts and the High Court respectively. Those still in force are set out in a schedule to CPR.

Enforcement action	CPR/ authority	Effect/procedure
Warrant or writ of execution (taking control of goods – 'TCG')	CPR 83–85 and the Taking Control of Good Regulations 2013 SI No 1894	The 'taking control of goods' (TCG) procedure replaced the old writs and warrants of execution as from 6 April 2014. A new requirement is that advance notice must be given before attempting to take control of goods to enforce a judgment. Seven clear days' notice must be given by enforcement agents (this includes High Court and County Court officers or private agents). The process permits the seizure and sale of the debtor's goods to satisfy the judgment debt. As a general rule, entry into premises to seize the goods cannot be forced. Certain belongings are exempt.
Attachment of earnings	CPR Part 70 and CCR Order 27 Attachment of Earnings Act 1971	An attachment of earnings order compels the employer of a judgment debtor to deduct an amount from his or her earnings until the debt is paid. The debtor is given notice of the application by the court with a form of reply. On receiving the reply a court officer may make an attachment of earnings order. A hearing may be listed if there is insufficient information for an order to be made. If an order is made without a hearing, both parties have the right to apply for a hearing within 14 days. Where a debtor fails to file a reply or attend a hearing an application may be made for the debtor to be committed to prison, provided service can be proved.

Enforcement action	CPR/ authority	Effect/procedure
Third party debt order	CPR Part 72	A third party debt order is an order that a person who owes money to the judgment debtor pays the amount of the judgment debt to the judgment creditor. It is generally used to obtain money directly from a person's bank or building society.
		The bank or building society is the third party. The court first makes an interim order without a hearing and without notice to the debtor. This order is served on the third party and specifies the amount of money that must be retained pending a final order. The interim order is served on the debtor after being served on the third party. The judgment creditor may apply for a hardship payment and, if he or she objects to the making of a final order, written evidence must be filed stating the objections. If no objections are made, or if the objections are not upheld, the order will be made final at a hearing and the third party must then pay the outstanding amount, plus the costs of the application, to the judgment creditor.

Enforcement action	CPR/ authority	Effect/procedure
Charging order	CPR Part 73	A charging order may be appropriate when a judgment debtor owns property, including his or her own home or premises let to a tenant.[46] An interim order is requested without a hearing and without notice to the judgment debtor.
		This can be registered at the land registry to prevent the judgment debtor transferring ownership of the property.
		The interim order is served on the judgment debtor, who must file and serve written evidence if he or she objects to the making of a final order. If no objections are made, or objections are not upheld, the order will be made final at a hearing. A charging order is a form of mortgage. If the judgment debtor does not pay, an application may be made for an order for sale and the judgment satisfied from the proceeds of sale, see below.
Order for sale	CPR Parts 73 and 8	If a final charging order has been obtained and the judgment debt is still not paid, an application may be made under Part 8 for an order that the property be sold.
Appointment of receivers	CPR Part 69	A receiver may be appointed by the court to preserve or manage property pending the resolution of a dispute. Generally, other methods of enforcement will be more effective. However, in a disrepair action a receiver could be appointed to receive rents from a number of tenants to pay for essential repairs.

46 This can be discovered by carrying out a Land Registry search. See para 4.139.

Oral examination

22.114   If the judgment creditor has insufficient information about the debtor's assets to decide on an appropriate method of enforcement an application may be made for an oral examination of the judgment debtor. This is summarised in the table below.

Action	CPR	Effect/procedure
Order that judgment debtor attend court	CPR Part 71	Application is made by request to a court officer. An order will be made without a hearing by a court officer. The order requires the judgment debtor to attend court to answer questions about his or her assets and income to enable the judgment creditor to choose the best way to enforce. The order should be endorsed with a notice warning the debtor that he or she may be sent to prison for contempt if it is not obeyed. The order should be served personally on the debtor by the creditor and travel expenses must be offered. At the hearing the debtor will be questioned by a court officer or a judge. If the hearing is before a court officer, the creditor *may* attend and ask questions. If the hearing is before a judge, the creditor *must* attend and conduct the questioning. If the debtor fails to attend the hearing the matter should be referred to a judge. The judge may make a committal order provided the order was served personally and an affidavit has been filed confirming service.

22.115   Each method of enforcement requires an application and fee. If successful, the creditor will usually recover the fee and a fixed amount towards any legal costs. Clearly, if the judgment debtor has no assets or cannot be traced, the creditor may be unable to obtain satisfaction of the judgment and it will be pointless to incur further court fees that are unlikely to be recovered from the debtor. This is why it is essential to have information about a defendant's means before commencing a claim if possible.

Enforcing injunctions and orders for specific performance

22.116 If a party does not obey an order that he or she must do or refrain from doing something, an application can be made for the person to be committed to prison for contempt of court. Committal proceedings are described in more detail at paras 10.173–10.177.

Judicial review proceedings

22.117 The above rules relate to private disputes. The High Court also deals with challenges to administrative decisions made by public bodies. The procedure to challenge such decisions is judicial review which is explained at paras 2.4–2.39.

22.118   Claims for judicial review are generally brought in the Administrative Court, which is a branch of the High Court. However, some are brought in the Upper Tribunal. 'Fresh' asylum claim[47] judicial reviews and immigration judicial reviews on human rights grounds must be brought in the Upper Tribunal. The Administrative Court also has the power to transfer judicial review claims to the Upper Tribunal. Claims by asylum-seeking children whose age is disputed are usually transferred to the Upper Tribunal if permission is granted by the Administrative Court.[48]

Costs

22.119 In civil proceedings the usual rule is that the losing party will be ordered to pay the legal costs of the winning party. The rules for criminal prosecutions (which may be brought by individuals) are different and are outside the scope of this book. The detailed rules about costs are contained in CPR Parts 44 to 48. This section examines the main issues advisers are likely to encounter. These are:

- the circumstances in which a successful party may not recover costs;
- the nature of the 'costs' that can be recovered;
- what happens when one party is legally aided;

---

47 That is, new claims made after initial asylum claims have been refused.
48 See the First-tier Tribunal and Upper Tribunal (Chambers) Order 2010 SI No 2655 art 11(c)(ii) and Tribunals, Courts and Enforcement Act 2007 s15(1).

- how the amount of costs claimed is controlled;
- when costs can be ordered against someone who is not a party;
- when costs may be ordered against a party's representatives.

When might a successful party not recover costs?

The general rule

22.120 Under CPR the court has a general discretion as to whether to make an order for costs at all.[49] If the court decides to make an order about costs, 'the general rule is that the unsuccessful party will be ordered to pay the costs of the successful party; but ... the court may make a different order'.[50] In deciding what order to make, the court must have regard to all the circumstances, including:

- the conduct of all the parties;
- whether a party has succeeded on part of his case, even if he or she has not been wholly successful; and
- any payment into court or offer to settle the case.

22.121 The court can order that one party pays a proportion of another party's costs; pays costs from or until a certain date; pays costs incurred before proceedings have begun; pays costs relating to particular steps taken in the proceedings; or pays costs relating to a distinct part of the proceedings.[51]

Conduct of the parties

22.122 This relates to conduct in relation to the proceedings, not generally. It would include such conduct as refusing to consider mediation as an alternative to litigation. However, there may be good reasons to refuse mediation and it is for the unsuccessful party to prove that it was unreasonable to refuse to mediate.[52]

Partial success

22.123 In some cases a party may succeed on one issue but not on another. In such a case the court may order that a proportion of the costs be paid by one party to the other or that each party recovers costs

---

49 CPR 44.2(1).
50 CPR 44.2(2). However, the general rule does not apply in Court of Appeal cases in relation to probate or in family proceedings: CPR 44.3(3).
51 CPR 44.2(6).
52 *Halsey v Milton Keynes General NHS Trust* [2004] EWCA Civ 576, 11 May 2004.

in relation to the issues on which they were successful. These are known as 'split costs orders'. Alternatively the court may order that each party pays their own costs or make no order for costs (which has the same effect).

Offers to settle

22.124 Offers made under CPR Part 36 will usually carry automatic consequences in relation to costs. These are described at paras 22.69–22.73 above. However, when deciding what costs order to make, the court will consider attempts to settle made by the parties, even if not made in accordance with Part 36. A party who has refused a reasonable offer to settle may be unable to recover all of the costs incurred even if successful.

Costs orders made before final hearing

22.125 Hearings may take place to decide procedural issues before the final hearing. This can happen if the parties do not agree about the steps to be taken to prepare for the hearing. Also, in some cases, an urgent injunction may be sought. Any application made during the course of proceedings will require a further court fee to be paid. Also, the parties may incur legal costs in making or opposing an application. The court will usually make some kind of costs order relating to the application and hearing. The following is a list of the kinds of orders that may be made:

- *Costs in the cause (or case)* This means that the costs of the particular application/hearing will be paid by the unsuccessful party as part of the overall costs at the end of the case.
- *Costs of the defendant/claimant to be paid by the claimant/defendant (sometimes expressed to be 'in any event')* This means that the party who has been unsuccessful must pay the other party's costs of that particular application/hearing regardless of who is successful at the end of the case.
- *Costs reserved* This means that the costs of the particular application/hearing will be decided at a later date. If they are reserved to the end of the case this leaves open the possibility of arguing that the party who is ultimately successful should nevertheless have to pay the other party's costs of the particular application/hearing.
- *No order for costs* This means that each party pays his or her own costs for the particular application/hearing. An order may also state expressly that each party should pay his or her own costs. If

an order makes no mention of costs the general rule is that this is the same as 'no order for costs', subject to some exceptions.[53]

What costs can be recovered?

22.126 The costs that one party may be ordered to pay to another include:

- *Legal fees:* the fees for the work of the party's legal representatives (solicitors and barristers).
- *Disbursements:* fees paid to other professionals or agencies, including court fees and expert's fees.
- *Expenses:* the travel expenses and loss of earnings for the party and any witnesses attending court.

Barristers' and solicitors' charges

22.127 Solicitors' fees are calculated on the basis of the amount of time spent and the number of routine letters and telephone calls made. Barristers usually charge a fee for each piece of work (for example, drafting a defence, attending a hearing) but this is also calculated on the basis of how much time the work takes. The court may reduce the amount recoverable from the losing party because the rate is considered too high or the time claimed excessive (see paras 22.143–22.148 below).

Litigants in person

22.128 A person who conducts his or her own litigation is entitled to recover:

- the necessary disbursements and witness expenses; and
- an amount for the time spent preparing the case.

22.129 There are two possible ways for a litigant in person to calculate the amount to be claimed for his or her time. A person who can show actual financial loss (for example, a self-employed person who lost income as a result of time spent on litigation, or an employed person who had to take time off work) may recover costs on the basis of the lost income. In the absence of actual loss, there is a prescribed rate, currently £18 per hour. A litigant in person can claim this amount for each hour of his or her time spent preparing the case, subject to the court's overall discretion to disallow claims for excessive amounts of time.

---

53 CPR 44.10.

22.130 Additionally, there is an overall limit to the amount of costs recoverable by a litigant in person: the costs allowed cannot exceed two-thirds of the amount that would have been allowed had a legal representative been instructed.

Success fees

22.131 Representation in civil proceedings can be funded under a conditional fee agreement (CFA). A CFA generally means that the lawyers will only receive payment if the claim is successful and costs are recovered. It is usual that under a CFA, a success fee is charged, which is a percentage increase on the usual level of fees to reflect the risk that no fees are recovered at all. Until April 2013 success fees were recoverable from the losing party. For CFAs entered into after 1 April 2013 any success fee agreed must be paid by the client (usually from the damages recovered) and cannot be recovered from the opponent.

What happens when one party is legally aided

22.132 A party may be granted legal aid to bring or defend proceedings. The granting of a legal aid certificate means that, instead of that party being responsible for paying his or her own solicitor's costs, the Legal Aid Agency (LAA) is responsible. However, the fact that one party is legally aided should not affect the court's decision when considering a costs order. The usual rule, with some exceptions, still applies: if the legally aided party is successful the other party should be ordered to pay his or her costs. However, the existence of the certificate does have implications for the way costs are assessed. The possible outcomes are described below at paras 22.133–22.137.

The legally aided party is successful and the other party is ordered to pay costs

22.133 In such a case the losing party may not be responsible for paying all of the winning party's costs. This may be because some of the costs are considered to relate solely to obtaining legal aid or because the court has previously made an order that both parties pay their own costs of a particular application or hearing. In such a case the solicitor can claim these costs from the LAA, while claiming the majority of the costs from the other party.

22.134 In all cases where the LAA pays costs to the legally aided person's solicitor this sum will be deducted from any damages or money

awarded. This is known as the 'statutory charge'. See below at para
22.168.

The legally aided party is unsuccessful

22.135 Where the legally aided party loses the case, the court will usually
make an order that he or she pays the costs of the successful party.
However, the amount they must pay must not exceed what is reasonable, having regard to all the circumstances, including the financial
resources of the parties and their conduct in the litigation.[54] In practice, enforcement of the costs order will usually be impossible and
the order itself should provide for enforcement to be stayed. This
leaves open the possibility of future enforcement if the financial position of the legally aided person changes. An assessment of the person's means is required before the order can be enforced and the
actual liability would be limited to any amount they could pay. This
is referred to as 'costs protection', ie a party who has legal aid will not
normally have to pay the costs of the opponent.

22.136   In certain circumstances a successful defendant may claim costs
from the Lord Chancellor (ie the LAA).[55]

Partial success or case settled and court makes no order for costs

22.137 'No order for costs' means that each party is responsible for his or
her own costs. In relation to a legally aided party this means that his
or her solicitors claim the whole of their costs from the LAA. If the
assisted person has been awarded money or property by the court,
the statutory charge will apply.

Controlling the amount of the costs

22.138 There are three ways the amount of costs to be paid may be determined, see paras 22.139–22.148 below.

---

54 See s26 LASPO 2012. The wording is different from that under the Access to
Justice Act 1999 (which s26 replaced) but the government indicated that s26
did not change the existing provision in relation to costs protection for legally
aided litigants.

55 The criteria for orders to be made against the Lord Chancellor are complex and
depend on when the certificate was issued.

Fixed costs

22.139 Some applications and claims are subject to a 'fixed costs' regime. This means that a set amount can be claimed for solicitors' costs. The amount can only be claimed if a solicitor is actually instructed. This is distinct from the fee paid by the party to the court. For example, there are fixed costs for an accelerated claim for possession brought against an assured shorthold tenant: the court fee is, at the time of writing, £280 and provided the landlord instructs a solicitor to complete the claim form, an additional fixed amount can be claimed for the solicitors' costs.[56] It should be noted that these fixed costs apply only if the matter is decided without a hearing. A defendant who raises an argument that results in a hearing being held risks being ordered to pay additional costs if unsuccessful.

22.140 The proceedings that are subject to fixed costs are listed in CPR Part 45.

Summary assessment of costs

22.141 In relatively straightforward cases a court may do a 'summary assessment' of the costs of the successful party at the end of the final hearing (or in some cases at the end of an interim hearing).[57] A party seeking costs must serve on the other party a summary of the costs claimed at least 24 hours before the hearing of an application and 48 hours before the trial.[58]

22.142 Costs being claimed by a legally aided party cannot be summarily assessed because the court must carry out a full, or detailed, assessment of the amount to be paid by the LAA.[59]

Detailed assessment of costs

22.143 In more complex cases the amount of costs to be paid by one party to another will be subject to 'detailed assessment' by the court. In most cases when a person has legal aid the court must do a detailed assessment of the solicitor's claim for costs (unless the costs are below a certain level in which case the LAA will do the assessment).

22.144 As between the two parties, there is a procedure to be followed to determine the amount of the costs. This involves the following steps, see paras 22.145–22.148 below.

---

56 The amount varies depending on who serves the claim form.
57 CPR 44.9(2).
58 CPR 44.9(5). The summary must be in a certain format.
59 CPR 44.9(8).

Serving the bill

22.145 A bill is prepared in a specified format, setting out in detail the amounts claimed. This is served on the paying party with a notice stating the total amount payable if the paying party fails to respond or if the costs have to be assessed by the court.

Responding to the bill

22.146 The paying party's solicitors should respond within 21 days with 'points of dispute', setting out their objections to the costs, eg the rate being charged, the time spent or particular work claimed. If they fail to do so, the receiving party's solicitors can apply to the court for a 'default costs certificate'. This entitles the receiving party to be paid the full amount of the costs claimed.

Assessment hearing

22.147 If points of dispute are served and no agreement about costs is reached, the receiving party's solicitors must apply to the court for an assessment. This is done on the papers initially by a costs judge. The judge will decide how much the paying party must pay. If either party wants to challenge the provisional assessment a hearing can be requested. Fees are payable both for a provisional assessment and an assessment hearing. In addition, one party may be ordered to pay the other party's legal costs incurred in dealing with the process of assessment.

22.148   In practice, the parties usually negotiate on a 'without prejudice' basis to agree the amount of the costs in order to avoid incurring further fees and legal costs.

Costs against someone who is not a party

22.149 It is possible for the court to order a person who is not a party to the proceedings to pay the costs of one or all of the parties.[60] The person against whom costs are sought must be added as a party to the proceedings, for the purpose of costs only, and must be given a reasonable opportunity to attend a hearing at which the court will consider the matter. An order may be made where it is alleged that the proceedings would not have been necessary but for the actions or default of that party. An example is the County Court case of *ASRA v*

---

60 CPR 46.2. The rule does not apply when the court is considering an order against the LAA or a wasted costs order: CPR 46.2(2)(a).

Coke[61] in which the London Borough of Newham was ordered to pay the costs of both parties in a claim for possession; the claim had been brought because of the authority's failure to deal with the tenant's claim for housing benefit.

Costs ordered against a representative/wasted costs orders

22.150 'Wasted costs' means any costs incurred by a party 'as a result of any improper, unreasonable or negligent act or omission on the part of any legal or other representative or any employee of such a representative'.[62]

22.151   The court may order that the legal or other representative must pay the whole or part of the wasted costs.[63] 'Legal or other representatives' are defined as those exercising a right of audience or right to conduct litigation. This includes solicitors, barristers and lay representatives exercising rights under the Lay Representatives (Rights of Audience) Order 1999.[64] However, the court clearly has the power under CPR 46.2 (costs orders in favour or or against non-parties, see para 22.149 above) to make an order against others who are informally representing a party. Many advice agencies assist people with litigation although they are not on the court record and do not have rights of audience or representation. Such agencies should ensure that they are not inadvertently placed on the court record as formally representing the party and should generally not agree to receive notices and correspondence from the court on behalf of a client. If notice of a hearing were sent to the agency direct and the client not notified, the agency could be ordered to pay any costs wasted as a result.

22.152   If the court is considering making a wasted costs order, it must give those against whom the order is to be made a reasonable opportunity to attend a hearing to give reasons why such an order should not be made.[65]

22.153   It is not necessarily 'improper, unreasonable or negligent' to act for a party whose claim is bound to fail. However, a representative

---

61 Reported in June 2001 *Legal Action* 31.
62 Senior Courts Act 1981 s51(7). It also includes costs 'which, in the light of any such act or omission occurring after they were incurred, the court considers it is unreasonable to expect that party to pay': s51(7)(b).
63 Senior Courts Act 1981 s51(6), CPR 46.2.
64 SI No 1225.
65 CPR 46.8(2).

who acts in a claim which is an abuse of process, or is dishonest may be at risk of a wasted costs order.[66]

Legal aid/public funding

22.154   The legal aid scheme was introduced to ensure that people with limited means could be represented in legal proceedings. It is currently administered by the Legal Aid Agency, an executive agency of the Ministry of Justice. The scope of legal aid in civil cases was drastically reduced by the Legal Aid, Sentencing and Punishment of Offenders Act (LASPO) 2012, which came into force on 1 April 2013.

22.155   The following table sets out in broad terms what is in and out of scope, relevant to housing cases:[67]

Area of law	In or out of scope
Defending possession claims	In scope unless claim is against trespassers – where no argument that occupation started as trespass.
Anti-social behaviour cases	In scope where a local authority or other social landlord is seeking an anti-social behaviour injunction.[68]
Homelessness	In scope.
Transfers and allocations	Out of scope (unless judicial review).
Disrepair – order for works	In scope only if serious risk to the health and safety of the occupiers.
Disrepair – damages only	Out of scope.
Unlawful eviction and harassment	Injunction application in scope, damages claim out of scope.

---

66   *Tolstoy-Milosalvsky v Lord Aldington* [1996] 2 All ER 556.
67   More detail is given in the chapters dealing with each area of law.
68   Criminal legal aid is also available to defend criminal prosecutions for anti-social behaviour. New guidance will be needed when the ASBCPA 2014 comes into force.

Area of law	In or out of scope
Housing benefit	General advice and appeals to First-tier Tribunal out of scope. Judicial review, in scope.
Transfers on relationship breakdown[69]	Out of scope.
Judicial review	In scope but limits on payment for pre-permission work (see para 22.173).
Community care – all accommodation duties	In scope.

22.156   Note that even if an area of law is still in scope, legal aid will only be granted if the case passes a 'merits' test (see below at para 22.164).

22.157   Currently in relation to civil proceedings a person may be assisted in one of two ways: under the Legal Help scheme or under a legal aid certificate.

Legal Help (and Help at Court)

22.158   Under the Legal Help scheme advice and assistance can be given in relation to those legal issues that remain 'in scope'. In all cases the provider of the services must be satisfied that there is likely to be 'sufficient benefit' to the individual to justify the cost of providing the legal help.

22.159   The Legal Help scheme covers advising orally and in writing, corresponding on the person's behalf and obtaining expert evidence. The fees are fixed and vary according to the category of law. Expenses such as interpreter's fees and expert's fees can be claimed in addition to the fixed fee. If the amount will exceed three times the fixed fee, hourly rates can be claimed.

22.160   In most cases the Legal Help scheme does not cover representation at court. However, 'help at court' can be provided in possession proceedings where the only issue is the amount of any arrears, the rate of repayment of arrears and/or whether a warrant of possession should be suspended.

---

69   This is subject to exceptions when a party has been the victim of domestic violence and can provide specified forms of evidence of this.

22.161　The means assessment is conducted by the adviser who must obtain and keep on file the evidence of means.[70]

Legal aid certificates

22.162　A certificate may be granted to cover representation in specific court proceedings. An application can be made on behalf of a prospective claimant or a defendant in a claim that has been issued (but not in anticipation of being a defendant). The certificate is issued to a specific firm or organisation to represent the assisted person. To be eligible for a public funding certificate, the applicant must satisfy both a means test and a merits test. The firm or organisation must have a contract with the LAA to provide the type of service covered by the certificate.

22.163　The means test is similar to that applied for Legal Help but people whose income is above a certain limit may be granted a certificate subject to payment of a financial contribution. The contribution must be paid by the assisted person every month for as long as the certificate is in force.

The merits test

22.164　In addition to the person passing a means test, the case must have sufficient merit. A cost benefit test is applied, balancing the prospect of success and the likely benefit to the assisted person against the anticipated costs of the proceedings. The test differs according to what is at stake.

22.165　The merits test must be applied continuously as long as the certificate is in force. Any offers to settle a claim must be reported to the LAA and if a person is considered to be acting unreasonably in his or her instructions the certificate may be terminated.

Emergency funding

22.166　An emergency certificate may be granted to cover urgent work such as an application for an injunction or to represent a person at an imminent hearing. Most firms and organisations will have 'delegated powers' to grant emergency funding as soon as the application forms are signed. The forms must be submitted to the LAA within five working days. The extent of delegated powers depends on the

---

70　An eligibility calculator is available on the LAA website.

area of law, but for most cases involving a person's home delegated powers are available.

Limits of certificates

22.167 Public funding certificates are limited to taking certain steps within proceedings and extensions of the scope will be needed at various stages as the litigation progresses. A certificate will also limit the costs that can be incurred under a certificate and for complex cases that are not resolved quickly it will be necessary to make several applications for the scope and costs limits to be extended. At all stages the LAA must be satisfied that the cost benefit test is met.

The statutory charge

22.168 The statutory charge refers to the right of the LAA to recover the costs it has incurred in funding litigation. It applies where there is an award of property or money to the legally aided person. If the person is successful in the litigation the court should order the other party to pay the assisted person's legal costs. If all of the costs are recovered from the other party there should be no claim for costs against the legal aid fund. Therefore the statutory charge will not apply, although it does mean that a solicitor cannot release damages to the client until all of the costs have actually been paid by the other side.

22.169   In some cases not all of the costs can be recovered from the other party (see para 22.137 above). If this happens and some of the costs are claimed from the LAA, the amount claimed will be deducted from any money recovered by the legally aided person. Where property is recovered or preserved the LAA may register the amount owed as a charge on the property and payment must be made when the property is sold.

The Exceptional Case Funding Scheme

22.170 LASPO 2012 s10 provides for legal aid to be granted in cases that are no longer in scope, where the Director of the LAA makes an 'exceptional case determination'. Such a determination should be made where it is necessary to provide legal aid because a failure to do so would be a breach of the individual's rights under the ECHR, or 'any rights of the individual to the provision of legal services that are enforceable EU rights.' Alternatively, where it is appropriate to grant legal aid having regard to the risk that a failure to do so would be such a breach.

22.171   When LASPO 2012 was being introduced the government estimated that some 3,700 cases each year would be granted funding under the scheme. In fact in the first year of operation 1,519 applications were made and only 57 granted.

> *Gudanaviciene & Others v Director of Legal Aid Casework & Another*[71] was a challenge by six claimants to decisions to refuse exceptional case funding and to the lawfulness of the LAA's guidance. All were immigration cases. The Court of Appeal held that the Lord Chancellor's guidance on exceptional funding was incompatible with article 6 of ECHR and the Charter of Fundamental Rights of the European Union, in indicating that a refusal of legal aid would amount to a breach of the applicant's rights only in rare and extreme cases. The guidance was also incompatible with ECHR article 8 in immigration cases.

22.172   Assistance to individuals and advisers wanting to apply for exceptional cases funding, the Public Law Project offer assistance. See: www.publiclawproject.org.uk/exceptional-funding-project.

Judicial review

22.173   As from April 2014 new rules were introduced by the LAA which mean that although legal aid is available for judicial review claims, payment to the claimant's legal representatives will not be made in cases where permission is not granted. For cases that are settled prior to permission, but with no order for costs, the LAA has discretion to allow payment. The regulations introducing these rules were challenged in the case of *R (Ben Hoare Bell & Others) v The Lord Chancellor*[72] and on 3 March 2015 the High Court declared them to be unlawful. The regulations were quashed but the Lord Chancellor introduced new regulations immediately to achieve the same end.

The 'telephone gateway' and future proposals

22.174   When LASPO 2012 came into force some areas of law were made subject to the mandatory 'telephone gateway' scheme under which a person cannot immediately obtain face-to-face advice but must

---

71   [2014] EWHC 1840 , and [2014] EWCA Civ 1622, 15 December 2014.
72   [2015] EWHC 523 (Admin), 3 March 2015.

contact a telephone contact centre initially. The contact centre will determine whether the person is eligible for legal aid and, if so, any initial advice will usually be given by telephone. However, the contact centre can authorise the person to obtain face-to-face advice if appropriate (eg a vulnerable client and/or a lot of documents to consider). The areas of law are currently: debt (where the home is at risk); special educational needs; and discrimination cases. It is proposed that the telephone gateway will be extended to other areas of 'in-scope' cases.

22.175   The service is called Civil Legal Advice (CLA) and the telephone number: 0345 345 4345.

Tribunals

22.176   Some housing disputes are heard not by courts but by tribunals. Tribunals are decision-making bodies set up by statute to resolve particular kinds of dispute. Legal aid is not available for representation at most tribunal hearings.

22.177   Most tribunals are now incorporated into the First-tier Tribunal which has six chambers. Appeals from the First-tier Tribunal are generally made to the Upper Tribunal.

22.178   The Residential Property Tribunal Service is part of the Property Chamber of the First-tier Tribunal. Its work includes:

- rent cases: disputes about rent levels in the private sector, see paras 4.182–4.196;
- leasehold disputes: eg service charge disputes, applications to dispense with consultation and appointments of managers, see chapter 5;
- Housing Act 2004 cases: including appeals by landlords and tenants in respect of statutory notices served by local authorities, see chapter 11;
- park homes cases: disputes about the management of mobile homes.

22.179   The following First-tier Tribunals may also be relevant to housing advisers:

- the Information Rights Tribunal (Part of the General Regulatory Chamber), which deals with disputes about access to information under the Data Protection Act 1998 and the Freedom of Information Act 2000, see paras 2.101–2.113;

- the Asylum Support Tribunal (Part of the Social Entitlement Chamber), which deals with disputes about asylum support, including accommodation;
- the Social Security and Child Support Tribunal (Part of the Social Entitlement Chamber), which deals with welfare benefit entitlement, including housing benefit.

APPENDIX 1

HM Courts and Tribunals Service

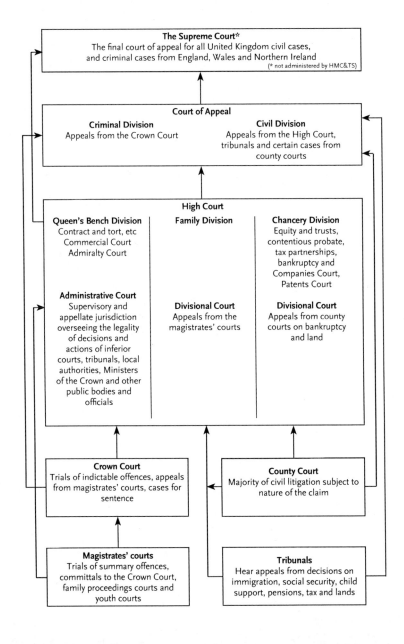

The Supreme Court*
The final court of appeal for all United Kingdom civil cases,
and criminal cases from England, Wales and Northern Ireland
(* not administered by HMC&TS)

Court of Appeal

Criminal Division
Appeals from the Crown Court

Civil Division
Appeals from the High Court,
tribunals and certain cases from
county courts

High Court

Queen's Bench Division
Contract and tort, etc
Commercial Court
Admiralty Court

Family Division

Chancery Division
Equity and trusts,
contentious probate,
tax partnerships,
bankruptcy and
Companies Court,
Patents Court

Administrative Court
Supervisory and
appellate jurisdiction
overseeing the legality
of decisions and
actions of inferior
courts, tribunals, local
authorities, Ministers
of the Crown and other
public bodies and
officials

Divisional Court
Appeals from the
magistrates' courts

Divisional Court
Appeals from county
courts on bankruptcy
and land

Crown Court
Trials of indictable offences, appeals
from magistrates' courts, cases for
sentence

County Court
Majority of civil litigation subject to
nature of the claim

Magistrates' courts
Trials of summary offences,
committals to the Crown Court,
family proceedings courts and
youth courts

Tribunals
Hear appeals from decisions on
immigration, social security, child
support, pensions, tax and lands

APPENDIX 2

Tomlin Order

IN THE ...... COUNTY COURT

CLAIM No:

BETWEEN:

Claimant

and

Defendant

CONSENT ORDER

UPON the parties having agreed terms of settlement BY CONSENT

IT IS ORDERED that all further proceedings herein be stayed upon the terms set out in Schedule 1 hereto save for the purpose of enforcing or carrying into effect the said terms, with liberty to apply for that purpose.

IT IS FURTHER ORDERED that there be no order for costs save for the detailed assessment of the Defendant's public funding costs/the Defendant shall pay the Claimant's costs, such costs to be subject to detailed assessment if not agreed/alternative provision for costs.

SCHEDULE 1

1

2

3

We hereby consent to an order in the above terms:

Claimant   Defendant

or Claimant's solicitors   or Defendant's solicitors

Index